Chief Joseph

Trail of Glory and Sorrow

Chief Joseph
TRAIL OF GLORY & SORROW
by Ted Meyers

hancock house

ISBN 978-0-88839-743-0
Copyright © 2016 E.C. (Ted) Meyers
Printed in the USA

Library and Archives Canada Cataloguing in Publication

Meyers, Edward C., author
Trail of Glory and Sorrow: Chief Joseph of the Nez Perce vs
The Army of the Northwest / by E.C. (Ted) Meyers.

Includes bibliographical references and index.
ISBN 978-0-88839-743-0 (paperback)

1. Nez Percé Indians--Wars, 1877. 2. Joseph (Nez Percé Chief),
1840-1904. 3. Howard, O. O. (Oliver Otis), 1830-1909. I. Title.

E83.877.M49 2016   973.8'3   C2016-900022-2

All black and white photos are courtesy of The Canadian National Archives, Ottawa, Ontario, from The Edward Sheriff Curtis Collection. (Unless otherwise noted all photos were posed for Mr. Curtis by Nez Perce warriors of the Idaho Nez Perce who had survived the war. The poses reenact conditions and situations in the war and were taken in 1911. The (undated) photos of Chief Joseph, Yellow Bull, Black Eagle and Raven Blanket are also from the E.S. Curtis Collection.) All other photos are from the author's personal collection.

All rights reserved. No part of this publication may be reproduced, stored in a retrieval system or transmitted, in any form or by any means, electronic, mechanical, photocopying, recording, or otherwise (except for copying permitted by Sections 107 and 108 of the U.S. Copyright Law and except for book reviews for the public press), without the prior written permission of Hancock House Publishers.

Editor: Theresa Laviolette
Production: Mia Hancock
Cover Design: Ingrid Luters, Mia Hancock

HANCOCK HOUSE PUBLISHERS LTD.
19313 Zero Avenue, Surrey, B.C. Canada V3Z 9R9
(604) 538-1114 Fax (604) 538-2262
HANCOCK HOUSE PUBLISHERS
#104- 4550 Birch Bay-Lynden Road, Blaine, WA
U.S.A 98230-9436
(604) 538-1114 Fax (604) 538-2262
www.hancockhouse.com

All black and white photos are courtesy of The Canadian National Archives, Ottawa, Ontario, from The Edward Sheriff Curtis Collection. (Unless otherwise noted all photos were posed for Mr. Curtis by Nez Perce warriors of the Idaho Nez Perce who had survived the war. The poses reenact conditions and situations in the war and were taken in 1911. The (undated) photos of Chief Joseph, Yellow Bull, Black Eagle and Raven Blanket are also from the E.S. Curtis Collection.)

All other photos are from the author's personal collection.

Table of Contents

Author's Note 9
Quotes 11
Preface. 13
Introduction. 25
Prologue 59
Chapter 1 The Making of a Chief. 63
Chapter 2 In the Future Lays the Past 71
Chapter 3 Thieves' Treaties 77
Chapter 4 Ebbing Tide. 87
Chapter 5 Prelude to Lapwai. 111
Chapter 6 The Lapwai Council. 133
Chapter 7 The River Spirits are Angry 157
Chapter 8 Disquiet Amid Disarray. 169
Chapter 9 Prelude to Disaster 187
Chapter 10 Anatomy of a Failed Mission. 205
Chapter 11 Battle at White Bird Canyon 223

Chapter 12 Waiting Game 241

Chapter 13 Cottonwood and Clearwater. 261

Chapter 14 The Weippe Conference 297

Chapter 15 Fort Fizzle: The Battle That Never Was. 307

Chapter 16 Pursuit Continues. 319

Chapter 17 Disaster at Eschuchilpan 385

Chapter 18 Battle at Camus Meadows 405

Chapter 19 Yellowstone 425

Chapter 20 Close Calls at Canyon Creek. 439

Chapter 21 Humiliation at Yellowstone 457

Chapter 22 Tightening Net 469

Chapter 23 Siege at Snake Creek 483

Chapter 24 Aftermath 525

Appendices

A. The 1863 Treaty. 571

B. A Tense Night at Fort Walsh 577

C. Authenticated Battle Casualties 583

D. Rogue Missionaries among the Nimipul. 591

E. Arthur Chapman: A Villain of the Piece 621

F. Joseph's 1879 Speech to the Senate 631

G. Anatomy of Treachery and Deceit. 635

H. Those Not Forgotten 641

I. Inter-tribal Animosity and Distrust. 655

J. Religious Denominations in Charge 661

K. Tribe Names 665

L. Warriors' Names 669

 M. Recent Thoughts on Joseph's Motives. 673
  Timeline 679
  Bibliography
   Biographies & Histories 689
   Articles. 694
   Documents 695
   Magazines 696
   Newspapers. 696
  Index 698
  Acknowledgments 711
  About the Author 713

List of Maps (drawn by author)
 1. Nez Perce Reservation, 1855 and 1866 714
 2. Battle at White Bird Canyon, June 17, 1877 715
 3. The Big Hole Battlefield, August 9–10, 1877. 716
 4. Canyon Creek Battle, September 13, 1877 717
 5. Bear's Paw, First Battle, September 30, 1877,
  9:00 a.m. to 12:30 p.m. 718
 6. Army attack and Nez Perce defensive positions
  at Bear's Paw, September 30, 1877, 3:00 p.m. 719
 7. Bear's Paw positions until final surrender,
  October 5, 1877 720

This book is for
Maureen, Scott & Craig

Author's Note

Because my knowledge of the Nez Perce language is limited to only a few phrases, I obtained as much English translation for names and places as I could from various people who are familiar with the language. Nez Perce (as are most First Nation languages) is extremely colorful and complex, with most names and places having several translations. For instance, the name of the Piqun-in chief, Tool'hool'hool'zote, has been translated both as "Sound" and "Speaking Eagle." Also, some names in Nez Perce are complete sentences. Heinmot'tooyalakekt, Chief Joseph's proper name, is an example, with one translation being "Thunder-that-rolls-from-the-mountains-to-the-valley-then-returns-to-the-hills," and another, "Thunder-traveling-to-loftier-mountain-heights." There are even more examples. Lapwai translates as, "The place of butterflies" and also "Butterflies gather here." The list is long.

Pronunciation also poses a problem, so, in order for the reader to find the names easier to say, I have divided each into punctuated segments. I can only hope my efforts—although I am ungifted with linguistic acumen— are helpful and not offensive to those who do have a good command of the language.

Throughout the text I have endeavored to identify animals and birds with their Nez Perce names, which will appear in brackets. For example the Nez Perce owned two types of horses, the large, husky Appaloosa [ma'min] and the agile, tough prairie mustang [sik'em] used in hunting and in battle. Readers will get the idea as they progress.

I used the present-day names of the various tribes throughout the text but, as today's names often have little resemblance to their originals, for those readers who may be interested I bracket the original names at their first appearance. Also, Appendix K offers more detail to the original names of tribes regarding meaning, reason(s) why the change was made and who—or which group—instigated the change(s). Some original names are not mentioned because I was unable to obtain them. Also, although I researched everything as carefully as possible, I found tribes, bands, people and places often have more than one translation; and because the American Natives had no written languages spelling is often different and in some cases, as in the Cayuse and Chinook tribes, their original languages are today unknown. If a reader finds an error I take complete responsibility and apologize in advance. For any errors that may be discovered I would appreciate very much having a note dropped to me through the publisher so I will be able to correct my own files.

Quotes

"I think that in his long career, Joseph cannot accuse the government of the United States of one single act of justice."
—Anonymous American officer,
quoted by R.K. Andrist in The Long Death.

"I cannot understand how the government sends a man out to fight us as it did General Miles and then breaks his word. Such a government has something wrong with it."
—Chief Joseph, 1879.

"I have carried a heavy load on my back ever since I was boy. I learned then that we were but few while the white men were many, and that we could not hold our own with them. We were like deer. They were like grizzly bears."
—Chief Joseph,
quoted in the North American Review, 1879.

(Pointing to the sun) "From where the sun now stands I will fight no more forever."
—The final line of Chief Joseph's surrender statement on 11 October 1877.

"He who draws his courage from fire water often ends trembling in fear."
—During a discussion on whisky.

"A big name often stands on small legs."

"Eyes will reveal what tongues try to hide."
—On deceitful promises. Possibly a reference to Washington negotiators.

"The hand is cursed that scalps the reputation of the dead."
—On speaking ill of former foes.

"The finest fur can cover the toughest meat."
—On discussing outward appearances.

"It is wise to look twice at men with two faces."
—During a discussion about missionaries.

"If a man can get the last word with a mountain echo he may do so with a squaw."
—On relationships with women.

"The Great Spirit Chief must have been looking the other way and did not see what was happening to his people."
—On discussing the fate of the Nez Perce from 1855 onward.

"I have heard talk and talk, but nothing is done. Good words do not last long unless they amount to something. There has been too much talking by men who had no right to talk."
—To the US Congress in 1879.

Preface

The most difficult task facing any history detective is sifting through facts, legends, fiction, fabrication and half-truths. Sifting is also necessary to separate biased accounts from well meaning, but often misplaced, sympathy. The flight by more than 800 Nez Perce men, women and children on a long, circuitous trail from Oregon to within 40 miles of their perceived safety in Canada is one of the most perplexing and exciting chronicles of the Old West. The history of Joseph, Ollokot, White Bird, Husis Kute, Looking Glass and Tool'hool'hool'zote, the band chiefs who led them and formulated strategies that humbled and embarrassed a large army, is not only exciting, but intriguing. Equally interesting are the accounts of the war chiefs who put the tactics into play and the warriors who carried them out.

The truth of the Nez Perce War, differing vastly as it does from one version to another, lies somewhere between two extremes. Some writers, in particular those heavily biased either for or against the North American Native people, have used the 1877 Nez Perce War as a vehicle for fictional stories, altering facts to suit their story lines. They told of running gun battles, heroism, cowardice, murder, terrible slaughter, acts of mercy, treachery, military blunders and brilliant tactics. Some personified the soldiers of the pursuing Army of the Northwest as gallant knights dauntlessly defending settlers' lives from Nez Perce warriors they portrayed as lawless rebels without a legitimate cause. They painted into their portraits of prose vile renegades who murdered and scalped dozens of helpless civilians. That a renegade gang of about fifteen young warriors did, over a span of three days (June 13–15), kill and injure fourteen settlers is, unfortunately, very true—but the tales of scalping are all false. In all their long history the Nez Perce shunned the taking of scalps.[1]

In fact, during the 1877 uprising the only scalping done was by Cheyenne, Bannock and Crow scouts in the employ of the US Army. The worst occurred in the days following the battle of the Big Hole River when Cheyenne and Bannock scouts roamed the battle site scalping the remains of Nez Perce women and children killed in the fighting. Some went so far as to open shallow, hastily dug, graves to mutilate the corpses. Appalled by these atrocities, official US Army historians and many soldiers who later published accounts of the chase commended the Nez Perce warriors for their chivalry in battle. They expressly mentioned the declination to further harm the wounded or scalp the dead. They also noted that soldiers and civilians taken prisoner were in general treated kindly and with dignity.

The army historians' findings plunged biased writers into a quandary. How could they equate their fictional tales of savagery with official claims of chivalry? They did both by continuing their depiction of some rebels slaughtering defenseless settlers, raping women and killing innocent children (never citing a single source or giving names) while grudgingly crediting others for saving many from the savagery of their companions; exciting fiction, but untrue.

During the post-war period a printing frenzy lasting several years allowed journalists, such as the author of an article that appeared in the *Century Illustrated Monthly Magazine*[2] in May 1884, to expound views of the war based not on prejudice, but on ignorance of its history. These journalists credited Joseph with far more tactical brilliance than was warranted by facts. Perhaps it was inevitable that the *Century Illustrated Monthly Magazine* would adjudge what the editors felt to be the ultimate recognition to Nez Perce elan in warfare. They bestowed upon Joseph the title "Napoleon of the Plains," which was quickly followed with yet another sobriquet, "The Red Napoleon."[3] Joseph never commented on either.

Canadian writers, particularly during the hey-day of the 1920s and 1930s pulp magazines,[4] were no less guilty in altering facts and inventing situations to suit their storylines. Some wrote of Canada's warm welcome and offers of sanctuary to the Nez Perce refugees who managed to cross the border with Chief White Bird. The truth is quite the opposite. When those oppressed Natives crossed the border Canadian officials wanted nothing to do with them. Ottawa bureaucrats, on orders from their political masters, had already spent the better part of the previous year in futile attempts at convincing Sitting Bull, shaman of the Hunkpapa Sioux, that a return to Montana was in his and his followers' best interests. Sitting Bull disagreed. Ottawa finally told the Sioux they could remain but not to expect treaties or land grants; neither should they expect, nor even request, emergency supplies for sustenance.

Ottawa dealt with the Nez Perce refugees in exactly the same reprehensible manner. Ottawa allowed sanctuary to White Bird and his followers but refused even a meager allotment of food staples that would have helped them over the oncoming winter. Had it not been for Sitting Bull and his Sioux followers, a number of white settlers, nearby townspeople and members of the North West Mounted Police White Bird's people would likely have perished long before the arrival of spring. Ottawa politicians and their underlings absolutely did *not* welcome the Nez Perce; and they steadfastly ignored or denied all entreaties made by enlightened Canadian officials assigned to the Northwest Territory.

Two NWMP officers, Inspectors James Walsh and James Macleod, spoke out for the Nez Perce. In fact, Walsh often used funds from his own allotment to buy flour and sugar for the Natives. He also expelled an Indian Agent from an established reservation for cheating the Indians in trade. Ottawa bureaucrats went so far as considering prosecuting Walsh on a charge of embezzlement, alleging the officer had withheld supplies from his own men in order to give sugar and flour to the Indians. All thoughts of charges were quickly and quietly dismissed when police personnel came forward to declare they had voluntarily donated their own rations to the cause.[5]

For years the lives of the Nez Perces in Canada were nothing short of a desperate struggle for survival. To his everlasting discredit, Prime Minister John A. Macdonald not only refused to act on reports sent by territory officials but made determined efforts to keep information in those reports from the public. His policy of silence ensured the vast majority of Canadians remained unaware of a Nez Perce presence in their country.[6] Canada has nothing to be proud of in her treatment of the wretched remnants of Joseph's tormented people who sought refuge in the "Land of the Grandmother."[7]

Most conflicts begin with a series of betrayals, disagreements, mutual distrust and bullying tactics by the stronger faction. So did the 1877 uprising. All-out fighting generally is set in motion when one side fires upon the other, and it matters little who fires the first shot. The Nez Perce uprising followed that pattern very closely. In this case, Washington took the first serious action when, in March 1877, the Army of the Northwest (Columbia Division) was ordered to compel the non-Treaty Nez Perce bands and a neighboring Palouse band[8] to resettle at Lapwai. It was this edict that precipitated the war and its tragic results. That meeting resulted in the chiefs' grudging agreement to resettle at Lapwai no later than June 30. The chiefs returned to their villages, General Howard remained in Lapwai to await developments, and platoon commanders in various forts here and there nervously awaited orders.

However, compliance was far from guaranteed as opposition continued from two powerful and influential chiefs. White Bird did not believe Washington could ever be trusted under *any* circumstances, while the other, Tool'hool'hool'zote, the Piqunin chief, wanted nothing to do with the confines of reservation life. Both believed suitable land could be found in isolated valleys of the Bitterroot Mountains. They advocated resettlement in Montana. Joseph, the third chief of influence, was hopeful that a more suitable treaty, one that would restore the Wallowa Valley and the

Salmon River area to the Nez Perces, could yet be negotiated. He was willing to temporarily resettle his people at Lapwai while talks on the subject continued.

White Bird and Tool'hool'hool'zote eventually, albeit with great reluctance, prepared their people for the journey to Lapwai. On June 5 the three bands assembled on the shores of Lake Tolo, a mere fifteen miles from the reservation's southern boundary, for a final discussion on the subject. Following several days of heated and often bitter debate agreement was reached: all would go to Lapwai. On June 11 preparations began for the final walk to Fort Lapwai. The walk would begin on June 15 and would take about ten days.

Their well-laid plans were shattered when, on June 13, three heavily armed young men from White Bird's group rode out of camp bent on vengeance against some White cattle rustlers who had stolen cattle and horses from the band's herd. A dozen others joined them the next afternoon. During the following three days the renegades rode amok throughout the area making sporadic raids on farms and settlements. The large group on the shore of Tolo Lake waited fearfully amid conflicting rumors of imminent attack by the army and Howard's intention to await further developments. Even then there was no immediate outbreak of fighting. During that suspenseful time the two rumors traded priorities while the bands remained in several scattered areas near the lake, unsure whether or not to continue to Lapwai. The fuse leading to the powder keg was slowly burning to the final explosion.

What is *not* confused—in fact is very clear—is that it had been the White rustlers—against whom the renegades were venting their rage—who had already lit the fuse to the powder keg.

The smoldering fuse reached the powder keg on June 17 when a small group from Joseph's camp was fired upon as it approached the army line under a white flag. The explosion came minutes later with an all-out attack launched by the army. The three incidents combined to become the deciding factors in the uprising.

Had there been only one incident it is doubtful war would have erupted. Joseph considered the theft of livestock a matter that could be resolved through negotiations. Even the young warriors' belated retaliation against the rustlers was considered negotiable. What determined the point of no return was the army's uncalled-for attack at White Bird Canyon.

The Nez Perce warriors fought back and when the rifles fell silent the battlefield was littered with dozens of soldiers dead, dying and wounded. The Nez Perce had suffered but two injuries, both minor, in a decisive, but Pyrrhic, victory. Now even Joseph knew Lapwai was no longer an option. The only remaining choices were two: await the certain coming of many soldiers and fight and die in a last ditch battle, or take immediate flight for dubious safety in Montana. The Nez Perce chiefs opted for flight.

The trek of the Nez Perce proved a Herculean endeavor. Suffering, particularly among the non-combatants, was immense; the fighting prolonged and bitter. While most of the Nez Perce victories were absolute, others were less than total. The major battle at the Big Hole River was at best a draw.

Many early accounts of the fighting are little more than fiction, such as an account of how Joseph bypassed the army at a barrier that became known derisively as Fort Fizzle.[9] Some American writers claimed a great battle took place there but the official historian of the First Cavalry Division mentions only, in a terse notation, the barrier's commander, Captain Charles C. Rawn, met with Joseph and that the Bitterroot Militia, which was stationed at the barricade, had sustained "heavy losses…" Without further comment to guide them, many writers of the day assumed the reference indicated dead and wounded and spun their tales around that supposition. Writers in later years copied those stories, but none explored army files for verification. In his own account of the situation Rawn makes only brief mention of the meeting and the Indians' escape. In fact, the militia's "heavy losses" had all been through desertions.[10] Army records list no casualties at all for Rawn's command. The alleged battle simply did not happen.[11]

Throughout the entire four-month campaign the army largely fought poorly under generally inept leadership. There were a few occasions in which the army claimed victory, but the claims are all suspect and were eventually disproved. The army "victories" had come about only because the Nez Perce fighters had simply drifted away, leaving the site to the soldiers. The Battle at Cottonwood is one example.

In all the major battles and sixteen lesser engagements the army failed to gain a single genuine victory. The army can claim as a victory only the final encounter at Bear's Paw, because in any war when one side surrenders the opposing side wins. The Bear's Paw siege, for that is what it became, can justifiably be considered a stalemate.

Consequently, the US Army won the war, but it was victory by default. On the other hand, the Nez Perce war chiefs clearly emerged the better field generals and the outnumbered warriors remain unchallenged as the best fighters.

None of these successes, however, could have been achieved without the sub-chiefs who not only carried out the devised plans but often added their own innovations. Neither could there have been success had the warriors been unable or unwilling to fight against odds conservatively estimated above eight to one.

Through their clear victories the Nez Perce chiefs emerged head and shoulders above any of their opponents as the better tacticians. Their well-laid strategies caused such trouble and frustration that almost to a man the army conceded it had been beaten by maneuvers none had imagined possible from the minds of non-military men. Nonetheless, many able generals have won many battles only to eventually lose the war,[12] and Chief Joseph joined their ranks. As a result, he and his people lost their final bid for unimpeded freedom and the right to live in the land of their choice.

There was inordinate over-confidence on the part of army commanders, notably General Oliver O. Howard. Most, if not all, of the officers failed to consider the lack of training and inexperience of the green recruits under their commands. None foresaw the failings of their gun-shy horses. By considering their troops superior fighters and believing no Indian was capable of fighting over a prolonged period, they paid a savage toll. The army's two weakest links, Colonels Sturgis and Gibbon, each suffered humiliating defeats at crucial points when victory at either venue would have ended the war then and there.

The Nez Perce chiefs also had weaknesses in which errors and omissions played major roles. Misguided was the trust Looking Glass placed in promises made by Crow chiefs who had pledged undying support in 1873, only to renege on those promises in 1877. Looking Glass, though acknowledged in bravery and military acumen, made no less than four costly major errors. His first came close to ensuring early and total defeat, while his next two combined to deny the Nez Perce a chance at safety in Canada. The fourth cost him his life. Chiefs White Bird and Tool'hool'hool'zote naively thought freedom could be found in the valleys of western Montana. Joseph further weakened the chain through trust of white men and his belief that an honorable peace could be negotiated.

Because his life had been fashioned within Nez Perce laws that forbade any chief from overriding decisions made by another, he never understood that a white general (which he equated with a chief) could not negotiate a treaty or accept surrender without having final approval of the agreed terms. Neither could he grasp that nothing promised by a general was binding upon his political masters in Washington. Joseph, though well aware of Washington's perfidious history with treaties and other promises, erred greatly in his naive belief Washington would respect the terms of an honorable surrender.

For the non-Treaty Nez Perce the war ended tragically—and the tragedies continued into the years ahead.

For the army the war produced heavy casualties, intensely humiliating embarrassment, ridicule in the nation's press and a great deal of derision from the citizenry. It also proved extremely costly from the taxpayers' viewpoint.

The war ended any doubts that may have been held about the treachery capable by Washington politicians and bureaucrats in charge of the Department of Indian Affairs. Even ordinary Americans, few of whom cared not one whit about Indians, expressed dismay. An unidentified army officer best summed up Washington's image when he sarcastically commented, "*I* think that in his long career, Joseph cannot accuse the government of the United States of one single act of Justice."[13]

Nevertheless, the Nez Perce Nation survived to gain a place among the wealthiest and most respected tribes in America. A very slow reform that remains a work in progress began when Washington, under force of public opinion, changed its policies to eventually recognize Indians were indeed Americans with rights. Today, with all the evidence considered, there is still no way to determine the ultimate victors. Perhaps there is no final single victor. Though final evaluation lies yet within the future, it may well be the nation as a whole that will be deemed the winner. How much of this achievement that can be credited to Chief Joseph is the subject of this book and will be discussed in the pages below.

[PREFACE ENDNOTES]

1 The Nez Perce had ceased the practice at least a hundred years before and, so far as is known, had never scalped a white person. In fact the last known incident of a Nez Perce warrior taking a scalp was during a victorious war against the Blackfeet in 1855. Chief Looking Glass the Elder, then past 70 years of age, had ridden with the war party and returned with the one grisly trophy. It was a singular event. [*American Indian Warrior Chiefs,* 109.]

2 *Century Illustrated Monthly Magazine,* May 1884, 136–42.

3 *Ibid.* Volume 27, October 1884.

4 Many of these magazines (e.g., *Ranch Romances, Western Trails, Far West, Dynamic Western, Northwest Romances,* and others) are still available as collectors' items, at prices ranging from $5 to $50, from various internet sources (e.g. Ebay) and secondhand bookstores. Some of the stories within were considered, by the standards of the 1930s and 1940s, as being quite lurid with purple prose. All are greatly exaggerated. [Author's files.]

5   *Sitting Bull's Boss,* 189–92.

6   Many Canadians still believe the Nez Perce who managed to escape to Canada were given land and assistance, a presumption that persists because some of White Bird's band eventually assimilated with the Piegan tribe near the present town of Brockett, Alberta. They are always surprised to learn what really happened. [Author's files.]

7   There being no word in their language for king or queen, the Nez Perces sometimes referred to Queen Victoria as "the Grandmother" and sometimes as "the Great White Mother," the latter because they thought Queen Victoria held similar authority in Canada to that of the US president whom they called "the White Father."

8   Despite a commonly held belief, this band of the Palouse tribe was *not* a Nez Perce band. They had resided within Nez Perce territory for years and had become so intertwined in matters of commerce, marriage and cooperation they had come to be thought of as part the greater tribe. [Curtis, Edward, *The North American Indians,* Vol. 8, Norwood, Massachusetts (1911).]

9   A bemused reporter for the Helena, Montana newspaper bestowed the name on the barricade, and the name stuck. Today the location, but not the barricade, remains as a tourist site.

10 The term "deserters" in this case does not mean the men ran away rather than fight. Many who departed simply went home to tend to their farms or businesses. Others were well acquainted with the Nez Perce from past buffalo hunts and saw no threat in their passing through. Whatever their individual reasons, the militia members elected to leave in peace. During the following days the

Nez Perce returned that respect when they passed by the Montanans' towns and villages.

11 Chief Joseph, referring to Fort Fizzle in an address to Washington dignitaries in 1879, recalled a few shots being fired as they by-passed the barricade over a trail high on the mountain. He also admitted to having broken the truce Rawn and he had agreed upon so they could discuss the situation further. Leaving in the pre-dawn darkness had been Joseph's and White Bird's decision, an action that was, technically at least, a breach of the truce. Joseph's account of Fort Fizzle rings true and, as Rawn *never* contradicted it, can be safely accepted without further debate.

12 "There are lucky generals and there are unlucky generals. The unlucky ones lose battles and make excuses. Lucky generals win and are not required to make excuses." [Attributed to Napoleon Bonaparte, but may be apocryphal. Author.]

13 Quoted from R.K. Andrist in *The Long Death*. (Anderson, Ian, *Sitting Bull's Boss,* 140.)

Introduction

History clearly shows the uprising that became known as the Nez Perce War of 1877 was neither spontaneous nor long planned but the result of decades of mistrust and treachery. History and recorded facts clearly show Chief Joseph and the other four chiefs involved did not one day simply decide to take their people on the long, arduous journey that lead to their ultimate sorrow. Quite the contrary; the war and its aftermath began years before—as early as 1834—the result of four decades of betrayal, deceit that included land-grabbing, a rash of broken promises, the breaking of two formal treaties, and the continued refusals by various Washington departments to honor agreements negotiated with, and accepted by, the Nez Perce tribe.

To fully understand the reasons that lead to the so-called Nez Perce War of 1877 it is necessary to gain some insight into the history of the tribe, the people, the origins of their traditions, the rebellious bands and the series of events that preceded the crisis.

The proper name of the Nez Perce nation is *Nimipu* (pronounced Nee'mee'poo), which means "The People."[1] Over time the nation grew larger, extended its territory, then fragmented into bands of varying sizes. There is no way of knowing how many bands there were during the long history of the Nimipu, but around 1800 there were estimates of twenty-five bands; by 1877 there were probably fewer than fifteen. By 1855 very few bands were still identified by their original names, which had been derived from areas of residence, traits, customs peculiar to an individual band, and sometimes the name of an original or notable chief. Many had already adopted the English or French names imposed upon them by trappers, explorers and settlers.

The majority of Nez Perce bands did not join the rebellion in 1877, but the large Alpowai [People of the Butterfly Place] supported the cause morally. The names of the bands involved in the Rebellion of 1877 are listed below with their original names and their meaning, when they could be defined, in brackets. Details of band and tribal names, with explanation of how and why the names were Anglicized, are in Appendix K.

Wellamotkin [named for Chief Wellamotkin].[2] It was also known, although rarely, as the Willewah [Wallowa Valley] band, but by 1870 was generally called the Wallowa Band. After 1867 this band included the survivors of the Canyon Band[3] who had merged with the Wellamotkins for protection following a raid by a hostile Snake war party in which their chief was killed.

Asotin, aka Kam'nakka [Clear Creek People]. The group involved in the rebellion was a small segment of the greater Asotin band.

Lamtama [after the river flowing into the Salmon River]. The Lamtama Band was also called the Salmon River Band.

Piqunin [People of the Snake River][4]

Palu [People of the Rocks]. A small band of the greater Palouse tribe. This band lived under the protection of the Nez Perce.[5]

Inter-marriage between bands and even between tribes was neither uncommon nor discouraged because marriage helped form alliances of peace and cooperation. As a result the Nimipu were closely allied or related to the Umatilla [River People]; Kalispel [Camas People] aka Pend d'Oreille [Wearers of Earrings]; Wallawalla [People of Many Rivers]; Schitsu'umsh [We Who are Found Here]; Skitswish [The People] aka Coeur d'Alene[6]; Sihgomen [Sun People] aka Spokane; Tet'aw'ken [We Persons] aka Cayuse; Wanapum [Of the River]; Klickitat [People from Beyond the Mountains][7]; Qwulh'waipum [Prairie People]; Waptailnsim [People of the Narrow River] aka Yakima.

Some of the bands spoke dialects rooted in the Penutian language group while others spoke a Sahaptian dialect. These were considered Plateau Indians. Others were thought of as Plains Indians because their languages were similar to Selish, also called Salish[8] and Chinook (and also referred to as Flatheads by early explorers and settlers).[9] It is very difficult to pinpoint the roots of all Indian languages decisively because lines cross many times over. For example, the group of languages known as Athabaskan extends from the sub-Arctic into Mexico. This circumstance makes it possible, once differences of dialect are overcome, for the Apaches[10] [Ndee, "The People"] in Arizona and New Mexico to converse with the Beavers [Dunne'za, "Real People"] and the Carriers [Dakelh, "Water Travelers"] of northern Alberta and BC.[11]

Tribal names are also difficult to define, as over the decades many changed, some several times, and many modern names have neither resemblance nor connection to the originals. One example is Nez Perce. In 1807 the Nimipu received their modern name through a misunderstanding of customs by associates of the Canadian explorer David Thompson [1770–1857].[12]

In 1805 Thompson and companions were camped on the shores of Lake Windermere[13] in eastern BC. Thompson was idly wondering where to go next when a minor rivulet gurgling its way to freedom from the lake caught his eye. His curiosity piqued, he decided to follow it a distance to see where it might lead. Preliminary observance determined it was on a southern course and that it was rapidly widening. Thompson realized he had discovered the source of a river that he assumed was probably minor, but he decided to follow it further to determine if this new find might have some importance. He and his companions set out, and as the days passed Thompson's "minor river" continued to increase in width and force. Many weeks later they become the first white men to cross Latitude 49°N from just west of the Rockies. In so doing they opened Idaho's first northern portal. In 1807 Thompson came to the end of his latest survey. While he had first presumed this would be a "minor" river, he had in fact discovered, surveyed and charted the entire length of the mighty Columbia River.

Thompson and his associates encountered many bands during the two years (1805–1807) they spent charting the Columbia River. Near the Lower Columbia River Basin they spent some time with a band they thought was Nimipu. The males pierced their noses in order to insert horizontal skewers made of dentalium,[14] so Thompson's French speaking associates assumed that all Nimipu bands followed this practice. They were mistaken, both about the name of the band (it has never been discovered to which tribe the band belonged) and about the nose piercing, as Nimipu males are not known to have pierced their noses for any reason at any time. However, as a result of the explorers' nescience the Nimipu were erroneously named Nez Percé (pronounced Nay-Pair-Say: literally "pierced noses"). Over time the spelling was Anglicized to Nez Perce (pronounced Nes Purse). Within a few more decades the Nimipu themselves adopted the Anglicized pronunciation and today generally refer to themselves as Nez Perce. Why the Nimipu adopted the erroneous name is unknown.

Thompson's opening of Idaho's northernmost trail led to a further influx of Canadian trappers to add to those who were arriving via Montana and southern Alberta. As had earlier trappers who had come via eastern trails, the newcomers also become friends with the Nez Perce, trading with them freely and honestly. Because of mutual trust there was very little trouble.[15]

For hundreds, perhaps thousands, of years the Nimipu and their equally powerful neighbors, the Selish, shared a large portion of the upper Northwest plus a small northern area of what is now Utah, the Western Shoshones [Tukuaduka, "Sheep Eaters"] and the Utes [Nuut'siu, "The People"] holding the greater area. So vast and diverse was the area it stretched west from Montana's Bitterroot

Mountains to the Coastal Mountains. While the Nimipu ranged mainly in Idaho and the eastern parts of Oregon and Washington, the Selish also extended their range into southern British Columbia. Thus, the two tribes controlled much of the flat plains, lush grasslands, high plateaus, sere deserts, heavily timbered valleys and rivers that coursed from the Rocky Mountains to the Cascades.[16] Many rivers, some gently flowing, others raging maelstroms, flowed through the numerous valleys.

Although Nimipu bands ranged far and wide, the majority stayed within the plateaus and valleys of northeastern Oregon and Idaho encompassed by the Bitterroot, Clearwater and Blue Mountains. A vast grassland in Idaho, now called Camas Prairie, owes its name to a prolific plant the Nez Perce called "kamas."[17] It was a principal harvesting area because of the kamas plant's nutritious root and medicinal blossoms.

Six rivers flow through the land that once belonged to the Nimipu, all traveling diverse directions and distances before becoming one. Three—Grande Ronde, Powder and Salmon, each flowing different routes—merge into and become part of the powerful Snake River[18] as it rushes northward. Just south of the present city of Lewiston the Clearwater River, flowing from the east, joins the Snake. Continuing westward the Snake meets and becomes part of the great Columbia River that has travelled southward from its headwaters at Windermere Lake, BC, through the Columbia Valley to its rendezvous with the Snake. From the point of confluence[19] those six great rivers, now called The Columbia, rush a distance south before turning westward on the final leg to the Pacific.

There were occasional territorial clashes with the warlike Snakes, the Shoshone and the equally hostile Bannocks [Panaiti or Bana'kwut, "Northern People"].[20] The Nimipu, despite a nonaggressive nature, emerged the victors more often than not. There were also long periods of peaceful coexistence during which wiser chiefs made treaties that allowed their people to enjoy peace and good fortune. Overall, the passing centuries saw the Nimipu flourish and increase in population.

According to Nez Perce accounts and recorded American history, the first contact between Nez Perces and white men occurred in late 1804 when the Lewis and Clark expedition stumbled out of blizzard into one of their villages. The Nez Perce account, if true, shows the initial meeting did not start in particularly amiable fashion.

Winter's fierce grip was already upon the land when a group of dirty, shaggy-haired creatures stumbled out of a snowstorm into a Nez Perce village. So matted and dirty were their coats it looked as if they were large fur-bearing animals. They were so incredibly filthy and smelled so terrible the fastidiously clean villagers[21] looked upon the group as aberrant mutants descended from bears that had mated with wolves. Their first thought was to destroy these strange animals.

Village elders were debating the matter when a woman saw the group huddled around a fire trying to get warm. She declared they were humans. Then, realizing her people had never seen a white man, she reminded the elders of how, when and why she had been adopted into their band. Many years before, her story goes, at a very young age she had been seized by a Sioux war party who sold her to a Delaware band [Lenni Lenape "True People"] who took her east. After two summers she was rescued by soldiers who took her to a white family on a nearby farm. That family arranged for her return to Montana and from there she found her way to her homeland in Idaho. Though she remembered she was Nimipu, she could not remember her original name, her family or the band to which she had belonged. Luckily she found refuge with this band and was adopted into a family. Because she was unable to remember her original name her new family named her Watkuweis [Returned-from-far-away].

Watkuweis persuaded the elders to spare these men because she was convinced Whites were good people. The strangers were given food and shelter, and over the next days regained their health on a diet of kamas, smoked fish and buffalo.[22] The group stayed throughout the winter and resumed their journey the following spring. In fact, had it not been for Watkuweis' appeal and the Nez Perces' ongoing assistance, the "bear-wolves" would have become just another group of explorers to perish in the vast ranges of western mountains, and the Lewis and Clark Expedition would never have gained its fame.[23]

Whether Watkuweis saved them or not, it has long been undisputed that had it not been for Nez Perce help during the harsh winter of 1804–05 the Lewis and Clark expedition would have perished. As Lewis and Clark made their way through the territory towards the Pacific they estimated the tribe tallied well above 6,000 men, women and children. By 1850 less than half that number could be counted. Disease and other evils introduced by white men (including a number of atrocious murders of Natives, of which all but one went unpunished)[24] had exacted an appalling toll.

Four areas of the tribe's vast holding became crucial bones of contention in events leading to the 1877 uprising. The major areas were Oregon's Wallowa Valley,[25] two large areas in Idaho and a smaller one in north-eastern Washington. Laying claim to these particular areas respectively were the Wellamotkin, Lamtama and Piqunin, plus the small above-mentioned band the Nez Perces knew as the Palus. All four were in more-or-less permanent encampments except the Wellamotkins who, because they divided each year between summer and winter camps, were considered semi-transient. From spring until late summer or mid-autumn they lived in the Wallowa Valley, devoting their time and labor to harvesting the abundant plants and roots growing there. This harvest provided their winter sustenance. The band wintered in the adjoining Imnaha Valley.

All four bands sent warriors eastward to Montana each spring to hunt the wide-ranging qoq'a'lx [buffalo], an encroachment not tolerated gladly by Montana's permanent inhabitants. These were the Sioux known as Dakota and Lakota [Allies][26] and the Cheyenne [Tsitsistas, "Red Speakers"], who claimed most of Montana and the Dakotas as their lands. Other claimants were the Sisika [Blackfeet] and their confederacy of tribes in northern Montana, southern Alberta and Saskatchewan. Known as the Blackfeet Confederacy[27] it was a large, but loose, coalition. While all resented encroachment, so greatly respected were the Nez Perce warriors' fighting ability they rarely made a challenge. Thus, the Nez Perces hunted when and where they pleased; but when the hunt ended they returned to their own lands, never claiming any of the vast prairies. They considered Montana a great place to hunt, but not a desirable place to live.

Nez Perce hunters also frequented the traditional lands of the Absaroke[28] [Bird People] known to Whites as the Crows. The Crows also claimed a large area of Montana but made no effort to drive off the Nez Perce hunters, who repaid the Crows' hospitality by assisting them in fending off attacks by the Cheyenne and Sioux. In 1873, when a combined force of Crows and Nez Perces delivered a decisive defeat to Cheyenne and Sioux raiders,[29] the Crow chiefs, to acknowledge their gratitude, vowed they would never deny assistance to the Nez Perce, should help be needed. As future events proved, the Crow chiefs had either spoken in the heady glow of victory or with forked tongues. In 1877 they reneged on their promise, effectively denying the Nez Perce any chance of settling on their lands. Another consequence of their treachery was a delay that contributed to the Nez Perce being unable to reach safe haven in Canada.

Sometime during the 17th century, Indians of the plains and northwest saw their fortunes increase with the arrival of large animals never before seen in their lands. These animals were, of course, horses; they captured many, using them at first to pull heavy loads, such as bundles of buffalo hides, lodge poles and other items, on a type of frame sled.[30] And when it was discovered horses could be ridden, warriors and hunters became very mobile indeed. The Nez Perces called the strange creatures *ma'min* [big dog].[31] They became expert equestrians, a skill that changed their strategy in hunting and later in warfare.

When the Palu began to crossbreed various ma'mins they either inadvertently, or by design, developed an entirely new breed of beautiful, broad-chested, powerful animal with uniquely spotted hindquarters. They called this breed Appaloosa.[32] The Palus shared their new animals with the Nez Perces, who soon became owners of large herds. Just as an individual's wealth was determined by the number of horses he possessed, so a band's wealth was likewise defined by the size of its communal herd.

When trappers, explorers and settlers arrived they recognized the quality of the Appaloosa and offered to trade goods and commodities for horses. The Nimipu quickly realized how valuable were their animals, and white men equally as quickly learned Nez Perce men were no slouches in the fine art of horse trading. The currency of trade and commerce became guns, iron utensils, practical tools, rope, twine, cloth and other clothing material of good quality. The latter items held special appeal to the women who also became expert in the dealing and trading of horses.

Unfortunately, the trappers and explorers also introduced as items of commerce and trade Hudson's Bay rum and rye whiskey, plus myriad other vices. They also seriously interfered with an established societal structure when they and Nez Perce women united in what came to be known as "country marriage." In many cases the unions proved lasting[33] but there were also many that did not. Through death and desertion many women, almost always with children to look after, were left to fend for themselves. Fortunately for them, the Nimipu social and family structure was geared to the care and protection of women and children. There is no evidence of prejudicial attitudes or enmity having been levied by their peers against women or their children, who by circumstance had suffered marital misfortune.[34] The nuptial arrangements also gave North American vocabulary a new word: "squawman."[35]

Idaho, Oregon and Washington territories were all part of British North America by the time Nez Perces began trading with white men. Because they mainly dealt with Canadian trappers, they referred to themselves as "British Indians."[36] This was a commercial alliance, not allegiance to Britain. Neither was it a military accord, for Nez Perce warriors did not normally ally themselves militarily with anyone.[37] Regardless, they never hesitated to assist anyone encountering difficulties with Sioux, Cheyenne or Blackfeet war or hunting parties.

Cracks in the alliance first appeared with the amalgamation of The Hudson Bay Company and The Northwest Company. It widened further upon the arrival of John Jacob Astor's Pacific Fur Company. Eventually Nez Perces switched their alliance to the

Americans, a change almost certainly attributable to the attitude of managers in charge of Astor's trading posts.

Pacific Fur Company managers, as had those of the Northwest Company, treated Nez Perce traders as equals in business matters,[38] while HBC managers rarely afforded Natives equal status in any capacity. With the arrogance customarily displayed towards non-Whites by the English of that era, HBC managers, most of whom were from England,[39] regarded Indians as inferior. Individual trappers[40] got along well with their Nez Perce counterparts who in turn willingly helped newcomers.[41] Their reputation as honest traders and the most generous of all the tribes became well known. Over the years the Nez Perces were considered the most highly respected of all the northwest Natives.

Canadian trappers shared the cherished trapping grounds equally with Americans until 1846 when The Oregon Treaty was signed. With its signing, London ceded the huge territory to Washington. The HBC closed its trading posts. Most Canadian trappers and many explorers and adventurers retreated north of the Medicine Line.[42] They left, as evidence of their lengthy tenure, names they had given to Indian bands (Nez Perce, Cayuse, Pend d'Oreilles), towns (Thompson Falls, Havre) and cities (Le Grande, Coeur d'Alene, Ogden[43]), rivers (Grand Ronde, Snake, Columbia), dozens of lakes, mountain ranges such as the Grand Tetons,[44] mountain peaks and other sites. All serve as memorials to British and French influence through the long presence of Canadian trappers, explorers and adventurers.

It was during this period of adaptation that relations with Whites began to change for the Nimipu, little of which was favorable to the Natives. Until the Oregon Treaty was signed and ratified, few had paid much attention to a new influx into the mountains and valleys of Idaho and Oregon. Miners and prospectors began arriving, to be followed by farmers and ranchers. This general invasion did not bode well for either trappers or Natives, although it was not responsible for sounding the fur trade's final death knell.[45] That did not come until after 1842 when the northwest's major economy passed to mining, which in turn lessened in importance, then gave way to ranching, farming and forestry.

Meanwhile, as the flood of white settlers continued their relentless thrust across the boundaries of their traditional lands the Nez Perces were pushed aside. Inter-relations continued to co-exist between the two cultures, but were cooling. Where trappers had respected Nez Perce boundaries, farmers and ranchers, both factions coveting the land, did not. Farmers desired the loamy soil that yielded easily to the plow. Ranchers craved the water and lush grassland. Neither cared that the Nez Perces considered the land theirs, a sacred gift from *Ahcum'kinima'mehut* [Great Chief in the Sky Above],[46] who was also known as *Han'ya'wat* [Creator].

Ranchers and farmers notwithstanding, among the worst of the tragic events to befall the original residents was the arrival of the first of a dishonorable trio of missionaries.[47] In 1834 the first, Rev. Jason Lee,[48] a Methodist minister, arrived in Oregon. He had been sent to establish a mission to administer to the Willamette tribe. He was there a very short time before he discovered land accumulation could be a truly lucrative sideline. With that discovery the gospel train jumped the tracks, the engineer having been overcome by the heady vapors of perceived wealth.

Lee quickly took advantage of a treaty signed in 1818 that gave the US and Britain joint control over occupation of the Northwest. British subjects and American citizens held equal rights in claiming Oregon land, and the Canadian-born Lee, a British subject, began laying claims to vast tracts of land. This garnered him a vast acreage of the Willamette Indians' traditional lands. By 1838 he held title to so much, he traveled east to recruit settlers who would return with him and buy the land. His enticement policies were highly successful and upon his return the following year his "colonists" quickly occupied the land he had usurped from the Willamettes. The transition from humble minister to real estate baron was complete. As L.V. McWhorter laconically observed,

"The saving of heathen souls was foregone, and the gospel wagon sidetracked as a thing of cumber. Mammon had invaded the synagogue, and its keepers grew busy laying claim to, and staking, from six hundred and forty to one thousand acres each of enchanting Indian domain."[49]

By 1840, the Willamettes, already decimated by diseases contracted from Spanish and British sailors and the ill-treatment received at the hands of Lee's assistants,[50] had been robbed by Lee's colonists of nearly all the land they had once called theirs. For Lee, the acreage he sold amounted to a vast personal fortune.

In 1842, Lee's failure to tend to mission work came to the attention of his Methodist superiors and he was fired. He returned east, but his new wealth gave him little enjoyment. He was stricken with a debilitating ailment and died three years later at age 42. In his final weeks, aware he was near death, he attempted to salve his conscience by telling all who would listen that he had saved the immortal souls of countless numbers of Willamettes. Few were those who listened; even fewer believed him.

The first man of this ill-famed trio to have a *direct* effect on the Nez Perce bands arrived in the person of Dr. Elijah White.[51] He, second of the larcenous clerics, was a physician assigned by the Methodist Church to reinforce Lee's Willamette mission with medical services. White, however, no sooner arrived in Jason Lee's bailiwick when he, too, began eyeing land with mercenary interest. He also began to claim acreage. Lee realized White was becoming a real estate rival so he fired him, explaining to his superiors as being necessary because White was "morally unqualified for the position."[52]

White returned east but reappeared in 1843 bearing an official letter affirming his commission as Indian Agent for the entire Oregon, Washington and Idaho areas. He also had with him 112 settlers to whom he, in his new capacity as Indian Agent, promptly granted homesteads on Indian land—for a fee, of course. The Letter of Commission, though official, was so ambiguously worded it did not specify the limits or restrictions of his authority. These omissions he worked to full advantage.

For several years he freewheeled and dealt with any matter that came to his attention. To his credit, he did successfully settle some disputes between Whites and Indians, but just as often ran afoul of both races. Many were those who objected to the heavy-handed rules he had made up of his own volition. Within a few years so many complaints piled up they could no longer be ignored; his stewardship was investigated and he was deemed unfit for the position. Still, much time passed before he was fired. When that happened he went to Washington to appeal his case. He was rehired in 1861 as a Special Indian Agent and returned to Oregon with a letter of reinstatement bearing the signature of President Abraham Lincoln. He was shortly fired again, but by now he was a very wealthy man beyond caring what Washington thought of him. He moved to San Francisco, resumed his medical practice, which he operated for almost fifteen years, and when he died he left many documents and records with the Bancroft Library that have proven useful to historians.[53]

While Lee was prospering in real estate larceny and White was preparing to see his own ventures pay off, the third of the thieving theologians arrived among the Idaho Nez Perces in the person of Henry Harmon Spalding. He arrived in 1836, coming to Idaho as he put it, "to bring the true religion…to the Nez Perce pagans…;" his "true religion" being Christianity as interpreted by the elders of the Presbyterian Church (unless their interpretation disagreed with his). The methods he employed for the conversion of souls were part John Calvin, part John Knox, part slave driver and part confidence man. He did not, however, possess the great level of greed for real estate as had Lee and White. While Lee and White grew wealthy in land theft, Spalding remained content in building a personal empire. By 1843 he was well on his way to achieving those aims, but in so doing he sowed many seeds of discontent that eventually blossomed into weeds of ultimate ruin for those he had hoped to subjugate. His desire for empire turned his would-be subjects against him. An uprising in a neighboring mission so unnerved him that, fearing for his life, he abandoned his mission and fled.

With the Treaty of Oregon ratified and British influence gone, Washington officials began a systematic shredding of the trust still remaining between Whites and the northwest Indians. They began by sending emissaries to talk with Nez Perce chiefs about treaties and reservations. At first they concentrated their efforts on the

Salmon River and Wallowa Valley chiefs. When they showed no interest, talks shifted to chiefs considered more malleable. Though Washington ceased direct talks with the disinterested chiefs, emissaries continued to press for meetings. The requests were always declined.

In 1845, as part of their strategy, Washington approached Indian Agent White to help convince the tribes in the vast territory to consider moving onto reservations. To deal with the Nez Perce bands, White turned to Spalding whose artful manipulation had gained him control over six influential chiefs he had converted.[54] Although three—James and Ellis and Old Joseph (chief of the Wellamotkins)—had turned against him (as Mrs. Spalding put it in a letter to a relative, "they returned to the blanket"[55]) he still had three—Lawyer, Timothy and Jason—he could count on.[56] To them he began extolling the benefits of resettlement on a reservation and the three dutifully proselytized the proposal among their bands, as well as others. Spalding did his work well; so well, in fact, his three puppet chiefs, sensing their own fiefdoms were in the making, continued to cooperate with Washington even after he had departed.

Around 1850, in order to further their soon-to-be-announced proposals, Washington's emissaries began their own proselytizing by tossing out hints that reservations meant large lump sum cash payments, several years of generous annual payments, spacious reservations for each band (many hundreds of square miles for some) plus fishing rights on rivers and lakes outside reservation boundaries.

In late 1854, sensing the time was ripe, Washington presented to all the chiefs of all the northwest bands an official notice that a Grand Council was to be convened to discuss a treaty to create reservations for all the tribes. The concessions the government was promising were neither grudging nor scrimping. In fact they were extremely generous. It looked good on paper.

For the Nez Perce nation alone Washington promised a huge reservation in northern Idaho centered at Lapwai [Place-of-the-Butterflies]. As proposed, the reservation's western boundary extended from the Snake River (just south of Sheep Mountain) to Oregon's Grande Ronde River then northward through Washington to the Moscow Hills. It then skirted northeastward (past Beals Mountains to Badger Peak) before swinging south along the western edge of the Bitter Root Mountains to the southern boundary, which followed the south bank of the Salmon River to the Little Salmon River south twenty-five miles before swinging west almost thirty miles to the Snake River. The reservation's total area encompassed nearly a third of what is now northern Idaho, the Wallowa Valley in Oregon and a wide strip of eastern Washington. In area it exceeded 26,250 square miles (42,000 sq km)—almost 4,150,000 acres (see map).

The proposal's downside, so far as the Nez Perce chiefs were concerned, were prohibitions on travel beyond the reservation's limits, which meant an end to the Montana buffalo hunt. While the prohibitions did not sit well with some bands, others saw them as no problem. This disagreement created a deep rift that was never resolved.

The Great Council, held at Walla Walla, resulted in the Treaty of 1855. It was signed by fifty-eight band chiefs—all the northwest tribes except the Palu, who refused to attend. The signatories included all the Nez Perce chiefs—including those who had been opposed to the treaty. A sizable majority of the Nez Perce chiefs were pleased, but it was the Washington bureaucrats who were the most pleased. Washington's secret agenda of a massive future land grab had begun on a very positive note.

Included among the opposition had been many traditionalists alarmed at the inroads Christianity was making against their ancient religion, Wéset. The matter, however, became a non-issue with a large segment continuing in the traditional ways. All went well until the introduction of reforms to Wéset by a strange mystic and renowned medicine man of the Wanapum [River Dwellers] tribe named Smoholla [Prophet]. He furthered the split, with far-reaching consequences.

To his followers, called Smokellers [Dreamers], Smoholla preached a revised version of Wéset. He combined the powers of Han'ya'wat [The Creator] and those of the supernatural spirits, usually portrayed as Coyote, Bear and Eagle, with the power of dreams, which he declared revealed omens and prophesies. By about 1860, Smoholla had gathered a significant following among traditionalists, including influential chiefs such as Big Thunder (the former James), White Bird, Tool'hool'hool'zote and Joseph the Elder. Naturally, the missionaries railed against Smoholla. Prior to the appearance of the Dreamers, Wéset and Christianity had co-existed reasonably well. The political rift in the tribe, however, was so widened by the onset of Dreamer philosophy that it presented Washington with the perfect scapegoats: when troubles arose they simply leveled all the blame squarely on the Dreamers.

In 1863 Washington, again abetted by the missionaries and their three pliable chiefs, presented the Nez Perce chiefs with an agenda of amendments to the Treaty of 1855. The new proposals called for a staggering 90 percent reduction in the original land grant. This caused great concern among the so-called Upper Nez Perce bands. They had been the most outspoken among those opposed to the 1855 Treaty and their objections to the new proposals were intense and strident. This presented an ideal opportunity to blame the Dreamers for the opposition and they were quickly labeled "unreasonable malcontents."[57]

When talks eventually commenced, and after tumultuous debate, the result was a new agreement titled the Treaty of 1863. The proposal was carried because enough chiefs were swayed by added promises, but the margin of majority was greatly reduced. By signing away 90 percent of their land the Nez Perce tribe was left with 2,362 square miles (3780 sq km) and had lost access to the promised lakes and rivers agreed to in 1855. The signing chiefs victimized not only their brothers but themselves as well—although they did not realize their losses until 1868 when it too late. All who voted for the proposal were domiciled within the 10 percent that was left of the original reservation. None would be affected except for an off-shoot of the Asotin band who would relinquish a small amount of land. Nonetheless, the Treaty of 1863 caused all things to change forever. The final realization of what had been lost came twenty-six years later. In 1889 Washington completed the theft when Congress, unilaterally and without notification, removed the remaining 10 percent through an Act of Congress called Allotment.

The bands signing the Treaty of 1863 became officially known as Treaty Nez Perces. Previously they were called Lower Nez Perces. The three bands that had repudiated the amended treaty and refused resettlement at Lapwai were now designated non-Treaty Nez Perces whereas they had been previously referred to as Upper Nez Perces.[58] The Wellamotkin band remained in the Wallowa Valley while the Piquinin and Lamatta bands stayed in the Salmon River area. The Palu, the band that was usually considered Nez Perce, remained in eastern Washington where the boundary had been set in 1855. Wéset bands residing within the new Lapwai boundaries, particularly that of Chief Big Thunder, quietly supported the non-Treaty bands but his support was strictly moral. No members of the Lapwai bands, however sympathetic they professed to be, joined the 1877 rebellion except some twenty-eight Asotin warriors and their families who joined Chief Looking Glass—and their participation was purely the result of an army officer's blunder.

After 1863, there followed a period of respite. To Washington, the agitation churning around the revised treaty was nothing compared to the turmoil of the Civil War (1861–65). With war occupying most of the government's time, a hiatus resulted for the non-Treaty bands. The war ended with the surrender of the Confederate States of America, but there was no immediate effort to enforce a move to Lapwai. For the next twelve years relative peace followed, with only slight outbursts of unrest and dissatisfaction. One such incident was a threatened revolt in 1868 within the Lapwai reservation by the Treaty bands. It was quelled when Washington sent a special envoy to deal with the complaints.

Trouble came very close to erupting again in 1874. War loomed when a huge tribal council was convened at Lapwai. Brought together were some 1200 tribesmen from all the bands—Treaty and non-Treaty. A rowdy affair, it lasted ten uneasy days. Only the ominous presence of several companies of cavalry under command of Captain Jefferson C. Davis (1828–79)[59] kept it in check. In his reports, Davis held to the official line by maintaining the unrest was fomented by general dissatisfaction—and the constant drumming—of Dreamers. He also blamed fiery speeches made by renegade chiefs and their shamans.

Though the council ended peacefully, nerves, in particular those of white settlers, remained on edge. Later that year word reached the recently appointed Commander of the Department of the Columbia, General Oliver O. Howard (1830–1909), that the Wallowa Valley Band was becoming very restless. He quickly dispatched several units of the First Cavalry Division under command of Major John Green from Fort Boise to the valley. Green was pleased to report the perceived restlessness was nothing more than the regular commotion of the band leaving for their winter residence in the Imnaha Valley. Green and his troops, nonetheless, remained until the entire band had departed.[60]

1875 passed peacefully, but the following year saw an incident that could have easily sparked a general uprising. In 1876 a member of the Lamtama band, Tipyahlahna Siskan [Eagle Robe] was shot and killed by Lawrence Ott, a white farmer. A claim that Ott was infringing on Eagle Robe's land ended in a confrontation. Both men drew pistols and fired. Ott's aim was better and Eagle Robe fell dead. Ott was ordered to stand trial in which he entered a plea of not guilty, claiming self defense. The proceedings were barely underway when witnesses, most of whom were Lamtamas, gave conflicting statements as to which man had fired first. The judge released Ott on the grounds of insufficient evidence, an action that caused so much unrest the Lamtamas threatened to take unilateral action against Ott. Howard, fearing the situation was getting out of hand, requested Zacharias Chandler, Secretary of the Interior for Indian Affairs, to "send a delegation immediately to hear and settle the matter before war is even thought of." Chandler hastily sent a special commission to Lapwai.

In November the commission (General Howard had been included as a member) met at Lapwai with Indian representatives and a variety of witnesses, White and Indian. The commissioners, however, completely ignored the initial dispute, the shooting, the trial, the acquittal and everything else they were supposed to be investigating. Instead, they spent the entire session attempting to convince the non-Treaty Nez Perce bands to move to Lapwai. The commissioners ended the hearing by accusing Lamtama Dreamers of being agitators, intent on fomenting war. The commissioners, in their final report that Howard dutifully signed to make it unanimous, went on record as recommending an indictment be issued against the Dreamers even though the only Dreamers involved had been the deceased and two or three of the many witnesses.

No indictment was issued, but to the Nez Perce bands (and no small number of white observers) it was the commissioners who stood indicted. Had Ott been killed and Tipyahlahna Siskin arrested, they argued, there would have been a trial regardless of who had fired the first shot; and should the Indian be subsequently acquitted and a hearing convened, the commissioners would have been no less biased and would have dwelt solely on the acquittal. The governor of the territory actually disagreed with the commission's finding, but did not move to appeal the decision. The incident, or at least its memory, was to have much to do with the 1877 uprising.

The final phase of change crashed onto the scene in April 1877 when Washington decreed *all* Nez Perce bands must immediately accept residency on the Lapwai reservation. It did not matter whether they went voluntarily or were resettled by force—they would go to Lapwai. Although the general consensus amongst those involved was to refuse the order, Chief Joseph and his brother Ollokot (both of whom had been chosen co-chiefs by elders on the death of Old Joseph), were in favor of a peaceful move because Joseph was convinced the eventual return to the disputed lands could be negotiated.

Two meetings with General Howard were convened at Walla Walla with both ending without resolve. A final meeting with the general was later convened at Lapwai. It ended in agreement for resettlement and the bands began the journey. All would have ended well had it not been for two events. The first occurred when several white settlers stole horses and rustled cattle owned by Joseph's band. The second occurred the day before the final leg of the journey was to have commenced. An ill-advised Tel'lik'leen, a ceremonial ritual with warlike undertones, was staged by Chief White Bird's Lamtama band. An incident involving a horse and a pile of kamas roots stirred memories of the slain Eagle Robe. This prompted some young warriors, intent on avenging the killing, to find Lawrence Ott and kill him. Along the way they decided to also punish several others who had mistreated Indians from time to time. Ott escaped, but four farmers were killed and a fifth wounded. In the rampage that followed, farm animals were killed and several houses plundered and burned.

This outlawry prompted General Howard to dispatch army units from Fort Lapwai to ensure peace was kept. Perhaps he did not fully realize the volatility within the Nez Perce camps and he went a step too far. He ordered the arrest of the young warriors "by any means possible…" which the army's commander interpreted as authorization for a full-scale attack. Totally mishandling the situation, the attack he launched left the Nez Perce warriors no alternative except to fight.

When the shooting stopped some two hours later, the soldiers had been routed, were in total disarray and in full panic retreat. The battlefield, which extended over quite some distance, was littered with dead, dying and wounded soldiers. Many of those who had retreated, though safe, were seriously injured, with one or two dying later. Only two Nez Perce warriors had been wounded, neither seriously.

It was at this point Joseph and his fellow chiefs realized Washington had never intended to discuss the return of their ancestral lands. The decision was made to move the bands to Montana. What lay ahead for the non-Treaty Nez Perces was a long trail of sorrow and for the US Army of the Northwest a series of humiliating defeats.

The Nez Perce War had begun.

[INTRODUCTION ENDNOTES]

1. In most North American Indian languages the name each nation gave itself (e.g. Absaroke, Nimipu, Selish, Nk'meep) usually translates as "The People" or refers to the area in which they lived.

2. This was Chief Joseph's grandfather. Joseph's father was also named Wellamotkin, but was more commonly known as Tuekakis, and after 1836, as Old Joseph.

3. When a Snake raiding party killed their chief, the survivors of the Canyon Band (original name is lost to history) fled to the Wallowa Valley and sought the protection of Chief Tuekakis. Later, rather than elect a new chief and return to their old land, they decided to stay as part of his band. Although they became fully a part of the band they, preferring to remain in the Wallowa Valley year around, never went on the yearly trek to the winter site. They participated with Chief Joseph in the war of 1877. *[www.nezperce.com]*

4. Although Piquinin means "People of the Snake River" the band was Nez Perce with no relationship to the Snake Tribe, which is a band of the Shoshone nation. In fact the two were sworn enemies.

5. The Palu were also known as Naham but no reason for this has been mentioned in Palu sources. Many Whites thought the Palus were Nez Perce because they spoke Nimiputímt, the Nez Perce language. In truth it was only because that Palu band had lived under the Nez Perce protective umbrella so long they had acquired Nez Perce traits and customs. They considered themselves Palouse.

6. French trappers named this tribe Coeur d'Alene, which means "heart of an awl." This is thought to have been French slang depicting a "sharp trader"; an alene [awl]

is a tool with a very sharp point used mainly by leather workers. *[www.native-languages.org/originalnames.html/]*

7   Klickitat [People from Beyond the Mountains] but the name the Chinooks called them was the Qwulh'waipum [Prairie People]. That was erroneously assumed by Whites to be the proper name.

8   The correct spelling and pronunciation is "Selish" but modern usage has changed it to Salish. Usually connected with the Salish are Flatheads, Spokane (Spokan); Coeur d'Alene (Skitswish); Cayuse [Tet'aw'ken]; Pend'Oriele (Kalispel), Okanagan (Nk'mip); Nicola; Sanpoil; Colville; Lake (Senijextee); Lillooet (Ntlakyapamuk); Shuswap; Columbia (Methaw); and Wenatchee.

9   The original Chinook tribe is long extinct and their original language mostly forgotten. Versions still exist, however, one of which is the Chinook Jargon, the Lingua Franca of the old trading days. Consisting of some 800 words and a simple grammar structure (mostly first person, present tense) it was used as communication between northwest Natives and white trappers. Nowadays very few speak or understand it, but a number of its words are found in modern English. It can be found in place names in British Columbia and the US northwest states. *[www.native-languages.org]*

10 The name Apache is only partly an Anglicized name. It was given to the Ndee by the Zuni Indians, who called the Ndee Apachou, meaning enemies. *[www.greatamericanlegends.com/]*

11 The different bands of the Apache tribe of the US southwest had trouble conversing with neighboring bands because of dialects unfamiliar to each other. For instance, Cochise was unable to talk with Geronimo or

Vittorio, but would have been able to talk to a Beaver or Carrier despite the difference of several thousand miles.

12 Canadian David Thompson, (April 30, 1770–February 10, 1857) explored a huge area of the Canadian west as well as the US northwest over a period of forty-eight years. He was the second white man to cross the Canadian Rockies (Alexander MacKenzie was the first). He charted the Columbia River from its source at Lake Windermere in northern BC to its outpour into the Pacific Ocean near Portland, Oregon. Prior to 1807 he had opened trade deals with the Blackfoot tribes. After leaving the west in 1816, Thompson spent many years (1817–1827) mapping Ontario and surveying the Canadian/US border as far west as the present boundary of Manitoba/Minnesota. His charts of Lake Superior were so accurate very few changes (all minor) ever became necessary. He then turned his attentions to Maritime Canada until 1840. From 1842 through the remaining years of his life little is known except that he had returned to Montreal where he died in obscurity. Although his maps and notations were widely used for many years, he received little recognition until c.1898 when Joseph B. Tyrell discovered his original papers, a huge hand-drawn map of his surveys, plus a complete narrative of his adventures. These were published in 1916 and since then Thompson has been given the recognition denied him during his lifetime. Rivers, towns and valleys bear his name. [Various Canadian publications.]

13 Lake Windermere lies at 50°31'02"N; 116°01'46"W and feeds the Columbia River, which proceeds south between the Purcell Mountain range on its right and the Monashee Mountain range on its left before capturing the Snake River at 46°02'N; 117°W from whence it proceeds to Oregon's shoreline. From its beginnings at

Lake Windermere to its terminus at the Pacific Ocean the great river courses a distance of 2200 kilometers (1243 miles).

14 Dentalium is the hard, fossilized shells of marine animals (snails, shrimps, urchins etc.) that existed during the Pleistocene Epoch. Very beautiful ornaments are produced when the shell is carved and polished. All Nimipu bands used dentalium, which produces an ivory-like sheen, for making ceremonial objects, incidental artifacts and trade currency.

15 The only trouble was between the HBC and the Northwest Company, but in later years the merger of the two companies forced the French- and English-speaking trappers to work side by side as employees of the HBC. This made life easier for the Nez Perce. [Author's files.]

16 These rivers were generically referred to as Uchuck [Great Water] in the widely used Chinook Jargon. [www.indianlanguages.com]

17 The bulbs of this plant *(Camassia quamash)* were once the staple food of the Nez Perce, second only to salmon. A member of the lily species, its bulb was prepared for eating in much the same way as the modern potato. Camas grew throughout the northwest and was harvested by many tribes. *[www.ehow.com/]*

18 According to one legend the Snake River was misnamed by the first white explorer to set eyes on it. He asked his Shoshone guide what the river was called. The guide replied in sign language meant to indicate, in effect, "river of many bends and turns." The explorer misunderstood the signs and thought his guide's undulating hands and arms were describing a snake in motion. Whether this story is correct is difficult to determine. It does sound plausible, however. [Author's files.]

19 The point of confluence is now submerged in a series of reservoirs, part of a dam system built years ago.

20 Scottish trappers translated Bana'kwut as Bannock because those Natives ate flat bread that resembled bread Scots call bannock.

21 Nez Perces bathed as often as possible, sometimes twice a day, because their traditional religion, Wéset, taught that clean water, warm or frigid, cleansed not only the body but the spirit. Thus, they cared not if the water at hand was a lake, a river or a stream; nor did they care if the water was warmed by the summer sun or chilled by the icy breath of the North Wind Spirit. Following the surrender in 1877, the bedraggled Natives from the Bear's Paw surrender astounded their guards and some onlooking citizens by shedding their ragged clothing and plunging into the frigid waters of the Missouri River for a communal bath. [J. Diane Pearson, *The Nez Perces in the Indian Territory*, 56–58.]

22 According to entries in diaries of members of the Lewis and Clark expedition, their first reaction to Native food was not pleasant. The food was too rich in protein and the unfamiliar diet upset their digestive systems. After several days they eventually got used to it, they all wrote, and thereafter enjoyed it.

23 This account is not verifiable. Nez Perce storytellers are adamant in averring to its truthfulness, but a thorough reading of the Lewis and Clark journals and diaries (a massive 1100 pages) fails to reveal any mention of this encounter. However, it is unlikely that anyone of that party would have been anxious to report such a predicament. On the other hand, the story may be true but relates an encounter with a different group. As we know, legend has a habit, over the years, of combining one account with another. This may well be the case

here. [*Lewis & Clark Journals 1804–1806,* National Archives, Washington, USA.]

24   Between 1855 and 1885 in excess of 35 random and wanton murders of Nez Perce men and women by white outlaws, ranchers and miners are recorded, plus no less than four hangings ordered by army officials on grounds of "on suspicion," which covered anything from alleged theft to perceived conspiracy. Of the civilians who were involved in the 35 murders only one was tried for his offence. According to Ora B. Hawkins, Idaho State Historian, in a letter to L.V. McWhorter, dated 21 May, 1941, James Picket was tried in the 1st Judicial Court (Idaho County) in May 1873 for the murder of a Nez Perce woman. He was found guilty and sentenced to death. The judgment was affirmed by the Idaho Territory Supreme Court in 1874. There is, however, no record showing the sentence was ever carried out. [McWhorter, *Hear Me My Chiefs,* 116–131. See also fn#15 on page 126.]

25   In the Nez Perce language Wallowa means "Valley of Winding Rivers."

26   In the Souxian languages both words mean Allies.

27   This much feared Alberta–Montana confederacy, which controlled the western regions, was made up of Sisika [Blackfeet], Peigan [Short Robes] and Kainai [Many Chiefs] aka The Blood. Sometimes thought of as members—but were not—were A'aninin [White Clay People] (Gros Ventre); Lakota [Allies] aka Assiniboine [Cooks With Stones]. The two latter tribes resented the intrusions nonetheless. The Assiniboine excepted, Nez Perce hunters were rarely troubled by Blackfoot tribes, mostly out of respect for their fighting prowess.

It was thought for decades the Blackfoot were so-called because they blackened their moccasins with soot from their campfires. This is erroneous. The name comes from an Indian word meaning Black Legs. (Touchie: *Bear Child*. Passim.)

28 The rugged Absaroke Mountains range is named for the Crow nation.

29 The Battle of Pryor River, 1873. The defeat was so decisive the Sioux and Cheyenne never again launched an attack against the Crows. *[www.nezperce.com]*

30 The device was similar to what Whites called a *travois* in which two poles of even length were bound at the top with one or two short poles as cross-members. The result was an A-frame. These devices were used for hauling by fur trappers, but whether they introduced it to North American Natives or the introduction was the other way around, no one is certain. It seems very reasonable to think both cultures had invented it independently.

31 Horses were unknown in North America until introduced by Spaniards c.1520. The horses that appeared in the northwest were of various breeds, mostly escapees from Spanish, English and French explorers. The feral herds worked their ways westward and became known as mustangs. Captured and tamed, the horse changed the Indians' way of life in many ways. Because there was no Indian word for horse, and most Indians first thought them to be a species of dog, many tribes labeled them "big dogs." The Nez Perces acquired horses late 16th century.

32 Named for the Palouse tribe, the first to breed the "spotted horse," Appaloosa means "of the Palu." The breed is internationally famous and much sought after.

33 Some notable explorers and trappers whose marriages with northwest Indian women had clerical blessing or otherwise lasted the lifetime of one of the spouses include Alex Potts, Peter Skene Ogden, William Craig,

David Thompson, James Douglas, John "Kootenai" Brown, Andrew Garcia and Arthur Place. [Author's files and various sources.]

34 A number of Nez Perce residents of Idaho and Washington have surnames denoting their grandfathers were Canadian trappers or traders. [Author's conversations with various Nez Perce contacts.]

35 This was not a new word to the Nimipu as they had an equivalent word that referred to, but did not explicitly define, hermaphrodites. Although hermaphrodites were not unknown among Native people, no one knew if such a person should be considered male or female. Thus, they were considered, "People-with-Two-Spirits." A word was coined indicating a person who was at the same time a man and a woman. The Nez Perce word is not listed in their modern dictionary, but it was likely similar to one of other known words in Penutian or Sahaptian languages: Winkte [Sioux-Lakota] or Heemaneh [Cheyenne]) Both translate to English as "squawman."

There is no evidence of outright malevolence, discrimination or persecution against them. Nez Perces treated them without prejudice; in some bands they were considered almost sacred. Some families considered it good luck omen if such a child was born into it. There was at least one such person in Chief Joseph's band. He would join the warriors some days for hunting and on others would work with the women. One Nez Perce woman related the situation as being on "a day-to-day basis. No one knew what he would be until morning when he would emerge from his teepee dressed either as a warrior or a woman."

To white people, however, "squawman" had a very different and often derogatory denotation. Their definition came about when intolerant white men and women (one being a biased Ursaline nun who was also her convent's official historian) seized yet another opportunity to place a discriminatory label on white men who chose to marry an *esquao*—another authentic Indian word. Over the years esquao was Anglicized to squaw and used by some whites in a derogatory fashion. Esquao, a familiar word in many Indian languages is a noun meaning woman, single or married. [McWhorter. *Hear me My Chiefs*. See also: www.audioenglish.net/dictionary.]

36 When Sitting Bull and his people fled to Canada in 1876 he, citing the circumstances of the Santee Sioux who had settled in Manitoba, c.1825, claimed his Sioux followers were also "British Indians" but his claim found no favor with Ottawa. [*Sitting Bull's Boss*, 110–11.]

37 In 1847, in an unfortunate but isolated episode, a small group of disgruntled braves from a never-identified Nez Perce band joined with a Cayuse band that killed and wounded many residents of the Whitman Mission near the Walla Walla River. This was the action that so frightened Henry Spalding that he and his wife fled Idaho. His flight necessitated the temporary closing of the Mission in Lapwai.

38 One of the more notable of the American managers was the infamous Alexander Harvey. Although remembered mainly as a psychotic killer (he shot and killed a trapper when he, wrongly, thought the man had stolen one of the post's pigs), and was equally renowned for mistreating his employees, he always treated Indians fairly in his dealings with them. [Meyers, *Wild Canadian West*, 113.]

39 Scottish and Irish HBC managers, on the other hand, were nearly always respectful toward Indians and traded fairly with them. Perhaps this was because they were also often looked down on by their English counterparts.

40 Unfortunately, the trappers introduced their new friends to several evils, not the least of which was whiskey and rum. Later, when the infamous whisky runners from Fort Benton found the trails leading to Canada had been closed by the NWMP, they expanded their trade beyond the Bitterroot Mountains; alcohol began to flow overly freely. Despite the chiefs' efforts to stop the runners' nefarious trade, alcohol became a problem among the more vulnerable youth. [Debo, Angie, *A History of the Indians of the United States,* 108.]

41 Generally, Indian nations willingly gave help to Whites upon request. The problem lay in the paranoid fear Europeans had of Indians, whom they perceived as savages. The famed Donner Party came to grief in the mountain pass that now bears its name only because they were too afraid of the Utes (generally a friendly tribe) to ask for help. The Utes watched the long line of wagons snake across their lands and would have helped—*but they were never asked.* [Author's files.]

42 The Plains and Plateau Indians referred to the international border (49°N) as the Medicine Line. This was because they felt "good medicine" existed north of the line and "bad medicine" existed to the south. They were, of course, comparing harsh treatment they often received from the US Army to the more moderate approach in dealings with Canadian settlers and officials.

43 Ogden, Utah is named for Peter Skene Ogden [b. Montreal, 1790; d. Oregon, 1854]. Born of American parents who had moved to Canada prior to the 1776 revolution, he became an employee for the HBC and went west. He spent his entire life as a trapper, adventurer and explorer, earning great renown in Canada's Northwest Territory, BC, Idaho, Utah, Oregon and Washington. He was a highly respected friend of many northwest tribes, including the Nez Perce. Ogden's

consort of many years (they refused to marry) was Julia Mary Rivet [1785–1886] daughter of a Canadian trapper and a Nez Perce woman. Julia was a widow whose first husband had been a Salish chief. She became equally famed as an adventurer who could outride and outshoot any man. Ogden's death left Julia heartbroken. She left Oregon for BC to settle near family members at Lac le Hache. Her grave is there. [Cline, Gloria Griffen, *Peter Skene Ogden and the Hudson's Bay Company*; Thrapp, Dan, *Encyclopedia of Frontier Biography*, 1075–6; Binns, Archie, *Peter Skene Ogden: Fur Trader.*]

44 Americans often become slightly embarrassed when they are informed of the meaning of the name of those mountains. French-Canadian trappers, a risque lot generally, decided that particular range of mountains reminded them of womanly breasts. *Teton*, a French noun, means breast. In French-Canadian dialect it is used more as a slang term to describe a very ample bosom of a full-figured woman. Thus, *Les Grande Tetons*. English slang is similar. [*Collins Gem French Dictionary*, 385.]

45 The Napoleonic Wars (1796–1815) plunged the European market into such drastic descent the fur trade all but disappeared. Trapping quickly declined in economic importance, recovering only slightly after that war ended. By 1842 fashion changes saw beaver hats give way to silk toppers and the trade in beaver fur was finished. The market once again collapsed, never to recover to any great extent.

46 In fact, "Great Spirit Chief Above" is an improper translation that came into usage through repetition and missionaries' lack of understanding, or refusal to learn, the Natives' various languages and dialects. The Plains, Plateau and Coastal Natives rarely, if ever, referred to their deity as "Great Spirit." To the Sioux, for instance, their deity was "The Everywhere Spirit" and to the

Kwate, a coastal tribe, he was "The Changer." To the Nez Perce, both *Ahcum'kinima'mehut* and *Han'ya'wat* meant simply "Creator."

47   Missionaries did untold damage over the years, mostly through ignorance and fear of the Natives' beliefs and the meanings of their religions' rituals. They criticized the Indians' practice of having several wives (totally oblivious to the reasons) and were met with reminders from their Native converts that "the Sky Book [Bible] tells us Solomon had 700 wives." Their prejudicial insistence that converts must have their hair shorn (to distinguish them from Traditionalists and Dreamers who kept their hair long) resulted in a slowing of conversions. Finally, one exasperated Indian chief told a missionary, "If the Creator had a rule that long hair would exclude people from entering his heaven he would have created all persons bald." Conversions also slowed because Natives had trouble envisioning a supposedly benevolent god who would doom anyone to an eternity in a dark land of intense fire and suffering. Their Creator did not have such an afterworld. Many Natives returned to their former beliefs—or as the missionaries lamented, "returned to Egypt" or "went back to the blanket." Notables include many important chiefs and one James Reuben, a Nez Perce warrior who had converted and was later ordained as a Presbyterian minister. He, too, eventually "returned to Egypt." [McWhorter, *Hear Me My Chiefs,* Ch.1V, 50–74. See also: Appendix J.]

48   Jason Lee was born in Stanstead, Quebec, Canada on June 28, 1803. He became a minister in 1825. Clifford M. Drury, a leading historian of Protestant missionaries and missions of the northwest, determined him to be "a good man, but he made mistakes of judgement." Lee married twice, both mates predeceasing him, and he had one daughter. He died in New York on March 12, 1845. In

1906 his remains were reburied at Salem OR. [*Dictionary of American Biography*. Information by C.M. Dury.]

49 McWhorter, L.V., *Hear Me My Chiefs,* 53.

50 Lee visited the missions run by Spalding and Whitman in 1837 at which time he advised them to use harsh methods to punish miscreant Indians. He wrote in a letter to Daniel Lee, a nephew, that Spalding "has had troubles with [his converts] but the truth is they are *Indians*. Both Mr. W. [Whitman] and Mr. S. [Spalding]… when their people deserve it let them feel the lash." Lee had long before instructed his own co-workers, "Let not the Indians trifle with you, let them know that you must be respected, and when they intentionally transgress bounds, make them feel the weight of your displeasure." He was referring to the use of the whip. [Drury, C.M., *Henry Harmon Spalding*, 180.]

51 White was born in New York State, c. 1805. He became a physician in 1837. Following his eventual dismissal (1861) as Indian Agent, he moved to San Francisco to resume his medical practice. He died there in March 1879 at age 74. [*Encyclopedia of Frontier Biography* Vol. 3 P–Z.]

52 Gray, William H., *History of Oregon* (New York, 1870), 176.

53 Gray, *History of Oregon* (New York, 1870).

54 The six were: Old Joseph, Lawyer, Timothy, Jason, Ellis [Sparkling Horn] and James [Big Thunder]. Spalding had earlier used the despotic White, who had more influence in Washington, to have Ellis appointed to the illegal position of Chief of the Nez Perce. About 1840 Ellis bolted from Spalding's control and moved his band to Montana. Spalding had the title transferred to Chief Lawyer. In 1843 James also defected.

55 "Blanket Indians" was a derogatory term coined by Whites when referring to unconverted Natives and those who had apostatized to their traditional beliefs.

The origin is not known. [Anthropology.si.edu./wrenstead.hml/]

56 Of the original group, two had renounced Spalding. Chief Taawis Simmen [Sparkling Horn] whom Spalding had renamed "Ellis," took his people to Montana where smallpox decimated them. In 1843, Iname'to'omshila [Big Thunder], renamed "James" by Spalding, returned to the traditional Wéset beliefs.

57 This term was used often by General Howard in his reports of various meetings he had with Nez Perce chiefs of the various bands. He used it first in reference to Tool'hool'zote, but later included all the non-Treaty chiefs.

58 Upper and Lower was strictly a geographical designation based on locations of the groups' residences. The Upper group inhabited land where rivers began their courses to the lower areas. Lapwai lay within the lower region.

59 Jefferson Columbus Davis (not related to Jefferson Davis, the CSA President) had recently (1873) subdued the Modocs at Lava Beds, California. He had been in the army since 1846 when he joined as a private and had climbed the ranks steadily. He was a brigadier-general when he shot and killed his immediate superior, General William "Bull" Nelson (1824–1862), following an argument in a Louisville hotel on September 29, 1862. Because of his military abilities and political influence he was never charged with the murder, despite the evidence that Nelson had been unarmed. However, he was denied further promotion. He was later (1865) breveted Major-general of Volunteers, but the next year was demoted to colonel and sent to Alaska. He was still in the army when he died, in Chicago on November 30, 1879, at age 51. [US Army records, Washington; and *The Harper Encyclopedia of Military Biography,* 209.]

60 Howard, *The True Story of the Wallowa Campaign,* 54–63.

Prologue

Spring 1840

Wala'mute'kint, sometimes called Tuekakis[1] by his people, age fifty-four, chief of the Wellamotkin band[2] of the Wallowa Valley, waited with no small degree of impatience several yards from his tepee while village women within fretted over and administered to Khapk'haponimi[3] [Strong Leader of Women], his primary wife.[4] She was about to give birth and Wala'mute'kint hoped this child would be a boy, a companion for Sousouquee[5] [Brown] his eldest son who, at the moment, was noisily engaged in a game with a playmate, another two year old. He could do nothing but wait because the expectant father was not allowed within—or even near—the tepee. The process of childbirth lay strictly within the purview of village women and only if the birth became complicated would a tewats[6] [medicine man] be called.

Thus, having nothing else to do, Wellamotkin whiled away the time before a small fire smoking dried leaves of kinnikinik (a plant familiarly known today as the bearberry plant). Between puffs he intoned songs of praise to Han'ya'wat [The Creator] who was also known by other names, including Tah'Mah'Ne'Wes[7] [Spirit Chief

Above]. His songs asked Han'ya'wat for a son who would grow strong, be blessed with wisdom and who in time might take his place as a chief of the Wellamotkin band. From time to time elders joined him to share his kinnikinik, discuss tribal affairs and comment on the advantages of fathering strong sons.[8]

While Wala'mute'kint sang his songs of praise he did so with a certain nervousness. He was keeping an eye peeled for any sign that he who called himself The Reverend Henry Harmon Spalding might be approaching.

Wala'mute'kint had brought his band to the Lapwai Valley in 1837 when the strange, bearded man in a black suit had arrived with his wife. The pair spoke convincing words they read from a black book and several chiefs had listened. Some had fallen under his spell and exchanged their belief in the old traditions for this man's new religion. Wala'mute'kint had also listened, had learned to sing songs of praise to Spalding's deity, had allowed water to be poured on his head and had accepted a new name—Joseph. But he was also determined to keep some of the old traditions, of which Han'ya'wat was one. Spalding would not approve, so Wala'mute'kint would listen for the snap of a twig or the twitter of an alarmed bird that might signal the approach by Spalding.

Finally Wala'mute'kint heard a lusty wail and knew his child had arrived. The sun seemed to rest a moment atop a majestic mountain peak. This seemed an omen that the child's life would be filled with hope and good fortune. Soon the junior of his two wives emerged from the tepee to inform him the wail belonged to a healthy boy of sturdy build and good weight.

Later, when Wala'mute'kint was allowed a first look at his new son, he was pleased with what he saw.

[PROLOGUE ENDNOTES]

1   The British writer, Jason Hook, author of *American Indian Warrior Chiefs,* misspelled Old Joseph's informal

name as Teukakis and some other writers followed his lead. Old Joseph's informal name among his people appears to have been Tuekakis but correspondence between contemporary officials identified him more often as Wala'mute'kint, his proper name. It is uncertain why Hook misspelled the name. A teukakis, in the Nez Perce language, is a tool used for digging kamus roots.

Where the name Tuekakis originated is hard to place. It is mentioned in two of the more important Nez Perce history sources and therefore has found its way into lesser works. Whether, or even why, this important chief had several names is not established, but I will stay with his original name unless referring to him as Joseph the Elder or Old Joseph. [Author]

2   A band often took the band chief's name as its identifier, thus the Wellamotkin band had been named for Wala'mute'kint's father, the grandfather of Young Joseph. In many studies of the 1877 war the band is referred to as the Wallowa Valley band.

3   Joseph's mother was Khapk'haponimi [Strong Leader of Women] but when Wala'mute'kint converted she was also baptized by Spalding, who renamed her Arenoth. How long she kept that name after the family returned to their traditional beliefs is not known. The meaning and origin of Arenoth has so far been elusive and has not been discovered by this writer. To Spalding it must have had some religious connotation.

4   Wala'mute'kint during his lifetime had several, perhaps as many as five, wives. Under tribal law the allowable number of concurrent wives was determined by a man's wealth and his ability to support them. This was general among western tribes.

5   Wala'mute'kint's first son was fated to die in 1865. His name, Sousouquee, was also spelled Cecushcue according

to the Rev. Mark K. Arthur, a Nez Perce whose original name was Kul'kul'star'hul. As a seven-year-old boy, Arthur survived the 1877 trek and later was ordained a minister in the Presbyterian Church. He was appointed minister to the Lapwai reservation church around 1905.

6   Although many tribes limited the position of tewats or shaman to males, in the Nez Perce bands it was possible for a tewats to be a woman. Tewats would assist at troublesome births as they knew which herbs to use and were considered to have knowledge denied to others. [www.nezperce.com]

7   Each tribe, and some bands, had different spellings and pronunciations for their deity. Because they all refer to the same Great Spirit it is not necessary to know them all. I have chosen to use Han'ya'wat, as this was the most common reference found throughout my research of the Nez Perce bands. [Author's files]

8   Two years later he would be further blessed with the birth of a third son he would name Alokat [Young Mountain Sheep]. When Alokat became a warrior he was renamed Ollokot [Frog] to honor his uncle and his maternal grandfather. As the Frog Spirit was considered very powerful among traditionalists, to be named such was a great honor. Upon the death of Old Joseph, both Ollokot and Young Joseph were elected co-chiefs, with Ollokot becoming the band's war chief. Old Joseph reportedly sired two more sons and two or three daughters with later wives, but nothing at all is known of these children or their mothers. In fact, very little is known of any of his wives except for some information about his first two wives, and that one of his later wives was named Tayám [Summertime].

[CHAPTER 1]
THE MAKING *of a* CHIEF

Naming a newborn in many plains and plateau bands was the traditional prerogative of the mother. She would bestow upon the child a name representative of some identifying feature or action of the first person, animal, bird or situation she saw upon emerging from the tepee.[1] Original names were rarely permanent, as an individual often changed his or her name following some incident, brave deed or significant event in which the individual was involved. Some names, particularly among warriors, would change several times.

However, the naming of a son who might someday take his father's place as the band's chief was the father's entitlement. In compliance with this tradition, the following morning Wala'mute'kint ventured into the forest to one of several sacred places for a period of meditation and communication with his Wyakin, the personal spirit who guided his life.[2] He asked the Wyakin to intercede with Han'ya'wat for a sign that would enable naming his newest man-child. The day passed until the sun began its slow descent behind the mountain peaks.

Suddenly, from the mountains came a sound not unlike that of a thousand war drums. With a great rumble it coursed outward, rolled across the valley before it seemed to pause for a moment before rolling back to the mountains. Wala'mute'kint realized this was the sign he awaited. The Thunder Spirit had moved from the mountains and entered the valley; then, satisfied that all was well, returned to his mountain home. Wala'mute'kint knew his child's name must honor the Thunder Spirit, for it had told him his new son would have no fear of travel yet would always know his home.

Wala'mute'kint returned to the village where he sought out his brother, a warrior chief named Ollokot [Frog][3] to whom he related the sign. The two discussed it and his brother agreed. Then they met with the village elders who also agreed it was an omen. Thus, it was determined the name to be bestowed upon the child would be Heinmot'tooyalakekt [Thunder-Rolling-From-Mountains-and-Returning].

With this first important item of business settled, Wala'mute'kint announced a great celebratory feast. Warriors hastened to select the fattest cattle from the band's vast herd to roast slowly over glowing coals in fire pits. Others rode to scattered villages to issue invitations to all to attend. Women hurried about selecting the finest roots and sundry vegetables from the supply caches with which to complete the great repast. No Nez Perce was averse to enjoying a celebration, and it was only fitting that a future chief be welcomed into the world in the grandest possible style. Such a festival, always a great event, would be attended by the entire band, plus many guests from neighboring bands that would travel a distance to participate. The merrymaking was to last several days during which a vast amount of food was consumed. The visitors viewed and admired the latest arrival to the band. Gifts were distributed to the guests.[4] The days' festivities included sports, displays of personal strength, and games played by children and adult men. Included were the ever-popular horse races. In the early evenings they gambled in their favored games of chance. Late evenings were times of ritual dancing and singing songs of thanksgiving to Han'ya'wat for sending to this Nez Perce band such a child. All assured Wala'mute'kint his baby son would one day be a chief.

Days later, with festivities ended and the last guest departed, Chief Wala'mute'kint presented his child to the Reverend Spalding to have the water poured on his head. Clearly displeased that the celebration had been held with heathen trappings of the old traditions, the glowering clergyman stoically curbed his displeasure, baptized the newest member of the band and then bestowed upon him a new name—Ephraim.

Wala'mute'kint did not like the new name and said so, but Spalding refused to change it. The old chief then returned the baby to the women, for to them would fall the responsibility for the little one's training and care for the next couple of years. When he entered his third year of life young Ephraim was returned to Spalding for enrolment in the mission school—and it was at this point where the youngster showed indications of having a mind of his own. He steadfastly refused to answer to his Biblical name, which did not sit well with either the Reverend Spalding or his wife, the brooding Eliza.

To Spalding's credit, he did discuss this show of rebellion with Wala'mute'kint and the child's name was changed to Ibrahim (which immediately drew the chief's veto) and then to Abraham. The little boy, however, again refused to answer to this name, a situation that lasted several weeks until Spalding conceded by renaming the boy Joseph. Normally, the feelings or opinions of a two-year-old child would neither be considered nor would it result in such a series of changes, but even Spalding had to admit this child was determined. His observation proved correct when the boy accepted his final Biblical name.[5]

Since two Josephs in the same family seemed complicated, Spalding began to refer to Wala'mute'kint as Joseph the Elder and his son as Joseph the Younger. Within months white acquaintances of the tribe began to call the pair Old Joseph and Young Joseph. The names became permanent.

Young Joseph spent the next two years in attendance at the mission school, but whatever subjects he might have been taught, one was not English. His grasp of the language never advanced beyond a very basic conversational level. This may have been as simple a matter as not wishing to learn the language, because as an adult he was far from illiterate. From his early teenage years he proved himself fluent and eloquent in Nimiputímt, his native tongue. By his early twenties he was equally fluent in several dialects including the Chinook jargon,[6] the lingua franca of the northwest.

The future chief's education, however, did not truly begin until 1845, the year Wala'mute'kint fell out with Spalding. He removed his band's children from the mission school and returned to the Wallowa Valley. Neither the break nor the move was impulsive. From 1843 the old chief had viewed with increasing alarm the harsh treatment Spalding had begun to inflict upon his converts. Kind words and friendly persuasion had given way to the whip and the boot. Spalding, influenced by Lee and White, both of whom considered Indians better controlled through punishment than moderation, had returned to methods he had learned in earlier days at an eastern reservation.[7] By 1844, the whip became the symbol of Spalding's authority and it was laid onto the backs of anyone he considered rebellious or unruly. Whipping included women and children, to the dismay of most of the chiefs, for in Nez Perce society only miscreant males were subject to corporal punishment, and even then such treatment was rare.

By 1845 Wala'mute'kint had seen enough, as had his fellow chief and friend, Inametoom'shila [Big Thunder], who had been renamed "James" by Spalding. Both sought the advice of William Craig,[8] a trapper married to Inametoom'shila's daughter Pah'tis'sah, whom Craig called Isobel. Although Craig later saved Spalding's life, he was certainly not his friend. Craig had also seen the rising violence and was growing increasingly concerned. When informed the children were being subjected to Spalding's wrath he confronted the missionary, but Spalding refused to talk with him. Craig advised the chiefs to withdraw their children from Spalding's influence. Inametoom'shila acted immediately but Wala'mute'kint delayed his decision until later in the year when finally he, too, had seen enough.[9]

Once the band returned to Wallowa, Young Joseph was returned to the women and shamans and his education as a future chief began. During the next several years he learned the skills, customs, laws and mores necessary for success within the Nez Perce social structure. When he was older he was given to the warriors who taught him to hunt, trap[10] and use the weapons available to them, including firearms that were beginning to open the next chapter in the history of the northwest. He learned to make arrows and tools, as well as to construct the elaborate and beautiful ceremonial bows made from the horns of the Dahl ram.[11] He learned to handle and care for the Appaloosas [ma'mins] and the hunting and war horses [sik'ems]. He was taught to herd and care for the huge cattle herd owned by the Nez Perces.

When he was about age twelve he was sent into the woods to meet his Wyakin and was then initiated into the warrior ranks in the ceremonial Sun Dance. Although he was considered a warrior, there is no evidence that he participated in major hunts, and there are no indications he ever went on a raiding party. His future as a band chief was equivalent to what white society refers to as a civic administrator. As such, he would be primarily responsible for the safety and well being of children, elders, women and others who were not warriors. In order to learn the finer points of this important task he was required to remain close to home. Diplomacy and mediation were considered tasks more important for a band chief than hunting buffalo or counting coup over fallen adversaries.

The young man learned his lessons well, and when the time came he was fully prepared to step forward and take his place as chief of the Wellamotkin Band. History shows he did his work well. Had it not been for the treachery and deceit of white settlers and ranchers, aided and abetted by Washington politicians and bureaucrats, he would have, in all probability, led his people to a negotiated and lasting peace within white society. Unfortunately, treachery and deceit is akin to cancerous cells; if allowed to develop they do so without restraint. As Joseph and his fellow Nez Perce chiefs were soon to discover, such a condition is impossible to stop.

[CHAPTER I ENDNOTES]

1   This procedure resulted in such names as Soaring Eagle, Bird Alighting, Running Deer, Pretty Wolverine, Good

(or Bad) Young Man and Standing Wolf. [*Compendium of Indian Names,* several editions.]

2 Each man and woman had a personal guiding spirit the Nez Perces called a Wyakin. The Wyakin's totem was usually a simple item—a feather, a piece of fur or even a stone with some remarkable feature. The totem was kept close to its holder for a lifetime. Wyakins were believed to guide individuals through life, making it more like intuition than comparisons to Christianity's guardian angels or the benevolent Djinns of Islam. [*Oxford Encyclopedia,* 1998.]

3 To be named for the Frog-god was a great honor. The Frog Spirit held a high place in the spiritual hierarchy of the northwest Indians. Frog-god was not far below Coyote-god in importance as an ally and advisor to the Great Spirit. [*Legends of the Northwest;* see also: Meyers, E.C., *Totem Tales,* Surrey, BC: Hancock House, 2005/2008.]

4 While such parties were similar throughout all tribes and bands, there were variations—some very extreme. In the northwest such a gathering became known as a potlatch, from the Nootka word *posh'tl* (giving). Though similar in that the guests were given gifts, those by plains or plateau bands differed greatly and Nez Perce bands never indulged in such excesses.

At a potlatch, the host lavished gifts upon his guests, but as the decades passed giving got completely out of hand. By the mid-1800s bands were bankrupting themselves trying to outdo all others. In their zeal to show their great wealth, eventually a point was reached where hosts gave away their band's elaborate canoes and all their stored food. The extravagance caused hardship and starvation during the coming winter. The final atrocity—the killing of slaves to impress rival chiefs—forced Washington and Ottawa to put a stop to the potlatch.

Lately the potlatch has been resumed, but is now extremely moderate in scope. Usually held on a weekend, the modern potlatch is a gathering for fun and games, without any lavish waste, to which the general public is invited. (The word has entered the English language as "potluck" referring to a supper gathering where each guest will bring an offering of food for sharing.) [Meyers, E.C., *Children of the Thunderbird*, 155–158.]

5   In modern terms the encounter would be considered a "shutout win" and scored: Joseph 1, Spalding 0).

6   Chinook Jargon was derived from the Chinook language, as for centuries it had been the Chinooks who were the foremost traders among Indian tribes. The jargon was a trading language of about 800 words spoken in a simple grammar, mostly in the present tense. It is little known now and very few are able to converse in it, but many words have found their way into modern English slang and place names of rives and lakes. [http://nativeamericanfirstnationshistory.com/]

7   Spalding's first mission following his ordination had been in the east at an Osage reservation. He was there only a few months before complaints decrying his cruel treatment of his charges began to be lodged against him. Before church authorities could act on the complaints, Spalding joined the group assigned to the northwest, which resulted in his arrival among the Nez Perces.

8   William Craig [b. Virginia 1807; d. Idaho 1869] though a nominal Christian, had no use for such men as Spalding, Lee and White. He despised their methods and opposed them at every turn. Craig spent his life helping his Indian friends, and to this day is remembered by many as the "Father of Idaho." [Baughman, "Such Deeds of Darkness," *Idaho Yesterdays*, Vol. 46, Spring/Summer 2005.]

9   Stories that Wala'mute'kint had fled with his band

following a disagreement with Inametoom'shila [Big Thunder] are untrue. There had been a disagreement, but it had been with a medicine man of a small band. The shaman's Nez Perce name translated to Loud Thunder and it was the similarity in the names Big Thunder and Loud Thunder that had caused confusion among early researchers. Loud Thunder had long objected to the Wallowa Valley's people occupying space at Lapwai and had made several verbal attacks against Wala'mute'kint. Finally, when his words escalated to dire threats of physical injury or death against him, Wala'mute'kint decided it was time to leave. [Author's files.]

10 The Nez Perces refused to trap beavers despite offers of above average payment from trading post managers. The reasoning behind this is not fully understood but may lie in the legends of the Nimipu. Beaver in legend was considered a sacred animal, but why that was is never explained. [Author's files.]

11 For detailed information how these ceremonial bows and other artifacts were made visit the Nez Perce internet site and follow the links. *[www.nezperce.com/]*

[CHAPTER 2]
IN *the* FUTURE LAYS *the* PAST

There were many reasons for the elder Joseph resuming control of his children's spiritual upbringing. He had become alarmed at the increasing influx of missionaries into his valley, seeing them as not only too many, but too divergent in their teachings. The disparity bothered him, as he had been unable to understand the god he had temporarily accepted under Spalding's influence and now he saw even more conflict among the newcomers. He was much disturbed when this god's followers fought with each other, mostly verbally but sometimes physically, over which group was most favored, and it troubled him that Han'ya'wat should be displaced by a god whose adherents resorted to violence when debating opinions.[1] Eventually his concerns influenced his sons. Still, although Old Joseph considered the new teachings antithetical and he returned to the traditional Wéset,[2] he felt his people should be free to make their own decisions. Thus, from 1848, he made no effort to prohibit his people from visiting with missionaries. There was, however, one major proviso and several lesser caveats that had to be honored, one of which stipulated there would be no coercion to convert others. Pragmatic missionaries, feeling time was with them, respected his conditions. They were proven correct, for as the years passed pressures exerted on the unconverted came less from missionaries than from family members, particularly the women who held great influence among families. In 1864, however, he banned all missionaries outright because the conditions he had set were being broken. Missionaries attempting to visit his various camps were turned away.

Once Old Joseph's relationship with Spalding and the mission school[3] was fully terminated and he returned to the Wallowa Valley, his entire band returned to the beliefs of the Wéset. Old Joseph told the shamans to resume their interrupted responsibility for the band's spiritual guidance and the elders again educated the children. Life quickly returned to the normal ways of the old traditions and probably would have remained so had it not been for the unheralded appearance of a strange little man, a revisionist who called himself Smoholla [Prophet].[4] This self-appointed Moses headed a sect called Smokeller [Dreamers].[5] Their beliefs utilised traditional principals of Wéset, but also included a prophecy of a messiah warrior who would organize all the tribes and lead them to victory over the white invaders. In a very short time Smohalla garnered a huge following in many northwestern tribes. His most ardent disciple was Chief Skolaskin,[6] the penultimate chief of the Sanpoil tribe.[7] Though a number of White Bird's Lamtama band appear to have been influenced by the prospect of a messiah, the vast majority of Nez Perces accepted Smoholla's teachings but discounted the possibility of a messiah. Among those who dismissed the future messiah were Old Joseph and his sons. Nonetheless, with the exception of the messianic belief, nearly all the reforms inserted into Wéset by Smoholla were embraced by members of non-Treaty Nez Perce bands.[8]

Upon Old Joseph's death in 1871, Young Joseph ascended to the position of band chief. He kept the ban on missionaries in place and continued to refuse offers from Washington to build schools for the children. Despite Washington's repeated attempts, the offers were never accepted because they always contained the provision that missionaries would operate the schools.[9] It was during one of those meetings when Joseph famously made his comment concerning the need to look twice at men with two faces. Unfortunately, while he was looking twice at one group of such men he was not paying enough attention to a second group. This group, by far more insidious and possessing a longer reach, included two presidents, four secretaries of the interior, several dozen administrative officials, and hundreds of army officials, politicians and lobbyists for ranchers, settlers and miners. He should have kept an eye on those within the Bureau of Indian Affairs as well. All were conspiring against him and his people.

[CHAPTER 2 ENDNOTES]

1. The Nez Perce never worshipped Han'ya'wat per se, but they did sing songs of praise to him. They recognized him not as a god, but as the greatest of many spirits who, as such, held power over all good and evil. However, because his "medicine" had limits he relied on other good spirits to help him keep the natural world in order. To the Nez Perce and many other northwest tribes, Coyote-god was the second most powerful of the good spirits. On occasion, evil spirits might come close to defeating Han'ya'wat, but were never able to overcome the combined medicine of Han'ya'wat and his powerful allies. The legends of lore of most western Indian tribes follow this formula for explaining how the earth evolved. [Meyers, E.C., *Totem Tales* (2005/2008) and *Children of the Thunderbird* (1994), Surrey, BC: Hancock House.]

2. The Wéset is also called The Seven Drums Religion. [Pearson, J. Diane, *The Nez Perces in the Indian Territory*, 4, 58, 238, 243.]

3. William Craig undoubtedly influenced Old Joseph's decision, as he had never had any liking for Spalding (although he did save his life during the time of the Whitman Massacre) and was very much opposed to the ways and means he used. Craig, although himself a

Christian, was opposed to Spalding's insistence the Nez Perce convert to Christianity. [*Such Deeds of Darkness.*]

4. Early researchers thought Smoholla was of the Umatilla, tribe but this has since been disproved. The few vital statistics available for Smoholla reveal he was born in 1815 into Oregon's Wanapum [River People] tribe. Wanapum traditional territory was along the shores of the Columbia River not far from Oregon's The Dalles. Because their land was so close to their Umatilla neighbors, much inter-marriage resulted. His birth name was Wakwei [Arising-from-the-Dust-of-the Earth Mother]. He was considered bizarre as a youth because he displayed strange and arcane characteristics. Smoholla was almost a midget and severely hunchbacked, but he was a warrior who proved his bravery in several skirmishes with enemy tribes.

One day he suddenly left his village and was not heard from for several years. The day in 1854 he suddenly reappeared he announced he was the new prophet of the Wéset religion. He was no longer Wakwei; he was now Smoholla. Where he had been remains largely unknown, although there is some evidence he had been with a southwest tribe, possibly the Hopi. His belief in the imminent appearance of the messiah warrior was so similar to that of the Ghost Dancers of the Hunkpapa Sioux it indicates he had spent some time with them and may have been a disciple of Sitting Bull. He attracted followers as his teachings quickly spread far afield.

Smoholla died in 1895 while in residence at the Yakima Reservation but his religion continued and flourished for many years under the leadership of his son and a nephew. It was still popular in several reservations as late as 1975 when it began to diminish, but never totally disappeared. Its ceremonies and rites, sans the Messiah belief, are still performed in some northwest reservations.

5   The Dreamer sect emphasized omens seen in dreams that foretold events. [Author's files and other accounts.]

6   Skolaskin became Chief Joseph's *bete noir* during the first three years the Wallowa band spent at Colville. For all his enthusiasm towards the Dreamer religion, Skolaskin, while on his deathbed seems to have had an epiphany. His final years had been spent on the Yakima reservation where he spent much of his time proselytizing Dreamer beliefs. Suddenly, during his final hours he converted to Catholicism, a truly surprising decision considering his lifelong devotion to Smoholla. The Sanpoil chief who succeeded Skolaskin was called Jimmy Jones. [Author's files.]

7   Although called Sanpoil by Whites, the band's true Indian name is Nesilextch'n and also N'pooh'le. Why French-Canadian trappers renamed the band San-poil is uncertain. The French word "sans" means "without," and "poil" means "body hair" (or in animals, "fur"). The root language of this tribe is Salishan. Their traditional lands stretched along the banks of Washington's Sanpoil and Nespelem rivers near the Big Bend area. Both are tributaries of the Columbia River. [*Collins English-French Dictionary,* 293 and 349; see also: www.sanpoil.com]

8   Another religion that appealed to Indians in the mid-1800s and remains popular with various tribes along the Pacific coast is an adaptation of the Christian cult Society of Believers, commonly called Shakers. Although not affiliated with the Society of Believers, the Indian Shakers adapted many of the rites and ceremonies of Indian traditional religions to Shaker rituals. It held appeal to those opposed to Christianity and still has numerous followers within a number of Indian communities of the northwest. [www.canadianenclyclopedia.com/index and Author's files.]

9   With the passage of time, Christianity in all its

variegated forms supplanted the Wéset. In fact, one requirement for repatriation to Idaho from their Oklahoma exile in 1884 was conversion to Christianity. Those who declined to convert were sent to the Colville Reservation in Washington. Sixty more years passed before American Natives were granted freedom of religion and another decade elapsed before they were proclaimed American citizens.

[CHAPTER 3]

THIEVES' TREATIES

What treaty that the whites have kept has the red man broken? Not one. What treaty that the white man ever made with us has the red man broken? Not one.
—Chief Sitting Bull, 1881

I never led an expedition against the Indians but that I was ashamed of myself, ashamed of my government, and ashamed of my flag: for they were always in the right and we were always in the wrong. They never broke a treaty, and we never kept one.
—"Buffalo Bill" Cody.
[To Ernest Thompson Seton at a Boy Scouts of America banquet in Washington DC, December 15, 1915]

The Treaty of 1855

In 1853, the US Congress, anticipating the eventual granting of statehood to Idaho and Washington, split Montana Territory to establish a new territory, which was then divided into two districts. A side effect was the fragmentation of the Nez Perce homeland into three, widely separated areas. With the majority of the Nez Perce tribe now within Idaho, the federal government saw the beckoning finger of advantage. It was deemed expedient to hasten settlement of all bands within Idaho at the same time, including the Palu band. The Secretary of the Interior quickly moved to localize them within Idaho proper.

It also seemed expedient to arrange treaties simultaneously with every tribe, large and small, within the entire northwest, east of the Cascades and west of the Rockies. The quickest way to achieve this would be to gather the dozens of tribes together in a single, extraordinary conference in which all the tribes would negotiate a treaty. Terms would be discussed and formalized. At the same time the creation of three major reservations would be accomplished. Each reservation would bear the name of the tribe of greatest size and importance—Umatilla, Yakima and Nez Perce. Within these great reservations lesser tribes would be granted areas in ratio to their population. Plans were drawn up but because of the dozens of tribes involved the task proved far more difficult to arrange than it had been to envision.

Because it was the largest, Washington felt the Nez Perce tribe held the key to success or failure: if they agreed, the others would likely follow their lead. With that in mind, Bureau of Indian Affairs (BIA) officials set about recruiting missionaries willing to work towards convincing the Nez Perce chiefs of the advantages of an agricultural, sedentary life within a guaranteed land. The missionaries in the Lapwai area, like their colleagues elsewhere, were more than eager to assist.

The Lapwai mission turned full attention to three chiefs: Lawyer, Timothy and Jason, all pro-white Christians. Although Henry

Spalding had deserted his post at the mission in 1847, up until then he had done a complete job of indoctrination on the three and these chiefs had remained steadfastly loyal to his vision of acculturation of all Nez Perces to white society. The three worked diligently to persuade their colleagues to accept the concept of a binding treaty on a fixed reservation.

Following a number of delays, the conference was finally scheduled for early spring of 1855. It was to be chaired by Isaac Ingalls Stevens (March 25, 1818–September 1, 1862)[1] who had recently been appointed governor of the newly formed Washington Territory. Because he had trouble contacting all the numerous tribes, the first date proved untenable, so the council was rescheduled to convene on May 24.

That date also had to be cancelled when the tribes involved engaged in inter-tribal bickering, beginning with an argument concerning the size of the ceremonial fire. It spread from there to a squabble about arrangement of delegates' seating near the fire. That was solved and then the dispute rekindled when each tribe wanted its own chiefs to have the honor of speaking first. Finally, Stevens managed to deal with all the differences and the vast array of Natives headed for Walla Walla.

Preliminary proceedings commenced in the morning of May 30, but immediately ran into another squabble, this time over the protocol of the ritual smoking of the sweetgrass pipe. Again, each tribe wanted the honor of lighting the pipe. Eventually that problem was ironed out but, because each chief and all the delegates[2] were required to take a puff or two, the ceremony took up the better part of the day. Actual talks, therefore, did not commence until mid-morning of May 31.

Attended by delegates from every tribe in the vast territory (with the exception of the Palu, who had declined the invitation) plus the many warriors, elders, shamans and assorted families who came as observers, the total attendance exceeded 5,000. It proved an unwieldy number.

Because several tribes were avowed enemies and others harbored suspicions of other tribes' motives, at times events came close to erupting into open conflict. With the combined efforts of Governor Stevens, his small army escort and several peaceable chiefs, order was maintained—not without difficulty—throughout the lengthy session.[3]

Governor Stevens was the first to speak on behalf of the United States. He painted a very rosy picture of the life being enjoyed by eastern tribes who had accepted reservation life. He made no mention at all of the many treaties signed that had been broken or amended in various ways. He did not tell them the original assigned land had been whittled away acre by acre until in some case no land was left. Neither did he tell them of the Indians who, being left landless, had to move onto other reservations. He lied outright about how the Cherokees had been forced out of Georgia into their new land in the Indian Territory. Instead, he told the gathering how the benevolent white father [at the time of the migration, Andrew Jackson was president] had moved them in order to protect them from bad white men; but he did not mention Jackson's malevolent hatred of Indians. Stevens painted a picture of honorable and solicitous dealings in helping the Cherokees over twenty years to establish their own country, form their own government, enact their own laws and build their own schools. He did not mention the facts that had led to their vacating their ancestral lands for their new home. Stevens, as he had before and would do again, was willing to tell the most outrageous lies to gain the needed marks on treaty papers. He knew full well on the day he spoke his glowing words of welcome the 1855 Treaty would be broken in the same despicable manner as had a hundred previous treaties.

As the next ten days progressed, most of the talks centered around distribution of land. Stevens' orders were to ensure each band had land apportioned according to its population; and as well he was also to consider the land already under white settlement. His orders were to specify assurances that future settlers would not encroach on reservation land. As events transpired, that concern was no more than lip service. Neither settlers nor the federal government had qualms about appropriating reservation land.

As the largest tribe, the Nez Perce reservation was entitled to the most acreage, a decision fully supported by most Nez Perce chiefs. There were those, in particular Chief Eagle-from-the-Light and Chief Apis Wahykits [Flint Necklace] aka Looking Glass the Elder, who opposed it. Naturally, many small tribes had no enthusiasm to the proposed allotment ratio, so that set off more disputes. These dissenting chiefs wanted separate meetings in order to deal exclusively with the matter of each reservation remaining within traditional holdings. Stevens assured them all that traditional lands would be honored. The chiefs eventually accepted this as having been spoken sincerely. It took time to settle many smaller complaints, but Stevens pacified the concerns of smaller tribes with assurances. Before three years had elapsed all would come to regret their acceptance.

Throughout the meeting and the threats of potential melees, Nez Perce chiefs remained totally peaceful. They could afford to because their warriors were in the majority, but by treading cautiously they avoided conflicts. Regardless, at times they came close to becoming involved in disputes, one example being the spread of a rumor concerning an alleged Cayuse plot against Stevens and his entourage. Upon hearing the rumor, Chief Lawyer sought out Stevens to offer his protection by relocating his campsite beside Stevens' camp. The Cayuse chiefs denied plotting against anyone, and indeed there had been no such plot. Lawyer, according to Nez Perce reports, was merely playing his usual political games in an effort to curry favor.[4]

Finally, on June 11, the conference came to an end. Governor Stevens and all the various chiefs including all the Nez Perce chiefs[5] finalized and signed the Treaty of 1855, although at least ten dissenting chiefs signed with varying degrees of reluctance. One objection concerned prohibitions on hunting and travel outside the reservations. The ten signed only because of the Nez Perce reservation's huge area and Stevens' personal assurance that no white man would ever be allowed to settle within the boundaries without the express permission of the Nez Perce chiefs. In fact, so far as those chiefs—and several from other tribes—were concerned, the travel and hunting prohibitions were really moot. None had any intention of obeying the restrictions.

Within a few years the compliant chiefs who thought they had gained the upper hand in the negotiations realized they had not profited at all. Washington had, in effect, emulated the farmer of fable who, when his mule stubbornly refused to pull his wagon, dangled a carrot on a stick just inches from mule's mouth. The Nez Perce chiefs—as did all the others—reached for the carrot but, like the fabled mule, failed to grasp it.

The reward the Nez Perce chiefs thought was within their grasp had been the treaty's clear statement that committed the federal government to pay the Nez Perce tribe $200,000[6] annually for 25 years.[7] The government would also, through resident Indian Agents, supply many basic staples such as sugar, coffee, tea, flour and salt. Other amenities were promised as well, including clothing and rifles and ammunition for hunting. Also included was a monthly allotment of tobacco. The federal government, the treaty promised, would supply the Indians all tools and implements needed to assist in the transition from their semi-nomadic past to a better future based on ranching and agriculture.

Within a few months the chiefs also began to realize Stevens' assurances against encroachment by Whites were meaningless; and only a slightly longer time passed before they saw most of the other promises were also empty. It had clearly been a land grab. The pact was later dubbed the Thieves' Treaty.

With the treaty safely signed but not yet ratified by Congress, Washington embarked upon what had become its stock in trade in dealing with treaties. Terms were changed unilaterally while others were simply erased or ignored. The bureaucrats began systematically whittling away at the terms on which Governor Stevens and the chiefs had agreed. The next step of amendment was the annual payments of the promised annuity: they became sporadic, were usually short of the agreed amount and some years produced no payment at all.

Meanwhile, the three chiefs who had orchestrated the agreement reaped their rewards, which included positions of influence within the Lapwai reservation, very heady stuff for each. None had ever enjoyed any influence outside his own band, but now each had the opportunity to develop a personal fiefdom. Lawyer probably gained the most. Prior to 1855 the most reward he had earned was the irrelevant title Head Chief of the Nez Perce, initiated by Spalding in 1843. First bestowed upon Chief Twvish Sisimnen [Sparkling Horn] (1809–1848), who became "Ellis" when Spalding baptized him,[8] Chief Twvish Sisimnen relinquished both the title and his baptismal name in 1846 when he angrily fell out with Spalding. The title had impressed no one. The reason for disdain was simple: under Nez Perce law there was such position as tribal chief. In fact, it was absolutely proscribed.

When Ellis quit, Lawyer was given the appointment. It was also met with total indifference because few within the numerous bands held Lawyer in any great respect. Nonetheless, though aware the title was without cogency, Lawyer felt honored that his bureaucrat masters had bestowed it upon him, so he accepted it. When Washington decided it deserved a small monthly salary he found some enjoyment as well, despite there being more than a few months when he received no payment. The check, it appears, was often "in the mail." Nonetheless, he managed to exploit the title to the point where eventually it gained small acceptance. Lawyer is mostly remembered for having done so much in assuring the Nez Perce chiefs would sign the treaty.

The 1855 Treaty was rigged from the start. Washington, realizing the Nez Perce chiefs held the key to success, decided all that was needed to entice acceptance would be to offer them an extremely large area in Idaho plus Oregon's Wallowa Valley. With that settled and the majority of the tribe sequestered in Idaho, the business of decreasing the reservation's size could begin in earnest. The bureaucrats sat back to plan the next move.

As history clearly shows, the federal government had decided even before the republic was three years into its existence that any reservation created through treaty could eventually be greatly reduced. Washington saw no reason why the Treaty of 1855 should be an exception. By 1863 the final part of the original plan was ready for implementation. The Nez Perce would be totally subdued, and the cost would be negligible.

[CHAPTER 3 ENDNOTES]

1   Isaac I. Stevens was born at Andover, Massachusetts. He was a brilliant negotiator, a gifted military officer, a courageous soldier. His term as governor of Washington Territory provided a blight on his record. During that term, following the signing of the Treaty of 1855, he embarked on policies that are considered the reasons for a number of Indian uprisings. His reasons for declarations of martial law and his actions under those edicts have diminished his prior resplendence as governor. He was killed in the Civil War battle at Chantilly, Virginia. [Thrapp, Dan, *Encyclopedia of Frontier Biography,* Vol. 3 P–Z, 1366–1377.]

2   The chiefs and delegates sat before the ceremonial fire in a semi-circle 45 rows deep. [Howard, Helen A., *The Saga of Chief Joseph,* 50.]

3   For a very interesting full account of this conference the reader is encouraged to obtain a copy of Helen Addison Howard's *The Saga of Chief Joseph* and read Chapter 1V "The Council Smoke of 1855," pp 45–57.

4   General Joel Palmer, at the time an officer with the army detachment assigned to guard Stevens and the other Whites, denied there was such a plot. So did A.J. Splawn, who lived with the Yakima Indians for over fifty years. Both men, in separate accounts, accused Chief Lawyer of trying to curry favor with Stevens. McWhorter also scoffed at the story. He was told by a Nez Perce who had also been there that Lawyer offered to protect Stevens and the white camp "only to save his own hide..." Lawyer had heard the rumor and had believed it but, apparently, he was the only one who did. No one else believed the Cayuse chiefs were planning to harm the white men. [Palmer letter to Major-General John Wool, Commander of the Dept. of the Pacific, 21 November

1855, House Executive Documents Vol. X1, No.93, 34th Congress, 1st Session, 115; Splawn, A.J., *Ki-mi-akin: the Last Hero of the Yakimas,* 28. See also: McWhorter, L.V., *Hear Me, My Chiefs,* 95.]

5   Besides the large Nez Perce delegation, the conference also included Umatilla, Walla Walla, Cayuse, Klickilat, Yakima, Spokane and several smaller tribes, with total attendance over 5,000. The conference was initiated as one to serve as a peace conference, an assignment of territory and agreement of the actual treaties to be signed individually.

6   About $3,700,000.00 by modern standards. In the mid-to-late 1800s a dollar's buying power was about 17 times that of the dollar during the mid-to-late 20th century.

7   Washington used the promise of money in every treaty it ever proposed, usually very generous amounts. It also used the same stratagem in proposed amendments to existing treaties; but it was never more than a ploy, for rarely was money forthcoming except in small amounts, and it never did total the promised amounts. Neither were annuities ever paid for the agreed duration of their terms. [Author's files]

8   Chief Ellis was born in the Kamiah area of Idaho. He accepted conversion and was a staunch follower of Spalding until he fell out over the latter's cruelty and introduction of the Book of Rules. Dr. Elijah White, the first Indian Agent appointed to the Nez Perce tribe had, at the request of Spalding, appointed Ellis Head Chief of the Nez Perce (c.1844). At the same time White named Old Joseph as Ellis' sub-chief, but Old Joseph refused it. White's selection of Ellis, who had been educated during the 1820s at the Anglican Church's Red River Mission school (now called St. John's-Ravenscourt College Prep School) in Manitoba, Canada, was apparently based on Ellis' education and fluency in English. When Ellis fell

out with Spalding he resigned the title of Head Chief and exiled himself to Montana where he died in 1848, either of measles or while hunting buffalo, but no one knows for sure. He may have been Chief Lawyer's cousin and there seems to have been some jealousy between the two. [Thrapp, Dan, *Encyclopedia of Frontier Biography*, Vol. 1; see also: *Hear Me My Chiefs*, Chapter IV, 68–9.]

[CHAPTER 4]

EBBING TIDE

1871 was the turning point for the non-Treaty bands, in particular the Wallowa band, for in that year Old Joseph died and with him passed many of the old traditions. Nez Perce bands were not strict adherents to primogeniture succession but the practice was often de facto. Elders would meet in council to argue the pros and cons of ratifying the late chief's wishes for his replacement.[1] In Old Joseph's case his eldest son, Sousouquee, possibly would have been his choice but he had been killed a few years previously.[2] Thus Young Joseph and Ollokot became the principal choices. Now it was up to the elders to decide. It was not an easy decision because both young men held qualities of the highest caliber.

    The position of band chief did not necessarily go to a proven warrior or a great hunter, nor was it expected to. In fact, Young Joseph was seen only as proficient in either category, whereas Ollokot was considered far above average in both. What impressed the elders was Joseph's expertise in civic matters. His education had never included participation in battles nor had he participated to any degree in buffalo hunts, for both endeavors meant absences of lengthy periods of time. Old Joseph had considered his son's time was better spent in learning the art of governance. The elders discussed the matter and arrived at a very sensible decision.

Because both Joseph and Ollokot were highly qualified in their own spheres of competence it seemed expedient to appoint them co-chiefs. Thus Joseph became the civic chief whose primary duty was dealing with the welfare of the people, while Ollokot was named warrior chief. He would supervise the teaching of young warriors and oversee camp security and safety.

As did all Nez Perce bands, the Wallowa Band had a number of sub-chiefs, most of whom were warriors. Each had earned his social rank through deeds in battle or leadership of hunting parties. Unlike other bands, however, the Wellamotkins had for several years recognized Ollokot as their war leader. His well-earned reputation for bravery and courage ensured the loyalty of younger warriors, and he had earned the respect of warriors young and old alike. As future circumstances unfolded he upheld the faith that had been placed in him.

In 1871 Ollokot was about twenty-seven years of age. Tall, handsome and muscular, he was famed for his sense of humor and was envied for his expertise in handling horses. As a rider he had few equals, and none could match his passion for horse racing. He was a constant winner in racing sessions held during special occasions. He also enjoyed gambling, as did most Nez Perce men; but unlike the majority of those who gambled, his participation in gaming was moderate. His weaknesses included occasional flashes of temper and a certain laxness in dealing quickly with young warriors who had displeased others, usually through an insufficient show of respect to superiors and elders. Lapses in civility were usually due to the famously lax Nez Perce concept of discipline.[3]

Joseph in 1871 was in his thirty-first year. Six feet tall and muscular of build, he presented an imposing figure. As was his brother, he was of lighter complexion than many of his fellow tribesmen.[4] His eyes, magnetic and piercing, indicated he missed nothing worth seeing. Because he spoke very quietly, some concentration was required to hear his words; interpreters quickly learned to listen attentively. Very rarely did he show agitation or impatience with the subject under discussion. His demeanor was usually calm, even sedate, although on rare occasions he showed some excitement during which his actions became animated and forceful. People were mostly impressed with his dignity, countenance, alertness and ability to discuss matters requiring dexterity with words. He was sparing with words, wasting little effort on flowery phrases so often favored by chiefs. During one of the final 1877 conferences a Washington emissary asked Joseph why the Nez Perce were divided into treaty and non-treaty factions. Joseph replied, "At the time the treaty [of 1863] was made we divided. The treaty was the cause. From that time we have been separated. We still remain so."

On the other hand, when debate required intellectual sparring, he was the match of anyone. Few were able to oppose him and none could best him in a verbal duel. On one occasion, when pressed for his stand on the matter of the Wallowa Valley being used only during the summer months, Joseph patiently explained. The land, he replied to the questioner, had been given to the Nez Perce people by Han'ya'wat to live on where and when they wished. They wished, he said, to spend summers in the valley and winters elsewhere for that was their right.[5] Only The Creator could tell him and his people they could no longer live upon the land as they pleased.

"If I thought you were sent by Han'ya'wat," he said, "I might be induced to think you had a right to depose me."

He then went on to say that Washington should not misunderstand him with reference to his regard that the land could not be sold or traded away.

"I have never said the land was mine to do with it as I chose. The one who has the right to dispose of it is the one who created it. I claim the right to live on my land and accord you the privilege of living on yours."

He then dismissed the issue with the terse statement, "We are not to be trampled upon and our rights taken from us. The right to the land was ours before the whites came among us."[6]

He presented a forceful, quietly dignified attitude to others but he also had a sense of humor, at times bordering on caustic. He always punctuated this by a quick, easy smile to allay offence. He also had a tendency to grin broadly when risible situations presented themselves.

He was considered extremely handsome by the many white women who had dealings with him, but there are no accounts that he was ever unfaithful to his three wives. Most historians agree the only white woman who did not like him to at least some degree was Kate McBeth, the acerbic lay missionary whose overall embitterment was caused mainly by her church's prohibition of women to attain ordination as ministers.[7] She disliked Joseph because she feared his influence over others and decided to become his personal nemesis. When she was assigned to the Lapwai Mission in 1878 (Joseph was still in exile in Kansas) she made it her mission to deny him access to Lapwai.[8]

Shortly after being approved as band chief by the elders Joseph began introducing changes, some far advanced from his father's rules. Although he never veered from the dogma of the Wéset, his edicts indicated he felt people should be free to choose their religious beliefs. He partly lifted Old Joseph's prohibitions against contact with missionaries by allowing his people to meet with them. However, he kept the old chief's prohibition against missionaries entering the villages. Those who wished to meet with missionaries had to journey to Walla Walla or Lapwai to do so. Few did, only partly because of the distances involved. He also made it clear that he would never consider Washington's ongoing offer to build schools for the children if it meant the schools would be operated by missionaries of *any* church. He viewed them all with equal disdain, distaste and distrust.

Old Joseph had so greatly opposed white encroachment into the Wallowa Valley he went so far as erecting stone cairns as boundary markers.[9] Chief Joseph was more accommodating. He steadfastly held to his belief that the land could not be sold or traded, but he did believe it could be shared. He allowed friendly white farmers to settle on his lands because he believed Whites and Natives could live in harmony. The sole exception was the Wallowa Valley; but in 1872 he eased the restriction by signing a formal agreement that allowed Whites to establish farms in certain areas.

He was scornful of the concept of reservations and segregation of the races, although it appears he favored some degree of separation. He viewed settlers not as encroachers but as investors in mutual cooperative endeavors, and encouraged and sought trade and commerce with them. He saw no need for formal contracts between individuals because he believed a man's solemn word was a bond of trust. A firm handshake was sufficient to finalize any deal.

For some time Joseph's belief in peaceful and shared prosperity proved highly successful. Unfortunately, he had failed to realize his beloved valley held areas of grazing and farming land too prime to keep white men from coveting it in its entirety. There was also the little matter of gold and silver and the grasp it had on white men. The Nez Perces had little regard for silver and even less for gold[10] using both mainly for embroidery purposes. They could not understand the strange hold the gleaming metals had over white men.

While both silver and gold were abundant throughout Nez Perce lands, the Wallowa Valley was totally devoid of either. Nonetheless, in their belief that all mountains held gold and silver, prospectors began to flood into the valley. Joseph objected to the trespassing miners and the shamans warned that white men burrowing deeply into the mountains were disrupting the spirits within. It was not wise to anger the mountain spirits, the shamans warned, because should the spirits become agitated they would cause rock slides and other disasters. Several times Joseph sent Ollokot and his warriors to order the miners to leave. They always complied but they always returned, usually within weeks.

Finally in 1873, naively believing he could trust Ulysses S. Grant[11] (1822–1885), the incumbent president whom he always respectfully called White Father Chief, Joseph appealed directly to him. In a letter asking for a stop to the flood of miners, Joseph asked Grant to issue a decree prohibiting the Wallowa Valley from exploitation. On June 16 Grant issued an Executive Order expressly forbidding mining in the valley and limiting settlement by white men to the specific areas outlined in the 1872 Agreement.[12] Grant's Executive Order immediately raised howls of outrage in Oregon, quickly becoming a chorus of voices from politicians and lobbyists of various interests.

Indeed, his yielding to Joseph in the matter was and remains surprising, considering his personal views of Indians and his negative opinions of their land claims. These views were a matter of record, because Grant had on several occasions made it very clear he considered white settlers' land claims held priority over Natives' claims. Grant's voice had long been heard among the many who cried out on matters of land and water rights, and he had long insisted that settlers' safety and rights meant Natives had to be severely restricted. Restrictions, he insisted, did not apply only to land allotment but also travel and movement. The extreme right of the political spectrum had suggested a time limit be imposed for settling the matter; some advocated annihilation of the entire Native population if a timely resolve could not be reached.[13] Such extreme measures were never acted on by Washington—at least not officially—although some of the army's actions indicate such decisions may have been made at command level.

A small number of settlers were supportive of the Indians' claims. Those few certainly wanted farm land but were willing to share it with the Natives; and few Natives harbored objections to sharing the land. Unfortunately, at the time in question sharing anything with anybody, even amongst themselves, was not part of the American psyche. Most wanted all the land—a forerunner of Manifest Destiny—and, moreover, they wanted the Natives, if not gone completely, at least confined to reservations. Advocates of strict segregation and confinement had highly placed allies in Washington.

One of the most vocal advocates of a tight policy on Indian affairs was Oregon's governor, Lafayette Grover (1823–1911). He was a staunch advocate of strict adherence to the law as it applied to Indian land. The ink creating Grant's signature had barely dried before Grover set out to persuade the president to rescind his Executive Order. The governor's lengthy letter in part reads:

> "Joseph's band do not desire Wallowa Valley for a reservation and for a home.[14] I understand that they will not accept it on condition that they shall occupy it as such... This small band wish the possession of this large section

> *of Oregon simply to gratify a wild, roaming disposition and not for a home."*(sic) [Underline included in original text.][15]

There was no truth in Grover's statement. While the Wellamotkins had never wintered in the valley they had certainly considered it.[16] The majority preferred winter in neighboring Imnaha Valley because it offered better shelter from winter storms and the ferocious wrath of the North Wind Spirit. They returned to Wallowa in March—or late February if the snows melted early—and from there teams of hunters ventured to Montana to hunt buffalo. When they returned months later it was with great quantities of smoked meat and many hides for tepee coverings and robes.[17]

For the others spring until autumn meant long hours of labor in the business of trade, commerce and harvesting. The long weeks were spent harvesting wild vegetables, cous and kamas roots and berries that grew profusely in the mineral-rich soil. Aside from the harvest of foods needed to last throughout the next winter, there were also plants, roots, bulbs and fruit to be eaten fresh daily. The valley supplied what was needed, including roots, leaves and flowers with medicinal qualities.[18] These were selected by shamans and medicine men. Ceremonialists also chose non-medicinal species for use in rites and ceremonies.

From streams and rivers fish were speared or netted to be smoked on cedar racks. Animals were trapped so their furs could be made into clothing or traded for goods. In mid-July, in order to enjoy a short reprieve from the heat of Oregon's summer, the band moved to higher elevations, returning to the valley floor in mid-August. By late September they would begin herding their horses and cattle into areas within the dense forest where they could safely shelter throughout the winter. Only the horses and cattle intended for barter or sales were taken to the winter camp.

At the first indication of snow, tepees were dismantled and once again the trek began to the Imnaha Valley and the winter camps. Elk, moose and deer would be killed during winter to supply fresh meat.[19]

Cattle brought from Wallowa to the winter camp were rarely eaten; they had more value when sold or traded commercially.

The Wellamotkin band's cattle sales, Grover wrote in his letter, had also become a main cause of vexation. It had been discovered after the 1863 Treaty had gone into effect that the Lapwai Nez Perces, being denied the annual buffalo hunt, provided an excellent market for beef. Each winter many of Joseph's people journeyed to Lapwai with their cattle. One result of this annual invasion by the free-wheeling meat merchants—often with their entire families—caused a huge increase in Lapwai's population. Had the visits been temporary the influx would have been barely noticeable, or at least acceptable, but far too many stayed far too long. In fact, in the view of many, most overstayed their welcome by many weeks. Most complaints centered on suspicions of the visitors helping themselves to supplies allocated for permanent residents. Those concerned complained, often vociferously, to the Indian Agent John Monteith.

While summers in Wallowa and winters in the Imnaha Valley comprised the mainstay of Governor Grover's complaint, he also made mention of the complaints from Lapwai. Later, he championed the disapproving Lapwai voices in a series of dispatches to Washington in which he demanded the non-treaty Nez Perce traders must "either live at Lapwai or stay away." His view echoed similar complaints by Indian Agent Montieth and a succession of commanding officers at Fort Lapwai. Equally prominent among the voices were those of resident missionaries who feared a resurgence of Wéset influence. Grover took up their complaints with grave insinuations about shamans proselytizing Wéset and chiefs agitating against the 1863 Treaty. The idea of reservations, he reminded Grant, was to provide Natives with a permanent home, but the Wallowa band showed little intention of seeking permanent residence anywhere.

Grover adamantly argued the Wallowa Valley could never be ceded legally to the Nez Perce band even by treaty. The government, he contended, was bound by federal law to impose the reservation system on all Native people. That alone, he reminded Grant, precluded granting the valley to Joseph because, in order to satisfy the law, Wallowa would have to be designated a reservation thereby becoming the band's permanent home. They would be legally bound to live there year round.[20] Because the Nez Perces lived in tepees, Grover declared, Wallowa's extremely harsh winter conditions would make their survival overly difficult. He pointed out settlers and ranchers, despite living in wooden houses heated by wood-burning stoves and fieldstone fireplaces, also had troubles surviving the winters. Although well equipped, he wrote, they were often hard pressed to cope with mid-winter temperatures. The Indians had only tepees and this alone, he insisted, meant they would be unable to endure Wallowa's harsh winter conditions. He carefully omitted mentioning the winter residence status of the Nez Perce Canyon band.

Grover's declaration of winter's harshness struck a chord with Grant who was certainly no stranger to the rigors of tent dwelling during inclement weather. He readily agreed the hardships imposed by the long winters would render life in Oregon's rugged grandeur extremely difficult. Had Joseph known of Grover's letter he would have been able to send a countering letter stating that winter in the Wallowa Valley was not nearly as harsh as the governor implied.

He would have agreed frigid winds produced a succession of blizzards from mid-November through February, and during December and January drifted snow often blocked trails and roads. He would not have denied there were few means of keeping trails passable and that inhabited clearings often faced isolation. He would have agreed with Grover that life during a Wallowa Valley winter was often harsh, but he would have added that lonely isolation and living in a tepee did not negate survival to people who over long centuries had adapted to every condition nature could produce.

Grover's missive convinced Grant the Nez Perces fear of winter conditions was the reason for their annual migration. Grant was never to know that Joseph was more than willing to live in the Wallowa Valley year around if need be. Neither did he know the Canyon Band remained there every winter rather than move to Imnaha. As Joseph said some years later, a tepee in the Imnaha Valley during winter was no more comfortable than a tepee in Wallowa.

It was after all, he noted drily, the same winter, the only difference being a distance of a few miles further west.

The governor's carefully prepared text and subsequent dispatches suggested Joseph's Nez Perce band should be forced to resettle at Lapwai not only because they wanted the Wallowa Valley as their exclusive summer residence but to ensure their survival. While Grover's letter implies a benevolent concern for welfare, it fails to hide its true objective. It was a lobbyist's implement for miners, ranchers, farmers and business interests, all of whom coveted the valley's fruitful soil, fresh water, lush grasslands and commercial potential.

None of Grant's cabinet welcomed the governor's views more than Oregon's elected representatives and senators. They could not overtly oppose Grant's Executive Order, nor could they override it in their respective legislative assemblies, but now they felt there was a way to have it rescinded. Using Grover's letter and messages as leverage, they began to lobby towards a successful result. Grover undoubtedly did more to change Grant's mind than all previous efforts combined.

Meanwhile bureaucracy had moved forward on another tack, one designed to hasten the day when Joseph and other non-treaty chiefs would quietly acquiesce to their inevitable enclosure within the Lapwai Reservation. In the age-old custom of land grabbers, emissaries were sent bearing gifts. A party of bureaucrats soon arrived at Wallowa to offer Joseph a magnificent gift. The White Father Chief, they told him, wished to build a school in his valley for the children. Joseph listened politely before asking who would manage the school. Who would be the teachers? Missionaries, he was told, had graciously consented to accept both responsibilities.[21] Joseph pointedly told them Nez Perce children did not require a school in a wooden house. The forest was their classroom. Neither did the children require guidance from white teachers. Tribal elders were their guides and their teachers.

Joseph had obviously anticipated Washington's strategy of converting children to white ways so that they, in turn, would convince their parents of the advantages of modern life. When asked why he was voicing such strong objections to such a splendid benefaction he curtly dismissed them with his famously short, often quoted, reply:

> "It is the Nez Perce elders who teach the young. They teach them in the ways of the Great Spirit Chief. His way is the Nez Perce way. Missionaries mean churches. Churches teach people to quarrel about the missionaries' god and the Great Spirit Chief. It is alright for men to quarrel about things of the earth from time to time, but it is not good to quarrel about their god and the Great Spirit Chief."[22]

Joseph had won another round. The bureaucrats quietly returned to Washington without requesting a further meeting and Grant's Executive Order, which in effect had granted him the valley, was in effect. But if he thought the situation had resolved itself, or that the battle was over, he was soon to learn otherwise.

Grant's Executive Order was being blatantly disregarded, usually by prospectors, but this time ranchers caused the trouble. In early spring of 1874, local ranchers, eyes firmly fixed on expansion, started looking for ways around the restraining order. With connivance of territory politicians, the ranchers began spreading rumors in Washington that Nez Perce warriors were rustling cattle and stealing horses. In fact, it was the ranchers who were stealing Nez Perce livestock. Because all Nez Perce animals were free-range it was a simple matter for a group of ranchers to round up dozens of horses and cattle in a short time. Herding them to various ranches, they branded the purloined hides with their own marks. Indians never branded, or in any way marked, their animals nor did they keep accurate records of the numbers within their herds. There had never been a need for such methods. Thus the ranch brands made Indian ownership impossible to prove.

Politicians dutifully spread the false rumors throughout the halls of government while bureaucrats within the Department of the Interior ensured the rumors reached the president's ear. Grant may have recognized them as lies, but Grover's letter had begun to impact upon him. Perhaps thinking he had indeed been hasty in his original proclamation, he convinced himself of the prudence in reconsidering the matter. By 1875, the ranchers' lobby had garnered enough support in both the House of Representatives and the Senate that Grant was persuaded to review his decree. Once again he showed that despite competence and courage on the battlefield, he had neither competence nor courage in matters pertaining to the duties of the nation's chief executive. Indeed, Grant's two terms of office proved him one of the nation's least effective presidents to that point in time.[23]

Now, in the final lame-duck months of his troubled presidency, Grant saw little use in playing champion to a group of Indians. He succumbed to pressure and rescinded the Wallowa Valley restriction order. Joseph and two other band chiefs were informed the three Nez Perce bands must vacate the Wallowa Valley and the Salmon River areas and report to Lapwai for permanent residency. Their answers were flat refusals.

Washington, upon being notified of the refusals, once again hesitated. Some officials, albeit a decided minority, were beginning to show support of Joseph and his allies' claims, and advocated delay. Others, mindful of previous encounters, had developed a healthy respect for, as well as a certain fear of, the doughty chiefs—greater than a fear of a handful of ranchers. As a result, both schools of thought arrived independently at one conclusion: there was no compelling reason to take immediate action in enforcing resettlement. Forced action would mean sending in the army, and few preferred that action, at least for the time being. It was decided prudent to await the pleasure of the incoming president that November elections had determined would be Rutherford B. Hayes (1822–1893). Hayes had been handed the presidency (considered by many historians almost a gift) through adroit manipulation of the Electoral College.[24]

On March 3, 1877 Grant handed over the trappings of power to Hayes[25] who moved into the White House and began appointing an entirely new slate of secretaries. Among the newcomers was Carl Schurz (1829—1906) who was named Secretary of the Interior for Indian Affairs. Schurz came to his new job as a champion of human rights, but soon reversed his thoughts in many ways. He had proposed a series of measures he hoped would alleviate much of the Indians' sufferings, but to his complete dismay and discouragement he quickly learned, when his advisements were declined, that President Hayes had no sympathy for Indians.[26] In fact, the new president considered Indians not only the main obstacle to progress in the west but also an impediment to border expansion.[27] Thus Schurz, during his four unhappy years as Secretary, was allowed to make a few minor changes in general policy towards some factions, but managed not a single amendment in favor of Indians.

Schurz eventually stopped efforts on the Indians' behalf and became instrumental in trying to force Joseph and his allies to accept Lapwai as their home. After the 1877 uprising was quelled and Joseph was in exile in Kansas, Schurz, the erstwhile humanist, blocked every effort to return the Nez Perces to the Northwest. At one point he colluded with Ezra A. Hayt,[a] the corrupt chairman of the Bureau of Indian Affairs, to place even more roadblocks in the way.[28] In 1881, Hayes left the White House, a one-term president. Carl Schurz left with him.

Bureaucrats in the Department of the Interior, realizing the new president was not going to instigate many major changes in policies set by Grant,[29] acceded to the demands of the Oregon lobbyists and sent another team west to convince Joseph to remove his people to Lapwai. When the delegation arrived at the entrance to the valley they were met by Joseph and a half dozen mounted warriors. Joseph, sitting tall on his horse, cradled his rifle horizontally across the crook of his left arm, the accepted sign of peace in the west. He rode slowly forward but did not dismount. He looked at each delegate individually. His piercing gaze probed directly and deeply into each man's eyes but he did not speak. The principal delegate invited him to sit and talk but Joseph declined saying he knew the purpose of their visit was to tell him to leave the valley. There was, he told him, no purpose to be gained by discussion. In

---

a   *For further details of Ezra A. Hayt see Appendix E.*

a short declaration he reaffirmed his refusal to move to Lapwai. As he had to those who had come before, he ended his statement in condemnation of the three chiefs he considered traitors:

> "no chief, Jason, Timothy, Aleiya[30] nor anyone else, had the right to surrender Nez Perce land. The Great Spirit Chief gave the Wallowa Valley to the Nez Perce and it could be shared but not sold nor bartered nor given away."

If the valley was taken by force, he told them, such an act would be in violation of the Great Spirit Chief's laws. Joseph fully believed this. The delegates, of course, did not. Once again an impasse had been created.

The emissaries' leader began to object but once again Joseph told the group to leave. Then he wheeled his horse and rejoined his companions. The warriors melted back into the wooded depths of their valley. Only the trilling of birds broke the silence of the quiet forest.

The bureaucrats had no sooner departed when Joseph sent a petition to President Hayes concerning the matter. He asked again why Grant had rescinded the original order and requested the new White Father Chief reinstate it in order that the Nez Perces might live peacefully in their hereditary valley. As they awaited the president's reply he and his people carried on with their regular lives.

Several weeks later Joseph received the president's answer. It came not in the form of a letter but as an army general bearing an utimatum.

[CHAPTER 4 ENDNOTES]

1   Some northwest tribes had hereditary chiefs, but in others the elders chose the next leader after meeting in council. Other tribes would swing from one practice to the other, depending on which frame of mind the elders were in at the moment. The Nez Perce tribes, for the most part, gave much consideration to the late chief's sons in making their decisions. Young Joseph, for example, was elected with very little discussion, but when he died in September 1904 the elders waited almost two years before electing Albert Waters, who was not of Joseph's immediate family, as his successor. The election of Ollokot, Joseph's brother, as the principle war chief, had also been unanimous. [Various sources.]

2   Sousouquee was killed by his friend, Wayouhyuch [Blue Legs] during a drinking session when Wayouhyuch felt Sousouquee was about to kill him. He survived the 1877 war and he and Joseph remained good friends.

3   A lengthy treatise could be written concerning discipline, and the lack thereof, within Indian ranks during periods of warfare. Discipline within Nez Perce warrior ranks was almost impossible to achieve at any time, and was particularly questionable during the 1877 War. A simple explanation is the doctrine of Indian warfare: A warrior's idea of military discipline was further removed from that followed by the US Army than was the American contempt for the European (particularly British) concept. An Indian warrior fought where, when, how—and if—he pleased. Their collective habit of leaving the scene in mid-battle was mainly responsible for the Nez Perce failure to decisively win the Battle of the Clearwater. That was a battle they could have easily won had all the warriors obeyed the suggestions of their chiefs. At no time in Indian warfare

were there rigid rules of war. There was never close-order formation fighting and only rarely were there charges on horseback. The Indian method employed stealth, surprise and ambush. Though effective, it was not conducive to good order and military discipline. [*Save the Last Bullet for Yourself*, passim.]

4   As a tribe the Nez Perce were in many ways dissimilar. Complexions ranged from very light to extremely dark. Facial features also differed, ranging from the rounder facial features of the Pacific Coast Natives to sharply angular features associated with many Plains Indians. Early explorers reported blond Natives among Nez Perce bands.

5   Claims made by Oregon politicians and lobbyists for ranchers that Joseph wanted the Wallowa Valley strictly for summer residence were completely false. On several occasions Joseph indicated he would live there year-round if the valley was declared a reservation. That statement, and many others, were ignored when it suited official convenience.

6   Board of Indian Commissioners, eighth Annual Report, 1877, 60 and 212.

7   Kate McBeth, though often referred to as a missionary, was a mission teacher not an ordained minister. Self-centered, opinionated and narcissistic, she disliked anyone who did not adhere to her personal brand of religion or who disagreed with her opinions. Jealous of anyone she could not outdo in discussion or debate, she was particularly fearful of Joseph for she envied his ability to command the respect of others. Kate was somewhat different from her older sister, Sue, also a mission teacher. Sue had also harbored a desire to become an ordained minister but realized it was not possible, so never went to great lengths to make that desire known. Kate resented the Presbyterian authorities' refusal to recognize female

abilities, and was greatly embittered at the prohibition of females as ordained ministers. Her acrimony heightened when she discovered Nez Perce men (whom she considered converted savages far below her station) had been ordained. In her bias she could not understand why an Indian could attain what she could not. Her acerbity came to a head in 1890 when her attitude compelled Archie Lawyer, a Nez Perce ordained minister, to leave the reservation's First Presbyterian Church. He immediately started the Second Presbyterian Church. To her chagrin, the Reverend Lawyer took most of the FPC's congregation with him.

8   McBeth was partially responsible for the placement of Joseph and his followers to Colville and was the key objector to Joseph's request to visit Lapwai to visit his daughter, and later manipulated more refusals for visits to Lapwai. Nonetheless, much to McBeth's choler and consternation, he was granted two visits. [Pearson. *The Nez Perces in the Indian Territory,* 249–50.]

9   These cairns were built at both entrances to the valley and at all trails leading into the valley. One large cairn was erected atop a hill so it could be seen from a distance. They were the old chief's versions of survey markers.

10 The Nez Perce only collected gold in small amounts in order to pay for trade goods. On the long trek through the Bitterroot Mountains in 1877 they carried a large enough amount they were able to pay for all the goods and materials they needed.

11 Grant was born Hiram Ulysses, but when he reported to West Point in 1839 to begin his military training he found, due to a clerical error, his application form listed his names as Ulysses (the name he went by) and Simpson, his mother's maiden name. He accepted the error, possibly to avoid the red tape of correcting it, and

was thereafter known as Ulysses Simpson Grant. [*Harper Encylopedia of Military Biography,* 91.]

12   Commissioner of Indian Affairs, Report for 1873, section 18. See also, Royce, *Indian Land Cessions, Pt. 2,* 864–65; and Bancroft, *History of Washington, Idaho and Montana,* 494.

13   In British North America a different policy was imposed and, although never official, the British pre-1867 intent was the same as the right-wing American segment. London advocated a policy of leaving treaty Natives more or less alone, and if the reserved land proved insufficient for sustenance the Natives could starve. This policy was used to great degree in the BC colony where Natives generally refused to sign treaties. [Archives of Military Academy, Kingston, Ontario.]

14   Grover was among those with convenient memories who could never recall hearing Joseph say he would be happy to live all year in the Wallowa valley. Grover's efforts to convince Grant to repeal his 1873 Executive Order were prompted by his sympathies with (and his financial interests in) the Wallowa Road & Bridge Company and the Prairie Creek Ditch Company, both of which had acquired improvement rights to the valley from the State. Grover also had the higher ambition of becoming a "king maker" in federal politics. In 1876 he supported presidential candidate Samuel Tilden (1814–86) and tried to influence the Electoral College Commission to replace a Republican member with an Oregon Democrat. His campaign failed and Rutherford B. Hayes was awarded the presidency by one Electoral College vote. After his tenure as Oregon's governor ended, Grover served several years as a senator for that state. He eventually lost his massive fortune through business mismanagement, and by the time of his death, at age 88, he was penniless and largely forgotten. [*The*

Courier, Vol. 28, issue 1, Spring 2004; see also: Howard, Helen Addison, *The Saga of Chief Joseph,* 94–6]

15 To read the full text of Governor Grover's letter, the reader is referred to *History of North Idaho,* 46–47. [See bibliography.]

16 The Canyon Band, a small group of 28 families, remained during the winters. When their chief was killed in a fight with a Snake raiding party, rather than elect a new chief they permanently joined Old Joseph and the Wallowa Band. For their own reasons, the Canyon people never wintered in the Imnaha Valley but lived in Wallowa year round. They journeyed with Joseph throughout the rebellion and then went with him into exile.

17 The buffalo was a truly utilitarian animal. Large bones became sharp utensils and implements. Small ones were turned into needles for sewing while the sinews became thread. Hooves, boiled with fish skins, rendered into a sticky glue of many uses. Very little of the shaggy beasts was ever wasted.

18 As did their counterparts in all North American tribes, the shamans of the Plains and Plateau Natives knew many remedies for such diverse ailments as diarrhea, acute indigestion, kidney problems and liver disorders. They stopped bleeding with the broad leaves of the burdock plant and could reduce fever with an extract of the bark of white pine and spirea. They were well versed in the use of the flowers and root of the augustifolia plant that we know today as echinacea. In many ways shamans were far ahead of western physicians of the era. [Cohen, Kenneth, *Honoring the Medicine,* passim; see also: Hutchens, Alma R., *A Handbook of North American Herbs,* passim.]

19 The warriors hunted only stags and bulls, as Nez Perce law forbade killing females, calves and yearling animals.

20 Joseph eventually made it officially known he would

agree to the valley as a confined reservation in which his band would live all year around. This statement, however, was ignored and given no official consideration. About 1897 he offered to buy acreage in the valley sufficient for his diminished band. Washington commissioned James McLaughlin, an Indian Office agent, to report on the feasibility of such a purchase. McLaughlin's report was negative, so the request was denied and Joseph was told he would not be allowed to purchase land. [McWhorter, *Hear me My Chiefs,* 547.]

21 Grant's policy granting missionaries and church groups the authority to appoint Indian Agents and run the educational systems on reservations had just gone into effect. The reservations were divided among the various groups. Due to corruption and other related problems the policy was quickly revoked when Rutherford Hayes took office. [See Appendix G.]

22 See *Chief Joseph: An Indian's View*. Reference to The Great Spirit Chief is that of the original translator. Joseph's word would have been Han'ya'wat [Creator]. The Nez Perce never referred to a Great Spirit, a term more common in eastern Indian tribes than any of the Plains Indians. To the Lakota Sioux he was The Everywhere Spirit.

23 Grant, who occupied the Oval Office for eight years (1869–77), had not been long in office before he began to show the signs that eventually proved him a weak president. He was easily swayed and lacked ability to judge character. In civilian life, both pre- and post-war, he continuously failed in business through his inability to distinguish between sound and poor investments. As commander of the Union army during the Civil War he had promoted inefficient officers to positions of high command. As president, he was such easy prey for dishonest advisors and unscrupulous appointees that

both terms were plagued by corruption and scandal, not the least of which were the infamous Union Pacific Railway and the Whiskey Ring scandals. [*Chambers Biographical Dictionary*, 653.]

24 Rutherford B (Birchard) Hayes, from Ohio, had been noticed by the Republican machine while a civil war major-general. After the war he practiced law and represented Ohio in Congress. In 1876 he was chosen as the Republican candidate for the presidency, running against the Democrat, Samuel Tilden. When the popular votes were finally tallied, the results from several states were disputed. The dispute gave the Republican-dominated Electoral College the opportunity to award the disputed states to Hayes, thereby electing him the 17th president by one Electoral College vote. His presidency was controversial and was a failure in general terms. When his four years expired he declined to seek re-election. [*Chambers Biographical Dictionary*, 696.]

25 Hayes' inaugural ball, March 5 1877, proved a much more pleasant affair than had Grant's second term ball, which to this day is considered the biggest flop in US inaugural history; and perhaps should have been viewed as an evil omen. Grant's celebratory gala featured fireworks (the only successful event of the evening) and a magnificent band for the dancers' pleasure. Also laid on was a spectacular buffet which would have been a marvellous repast had things not gone awry. Among the huge variety of food and drink the many groaning tables included 30 barrels of salads of various varieties, 15 roasts of mutton, 200 baked glazed hams, 25 stuffed boar heads, 2400 roasted quails, 65 roasted turkeys each 15 lbs. all plump and all deboned. There were 400 partridges, 100 chickens and 18,000 oysters of which 10,000 were fried, 4,000 were scalloped and 4,000 were smoked. There were 26,000 sandwiches made of assorted meats. 2500

loaves of bread and 8,000 rolls were available on which to spread 5,000 lbs. of wild game paté. For dessert there were ice creams, 400 huge pies, 150 large cakes, assorted pastries plus apples, oranges and grapes. Of course, there was also the customary tea, coffee and unlimited clarets and white wines.

Unfortunately, in the early afternoon the thermometer took a sudden, unseasonable plunge as an intense cold front swept down upon the area. The unheated building became a veritable icebox. The orchestra encountered difficulties playing the brass instruments while the guests, teeth chattering, sat huddled in their coats and robes. It was too cold to dance. The cold also proved too frigid to encourage guests (each of whom had paid $20 admission) to attack the magnificent buffet tables. Many left early and by 11:15 p.m. everyone, including waiters and musicians had gone home. [*Lang's Compendium of Culinary Nonsense and Trivia* (New York: Porter Publishing, 1980), 88–90.]

26 Hayes was not sympathetic to freed slaves, either. During his tenure, the Reconstruction Period ended and political power was returned to the southern states. These states immediately implemented a policy of segregation that lasted until the mid-1960s. Hayes wisely decided one term as Chief Executive was enough and declined to seek re-election. [*Chambers Biographical Dictionary*, 696.]

27 The concept of Manifest Destiny was by now very much alive within the United States, with Hayes a staunch supporter. That it eventually died out was not through Hayes' lack of initiative. [Author's files.]

28 Pearson, Dianne, *The Nez Perces in the Indian Territory*, passim.

29 Hayes did make one important change. In 1879 he revoked Grant's edict that had endowed each of several

church groups full financial responsibility for reservation affairs. When Hayes was shown the corruption rampant in various reservations (in particular the Quaker agency at Quapaw in the Indian territory) he turned full management over to the Bureau of Indian Affairs. The BIA immediately fired most of the church-appointed Indian Agents replacing them with their own Special Agents. [See Appendix G]

30   Joseph always referred to Lawyer as Aleiya, although few others did.

[CHAPTER 5]
PRELUDE to LAPWAI

GENERAL HOWARD'S DILEMMA

President Hayes' reply to Joseph came in the person of General Oliver Otis Howard (1830–1909).[1] With recent uprisings still fresh in public memory, Hayes did not want the kind of trouble another Indian war would bring. Neither did he have any intentions of giving Joseph concessions. Instead, he based his hopes for a peaceful settlement on Howard's reputation as a skilled treaty negotiator. Hayes hoped the general could engineer a peaceful settlement. He was also aware that no skills are unlimited, so he informed Howard he was to use every means at his command including force, if necessary, to convince Joseph and his allies to resettle at Lapwai. There was nothing uncertain about the order. The general was to meet with the chiefs and issue an ultimatum to the non-Treaty chiefs: the bands would resettle at Lapwai voluntarily or by force. There would be no variance from this final order.

Over the past two years, as commander of the army in the Department of the Columbia, Howard, whom the Natives called Atim'kennin (Arm Cut Off),[2] had visited Lapwai on occasion but had rarely dealt with the non-Treaty Nez Perces and had, in fact, little knowledge of them. In his first months in Oregon, Howard apparently considered the claims by Joseph and his fellow chiefs to their traditional lands as being morally right. Privately he confided to friends his opinion that "the government [would be making]...a terrible mistake in taking...from Joseph and his band of Nez Perces that valley [Wallowa]."[3] Unfortunately, in his own publications, though he often professed empathy with the Indians, a great deal of animosity is evident. Further, the many errors in Howard's narrations prove conclusively he never bothered to learn anything about the many tribes in his jurisdiction. His ignorance of Nez Perce society was profound to the point of being woeful.[4]

Howard knew nothing, and cared less, of the Nez Perces' hopes and expectations for their way of life. He knew nothing of Wéset or its rituals and failed to see the several obvious similarities between Wéset and his own Christian beliefs. He had only contempt for the Dreamers, considering them collectively as malcontents and troublesome pests. To Howard's thinking the only good Indian was a Christian Indian. As good a man as Howard was in many ways, he was at the same time bigoted and intolerant. A fundamentalist in devotion, he saw the Bible (more so the New Testament) as the ultimate authority in the rules of life. No other beliefs were acceptable. He considered the non-Treaty Nez Perce rituals so strange and ungodly they could have no place in proper society. Devoutly religious to the point of annoyance, Howard was often referred to with pointed sarcasm as The Christian Soldier and The Bible General; and there was irony in those titles for they had been bestowed upon him not by Indians but by his societal peers, both civilian and military.[5]

Many of his soldiers, in publications and private journals, voiced criticism over his handling of the pursuit of Joseph and his allies. Those critical of his management of the 1877 Nez Perce War were severe in their complaints of his reluctance to advance, hesitance in decision making and poor strategy against the warriors. Howard has long been subject to analysis by historians and garnered much, often very unfair, reproach from armchair generals, contemporary and latter-day.

Oliver Otis Howard was born at Leeds, Maine on November 8, 1830. He graduated from Bowdoin College in 1850 and attended West Point, graduating in 1854. He remained as an ordinance officer and mathematics instructor until 1861. He served during the American Civil War and engaged in several battles in which one, Fair Oaks, he lost his right arm. He remained in the army serving in several important capacities. When he retired in 1894 he moved to Burlington, Vermont where he continued to work for various religious causes, wrote several books and helped establish Tennessee's Lincoln Memorial University. He was in his seventy-ninth year when he died on October 26, 1909.

Hayes' ultimatum placed Howard in an uncomfortable position. The general, though certainly no stranger in dealing with Natives, had always been in a position to negotiate; and he had found Indians were usually willing to compromise. This time Hayes had made it very clear there would be no negotiation—and certainly no compromise. Howard had mixed feelings, for he did not favor force and had long since avowed he would never again be a party to a treaty he knew Washington would only disregard. He had already suffered that humiliation, which he considered a betrayal, and wanted no repeats.

Howard's decision had resulted from an assignment in 1872 that had sent him to Arizona Territory to talk terms with Cochise (c.1802–June 8, 1874), chief of the Chiricahua Apaches. Howard's efforts had produced an honorable treaty acceptable to both parties, but once Cochise was safely corralled and the treaty papers sent to Washington, Columbus Delano (1809–1896), Grant's Secretary of the Interior from 1870–1875, proceeded to rewrite it.

Delano broke every promise Howard had made to Cochise. His action was a sure admission to Howard there had never been any intention of allowing Cochise, or any other Indian for that matter, to be included in the making of terms. Whether President Grant had been aware Delano intended to rewrite the treaty is unknown, but it is a certainty that Howard was not a party to it.

Howard, for all his faults, was a man with principals much higher than Delano's. Furious when he learned of the unilateral amendments, he vigorously protested but his remonstrances were ignored at every level. Hoping to present his case directly to Grant, he went to Washington only to find he could not get past Delano. He was told bluntly the treaty would stand as amended—no ifs, ands, or buts. Delano so effectively barred the door to the Oval Office an audience with Grant proved impossible to attain.

Further disappointment followed when Howard learned fellow officers were beginning to refer to him as "the Indian lover." Finally, in order to keep him away from Washington, Delano had him transferred to the Department of the Columbia as commanding officer of The Army of the Northwest. Headquartered at Portland, Oregon, this took him about as far west as it was possible to be at the time and still be on the continent.[6] The transfer served its purpose and General Howard was effectively silenced.

The transfer did more than stifle the general's protests. It also meant his stock within Washington society, a necessary ingredient for future advancement, had plummeted, making him an all-but-forgotten entity.[7] His military career entered a stagnation period. It was then the embittered Howard swore he would never again accept an assignment to negotiate a treaty.

However, when notified he was to ensure Joseph and the other chiefs resettle on the Lapwai Reservation, his sense of duty clashed with his personal feelings. Honor forbade disobedience and he had no desire to resign his hard-earned commission to seek civilian employment. The only course was compliance, so he accepted it with no small reluctance and foreboding. Determined to keep the talks to a bare minimum, the unhappy general prepared to meet with Joseph and the other non-Treaty chiefs.

Resolved to do his duty, he made plans accordingly. Those plans and his views on the Nez Perce chiefs and warriors involved have appeared in several publications over the years, including his own books and papers.[8] His own post-1877 publications profess less empathy with Indians, but expressed more respect for their military capabilities.

History gives us three accounts, all flawed in various ways, of how the Lapwai Ultimatum came about. The first is incorrect and highly speculative, but still believed by many. It contends Howard was determined to avoid a repeat of the debacle of the 1872 Chiricahua Treaty. Knowing Grant's administration would end in March and that Zachariah Chandler[9] (1813–1879), who had replaced Delano as Secretary of the Interior, would also leave, there would be no changes in existing policies. There was, therefore, no sense in stating his case before Chandler. Howard instead hoped the inauguration of President-elect Rutherford B. Hayes and his new cabinet might make changes in the handling of Indian land claims. He was well aware that Hayes, though he cared little about Indians, did not want to fight them.

Following his March inauguration, Hayes announced his list of appointees for the various secretarial positions. Secretary of the Interior would be Carl Schurz (1829–1906).[10] Schurz accepted the appointment believing (a naive hope, as he quickly discovered) that he would be able to change Washington's attitude towards minority and ethnic groups. He hoped to bring about fairer treatment to Indians, and Howard also hoped Schurz's intentions would succeed. Knowing changes would not be forthcoming immediately, when he received his orders he decided to stall for time. He thought he could best achieve this by meeting with Joseph and the other chiefs, explain the situation, then deliver the terms which they could consider over the next few weeks. He would then await the results, leaving the president to do as he pleased should the chiefs continue to resist. Howard saw himself as a messenger, his days as negotiator behind him.

The second version, also accepted by many, is equally untrue. It states Howard, upon receiving his orders, journeyed to Fort Lapwai[11] in April and immediately informed Joseph, White Bird, Tool'hool'hool'zote[12] and the Palu sub-chief, Husis Kute,[13] whom he also erroneously believed to be chief of a Nez Perce band,[14] to attend a council on May 4. Joseph countered by inviting Howard to hold the conference in his village. Howard, having no intention of changing his pre-set course, declined the invitation. Changing the venue would not only be inconvenient, he was more concerned about what might happen when he delivered such disagreeable terms while isolated in Joseph's village. He informed Joseph the chiefs must come to Lapwai. Joseph sent word that he would comply.

The third version, though flawed, is much closer to the truth and generally accepted by historians. Howard did *not* order the chiefs to meet him at Lapwai. He merely informed the chiefs he wished to meet with them to discuss future events. As a result three councils were eventually held, the first two in April at Walla Walla, the final one at Lapwai in May.

The First Council

On April 1, Howard met with the chiefs at Fort Walla Walla where he was confronted with a proposal put forward by Joseph.[15] The proposal contended the projected move to Lapwai was unfair and odious for several reasons. It stated the non-Treaty chiefs were willing to join the Umatillas on their reservation in the neighboring Imnaha Valley. Joseph, however, was not there to present it. He had fallen ill with some never-disclosed ailment and was unable to travel, so Ollokot acted on his behalf. His presentation was reported as being so eloquent the proposal was met with a favorable response from Howard's delegation, which included Indian Agents and some chiefs of other tribes.[16]

Among those favoring the proposal were Narcisse A. Cornoyer,[17] the Umatilla tribe's Indian agent, and Young Chief, the Umatilla band chief,[18] who was Joseph's cousin and good friend. Others who favored the move to Imnaha cited basically the same reasons: both tribes spoke the same language, held the same religious views, were closely related through marriages and family ties. Both tribes were considered "Blanket Indians," vernacular of that era indicating they subscribed to the old traditions of hunting, fishing and harvesting of wild berries, vegetables and roots. Another important reason was none had any inclination to adapt to the white man's agrarian methods. Also, the Imnaha Valley reservation had a considerable area. Had the three Nez Perce bands moved there, the Lapwai reservation would have avoided an over-crowding situation. It was a move that made sense and, according to eyewitness reports, Howard also favored it. The witnesses all reported he agreed to forward the proposal to the Bureau of Indian Affairs (BIA). The main opposition came later via a letter to Howard from John Bochus Montieth,[19] the Lapwai Indian agent. Though Montieth was not present at the first April meeting his views were well known, as he had previously gone on record insisting the bands must move to Lapwai.

The talks that day, so far as Ollokot was concerned, had gone so smoothly that when he returned to Wallowa he informed Joseph the general had been most amicable and had listened to what the chiefs said. In fact, he told Joseph, he had been told by Howard that he was of the opinion the band should be allowed to stay in the Wallowa Valley, but should relocation be required it should be to the Umatilla reservation. A second meeting, presumably to iron out final details, had been arranged to be held over two days at Fort Walla Walla, convening on April 19.

Aftermath of the First Council
Joseph's proposal was vetoed out of hand by the BIA, whose officials had already decided (but not yet revealed their plans) to take the Umatilla reservation from them. Washington, in what had become its stock in trade, had unilaterally decided to break yet another agreement made at the Grand Council of 1855. Without consultation, and with no regard whatsoever for the Umatillas, the entire Imnaha Valley was to be ceded to white settlers.[20]

The veto caused Howard another dilemma, which he solved in the manner that was to become his fashion—complete and total denial. The general's many forthcoming denials and changes to the details concerning the 1877 uprising began at Lapwai on May 4 during his first discussion with Joseph. At that meeting he denied having agreed to a move to the Umatilla reservation. Ollokot, he declared, had either misunderstood the gist of his comments or the interpreter, identified only as Mr. McBain, had been incorrect in his translation. Nothing, he insisted, had been promised. His denials continued in his report to the Secretary of War and then were carried over in his first published book on the overall matter. In that first book, *Nez Perce Joseph*, published in 1881, he compounded his denial by stating there had been no discussions concerning either the Imnaha Valley or the Wallowa Valley. The only discussion, Howard insisted, had concerned relocation to Lapwai and an offer to tour the reservation. Howard wrote in *Nez Perce Joseph* that Chief Ollokot had obviously misunderstood; he had invited Ollokot to tour the reservation so he could determine for himself that a suitable land deal within the Lapwai Reservation could be worked out. He further averred he had told Ollokot to inform Joseph and all the chiefs they, too, were included in the invitation. Howard stated he was anxious for all to see firsthand the first-rate situation at Lapwai. Whatever Ollokot had inferred, Howard declared, the reality was only that the second meeting at Fort Walla Walla had been arranged—and was intended only—to discuss logistics for the move to Lapwai.

Howard's explanations were accepted by historians until L.V. McWhorter, a lifelong champion of the Nez Perce cause, uncovered evidence between 1926 and 1935 when he researched the entire uprising in depth. The new evidence came in the form of written accounts from two very reliable eyewitnesses in attendance at both Walla Walla councils: the Umatilla Indian agent, N.A. Cornoyer, and Captain W. Charles Painter,[21] commanding officer of the Oregon militia company assigned to the reservation. Both men indicated Howard had indeed been receptive to Joseph's relocation proposal. McWhorter also produced quotes from Nez Perce eyewitnesses he interviewed. All had been in attendance and all corroborated Ollokot's presentation of Joseph's proposal. All witnesses, Nez Perce and White, stated Howard had agreed it had merit and had promised to recommend it to Washington. Whether he actually forwarded it to Washington remains an open question as no deposition of

Howard's recommendation has been located to date in any Washington file.[22]

However, a letter, dated February 9, 1877, written by John B. Montieth (1836–1879), the Indian agent at Lapwai, does exist. Written to John Q. Smith, Commissioner of Indian Affairs, its defining line reads, "I have given Joseph until April 1, 1877, to come on the reserve peaceably."

That letter, written seven weeks *prior* to the first council, clearly indicates Montieth's opposition to any delay in moving the non-Treaty bands to Lapwai. His order to Joseph to move to Lapwai by April 1 was illegal. Rules in existence at the time prohibited Indian agents from issuing such orders without written approval from department commanders. Thus, without Howard's written approval, Montieth's order would have been declared invalid. No evidence exists showing Howard having issued approval. Montieth had obviously overstepped his bounds, but despite his later denial of any knowledge of the Umatilla proposal the letter stands as clear indication of his opposition to relocation of Joseph's band to any place other than Lapwai.[23]

THE SECOND COUNCIL

On April 19 the second Walla Walla council was declared opened and chaired, not by General Howard but by the general's aide de camp, Lt. William Henry Boyle (1837–1919).[24] Joseph was still unable to attend because of the above-mentioned illness, so Ollokot again took his place. Ollokot had come prepared to reinforce the advantages of relocation to the Umatilla reservation. He also intended to remind Howard that Joseph had previously informed the general of his concerns about the certainty of overcrowding Lapwai, which was already a problem and would become worse with an influx of more bands.[25]

Boyle, as chairman, indicated Ollokot should speak first. The gesture pleased Ollokot and the other chiefs for it added to their conviction that Howard had meant what he had said at the previous council. In his speech Ollokot opened with words of gratitude towards Howard. He thanked him for agreeing that the Nez Perces should live with their brothers the Umatillas. He then spoke of Nez Perce traditional and genuine friendship, kindness and cooperation the tribe had always shown white men over many decades. He closed by saying he looked forward to many more such years. When he sat down the chiefs were all smiles, convinced the meeting would end in success and harmony. They awaited Howard's appearance and his reply to Ollokot.

Howard, however, did not come forward to reply to Ollokot. He was not present. It was Boyle who stood up to reply. Never noted for a diplomatic manner Boyle delivered Howard's message in three curt, blunt sentences.

> *"You are not coming to the Umatilla reservation. General Howard orders that you move to the Nez Perce reservation. You are to get ready to move at once."*[26]

Having delivered his message, Boyle resumed his seat without a further word. The entire group, including the white observers, sat in stunned silence. Ollokot, who up to that minute had been in good humor, was taken aback. For a long moment he seemed speechless. Then he flew into a rage.

Rising to his feet he clenched a fist and pointing it directly at Boyle extended his index and forefinger. Ollokot, in sign language of the Plains Indians, was accusing Boyle of speaking with a forked tongue. Then Ollokot curved the two fingers downward indicating a snake's fangs. In this manner he had silently, and with contempt, accused Boyle of being akin to a viper. Then he spoke to him directly.

> *"Nesammemiek [liar], who are you? Where is Atim'kennin [General Howard]? He promised to come to this council. I, a chief, came to talk to a chief! General Howard sends one of his boys to give orders to a chief? I did not send one of my young men to talk to a chief! I am a chief and I came to talk to a*

*chief. Where is General Howard? General Howard talks with
forked tongue! He has lied to the Nez Perces! Is he ashamed
to talk to men to whom he has talked with a forked tongue?
Is he, a commander of soldiers, afraid? He has insulted me! He
makes me ashamed before my people! I am done!"*²⁷

He turned and departed to his campsite accompanied by his sub-chiefs.²⁸

Boyle's message was so tactless he may very likely at that moment have assured the future war. For his part, Howard, by choosing not to face Ollokot and the other chiefs, certainly instilled the distrust and unconcealed contempt the Nez Perce chiefs held for him from that moment forward.

Aftermath of the Second Council

Howard's accounts of the council are diametrically opposite to those of Painter and Cornoyer, and clash completely with the account given to Joseph by Ollokot upon his return to Wallowa Valley from the first council. Howard's report to the secretary of war concerning the second council is sparse and so meandering it is difficult to read. For these reasons the report has been transcribed verbatim with no corrections to either spelling or grammar.

> "*On the 19th, in the afternoon, Ollicut* (sic), *with several
> other Indians, makes his appearance at Fort Walla Walla,
> and excuses his delay, and explains that his brother is not
> coming, but that he himself wishes to have a talk with me
> in the presence of several of his people. Colonel Grover has
> a barracks room prepared, where the interview took place,
> commencing at 10 o'clock A.M. on the 20ᵗʰ.*
>
> *There were present Ollicut, Young Chief of the Umatillas
> the Dreamer before mentioned, and several other non-treaty
> Nez Perces. Besides my aids, several officers of the fort and
> some citizens were present. The Indian Agent, Cornoyer
> and his interpreter, McBain, participated.*

I explained the requirement of the government; that the Indians would be required to go on the reservation—some reservation; that the government had consented to allow Joseph and his people a yearly visit to the Imnaha Valley for hunting and fishing, but always with a pass from the agent.

The Indians seemed at first to wish to join the Umatillas, then it appears there was a project (probably originating with white men) to combine the reservation Indians of Umatilla with the non-treaty Nez Perces, thus joined the Wallowa and Imnaha country giving up the Umatilla reserve. But I replied the instructions are definite; that I should send troops very soon to occupy the Wallowa, and proceed to Lapwai in execution of my instructions.

Ollicut, who manifested a good disposition, was evidently afraid to promise anything, and I was aware that some representative of the Indian bureau should take the initiative in dealing with these Indians, so I was glad to have him ask to gather the Indians, all the non-treaties, tomeet me at Fort Lapwai during my coming visit."[29] (sic)

Howard's account of that day as published in his 1881 book, *Nez Perce Joseph*, is even more skewed and confusing than his report to the secretary. In the book the general has the council beginning on the 20th, conveniently forgetting the events of the 19th. He makes no mention of delegating the tactless Lieutenant Boyle[30] as chairman for the meeting. His book account differs from reality in other ways as well. The book's account, like the report to the secretary, is imprecise, lacks worthwhile information, while that which is mentioned is often incorrect. In the report, for instance, Howard mentions, without further comment, the presence of the Umatilla leader, Young Chief. In his book he states,

"Young Chief, the Umatilla friend and advocate, wishes some new lands in Wallowa that will hold them all

(Cayuses, Walla-Walla, Umatillas and non-treaty Nez Perces) in fellowship. Really matters did not look much like war."[31] (sic)

Writing in *Nez Perce Joseph*, Howard not only fails to make mention of the proceedings of April 19, he also makes no reference to reports written by other attendees. Nor does he acknowledge the existence of those reports.

Whether intending to contradict Howard, or just to add to the record, is unclear, but both the militia commander, Captain Painter, and Indian Agent Cornoyer,[32] independently related their accounts of the proceedings at both councils, and both asserted Howard had indeed told Chief Ollokot he would recommend the Nez Perces be relocated in the Imnaha Valley. Both Painter and Cornoyer wrote of feeling the general made the promise in good faith, but upon the rebuke from Washington could not bring himself to face Ollokot. Unwisely, he sent Boyle in his place.[33]

Other witnesses also declared they felt the usually doughty general, upon receipt of Washington's negative reply, could not muster enough courage to deliver the bad news in person. They felt he ordered Boyle to deliver the news of Washington's veto and to inform Ollokot and the others the bands must prepare for an immediate move to Lapwai.

So, questions arise. Which accounts are honest and correct? Did Ollokot really misunderstand? Did Howard lie to cover his tracks as best he could in hopes the entire mess would wash away over time? Did the interpreter, McBain, deliver an incorrect translation? To date no absolute consensus has emerged among historians or students of Old West history. It seems inconceivable that Painter and Cornoyer could both have been wrong. In the probability the truth may never be known, it must be left to individuals to form their own opinions in the knowledge that some opinions, having more value, are likely correct whereas others of less value are likely wrong.

In late April Howard informed Joseph, White Bird, Husis Kute and Tool'hool'hool'zote he would meet with them in council at Fort Lapwai on May 4. He expected the meeting to last a week.

[CHAPTER 5 ENDNOTES]

1. Oliver Otis Howard has become controversial in many ways. Some historians and biographers believe he was a rarity among US Army officers in that he treated Indians with fairness and compassion. Others consider him biased, unable to see the real problems they faced. None dispute his personal courage or that his career on the frontier was distinctive. Oliver Knight, a distinguished historian, is one who disputes the general's abilities in diplomacy. Knight wrote in *The Reader's Encyclopedia of the American West*, "The record indicates that the self-righteous Howard lacked the temperament, empathy, and knowledge to deal with the Indians effectively, in council or in the field."

    In this summary Knight is correct. Howard, a Congregational Christian fundamentalist in every way, allowed his religious bias to interfere at every step in negotiations with Indians. All that he offered or agreed to was planned with the Bible in mind. His troops, rarely a hallowed group, often grew tired of the Bible-inspired sessions he held for their education. Howard wanted to treat the Indians in a similar manner. Those who accepted Christianity, he believed, were worthwhile dealing with, but those who did not concur with his beliefs were mere savages and thus unworthy. Howard was not called "The Christian Soldier" without good reason. [Thrapp, Dan L., *Encyclopedia of Frontier Biography;* McWhorter, V.L., *Hear Me My Chiefs; The Harper Encyclopedia of Military Biography.*]

2. Howard lost his right arm during the Battle of Fair Oaks fought seven miles southeast of Richmond, Virginia from May 31 to June 1, 1862. The battle is also called the Battle of Seven Pines. [*Compton Home Library Encyclopedia*, "US Civil War Battles" section.]

3   Although Howard made the statement in 1875, there is no reason to believe he had changed his mind by 1877. [Author.]

4   Howard had no idea of the degrees of variance between band chiefs, sub-chiefs and warriors. Neither had he learned the differences between the civic chiefs, such as Joseph, and war chiefs, such as Ollokot. He never bothered to learn how to recognize the deep diversities that separated shamans from medicine men; and of ceremonialists he knew nothing. He thought, for instance, that Tool'hool'hool'zote was a medicine man and a sub-chief to White Bird when, in fact, Tool'hool'hool'zote was, and always had been, a band chief. He also thought White Bird was an hereditary chief when, in fact, he had always been a ceremonialist. White Bird was probably nearly sixty years of age when he had been thrust into the position of the Lamtama band's chief in what had been a matter of necessity. The Lamtama elders needed an immediate replacement for their recently deceased chief and chose White Bird. He accepted, but not without great reluctance. [Author's files; many other publications.]

5   Accounts of the 1877 pursuit, written in later years by some infantrymen, state that Howard refused to proceed on Sundays in order that the Sabbath be observed. There is no truth in these stories. Howard's numerous bivouacs necessarily included an occasional Sunday, but this was coincidence. Despite his religious fervor and convictions, he had no qualms about working on Sunday. Unless the infantrymen had a dislike of their general and hoped to discredit him further, the reasons for these charges remain unknown. [Author's files.]

6   Only Alaska, at 141°W is further from Washington than Oregon at 124°W. [*Rand McNally Atlas.*]

7   This was during a time when a social life was necessary

if an aspiring officer had any chance to rise in rank. Brevet-colonel George A. Custer had emerged from the Civil War as a hero of some renown and, because he had married into a prominent family, was able to use his marriage to advantage. Even after he was exiled to the frontier, his wife stayed in Washington and kept his name in the forefront. Such was her influence there were rumors that he might be touted as a candidate for the presidency. Howard, on the other hand, lacking a presence in Washington, had no champion to keep his name in the foreground.

8   Howard's writings often directly contradict those of others, including many eyewitness accounts of events. Several of his statements have been proven false and were obviously intended to increase his own prestige. Glaring errors can be readily seen in such works as his serialized article titled "Nez Perces Campaign of 1877," which appeared in the magazine *Advance* from January to October 1878. [Howard, O.O., *Nez Perce Joseph: An Account of his Ancestors, His Lands etc. etc.,* Decapo Press, 1972 (reprint); "The True Story of the Wallowa Campaign," *The North American Review* (July 1879): 53–64.]

9   Chandler replaced Delano upon the latter's sudden resignation in 1875. Grant fired Delano on October 15, 1875 for taking bribes for fraudulent land grants. [Salinger, Lawrence, *Encyclopedia of White Collar & Corporate Crime*, Sage Publication, California (2005), 374–375.]

10 Carl Schurz was no stranger to the troubles of the oppressed. Born in Germany he joined revolutionaries in 1849 in a bid to overthrow the regime. It failed and he was imprisoned. He escaped and fled to Switzerland from whence he went to the US. There he earned a law degree and in turn became a journalist and a politician. He was a friend of Abraham Lincoln and an avowed

abolitionist. He fought in the civil war as a brigadier general. As secretary of the interior he advocated improvements for minorities and sought fair treatment for Indians but saw little success in either venture, as President Hayes did not share his concerns. In later life Schurz opposed American involvement in the Spanish War and objected to the annexing of the Philippines as a prize of that war. One of his several quotes chided his adopted country for rushing into that war. "Our country, right or wrong. When right, it is to be kept right. When wrong, it is to be made right." [The Balch Institute for Ethnic Studies, Pittsburgh.]

11 The fort, the symbol of authority, was located in the reserve's northwest area. It housed a small detachment of soldiers, the Indian agent and other government employees. (See map.)

12 Tool'hool'hool'zote [Speaking Eagle] (1840–October 5, 1877) was chief of the Piquinin band. His name was pronounced Tuhul'huzut. A shaman and mystic as well as a chief, he was also referred to as "The Prophet." He was athletic, agile, extremely strong, and a good wrestler, often showing his prowess by easily defeating two strong men at the same time. He was admired and respected by his people and others within the Nez Perce community. Described as very dark, stocky, bull-necked and exceedingly ugly, with a matching demeanor, he was feared by white settlers, who called him "the Indian from Hell." He was equally feared by Washington bureaucrats because of his skills in oratory and debate, which he conducted with logic, conviction and intelligence. During the long trek from Idaho to The Bear's Paw he displayed above-average talent as a field general and tactician. Though he was adamantly opposed to the Lapwai terms of resettlement, he did eventually agree he would go there with his people.

13 Husis Kute [Bald Head] was one of Joseph's several cousins and was about the same age as Joseph. During fighting in the 1855 Yakima War an exploding shell fired by the army resulted in a loss of most of his hair. It did not grow back so he took the name "Bald Head."

He was not the Palu band chief; he was a shaman renowned for his eloquence. He was also a Dreamer ceremonialist and in this capacity was a sub-chief. The actual Palu chief was Hahtalekin, also known as Taktsoukt Ilppilp [Red Echo]. Hahtalekin was killed by a sniper at the Big Hole and it was at this point when Husis Kute became the band chief. [McWhorter, *Hear me My Chiefs*, 173; and Author's files.]

14 Howard's confusion over the chieftaincy came about through his abysmal ignorance of both the Palu tribal hierarchy and the Dreamer structure. Howard disliked Husis Kute intensely and showed his animus on page 19 of his 1881 book, *Nez Perce Joseph* in which he describes Husis Kute thus, "It could be said of him in the words of Scripture, 'His heart was deceitful above all things and desperately wicked.'" [McWhorter, *Hear me My Chiefs*, 173; and Author's files.]

15 No official minutes can be found of this council but enough supporting evidence shows it was held on March 1 and that Joseph's proposal was presented. It is also recorded in General Howard's supplementary report to the Secretary of War on the Nez Perce campaign. [Report of Secretary of War, 1877, I, 590.]

16 Why other chiefs were present has never been explained. Perhaps Howard felt they might help him explain to the Nez Perce chiefs that reservation life was to their benefit. It is known the Umatilla chief was agreeable to assimilation with the Nez Perce bands.

17 Narcisse Antoine Cornoyer was born to a Quebec family

named Cournoyer in Illinois in 1820 and died at Walla Walla, Washington in 1909. He changed his original surname slightly (probably for easier pronunciation) shortly after leaving Illinois for the California gold fields in 1849. Cornoyer later went to French Prairie in Oregon, fought in the 1855 Rogue River War and earned the rank of major which, as was the custom of the era, he kept as an honorarium in later years. He served as sheriff of Marion County from 1856 to 1860 and later served in various capacities including a lengthy tenure as Indian agent for the Umatilla Reservation. Very popular amongst the Natives, he was a staunch supporter of Indian rights all his life and was particularly critical of those who were not. His account of the February 1877 council, in which affiliation with the Umatillas with the non-Treaty Nez Perces was discussed, is a matter of record. [Helen A. Howard, *Saga of Chief Joseph;* Pearson, *The Nez Perces in the Indian Territory;* Greene, *Nez Perce Summer 1877.*]

18 A Cayuse chief, also named Young Chief, has been occasionally confused with the Umatilla chief. The confusion probably originated when the Umatillas were transferred to the Cayuse reservation. The Cayuse Young Chief had no dealings in the 1877 council. All references to him as a participant should be discounted. [Author's files.]

19 Upon his death, John Bochus Montieth (b. Kentucky 1836; d. Lewiston, Idaho 1879) was succeeded as Lapwai agent by Charles D. Warner.

20 The Umatillas first learned of this latest treachery several months later when they were informed they were to move immediately to the Cayuse reservation in Washington State.

21 Captain W. Charles Painter was promoted during the 1878 Bannock War to lieutenant colonel and appointed

commander of all Oregon volunteer militia groups. He fully supported the non-Treaty Nez Perces in their claims to their traditional lands. In 1877 he refused to command the Walla Walla volunteers when they were ordered to join Howard's army. He said later he could "live with the jeers of my countrymen but would have been unable to salve a nagging conscience." [McWhorter, *Hear Me My Chiefs*, 152.]

22 There seems some doubt in the contention by Cornoyer and Painter that Howard actually favored the move despite agreeing to send in a recommendation favoring it. In the autumn of 1876 the commission detailed to look into the situation in Lapwai had filed a unanimous report in which one of the recommendations included resettling the Umatillas on the Cayuse reservation. Howard was a member of that commission, so the question is raised as to why he would now favor Joseph's proposal. Two possibilities emerge: either Howard had forgotten the commission's recommendation or Ollokot had misinterpreted Howard's agreement to forward the proposal to Indian Affairs as acceptance. [Report of Secretary of the Interior, 1877, 611–12.]

23 John Montieth was another example of the attitudes rampant among church-appointed Indian agents. He was greatly biased against the people he was supposed to be assisting. In his opinion Indians were required by law to occupy their assigned reservations, an adamant belief he held because the churches were mandated by Washington to achieve that aim. If his church was to acculturate the Nez Perces to white society they were all required to live on the Lapwai reservation under agent administration. A corresponding, and equally logical, suspicion indicates Montieth was more interested in improving his own private fortune. The more Indians on his agency's roles meant more profit he could personally

realize. John B. Montieth has been considered by some as being honest in his earlier days and concerned for his charges; but he was much more the scoundrel than has been hitherto assumed. For all his intrigues, he did not long profit from his pernicious labor. He had but two more years to live. He died of consumption on August 7, 1879 [*Encyclopedia of Frontier Biography,* Vol. 2, 1000; and Author's files.]

24 William Henry Boyle was born November 13, 1837, at Bay Ridge, Long Island. Commissioned as second lieutenant on May 10, 1866, he was promoted to lieutenant the following year. He served as acting Indian agent at the Umatilla Reservation from 1870–71. He fought in the Modoc War in 1873 and it was during that war when he barely escaped a treacherous ambush as he sat under a flag of truce in cease-fire talks with a small group of Modocs led by Chief Curley Headed Jack. Several of his companions were killed. In 1877 he served briefly as aide de camp to General Howard. Following his unfortunate (mis)handling of the Second Walla Walla Council he was promoted to captain and was then stationed at Fort Lapwai but saw no action in the forthcoming war. Until his retirement, as lieutenant colonel, in 1900 Boyle served in various capacities. In 1904 he was promoted from the retired list to full colonel. He was 81 when he died on Apr 23, 1919 at Plainfield, New Jersey [Thrapp, Dan L., *Encyclopedia of Frontier Biography,* Vol. 1, A–F, 152–3.]

25 Joseph recalled in 1878 that he had earlier informed Howard that his own band's cattle and horses, which numbered in the thousands, would alone take up an inordinately sizeable portion of the already limited pastureland. The animals of the other three bands would take up the remainder and that number of animals

would cause serious problems for the present residents. [Author's files.]

26 H. Painter in a letter to McWhorter. [McWhorter, NP36, 1–33.]

27 Quoted by McWhorter from a letter written to him by Captain Painter, who was at the council. [McWhorter letters. File NP35, 1–33; and also McWhorter, *Hear Me My Chiefs*, 154–55.]

28 McWhorter, *Hear Me My Chiefs*, 152–155.

29 Report of the Secretary of War, 1877, I, 590.

30 Report of Secretary of War, 1877, I, 590.

31 Howard, *Nez Perce Joseph*, 43.

32 Captain W. Charles Painter, US Army and Mr. Cornoyer, the Indian agent for the Umatilla reservation, were the officers who wrote of the promise of relocation. [McWhorter, *Hear Me My Chiefs*, 151–54.]

33 To this day it remains unclear why Howard promised Ollokot that a move to the Umatilla reservation was possible. The general had been a member of the commission that had advocated the Umatilla lands be forfeited in favor of white settlers. He would not likely have forgotten that section of the commission's report. Either Painter <u>and</u> Cornoyer both misunderstood what Howard had said (and are thus wrong in their averments), or Ollokot had taken Howard's agreement to suggest the idea of a merger was a de facto agreement. Whatever had been meant does not excuse Howard for sending an underling on a chief's mission. [Author's files.]

[CHAPTER 6]

THE LAPWAI ULTIMATUM

If it is true that Howard was indeed a reluctant emissary, it now appears his promise of a move to the Imnaha Valley may have been nothing more than a ploy to stall for time. He likely suspected the chiefs would refuse any order to go to Lapwai and he certainly knew Washington would follow its normal fashion and veto the Imnaha proposal. Either way, he knew the final decision for action to be taken rested not with him, but with Washington. All that would then be required of him would be the scheduling of a meeting at Lapwai to dictate Hayes' final terms and set a deadline for relocation—in effect delivering an ultimatum. With the second Walla Walla council having so abruptly ended in acrimony there was no longer reason for delay, so he scheduled the Lapwai meeting for May 4 and sent word to Joseph and the others they must attend. He wanted a short, final meeting; he was in no mood for one of long duration.

Howard, at age forty-seven, no longer had the patience required for many days of seemingly endless hours sitting before a council fire, tolerating heathen ceremonies and smoking sweetgrass from a communal pipe. What may have been once tolerable was now nothing more than insufferable endeavor. He found nothing pleasurable in interminable discussion with chiefs whose vocabularies apparently did not include the words "immediately" or "forthwith." Howard had long before realized Indians had patience that could equal, if not surpass, that of the proverbial Oriental. He had also grown tired of their habit of agreeing to terms in late afternoon then changing several members of the negotiating team overnight. This, he had quickly learned, was a ploy to force amendments to agreements made the previous day. Often the entire team would change, forcing the talks to start anew.[1] Further, he was no longer able to conceal or control his irascible temper for lengthy periods. Howard had passed the stage in his life where he could be considered a patient man.

With no intentions of engaging in lengthy palaver, Howard now needed only to impress upon Joseph and his allies that peaceful resettlement on the reservation was obligatory. He hoped to convince them of this through persuasion, but, if necessary, through threats despite his awareness that protocol discouraged "showing the rifle" at such a meeting.[2] Erroneously thinking the chiefs' final decision would be up to Joseph he decided to deal with him by directing his comments to him whenever possible.[3]

On May 1, Joseph, Tool'hool'hool'zote, and Arthur L. "Ad" Chapman departed on the journey of seventy miles (110 km) to Fort Lapwai.[4] Chapman, a man Joseph thought he could trust—and too late would become aware of his true nature[5]—had agreed to act as interpreter. Tool'hool'hool'zote, because of his eloquence and skill in debate, was selected as spokesman. The riders were met near Lapwai by White Bird and Husis Kute of the Palu tribe who was representing his band.

Upon arrival at Lapwai on May 4 the delegation was warmly greeted by Ala'limya Takanlin [Cyclone Traveler] (1830–1877), chief of the Kam'nakka band, a branch of the larger Asotin band.[6] He was the eldest son of Apash Wyakaikt [Flint Necklace] who, since the days of the Lewis and Clark expedition,[7] had been known as Looking Glass to the white community because of the round polished mirror he wore as a necklace. In 1863, Apash Wyakaikt died and bequeathed both his pendant and name to his son. Ala'limya Takanlin then became known as Looking Glass and was elevated to band chief in unanimous acclamation by the Kam'nakka elders.

Both father and son had opposed the 1855 Treaty, but when the old chief decided to sign, his son continued in opposition. He opposed the Treaty of 1863 mainly over the band's loss of a small parcel of land. For centuries the Kam'nakkas had lived in the area of Clear Creek with its center located near the middle fork of the Clearwater River. In the 1863 land grab all their land remained within the revised Lapwai Reservation except for the disputed acres. Ala'limya Takanlin saw that as theft of a good hunting area. As late as 1877 he still wanted it back, and hoped its return could eventually be negotiated, but he had no intention of fighting over it. In his opinion, the contested ground was a matter of principal and for that reason he remained non-Treaty.[8] His elevation to band chief had placed him, as the non-Treaty leader of a treaty band, in a bit of a quandary. All in all he was in an unusual position.

While still in his late twenties, Looking Glass had become as famed as his father, but for different reasons. Having led many hunting parties into Montana, he was considered among the foremost of the great Nez Perce hunters. He had spent so much time in Montana on those hunts he became well known to Sioux, Cheyenne and Blackfeet alike. Inevitably his involvement in skirmishes with all three factions served to increase the respect held for him. The Sioux in particular became so highly respectful of his fighting prowess he gained lasting fame within their circles. In 1873 in the final and decisive Battle at Pryor Creek, he allied with the Crows against the Sioux-Cheyenne coalition. In that battle the coalition was soundly defeated and his fame increased. Because warriors showed other great warriors respect and never held grudges, Looking Glass was free to travel unmolested throughout Montana. He became so famous, a Sioux band in the Bear's Paw region, enthralled by his remarkable singing voice, honored him with a Lakota name—Ta-siyag'nupa [Meadowlark].[9] As an individual he struck an imposing figure; though not overly tall he was athletic and agile. He exuded confidence that many considered arrogance.[10]

White historians of the 1920s referred to Looking Glass as Joseph's best friend, but interview statements in 1926 by Nez Perce men who knew both makes this increasingly doubtful. They all agreed the two were friendly but Joseph disliked his haughty manner, which was most noticeable in his dealings with those of lesser status. Looking Glass was a chief and expected others to remember that at all times.

All in all, Looking Glass is not kindly remembered by Nez Perce historians. They have determined it was he who must bear the ultimate responsibility for the failure to reach Canada and the safety that had come so close. Nez Perce survivors of the 1877 ordeal were unanimous in this opinion when they spoke with L.V. McWhorter during 1927 and 1935. All considered his leadership during the 1877 war a dismal failure because he made too many critical errors.[11] Some criticized Joseph, White Bird and Tool'hool'hool'zote as well for electing him overall war chief; most felt White Bird should have been appointed to that position. They all thought Looking Glass's refusal to heed advice was the prime factor in the disaster at The Big Hole. They were also critical of his decisions that delayed progress on the northern route from Yellowstone. Everyone agreed the two extra days he insisted upon staying at Snake Creek was the reason for the surrender at Bear's Paw.[12] Had he not insisted on the delay the entire group would have safely reached Canada.

When the events in 1877 began to flare, Looking Glass faced a dilemma, one he really did not know how to manage. During the Lapwai Council he became aware of the need to make a decision, but remained uncertain of what direction to take. He supported the dissenting chiefs, but his predilection to neutrality was obvious. Following the conference his predicament became steadily more tenuous as his indecision grew. If he joined Joseph and White Bird in what might become open revolt he could count on only thirty seasoned warriors. Equally important was his awareness the majority of his band did not support the dissenting chiefs. While there is no doubt that on May 4 Looking Glass intended to support Joseph in his claim to the Wallowa Valley, it is equally obvious the support was offered in hopes of gaining Joseph's support in his own quest. He never got the chance to reveal what may have been his original plan, for the series of tragic circumstances that followed rendered it moot. His fervent greetings to Joseph, however, indicated eager support—and it was that fervor which immediately captured Howard's attention.

Looking Glass, it is now apparent, would never have joined the revolt had it not been for two senseless errors. The first was made when Howard misinterpreted Looking Glass's greeting on Joseph's arrival. The second, by far the more serious, occurred July 1 when one of Howard's ambitious officers in command of a volunteer militia company of trigger-happy civilians failed to obey the orders he had been given. Those mistakes drove Looking Glass to his fateful decision.

THE LAPWAI COUNCIL: TWO VERSIONS

As Joseph Saw It
According to Chief Joseph, in an article published by *The North American Review* in 1879 (later incorporated and addressed by Chester Anders Lee in his excellent book, *Chief Joseph: The Biography of a Great Indian*[13]) he and the others arrived on schedule. The council began the next morning with the customary speeches of welcome and the passing of the sweetgrass pipe. Howard, with Arthur Chapman translating, read the terms of resettlement. Joseph, White Bird and the other chiefs, hoping the meeting would produce an honorable treaty, conferred briefly. They rejected the terms and made a counter proposal. They proposed new boundaries be drawn that would include Joseph's Wallowa Valley and the two Salmon River areas occupied by the Lamtama and Piqunin bands. Howard immediately rejected their proposal, and told the chiefs the terms he had presented were final orders not preliminaries to negotiations. There would be no discussion about redefining boundaries.[14] An uneasy silence followed before Tool'hool'hool'zote spoke.

The wily old chief maneuvered Howard into a lengthy discussion during which the general was worn down by a logic he had neither expected nor wished to hear. He soon began showing signs that his patience was wearing so thin as to be nearing the breaking point when Tool'hool'hool'zote casually asked, "What would white men do if foreigners came to them from across the great sea to demand the land be given over to them?"

"They would fight according to the laws of the nation," Howard responded.

"The Nez Perce nation would also choose to fight according to the laws of the nation," the chief replied.

Howard, taken aback, was momentarily without a reply but quickly recovered.

"The laws do not apply to Indians," Howard said.

"Why do the laws not apply to Indians?" enquired the chief.

"Indians are not citizens of this country," Howard replied, "so therefore the laws do not apply."

Tool'hool'hool'zote sat for a few moments eyeing the general with a steady glare. Then he sprung his carefully baited trap.

"If the Indians are not citizens of this land and the laws of this land do not apply to them then neither do the treaty laws," he quietly replied. "Either all laws apply or none apply."[15]

Tool'hool'hool'zote had quietly and effectively trapped Howard and the general knew it. He lost his composure and in a rage ordered soldiers to arrest the chief and place him in the stockade. Howard at that point abandoned all thoughts he might have had towards further talk. He called a recess.

As Howard Saw It

Howard's account, as can be expected, holds a view diametrically opposed to Joseph's. He states he was fully aware the message he was about to deliver would not be accepted gladly. He was also noted that he was fully aware that Looking Glass, though a resident of Lapwai, was in sympathy with the non-Treaty Indians. He therefore had resolved to watch that chief's actions closely. His account also contradicts Joseph's account of when the chiefs arrived. Concerning White Bird's presence, Howard wrote, White Bird did not arrive with the others. At Joseph's request the meeting was delayed four days to accommodate the tardy chief.[a]

Howard agrees with Joseph's account of the morning's events and his debate with Tool'hool'hool'zote—up to a point. He agrees he ordered the arrest of his tormentor but dismisses outright Joseph's claim that ordering the arrest was done in anger or that he acted in haste. A portion of Howard's account of the situation leading to the arrest has the backing, in part, of the official minutes. The minutes touch on the problem by mentioning it had its beginnings the previous evening with excessively loud drumming during a religious rite by the Dreamers. Howard's account mentions the incident. The noise, he wrote, brought complaints from residents, whereupon he had ordered the drumming be quieted. This order had greatly annoyed Tool'hool'hool'zote who had complied but not, in Howard's words "before indulging in a lengthy pout."

Tool'hool'hool'zote might have brought his "pout" with him to the meeting because, the minutes note, when the meeting began the chief, in his opening speech, caused the general to lose patience. Then, following their brief debate, he perceived the chief was drawing the crowd towards a frenzy He stepped in and took charge. The official minutes read:

"The rough old fellow [Tool'hool'hool'zote], in a most provoking tone, says something in a short sentence. The interpreter [Chapman] says, 'He demands what person pretends to divide the land and put me on it?' Howard says, 'I am that man. I stand here for the President, and there is no spirit, good or bad, that will hinder me. My orders are plain and will be executed. I hoped the Indians had good sense enough to make me their friend and not their enemy.'" (*sic*)

Howard's account, written much later, states,

"From various unmistakable signs (I am no novice with Indians) I saw immediately trouble was at hand. Joseph, White Bird

---

[a] *Joseph's article makes no mention about White Bird arriving late. [Author's note.]*

and Looking Glass endorsed and encouraged this malcontent [Tool'hool'hool'zote]. I must somehow put a wedge between them, so I turned [to Tool'hool'hool'zote] and said 'Then you do not propose to comply with the orders of the Government?'

He replied, growling and menacing, 'The Indians may do what they like, but I am not going on the reservation.'" (*sic*)

At this point, Howard wrote, he ordered the "malcontent" be "detained under the supervision of an officer [Captain David L. Perry]..." and he was "placed into the keeping of an armed guard appointed by Captain Perry, the fort commandant." A short while later, with Tool'hool'hool'zote out of the way, Howard proposed the chiefs join him in a tour of the reservation so they could all see for themselves that settlement at Lapwai was a good idea. The chiefs agreed to the tour.

The Tour According to Howard
According to Howard his personal invitation to tour the *entire* reservation was then extended. Joseph, White Bird and the other chiefs departed the following morning in the company of both himself and Montieth.[16] Howard scheduled the tour for period of seven days—but could take longer if needed—so the chiefs could speak with as many residents as they wished in order to determine their degree of satisfaction with reservation life. The tour would also allow them to inspect land Montieth had already set aside for them and their people.

Over the next week the chiefs were shown farms in various stages of cultivation. They saw herds of cattle and horses grazing contentedly in grassy fields. Howard, knowing Ollokot's great influence over the youthful warriors, put special effort towards convincing him to resettle at Lapwai. He also obviously spent much time with Joseph for he wrote,

"[I] spent a long time giving [Ollokot and Joseph], in the kindest manner, the benefit of my counsel."

Howard wrote emphatically that Ollokot had been very favorable towards a move to Lapwai when the two had met earlier at Walla Walla. This, however, disagrees with Joseph's belief of his brother's impressions of the Walla Walla meetings.

Each chief was shown the land Montieth had tentatively assigned to them but were informed, should they not like the property, they could exchange it for vacant land elsewhere. Howard wrote later that White Bird's selection was choice acreage adjacent to the farm held by Looking Glass. Howard was adamant that White Bird quickly agreed to sign the papers which would give him title to the land.

Howard stated that Joseph explained his band did not wish to be dispersed as individuals but preferred to retain their communal lifestyle. He requested an area large enough to accommodate the entire band. He was shown an extremely large tract of prime acreage. This he agreed to accept and Howard told him the deal could be made but it would be necessary to dispossess several families already settled there. According to Howard, Joseph made no objection to the evictions.

The Tour According to Joseph
By Joseph's account the tour began in good order. He and his sub-chiefs were pleased with what they saw and, for the most part, the residents they spoke with expressed satisfaction with their lives and holdings. As the party rode through the northeastern reaches of the reservation, Joseph wrote, he saw an extremely large tract of land that he liked. It could easily accommodate his entire band, allowing it to remain intact. Joseph indicated he would be willing to accept it on behalf of his people. Howard agreed, but then he said the agent would have to relocate some families who were the present occupants. Joseph, unaware the land already had residents, told the general he could not agree to such a thing.

He was later shown suitable acreage near Kamiah, equal in good measure and value to the first shown. Located further east in an uninhabited tract of several square miles it was good land bordered on the east by the Clearwater River and to the south by Lawyer Creek, both good sources of fresh water. Joseph agreed it was suitable, as it would allow adequate acreage for each family.

It appears, therefore, that Joseph, White Bird, Ollokot and the others were amenable to accepting land on the reservation. Their choices were acceptable to both Howard and Montieth. Also satisfied was Joseph's desire for acreage where his entire band could settle in a spirit of social economy. Although it would incorporate a single area of several square miles, making it in effect a community within a community, this apparently was no hindrance to agreement. Montieth said he would assign the land near Kamiah as a community holding and the deal was pronounced mutually acceptable. At that point, according to Joseph, it appeared he and Howard had reached an arrangement.

The Tour's Aftermath According to Howard
Upon the group's return to Fort Lapwai everyone seemed satisfied, so Howard released the apparently repentant Tool'hool'hool'zote from the stockade. Howard wrote later he had received a solemn promise from Tool'hool'hool'zote that he would cause no more trouble and would "behave better and give good advice [to his people]."[17]

On May 14, Howard reconvened the meeting for the purpose of tying up loose ends only to realize the chiefs (he of course blamed Joseph for the change of mind) were not going to accept the terms without further thought. Having no intention of allowing anyone extra time to think matters over, he spoke only long enough to inform them they had thirty days in which to gather their people, round up their livestock and report to the reservation. The deadline for entering the reservation, he told them, was June 15 and there would be no further discussion. So far as Howard was concerned final agreement had been reached. He then adjourned the council.

The Tour's Aftermath According to Joseph
In his 1879 article, Joseph insists he appealed to Howard for more time before moving. He estimated his band would require three months to make the move considering the logistics involved. He estimated the cattle alone would require several weeks for round-up and even then some would be left behind for collection later. Even three months would be difficult, the equivalent of compressing six months work into three. Thirty days was not nearly enough time.

"Let us at least have until Piqun'mauqal[18] [when fish return to spawn]," Joseph pleaded. "Our stock is scattered throughout the hills and the river [the Snake] is running very high."

Howard, according to Joseph, was still rankling from his encounter with Tool'hool'hool'zote. He angrily told Joseph he had thirty days and not one day more.

"If you let the time run over even by one day," he warned, "the soldiers will drive your people [to Lapwai] and all your cattle and horses…will fall into the hands of white men."[19]

Joseph and White Bird realized they had no choice but to obey Howard's orders or risk the stockade for who knew how long. It was this ultimatum that caused them to accept the time limit.[20] Joseph was deeply offended by Howard's refusal to consider his request for an extension. He felt his only choice was to inform Howard he would obey the order and report to Lapwai within thirty days.

"We shall leave the Wallowa Valley as you order," Joseph told Howard. "Will you allow Tool'hool'hool'zote to be released from your prison?" (Howard, as noted above, insisted the chief had already been released, but Joseph clearly says he was still in the stockade and was released on his appeal.)

Howard took only a little time considering Joseph's request for release and Joseph felt this was because the general had no real desire to keep the old chief in the stockade. The general, Joseph thought, had come to look upon the chief as his personal *bete noir*, so keeping him in captivity would likely produce a martyr who would cause further problems. He ordered the release whereupon the delegation mounted their horses and departed.

According to tribal legend (possibly apocryphal) the chiefs rode out of Lapwai proudly. Joseph stopped as he passed Chief Jason. Shifting position on his horse in order to gaze fully on the discomfited man, he cradled his rifle across his arm in a decidedly non-peaceful angle, stared down at Jason for a long moment with such undisguised contempt the older man, visibly frightened, hung his head and averted his eyes. Then Joseph, having spoken not a single word, rode away. Words had not been necessary. The message was clear.

Chief Timothy, the legend continues, having claimed illness, had not attended the meeting. His true reasons are easily guessed.

Chief Lawyer had died the previous year (January 7, 1876) but had he lived to meet Joseph that day it might have been an interesting confrontation.

Because versions of the proceedings differ so greatly it is difficult to determine an accurate summation. Howard replied to Joseph's accusative article by writing a rebuttal. He stated Joseph had been amenable to resettlement at Lapwai but had desired land already occupied. Dissuaded only through Howard's gentle argument, he eventually accepted the offer of equally valuable land near Kamiah. According to Howard, when Joseph agreed to the offer new papers were drawn up for signing. Howard also wrote that Joseph had *never* voiced objections to the thirty days deadline nor had he requested an extension. Neither, said Howard, had White Bird. Howard further wrote that Tool'hool'hool'zote, although still adamantly against resettlement, had promised to advise his people to accept resettlement. Looking Glass was already settled within Lapwai and White Bird had chosen acreage right next door to his farm. The Palouse chief (who is nowhere mentioned in Joseph's account)[21] also chose a fine piece of land for his people and had signed the papers. He alone, said Howard, had objected to the thirty-day deadline and had been allowed a further five days, which he accepted. However, Howard quickly withdrew the extension *and* the land offer, "because of something Kool'kool'cute (*sic*) said that indicated he was attempting to conceal his true intentions."[22]

Howard then returned the papers to Montieth telling him to give the land to someone else if the Palouse band did not report within the time limit.

Howard also wrote there was "a general joy..." among the Treaty Nez Perce, the non-Treaty Nez Perce and the white settlers at the peaceful outcome of the talks. When he wrote his article he either did so with tongue-in-cheek or was dreadfully naïve—or, what is more likely, was trying to cover errors he made in his reports to the secretary of war. If he truly believed the uncertainties of the past years were at last laid to rest, he deceived only himself, because no one else on either side ever mentioned—or even hinted at—"a general joy" or anything remotely akin to it having descended upon the various groups.

In fact, considering the social and political situation existing between the Nez Perce factions at the time, it is difficult to accept Howard's claim that Lapwai residents greeted the outcome of the talks with anything approximating "a general joy." He would surely have been aware of the opposition many Lapwai residents were expressing about the admittance of the non-Treaty bands. The majority did not want them in Lapwai at all and Howard had to be fully aware the majority of non-Treaty Indians were less than happy, despite having agreed to live on the reservation.

Lapwai residents had no great liking for their non-Treaty brothers for a number of reasons. Many begrudged their affluence, which was easily evaluated by the vast herds they owned. Their feelings towards the Dreamers were the direct opposite of tolerance. They feared the Dreamers would influence the young men who had grown restless over restrictions forced on them by reservation life. Envy was also felt for the unfettered freedom of spirit displayed by the non-Treaty Indians. The residents of Lapwai certainly did not share Howard's feeling of "a general joy."

Chiefs Jason and Timothy, for reasons political, were also fearful of the impending influx. They had established themselves as overall leaders, and various lesser chiefs who had attached themselves to their coattails had also carved tiny niches in the larger fiefdom. They all knew Joseph and White Bird were influential and could quickly upset the delicate balance of power. None wanted disruptions to the status quo. The Lapwai chiefs were not consumed by Howard's "general joy." The only chiefs of substance who would have welcomed the newcomers were Looking Glass and Big Thunder.

The Lapwai missionaries were fearful of the non-Treaty chiefs but held more dread of the grassroots Dreamers. The struggle for Native souls had been difficult enough, and the missionaries knew many of their converts were holding to their adopted beliefs by very slender threads. A religion such as that proselytized by the Dreamers could find fertile ground on which to cast the seeds of discourse, particularly among the young. For untold ages Nez Perces had been influenced by spirits and supernatural birds and animals they believed had once ruled the land, rivers and forests. Coyote-god, the right hand of the Great Spirit Chief, still held sway over the lives of many elders. Still popular was the prophetic power of the shamans. During that unsettled era the winner in a contest between Coyote-god and the Holy Ghost was impossible to predict. The missionaries were not anxious to see several hundred Dreamers running loose among their impressionable flock. They did not share Howard's feelings of "a general joy."

The only ones who could be said to be happy were the white settlers, ranchers and business interests. With all the Nez Perce bands confined in a controllable area, a sizeable region of untold wealth would soon be up for grabs. Invaluable acreage hitherto unavailable would immediately become farmland and free-range grazing for the ranchers' cattle and horses. Land values would rise with the expected influx of settlers. Forests would open to logging. Mountains would be free for mining. White men were the only ones expressing satisfaction, although not one of them ever mentioned it in Howard's quaint terminology.

Joseph's account of the conference's outcome again differed from Howard's "peaceful outcome" and the feeling of "a general joy." When he returned to the valley he was dismayed to see units of soldiers already bivouacked there. Even warriors less astute than Joseph easily determined the strategic placement of the soldiers' camps. The army was obviously in place to ensure the Indians moved out quietly without delay. Even the least clever among the warriors saw that Howard had known ahead of time how the talks would end.

Once again betrayal had come to the Indians at the instigation of the White Father Chief. When Joseph wrote[23] his 1879 article he not only tacitly accused General Howard that his handling of the conference showed he had lied out of hand, but that both Hayes and Grant had in turn been treacherous. All three were therefore no less perfidious than any other white man intent on stealing the Indians' land. Preordained treachery was not Joseph's imagination. Howard had indeed manipulated the proceedings to suit Hayes' agenda.

In the aftermath of the conference there began a series of mistakes and mistaken beliefs, not unusual given the aura of mistrust so prevalent at the time. Joseph himself was to dwell for years on his misunderstanding of Howard's reaction to the fervor Looking Glass exhibited when he greeted the chiefs. Joseph believed Howard had come to the conclusion that Looking Glass was in a conspiracy with others against the established reservation chiefs. Joseph was correct only in his belief that Howard had noticed the greeting. He was wrong in his belief the general was convinced conspirators were planning rebellion.

Also, somewhere along the way Joseph had become convinced Howard had issued orders for Looking Glass to be arrested and lodged in the stockade pending an investigation into the matter. The facts in the case were that Looking Glass, while not particularly happy in the confines of Lapwai, was not part of any conspiracy, nor was he about to lead a rebellion. Even had he wanted to revolt, he would never have succeeded in recruiting enough followers. There was no thought towards such a venture within his own band, and none whatever within others. Joseph had believed a fiction and had accepted it as true because shortly after the conference ended, Looking Glass, his family, and a number of warriors and their families had quietly left their homes. It was this that had led to the rumor that he was escaping the arrest Howard had ordered.

What actually happened had come about on a whim. Looking Glass, thinking he could perhaps re-open negotiations on his lost parcel of land, decided to move closer to the disputed area. He gained the agreement of several tribesmen and they, making their way through the forest to Clear Creek, occupied a campsite near their ancestral camping place. Looking Glass and his followers erected tepees indicative of a permanent camp along the banks of the Clearwater River—but still within the borders of Lapwai. There is no indication they had plans to travel elsewhere and Howard, as events show, had already dismissed his suspicions of Looking Glass as a conspirator. As fate would have it, however, the campsite was close to Tolo Lake; too close, as unfolding events were to prove. When the non-Treaty bands arrived at the lake in June the always-affable Looking Glass rode over with some warriors and, in his capacity as a non-Treaty chief, joined the conference. By this singular move he placed himself nearer to the fateful decision he was to be forced to make on July 1.

Joseph's account of Howard's reaction to Looking Glass' perceived mutiny runs contrary to established facts. Howard had *never* believed Looking Glass intended to join Joseph in a revolt, and he had said so in a conversation with one of Lapwai's chiefs.[24] It was not until June 28, with Joseph and the others already in open revolt, that Howard ordered Looking Glass be arrested. This order was issued only after Howard had been informed that several warriors from Looking Glass' band had pillaged some settlers' homes. His informants had misidentified the renegades. Howard may have had doubts of the informants' identification but had no way of knowing it was false, so he had to take the report seriously. Howard's doubts appear clear because he dispatched an officer and a company of infantry to the Clear Creek camp. The officer was under direct orders to detain Looking Glass and those with him. He was to escort them to Mount Idaho for safekeeping under the protection of the militia commander. That would end any chance for Looking Glass to join Joseph.

Howard later explained his orders, though made verbally, had been explicit. He had given no authority whatever for an attack on the camp.[25] The unit's commander disregarded the orders and launched an attack. By his brash action he forced Looking Glass into his fateful decision.

Thus, the events of the Lapwai Council—and the consequences arising from its aftermath—remain shrouded in uncertainty amid conflicting versions. In Howard's defense, it should be noted that while he certainly resorted to less-than-ethical tactics, he did make serious offers to Joseph and the others. It is equally certain the offers had been accepted. Some of Howard's other orders had not been so well understood, or perhaps had been poorly translated. It is equally possible some errors were conveniently forgotten by Howard, who refused to admit making them.

Perhaps Joseph did not complain about the thirty-day deadline but, considering the Snake River's condition at the time, logic dictates he would have requested an extension. Joseph and others always insisted he had, and all were equally adamant his request had been denied. This begs the question: why would Howard refuse Joseph extra time yet grant Husis Kute, who had no rivers to traverse, the same request, albeit for only five days? Howard's writings offer no explanation.

Other questions remaining unanswered are whether Tool'hool'hool'zote was released from the stockade through Howard's act of consideration or through Joseph's supplication. This also will never be resolved, the only certainty being that he was released and he did leave with the others. Did Joseph ask for land already settled or did Howard offer it? This also will never be known. The two accounts of the entire council proceedings are of the "he did, he did not" variety, the word of one man against that of another. These are questions to which the answers are lost in the mists of time.

There are, on the other hand, some recollections that give a certain credence to Howard's accounts of the council proceedings and its aftermath. Some independent accounts of the proceedings agree, at least to some extent, with those of the general. Still, it is exceedingly difficult to believe Howard over Joseph, whose account is backed by others, among them Captain Perry and Agent Montieth, both of whom took notes during the proceedings. Perry, though he was Joseph's formidable foe during the early fighting, later wrote in his favor. Montieth was no friend of the chief and he left no writings outside of agency reports, but in one report he backs Joseph. It is also possible—perhaps probable considering the dubious fiber of his character—that Chapman translated incorrectly from time to time. Many translators were less than trustworthy in that era, with Chapman standing first among those deemed exceedingly untrustworthy.[26]

Joseph's versions of events following the Lapwai Council, the departure from Wallowa, the initial skirmishes, the major battles and the pursuit itself read differently from Howard's. This is mainly because Joseph's accounts contain a vast array of eyewitness facts, his own and others' which give substantive credence to his narratives.

Howard, on the other hand, was only once during his pursuit ever closer than two days march and was often behind two to three weeks. Aside from the engagement at the Clearwater River, he never participated in a major battle. Of that encounter, which Howard claimed as a victory, he so greatly exaggerated the outcome his entire account is shrouded with doubt. The only important skirmish in which he was directly involved was at Camus Meadows, and that ended in defeat, which put him even further in the wake of the fast-moving tribesmen. He was so late arriving at the Bear's Paw he saw no action there. Thus, only twice was Howard or anyone in his company in a position to provide eyewitness accounts.

Thus, Joseph's accounts of the three councils, Lapwai's aftermath, the causes of the rebellion, the great trek, and the battles and skirmishes must be awarded more weight than Howard's. Joseph was an eyewitness at all times. Howard, with the two abovementioned exceptions, was not.

[CHAPTER 6 ENDNOTES]

1   This ploy is still used to this day by First Nations' negotiators in talks with state, provincial and federal governments on both sides of the border. It is particular-

ly popular in discussions pertaining to mineral, fishing, hunting and timber rights. [Author's files.]

2   Although Howard, in his 1881 article and subsequent writings, had made no mention of weapons at Lapwai, in 1907 he suddenly recalled the Indians were armed at Lapwai. He wrote, "every Indian appeared to have… some weapon at hand…"; and also, "At that instance some of the Indians were on the point of plunging their knives into my breast, but Joseph and White Bird both counseled delay." [Howard, *My Life and Experiences Among Our Hostile Indians*, 254 and 256.]

3   Howard, in his woeful ignorance of Nez Perce law, always considered Joseph the leader of the non-Treaty bands. He never realized, even with the passage of years, that Joseph was a civic chief, nor did he realize that Joseph had never encouraged the rebellion. [Author's files and many other sources.]

4   General Howard wrote later that White Bird arrived four days late and that the conference had been delayed at Joseph's request. Joseph, however, clearly states White Bird arrived with him and in no way delayed the opening.

5   Joseph's trust in Chapman was misplaced, as he was to discover over the next several years. Chapman led a group of militia during the Battle at White Bird Canyon. Reports confirm it had been he who fired upon a group of Indians as they emerged under a white flag to parley. Chapman later assisted Howard in tracking the Nez Perces during the flight. Chapman gained salaried employment as a federal translator and was assigned to serve as Joseph's interpreter during his exile in Oklahoma and his visits to Washington. It was during this latter period that Chapman's perfidy became clear to all. [For a biographical sketch of this thoroughly despicable man see Appendix E.]

6   The Asotins were actually under Chief Jason, but Old Looking Glass had separated his band from Jason over the latter's alliance with Spalding. The break became complete when Jason supported the Treaty of 1863, which Young Looking Glass opposed. [McWhorter, *Hear me My Chiefs*.]

7   The Lewis and Clark Expedition [1804–06] is a somewhat over-ballyhooed event. Granted, it has historical value in that it opened the northwest to American expansion and charted a large area of previously unknown territory; but it has become blown out of proportion owing to the American penchant for creating legends from ordinary feats. The "unknown territory" was far from unknown except to Americans. Much of the northwest was already well covered by Spanish, British and Canadian explorers. Simon Fraser, a Canadian from Cornwall, Ontario, covered much of the west to the Pacific coast during 1805–8; and before him Alexander Mackenzie, a Scotsman domiciled in Canada, had already mapped vast areas north of the 49th parallel. In 1792–3, Fraser became the first white man to cross the Rocky Mountains into BC. The Lewis and Clark expedition was actually a Johnny-come-lately affair. In fact, had it not been for the Nez Perces and Sacajawea, a Shoshone woman married to a Canadian guide, the entire expedition would have perished in the Idaho mountains during its first year. Fraser and Mackenzie had required no such help. [*Chambers Biographical Dictionary*, 7th Edition (2002); also: Author's files.]

8   Looking Glass emphasized his opposition by participating in the short-lived Lapwai Rebellion of 1868.

9   Conversation with Park Ranger Jim Magera at The Bear's Paw Battlefield Memorial Site, September 19, 2009.

10 This arrogance appears quite visible in the 1871

photograph taken by William Henry Jackson, the noted frontier photographer.

11   His first disastrous error was insisting the Crows could be counted on for help. Over White Bird's objections Looking Glass convinced the other band chiefs of the sincerity of his one-time allies. The long southern detour in search of the Crow chiefs led to the Big Hole disaster. That error alone conclusively fixes his failed leadership as the decisive factor in the ultimate defeat. [Author's files.]

12   Snake Creek lies just forty-three miles from the border, less than two days easy travel.

13   Lee's account was taken from an article written by Lt. Charles Wood, General Howard's aide de camp. (See: Bibliography.)

14   Howard's eventual written version of the negotiations differ greatly from those of Joseph, Yellow Wolf, Howard's aide de camp and many others involved. (See: Howard, Oliver O., "The True Story of the Wallowa Campaign," *The North American Review*, July 1879.)

15   The chief was correct, but at the time there were no sympathetic organizations to forward the case. The non-Treaty bands could have overturned the 1855 treaty in 1863 when Washington pushed through the reduction of the boundaries because the revision, indeed the original treaty, was illegal—but the Indians did not know it. [Author's files.]

16   John B. Montieth, the Indian agent at Lapwai, was an appointee of the Presbyterian Church, which, under the Grant administration, had instituted its so-called "Peace Policy." Montieth was particularly unhappy with the non-Treaty Indians' annual winter sojourn on the reservation, seeing it as a Dreamer plot to re-convert others back to the Traditionalist beliefs.

17 Howard, O.O., *The True Story of the Wallowa Campaign*.

18 The annual fish migration began in September. (The Nez Perce calendar divided a year into natural phases.) Joseph was asking the trek to Lapwai be delayed to the end of August.

19 Howard, it should be noted, was under direct orders to issue this ultimatum. It was the Washington officials who had insisted on a thirty-day limit.

20 Whether at this point they were fully resigned to resettlement is difficult to assess. It appears Joseph, Ollokot and Husis Kute, the Palouse spokesman, were resigned, but others not so much. They may have discussed the matter previously to consider what they could do should Howard prevail, as he obviously had, but now realized negotiations had never been on the agenda.

21 According to Joseph, the Palouse chief and his warriors joined the war only after fighting had commenced. Joseph intimates the Palouse were drawn into the fighting because they believed Lapwai land had been treacherously denied them.

22 Howard, perhaps thinking of his *bete noir*, Tool'hool'hool'zote, misspelled the Palouse chief's name in all of his accounts. [Author]

23 Because there was no written Nez Perce language Joseph did not "write" his own statements. These were transcribed by others from his direct statements at interviews, congressional hearings, and conversations with influential people who had taken interest in his case. [Author's files]

24 June 24, 1877. [Box 1, entry 897, part 3 1877, US Army Continental Command Archives.]

25 Howard. *Nez Perces Campaign of 1877*, published September 19, 1878.

26   In September 1877 the Sioux chief, Crazy Horse, who had recently surrendered, was imprisoned at Camp Robinson, Nebraska. He was approached by General Terry and asked if, for future considerations, he would lead his Ogalala warriors against Joseph. Crazy Horse, speaking through a translator, Frank Grouard, replied, "I will fight until not a single Nez Perce remains alive." Grouard told Terry Crazy Horse had said, "I will fight until not a single white man remains standing." Terry was infuriated. He ordered Crazy Horse returned to the jail. Confused by Terry's reaction, he struggled against his guards and was shot and killed. It is thought by many that Grouard deliberately misinterpreted the reply because of a long-standing hatred of Crazy Horse. It is highly possible Chapman did the same thing at Lapwai. As events unfolded over the next six years, it became clear that Chapman was not above giving misleading information if he thought he could profit from it. [Thrapp, Dan. L., *Encyclopedia of Frontier Biography*, Vol. 2, G–O, 692–3. Also, many others sources available.]

[CHAPTER 7]

THE RIVER SPIRITS are ANGRY

When he returned to his village, Joseph set about the onerous task of telling his people they must leave their beloved valley. First, though, he had to allay their fears over the presence of soldiers, no easy undertaking as some of the young warriors were already muttering about driving them out. They settled down when Joseph assured them the soldiers were not there to cause trouble. Still, he remained concerned, knowing any spark could ignite a flame among hot-headed members of his band. Just one wrong word or a misunderstood gesture from a soldier could set the entire area ablaze.

At this point, though resigned to resettlement within the thirty-day limit, his primary concern was how best to accomplish the logistic nightmares that were sure to be encountered in meeting the deadline.

For a number of years some researchers also believed Joseph had agreed to assimilate the Piquinins into his band at the request of Tool'hool'hool'zote, who had told Joseph his band could go to Lapwai but he would not go with them.[1] Once the Piquinins were settled they could elect a new band chief. However, this has never been confirmed; it is only known that Tool'hool'hool'zote did leave his band for a time.

The Piquinin band numbered less than 180 individuals, which

included about thirty warriors; but no figures are available for summation of females, elders, children or non-combatant males. They inhabited an area situated along the Idaho (east) bank of the Snake River,[a] with their immediate neighbors being White Bird's Lamtamas, while the Wellamotkin band lived in Oregon several miles west of the Snake River. Geographically, it would have made more sense for Tool'hool'hool'zote to have approached White Bird with his request.

Why Tool'hool'hool'zote had not asked White Bird to absorb his band—if, indeed, he had asked anyone—remains a puzzle; and no reason for his leaving his band was ever forthcoming, either. It is only known that he rejoined his people at Tolo Lake. Perhaps he had simply decided to remain alone in the wilds for a time. In any event Joseph was not required to take in the Piquinins. If the suppositions are verifiable—the Piquinins did accompany the Wellamotkins to Tolo Lake—where they made contact is not known, but certainly it was not in Oregon. None of them would have dared a river crossing knowing they would have to cross again within a few days. Looking at the geography and logistics, it seems unlikely the story of a proposed union of the two bands is true.

Joseph's immediate concern and major problem was how to cross the Snake River.[2] Going around this natural barrier between Oregon and Idaho was prohibitive, so a crossing had to be made at some point and expediency dictated the crossing be reasonably close. As Joseph had warned Howard, the river was in full and raging flood. Icy water—the late melt-off of winter snow high in the mountains—cascaded via dozens of mountain streams, filling the river to capacity. Even at its widest, the flatlands far to the west, the river's banks were hard-pressed to accommodate the pounding torrent. Normal fording places were flooded. Treacherous eddies, deep and swirling, produced cross currents and undertows capable of pulling humans and animals below the surface. Any living thing losing footing in the churning water would be swept quickly away

---

a   See map: *Nez Perce Territory in 1877*.

to probable death through drowning or being battered against jagged rocks. The odds of crossing safely were definitely not favorable. Scouts were told to ride as far as necessary to find any fording place offering even a modicum of safety. Joseph had doubts such a place could be found. The river was a roiling monster. Clearly the river spirits were angry.

Crossing the river would be just the first phase of the journey. Once that had been accomplished—if indeed it could be—ahead lay a difficult trek to Eewatham[3] [Small-Body-of-Water], a solitary lake on Camus Prairie, the agreed place of rendezvous. While the walk itself would take only two to four days, dense forest and heavy brush lay between them and the flat lands of Camus Prairie. Tall weeds, thorns, gravel and sharp stones underfoot awaited them. It had been decided the three Nez Perce bands would join with the Palu band there to meet in council before moving on to the reservation proper.

The council would be held at Tepahlewam [Split Rocks], an unusual rock formation near the camping grounds at Eewatham. When and why the decision for yet another council had been made has never been fully known, as reporting to Lapwai singularly would have been much easier with less travel involved. Credible reasons have been suggested from time to time, with one implying that reporting en_masse was simply a way to show solidarity. Another, it is suspected, was to allow the four chiefs to make a final decision about whether to obey or defy the government's order.

Tepahlewam had once been considered sacred by shamans and tewats [medicine men], but with the passage of time the sacred status had dissipated. The lake, now known as Tolo Lake,[4] became a popular site for Nez Perce bands to gather each summer to visit and exchange gifts. The annual gatherings were celebrations lasting several days, the lakeshore a playground for happy, laughing children, while games, sports and archery events occupied the adults. There were also opportunities to gamble, the popular sideline of many adult males. A highlight of the festivities was the ever-popular horse races. Not all was play. Business deals were finalized and band chiefs discussed inter-band topics. The women spent mornings harvesting roots and bulbs and afternoons in visits and gossip. Evenings were reserved for participation in ritual dances and ceremonies. Adults and older children, dressed in ceremonial garb, participated. The gatherings ended in 1863 when the revised treaty no longer allowed travel beyond the new borders.

But before Joseph could even consider thoughts of Tepahlewam, he had to solve the immediate problem of a very dangerous river crossing. He was not surprised when scouts returned to reveal the usual fording places were not even reasonably safe. This necessitated a delay in his planned departure, which he feared would hinder arrival at Lapwai. He had no doubts Howard would exercise his threat to have the army take total charge of the move, and that would mean the loss of all their livestock. Of course he knew the soldiers would not be able to get the people across the river either, but they would corral everyone into some canyon forcing them to stay there until the river quieted enough for a crossing to be made. Joseph knew the soldiers would never allow the time needed to herd many hundreds of animals on an enforced journey, thereby fulfilling Howard's grim prophecy of farmers and ranchers seizing them. Joseph knew crossing was imperative, and it must be made quickly. With each wasted, passing day he grew more concerned.

Finally scouts returned with reports of finding two locations considered safe. Joseph ordered departure to begin the next morning. The exact day on which they started their sorrowful journey is not certain, but it is known they broke camp near the end of the third week of May. A report from army scouts reached General Howard at the beginning of the month's final week.

> *"Joseph's band, accompanied by the Pikunin (sic)...[have struck their tepees] and are now driving large herds of horses and cattle towards the river."*[5]

General Howard, who had remained at Fort Lapwai to await developments, was pleased to learn the bands were moving. With Joseph heading toward the Snake River and White Bird moving north he assumed the chiefs had decided to report to Lapwai as directed. He slept a little easier that night.

Joseph, on the other hand, neither slept well that night nor would he for several more. The exodus may have been underway to Howard's satisfaction, but Joseph was greatly worried. Fearing the problems he knew lay ahead, he hurried the dismantling of the camp and got the people underway, hoping the river spirits had not increased their anger during the night.

Joseph had also considered the danger involved should a simultaneous arrival of humans and animals take place at the river's edge. He placed the drovers under orders to keep the herds already rounded up[6] well back until progress showed separation of at least one day. Only then should they begin moving the animals. If the drovers welcomed the absence of their chief's fretfulness, they were equally pleased by the lack of restiveness among the horses. A number of the numerous mares in the herds would soon be in estrus and that meant the stallions would become difficult to keep in check. Controlling a moving herd under such circumstances would be a very difficult task.

Joseph had been pleased when progress to the river[7] produced neither mishap nor delay; but on arrival a setback, which was to have far-reaching effects, was encountered. Considered reasonably safe only a day earlier, the site was now dismissed as too dangerous. The trek continued to the second location, but that proved no better. Scouts began looking for other sites and eventually found a ford at a place called Dug Bar. This they determined was placid enough to permit a reasonably safe crossing. The long line began its detour to Dug Bar.

Unfortunately, during the delay at the rejected crossings, the animal herd, still tightly herded, had begun its own journey. When the drovers received word to delay the advance they encountered increasing problems in slowing momentum. As a result the herd moved closer, so separation was reduced from the preferred one day to a few hours.

Dug Bar, though less treacherous than the ford they had just left, still presented a less than comfortable margin of safety. Regardless of risk, it was here the crossing would have to be made, but it would take much longer than first thought. Joseph's worry increased further when news of the approaching herd was brought to him.

The Nez Perces certainly knew how to cross rivers with all their goods and belongings, but moving dozens of women, babies, small children and elderly people (some of whom were sick or infirm) across that swirling water with its treacherous eddies and cross currents was intimidating. Crossing with hundreds of animals was a totally different situation, so the imminent cheek-by-jowl arrival of unpredictable horses and hundreds of easily spooked cattle was daunting. Joseph needed no time to decide only the horses, nimble and intelligent, could manage the risky transit. Plodding cattle, dull of mind and lacking agility, had little chance of survival under such conditions. Joseph and all his able-bodied men set to the task, knowing they had hours of hard work ahead of them. No doubt he envied White Bird whose band, living as it did along the northern bank of Idaho's Salmon River, did not even have to face the challenge of a crossing that river. Though the Salmon was also in flood, its flow was relatively tranquil when compared to the fury of the mighty Snake.

Joseph ordered the cattle to be herded to pasture some distance away. There they could be tended under the care of a few older boys until the people had crossed in their entirety. The horses were also pastured except for several that were cut from the herd to assist in the crossing. Once all the people were safely on the other side the herdsmen would bring forward the remaining horses in small, manageable groups.

It was with the gravest trepidation the people contemplated the perilous crossing. Serious innovation was called for but none could recall when such intense excogitation had been required. Treks to and from winter to summer camps had never involved crossing the Snake. When the river had to be crossed, fording sites were used after the water spirits had returned to their rest and the waters had calmed. In fact, within living memory of even the oldest men and women the Snake had never been crossed in large groups at this time of year. Neither had anyone ever crossed accompanied by so many animals. Several elders, all very old, came forward. Recalling tales they had heard as children, they revived methods of how a crossing involving the least risk could be made.

Under their tutelage tepee covers were formed into large bales then tied tightly together to form rafts. Lodge poles secured to their sides provided extra buoyancy. Horses tethered alongside each raft would act as buttresses against the current. Elders said they would test the safety of the rafts by crossing first. If all went well the women and children would follow. Finally the warriors would make the crossing.

Strong men grasped the ropes that bound the hides and, acting in unison with the horses, moved the rafts forward one by one with lines tightly closed and barely two feet between. Each of the makeshift rafts was eased into the churning water. Men swimming beside the rafts held tightly to the ropes controlling the horses. Close proximity enabled the swimmers to prevent any raft from breaking out of line to be lost in the swirling waters. The rafts made many crossings before all the people had safely reached the opposite bank. Many warriors made several crossings each to swim alongside while shouting encouragement to the children, all of whom were understandably frightened. In this manner the people conquered the mighty Snake River and its bone-chilling water to gain safety on the far bank. It was not a fording they would have attempted under normal circumstances.

It was late afternoon before the last feet touched ground on the opposite shore and the crossing was complete. Though it had taken longer than initially estimated, the far side had been gained with few incidents. No one had been swept away, no one had drowned, there had been no serious injuries, and no horses were injured or lost to the flood. Then, as the people milled about on the shore, there occurred on the recently vacated bank what could have resulted in calamity. When they realized what was happening they quickly vacated the area, rushing to gain higher ground.

In anticipation of their own crossing the drovers handling the remaining animals had again begun moving the herds closer to the river. Such were the numbers the handlers were unable to keep them under control. As the animals in the rear pushed forward into the confined area, those in front were forced into the water and all plans for entry in small groups went awry. Crowded together as they were there began a mad plunge into the roiling water. In the milling and pushing some stumbled and fell, to be trampled in the crush of those coming behind. Some cattle were swept downstream by the current and lost, but most survived and were later recovered. The horses fortunately all managed to cross safely to clamber ashore on the opposite bank. What could have ended in a terrible disaster was averted only because the human crossing had already been completed.

This incident has been attributed squarely to criminal actions by a group of local white settlers, reportedly a dozen or more. They had been watching the exodus from a distance and then rode into the farthest fringes of the pastured herds. Some began "cutting out"[8] and driving off large numbers of cattle. The drovers wisely offered no resistance, thereby avoiding a general gunfight, but unwisely hurriedly rushed the bulk of their charges to the river.

The cattle that survived the crossing never progressed beyond the Salmon River.[9] Joseph decided they should be left in pasture for later retrieval, a plan that would have succeeded had it not been for the events of the next few days. When fighting broke out, the herd was abandoned. Over the next weeks, settlers and ranchers took the entire herd, a loss the Indians would never regain. As a result, during the long trek that followed, not a single cow or steer accompanied the Indians.

However, their horses all crossed the two rivers safely and, despite losses along the way, the Nez Perce rebels retained a fairly large, though diminishing, herd until the final surrender at The Bear's Paw. Many horses ran off during the initial minutes of the disastrous Battle of the Big Hole River, but most were recovered. Several dozen were lost along the trail to Crow and Bannock marauders. A few, no longer deemed useful, were abandoned along the way. A large number (some 300) accompanied White Bird's escapees on their successful flight to Canada. Of the two hundred or so that remained with Joseph, some were released into the woods before the surrender. Those remaining were confiscated by the army.

With the river crossing behind them, camp was made in a sparse, craggy defile now called Rocky Canyon. Joseph decided to remain two days in the canyon so his tired people could rest and the animals could graze in a nearby field. The rafts were taken apart so the hides could dry. That first evening as the sun began its descent, army scouts watching from a distance realized Joseph intended to stay awhile. They departed for Fort Lapwai and on June 2 reported the details of their surveillance to Captain Perry. He in turn briefed General Howard on the latest developments.

[CHAPTER 7 ENDNOTES]

1   This, if true, is further proof that Tool'hool'hool'zote was indeed a band chief and not a medicine man or shaman, as thought by early researchers. Only a band chief had the authority to make such a deal. [Author's files.]

2   The Snake, 1,040 miles (1,664 km) in length, though a river in its own right, is also the longest tributary of the Columbia River. While very wide in places, it is dangerously narrow in others where steep cliffs rise. The section Joseph had to traverse is twenty-five miles (40 km) south of the Washington/Oregon boundary. The Snake River's run of 200 miles (320 km) where it cuts through the Blue Mountains and the Salmon River Mountains marks the Oregon-Idaho border. The section of the river Joseph could safely cross has dozens of rapids. In 1877 all were more than normally treacherous because of the heavy spring runoff.

The river got its name through a misunderstanding. When the first white explorers asked a group of Natives the river's name the Natives replied in Plains Indian sign language. They moved their hands forward in a series of undulating motions. This means "many fish swimming." The explorers misinterpreted the sign by thinking the motions meant "snakes," hence the name. [www.tomlaidlaw.com/otkiosks/snake.html]

3   Eewatham had been molded thousands of years in the past, possibly from the impact of a huge meteorite.

4   Although the traditional Nez Perce name for the lake was Eewatham, it was renamed Tolo Lake for a Nez Perce woman named Too'lah (also known as Aleblemot) who warned the Slate Creek settlers of the renegade Lamtama youths. She then rode to Florence to get assistance. A monument erected in her honor in 1939 stands in Red Rock Canyon. [Elsensohn, *Pioneer Days in Idaho County*, Vol. 1, 281–82.]

5   This report is undoubtedly the source of the above-mentioned rumor of the agreement between Joseph and Tool'hool'hool'zote. Why the army scouts reported the presence of the Piquinin is confusing. No one else reported their presence, and it is illogical to think the Piquinin band, knowing they would have to cross again with Joseph a few days later, could have crossed when Joseph could not. A more plausible answer might be that a Piquinin hunting party, stranded in Oregon, sought shelter with the Wellamotkins. [Author's opinion.]

6   A number of riders had also been dispatched in small groups to retrieve animals still at large. It was a truly formidable task that would continue for several days, but there was still time.

7   Various campsites used during the traverse to the river have been marked by plaques and can be seen from the Buckhorn Springs Lookout, Joseph Canyon Viewpoint and Tom'mah'talk'ke'sin'mah [White and Fluffy Soil]. Located near the town of Enterprise, it is an area where groups of Nez Perce families camped along Trout Creek

to catch the spring run of salmon. Hunters also visited the nearby salt licks that attracted game animals. [www.ourheritage.net]

8   The term "cutting out" denotes selection of preferred animals as opposed to a general "round-up," the indiscriminate capture of an entire herd. In the Old West a "round-up" included all steers, horses or cows encountered. Afterwards, the animals were sorted by brands and were expected to be released or returned to their rightful owners. An animal lacking a brand was called a "maverick" and could be kept. [Author's files.]

9   The necessity of leaving the cattle on the far side of the Salmon River, the subsequent fighting, and the theft by settlers meant the fleeing Nez Perces had no cattle left that could be used as a source of emergency food on their long trek. Reports by some militia members at Fort Fizzle of seeing many steers with the Nez Perces have no basis in fact. According to Chief Peo'peo'Tholket [Bird Alighting], much of the greater herd was left at the Snake and the Salmon Rivers and was taken by settlers. The herd that did cross the Snake was brought only as far as the Salmon River. These animals were left there under the care of a few men who were so hurriedly recalled to join the trek they could not bring the cattle with them. This herd, too, was systematically stolen by ranchers and farmers. Reports of driving a large herd of cattle through Montana is total fiction. The horses on the other hand were relatively numerous, but there were no cattle and thus no readily available meat for food. [McWhorter, *Hear Me My Chiefs,* 176.]

[CHAPTER 8]
DISSENSION AMID DISARRAY

The Lake Tolo councils in 1877 witnessed prolonged and rancorous debate among the leaders of the different bands regarding their imminent movement onto the reservation.
—Jerome A. Greene, *Nez Perce Summer*, 1877.

Some of the optimism General Howard had felt on June 2 dissipated by several degrees a few days later. On June 5, scouts reported Joseph's band had left Rocky Canyon and had proceeded twenty miles east where a crossing of the Salmon River was accomplished. They later reported the direction traveled was now east, not north towards Fort Lapwai as expected. He was further disturbed when he began receiving reports that all the bands were traveling away from Lapwai. A quick look at a map indicated the routes of progression would converge at Tolo Lake. This caused him no small amount of annoyance and anxiety, for such a convergence meant the chiefs were intending yet another of their seemingly endless councils.

The thought of another inter-band parley discomfited Howard for he was well aware of the Indian predilection for changing their collective minds, often on a mere whim. He began to fear his carefully laid plans might be unraveling. He drew but small comfort when informed the bands would still be within fifteen miles of the reservation's southern boundary. Regardless, the general could not help but wonder why they were venturing to a point so far east when the most logical contact point would have been where the Fort Lapwai Trail joined the main road connecting Mount Idaho and Lewiston. Still, the nearness to the reservation's eastern expanse gave him some comfort.

Because the overall picture was still unfolding as prefigured, at least temporarily, there seemed at least a reason to relax. Convergence in one spot by a great number of people, the majority of whom were elders, women and children, should be easy enough to contain. With the added encumbrance of hundreds of animals (he had not yet learned of the cattle left behind), the advantage lay with the army. For some added insurance he placed the Fort Lapwai detachment on immediate alert[1] then informed several militias within a wide radius as far south as Fort Boise to go on short notice alert.

An officer experienced in logistics was called in. A quick estimate enabled him to inform Howard the final convergence was in all likelihood Tepahlewam, a former meeting site near Tolo Lake. The final leg of their trek into the reservation proper would take no more than two days and no more than another seven to reach Fort Lapwai. Both entry and reporting dates were well within the respective deadlines.

Howard now shifted his concern to ensuring the Indians enter the reservation proper no later than the June 15 deadline. So far as it concerned Howard, once inside the reservation they could take their own time to report to Agent Montieth who could then begin placing them on their assigned acres. Seeing resettlement was now nearing its successful completion, he informed Captain Perry he would depart for Portland the day after the Indians entered the reservation. Within hours, however, his natural tendency for caution returned. Instead of Portland, he decided to go only as far as Fort Boise and wait there a few days just to make sure all was still going well.

Following the successful crossing of the Snake River,[2] the people and the horses, well rested by their two-day sojourn in Rocky Canyon, moved quickly along the next leg of the journey. Following were teenage boys assigned to herd the cattle that had managed to cross the river safely. Upon reaching the next obstacle, the Salmon River, Joseph saw it did not pose the intense perplexities encountered at the Snake. It did, however, hold enough risk to warrant leaving the cattle at pasture on the river's south bank. They were left under the protection of some warriors who were instructed to herd them across the river as soon as a crossing could be safely made and proceed independently to Lapwai. With that matter resolved, the long line of men, women and children began a safe traversal. When the people had crossed, the horses followed and the trek continued.

Following an uneventful four days they reached Tepahlewam to be met by White Bird whose band was encamped near the canyon that bore his name. Later that afternoon Looking Glass and a few of his warriors rode in from their camp near the delta formed by Clear Creek, the Clearwater River and the Middle Fork.[a] A few hours later Husis Kute with sixteen warriors and the majority of the Palouse band entered the area. Their aged band chief, Hahtalekin,[3] arrived the next day with an additional sixteen warriors plus several members of a Cayuse band who had joined him for reasons, never explained, of their own.[4] This addition completed the Palouse camp and brought to a final count about 191 men capable of bearing arms.[5]

There were others, not of the warrior class, who proved capable of fighting but their contribution is not fully known. These included older, middle-aged men past the age of combat readiness whose fighting endurance had limits, and youths whose day had

---

a   *For locations of the various camps, see maps.*

not yet come, as well some teenage boys with limited qualifications. How effective these males were during the various encounters with the army remains unknown. As none were considered warriors few, if any, were chosen to participate in war parties. There were instances, particularly during the Big Hole battle, where women took up arms when some soldiers managed to infiltrate the village.

Research shows the total number of able-bodied warriors in all the bands probably never numbered above two hundred, and only the one hundred and fifty-five Nez Perce warriors have been identified. In most cases the roles of those identified have been established to some degree, as have the exploits of others who also bore arms from time to time. Most of those unidentified were of the Asotin and Palu bands. Because not all the warriors fought in every battle or skirmish—the major fights at Big Hole and Bear's Paw being exceptions—they rarely assembled as a cohesive force. Nonetheless, all the identified warriors stand in Nez Perce histories as having contributed in one way or another. Those contributions will be dealt with in future pages.

The next day Tool'hool'hool'zote arrived and took charge of his band. Thus, the non-Treaty chiefs once again gathered to discuss the final phase of their entry into Lapwai.

Tepees spread across a wide area creating a huge village housing a population numbering well over 800.[6] The number increased over the next few days as friends and relatives, defying the no-travel ban, began arriving from Lapwai. These visitors, though intent on welcoming the newcomers, also intended to prepare them for the hostility they were certain to encounter from Lapwai residents who did not want the non-Treaty Indians for neighbors under any circumstances.

While the people rested and visited, the chiefs met in council.[7] It was at this point a dismaying atmosphere began to develop. While Joseph, Ollokot, White Bird and, judging from his unexpected return, even Tool'hool'hool'zote had resigned themselves to Lapwai, many Lamtama and Piquinin warriors and their war chiefs were having serious second thoughts. Acute dissension now entered the picture as the overall mood began to change. Dissatisfaction against enforced resettlement began to appear first among the elders, few of whom expressed optimism for success or wanted to surrender the freedom of the old ways. This embitterment had spread to younger men, who had the most to lose considering the restrictions life on a reservation would bring. Few could be found in favor. Among the chiefs there was only resignation bordering on lethargy. Neither White Bird nor Tool'hool'hool'zote shared Joseph's belief a return of their land could be negotiated. Though both chiefs were resigned to life at Lapwai, neither did anything to restrain the discourse of public opinion now humming within their respective bands.[8]

The Palu chiefs subscribed to the views espoused by Joseph and Ollokot, but the Cayuses who had joined them were less favorable. Looking Glass supported Joseph's views.[9] To Joseph and Ollokot it was becoming more and more apparent that some warriors under White Bird and Tool'hool'hool'zote were close to defying the order to enter Lapwai. It was also becoming obvious they were wielding their influence amongst others. The direction a final vote would take depended greatly on the influence exerted by lesser chiefs, so Joseph and his brother, hopeful of swaying the vote back towards Lapwai, sought to influence enough chiefs to their points of view. For several days the debate was mainly thrust and parry with Ollokot, highly influential among the war chiefs, lobbying in favor of Lapwai. Using measured counseling, Ollokot convinced many the move was not only pragmatic it was wise. Several Lamtama and Piqunin chiefs began to consider his point.

The only accounts of this fateful conference survive through interviews that survivors of the revolt granted to writers many years later,[10] but from these interviews much can be learned of the proceedings. Probably the most important revelations came from Yellow Bull and Yellow Wolf, both generally considered as the most important of the sub-chiefs interviewed. They gave accurate accounts, first to Walter Camp and later to Lucullus McWhorter[11] casting excellent light upon what had actually transpired, not only at Tepahlewam but throughout the entire trek. Both related in detail the proceedings from the meeting at Tepahlewam, the long trek to Bear Paw, the ensuing siege and the years spent in exile.

Serious debate, often acrimonious, raged among the factions. Ollokot argued acceptance of resettlement was better than seeking a dubious freedom in some illusive Elsewhere Land.[12] That no one had any perceivable idea of where this Utopian demesne might be located carried weight. Even Tool'hool'hool'zote, irrespective of his supposed powers of prophesy, was unable to visualize its location.

Looking Glass counseled the move to Lapwai as best but contended, should migration become necessary, Montana would be their best destination. He was certain a promise made to him by Crow chiefs following the combined Nez Perce/Crow victory over the Sioux/Cheyenne coalition three years previously assured their cooperation and support. White Bird, always suspicious of treaties and agreements, regardless of perceived sincerity, was not enthusiastic. Promises made during heady celebrations of victory, he countered, were rarely substantial. Looking Glass dropped the subject. As events unfolded he revived it later in Montana.

Back and forth the pendulum of opinion swung. White Bird proposed and argued for resettlement in Canada, as he feared grave danger would stalk the bands in Montana. He felt they would be safer in "The land of the Grandmother" where the U.S. Army had no jurisdiction. He also felt a return of their lands could perhaps be negotiated from Canada. Very few others, including Joseph and Ollokot, favored the idea and it was discarded.

White Bird, proper name Peopeo Kiskio'hinih [White Pelican or sometimes, White Goose], was at the time probably seventy-two years of age, having been born in Idaho about 1805. He had been a warrior and a hunter, and then became a ceremonialist and a shaman. The oldest of all the chiefs, he was also the most experienced in life's struggles. He did not trust or respect any of Washington's emissaries, considering them men who would promise anything and then break those promises at will. He was a reluctant chief who had been drafted into the position when the band elders could not decide on a successor. Thinking it was a temporary solution, he had accepted the position only to find it was considered permanent. It was White Bird who devised most of the strategies and tactics that defeated or humiliated Howard, Sturgis and Gibbon. His greatest weakness was putting too much faith in what to expect should the bands reach Canada. He also had trouble controlling his younger warriors who had developed a taste for whiskey, as he had no warrior chief such as Ollokot to keep them in check.

Meanwhile, the chiefs seemed unaware of other meetings being held on the camp fringes. Around their own campfires young warriors were darkly advocating all-out war. Most realized such action was tantamount to a final stand, but the desire to live free overrode the prospect of a confined life. The young warriors, often less than discreet, were unknowingly overheard by a visiting Treaty Nez Perce. While passing one of these meetings he overheard the discussions and decided to inform the authorities. He departed for Lapwai the following morning where he immediately sought out an army officer and reported his news. Within the hour Captain Perry was informed of what was transpiring.

While chiefs talked and young warriors conspired, the women, oblivious to meetings, perhaps even disinterested, busied themselves with their never-ending daily chores. They gathered roots and kept watch over the children playing noisy games. They would go wherever and whenever the chiefs, husbands and sons dictated. They had no official voice in such matters, but no doubt could offer some counsel within the confines of their tepees.

To this day the prolonged discussion amongst the chiefs raises questions. Speculation seems reasonable in presupposing the subject of migration had been discussed prior to the May conference at Lapwai. It also seems logical to think the chiefs had decided to delay their final decision pending results of their gathering at Tepahlewam. There is merit in this conjecture, as not only was Tepahlewam in close proximity to the reservation, it also accessed trails leading to Bitterroot Mountain passes into Montana. There were also those leading north to Canada. On the other hand, should the decision be to go to Lapwai, a walk of less than two full days would put them inside the reservation, and Fort Lapwai would be reached within six. Thus, all possible destinations were relatively easy to reach. Even Canada, being the furthest, required only slightly more than fourteen days including suitable rest periods.

Another advantage in holding the conference at Tepahlewam was that it would allay fears the authorities might have that the bands were not intending to report. General Howard had certainly felt easier when he learned of Tepahlewam's proximity to the reservation. That the meeting at Tepahlewam seems to have been deliberately contrived certainly appears verifiable because the bands all had traveled widely diverse trails. For White Bird, Tepahlewam was close to his route; but Joseph had to turn east over four days. The Palu not only traversed many miles from their land in Washington, they actually passed a few miles south of Fort Lapwai in the process. These detours indicate clearly the conjunction was in no way coincidental. The convergence suggests it was intentional as a means to further discuss migration. Without such prearrangement the bands would likely have proceeded to Lapwai independently and directly.

For Joseph, it perhaps had been against his better judgment to have allowed himself to be swayed by White Bird and Tool'hool'hool'zote that a final conference was needed. The Palu chief, on the other hand, had little choice but to follow the others. He believed that Howard, by taking back the paper Husis Kute had signed, had nullified their part in the Lapwai agreement. The Palu believed they now had nowhere to go.

In fact, when Howard returned the paper to Agent Montieth he told him to honor the agreement if the Palu reported within the specified deadline. However, he failed to mention that important provisionary detail to Husis Kute. Was this omission intentional? Howard was not above dishonorable conduct. He certainly felt intense dislike for Husis Kute, describing him as, "a wily chieftain about the age of Young Joseph (he meant Ollokot). It could be said of him in the words of Scripture, his heart was deceitful above all things and desperately wicked."[13]

But Husis Kute was neither deceitful nor wicked. He was a brave warrior who had fought in the 1855 Yakima War. He opposed war, but was forced into the 1877 revolt because of Howard's animosity towards him.

Joseph's optimism for resettlement in Lapwai began to reemerge during the third day of the talks when he saw some lesser chiefs beginning to lean his way. He and Ollokot bolstered their argument for Lapwai by voicing concerns the army would launch a relentless pursuit should the bands not report. This would mean having to engage in a series of running battles that few wanted to fight.

Joseph had particular grounds for concern—more than 600 reasons. He was in charge of hundreds of women, elders, children and various other non-combatants. He had no desire for war. In fact, despite the reputation he garnered as being a military genius and brilliant tactician, he was neither. By both demeanor and sentiment he was no advocate of war, and there is evidence he had no personal experience in warfare prior to 1877. He is not known to have been part of even so much as a small raiding party. Joseph was very much a pacifist[14] anxious to solve problems through discussion and compromise. The role of warrior chief had fallen to Ollokot in order that Joseph might remain at home to fulfill his role as civic chief. His concern was and always had been the welfare and prosperity of his people.

Regardless of his arguments, the final decision would be made by majority vote, and if that was to migrate he would then face a difficult decision: he could either lead his band to Lapwai and a new life, or to Montana and whatever destiny awaited them. It was not a decision he wished to face, so with great nervousness he awaited the final vote.

Agreement was reached mid-day on June 10. The bands would report to Agent Montieth on June 30, as ordered by Howard. Cognizant of their obligation to be within the confines of the reservation no later than June 15, they agreed departure would commence during the early morning of June 13. Their agreed pace of progression was deliberate, for it allowed just enough time to report to Montieth and claim possession of their assigned properties before the month-end deadline. Though a mere token, in reality it was seen by later researchers as symbolic—a final statement of reluctant submission to Washington's odious betrayal. The next two days would be spent preparing for the start of the journey.

Joseph has been long considered the architect of the Tolo Lake agreement, and he was further credited with scoring a diplomatic coup in achieving it. This was not the case, but as his legend grew it added yet another chapter to an enduring myth. The outcome had come about through Ollokot's arguments and persuasions. Joseph's lack of input becomes clear when it is remembered that his oft-vaunted status as "Chief of the Nez Perce" and "the most important of the Nez Perce leaders" are éclats bestowed upon him by writers, mostly white, extolling his exploits. That he was indeed a great chief is beyond question and needs no fictionalization by admiring writers, but he was never "Chief of the Nez Perce." In the long history of the Nez Perce there was never such a chief until the day Washington bureaucrats decreed one was needed.

Aside from whatever influence might be exerted through personality or reputation each chief was equal. A chief's vote in council was singular, holding no extraordinary importance, one opinion no more authoritative than that any other. In previous councils Joseph's proposals had sometimes been rejected, sometimes approved, and at other times his vote had broken a stalemate. In general practice, and Nez Perce law, there existed only the understanding that proposals that gained acceptance by majority vote would be respected but not necessarily accepted. There was no obligation on a chief to adopt the proposal for his own band. It all came down to a matter of personal choice. The Nez Perce people had been for many centuries living in a democratic system of their choice.

The American version of democracy was as alien to the Nez Perces as was that of the Nez Perces to Americans. For centuries the Nez Perces had utilized their own concept of democracy, one that held no provision for a chief superior above all others. Chiefs were forbidden to impose obligations on other chiefs. No chief could speak for another without that individual's permission. No chief could interfere in the affairs of other bands. It was forbidden to issue orders to a member of another band without the band chief's consent. A warrior could not seek out another chief in hopes of gaining a more favorable decision than one made by his own chief.[15] And, as much to the point, no warrior was required to acquiesce to his chief's wishes if he chose not to.

This lack of a tribal chief was to a great extent one of the major factors in the overall tension between the Nez Perce and Washington. Americans even then were deeply inured in their belief that no society can function properly without an overall leader (preferably an elected president) or at the very least an acceptable appointed figurehead. They never grasped the success of the Nez Perce system. Americans had an elected president, ergo the Nez Perce also required an acceptable alternate, a tribal chief. It was this belief that had first inspired Washington to force such a figurehead upon them in the person of Taawis Simmen [Sparkling Horn], known as Ellis to the missionaries. The Indians ignored Ellis, and he himself had no real interest in the appellation. When he abdicated the title, Washington's second appointee was the generally unpopular Hallalhotcuut [Knower of Laws], also called Aliyea, which Whites interpreted as Lawyer. That appointment was also met with disinterest. Lawyer, however, was undaunted. Despite both appointment and title going generally unrecognized within the tribe, he proved less thin-skinned than Ellis. He rode out his appointment and actually achieved some small degree of success for his efforts.

Joseph was only a band chief, one among many. Like all band chiefs before and since, he had neither special authority nor status outside his own band. That he possessed diplomatic skills is unquestioned, but these brought him fame during the years *following* the surrender. Prior to 1877, civil servants sent to negotiate with him on various subjects listened to him, but he is not known for any major achievements; while he was respected by many, he was not considered important. In 1877, his age alone would have barred him from becoming the war leader (which went to Looking Glass) but there were other reasons as well. He was the only one among them without fame as a buffalo hunter; he had no experience in tribal warfare, and had never participated in a raiding party. His later fame came through circumstance. He was the only band chief to survive the war, aside from Husis Kute and White Bird. Husis Kute, because he was Palu had no say in post-war Nez Perce affairs, and White Bird was in exile in Canada. Therefore Joseph was the only chief who could relate in detail the execution of the war. Whatever ability he showed in battle leading to the final siege at Bear Paw he learned from Ollokot, who in many ways had become his mentor and guiding light.

When the meeting ended, Looking Glass and his warriors returned to their Clear Creek village in the reservation. Husis Kute returned to the Palu camp to inform his band chief of the decision and prepare his people for departure. Tool'hool'hool'zote also departed for his camp to oversee his people's preparation for decampment. White Bird returned to White Bird Canyon where he informed his people they would be going to Lapwai. The young warriors were displeased and said so, but he soothed their displeasure by telling them that during late afternoon of June 12 a tel'lik'leen would be held. This was a ceremony, in effect a parade, held ostensibly to honor past and present warriors, past wars and great deeds. In this case it appears primarily intended as a morale booster, perhaps a commemoration to the land they were leaving. Considering the only participants were members of the Lamtama band, the event was clearly, and solely, White Bird's decision. It was possibly the worst decision he had made during his life to that point.

No other chief became aware of the event until the morning of the 13th, when it was too late. Despite fictions suggesting otherwise, there is no evidence showing Tool'hool'hool'zote knew anything about it. Neither did Looking Glass or Husis Kute, as no warrior from any of the other bands participated. Certainly Joseph knew nothing of it. He and Ollokot, pleased with the peaceable ending to the fractious conference, had departed within an hour of the council's ending for the Salmon River, intending the next day to butcher enough cattle so the band would have sufficient meat for their journey to Fort Lapwai. They took with them several women to help in the task. When they departed Tolo Lake all was serene and peaceful.

During this time Captain Perry was at Fort Lapwai waiting uneasily for word from scouts that the Indians were about to begin making their way to Lapwai. Perry hoped they would start soon, as the atmosphere was always tense under such conditions. His own tenseness changed to nervousness when he was informed of the aforementioned eavesdropper's unsettling information that some young warriors were plotting to go to war. Perry sent a note informing Howard who was at Lewiston meeting with that area's detachment commander. Howard replied he would deal with the matter when he returned on the 14th, but that Perry should place his troops on full alert.

[CHAPTER 8 ENDNOTES]

1. In modern military parlance such alert modes are color coded as Yellow (stand-by) or Red (Action Imminent). In that era they were simply orders to "Stand-by" or "Boots and Saddles."

2. Joseph crossed the river near the point of land famed in the Nez Perce creation legend "When Coyote Defeated the Swallowing Monster." A huge rock, representing the heart of the monster, has become a famed landmark and a popular tourist attraction.

3. Hahtelekin, the Palouse band chief, was also known as

Taktsoukt Ilppilp [Red Echo]. He was killed at Big Hole, whereupon Husis Kute assumed overall command of the Palouse band. [*Nez Perce Summer 1877*, 130.]

4   The total number of Cayuse tribesmen who allied themselves with the Palouses was never fully known. Many were with Joseph in exile but no mention has ever been made of any escaping to Canada with White Bird. These Cayuse tribesmen are covered briefly in Angie Debo's *A History of the Indians of the United States* on pages 148–58 and also on page 271, but she mentions nothing of reasons why they became involved in the 1877 Nez Perce War. They are also mentioned in Helen Addison Howard's *Saga of Chief Joseph* on pages 58–63, 99 and 376 but without names or reasons for participation mentioned. The Cayuse presence as part of Joseph's group is acknowledged passim by J. Diane Pearson in her book, *The Nez Perces in the Indian Territory*, but again numbers, names and pertinent details are not given. It is known some went to Colville with Joseph, but where others went remains unknown.

5   Though numbered among the 191, the Palouse warriors did no fighting in Idaho either at White Bird Canyon or Clearwater; and Looking Glass did not join the rebels until after the Clearwater battle. [McWhorter, *Hear me My Chiefs*, 185.]

6   Howard's reports estimated about 700 were non-combatants but Nez Perce records indicate the number who could be classified as non-combatants, women, children and elders, was closer to 600. [McWhorter, *Hear Me My Chiefs*, 185, fn27.]

7   The McWhorter interviews during 1932–35 with the 1877 survivors cast doubts on whether Joseph was even included in the Tolo Lake council. This, some insisted, was because Joseph was not a war chief so it was Ollokot who represented the band. If this is true

then Joseph would have had only limited influence in discussions on whether to go to Lapwai or Montana. Others think it unlikely he would have been excluded. Exclusion does, however, seem plausible because much of the heroics attributed to Joseph are from the pens of adoring fiction writers. It is acknowledged as fact his influence in the fighting phase of the exodus was far less than previously thought. [McWhorter, *Hear Me My Chiefs,* 178–82.]

8   Under the conundrum of Nez Perce law, chiefs determined final decisions arrived at in councils, but Nez Perce philosophy allowed individuals freedom to do as they pleased. Thus, while chiefs often possessed enough control that tribesmen usually complied with their chiefs' decisions and advice, no chief wielded dictatorial or absolute powers. If an individual did not wish to obey his chief he was free to disregard him. The same freedom of choice applied to chiefs. While most were inclined to concur with a council decision arrived at through majority vote, the dissenters could disregard the decision. The same philosophy guided individual warriors. In battle each made his own strategy, fought in his own way and took orders from no one unless he felt like it. Moreover, if on a particular day he did not feel like fighting he did not have to. Should he join the fray, if at any time he felt like leaving the battle he could do so. The overall thought was succinctly symbolized by one warrior in yet another way of expressing the adage that discretion trumps valor: "To be killed today means there is no fight tomorrow." *[Leave the Last Bullet for Yourself.]*

9   Although he was a non-Treaty chief, his band had treaty status and was in residence at Lapwai. The authorities tended to regard him as a Treaty chief. It is certain that

Looking Glass did not share their consideration but he often seemed ambivalent on the subject. [Author's files.]

10   Many such accounts survive. Young Two Moon's account, as told to George Bird Grinnell in 1908, and that of Mrs. Shot-In-Head, are of interest. Other accounts are also available for viewing in various archives and collections. [See: Bibliography.]

11   McWhorter has become generally considered the definitive historian among white researchers of the Nez Perce. His writings, which cover many years, remain main sources of material covering the events of the uprising and its aftermath from 1877 to 1935. Of course, since McWhorter's day, new evidence has emerged. However, new facts rarely dispute those he uncovered during those years now long past. In most cases they confirm his findings.

12   In general, Indian languages were—and are—descriptive, flowery and unique. Because their world was limited, little was known about places far away. As a result, places beyond their horizons were referred to by what <u>was</u> known of them. The Nez Perce, for instance, called Montana "Land of the Buffalo," while Canada was referred to by several tribes as "The Grandmother's Land," the grandmother being Queen Victoria. Most tribes knew nothing about other lands except that such places did exist. In general they were referred to as "Elsewhere Land" and, sometimes "The Beyond Lands."

13   Howard, *Nez Perce Joseph*, 19.

14   Giving credence to Joseph's pacific nature is this fact: he fired at the Indian who had killed his brother but did not hit him—and he did not take a second shot. Joseph, an acknowledged marksman with both bow and rifle, would not have missed had he intended to kill the man. Further, they later became good friends. [Author's files.]

15 This was among the many weaknesses in Nez Perce law and more than anything else it led to the near-defeat at Big Hole. Had the warrior been allowed to voice his fears to another chief as well as Looking Glass the army attack would not have happened as it did. Alerted warriors would have ambushed the troops on their approach.

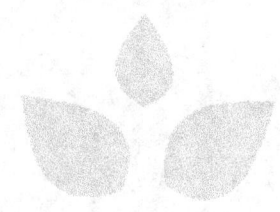

[CHAPTER 9]

PRELUDE to DISASTER

The tel'lik'leen and an angry outburst by Heyoom Moxmox [Yellow Grizzly Bear],[1] an elder, combined to furnish the catalyst leading to the Battle at White Bird Canyon. Normally a tel'lik'leen was little more than a sort of "bragging" rite, a simple parade involving a formation of mounted warriors riding a circle around the camp. During the circuit's progression each rider could choose to call out his deeds or remain silent, the honor being in participation, not self-adulation. The two positions of greatest honor involved three warriors selected by their peers to bring in the circle of warriors. A single rider in the lead represented the bravest warrior because in actual warfare the leading rider was considered to be in the greatest immediate danger.[2] Two riders on one horse denoted the rear guards, also considered a very dangerous position in actual warfare.[3] When the circle was completed, the leader and rear guards retired to the background.

Nez Perce accounts indicate that on this afternoon the riders had commenced the encirclement of the camp boundary and all was progressing routinely. Then, the horse bearing the rear guards, Wahlitits [Shore Crossing] and his cousin Sarpsis Ilppilp [Red Moccasin Tops], shied sideways. Before Wahlitits could bring the horse under control its hoofs had scattered a pile of cous roots[4] that Yellow

Grizzly Bear's wife was drying. As his wife scurried about retrieving the roots, the old man angrily berated Wahlitits over his perceived inability to control his horse. His anger growing, he questioned the young man's participation in the ceremony and accused the youth of entering the ceremony under false pretenses, saying he had no right to be in the ceremony for two reasons: he had no heroic exploits to his credit, and what was worse, he had made no effort to avenge the killing of his own father. He, therefore, had no place in a tel'lik'leen.

Wahlitits was the son of Tipyahlahna Siskan [Eagle Robe] who had been killed three years previously in a gunfight with Lawrence Ott, a white farmer. Wahlitits was loudly berated by Yellow Grizzly Bear.

"What right have you to ride in a tel'lik'leen when the man who killed your father remains alive? You are playing at being a Brave," Yellow Grizzly Bear thundered, "yet your own father's murderer remains free. Why do you not go out and kill the murderer? Then you would have an exploit to relate."

Yellow Grizzly Bear well knew Ott, though ordered to stand trial, had been acquitted when witnesses to the shoot-out, all Nez Perces, could not agree which man had drawn and fired his weapon first. The old man's anger over his scattered cous roots had clouded his mind to that fact. To his way of thinking, Eagle Robe had been killed by Ott and his death had not been avenged.[5] So far as he was concerned his friend had been murdered and his killer had walked free. Wahlitits, flustered, recoiled in embarrassed surprise.

"You will be sorry for your words old man," Wahlitits shouted as he dismounted and ran from the circle.[6]

Chastened, thoroughly humiliated, he retreated to his tepee to brood in solitude.[7] He was shortly joined by Sarpsis Ilppilp. Early the following morning the two prepared to ride from camp. Before leaving, however, they went to the tepee of Wetyemtmas Wahyakt [Swan Necklace], another cousin, and asked him to accompany them. Whether they told him why they wanted his company is unknown (his widow said years later he thought he was to have been the horse holder) but he agreed to go with them. The three mounted their horses and left the camp.[8]

Early the following afternoon (June 14) Swan Necklace returned to the camp alone, riding a roan horse stolen from Henry Elfers, their second victim, Richard Devine being the first. He told the news of the killings. At that point a young warrior named Hemackkis Kaiwon [Big Morning] rode the roan around the camp's perimeter in imitation of a tel'lik'leen. He loudly called out that white men had been killed near the Salmon River and showed off the roan as proof. He told of how the three had sought to avenge Eagle Robe. They had searched for Lawrence Ott but he had not been at his ranch.[9] Since they could not find Ott, he told his audience, they had instead sought out five other white men known to have mistreated Indians over past years. They killed four but a fifth man, though wounded, had escaped. Big Morning was finishing his narrative when Sarpsis Ilppilp, Wahlitits and his wife rode into the camp. Wahlitits confirmed what Big Morning had told his listeners but he was *not* inviting them to join him. He turned to leave when at that moment Leepet Hessem'dooks [Two Moons] rode through the camp urging every able man to join the two men.[10] Most returned to their tepees, but between twelve and sixteen young men,[11] many fortified with whiskey that had been supplied by a visiting trader, rushed forward intent on joining him.[12] Minutes later the group, vowing to locate Lawrence Ott,[13] rode from the camp with wolf howls and war whoops.

Had White Bird been in camp he might have succeeded in stopping them, perhaps might have even prevented Big Morning and Two Moons from holding their impromptu court, but his whereabouts remain unknown. As a result, his absence gave rise to erroneous claims by Idaho settlers that he, not Shore Crossing, had led the group.[14]

Word of the gang's departure spread quickly, causing pandemonium that increased by the minute until it reached all the camps at Tolo Lake, electrifying the entire gathering. Panic ensued. All knew the killing of four settlers was certain to bring retaliation; and now it appeared the killing was going to accelerate. Certainly Howard's soldiers would be sent against them. Most had no idea of what they should do or where to go; their only thoughts were to get away from the area as quickly as possible. Those whose chiefs were in the area had some guidance, but others did not and it was these who were most greatly affected.

Looking Glass had returned to his Clear Creek camp immediately following the final vote on June 12, but hearing the developments decided he would not likely be involved in any action Howard might take. Thus, he did nothing. Husis Kute quickly moved his camp to a South Fork location inside the reservation proper. Tool'hool'hool'zote, already camped near White Bird Canyon stayed where he was. The visitors from Lapwai, fearful of being caught up in the fighting should Howard retaliate, scurried back to Lapwai with all possible haste, taking with them some unattached non-Treaty women and their children. Within hours the shores of the lake stood almost deserted. Only Joseph's band remained, minus one youth named Lakpee'aloot [Two-Flocks-of-Geese-Alighting-on-Water] who had departed to join Shore Crossing's renegades.[15]

Upon hearing the first reports, several warriors rode to inform Joseph the disastrous news. During the morning of the 14th they intercepted him, Ollokot and the accompanying women returning with twelve packhorses heavily laden with freshly butchered beef. Leaving the packhorses to be handled by the riders and women, both chiefs rode at full gallop to the lake. Meanwhile, White Bird had moved the Lamtamas into more defensible confines within the canyon.

When Joseph rode into the Tolo Lake camp he was aware only of the three renegades and the killing of the four farmers. He had yet to learn others had joined the trio and already the large gang was engaged in a rampage of killing and wanton destruction. Had he known, he might have taken a different course of action, one which would not have nullified all possibility of restoring the delicate balance that had been had so carefully achieved. He knew only of the original three and that the other bands had scattered.

Joseph quickly gathered his people, dismantled the camp and hastened northward hoping to find security with Looking Glass within the reservation.[16] It was not to be. Before they could set up camp Looking Glass arrived, and he was not in the least receptive. He blamed the renegades' actions on White Bird and Tool'hool'hool'zote, but considered Joseph equally guilty through association. He told Joseph bluntly he was not to camp anywhere near his village.[17] Joseph complied, but rather than move more deeply into the reservation, he unwisely retraced his steps south and rejoined White Bird.

As Joseph and his band trudged southward from Clear Creek he and Ollokot mulled their next move. Still unaware of the true gravity of the situation, Joseph may have debated with his brother the wisdom of proceeding with all haste to Fort Lapwai. Perhaps a peaceful settlement might still be possible, but apparently neither found solace in the thought. Joseph was right to be concerned, for his understanding of white men was such he was fully convinced, simply because his name was the most familiar to them, they would blame him for everything that had happened. He also felt he would be blamed for everything which might follow. Future events would prove his fears correct.

The rash actions of the original youths and the escalation by the others had seemingly destroyed any chance of the move to Lapwai. The chiefs now faced a second dilemma. All were aware the authorities would demand the renegades be turned over for trial. They were naturally averse to surrendering the young men, but had the trouble ended with the original actions they might have complied while hoping for an unlikely event—fair trials. It was Two Moon's and Big Morning's recruitment of the others and the rampage that followed over the next two days that cast the final dice. Not only was Joseph's hope for peaceful resettlement doomed, but he was forced into a war he did not want.

There has been some interesting hypothetical contemplation of what the outcome might have been had Joseph considered returning to the Wallowa Valley to await developments. Such a move was not impossible, for although the band had traveled many miles over a circuitous route they were still a relatively short distance from Oregon—less than three days.[18] During the early days of the campaign Howard did think that was happening, but if Joseph had considered such a move it would have been a passing thought. A return meant re-crossing the Snake River and, because the first crossing had succeeded mainly through good luck, a second attempt would not likely be successful. As well, he felt committed to the majority so could not in good faith unilaterally desert his allies, although remaining was as dangerous as flight, if not more so.

As his journey to White Bird's camp continued, Joseph contemplated the issue and decided a flight to freedom might succeed should Howard launch an attack. Having reached that point of view he thought sanctuary might be found in some valley in the Bitterroot Mountains. Joseph wrestled with his uncertainty as he shepherded his people southward.

The Anxious Hours

Upon arrival at White Bird Canyon, camp was made and all settled into a period of uneasy waiting. There was some good news awaiting Joseph: scouts informed him some of the band's cattle previously rustled by settlers had been retrieved and had rejoined the main herd. Food would be no problem. Alas, that good news would also become yet another dashed hope.[19]

The next morning Ollokot requested another council. He was concerned because many of the youthful warriors, inspired by the brash actions of the Lamtama renegades, were advocating a preemptive strike against the soldiers they now knew had departed Fort Lapwai. Ollokot, who still favored resettlement at Lapwai over military action, had managed to subdue the warriors' enthusiasm but felt a statement by the combined chiefs would permanently stifle the idea. The chiefs concurred and told the young hotheads that to set into motion a general conflict would turn the entire white population against them. Such a war, they were told, was one the Indians could never win, and to start one was futile in the extreme. Once again reason prevailed. Joseph explained the decision some years later.

> *"The white men were many and we could not hold our own against them. We were like deer. They were like grizzly bears. We had a small country. Their country was very large.[20] We were content to leave things as the Great Spirit Chief had made them. They were not, and would have changed the rivers and mountains if they did not suit them."[21]*

Knowing they held no influence against that of the chiefs, the young men quietly dispersed.

If the warriors were devoid of sensible plans, neither had White Bird, Tool'hool'hool'zote and Joseph any real idea of what to do. This new situation was one none had foreseen. The chiefs felt there were now but two choices, both a gamble. They could gather their people now and go directly to Lapwai, leaving the renegades to fend for themselves; or, fully prepared for a running battle, they could hurriedly press northeast into Montana. None wanted a retreat to Montana, but unconditional surrender at Lapwai was equally distasteful. They also were reluctant to abandon the renegades. They knew Howard would demand the renegade warriors be turned over to the authorities for trial, and no one had doubts about the outcome of the trials. The settlers would demand the raiders be hanged, a demand the authorities would surely sanction. Joseph favored a wait-and-see policy to determine what would transpire when the army arrived. He felt a parley with the army commander might be possible. Perhaps the impasse could be settled peacefully.

White Bird, Joseph, Tool'hool'hool'zote and the other chiefs discussed the situation and once again Joseph prevailed. A decision—with conditions—was made to await developments. White Bird was not optimistic such a parley could be arranged. Neither, apparently, was Joseph, for after further discussion it was decided if a parley was denied, or if no guarantee for safe passage to Lapwai could be obtained, they would fight their way to freedom. Once again the warriors were called together. How much they were told of the proposed plans has never been authenticated, but some historians feel there was a plan of battle while others are not so sure. The dissenters are supported by Indian history, which shows their mode of fighting never included large scale or long-range planning.

If there was a plan of battle it was simplicity in the extreme: should the army attack they would fight; and if victory in the initial battle should be theirs, immediate flight would be undertaken either to Buffalo Country [Montana] or to "The Land of the Grandmother."[22] Either destination was fraught with danger and uncertainty.

It was Joseph who determined how travel must be made. Separate groups would be formed. Non-combatants—women, children and elders—would travel together as one group and move quickly. He did not want them becoming entangled with the warriors and end up in the shooting. A second group of young teens, for the same reasons, would herd the horses at a safe distance.[23] The third group, the warriors, would trail in rearguard defence, move forward as scouts and supply defence for the non-combatants. They would be on constant alert, fully prepared to fight and for the most part hidden. In order that evasive changes in directions could be made quickly, scouts must venture far afield and quickly return at the first sign of soldiers. They were to use signal smoke if necessary to hasten messages. Concern for their horses was paramount, but if it became necessary to ruin a horse in getting news to the chiefs that was how it had to be. The assembled warriors, many jubilant in their excitement, agreed and hurried away to prepare themselves for possible battle. They all knew what to do.

White Bird and Joseph were not particularly concerned about the civilian militia but were well aware that if they hoped to defeat the cavalry and the hundreds of foot soldiers who would be sent against them there could be no slackness in vigilance. They knew the infantry's weaknesses well. Over the years they had observed the soldiers' inability to move easily among the trees and had noted their tendency to tire in the heat of the sun-baked prairies.[24] The Nez Perce name for the infantry was "walk-too-much-soldiers." They also knew from observance their lack of shooting skills. They were well aware their own warriors possessed exceptional superiority in both endurance and marksmanship. The main problem was the warriors lacked good rifles. This was a problem that would soon be solved.

The Soyappo soldiers[25] [cavalry], on the other hand, were viewed differently, and deservedly so. Though the cavalry had many young riders lacking in expertise, there were many good riders with experience who did not fatigue quickly. However, the similitude in horsemanship between a Nez Perce warrior and a cavalryman ended there. Nez Perce warriors fought as equally well on foot as astride a charging horse, whereas the cavalrymen, once out of the saddle, were prone to the same weaknesses as those in the infantry. The weakest links in any cavalry unit of that era were twofold: first was the plethora of new recruits rushed into service with little basic training or practice with firearms; second were the horses. They were of poor quality and were poorly trained. The Nez Perce chiefs were cognizant of these weaknesses.

They also knew the cavalry generally engaged in full force charges over a wide front, something mounted Nez Perce warriors never did. During full frontal charges cavalrymen were forced to fire on the move, nullifying the ability to shoot accurately. Adding to the disadvantages were their horses' skittishness and penchant for shying in nervous reaction to gunfire. Nez Perce riders on the other hand very rarely fired while moving. Riding to rifle range they dismounted in order to fire from a kneeling position. They would fire once, occasionally twice, and as a result their shots were accurate. Then, quickly remounting, they would ride swiftly out of range.

Making matters even more advantageous for the Nez Perce warrior was that his sik'em [war horse], tough prairie mustang of uncertain lineage, was far superior to any army mount. Trained for use by buffalo hunters, they were not afraid of the sound of gunshots. They remained still in the midst of battle and were often observed placidly munching on grass quite untroubled by the confusion around them.

In contrast, the cavalry horse balked, shied from gunfire and often ran away at full gallop, his inexperienced rider either hanging on for dear life or on the ground, having been thrown.

Among their other talents in horsemanship the Nez Perces were gifted with perfect balance.[26] Nez Perce riders were able to become small targets by hanging from their horses' sides, one leg crooked over the steed's back, a feat the Soyappo could not duplicate. Yet, regardless of superior horsemanship and marksmanship, long-running gun battles had never been utilized by Nez Perce fighters and were not part of the chiefs' plans. Such battles were of attrition, which meant casualties that were not replaceable. The Nez Perce chiefs, unlike General Howard, had no sources of reinforcements at their disposal.

The sun was still low on the horizon the following morning when Joseph, greatly worried about retaliation for the killing and plundering, ordered his band to regroup and decamp quickly. He planned to move the non-combatants to safety away from the canyon in case Howard decided to attack without warning.

There was still no decision on where to go should flight become imperative. White Bird alone had spoken of Canada. The others leaned towards some valley in the Bitterroot Mountain range. They worried that Canada posed too many questions. Would the people be welcomed? Would the "Redcoat pony soldiers" [Northwest Mounted Police] let them cross the medicine line? Could they trust "The Grandmother" to give them sanctuary or would she prove as perfidious as the "White Father Chief" in Washington? There were also questions about white settlers. To what extent did Canadian white men respect Indians? How did their attitude compare with that of American whites?

Howard, having returned from Lewiston, had begun receiving confusing reports from scouts about having seen Nez Perce raiders in several scattered locations in the vicinity of the town of Mount Idaho. He immediately ordered the already alerted troopers to prepare for immediate departure. He also alerted the Mount Idaho Volunteers, a militia of some 100 members, to prepare for deployment. This group, eager and anxious for action, prepared for a rendezvous with the large troop about to depart Lapwai under the command of Captain David Perry.

Howard, Perry, the troopers and the militia all were of one thought—there would be no major difficulties encountered in subduing Joseph and his followers. Those who formed the militia were the most optimistic. Their attitude was expressed as, "What Indian can possibly overcome a well-armed white man?" They were soon to find out.

[CHAPTER 9 ENDNOTES]

1   Although all agree to the authenticity of the events, there are several differences of opinion in the name of the elder. Helen Addison Howard wrote his name as Heyoom Moxmox [Yellow Grizzly Bear] while McDermott (in 2006) names him Yellow Grizzly with no Nez Perce name. Jerome Greene states his name was Hahkauts Ilpihlp, which translates as Red Grizzly Bear. Greene cites Nez Perce records as his source while others cite no or various sources. Camille Williams, an authorized Nez Perce historian of the 1930s, states his name was indeed Heyoom Moxmox. Therefore, I will follow Camille Williams' translation.

According to J. Diane Pearson [*The Nez Perces in the Indian Territory*, 289] an elder named Red Grizzly Bear was with Joseph in exile but was eventually repatriated to Lapwai. Whether Ms. Pearson felt Red Grizzly Bear and Yellow Grizzly bear were the same person is not known. According to McWhorter, who quoted Williams, Yellow Grizzly Bear was a member of the Clearwater band, took no part in any battles, was exiled with Joseph but died at Kamiah some years after his repatriation to

Lapwai. Why a member of the Clearwater band was with the Lamtamas has never been explained. [Author's files.]

2 In this particular parade the lead rider was Two Moons, who two days later would exhort others to join him on the warpath and later figured prominently in several battles, including the Battle at Bear's Paw. [McWhorter, *Hear Me My Chiefs*, 189.]

3 The two selected as the rear guards were Wahlitits [Shore Crossing] and his cousin, Sarpsis Ilppilp [Red Moccasin Tops] with Wahlitits holding the reins. Both would lead the renegades—and be denounced for it by their elders—but would later redeem themselves in battle at the Big Hole. [ibid.]

4 Cous is highly nutritious. It is also called biscuitroot because when the roots are dried, ground and powdered into flour, they make excellent, very tasty, flat cakes.

5 In the traditions of the Western Indians (also, apparently, the Nez Perce) avenging the murder of a family member was not uncommon. There was no time limit, but it was expected to be accomplished. Some acts of vengeance are the stuff of legend. When Alexander Potts, a Scottish HBC trading post manager, was murdered by an enraged Indian trapper, his son, Jerry, was only two years old. The killer escaped but his identity was known to Jerry's mother, a woman of the Blood tribe, who related the details to her son. When Jerry was about fifteen he began his search for the man. Two years later he located him in an Indian village near Kalispell, Montana and killed him. Several years later he also avenged his mother and brother, both of whom had been murdered by Gros Ventre men during a drunken revelry at Alberta's Fort Whoop-up. [Meyers, E.C., *Wild Canadian West*, 112–113.]

6 The above is one of several versions of the event, but all are similar and closely resemble this version quoted

by Lucullus McWhorter's interview with Two Moons who witnessed the exchange. Another version claims the challenge from Yellow Grizzly Bear came *before* the ceremony started. Yet another states the insult was from a young woman Shore Crossing had seduced and then jilted. Two Moon's account is considered correct. [See: McWhorter, *Hear me My Chiefs* (1952 edition), 188–190; also, Curtis, *The North American Indian,* Vol. 8 (Seattle, 1911), 164.]

7   In differing accounts of the situation, Yellow Bull, Too Moons and Joseph all stated the youth had fortified himself with alcohol. Others, however, including War Singer and Yellow Wolf, claimed Shore Crossing was strictly teetotal and never drank alcohol at any time. Others concurred. [McDermott, John D., *Forlorn Hope: the Nez Perce Victory at White Bird Canyon,* 4, fn 2 and 3.]

8   Swan Necklace was known as John Minthon when his wife told this to Camille Williams, an official Nez Perce historian. Williams relayed it to McWhorter in a letter c.1935. [*Hear Me My Chiefs*, 190–91.]

9   Ott had gone to the town of Florence on business two days previously and while there had fallen ill. Unable to travel, he did not return to his ranch until after the fighting had commenced. A story that he eluded his pursuers by disguising himself as a Chinese panning for gold is fiction.

10   General Howard erred when he stated it was White Bird who rode through the camp advocating war. Contrary to Howard's claim, as well as officials' and others' reiteration on the subject, White Bird was vehemently outspoken in his opposition to fighting. [Howard, *Nez Perce Joseph,* 105–6.]

11   [Camille Williams to McWhorter, *Hear Me My Chiefs,* 194–5.]

12   The names of these men are not complete, but seven have been identified. Yellow Bull, Bare Feet, Red Elk, Stick-in-the-Mud, Big Morning and Strong Eagle were all from White Bird's band. The seventh, Lakpee'aloot was from Joseph's band. Strong Eagle was shot and killed by Cheyenne scouts at Bear Paw. [Author's files.]

13   Reports that White Bird and Tool'hool'hool'zote had ridden with them have long since been discredited but still appear from time to time. Neither of these chiefs led the renegades. In fact, White Bird was enraged at the news when he heard it and none of Tool'hool'hool'zote's band was involved in any way.

14   Helen Addison Howard apparently believed without question the Idahoans' accusations that White Bird and Tool'hool'hool'zote had inflamed the young men. In *Saga of Chief Joseph*, she devotes chapter 10 to the subject under the title, "Chief White Bird's Murders," somewhat ambiguously citing McWhorter, Yellow Bull, Dunn, Curtis and Macdonald without mentioning *their* sources. She does not claim to have uncovered any original sources of her own. Only once, on page 140, does she actually name White Bird (without citation) as responsible for inflaming the young men. Throughout her book she has not one cordial word for her favorite "malcontent," Chief Tool'hool'hool'zote. [Howard, Helen A., *Saga of Chief Joseph*, chapter 10, 134–7.]

15   Lakpee'aloot is known to have made a hasty departure from the renegades upon realising the mistake he had made in joining them. He rejoined Joseph, fought in several skirmishes and surrendered with him at the Bear's Paw. He eventually returned to Lapwai, later attended the Carlisle Indian Mission School and then returned to Lapwai under the Christian name Philip Walker. [Pearson, 289.] Also among the surviving renegades was Swan Necklace who, under the alias of John Minthon,

lived at Lapwai in quiet anonymity into the late 1920s. His original partners were both killed at the Big Hole. [*Forlorn Hope*, 11 and 162.]

16   Stories that Chief Joseph, a six-shooter in each hand, rode back and forth throughout his camp threatening to shoot any warrior who intended to join the renegades is absolute nonsense, a tale of pure fiction. Joseph did no such thing. Joseph was never known to own one pistol, let alone two, and evidence confirms he would never have staged such a performance under any circumstances. Such tales are best left to Hollywood, where it may have actually been invented for a "B" movie at some time. [Author.]

17   This singular act by Looking Glass fairly well nullifies the claims of some researchers that Joseph and Looking Glass were the best of friends. It does however cement contentions that Looking Glass supported Joseph at the Lapwai Council only to gain support for his hopes of regaining his own lost territory. [Author's files.]

18   Until Looking Glass was appointed to overall leadership as chief guide, Joseph's group was averaging twenty-five miles per day, an incredible pace considering the numbers and hardship involved. Under Looking Glass the _entire_ group averaged no better than fifteen miles per day.

19   Within weeks white farmers and ranchers stole all the cattle (as well as several horses) that had been left near the river. Overall, the Nez Perce bands lost thousands of animals to white rustlers, a loss they never recovered. [Author's files.]

20   In this statement he was referring to supplies and reinforcements. The Nez Perce had neither the means of replacing fallen warriors or replenishing diminished food

sources. The army, on the other hand, faced few lasting problems with either.

21 "An Indian's Views of Indian Affairs" by Chief Joseph. (*The North American Review*, Vol. 128 (1879), 420–3.)

22 Nez Perce called Queen Victoria "The Grandmother" for the same reasons they called the US President "White Father Chief." The words queen and president were not part of their vocabulary.

23 First plans called for inclusion of cattle, but as events unfolded there were no cattle to consider as all their bovine stock was systematically stolen by settlers.

24 Although no one thought much about it at the time, Perry recalled years later that he had seen White Bird and other war chiefs spending much time in Lapwai watching the soldiers during their training periods. He remembered seeing one of the chiefs intently observing a howitzer gun crew going through their routines of setting up, loading and firing the gun. He thought nothing of the interest at the time, but after the White Bird Canyon defeat he realized it had been much more than idle curiosity. The chiefs had also been observed watching the infantry at their drill sessions as well as the few occasions when they had firing practice, and they had also watched gunners practicing with howitzers and Gatling guns and seemed attentive to their operational routines. As a result, Nez Perce chiefs had become well versed in army battlefield formations and routines. [Numerous sources mention of these incidents: *The Diary of Sgt. Michael McCarthy*; Helen A. Howard's *Saga of Chief Joseph*; reports of Captain Perry; reports of Indian Agent Montieth.]

25 Literally "long knife soldiers," a reference to the swords or sabers used by cavalry officers. ["Learning the

Language," a segment on the Nez Perce website *www.nezperce.com*]

26 Perfect balance seems a trait among all North American aboriginal people. The Mohawks of Ontario, Quebec and New York, for instance, are so sure-footed they have always been in great demand as construction workers on high-rise skyscraper projects. These workers can walk, quite fearlessly, along the swaying girders being raised and lowered into place. Two centuries ago the Nootka people of the northwest Pacific coast hunted Orcas by steering canoes alongside the whale where a hunter would leap to the mammal's back and remain balanced there while killing him with spear thrusts. [Author's files.]

[CHAPTER 10]

ANATOMY of a FAILED MISSION

I think we shall make short work of it.
—General O.O. Howard

The Nez Perce War began at White Bird Canyon after Lamtama renegades ravaged the countryside for two days, murdering several white settlers, killing livestock, and burning houses and barns. These things they did in retaliation for previous abuses against their people and for recent thefts of their horses and cattle. The chiefs now had no choice but to prepare for war.

On June 14, at 8:00 PM, Captain David Perry rode out from Fort Lapwai at the head of three fully manned, well-equipped companies of infantry and cavalry. Their destination was the town of Mount Idaho from where they would begin their assignment of locating the non-Treaty Nez Perce bands and then escort them to Lapwai. Their estimated arrival at Mount Idaho was early afternoon of June 16. Each of the 103 soldiers and scouts (two civilians and several treaty Nez Perces) carried the basic rations of hardtack biscuits, navy beans and dried bacon sufficient for three days. Following were pack animals[1] and wagons loaded with extra rifles, ammunition, blankets, clothing, oats for the horses, and food and water for an additional five days.

Howard had overseen the departure and was pleased to see all was going well, but in order to ensure his orders were fully understood he called Perry to the porch for some final, explicit instructions. He and Perry took chairs on the porch while Howard ran through his instructions. The general reminded Perry that when Joseph was located and he had spoken with him and his allies the first order of business was the arrest of those who had killed the settlers. They must be placed with no delay under armed guards and brought with all possible haste to Fort Lapwai. The rest would then be escorted at a normal pace by the most direct route to the reservation and turned over to the Indian agent. Howard reminded Perry to use utmost discretion in dealing with Joseph and the other chiefs. Howard was hopeful of avoiding battle but told Perry should the chiefs refuse to obey him, or if his troops were fired upon, he could use whatever force he deemed necessary to enforce compliance. He also cautioned him, should fighting become necessary,[2] not to rely heavily on the militia that would join him at Mount Idaho.

With the command ready to mount up and move out Perry stood and saluted.

"Good-by, general," he said.

"Good-by colonel,[3]" Howard replied. "You must not get whipped."

Perry, obviously certain the encounter would end successfully within the eight allocated days, responded with certainty, "There is no danger of that, sir."[4]

Departure, which had seemed imminent, was now delayed for some time as riders experienced trouble getting their mounts under control. The horses shied, bucked and refused to settle down. After much cursing and the use of whips the riders were able to reestablish their authority. Finally the lines began to move out. Howard watched as the long blue line disappeared, engulfed by darkness.

The general, like Perry, held few doubts of his force's ability to achieve the intended goal. Nonetheless, the last minute contumacious display exhibited by the horses, and the difficulty their riders had in settling the dispute, caused concern. Cavalry soldiers unable to handle horses were not a sight to inspire optimism. Howard was to write years later he was aware new recruits were not being advanced to a sufficient degree beyond their basic training, and this included horsemanship. That had concerned him. He was no less concerned that none had received more than the most rudimentary training in rifle and pistol marksmanship.[5] The horses' behavior was also worrisome. Their conduct that evening was very definitely a sign of poor training. Howard also had long been concerned about the quality of horses being supplied to the cavalry.[6] His complaints, however, had gone unanswered.

Thus, though the early difficulties that evening went unnoticed as omens, they were perhaps indicative of troubles lying ahead. Still, to Howard's mind, the saving grace was that all but one officer and all the NCOs were highly experienced in battle. As generals throughout the centuries have learned, often to their sorrow, Howard was well aware victory depended upon the ability of the NCOs to draw the best from untried men. All the NCOs of both companies had demonstrated ability in motivating their subordinates. He also had no doubt about the overall regimental pride inherent in all involved. These men were heirs to the First Cavalry Regiment's hard-won battle honors, as well as those of their respective companies. That was all very well, but aside from the officers, NCOs and the few veterans in the lower ranks none of the green recruits had contributed to the earnings of those honors. None had experienced battle even in minor skirmishes. He could not help but be concerned about how they would react should a fight ensue. Howard hoped Joseph would not test them by rebuking Perry's demands.[7]

Perry, on the other hand, harbored no doubts, as his optimistic assurances to General Howard attest. He was well aware both companies F and H[8] of the First Cavalry Regiment, 103 strong, had only a handful of veterans seasoned in the Civil War and Indian campaigns, but he had the utmost faith in those in positions of command.

H Company was commanded by Captain Joel G. Trimble (1832–1911) from Philadelphia. At age forty-five he was the oldest of the four officers and an officer of proven ability. A veteran of the Union Army since 1855, his service with the army went beyond those twenty-two years. In 1849, at age seventeen, he signed on as a civilian scout and served in that capacity for six years before joining the regular force as a private. He took a brief leave-of-absence in 1860 to ride for the Pony Express, returning to army duties in August. When the Civil War began he was still a private but combat brought him changes in fortune. Throughout that conflict he fought in many campaigns where his bravery and ability were noticed and he began to climb steadily through the ranks. By the war's end he had achieved the rank of 1st lieutenant. Trimble remained in the army, was assigned to the western command and now, in 1877, was a veteran of many campaigns against the Plains Indians during which he was promoted to the rank of captain. Perry put great trust in his ability.

Trimble's second in command was 2nd Lieutenant William Randall Parnell (1836–1910), a bona fide soldier of fortune. A native of Ireland, Parnell was eighteen years old when he joined the British Army's 4th Hussars. He rode with the Hussars for six years, saw action in several European campaigns, and then transferred to The Lancers in 1856 in order to participate in the Crimean War. He was among the first to enter Sebastopol following that city's surrender. His greatest moment came when he took part in the ill-fated charge of the Light Brigade where his Irish luck proved its worth. Though wounded, he emerged from that disaster, one of the few survivors. For his gallantry he was promoted to the rank of captain. When the Crimean War ended Captain Parnell became bored with the between-the-wars life of the Officers' Club. He resigned his commission in 1860 to immigrate to the United States, hoping to participate in the American Civil War, which seemed imminent. He joined the Fourth New York Cavalry, a militia unit. Because of his battle experience he was elected by the unit to serve as a 2nd lieutenant. Throughout the Civil War this man of adventure and action fought gallantly in no less than ten major engagements and seven lesser actions.[9]

When the Civil War ended he applied for transfer from the New York Militia to the regular army. Accepted as a 2nd lieutenant he was transferred to General George Crook's southwest command where he saw action in several Indian campaigns. From there he went to the Army of the Northwest where he remained until 1878 when his many battle wounds finally caught up with him. He retired as a captain with a full pension. In 1897 his years of service were belatedly recognized when he was awarded the Medal of Honor. The citation reads: For Gallantry at White Bird Canyon.

Arguably the best NCO in H Company was First Sergeant Michael McCarthy[10] (1845–1907). A native of St. John's, Newfoundland he moved to the United States at age twenty-one to enter the Union Army. He participated in several campaigns along the Mexican border, and then saw action in various Indian encounters, particularly during the Modoc War.[11] His superiors had noticed him when he helped capture the Modoc chief, Captain Jack. His heroism at White Bird Canyon earned him the Medal of Honor. He was the regimental quartermaster sergeant when, in 1879, he was offered a commission if he would transfer to the National Guard. He eagerly accepted and served another twenty-three years before retiring as a full colonel. McCarthy was always very proud of his climb from private to colonel.

F Company was about the same in across-the-board experience. This was Perry's company, but because he was now the overall commanding officer, First Lieutenant Edward Theller†a (1833–1877) who had been seconded from G Company, 21st Infantry Regiment, assumed temporary command of Perry's Company. Theller, though a career officer, had limited combat experience. He had seen a little action during the Civil War and had participated in two western campaigns. Regardless, despite being the least experienced of the four officers, Perry had confidence in his ability.

---

a   A †beside a name denotes the man was killed in the Battle of White Bird Canyon. Only officers and NCOs are so noted. Privates and scouts killed are listed in Appendix B dealing with Army casualties.

Theller was respected for his work ethic and ability to manage enlisted men. He did, however, have one weakness that had not gone unnoticed. He was overly fond of gambling, his preferences being horse races and stud poker.[12] These frailties led him into questionable familiarity with Lewiston gamblers, a relationship that had very much worried an officer assigned from HQ to conduct a general inspection of the department's personnel. He had recommended to General Howard that Theller be transferred "far away from Lewiston..." as reassignment would be "for his own good."[13] Howard never acted on the recommendation.

F Company's senior NCO, First Sergeant Alexander M. Baird (1845–c.1920), was born in Scotland but was a small child when his parents came to America. In 1861 he joined the Union Army as a sixteen-year-old private. Assigned to E Company, Fifth Connecticut Infantry, he fought throughout the Civil War,[14] emerging as a battle-hardened veteran. Choosing to remain in the army, he was sent west where he saw action against the Plains Indians. Following his Nez Perce War experiences, none of which were outstanding, Baird, having decided to homestead in Montana, resigned from the army the following February. In August he posted his claim on choice acreage where for the next twenty years he grew grain, raised horses and cattle, accumulated more land and prospered. In 1896 he entered politics, serving as a State councilman for a single four-year term. Over the following years he achieved much notice for exploits and endeavors on a local basis. Baird became a celebrity in Montana, mentioned in various magazine and newspaper articles, all of which are now archived in the Montana Historical Society at Helena.

Perry, besides McCarthy and Baird, also had the services of three other highly qualified sergeants: Patrick Gunn†, Thomas Ryan† and Charles Leeman, as well as eight experienced corporals. In H Company these were Roman D. Lee†, Michael Curran†, Frank Powers and Michael Milner. In F Company the corporals were Charles Fuller, Thomas Fanning, Joseph Lytte and John L. Thompson†. The remainder of the force, privates all, was a commingling of nationalities: twenty-three Irish, thirteen Germans, six

English, five Canadians and three Scots, for a total of fifty. American privates numbered fifty-six, of whom fifty-three participated in the upcoming battle.[15]

The troopers had barely lost sight of the fort when the beginnings of misfortune fell upon them. When the column turned east from the main road to the trail leading to Tolo Lake[16] they found it barely passable. The hilly terrain was so overgrown with underbrush, delays became inevitable. The darkness of the moonless night made progress even more arduous. Pack mules and the horses pulling the supply wagons were greatly hindered by thick brush. Adding to the woes, the wagons' axles often scraped on the mounds between the deep ruts. Perry was forced to call halts at intervals to allow the wagons to catch up.

The stops caused him to fall so far in arrears of his estimated time of advance it was nearly 10:00 am before the weary soldiers and the tired animals reached a deserted farm. They had been riding for almost fourteen hours and Mount Idaho was still several hours distant. Perry called a halt to give everyone a chance for a hot breakfast, as only dry biscuits had been eaten during the night. With the horses settled in a grassy field, the troopers took a quick nap while cooks prepared bacon, heated biscuits and brewed pots of strong coffee.

Shortly after noon the force was once again on the move. Around 3:00 pm they were met by "Ad" Chapman and seven riders who had come from Mount Idaho. Chapman, acting out his contrived role of military expert, told Perry his "scouts" had informed him Joseph had joined other chiefs and all were camped at White Bird Canyon. He stated it appeared they were making preparations to leave the following day, but he could give no indication of when or which direction they intended to follow. Chapman and his riders, all eager to offer Perry further information, remained with the soldiers the rest of the afternoon.

The sun was setting as the troop entered the deserted village of Grangeville. All around was stark evidence of the renegades' raid. Dead horses and cattle, empty boxes and burned wagons, all plundered and some still smoldering, were mute testimony to the carnage. Perry decided to spend the night there in order to further rest his men and horses, all of whom were near total exhaustion. Despite Chapman's opinion that Joseph was planning departure, he announced his decision was to continue to Mount Idaho in the morning. He would meet with the militia commander, then return to Grangeville from whence he and a small party would ride to the canyon to hold council with Joseph. While the troopers unsaddled, set up sentry posts and prepared for a night's sleep, Perry continued his talks with the civilians. It was at this point the civilians told Perry the non-Treaty Nez Perces, whom they claimed to know well, were nothing more than a pack of cowardly scoundrels who would never fight unless they could do so from ambush. They assured Perry the Indians could be whipped by the militia alone if a few more rifles could be mustered.

It is uncertain if Perry believed this,[17] but when Chapman offered to go to Mount Idaho and recruit civilians willing to fight, Perry authorized him to enlist a company of volunteers. Chapman also claimed knowing a guide who was conversant with White Bird Canyon's area and terrain. With his usual penchant for boasting, Chapman assured Perry he could raise not less than twenty-five, and probably thirty, men and would have no trouble whatever locating the qualified guide. Chapman and his companions then departed, but when they rejoined Perry at the canyon the following morning he had with him only ten men—including the original seven.[18] He had not found the promised guide.

Instead of getting some sleep, Perry spent time mulling over the situation. The information he had received from Chapman was causing him uneasiness and he began to worry that perhaps he was allowing Joseph to escape. Though he had authority from Howard to use his own judgment about when and where to apprehend Joseph, he began to fear he might be waiting too long. He also worried that should the bands leave the canyon before he got there, they would escape into the heavily timbered woods where they would be hard to find. He was well aware tracking would be very difficult, and his quarry might very well escape completely. After all, he reasoned, they knew the country and he did not. His lack of knowledge of the area was to have a dire effect on his thinking.

During his time at Fort Lapwai Perry had never ventured into the rural area to acquire comprehensive cognition of the surrounding landscape. Because he had never gone to nearby Camas Prairie he lacked knowledge of that area's geography. Having never been to White Bird Canyon he knew nothing of its terrain or topography. He had also begun to consider the civilians' boasts of being able to defeat the Indians without help from the army. The statement worried him the more he thought about it because, as matters stood at the moment, he saw the entire situation reaching a point where some settlers might band together to take matters into their own hands. Being well aware how vigilantes had a habit of letting things get completely out of control, he feared friendly, settled Indians would find themselves in great danger. Vigilante action would also bring down extremely severe criticism from Washington. Worry of what might happen if he allowed Joseph to elude his grasp was also beginning to prey on his mind.

Darkness was already spreading its cloak to smother the light when Perry made the first mistake of several he was to make during the next eighteen hours. He decided he must go directly to the canyon. He would not remain at Grangeville overnight nor would he go to Mount Idaho in the morning. Instead he would proceed immediately to White Bird Canyon. While the distance was only sixteen miles, darkness would make it about a six-hour ride, hazardous in the dark but justified. He dispatched a messenger to Mount Idaho with orders for the militia commander to muster his men at once, move out as soon as possible and catch up with the army either on the trail or at the canyon. Perry felt the two forces could rendezvous before dawn if the militia moved quickly.

Before formulating his final plan, however, he would confer with his officers for their opinions because they knew their men well. His main concern was the degree of exhaustion they and the horses had already reached. He summoned the officers, outlined the situation and explained why he felt the decision he wished to implement was necessary.

While Perry and his officers conferred, the soldiers went about preparing their own meager suppers of boiled beans and biscuits.[19] As they rested and watched the beans boil, Perry explained to Trimble, Theller and Parnell the need to forego the rest period and depart at once. Following discussion, the three, while not wholly enthusiastic, were unanimous in agreeing the troop should depart at once. Just short of nine o'clock, with darkness already engulfing the land, Perry summoned his bugler to sound "Boots and Saddles."

When the bugle sounded the soldiers hastened to capture and saddle their mounts. Perry then spoke with them about the plan and informed them only basic necessities would be taken. They should, however, wear their greatcoats for warmth. Extra ammunition would be issued, but the rest of the gear was to be left in wagons for retrieval upon their return. A sergeant and two privates were then detailed to remain as guards while the others mounted up, formed two ranks and awaited the order to move out.

Word had come to the Nez Perce camp in the early morning of June 15 that about one hundred soldiers had departed Lapwai. That number of troops was considered a clear indication Howard intended to launch an attack. Had Joseph and White Bird known Howard's actual intention they would likely have awaited Perry's arrival and complied with his orders; unfortunately, there was no way for them to know. All they knew for sure was the soldiers would likely arrive in two days, still plenty of time to formulate a defense plan in case Howard did attack.

The chiefs met, made defensive plans and had finalized their decision about the same time Perry's force was leaving Grangeville. Thus, early on the morning of June 17, when scouts rode into camp with news of the army's approach they were ready for whatever might transpire. As the troops came within sight White Bird called the warriors together to direct them to previously arranged defensive positions.[20] There was nothing to do now but wait.

It had been a long night, but because the file was not encumbered by slow supply wagons (only a couple had been brought along) the sixteen miles were covered without mishaps or undue delays. Dawn was still a couple of hours off when the column reached rising ground above the trail leading downward to the canyon. Perry told his men to dismount and make themselves as comfortable as possible, but they were to stay awake and alert. Under no circumstances were there to be any fires or smoking. The order to stay awake was almost immediately disobeyed as total fatigue overcame the men. They had been on the move almost constantly, they were hungry, none were sufficiently rested and most were already napping in their saddles when Perry called a halt. Upon the order to dismount the men lay down in the grass where many soon fell sound asleep. Sgt. McCarthy and the corporals were kept busy patrolling the area, waking men and trying to keep them awake. The doughty sergeant later wrote in his diary that in many cases the weary horses had also lain down beside their riders and soon were fast asleep.

In a 1902 interview with Cyrus Brady, an editor with McClure Publishers, Parnell (then a retired captain) said at one point a careless soldier struck a match to light his pipe and before Parnell could shout at him to douse the light an eerie howl broke the silence of the darkness. At the first glare of the flame the howl had emanated from bushes quite some distance away. He described it as a series of yaps with a final trailing note. Others had also heard it with one soldier describing it as a frightening sound "enough to make one's hair stand on end." For the remainder of the night the men, shivering in the darkness, huddled in their greatcoats trying to stay awake. Parnell told his interviewer the howl had undoubtedly been a signal from an Indian lookout.[21]

Parnell also stated Perry himself was soon to fall victim to fatigue. He seemed fine up to and during the battle until it started to go badly. It was when the general retreat began that he began issuing unusual orders. Parnell told McClure that Perry became very confused about the time of day. The retreating soldiers had gained higher ground when the warriors stopped advancing. Perry, thinking they were regrouping to begin a second attack, ordered the troopers to hold their positions until darkness fell at which time the Indians would retreat for the night. Parnell, who was also thinking the warriors might launch another attack, informed Perry that holding the present positions would be impossible as the soldiers could never hold out until dark. Perry objected saying darkness was but an hour away. Upon hearing this Parnell indicated his watch saying to Perry, "Captain, it is now only a few minutes past seven in the morning, and we cannot hold out that long." To which Perry replied, "My God! I thought it was near night!"[22] Thus, the retreat continued.

There had been other signs of severe fatigue as well, according to Frank Allen, a civilian volunteer during the entire campaign. Years later Allen, who was very familiar with army routine, told how the cavalrymen, following custom, had made the long ride with loosened saddle cinches. However, he said, before the descent down the long hill to the canyon commenced most forgot to cinch the saddle straps—and the usual reminding order to do so was never given. As they reached lower ground the gunfire erupted and the horses reacted in fright, whirling and bucking. The saddles slipped and turned, pitching riders to the ground. That alone, said Allen, had told him Perry was overly fatigued. He was not alert enough to notice his men were too tired to tend to the important business of fighting. Allen's statements were later challenged by John Schorr who, as a private, survived the battle and eventually attained promotion to sergeant. He refuted Allen's statement, replying. *"So far as I know*[b] we all looked after the cinches, as it is a darned poor caval-

---

[b]   *Italics added. [Author]*

ryman that neglects to cinch his horse properly."[23] Schorr's rebuttal stopped short of denying Allen's statement outright, so his refutation was taken by many as being more in defense of fallen comrades than admitting to the correctness of a civilian's criticism of the army. Military people, active or retired, past and present, very rarely admit a civilian might be correct.

They were joined by the militia when the sun was in its very earliest moments of rising. Upon the militia's arrival Perry rode to a vantage point where he could observe the scene below. Though he could see little from that distance, he saw enough of the almost idyllic scene to cause him to believe the Indians would offer little, if any, resistance. Despite the wolf's howl, which he had also heard and had felt was a signal, it seemed to him no one was concerned over his arrival. That was good. He could wait. There was plenty of time.

Perry outlined his plan to the officers and then dispatched a message to Howard in which he predicted a quick settlement. The message pleased Howard, who assumed Perry was preparing to parley with Joseph. He in turn dispatched messages to Portland and Washington that included guarantees of speedy escort of the Nez Perce bands to Lapwai. He punctuated his telegrams with the optimistic ending: "I think we shall make short work of it."[24]

Perry did indeed intend to parley with Joseph, and had good reason to feel optimistic of the outcome. He also felt optimistic of the outcome should Joseph prefer fighting to talking. The regular army, combined with the militia, gave him more than sufficient manpower to enforce his orders. His only doubt seems to have centered on Chapman's group, because he relegated it to a secondary position to the rear of Company H. That he also harbored doubts about the members of the Mount Idaho militia seems apparent. He assigned them to the left flank of F Company as a support column. They would be out of the way, their activity minimized, but still able to support the flank. As the morning developed he regretted not keeping them in reserve also.

As Perry viewed the scene below, he could not help but consider the situation as being well in hand. All that was left to do was to meet with Joseph and tell him of Howard's decision. Unfortunately, as so often happens in any military campaign, at this point he made another error in his series of blunders. Perhaps because of the onset of fatigue he did not follow protocol; had he done so, he would have left his soldiers where they were. Then he and three or four officers and NCOs would have approached the village under a white flag. If he had done this he would have had his meeting without encountering any trouble. In fact, the chiefs were awaiting that move in hopeful anticipation. Instead, Perry signaled the three columns to proceed down the narrow pathway to level ground below and assume battle formation. Perry had not considered Murphy's Law, the number one caveat of warfare: "If there is anything that can go wrong it invariably will."

[CHAPTER 10 ENDNOTES]

1 Wagons with supplies had not yet arrived from Lewiston by the time Perry was ready to leave, so he left with what he had plus some pack mules. By the time the Lewiston supplies arrived the White Bird Canyon battle was over. Those supplies arrived with Howard and his reinforcements on June 25. [Greene, *Nez Perce Summer 1877*, 44.]

2 While Howard generally showed an abysmal ignorance of the Nez Perce (he believed a settler's claim that the renegades had been marauding and rustling for years), he did dismiss as idle braggadocio various militia leaders' claims that armed settlers could defeat an Indian force without help from the army. [*Nez Perce Summer*; *Hear me My Chiefs*; *A Forlorn Hope*, and other accounts passim.]

3 In referring to Perry as "colonel" one wonders if Howard was obliquely hinting promotion would be an award for a satisfactory outcome of the mission.

4 Howard, O.O., *Nez Perce Joseph*, 99.

5   Not until the 1880s was rifle practice increased. To that point, because ammunition was scarce, rifle range drills were limited in occurrence. Recruits were often issued only three rounds per session. [Rickey, Don, *Forty Miles a Day on Beans and Hay*, 103–105.]

6   US Army horses were purchased, for the most part, from traders, ranchers and friendly Indians. Training was often less than deemed adequate. Many were of poor quality and lacked the stamina for long hours on patrol and lengthy miles on the trail. Furthermore, few were trained to remain calm during periods of action amidst the noise and ruckus of battle. As a result many panicked at the first sound of gunfire. Horses that proved inadequate were given over to company and regimental quartermasters for use with supply wagons when mules were unavailable.

7   Howard held, and would always hold, his belief that Joseph was the overall leader of the five bands. He had never bothered to learn the roles of the other chiefs and, in fact, knew little of them beyond their names. He never believed that Joseph was not a war chief or that he had little to do with the planning, conduct and execution of the war. [Author's files.]

8   There were diverse nationalities in the private ranks of both companies. In H Company, for example, 15 were from Ireland, 3 from Canada, 8 from Germany and 4, one apiece, from England, Denmark, Austria and France for a total of 29. Only 24 were American. [Company H muster rolls, US Army archives, Washington, DC.]

9   Among the major battles in which Parnell was engaged were those at Fredericksburg, Cedar Mountain, Aldie, Cross Keys, Brandy Station and Upperville. He was wounded and captured by Confederate soldiers at Upperville (June 21, 1863) but recovered enough after only 10 days to escape. After a lengthy and arduous

trek northward he located and rejoined his command. Though wounded several more times, often seriously, Parnell always recovered to fight again. [Thrapp, D.L., *Encyclopedia of Frontier Biography*, 1116–7.]

10 Michael McCarthy (1845–1907), the first sergeant of Company H, was one of several NCOs who had not been born in the USA. McCarthy wrote in his diary (on page 102) of not being particularly impressed by the Irishman Parnell, of whom he wrote: "the first Lt. [Parnell], an ex English dragoon guardsman who claimed a high degree of skill in H.B.M [Her British Majesty] service. The ex British dragoon was not in it, when it came to campaigning and physical endurance." (*sic*). He did, however, admit Parnell was a fine soldier although he did not measure up to others in riding skill or endurance. McCarthy was possibly not aware of many wounds Parnell had suffered which certainly could have affected his endurance.

11 Registry of Enlistment, 1896–74 [Records of the Office of the Adjutant General, Record Group 94.]

12 Gambling was widespread throughout the army. Brevet-colonel George A. Custer was known to lose $1,000 on a horse race and think nothing of it. He usually tempered his losses by being able to boast a few days later of winning $600 at poker. [Author's files.]

13 Brown, Mark H., *Flight of the Nez Perce*, 121–122.

14 The regiment was heavily engaged in the battle at Cedar Mountain, August 9, 1862 in which it suffered serious losses. Of its 380 enlisted men, 180 were killed and dozens wounded. Most of its officers were captured, including the commander, a Col. Chapman (no relation to "Ad" Chapman), his 2i/c Lt. Col. Stone, and the adjutant Major Smith. At that point Captain Henry W. Daboll assumed command and led the shattered force

throughout the remainder of the fight and eventually to safety. [*Hartford Courant*, August 16, 1862.]

15   Two privates and one sergeant were left at Grangeville to guard unneeded supplies and equipment left behind. The names of the three have not been identified. [McCarthy Diary, June 16, 1877.]

16   Normally they would have stayed on the main road all the way to Mount Idaho, but a sweep past the lake was deemed necessary to round up any Indians who may have stayed in the vicinity. In retrospect the detour was a waste of valuable time. [Author's files.]

17   Likely Perry did not believe the claim, for by now he had become aware that Chapman was more swagger than substance. Though he had not bothered to learn much about the Nez Perces or the land in which they lived, he did know they were neither cowards nor backstabbers. Except for Chapman's warning of the possibility of Joseph planning a dawn departure, how much of Chapman's information he considered vital is unknown. [Author's files.]

18   *Lewiston Teller,* July 28, 1877, 4.

19   Daily rations for troops on the march had no variance. A daily menu was typically hardtack, bacon and coffee for breakfast, salt bacon and hardtack for lunch and boiled beans and hardtack for supper. The beans were what are generally known as navy beans and take several hours to boil to softness. Cooks would, when in bivouac, begin the preparations for supper by mid-afternoon. This procedure, however, was not possible when on the move, so supper was often delayed until well into the evening. [Rickey, *Forty Miles a Day on Beans and Hay,* 248–51.]

20   Canyons are often spectacularly deep, wide and heavily wooded. They should not be confused with arroyos, which are vertical sided, flat-floored deep gullies

common in arid and semi-arid climes. Canyons are generally wider than arroyos. [*Oxford Encyclopedia,* 81 and 249].

21   The howl was not from a scout. According to all Nez Perce accounts the scouts had all returned to the camp by that time, as there was no need to stay out. Perry's location was known and the militia from Mount Idaho had already been reported as being on the move. [McWhorter et al.]

22   Brady, *Indian Fights and Fighters,* 106.

23   McWhorter, *Hear Me My Chiefs,* 253 fn32.

24   First Cavalry Division records, 1877. [US Army Records, Washington Archives.]

[CHAPTER 11]

THE BATTLE at WHITE BIRD CANYON

A forlorn hope is a desperate mission undertaken by a few men with little chance of success.
— JOHN D. MCDERMOTT[1]

They were dropping like hunted birds.
— EELAHWEEMA [ABOUT SLEEP].[2]

Joseph, Tool'hool'hool'zote and White Bird,[3] watching the soldiers descend the incline, felt they were witnessing a plan to attack rather than to parley. They were even more upset to see the number of Treaty Nez Perce warriors acting as scouts for the army. The chiefs were not alone in their concerns; some of their warriors also counted the numbers of Nez Perce men with the soldiers. Joseph was further dismayed when informed of the presence of Chapman and his group.

White Bird and Joseph were well aware that in other areas the army had used sudden charges by cavalry as the principal tactic of attacking villages. Against that possibility Joseph had already hidden the elders, women and children—and horses not needed at the moment—across White Bird Creek some distance along the south bank. White Bird and Tool'hool'hool'zote had concealed warriors amidst the trees and underbrush along the north bank and both sides of the canyon's trails. One group, under the leadership of Leepet Hessem'dooks [Two Moons], had moved to a wooded area to the east of the trail, while Ollokot and fifty warriors stationed themselves behind a huge outcropping of rocks on the west side of the flat land. A third group had ridden to a heavily wooded glade, tethered their horses behind protecting rocks and then hid in the brush. All waited quietly as they watched the troops descend the incline, a sloping trail through a deep, narrow gorge.

Confusion arose among the army files as the trail narrowed near the valley floor. Reaching end of the trail, the troop came onto a wide, flat area bordered on the east by a low butte that extended to a broken terrain; to the west uneven terrain linked to a mountain range (the White Bird Divide) from the north. The militia volunteers began to partially merge with F Company, causing forward momentum to slow. The soldiers slowed to make room for the militia, but H Company on the right flank continued forward. Soon a gap of several yards opened and the once unified troop was now broken. F Company regrouped but the militia did not reclaim an orderly file. It continued its progress, not stopping until it was very close to the creek.

The warriors watched intently as the army moved closer, H Company to the right, F Company on the left. The militia however, by advancing too close to the creek, had opened a wide gap of several strategic yards and by so doing placed themselves in a very vulnerable position. The warriors were quick to assess the advantage offered. As the files branched out, Lieutenant Theller and eight of his men who had ridden ahead as an advance guard took possession of a swale to the left of F Company. Further to Theller's left was a knoll on which the militia positioned itself. The remaining soldiers stopped and loaded their carbines. Perry's entire command was now stretched along a ridge, exposed precariously and with no force in reserve.

Perry appeared in no hurry to proceed closer, which suggested to Joseph he was awaiting an indication from the chiefs they wished to talk. A truce party of six riders,[4] led by a brave named Wetti'wetti Howlis [Vicious Weasel],[5] was sent out under a white flag. All accounts agree Vicious Weasel was only to enquire of Perry if he wished to meet with Joseph and White Bird.

The six, shielded by brush and rocks, had covered about half the distance to where Perry stood when they emerged from behind a rocky formation. Suddenly a shot rang out, quickly followed by a second. It is recorded and fully verified in *all* accounts the shots had been fired from the rear line by Arthur Chapman.[6] This disregard for the white flag, long recognized on the western frontier, was a flagrant violation and the second shot was a violation of decorum. Chapman's marksmanship was, fortunately, poor and both shots missed. The six riders wheeled their mounts in hasty retreat. Perry's opinion of the rash action was never recorded, but apparently it convinced him he held the advantage. He ordered an immediate advance in preparation for an attack in full force. This decision was one for which two-thirds of his force were to pay dearly.

The warriors had watched in anticipation as the six emissaries rode towards the army lines. When they heard the shots and saw the riders wheel in full flight, the warriors tensed for action, awaiting the signal to open fire. White Bird raised his arm then brought it down in a slashing motion. The soldiers of The Army of the Northwest were about to be introduced to a style of warfare none had seen before. They were to learn that in this war there would be no riding roughshod through unaware villages shooting down helpless women and children, as had been the custom against Paiute and Shoshone villages further east. They would learn that every bush and rock concealed sharp-eyed braves, some of whom had modern carbines and rifles that fired bullets that did not miss. The rest had muzzle-loading vintage muskets that fired deadly .55 caliber miniballs, or bows whose barbed arrows carried death or painful injuries.

The first shots, from the bushes and rocks on the right, raked H Company with rapid volleys of withering fire. Several soldiers, including trumpeter Frank A. Mitchell, were shot from their saddles in that first volley, while others were tossed to the ground by horses bucking and twisting through fright or wounds from bullets and arrows. Perry immediately ordered F Company to move forward into "line front" while Captain Trimble moved H Company into "line right." Nez Perce horses, ridden by warriors hanging unseen from their sides, exploded from the bushes kicking up great clouds of dust. Crossing the outlying fringes of the field, the riders began firing volleys into the flanks.

As his men began falling from their saddles, Perry realized there was no longer any possibility of fighting from horseback. He ordered his bugler, Private John Jones, to sound "dismount." Jones only blew a few notes before he was knocked from his saddle with a bullet in the chest, shot by an old warrior named Otstotpoo [Fire Body].[7] Nevertheless, the men understood and quickly dismounted. While handlers rushed the horses into Theller's swale, both companies moved to "line front." F Company hurriedly moved left to abut Theller's position, while Captain Trimble's H Company moved into line on Perry's right. As Perry's troops hastened to form their defensive positions, Ollokot's fifty warriors behind their rocky fortress unleashed concentrated and intense fire into the entire line. Their enfilade had no cessation. On the left, the right and in the rear, soldiers and militia fell. Within minutes the soldiers began a retreat, at first dropping back in orderly fashion, but still causing disorder among those intent on holding their ground. Suddenly, a group of sixteen mounted warriors appeared at full gallop from the left, a completely unexpected attack. Led by Two Moons they had been so well concealed not a single soldier had seen them. The hard riding warriors were upon the left flank before soldiers or volunteers could react. With war cries adding to the din, the attackers raced past, raking the entire flank with rifle fire before wheeling to the left and vanishing as suddenly as they had appeared, as if they were ghosts swallowed up by the sheltering trees. They did not go far. Within a few minutes they reappeared in another sector.

When the militia on the left flank broke and gave way, those to their right realized the Indians had taken total control of the area. The left flank began to collapse, the retreat becoming panic. Soon those on the right were also overtaken. This attack proved too much for the undertrained, undisciplined members of the Mount Idaho Militia. In panic retreat, they fled en masse up the trail, dodging behind anything offering cover or safety, however momentary or dubious it appeared. One young militiaman, a youth named Charlie Crooks, later reported there were unseen Indians at every turn, one so close he had called out in English, "You, Charlie Crooks, take your Papa's hoss and go home."[8] Young Crooks considered this advice too wise to be disregarded. He ran to the swale, retrieved his horse and went home. Farming, he decided, was safer than fighting.

The volunteers' retreat impacted on the regulars. The breach now meant any chance to advance was shattered. It was now a matter of standing and fighting from set positions or falling back to find cover. Any semblance of military discipline slipped away as more and more soldiers began to fall. Amid confusion, the columns became hopelessly intermingled. From his command position Perry watched aghast. Thoughts of the previous year's debacle at the Little Big Horn no doubt entered his mind. It is known from later written accounts that same thought had entered the minds of many of the others.

Perry and his officers were now helpless to keep control over the situation. As pandemonium among the troops increased, Perry realized his plans were rapidly disintegrating. Acutely aware of the danger of being surrounded, his troop seemingly out-gunned, and the casualties undeniably mounting, his wisest maneuver seemed obvious—his men must return to higher ground. That meant swinging the entire troop into an orderly retreat. He shouted an order for his remaining bugler to sound "retreat," only to learn the bugler was unable to comply; he had lost his instrument during the first minutes of the frenzied action. Orders could be given through hand signals, but, although workable at close range, hand signals are impossible to transmit over an area as wide as the front had become. Therefore, all commands now had to be delivered by runners. Frantically racing from one unit to another, the hard-pressed runners relayed verbal messages. Many valuable minutes were lost, and the delays added to the toll. Theller and Trimble were unable to regroup many of their men because many soldiers, having lost their bearings and devoid of leadership, did not receive the verbal orders. Theller and Trimble located as many of the lost as possible and began the move to higher ground.

Some soldiers, frightened and confused, rushed into the swale hoping to regain their horses, no easy task, as the horses were now kicking and rearing in efforts to escape the grips of the handlers. So many of the animals broke loose that within minutes the field was overrun with horses trying to escape the noise and the bullets swishing around them like angry hornets. Many were hit; some killed, others injured.

Had it not been for Sergeant McCarthy, Lieutenant Parnell and Captain Trimble, the entire force might have been lost. Perry, with the determined help of those three, somehow managed to regroup enough men that a rearguard action could be mounted to cover the general retreat. The defeat had been a debacle from the first shots, but did end in a more or less orderly retreat. Still, Perry's losses were heavy. Over 30 percent of his force had been wiped out in the first five minutes.

Captain Perry's decision to advance his entire troop into the canyon had been his third major error since leaving Grangeville. His first had been to go to the canyon instead of proceeding to Mount Idaho in the morning as scheduled. His second had been to rush his over-tired men and horses back to the trail without proper food and a night's rest. Had he followed the original plan the chiefs would have waited for him, as they had already decided not to fight. Among his minor errors had been failure to give proper regard to a report from a group of settlers fleeing to Idaho City. When he met them on his way to the canyon they told him of seeing, some two hours previously, a group of mounted Indians. They were uncertain whether they were Nez Perce because the riders stayed their distance paying them no heed. Perry, thinking the riders would now be many miles away, disregarded the intelligence. Those riders were, in fact, scouts who had been sent to shadow Perry. They had watched him the entire route of his advance from Grangeville to the canyon. It had been they who had alerted the chiefs of the army's approach—not the wolf howl or the lighted pipe as related years later by Parnell, Schorr and others (see: Chapter 10). Those tales were fictions designed by the troops and their officers as apologia for mistakes made.

Perry was to make one more major mistake that morning. The echoes of Chapman's shots had barely died away when soldiers hit by bullets from Nez Perce sharpshooters, began falling from their saddles, so he ordered the horses be moved to safety in the swale. This necessitated the use of many soldiers whose firepower was desperately needed on the line.

Other factors as well have emerged emphasizing the failure of Perry's campaign. Before the first shots were fired, the nature of horses caused a degree of disarray within the army ranks. A volunteer, Theodore Swarts,[9] later described the incident,

> "Approaching the canyon we saw...an Indian village of some ninety tepees and many horses roaming about freely. It was mating season and Stallions were snorting and fighting while the mares were running and squealing. This caused great excitement among our horses and they began to act skittish becoming hard to handle [by their riders]. The horses nearer to the front, one of whom was Perry's mount, then began to act up."[10]

The retreat, although carried out as rapidly as possible, quickly became even further confused. Since the units were now thoroughly entangled, NCOs quickly lost control of the situation. Confused soldiers, unsure of where they were supposed to be or which orders they should follow, became disoriented. One was Corporal Roman Lee. Wounded in the groin by a bullet fired during the first volley, he was helped from his saddle by comrades but was in such pain he could not think clearly. When the order to retreat came he got up, eluded the grasp of fellow soldiers and stumbled aimlessly toward the creek. His unsteady walk ended when he crossed the sights of a Nez Perce marksman. Lee was the first of the five NCOs killed that morning.

Theller, having regained a semblance of control over his own men, lost it again when he and seven others moved too far ahead of the main body. Quickly overtaken by Nez Perce riders, they were trapped in a rocky defile. All were killed. One of those riders was twenty-one-year-old Tipyahlahnah_Elassanin [Roaring Eagle] who was armed with an old muzzle-loading musket. He fired one shot then realized he had forgotten the ramrod in his tepee. Since the eight soldiers were now all dead he dismounted, discarded the useless musket and retrieved a carbine and cartridge belt from one of the bodies. As he rode away he found to his dismay the belt contained only a few shells. Now armed with a new rifle but with a nearly empty ammunition belt, he rejoined his comrades. When all the rounds were fired he returned to camp.[11]

From the woods and from Ollokot's rocks the withering fire continued without letup on the fleeing remnants of F Company. Many more minutes elapsed before another officer realized Theller had been killed. He took command and was able to bring about a return of order.

White Bird, seeing the confusion amongst the enemy and recognizing the advantage was now fully his, sent more warriors to harass the scattered fray. On foot, relying now on bows and arrows, they assailed the soldiers by moving quickly from bushes to bluffs to rocks. Soldiers told later of being caught completely unawares by this tactic. All they could do was run or try to fight their way to safety.

Later, when chronicling Joseph's deeds, a series of idolizing writers suggested the Nez Perce chief had developed amazing new strategies that at White Bird Canyon he had a chance to put into practice. The fiction served to increase his legend, but this was neither a new tactic nor the product of Joseph's alleged military genius. In 1935, a participant in the battle, Weyahwahtsitskan (who by then was generally known as John Miles), told Lucullus McWhorter why the soldiers had been so soundly beaten. He explained the tactic thus,

> "Unlike the trained white soldier, who is guided by the bugle call, the Indian goes into battle on his mind's own guidance. All the warriors, whoever gets ready,[a] mount their horses and go. In the charge against the soldiers' right flank,

---

a   Here Miles was referring to the Nez Perce "fight-if-you-wish" philosophy.

> *Wahlitits, Sarsis Ilppilp and Tipyahlahnah Kapskaps [Strong Eagle] were the first to start the charge [in order to draw fire]. Other warriors follow after them riding singly... hanging on the side of their horses...*

> "It is a bad mixup for the soldiers. They do not stand before that sweeping charge and rifle fire of the Indians. Their horses go wild and throw their riders, and many [soldiers] dash away in retreat... The warriors charging the left flank were a small force. Some were middle aged and some were past that time of life. They routed the volunteers from a rocky butte..."

> "None of the chiefs, Joseph, White Bird or Tool'hool'hool'zote were in this charging fight. Joseph did some fighting but he was not with either bunch of the charging warriors. He did no leading.[12]

The battle by warriors on foot, as Weychwahtsistkan explained it, was a simple study in classic Indian warfare; a matter of creep forward, take cover, shoot, depart quickly, take cover, shoot and again move on. This tactic was used mainly by warriors with rifles because, by firing and departing quickly, there was no chance for anyone to draw a bead on telltale smoke from the rifle. Those who worked with bows could stay longer because only rarely was their presence detected quickly. The battle, though it lasted almost two hours, saw the fiercest fighting in the first forty-five minutes when the bulk of army casualties occurred. The entire fight produced only two Nez Perce casualties that needed treatment and one that resulted only in bruises. None were serious enough to cause the three to quit and they remained in the fight to its final minutes. Claims by militia volunteers of inflicting casualties were all fabricated attempts to cover the unit's hasty departure. One such story is that made by the abovementioned Theodore D. Swart who claimed he shot and killed an Indian while defending Perry's left flank.[13] He did no such thing. He was, in fact, among the first to run.

It is not within the scope of this narrative to describe in detail the full specifics of the Battle at White Bird Canyon. Those have been well documented and expressed through several excellent books pertaining to the actual fighting from the viewpoint of both sides.[14] It suffices to state the battle lasted an intense one hour and fifty minutes; thirty-three soldiers of the First Cavalry Regiment were killed and twenty of the dead were from F Company. Included were two highly experienced sergeants and one veteran corporal. Surprisingly, only one from F Company, a private, was wounded, but his wounds were so serious he was unable to participate in any future actions of the war.

Despite the confusion and turmoil, H Company casualties numbered one wounded and twelve dead, plus First Lieutenant Theller (who was officially of G Company), the only officer to die in the battle. Two corporals were killed. The wounded man, like his F Company counterpart, saw no further action.

As for the Mount Idaho Volunteers, their departure had been so rapid none had been killed and only two wounded. The experience, however, took all the fight out of them. They all went home and none saw any further action. Arthur "Ad" Chapman and his ten companions deserted their post during the first salvo. None were seen again until Chapman reappeared several weeks later with Howard's army as the official translator.

It was reported that several of the Treaty Nez Perces who had been with Perry's forces as scouts were trailed and killed. This has never been officially verified and such retaliatory action was always denied by Nez Perce survivors of the war. Both Two Moons and Otstotpoo [Fire Body] admitted to having had the chance to kill two of the Nez Perce scouts. In a 1935 interview they said they did capture the scouts but declined to kill them, instead telling both to return to Lapwai and stay away from soldiers in future. Two Moons claimed the two scouts left immediately and stayed at home as they had promised.

"I did not want to drop any of these enemy Indians, not at all," Two Moons said to L.V. McWhorter.[15]

With so many dead and wounded, dozens missing, and the

Mount Idaho Volunteers in desertion, Perry's command totally collapsed. His entire force had been routed and rendered completely inoperable.[16]

With the soldiers in full retreat and the shooting over, Joseph, White Bird and Tool'hool'hool'zote hurriedly took stock of their own warriors. As battles go this had been not only a rout, but a classic victory with little cost. Chellooyeen [Bow and Arrow Case], who had been caught in a crossfire, and Espowyes [Heavy Weapon][17] had been the ones wounded during close-quarter fighting, but neither had quit. A tewats [medicine man] treated their wounds later with herbal applications while Espowyes' mother sang medicine songs over them to hasten recovery. The unidentified third wounded warrior needed no herbal treatment.

In retrospect, this victory for the Nez Perces, though total in all respects, could have been as great as that of the Sioux/Cheyenne at the Little Big Horn the previous year. That it was not can be attributed solely to a large number of Lamtama and Wellamotkin warriors who missed the battle or otherwise declined to fight. Joseph and White Bird between them had at least 120 able warriors while Tool'hool'hool'zote had about thirty. On that fateful Sunday morning all the Piqunin warriors went into battle, but a number of White Bird's and Joseph's, estimated at sixty-five, did not. The Nez Perce philosophy of "fight-if-you-wish" figures in this case. Most of the sixty-five who did not show up were suffering from debilitating hangovers from a drunken party the previous night and sleeping off the effect of whiskey looted by the Lamtama renegades during their raids. . Despite loud curses and many kicks from their comrades, those warriors slept through the entire fracas. Had they been in the fight, the addition of their weaponry would very likely have been sufficient to deal Captain Perry the same fate as that met by Colonel George A. Custer only a year before, and White Bird would have become as well known as Sitting Bull.[18]

The troopers on the other hand, although all showed up, also performed very poorly. During the retreat many discarded their rifles, cartridge belts and heavy great coats (probably to allow them to run faster). When the last soldier had left, the field was littered with equipment. The warriors, of course, were delighted and immediately set about collecting the spoils of war.

Darkness was already shrouding the area when personnel in varying degrees of distress, thirst, hunger and fear began stumbling into the staging area at Grangeville. Several made their way to Mount Idaho where they were attended to before being reunited with their units. It was late the following day before an approximate accounting of survivors was achieved. Several more days were needed to locate, identify and bury the dead, not all of whom had died on the field. Several managed to wander some distance before dying, so two full weeks passed before all the dead had been found and buried. While most survivors returned to the original departure point at Grangeville, others had dispersed over a wide range. A few had returned to Fort Lapwai. Horses that had run away remained missing for days, but many had been captured by the Nez Perces and became part of their general herd. The situation forced Perry to spend the better part of three days regrouping and assessing material losses.

As if a resounding defeat in battle and a casualty rate of over 30 percent was not a heavy enough cross to bear, Perry was not long in receiving more depressing news. In the pandemonium, the two supply wagons brought from Grangeville had been abandoned, their mules still in harness. A Nez Perce chief spotted them and dispatched some of his fighters to sweep down and claim them. The wagons were destroyed after being emptied of their contents, which were distributed among the bands, and the mules were led away to be later butchered for food.

That loss left Perry with only the supplies he had left in Grangeville. With no way of immediately replacing the items lost in the fighting, these had to do. Since there was very little food available, strict rationing was imposed. Rifles and ammunition were inadequate for replacement, so many soldiers remained unarmed. Perry sent an immediate dispatch to Howard informing him of the defeat, a list of known casualties and the loss of equipment and material.[19] He also had to tell Howard the Nez Perces had salvaged all the rifles, pistols and cartridge belts from the dead and injured[20] as well as the abandoned weapons, ammunition and clothing.

The lost wagons, a disaster for Perry, proved a boon to the Nez Perces: mules for food, rifles, ammunition, several days supply of field rations, some clothing, greatcoats and even a few blankets. The rifles, a great prize indeed, totaled sixty-three .30 caliber Springfield carbines, all the latest model, new and never fired. These were quickly distributed among braves who had been relying on bows and arrows, old rifles and ancient muzzle loaders. To augment this treasure, the wagons also yielded hundreds of rounds of ammunition. The warriors now had a surplus of fire power. The field rations, beans, bacon, biscuits and coffee, as well as the clothing, were quickly doled out to the women. The blankets went to the children and elders.

Immediately following the battle Joseph assumed charge of the non-combatants of all the bands. Aware of the need to vacate the area as quickly as possible, he pushed his charges onward to a safer place on higher ground. He knew progress would be slow because of the numbers of women, children and elders, of whom several were ailing. They would also be hindered by the slow pace of the horses that had to be herded. Nonetheless, by the time Howard and his reinforcements arrived at the canyon Joseph had moved to an area some distance away. He now had time to break the large group into smaller ones and to separate the horses.

To ensure progress be as fast as possible, he decided to maintain a pace that would keep them well ahead of the pursuit he knew would come. Joseph was aware his charges, especially elders and small children, would require adequate rest, so he decided on encampments for periods of two days between each long advance. He would also enforce a pre-arranged decision to keep his group segregated from the warriors except during full-scale stops. That strategy worked well until two disastrous decisions were made, neither of which were his doing. The first came on August 5 with the election of Chief Looking Glass to the position of head chief. The second was the August 9 encounter with Colonel Gibbon at the Big Hole River.

[CHAPTER II ENDNOTES]

1. Quoted from John D. McDermott's book *A Forlorn Hope*.

2. Eelahweema was a boy of about 11 summers. Not yet a warrior he helped in the battle by reloading rifles for snipers. As such he witnessed much of the fighting. [McDermott, *A Forlorn Hope*, ch. 9.]

3. Husis Kute and his Palu (plus the Cayuse warriors) were still in the reservation proper, as was Looking Glass and his Asotins. Thus, neither participated at White Bird Canyon. The Asotins would not become involved until July 1, following the Clearwater battle. Husis Kute and his band rejoined the others at Weippe prior to the move into Montana. [Author's files.]

4. Some early accounts claim Joseph accompanied them but they have been discounted. Neither Yellow Wolf nor any others with first-hand knowledge mentioned him and all agreed he was not in the party. [Author's files.]

5. Beyond leading the truce party at White Bird Canyon nothing more was heard of Wetti'wetti_Howlis until years later. It was thought he might have been among the unidentified killed at the Big Hole or in an ensuing battle. His name does not appear in either the "known casualties" or the survivors' lists, and neither is there any record of him being in Canada with White Bird or of accompanying Joseph into exile. No mentions of any later exploits appear in narratives or interviews

with Yellow Wolf or other Nez Perces who spoke with McWhorter, Elsensohn *et al.*

However, it seems he had been known to white settlers for many years as John Boyd. A few years ago a very interesting, undated clipping from the *Lewiston Tribune* came to light. In 1957 a surviving member of the Mt. Idaho Militia, an elderly man named Elmer Atkinson, in an interview with a *Tribune* reporter, mentioned that about 1935 a Nez Perce elder he knew as Johnson Boyd told him he had been in the war party that attacked the Rains Patrol, *and that he had fired the shot that killed Lieutenant Rains.* Whether Johnson Boyd was Vicious Weasel is hard to say, but the coincidence of names and age is very strong. [On file at Idaho State Historical Society, Boise.]

6 For years Chapman, Joseph's supposed friend and trusted confidant, denied having fired on the truce party but eventually admitted it; but he said he had fired only one shot. He then tried to justify his action with a lame excuse that one of the party had fired at him. No one believed him. [See: Appendix E.]

7 It was long-distance shot but Fire Body, an experienced buffalo hunter, was renowned for his marksmanship. [McWhorter, *Yellow Wolf,* 55–56.]

8 [McDermott, *Forlorn Hope,* 87.]

9 T.D. Swarts is not overly reliable as a source of information. A few days after the battle, obviously unaware no warriors had been killed, he claimed to have shot an Indian in the head, killing him instantly, after the warrior had shot him in the knee. The claim was debunked within days and in 1915 Frank Fenn, a fellow volunteer, who had helped Swarts escape, ridiculed the man and his stories. When interviewed by Walter Camp on Sept 19, 1915, Fenn claimed Swarts never

shot anyone except himself. His knee wound had been accidentally self-inflicted. [Folder 2, Box 2, Camp Papers. Howard B. Lee Library, Brigham Young University.]

10 Thomas D. Swarts. [Cited by Jerome Greene, *Nez Perce Summer*, 36.]

11 Comments of Roaring Eagle to McWhorter in 1935. [*Hear Me My Chiefs*, 251–52, fn 29.]

12 McWhorter, *Hear Me My Chiefs*, 248–9.

13 Ibid, 250.

14 Two of the best books on this subject are Jerome A. Greene's *Nez Perce Summer 1877* and John D. McDermott's *Forlorn Hope*. Both are a wealth of verifiable facts. Included are names and biographic information pertaining to individuals on both sides, as well as their actions and deeds. Both works are highly recommended to students of the struggles by American Indians against the Washington bureaucracy. [See: Bibliography.]

15 McWhorter, *Hear Me My Chiefs*, 248.

16 Howard, Report of the Secretary of War, 1877, 132–37. [Government Printing Office. Washington DC.]

17 Names in the Nez Perce language can have many meanings and dialect pronunciations. Espowyes, as one example, can also be pronounced "Auskehwus," "Askeeis" or "Ashhawus." Interpretation also has a variety of meanings. Besides meaning "Heavy Weapon" the name can also mean "Prying Open" or "Thread" or "Thin Cord." With a slightly different inflection, Espowyes can be translated as "Light in the Mountain." [McWhorter, *Hear Me My Chiefs*, 254.]

18 Narratives of several Nez Perce survivors as recorded by McWhorter and others. [McWhorter, *Hear Me My Chiefs*, 239–242; McDermott, *Forlorn Hope,* 81.]

19   Howard, in his official report to the Secretary of War (1877, I, 120) stated the Nez Perce force was double that of Perry's. In a later book, *My Life and Experience Among our Hostile Indians* (page 285) he increased the number of warriors to more than 300. In the following years historians and careless researchers used these claims as the basis for their own writings. Some increased the numbers until the Nez Perce warriors numbered nearly 400, thereby putting the odds at 4 to1 in favor of Joseph when, in fact, the odds were 2.5 to 1 against him. Howard made many claims that were untrue. In one he claimed Ollokot had tried to run away during the battle but had been restrained by others. In another he claimed Joseph had in his possession a glass (telescope) in which could spy on approaching soldiers. Howard was as adroit at creating fiction as were many of his officers. [Author's files.]

20   In keeping with Nez Perce custom there was no scalping. Wounded soldiers were never taken captive, killed or harmed in any way. Neither was their clothing removed as loot. One wounded soldier of the White Bird Canyon battle told of a warrior carrying an ancient muzzle-loading musket coming across him as he lay unable to move. The warrior spoke kindly to the frightened soldier assuring him no harm would come to him. Though he took the soldier's new Springfield carbine and ammunition pouches, he thanked the soldier and wished him well. Before he moved on he placed the musket beside the man as if in payment. [Author's files.]

[CHAPTER 12]

THE WAITING GAME

Following the victory at White Bird Canyon, Joseph showed the leadership for which he had been born. It was, however, leadership in organization that became his forte, not the pseudo fame as a military genius bestowed upon him in later years. That was done by admiring writers with too much imagination and not enough inspiration to search out the truth[1] and an adoring public who cheered the underdog. Joseph had indeed fought in the White Bird Canyon, as had the other two chiefs,[2] and it may have been here Joseph decided he must leave the bulk of defensive decisions to chiefs experienced in warfare. It is equally possible he had little choice because of the Nez Perce structure: only chiefs with experience in war and hunting could lead in combat situations. With such a situation now upon them, Joseph may not even have been included in future war councils, nor did he wish to be. He was not a warrior and, regardless of what so-called authorities have to say on the subject, Joseph himself summed up the situation when he said a few weeks later at the Weippe conference,

"*I have no words! You know the country; I do not.*"[3]

With those words Joseph acknowledged he was no war chief

and from that day forward would lead the non-combatants, but would fight as required.

Though it was at Weippe he acknowledged his responsibility for the non-combatants, it had actually been at White Bird Canyon that Joseph had fully accepted that responsibility. From that day forward he shepherded the women, children and elders considered too sick or too old to fight. He was not, however, a soft touch for he pushed his charges relentlessly, resting only when necessary and for the length of time that he himself decided was adequate. Moreover, his methods were always in the interest of safety. He kept to the forests and heavy bush and in this way eluded the army scouts so easily that at times the entire group seemingly disappeared into thin air. Thus it was they departed from White Bird Canyon leaving no trail to follow.

With the canyon battle behind them, White Bird, Ollokot and Tool'hool'hool'zote, the primary war chiefs, named the battle chiefs who would take charge of the various war parties. These were: Red Cloud, Red Scout, Yellow Wolf, Rainbow, Two Moons. Others such as Peopeo Tholekt would join later.

Captain Perry, still attempting to regroup his shattered force and having no means of mounting a pursuit, returned to Grangeville with most of his remaining troop to await his general's pleasure. When Howard, still at Fort Lapwai awaiting reinforcements, was informed of Perry's defeat, he retired to his quarters, remaining there for several hours. Once his initial shock subsided, he began drawing volunteers from local militias, as well as a full complement of regulars from Fort Boise. The reinforcements were ordered to proceed to Grangeville. Then, assembling the available troops within Fort Lapwai, he set out for Mount Idaho where he would establish his HQ. From there he would go to the canyon to help Perry reorganize.

On June 25, when General Howard arrived at the scene of Perry's defeat he was greeted with

the first of the many setbacks when he learned the Fort Boise group would be delayed. That fort's commandant, Major John Wesley Green, had mustered his troops but encountered problems in acquiring enough wagons to carry the supplies needed.[4]

Howard was informed the Nez Perces had abandoned the canyon on the 18th and had moved to Slate Creek and had crossed the Salmon River near Horseshoe Bend the following day and disappeared. He, therefore, set up a secondary headquarters at Horseshoe Bend in order to better coordinate the various units whose arrival he expected over the next few days. He dispatched Captain Trimble's unit to Slate Creek as an advance force should Joseph appear in that area.

But his woes increased as scouts continuously sent word they were unable to report sightings of Joseph and his charges. Neither had they seen any warriors, singly or in groups. He told the scouts not to return until they had some good news. With the Nez Perce rebels seemingly departed from the earth, all the beleaguered general could do was wait. Though anxious to begin the hunt for his elusive foe, Howard had no idea where Joseph was heading and there were so many places the rebels could go he feared beginning a pursuit that possibly would lead him in the wrong direction. He remained in bivouac to await the slings and arrows of outrageous fortune; they were not long in coming.

The debacle at White Bird Canyon and the unfavorable publicity Howard had feared it would foment was already beginning to attract a great deal of attention. Besides comments of reproach from his superiors in the war department, several territorial newspapers had begun to express ridicule in large, black headlines. Idaho editors were chastising him for doing nothing, while some in Oregon and the Washington and Montana Territories were beginning to empathize with Joseph. An already bitter pill was becoming even harder to swallow.[5] Howard, though smarting from the barbed comments, was unable to offer rebuttal. Thus, with no real choice but to remain at the canyon and await word from his scouts, he spent much of his time inventing excuses to placate Washington and keep editors at bay.

To add to his problems, as if the abuse from local newspapers was not enough, he was now faced with visits from eastern reporters sent west to provide on-the-spot coverage. Because the new arrivals had no way to interview Joseph, they turned their focus to the goings-on within the army. They converged on Howard's camp, which caused the besieged myrmidon more gloom than he could handle. How, they kept asking, can a small band of hitherto peaceable Indians tread all over the mighty Army of the Northwest? Finally, Howard refused requests for interviews, assigning his aide-de-camp, 2nd Lieutenant Charles E.S. Wood (1852–1944), the difficult task of parrying reporters' thrusts. Howard ordered his scouts to increase their diligence while he wrestled with his own dilemmas.

He sent the majority of his men to assist Perry's survivors in the sad, distasteful task of recovering and burying the dead.[6] The task took three full days as bodies of the fallen soldiers were scattered here and there along the battle field while others were in out-of-the-way places. It was an effort to locate those known to have been killed but not yet found.[7] There were also settlers to be located to determine how many had been killed in the renegade Indians' raids and give support to survivors. On June 25 he visited the nearby towns of Mount Idaho and Grangeville, met with civic leaders, and then visited wounded soldiers who had been placed in makeshift hospitals set up in local hotels. When he returned to the canyon it was to organize and oversee a reconnaissance of the entire area.

When he reached the battle site he saw soldiers in the shallow defiles, thick underbrush and ravines searching for their dead comrades while others dug graves. He was filled with anguish as he watched them go about their dreadful duties, made worse by the condition of the bodies which, after seven or eight days in the open, were already grotesquely disfigured and decomposed. That afternoon, to add to the problems of recovery, a violent thunderstorm struck with such force that everyone had to find whatever cover they could to escape the driving rain.[8] It was following this storm that Lieutenant Theller's body and those of the seven who had fallen with him were found in the enclave near the top of the retreat route. With great care the bodies were wrapped in cloth and interred in graves dug on the spot.[9]

During this period of retrieval several warriors were seen watching from a distant vantage point, but there were no sightings of large groups of Indians. Howard may then have suspected the Indian camp, even if his scouts hadn't been able to find it, was so close he could probably move against it within a day or two.

On June 28, the resupply wagons from Fort Boise arrived with replacements of supplies and equipment lost during Perry's defeat. With them came reinforcements consisting of four units of the Fourth Artillery (to be employed as infantry) plus C Company from the 21st Infantry Regiment. These replacements boosted Howard's command to almost 400. The following day, two Washington Territory volunteer militia units reported, one from Dayton, commanded by Captain Edward McConville, and one from Lewiston, commanded by a civilian, George Hunter. He dispatched Captain Perry to take a few of the Dayton volunteers to Fort Lapwai for more supplies. McConville's volunteers were sent to Slate Creek to replace Captain Trimble who, with his full company, was to rejoin Howard.

The afternoon of June 29, scouts reported having sighted Joseph's camp on the south bank of the Salmon River. Howard immediately ordered preparations for a forced march, his intention being to launch a surprise attack.

Howard was pleased at the thought of being on the move to what he thought would be the final resolution to the Nez Perce rebellion. It appeared he could finally apprehend his elusive foe and herd the rebels to Lapwai. Perhaps now the newspapers and his superiors in Washington would have to curtail their criticism, which had increased on rumors of Nez Perce rebels being reinforced by rebellious Natives from other tribes.

He had barely digested the good news of Joseph's sighting when bad news—false at it turned out—came his way. Chief Looking Glass, the report read, had swung his support to the rebels and was planning to join them; and survivors of a raid on a farm claimed the raiders were members of the Asotin Band. Whether Howard believed the report is unknown, but he could not ignore it and had no time for verification. He called in Captain Steven G. Whipple of the 1st Cavalry and gave him instructions to proceed to the Indians' camp and take Looking Glass and his warriors into custody and take them to Mount Idaho to be dealt with later. With that under control, Howard headed out with his troops to track down Joseph.

Conversely, the Nez Perce chiefs had been well apprised of Howard's doings all along. Their scouts were on continuous watch over Howard's camp. In fact, his quarry was not far away, just well hidden. Joseph and his non-combatants had re-crossed the Salmon River and were now camped on the south bank in a dense forest a mile or two from a crossing point known as Craig's Ferry.

Joseph knew the time for his own decision was rapidly approaching. Well aware his large group could not remain unseen for a great length of time, the next destination had already been decided. It was now simply a matter of when to move.

During those uneasy days he and the other chiefs debated the options. Joseph and Ollokot still argued in favor of taking the people to Fort Lapwai and accept whatever fate was in store for them, but White Bird and Tool'hool'hool'zote would have none of that. They favored a run to the Lolo Trail,[10] where they could cross the Bitterroot Mountains and find safety in Montana. Both held the mistaken opinion that because Howard's jurisdiction did not include Montana they would be free once they got there. Whether Joseph also thought that is unknown. Joseph had to consider his options carefully because his primary responsibility and his major concerns were the safety of the women, children and elders. The war chiefs were equally concerned for the warriors. They all realized the folly of sustaining lengthy battles on stationary fronts and were well aware such battles, regardless of success, nearly always meant casualties. They knew they had been lucky at White Bird Canyon and another such encounter could easily diminish their already outnumbered force. With no means of acquiring reinforcements, a war of attrition could not figure in their plans. The victory over Perry, the relative ease of their escape from the canyon, and Howard's failure to advance made clear to them that only by keeping on the move could they achieve their aims. Agreement was finally reached to move to Cottonwood, a long-time camping site near the Clearwater River just south of the reservation. There a final decision could be made. On July 2 the trek resumed.

Two other important decisions had also been reached. If Joseph was to keep his group and the horses well clear of the fighting, White Bird must lure Howard to places as far as possible from Joseph's group while staying within riding distance. White Bird felt certain he could achieve this through judicious deployment and dictating where, how and when fighting would take place. He decided his war parties would allow themselves to be seen, only to disappear when troops were dispatched to apprehend them. Even the stubborn Tool'hool'hool'zote agreed with the wisdom of the concept.

In order to ensure the two groups not interfere with each other, it was further agreed there would be strict segregation except during periods of encampment. Joseph was fully aware separation could be managed only if nobody strayed from set courses, and the best way to achieve that would be to keep everyone busy. He devised a plan that kept younger teenage boys herding the horses well ahead of the greater body. Women and girls, already responsible for the camp's equipment, would now also tend to the ill and wounded.

Healthy elders were another matter. In normal village life they taught children and supervised their play, activities that were now suspended. The children, therefore, would stay with the women for supervision by older girls. Elders were given the task of sorting and caring for the increased number of rifles and cases of ammunition, plus the material and equipment plundered in the canyon battle. For the remainder of the trek everyone would have assigned tasks because Joseph believed busy people could maintain acceptable levels of morale—a correct surmise as it turned out. The morale of the Nez Perce rebels remained high even to the sorrowful end of the trail.

Joseph speculated that once his charges arrived at Cottonwood, Howard's troopers would be far enough behind that a halt could be called and a council could determine a final destination. Because they would still be close to the reservation proper, he could make one final appeal to the chiefs that they go to Lapwai, surrender and resign themselves to life on the reservation.

Chasing Shadows — A Study in Futility

"We were in a bad fix, with no means of crossing the river. We could not cross like the Indians."
—Sgt. Michael McCarthy[11]

Howard's belief that he could move easily against Joseph displayed his total lack of knowledge of both the immediate terrain and the Indians' ability to traverse raging rivers and negotiate rugged valleys and ravines.

In addition, because Howard believed Joseph was the major chief, he was not yet fully cognizant of the role White Bird[12] was playing in the unfolding drama. He also misinterpreted the reason the warriors were watching. He thought Joseph had sent the warriors to stop his men from fording the Salmon River. Determined as he was to capture Joseph, and knowing he must cross the river to accomplish this, he decided to send sharpshooters to a nearby ridge. When the time was right for his remaining force to cross to the south bank they would provide cover for the crossing. He sent a message to Captain Trimble at nearby Slate Creek instructing him to place troops at all the trails along the river's north bank. This impediment, he felt, would halt fleeing survivors of the attack he was planning and which he anticipated would be successful.

When Howard was informed of Joseph's location, he decided

not to cross the river at Horseshoe Bend but instead cross at White Bird Creek, a point further upstream. His reasons were never disclosed, but the revision meant the troops had to move from Horseshoe Bend to a new camp on June 29.

The following morning the troops began the first of several attempts at crossing the Salmon River. Crossing proved more difficult than Howard had thought and his first few efforts were unsuccessful. The soldiers could not extend ropes across the roiling water, and without guide ropes they and their horses were unable to cross. The warrior scouts, who had also moved upstream, were obviously amused at the soldiers' efforts and made no effort to conceal their amusement. From across the river they baited the troops by waving red blankets and shouting invitations to come over for a good fight. It was an invitation the troops were unable to accept and Howard finally called off the venture. They would try again the following morning.

This time, possibly because there were no Indians to distract them, after a few attempts they succeeded. However, the ropes were not secured until evening, so the crossing was postponed until the following morning.

On the morning of July 1 the soldiers tackled the river. It was not an easy crossing, but, after hours of frustration and setbacks, everything and everyone had relocated to the river's south side. They set out westward towards the forest where Howard's scouts had reported Joseph was camped in a place called Deer Creek. Once again, though, Howard's lack of knowledge regarding the terrain had caused him to plan unwisely. The route he had to traverse Brown's Mountains was across a high trail known as Brown's Pass. The trail was very narrow and very steep. Ascending and descending would be the first in a series of perils. The second was that on the other side of Brown's Mountain the trail dissipated into an area of rugged terrain—meaning there was no viable trail.

Deer Creek was located at the far end of a narrow valley near a bend in the Salmon River as it plunges southward to its wild meeting with the Snake River. Howard had no knowledge of this area or its topography. Partly plateau, partly gorge and ravines, great breaks of pine forest and expanses of deep prairie grass hiding a broken surface were reasons enough for local settlers, none of whom he had consulted, to avoid traveling through it. All of this was further complicated by the meandering courses of the two rivers that forced trails to take many twists and turns. To this mix, Nature had added constantly changing weather patterns in which sudden, often violent, thunderstorms could make an always difficult journey extremely hazardous. Howard was unaware of all this, but was pleased to note Joseph's people, encumbered by some 1,500 horses, had made no effort to cover their tracks. Perhaps it was this stroke of what he deemed good fortune that made him overly optimistic. He may have worried a little had he been aware his progress was being watched by Nez Perce scouts who were keeping Joseph informed of the army's every move and setback.

On July 2, the force began the steep ascent to the summit of Brown's Pass. Those in the lead of the long column were almost to the summit when the first of several disasters fell upon them. An intense storm suddenly struck, complete with strong winds and driving rain. The trail promptly dissolved into a gumbo of mud made worse when the rain changed to sleet and hail causing the shale base to turn as slippery as ice. Unable to keep their footing, men stumbled and fell, sliding backwards into those following. Horses and the usually surefooted mules also had troubles keeping their feet. Soldiers managed to control the horses, but a number of heavily laden mules plunged over the steep cliff, killing several.

Few of the soldiers had experience with the ardors of wilderness campaigning, so most of their time was spent complaining as they, slipping and falling, tried with no success whatever to stay dry. The straggling ranks caused Sergeant Michael McCarthy to write in his diary that the entire command "was strung out all the way from base [on the Salmon River] to the summit of the divide [Brown's Mountain]." (See map.)

They had little success making headway; bone-chilling rain and sleet pounded the soldiers without letup.

Finally, they stopped where they were and waited out the storm, wet and miserably cold. The storm caused such delay in hours lost the time could never be made up, and as a result, progress over the course of the entire trek never averaged better than ten miles a day.[13]

At 4:00 PM on July 4, Howard received a scout's report that Joseph and the entire Nez Perce group had not gone through Brown's Mountain at all; they had re-crossed to the north side of the river. The Indians had actually decamped on July 2 and had crossed the next day. Once again the opposing forces were on opposite sides of the river. Still only halfway to his intended destination, and with much of his supplies lying with the dead mules at the bottom of Brown's Mountain, Howard realized there was nothing to do but return to White Bird Creek.

Howard was now relying on conflicting reports from several scouts. He came to believe the Indians had split into two groups. The main group, he thought, may have crossed the Snake River intending to return to the Wallowa Valley,[14] while a smaller group was deliberately leading him northward. He sent word to Major John Wesley Green, who he believed by now should be well on his way from Fort Boise with additional troops, to watch for and apprehend this southbound group.[15]

At dawn the next day, July 6, he marched his weary command back along the route they had just slogged over to the original fording point. Sergeant McCarthy described it in his journal as "A horrible retrograde march…" At one point Howard stopped the march in an attempt to cross to the river's north shore. In all, two more days were wasted. The attempt ended in yet another disaster when a hastily constructed raft containing all the force's remaining supplies was swamped by the raging current and carried away.

Sergeant McCarthy describes the futility of the attempted crossings:

> "We were in a bad fix, with no means of crossing the river. Our force, except our company, were foot troops. A part of the next day was spent in trying to swim the Cavalry and the horses across but it was a failure. A raft carrying the supplies was tried but it was a failure also. How a whole tribe of Indians with horses, women, papooses, etc., got

across was a puzzle. It is yet a puzzle. We didn't seem to have engineering skill enough to devise ways and means to cross and the command marched back two days' march to White Bird Crossing."[16] (sic)

Sergeant McCarthy never did find out how the Indians had crossed in safety, but it had little to do with engineering skills. It had, in fact, everything to do with knowing the land in which they lived. One of the ironies of the trek was that Howard's aborted and disastrous crossing attempt was only a very short distance from Craig's Ferry, which was where Joseph and his band of women, children, elders and all the animals had made a safe, uneventful crossing. Had Howard gone there, he very likely would have also crossed in safety. Such are the vagaries the gods of war use to amuse themselves.

Howard's headaches were not yet over. The next morning he received word of the ambush of Lieutenant Sevier M. Rains' unit near Cottonwood, but no further details. Not knowing the warriors involved were only a small group from Chief Rainbow's much larger war party, he dispatched the McConnell and Hunter volunteer units, neither with any experience in war, to depart Slate Creek for Cottonwood to hunt them down.

At this point, so early in the campaign, it is almost impossible not to feel sympathy for General Howard. All the hard work he had deemed would end in success had unraveled. Perry's devastating defeat had been a hard blow, and now Joseph had eluded him.

Howard was also bitterly disappointed when he learned Captain Whipple had failed in the quest to detain Looking Glass which he had thought would be handled easily. Now the certainty that Lieutenant Rains and his companions had been part of Captain Whipple's company was salt in his wounds. Worse was yet to come. Upon his return to the starting point near White Bird Creek on July 7 he was informed that not only had Captain Whipple failed in his quest to arrest Looking Glass, but the chief and his Asotin warriors were undoubtedly going to join forces with Joseph and White Bird.

It was a discouraged Howard who exhorted his tired soldiers to retrace their weary steps back across the river to White Bird Canyon. He was right back where he had started, except now he was many days behind Joseph. He had lost a number of his valued mules, had few supplies left and was in command of 400 soldiers beset by low morale and short rations. Major Green and his Boise unit was still among the missing, the Indian war parties were still winning their short sorties against his advance troops, and so far the civilian volunteers had shown no mettle—or, as an old western description of a lack of fighting spirit has it, "They lacked sand." All in all it was not an encouraging prospect.

There was nothing for him to do now but to bivouac his troops once again and await Perry's return from Lapwai with the wagons of new supplies and hope Major Green would eventually show up.

He would start out once again on July 10, but not with any great expectations. His scouts had again lost contact with Joseph and his people; and White Bird and his various war parties were still enjoying success with their hit-and-run tactics. Very likely over the next few evenings the Christian soldier importuned his deity with extreme sincerity during his nightly session of bedtime prayers.

From a distant hill White Bird watched the soldiers re-cross the river to their former camp and begin erecting their tents. There was now no doubt he and his allies had not only decisively won the Battle of White Bird Canyon but had also taken charge of its aftermath. It was now evident the soldiers would not soon resume the pursuit, so White Bird marshaled his forces and hastened westward toward the Clearwater River to rejoin Joseph. The Battle of White Bird Canyon, and the immediate aftermath of the failed pursuit, was to White Bird an omen that General Howard was to see worse days yet to come.

Perhaps the bedeviled general also saw it the same way. His army had not merely been defeated, it had been trounced by a group of usually peaceful Natives. His immediate misfortunes did indeed increase. While in bivouac, daily reports arrived telling of how his advance parties had been ambushed, of lost equipment, and all without inflicting a single casualty upon the attackers. These war parties struck often and hard, disappearing as quickly as they had arrived. They were like shadows, never heard or seen until too late. For the veteran of many Civil War battles it was a humiliating experience. Exasperated to distraction because his expected reinforcements were tardy with no explanation forthcoming, he was forced to stay where he was for two full weeks.

Howard, however, was still the disciplinarian and, because he believed Satan finds work for idle hands, he set his troops to tasks that kept them busy. He also had them disinter the dead who had been buried hurriedly in shallow graves where they had fallen and complete proper burials. This onerous task kept them busy but did little to raise their morale. Most of the bodies had decomposed to a state where retrieval and identification was difficult.[17]

Howard kept himself busy as well by spending his time analyzing why the canyon battle and the pursuit just concluded had failed. He knew his reports were not what Washington wanted to hear, especially when they acknowledged the Nez Perce warriors were far superior to their military counterparts as riflemen and riders. Also, he was forced to admit their horses were better trained than were those of the cavalry. To Howard it was obvious the army had not provided proper training for either soldiers or horses for the type of fighting they were encountering. Nez Perce steeds were well trained, stood still, and did not react to gunfire as did the army mounts that shied and pulled their riders in all directions. Howard also pointed out the Nez Perce economized on ammunition, did not pursue fleeing soldiers for any distance, and throughout remained in what appeared to be a disciplined and orderly structure. In a word, they reacted to situations unlike what was expected of Plains Indians.

The Battle of White Bird Canyon and the subsequent events caused General Howard to realize he was pitted against a far more formidable foe than he had imagined. He now knew Nez Perce warriors were willing to fight for what they believed were their rights. He also realized this would be no easy campaign. If he was to win, his strategy would have to change accordingly; but he had no idea of how to go about making changes. His one consolation at the time was a certainty that he had resources in manpower and supplies, a luxury unavailable to Joseph. If this was to be a war of attrition his greatest ally was time. At the moment, time seemed to be favoring the Nez Perces, and Howard worried that Joseph might emulate Sitting Bull and move directly north to the border.

Howard was also aware that if the uprising was not quelled before the first major blizzard, Joseph would find a formidable ally in "General Winter."[18] The Nez Perce, he knew, were well able to survive cold weather, whereas his troops were not. His solace lay in the knowledge that winter was still four months away. Nonetheless, the present delays could quickly add other major problems to those he was already finding more than he could handle. He was fully aware of the animosity felt towards him by no small number of Washington authorities—and the news of the White Bird Canyon defeat would not sit well with his critics in the capitol. How long, he wondered, would the war secretary wait before removing him from command and sending in a replacement? Such thoughts do not give generals restful nights and relaxed days.

This was also the period in which Joseph became generally credited with being the mastermind behind the Indians' great successes. He was the only chief well known to the army, the others having remained for years in the background. He was also the only one with an Anglicized name easily remembered by army telegraphers and civilians, including reporters. The other chiefs had kept their Nez Perce names, none of which was easily spelled or even pronounceable to the average soldier or reporter. Thus, whenever it became necessary to identify a chief it was Joseph they singled out. His name became famous, not because of any deeds he may or may not have accomplished, but because his was the only name that was easy to spell.

On July 6, when the group arrived at the Cottonwood site Joseph was informed Howard had eventually realized he was following a false trail. Joseph now knew of Howard's disastrous efforts to re-cross the river, that he had lost more of his supplies in this failed attempt, and how he abandoned the attempt and returned to his original crossing point opposite White Bird Creek.

Realizing Howard would be forced to remain there at least a few days, possibly more, Joseph decided a four-day rest was in order.

[CHAPTER 12 ENDNOTES]

1. Early writers did little, if any, real research; most relied heavily on articles and books published by members of the army, the militia and various generals. Howard's first two books, which were used extensively, contain so many errors and outright falsehoods as to be useless. There were also many writers of that era who had no inclination to allow facts to interfere with a good fiction. One of the guiltiest of these writers was the internationally acclaimed author, George Oliver Shields. [Author's files.]

2. According to Weyahwahtsitskan (known in later years as John Miles), all the chiefs fought during the battle. None led the charges, however, as that was not part of the Nez Perce style of warfare. Joseph fought sparingly throughout the entire exodus, but until Bear's Paw did no actual leading. [Interview in 1935 conducted by L.V. McWhorter.]

3. McDonald, Duncan, *The New Northwest,* January 10, 1879, Volume X, no. 28:2.

4. He was to be disappointed when they did finally arrive because the force was only a portion of those he expected. Major Green and his troops were still in Fort Boise, delayed through lack of supplies and a shortage of horses.

5. These were papers from Montana, the Dakotas and

Wyoming. Editors in Idaho and many in Oregon remained vehement in their opposition to the Nez Perce insurgents.

6   A detailed but unsettling account of this task is covered fully in chapter 10 of *Forlorn Hope*. [McDermott, *Forlorn Hope*, 115–129.]

7   Their discoveries included several settlers who had been killed and also several who had survived the initial attacks or had escaped prior to an attack by Shore Crossing and his renegades. Two such refugees were a woman and her small daughter. They were given food, blankets and an escort to safety.

8   Such storms, common to mountainous areas, are caused by collisions of warm surface air with the cold air of higher elevations. Held in by the high mountains, the currents cannot circulate freely and their collisions create thunderstorms that are often intense in their ferocity.

9   Theller and the others were later retrieved and buried in more suitable surroundings. Theller's body was subsequently interred in Arlington National cemetery as he had been awarded the Medal of Honor.

10 Although believed by many to have been named after Lolo, a legendary chief of the Salish nation, this is incorrect. An old prospector, Peter Lobdell, told L.V. McWhorter in 1928 the trail was really named for Joseph Lolo (or Lulu), a Canadian trapper who was killed there by a bear in 1852. Duncan McDonald, an authority on that part of the country, agreed with the basic story but said the victim's name was Laurent (pronounced Lawron) but the Indians could not come any closer to Lawron than Lolo. [McWhorter, *Hear Me My Chiefs*, 343, fn 1.]

11 Sgt. M. McCarthy's Journal, entry 14.

12 Howard had met White Bird, Ollokot, Looking Glass

and Tool'hool'hool'zote, but he had no idea of their reputations as war chiefs. He knew none of the other war chiefs. Indeed, few if any of the army's officers had even met Joseph and none knew any of the war chiefs. To add to the confusion, the army's signalmen were unable to spell the names of the various chiefs but all knew how to spell Joseph and they used his name throughout the entire summer as an identifier for all the chiefs involved. It was for this reason that Joseph became the only chief ever mentioned in dispatches to Washington or the army authorities. Thus, he became thought of as being the only chief of consequence. It was this simple expedience in message transmitting that contributed so greatly to his future, undeserved reputation as a war chief. [Author's files.]

13 When the army began its trek Joseph was encamped only about 25 miles (40 km) away from Howard's starting point 1.5 miles (2.4 km) west of White Bird Creek.

14 This thought was bolstered when the troops found several caches of supplies that had been left by the Indians along with several horses that had seemingly been left behind. Howard thought the caches and animals were there to be picked up by the southbound group.

15 Major Green would never have found the group even if it had existed. He and his troops had not yet left Boise.

16 According to Sgt. McCarthy, whose diary and reports contain a wealth of information pertaining to those anguished days, Howard's problems lay in several erroneous scouting reports, including the one that caused him to think Joseph was returning to the Wallowa Valley. Howard, in an attempt to cut off his quarry, pushed his men at a forced pace despite the adverse conditions. The group he was chasing turned out to be a group of hunters.

17 The body of Lt. Theller was found and re-buried with full honors on the spot of his defeat. Several years were to pass before initial criticism of that defeat was set aside. Theller was then lauded for bravery under fire. [Author's files.]

18 "Russia has two generals in whom she can confide – Generals Janvier [January] and Fevrier [February]." Attributed to Nicholas 1, (b. 1796), Tsar of Russia 1825–1855. Nicholas coined his quote to commemorate Russia's defeat of Napoleon in 1812 to emphasize how the French army literally froze to death during the Russian winter. It was later Anglicized to "General Winter" by the English publication, *Punch*. [*The Oxford Dictionary of Quotations*, 543.17.]

[CHAPTER 13]
COTTONWOOD and CLEARWATER

While White Bird, Tool'hool'hool'zote and Ollokot maintained rearguard positions, Joseph urged the large group of non-combatants forward. Protected by the forests and warriors patrolling the flanks, they plodded on toward the Clearwater River.

The Clearwater River and Cottonwood Creek provided the stages for the final four encounters between the Nez Perce warriors and the army in Idaho. Three encounters came to be known as The Cottonwood Skirmishes, while the fourth and final was the Battle of the Clearwater River. Though considered minor, the skirmishes were all definite victories for the Nez Perce warriors. However, the major fight, which lasted two days, ended in a surprising manner. The warriors had the army pinned down and seemed in a position to win when suddenly, for reasons that remained undisclosed for fifty years, they abandoned the fight. In all likelihood Howard would have suffered yet another devastating defeat, but the warriors' surprising departure enabled him to claim a victory. As it was, Howard's casualty list stood at forty. Thirteen fatalities occurred during the fighting (two of the seventeen wounded died within a few hours). Nez Perce casualties were ten, including four dead.

Just as General Howard was preparing to take his troops across the Salmon River in pursuit of Joseph, he received a report that Chief Looking Glass had joined the rebels. Realizing the need to neutralize Looking Glass as an added threat, he called in Captain Steven G. Whipple (1840–1895)[1] of the 1st Cavalry and gave him explicit instructions. Whipple was to take two mounted units from the cavalry, obtain two Gatling guns[2] and their operators from Mount Idaho, proceed at once to Looking Glass' camp, detain him and his warriors, take them directly to Mount Idaho and place them in detention under the protection of the militia commander. Howard envisioned a simple assignment. He might not have known of Whipple's penchant for getting things wrong.

Captain Whipple's Folly

Captain Steven G. Whipple had never been short of enthusiasm. This and hope for a long desired promotion to major were the forces that drove Whipple onward. He had many times been overlooked by the promotion board, despite the fact he had served the full duration of the Civil War in command of a militia unit. Perhaps a succession of promotion board members had been unimpressed by his spending the entire war in the mountains of California guarding against Indian restlessness that never materialized. No matter, for at war's end he remained in the army ever hopeful. Action, however, continued to elude him, for he had been assigned to a fort in Arizona Territory where the only activity had been an occasional patrol or a regimental inspection by some visiting general. He served briefly as an Indian agent, hardly a position where promotion could be earned. He had been happy when orders were received transferring him to the District of Columbia for assignment to the 1st

Cavalry Regiment. There had been no action there either, but now, with the campaign against the Nez Perce rebels getting underway, he saw his fortunes might perhaps increase. On June 29, when he was selected by Howard and presented with the task of arresting Looking Glass he was very pleased.

Following his conversation with Howard, Whipple assured the general he would leave Mount Idaho in plenty of time to arrive at Looking Glass' camp by dawn on July 1. He thought it would be an easy matter to quietly enter the camp at dawn and take Looking Glass prisoner; he also assumed that with their chief in custody the warriors would then surrender without incident.

Whipple selected two units (four officers and sixty-four men of the 1st Cavalry's E and I Companies) and then went to Mount Idaho to collect the Gatling guns. He arrived there in the early morning of June 30, but some trouble in procuring the Gatling guns delayed his departure so it was not until late afternoon when he finally got underway. Leaving with him was a company of twenty-five civilians from a local militia under their leader, Darius B. Randall.

There was still plenty of time to cover the twenty-five miles to the Indians' camp but Whipple, never a great navigator, took a wrong trail which caused a loss of three hours. He had not foreseen the possibility of troubles that might be encountered on the trail in the dark, and he had also underestimated the time needed to reach the camp. The time he lost by taking the wrong trail, plus delays encountered when the horses had trouble making headway pulling the heavy Gatling guns on the rutted trails, ruined his plan to arrive at the village before dawn. Whipple missed his estimated dawn arrival at Looking Glass' camp by nearly three hours.

With no surprise now possible, Whipple stopped his men on the crest of a hill some 450 yards east of Clear Creek. His troops dismounted and spread out, making their presence known while the horses were led to a flat plain just behind the hill. From there everything went wrong.

Whipple's report to Howard, as quoted by the general in a later book, states:

> "An opportunity was given to Looking Glass to surrender, which he at first promised to accept, but shortly afterwards defiantly refused, and the result was that several Indians were killed, the camp, with a large amount of supplies was destroyed, and seven hundred and twenty-five ponies captured and driven to Mount Idaho."[3]

Whipple's report was almost entirely fictitious, written no doubt to cover as many of his mistakes as possible. In the book Howard published in 1878 under the title *Nez Perce Joseph,* the report was quoted in part but embellished, possibly for the same reason. In later years, Whipple's version (and therefore Howard's) was contradicted by Peopeo Tholekt, an Asotin chief and a hero of the battles at Big Hole, Camus Meadows and Canyon Creek. Others who were in the camp that day substantiated his account.

When the soldiers arrived, according to the chief, Looking Glass was in his tent. As it was Sunday[4], many of the villagers, including most of the warriors, had gone to Weippe to attend the Dreamers' religious rites. Looking Glass was not a Dreamer so he was in camp. When Whipple "halloed" the camp and called for the chief to meet with him at the edge of the creek, Looking Glass was having his breakfast, so he designated Peopeo Tholekt to meet the officer and see what it was he wanted. He got his horse and rode across the creek to where a group of civilians [Randall's volunteers] were assembled. Whipple and his four officers were standing a little to the side. Peopeo Tholekt noted the civilians appeared to have been drinking and this alarmed him. He was met by J.A. Miller, an interpreter from Mount Idaho. Miller greeted him warmly speaking to him in Nez Perce. He said Captain Whipple wished to speak with Looking Glass. The chief told Miller that Looking Glass was eating his breakfast and did not wish to be disturbed. Miller spoke with Whipple who replied that he must speak with Looking Glass. Peopeo Tholekt was told to return to Looking Glass and tell him he must come to meet with Whipple. No one, the captain assured him, would be hurt.

Looking Glass returned his reply in the persons of Peopeo Tholekt and an elder, Kawan [Old][5] Kalowet who spoke better English than his companion. To signify peaceful intentions Looking Glass had a white cloth raised above his tepee.

Whipple ignored Looking Glass' reply via the two emissaries and, insisting on entering the camp, he and two officers rode across the creek with the two Indians. They went directly to Looking Glass' tepee where Whipple called out that he wished to speak with Looking Glass. Before Looking Glass could come out of the tepee, however, a shot rang out from across the creek. An old man, Temme Ilppilp [Red Heart], fell with a bullet in his thigh. At this the officers wheeled their horses and fled across the creek. A few seconds later a hail of bullets from across the creek rained down into the tepees. Indians ran to escape as the shooting intensified. Tahkoopen [Shot leg] was hit. With help from two others he made good his escape, as did Red Heart.

Shortly after the second volley the soldiers began a charge across the creek, shooting as they ran. Looking Glass and his people escaped into the woods, with a few warriors covering their flight. Resistance, however, was futile so the warriors also fell back. Among them was Peopeo Tholekt who received the first of the several injuries he was to suffer during the upcoming long weeks on the trail. By the time all the soldiers had reached the camp it was deserted. They began razing the camp and rounding up the horses and cattle.

When the soldiers finally left, the warriors returned to find a scene of indiscriminate destruction. Tepees set on fire still smoldered. Battered utensils, torn apart smoke racks, and kettles and pots holed by bayonet thrusts were scattered everywhere. The gardens were trampled, the vegetables ready for harvest destroyed. Nearly all the horses were gone. Every head of cattle had been taken away. Two women and one baby were dead, as was a teenage boy named Nennin Chekoostin [Black Raven]. The women were never identified and the baby, who had been drowned with its mother who had tried to escape by swimming the river, was never found.[6]

Looking Glass and his people set out to locate Joseph whom they knew would be at Cottonwood. However, they did not encounter Joseph's group until after the Cottonwood and Clearwater actions had ended. They were with them during the Weippe talks.[7] Whipple's unprovoked and treacherous attack on Looking Glass and his peaceful villagers had forced the Asotins into the war.

In all likelihood the first shots and the subsequent volleys were instigated by Whipple's civilian volunteers. Still, Whipple must be held responsible because a commander is in charge of his men and therefore accountable for their discipline—or lack of it—and Captain Whipple was not known for his ability to keep rogues in check.

Seeing there was no chance now of arresting Looking Glass, Whipple assembled his command and returned to Mount Idaho, no doubt composing the story he would tell Howard. On his arrival he dismissed Darius Randall and his volunteers.

Whipple did not have to face Howard upon his return, as Howard had already departed in his disastrous mission to overtake Joseph. He managed to get by with a message. He did not, however, emerge totally unscathed for his rash stupidity. Howard did not push the issue further ,but his displeasure can be seen in the message he dispatched to Whipple.

> *Your report of 2 July is just rec'd. I am glad you came upon the Indians but am sorry you did not succeed in capturing that band, for I counted much on it. I said to you verbally: "Go to the forks of the Clearwater, resting only a couple of hours at Grangeville, and capture them before they can move across the river." By the delay till night you allowed them to get the usual warning of your approach, and therefore they escaped. Perhaps I expected too much of your tired horses.[8]* (sic)

Howard then ordered him to take his command plus the two Gatling guns to Norton's Ranch and wait there for Captain Perry who would bring him supplies. He was to stay there and attempt to head off the Indians should they come his way. Howard's displeasure with Whipple obviously continued as his order also added:

> Leave no stone unturned to ascertain for me where the Indians are heading, and report to me as often as you can. I expect of the cavalry tremendous vigor and activity even if it should kill a few horses.[9] (sic)

THE COTTONWOOD SKIRMISHES
(JULY 3–11)

The Rains Encounter
On July 3, a war party—led by two able chiefs, Pahkatos Owyeen [Five Wounds] (their recognized battle chief), and Wahchumyus [Rainbow]—on its way to Cottonwood to rendezvous with Joseph approached the farm owned by settler Benjamin B. Norton. Situated not far from the clearing known as The Cottonwood, the farm—abandoned by Norton at the outbreak of the revolt—was now occupied by Captain Whipple and his troop, newly arrived following their debacle at Looking Glass' camp. Intending to use it as base of operations he had renamed it "Fort Norton." As the war party approached, Seeyakoon Ilppilp [Red Scout],[10] trailing as rearguard, saw two young white men watching from a nearby hill.[11] Quietly making a wide circle he moved in behind the two. Employing arrows, he killed one, later identified as Charles Blewett, but the other, William Foster, escaped into the woods. Red Scout did not pursue Foster but returned to his companions, told Wahchumyus of his encounter and the party continued on its way.[12]

It took Foster some time to get to Fort Norton[13] and as a result of his frantic ride he was almost as winded as his near-blown horse.

He panted out his story but his narrative apparently caused Whipple little concern. Foster could not confirm if Blewett was dead or had escaped. Neither was he able to give an accurate estimate of the number of Indians he had seen. Whipple felt the sixteen-year-old Foster, inexperienced as a scout, was exaggerating the situation so he decided a small detachment would be sufficient to deal with the Indians. If they were no longer in the vicinity the party would either find Blewett or recover his body. Whipple allowed Foster a short rest, then gave him a fresh mount and instructed him to lead a detachment to the area of the sighting.

The detachment he selected to accompany Foster consisted of Sergeant Charles Lampman and nine privates to be led by Second Lieutenant Sevier M. Rains. Once again, however, Whipple blundered—a habit he seemingly could not overcome. By paying too little attention to Foster's concerns, by believing the boy had seen a very small group of Indians, and by thinking eleven soldiers a sufficient number to deal with them, his continuing errors in judgment sealed the fate of all twelve men. This blunder, however, probably saved the rest of his company from disaster.

Between the time of Foster's frantic ride to escape Red Scout and his entry into Whipple's presence, Rainbow and Five Wounds had already discovered the camp on Norton's farm. Here was an opportunity that could not be overlooked, for they quickly determined the soldiers were unaware of the war party. The chiefs were also pleased to note the soldiers seemed unconcerned for their own safety. Concealed by the forest, the two chiefs quietly watched the soldiers digging foxholes and defensive trenches. As they labored they conversed loudly with one another, calling from one trench to the others. Most of their conversations included bragging of their cowardly attack on Looking Glass' camp.

Up to that point neither chief was aware of the attack against

Looking Glass, but they could hear the coarse vocalizing and that told them some of the story. This, the first news of the attack to reach Nez Perce ears, was received with anger. The warriors discussed amongst themselves quickly launching an attack.

High ground had given Whipple such a feeling of safety he had not posted even a solitary sentry. Thus, no challenge had been given when Foster rode in on his panting horse, and the few soldiers who looked up showed no interest. On the other hand, Red Scout, watching from the woods, recognizing both horse and rider, informed Rainbow this was the man who had escaped him earlier.

While Whipple basked in the supposed security of Fort Norton and the Nez Perce chiefs discussed a plan of attack, the warriors quietly prepared themselves for the expected battle.[14] When preparations and discussions ended they were informed the attack would be a sudden "hit and run" tactic that had been proving its worth since being first employed at White Bird Canyon and later by various war parties. There would be a charge by three groups, all mounted, sweeping in staggered attacks across the right and left flanks while the third would ride directly through the center.

Five Wounds and his men would attack the right. Rainbow's force would strike the left. The third group, led by Two Moons, would charge through the center. This tactic they felt would sever the camp, separate the soldiers and cause the greatest possible degree of confusion. The attack was to be swift—in and out with no time wasted—and would end before the soldiers had a chance to react. Success depended on initial surprise and swiftness of execution. The warriors mounted. Concealed by heavy stands of timber they gathered near the forest's edge.

Suddenly Rainbow spotted a small group of riders leave the encampment. He raised his hand stopping the advance in order to determine if the riders had been sent out because his force had been seen, or if they were a routine scouting party. When the group turned in an easterly direction, Rainbow suspended his impending attack and motioned Two Moons and his warriors to ride in pursuit. The others melted back into the protective forest to await their return.

Making full use of the trees, Two Moons and his group rode

towards the riders on an intersecting angle. Not until the Indians broke from the woods at full gallop did the soldiers see them. They wheeled to escape the onrush, but it was too late. Unable to retreat, they rode hard towards cover offered by an outcropping of rocks some 300 yards distant. Quickly overtaken,[15] two, perhaps three, of the party were struck down in the first volley of shots from the Indians' rifles. Firing as they rode, the soldiers managed to reach the rocks where they sought out positions of defense.[16]

The soldiers fought valiantly, but expert marksmanship by the Nez Perces quickly settled the issue. In less than ten minutes the entire patrol was wiped out. None of the war party had been hurt.[17] Amidst the acrid smoke of black powder the warriors rode in to count coup.[18]

The condition of the soldiers' bodies when found three days later (by Perry and H Company) showed all had fought to the utmost of their individual courage. This certainty had also been recognized by the Nez Perce fighters for they showed utmost respect to the fallen. When the shooting stopped and the warriors moved among the fallen they displayed respect by shunning the usual treatment rendered a fallen foe. The warriors removed a few uniform items. They took the rifles, pistols and ammunition but left untouched all personal effects. Rains' West Point class ring, which would normally be considered a prize, remained on his finger. No money, watches or personal articles were taken.[19] In fact, unusual compassion was shown, as McWhorter's interviews with surviving warriors revealed. One of the men was found barely alive from a multitude of wounds including a bullet hole in his forehead. The warriors were undecided what to do with him and spent several minutes in debate. Some wanted to take him to Joseph's camp for treatment by a tewats [medicine man]. Because there was no doubt the unfortunate fellow had a very short time to live, a vote was taken. He was humanely dispatched.[20]

As the warriors were preparing to depart, two returning scouts appeared with word that no other soldiers beyond those encamped at Norton's farm were in the immediate vicinity. Two Moons and his warriors returned to Rainbow and Five Wounds to report the details of the skirmish.

The sounds of battle, however, had been heard in Whipple's encampment, putting the soldiers on high alert status. Five Wounds and Rainbow, realizing their target was now fully cognizant that Indians were in the vicinity, called off the planned attack. They withdrew to continue on their way to the pre-arranged meeting with Joseph. Before nightfall they arrived at the campsite by the Clearwater River. There they awaited the arrival of Joseph's group, expected to arrive later that evening.

The army's official report, and all civilian accounts, of the battle referred to the defeat as The Rains Massacre. To term it a massacre was, and remains, incorrect. The entire fight, though it lasted perhaps eight minutes, was equal combat between two well-armed groups. The two sides were not precisely equal in number, as Two Moons' warriors numbered fourteen while Rains and his soldiers numbered twelve including Foster; but it was fought by the warriors in the open while the defenders had some, albeit tenuous, defense behind the rocks.

The Nez Perce called The Cottonwood (as it was known by Whites) by the name Cupcup. The name derived from an ancient, hoary cottonwood tree that for untold decades had stood in lonely solitude.[21] Cupcup had once been a rest site on a stagecoach route but was now only an ideal camping ground. When the stage owners diverted the route several years before, they left the buildings intact. Cupcup then became useful to white trappers as well as Nez Perce buffalo hunters going to and returning from Montana. Its several wells furnished water, cold and clear. Though in disrepair, the remains of barns and buildings offered dry shelter for horses. Stout railings of large corrals provided daytime security for horses and mules. Large stands of deciduous trees provided firewood. It was the perfect resting place for hungry, tired, travel-weary people. Those in Joseph's group were all of that.

Dusk was approaching when Joseph arrived with his group. Tepees were erected and supper was prepared. As darkness claimed the land, the tired migrants settled in for a night of rest under the watchful eyes of Rainbow's and Five Wounds' fighters. Joseph, still under the assumption that Howard was many days behind, decided the stay could be extended a few restful days. His was a supposition which would too soon prove incorrect.

During the days between his return to White Bird Creek on July 7 and his departure for the Clearwater on July 9, General Howard reviewed the cost of his fruitless search for Joseph. It had started on July 1 with an entire day plus the better part of a second attempting to cross the Salmon River. He then squandered five days wandering trails that inevitably led nowhere. Finally, when informed Joseph had crossed back to the opposite bank, it took two more attempts before succeeding in re-crossing the river. To the weary general the battle against unseasonable storms that included heavy winds, snow on the high passes and sleet and rain was beginning to seem unwinnable. The entire ordeal had been a nightmare for men and animals.[22]

A good example of the dangers Howard's force had encountered is found in a letter written in early July, 1877 by 2nd Lieutenant Harold L. Bailey. Having returned safely to the camp near White Bird Creek, Bailey noted,

> "Have just crossed the swift and dangerous Salmon River in a skiff with four other men and four oarsmen. The stream at this point is about 200 yards wide, with plunging current. By a great deal of labor and loss of time [this morning] a large rope had been stretched across [the river]

and a number of horses and mules were forced to swim the river...Some of them [swept off their feet by the current] were turned over and over and others got carried away down the stream, but I think all got over."[23]

Retracing his steps to his original camp, he spent many days awaiting the arrival of more replacements for his lost supplies and equipment from Boise. Meanwhile, the Nez Perce chiefs, instead of continuing the trek, remained at Cottonwood feeling safe in their belief that Howard would not become a threat again for at least two weeks. Perhaps Howard's force was not a threat at the moment, but three other forces were already in the area. The Nez Perce scouts, however, were watching their every move and several war parties were positioning in secluded places, awaiting the time when attacks could be effectively made.

Despite the setbacks, Howard regained some confidence when scouts began informing him on a daily basis that Joseph was seemingly in no hurry to vacate Cottonwood. When the supply wagons bearing replacement goods finally arrived, the general departed for Cottonwood on July 9. He could now set a direct course, as this time there were no rivers to cross or high passes to climb. He made steady progress, but not at great speed. The weather gods still conspired against him to such an extent—not to mention bad direction from "Ad" Chapman whose advice more than once led him down impassable trails—the main force found progress so difficult only a few miles were covered day-by-day.[24] Only small patrols were able to move in a timely manner.

Howard's full troop of now almost 500 foot soldiers, gunners and mounted soldiers of the 21st Infantry Regiment, 4th Artillery Regiment and 1st Cavalry Regiment respectively, doggedly slogged forward dragging heavy Gatling guns and Howitzer cannons. The columns of horses, mules, wagons and blue shirts extended beyond two miles at a slow pace in the attempt to gain headway through the tangled brush that overgrew little used trails. At one point a scout rode in to report having sighted what he believed were Joseph's encamped Indians. The scout was wrong. He had spotted a large war party led by Ollokot who were stalking a company of the Lewiston volunteers.

On July 9, an eighty-man patrol of the Lewiston volunteers, commanded by Captain Edward McConville,[a] came into sighting distance of Joseph's camp. McConville, unaware he was being watched, exercised extreme prudence and no further approach was made. Instead he moved to high ground on Doty Ridge, which the Nez Perces called Possossona [Water Passing][25] (and the army, for good reason, later renamed Misery Hill). McConville made camp there, had the horses hidden in nearby woods, and sent a messenger, John McPherson, scurrying away to locate Howard. McPherson was to give the general the volunteers' position and inform Howard that McConville would wait there for the general's arrival with reinforcements. Shortly after, he sent two more riders, George Riggins and Peter Malin, to Mount Idaho in case Howard might still be there. He and his troopers settled down to await the general and the expected reinforcements.

McPherson finally located Howard a day after the general had begun his march toward Cottonwood. Howard, however, felt McConville should be able to hold his ground without reinforcements. Besides, he had none to spare as Captain Perry had already proceeded toward Cottonwood with H Company to meet with Whipple. Then, in cautious afterthought, he notified Whipple (who, despite his fiasco of July 1, had apparently gained his general's absolution) to stay where he was, position his Gatling guns strategically, then meet and bolster Perry's force which was proceeding with cautious haste. In an extremely confusing patrol report to Colonel McDowell, his immediate superior in Portland, Perry wrote he had been very pleased when he met Whipple.

---

a   *General Howard and others indicate McConville was considered the equivalent of captain, whereas his militiamen who wrote accounts of Misery Hill refer to him as colonel. It is likely "colonel" was the honorary term common to that era. [Author]*

> "*Indians around us all day and very demonstrative. Last evening Lieutenant Rains, ten soldiers, and two citizen scouts were killed, and had not Whipple, with whole command, come to our rescue, my little party would have all been undoubtedly taken in.*"(sic)[26]

On July 4, Perry's H Company, a unit of some thirty soldiers, found the bodies of the Rains Patrol. After tending to quick burials and dispatching a messenger to Howard, they moved on for their meeting with Whipple. Within a few hours of their merger both companies were within observation distance of Cottonwood and Joseph's main camp. Perry's men dug in at a point to the rear of Whipple's company, which was dug in about halfway between Perry and the camp. There, for once following orders to the letter, Whipple had his infantrymen remain concealed while he positioned his artillery and Gatling guns on higher ground some distance away. Perry had brought sufficient blankets to assure warmth. They shared these with Whipple's men. The extra blankets were welcomed gifts. "Stay warm," Whipple told his men as he distributed the blankets, "and above all remain silent. No pipes, no drinking, no fires."

Joseph was fully aware of the various patrols that were approaching, for scouts had watched, waited while Whipple dug in, and took notice of the positions before sending word to Joseph. It was not long before several war parties took up positions at strategic points around the perimeters of the encampments. White Bird then began a policy of harassment.

For the remainder of their stay in the area Perry's and Whipple's companies were subjected to sporadic fire from groups of warriors firing into the entrenchments. When on the one occasion they came too close, the Gatling guns were brought into action, but the distance was too great for accuracy. The warriors noted the guns' range, allowing them to determine the limits of their advance.

Although there were no casualties on either side the first day, many soldiers prudently abandoned their foxholes for the safety afforded by ones further back. The morning of July 4 Perry and Whipple were introduced to a new tactic that caught officers and men completely by surprise. A large herd of horses, apparently riderless, emerged from the trees at full gallop as if in stampede. The herd raced across the left flank until it reached the midway point then, as if by magic, fully armed riders appeared on the horses' backs as the herd wheeled to attack an unprotected segment of the flank. Had it not been for alert Gatling gun operators, there would have been without doubt a number of casualties. The Gatling guns opened fire and, although the riders were not within range, the gunners succeeded in driving them away. Though it was not tried again, this ruse kept the soldiers on a thin edge of misgiving and nervousness. Occasional horses that wandered alone from the woods caused flurries of excitement.

The troopers' apprehension in no way decreased when unmounted warriors added to the uncertainty about what might happen next. Acting singly and in pairs, warriors employing brush and small bushes as camouflage were able to advance a yard or so at a time by crawling close to the ground. In this way they come within rifle range. Suddenly puffs of black powder would erupt from a tree or bush. This artifice, which worked well in the half-light of dawn, enabled undetected movement as the warriors moved stealthily from place to place. Several soldiers later reported having seen entire bushes and even trees moving, but their claims were dismissed as overactive imagination. The result of the deceptive ruses gave the impression of the Nez Perce being many in number. Both Perry and Whipple, fully convinced they were outnumbered by a huge margin, chose to remain dug in and make no attempt to advance or launch an attack. Their belief eventually worked its way into the mind of General Howard, as is evident in a number of his reports for July. In them he makes outlandish claims of up to 300 warriors or more from other tribes arriving to help Joseph.

The Brief War of the Brave Seventeen

Shortly after dawn on the morning of July 5 a volunteer group of seventeen citizens from Mount Idaho approached the army units. Under command of Darius B. Randall (he of the Looking Glass attack) they had departed Mount Idaho in the very early hours with the intention of assisting the soldiers.[27] The riders were less than a mile from Perry's entrenchment when they began crossing an area of open ground. They were spotted by one of Rainbow's war parties, a group of twelve to fifteen warriors,[28] who swept down from the rear quickly breaking the group's formation. Though the volunteers fought valiantly (earning for themselves the soubriquet The Brave Seventeen) the attack was so rapid the patrol was doomed. In fact, the fight was so short that Perry's entrenched soldiers, pinned down by hidden sharpshooters, were unable to help. They could do nothing but watch helplessly during the fifteen seconds it took for the seventeen volunteers to be reduced to twelve. Randall[29] and Benjamin Evans were killed in the first volley of shots. D.H. Howser was so seriously wounded he died later.[30] Charlie Johnson and Alonzo Leland, also fell, seriously injured, in the first volley. Both survived to return safely to Mount Idaho, but they were hospitalized for many days. Mauled, in total disarray but waging a fighting retreat, the surviving twelve with their dead and wounded escaped and returned to Mount Idaho. None ever ventured forth again.[31]

Their escape owed more to circumstance than heroics. All seventeen would surely have perished had Chief Rainbow not called off the pursuit when Weesculatat, also known as Mimpow Owyeen [Wounded Mouth] his battle name,[32] fell. He died that evening. A very able warrior, he was struck by several bullets during the initial charge but had continued to pursue and shoot as he went. Not until he fell from his horse was the chase abandoned.[33] This was quite routine in Indian warfare and, while it allowed the volunteers to escape, it also assured there would be no more Nez Perce casualties in that particular skirmish. In this, the Nez Perce lost a warrior of vast experience and exemplary leadership.

His son, Elaskolatat [Animal Entering a Hole], who was serving as a scout for General Howard under his Christian name Joe Albert, replaced him. A few days later he heard his father was dead. During the first day of the Battle of the Clearwater he suddenly dashed across to the Indian side. He drew fire as he ran from both sides—the soldiers firing because he was deserting and the Indians because he in an army uniform. He was later wounded in that battle, but not seriously enough to keep him inactive. He was wounded again at Canyon Creek, a thigh wound that did not heal in time to allow him to participate in White Bird's escape from the Bear's Paw. He stayed with Joseph in exile, eventually returning to Idaho where he died in 1926.

Another warrior, Wareyouh Teepmanin, was wounded when his horse was shot out from under him. He survived to fight again, but in several narratives concerning this particular skirmish he has often been mistaken for Mimpow Owyeen. A third warrior had also been slightly wounded but he remains unidentified to this day.

Late during the same day, with the volunteers having returned to Mount Idaho and the war parties seemingly departed, Perry dispatched a patrol that cautiously advanced closer to the main encampment. The officer in charge intended to have his men dig in and commence firing into the camp, but the patrol was stopped by a Nez Perce rearguard that had been watching the advancing patrol. When the warriors began sporadic salvoes, the patrol quickly retreated. Thereafter Perry and Whipple, content to wait for Howard, confined their soldiers to the foxholes and barriers.

Meanwhile, Howard was approaching the Clearwater. Having been hampered not only by his own delays but by his guide, Ad Chapman, his troops were also beset by groups of Piqunin warriors under the command of Chief Tool'hool'hool'zote. Although only twenty-two in number, these men—sharpshooters all—had positioned themselves at various points along the length of the drawn-out force. Working as teams, their sudden attacks from various sectors further delayed the advance.

Misery Hill (July 9–11)
Meanwhile, on Possossona,[34] which he later named Misery Hill, Captain Edward McConville [1849–1899][35] was experiencing the distinct feeling of having been abandoned. His intention had been to pin Joseph down until Howard's force could be brought up. Fully expecting the general would hasten to help, McConville had dispatched a messenger to find Howard and direct him to his position. When two days passed with no word from the general, he came

to realize nothing of the sort was about to happen anytime soon. In fact, he had good reason to worry. He was now surrounded by Ollokot's fighters and pinned down by their sporadic gunfire. His casualties had been slight during the first day when there had been a few minor injuries; but during the second day his men began to fare badly with two killed and another three wounded. The losses, plus unnerving harassment by unseen warriors, were proving too much for McConville. He decided he could not wait any longer for Howard.

McConville, although he had some experience in war, was never rated highly as an Indian campaigner. His main weakness was a habit of deploying insufficient scouts. On this latest foray his command would probably have blundered into total annihilation had he not received a timely warning. By good fortune, an independent scout named Elias Darr happened to encounter the troop. When Darr rode onto the scene the captain and his militia were riding blindly and directly toward Ollokot and his fighters. Again, it had not occurred to McConville to send riders far ahead for precautionary reconnaissance. As it was, McConville and his troopers were spared a fatal ambush, but exchanged it for a great and humbling embarrassment. Not only did they fail to subdue their foes, they lost their horses to them.[36] McConville, up to the middle of the second day, was actually convinced he held the upper hand and had the Nez Perces pinned down. This despite the fact his troops were being denied sleep, the result of an all-night barrage laid on by Ollokot's men on July 10, commencing about 1:00 AM and continuing until dawn. In his self-assured belief that he was winning, he laid plans for a final assault the next morning.

In the half-light of dawn on July 11 he ordered an all-out barrage of rifle fire be laid into the enemy camp. McConville then ceased the firing and waited for return fire in order to use muzzle flashes and smoke clouds to determine where he would concentrate his assault. To his surprise there was no return fire—and while he was contemplating this unexpected turn he was informed that his best forty-eight horses had disappeared during the night.

McConville, disgruntled but not wishing to think the unthinkable, dispatched scouts to track the horses while his remaining troops cautiously moved forward to the woods. When they reached the trees they realized there was no need for caution; Ollokot and his warriors had silently departed during the night. They had paused only long enough to silently make off with McConville's horses.

To make matters even less palatable for the hapless volunteers, besides the three killed and the four wounded (one died later from his wounds), they had nothing to claim in the way of courage. There was not a single shred of evidence indicating Nez Perce casualties. McConville never learned one Indian, Paktilek, had in fact been wounded—but not by gunfire. That warrior lost the forefinger of his right hand when the hand was crushed between rough bark of a tree and a skittish horse he was stealing.[37]

So ended the battle at Possossona, which in army records was later, quite aptly, designated as Misery Hill. Once again the army had been dealt a blow to its already diminished prestige and besmirched pride. With nothing left to do, McConville returned to Howard, reported his losses, manfully accepted, and fended off as best he could, the criticism that followed. To add to the agony of defeat, he and his soldiers had been forced to walk the entire distance to Howard's placement. The few horses the warriors had left were good for nothing more than transporting supplies and equipment.

As events transpired, however, McConnell fought again at a later date. And he had not failed entirely. By holding firm for two days he had delayed Ollokot's war party long enough to assure their arrival at Joseph's camp came too late to become fully engaged in the upcoming Battle of the Clearwater.

THE BATTLE OF THE CLEARWATER
(JULY 11-12)

The chiefs still thought they held the advantage and saw no need to leave Cottonwood. Camp life continued on a routine basis; but this time Joseph's optimism was badly misplaced. Howard and his 500 men, despite their setbacks and misfortunes, were actually a scant few hours' march from the Nez Perce camp. Joseph and his entire group were ripe for the taking—and he had no idea that Howard was so close.

This was the battle that began and ended in confusion and uncertainty. Unlike the unexpected attack at White Bird Canyon, the Nez Perce chiefs knew Howard would eventually arrive at Cottonwood and would attack. Regardless, had it not been for two unforeseen factors, the ending could have equaled, perhaps eclipsed, their victory at White Bird Canyon. The two factors that denied them victory at the Clearwater were the concepts held by a majority of warriors of how to wage war, and the chiefs' lack of a cohesive strategy. The factors combined to deny Joseph and White Bird a tipping of the scales in which the entire uprising might have ended in a settlement mutually agreeable to both sides.

While post-war analysis has generally determined this battle's outcome as little more than an impasse, Washington, at least for awhile, declared it a great victory. This short-lived belief came about as a result of Howard's reports to various superiors in which he fudged figures and misrepresented the situation within the Indian camp. Examples of his incorrect assumptions of Joseph's intentions permeate his ill-advised reports, one of which can be seen in the dispatch he sent to General Sully at Lewiston. Sully, in turn, forwarded it to headquarters in San Francisco. Wrote Howard,

> "If Joseph will remain one day longer burning houses and bragging of his victories, I will be able to strike him a blow..."[38]

In an effort to gain credit for his "victory," the general's reports also claimed his actions had resulted in many Nez Perce casualties, while downplaying his failure to advance following the battle. The delay, he stated, had as its cause the presence of reinforcing Indians, warriors from other tribes who were joining the Nez Perce fighters.[39] These reports and other narratives he wrote have been largely discredited by evidence that eventually surfaced. Evidence proved the major casualties had all been on the army's side of the line, and not a solitary Native had arrived from any tribe to reinforce the Nez Perce warriors. The reinforcements reported by Howard were, in fact, a couple of Asotin warriors newly arrived from Looking Glass' band,[40] two returning war parties headed by Ollokot and Rainbow, and Tool'hool'hool'zote's sharpshooters who had been harassing the army ranks along the trail to Clearwater.

In fact, the great legion of Indians from other tribes reported by Howard were exactly *two individuals, neither of warrior status or even capable of fighting*. One was an elderly Yakima named Owhi who, for unknown reasons, joined the group after it had entered Montana. How long he stayed with them is likewise unknown. The other was an ex-slave from some unknown tribe who had been granted sanctuary years before the rebellion. Because he had no feet and only one hand he had been renamed Sees'koomke [No Feet]. Sees'koomke, though a superlative rider, was totally incapable of fighting[41] and was used mainly as a messenger between White Bird and the various war parties.

Howard's imagination again ran rampant when he wrote of 400 braves riding in to aid Joseph against Colonel Gibbon at the Big Hole. This later fantasy was further embellished by George Oliver Shields, a true master at avoiding facts where fiction was more saleable. Shields added another fifty.[42]

When Ollokot and Rainbow rejoined White Bird at the Clearwater they were still buoyed by their victories over McConville and their delaying tactics of the Perry/Whipple companies respectively. Although their arrival at the Clearwater was too late to participate in a great fight against Howard, they did manage to initiate a rearguard action. By then the need for retreat had became necessary, so they combined to protect Joseph and his non-combatants who were now plodding steadily eastward away from the Clearwater River.

The Battle of the Clearwater was never an all-out clash between forces. It was instead a one-sided contest between the army's poor shooting and Nez Perce sharpshooters. The battle lasted two days before ending abruptly and surprisingly. Lieutenant H.L. Bailey wrote of the poor marksmanship of his own troop, blaming it on lack of target practice.

> *"[the Indians] succeeded in getting within one hundred yards of us when we suffered our many casualties and narrow escapes. [And] they had repeating rifles, which our soldiers were not to have for some time because they would shoot all their ammunition away at the first alarm."*

Bailey also blamed the army's allowance of only three rounds per man per month for practice. That the soldiers were less than inept is described by Bailey.

> *"A number of us saw a poor old horse, probably wounded, standing for some hours out in my front, and I suppose several hundreds of bullets were fired at him without apparent effect. That was one of the lessons I had about our shooting..."*[43]

The gist of Bailey's comments was that the army authorities were guilty of criminal negligence for sending such raw recruits into an Indian war. Bailey contended the army was well aware of the Nez Perce warriors' ability to shoot. To Bailey (who would later be promoted to colonel) the White Bird disaster had taught them nothing of what to expect from their untrained riflemen.

Tool'hool'hool'zote and his sharpshooters continued to keep Howard's 500 soldiers at an impasse. It was probably Tool'hool'hool'zote's greatest measure of glory when he and his twenty-two sharpshooters kept Howard pinned down and unable to advance for two days. They were assisted from time to time by Rainbow and some of his warriors, and working as teams they moved quickly from location to location keeping a steady fire into army positions. Confused and demoralized, many soldiers reached the point where they came to believe they were facing many dozens, perhaps hundreds of warriors. It is undoubtedly this stratagem that convinced Howard other tribes had arrived to join Joseph.

On July 12, Tool'hool'hool'zote withdrew his weary marksmen. Three had been shot. Wayakat [Going Across] had been killed and Yoomtis Kunnin [Grizzly Bear Blanket] had been mortally wounded and would die later that night. He had, however, stayed after the withdrawal and delayed the soldiers sufficiently so he was also able to return to the village. The third, Howwallits [Mean Man], had been wounded and would fight again. Naturally, it was expected other warriors would take their places, but that did not happen. Wottolen and those few who remained enabled Joseph to safely evacuate the non-combatants and proceed with due haste towards Kamiah.[44]

Wottolen and most others were convinced that had "the cowards" stayed to fight, Howard's soldiers could have been soundly thrashed or at the very least severely mauled.[45] There is little doubt that had the Nez Perce chiefs been able to bring all their warriors to bear as a cohesive force Wottolen's conjecture would have come to pass. Lieutenant Bailey's later writings clearly indicate that he would have concurred with Wottolen's views.

Howard eventually realized shooting from the Indian lines had eased significantly so he began moving his troops forward. Wottolen and his handful of warriors, unable to hold out any longer, were forced to retreat. It was this complete withdrawal that enabled Howard to pronounce his advance a victory. His reports to Washington claiming heavy casualties amongst the Nez Perces were probably an afterthought. It was certainly untrue.

During the retreat, Joseph's group, with White Bird's force riding as rearguards, was surprised by a company of infantry regulars who had managed to approach unseen from a different direction. The soldiers, sensing advantage, attacked. One Nez Perce fell in the initial volley while two received minor wounds. Quickly recovering from the surprise, White Bird showed he had several hitherto-untried tricks in his armory. Feigning retreat, he and his riders withdrew into the forest. The infantrymen, certain they now had their enemy in disarray, if not routed, took up the pursuit. White Bird, commanding his fighters in masterly fashion, remained always ahead but in view of the onrushing soldiers. The soldiers, having been drawn into the woods, suddenly discovered the Indians had disappeared—totally. Confused, but still in good battle order, they stopped to consider their next move; and it was while they were in this less-than-ready formation that White Bird's warriors unleashed a burst of rapid fire. It was enough to convince the soldiers to retreat and await the arrival of Howard and his large force. White Bird and his fighters once again had won a skirmish. As the retreating soldiers scurried out of range and then out of sight, White Bird rode to rejoin Joseph.

That thirteen soldiers lay dead and twenty-seven wounded, of which two would die within hours, would have given little consolation to Joseph and his chiefs, had they known. What they all knew was they must continue to move and that more battles lay ahead. They must first, however, gain access to the Lolo Trail if escape was to be attained. They were again within the reservation and it was at this time Husis Kute and his Palu and the remainder of the Asotin warriors joined them. The entire band continued northward without delay, intending to stop only when they reached a campground along at the eastern edge of the Clearwater River called Kamiah. A quick conference could be held there to determine their next move.

They reached Kamiah on July 13. During this overnight rest the vacillation continued. The division was between White Bird who wanted to go to Canada without delay and those wishing to go to Montana. Tool'hool'hool'zote argued in favor of Montana, but conceded that if no valley suitable for settlement could be found, they could then turn northward to Canada. Looking Glass (who had not yet proposed meeting with the Crows) favored Montana. Some favored returning to Lapwai and taking their chances there.

Others preferring the idea of finding refuge in Montana also agreed to the merits of going to Canada, as all were aware Sitting Bull with many Sioux warriors plus their women and children had found refuge there. They were certain the Nez Perce refugees could resettle their lives there as well. As a further incentive, Canadian explorer and frontier scout Duncan McDonald, who was of Scottish-Nez Perce ancestry and a longtime friend of the non-Treaty Nez Perce bands, was also at Kamiah and offered to lead the bands directly to Canada. His offer was rejected.[46]

Joseph did not participate in this conference in any way. Kamiah was a warriors' meeting and he did not qualify as a warrior chief. "I have no voice," he had said, but his voice was undoubtedly heard through that of Ollokot.

Among the chiefs favoring Lapwai there was general agreement that hardship and punishment awaited them should they surrender. They agreed Howard might prove reasonable, but none doubted his superiors in Washington would be inclined to dismiss lightly the defeats that had been inflicted on their soldiers.

It was finally decided to proceed the next morning to Weippe. They would have to engage in running fights much of the way, but all hoped Howard, who had continued in pursuit, would become wary again and stop the chase as he had done before. A decision was made to put as much distance as possible between themselves and Howard. They would go as far as Weippe because there perhaps they could take a few days rest, discuss the matters at hand and make a final decision.

As Joseph and his allies prepared to depart Kamiah, they knew at Weippe the decision would be final. A change of mind would not be possible.

Nez Perce casualties in the two-day Battle of the Clearwater numbered ten. Four had been killed: Wayakat [Going Across], Yoomtis Kunnin [Grizzly Bear Blanket], Heinmot Ilppilp [Red Thunder] and Lelooskin [The Whittler]. Six had been seriously wounded: Howwallitis [Mean Man]; Pahkatos Owyeen [Five Wounds]; Heinmot Hihi [Yellow Wolf]; Elaskolatat [Animal Entering a Hole]; Old Yellow Wolf and Kipkip Owyeen [Wounded breast].

So why had the warriors suddenly quit the engagement when they were on the verge of winning? That perplexing question remained long unanswered until the mid-1930s when surviving chiefs and warriors began to discuss with historians the events of 1877. Their revelations were astonishing. From their statements emerged an assessment that victory was theirs for the taking but it had been denied them by the cowardice of a large number of young warriors.

In a 1935 interview with L.V. McWhorter, Wottolen [Hair combed over eyes], a warrior of great courage and regard, placed the blame for the failed outcome squarely on the young warriors who he contemptuously referred to as "the cowards."[47] These young warriors, not an insignificant number, decided they did not wish to fight that day. They stayed away from the firing lines by retiring to the sweat lodges in the main camp. Their reasoning was this: Howard was not attacking, which meant he and his army had obviously been whipped. Thus, there was no need for a continuation of the fight. According to Wottolen, "the cowards refused to return" to the battle area.[48]

There was more to it, of course, than cowardice, for other events also factored into the overall situation. Perhaps individual cowardice was secondary to the Nez Perce battle philosophy of "fight-if-you-wish," an overall lack of cohesive strategy, lack of collective discipline and refusal to obey the chiefs. All these factors interacted in producing an indifference bordering on malaise. Added was the attitude held by the young warriors of there being no need to fight *because the army was not attacking*. Those individuals were quite happy to sit in the sweat lodges and drink whiskey they had obtained from traders or looted from settlers' homes. As Wottolen [Hair combed over eyes] noted,

> "There were cowards who refused to fight. Teeweeyownah [Over the point] said to us, 'Get ready! Let the young men mount their horses! We will go mix with the soldiers! We will make a desperate fight!' He then made to turn

their horses loose. He told the young men 'You go too often to camp. You are here to fight!' Some got mad. They told Teeweeyownah, 'You have no right to turn our horses loose!' Teeweeyownah then said [to the young men], 'You cowards! I will die soon! You will see hardships in bondage. You will have a hard time. Your freedom will be gone. Your liberty will be robbed from you. You will be slaves!' The cowards then left the fighting."[49]

Though the Nez Perce chiefs were denied a victory because of those called cowards, General Howard's unjustified claims of victory saved his job, but did nothing to hasten the end of the war.[50] His claim was doubted by many, and he garnered no plaudits from any quarter of the public or the press. Neither did it impress his superiors in Washington, although a decision to relieve him of his command was cancelled.

[CHAPTER 13 ENDNOTES]

1   Steven Girard Whipple was born in Vermont in 1840 but had moved to California at an early age, as by 1858 he was publishing a newspaper, *The Northern Californian*, and later the *Humboldt Times*. During the Civil War he commanded a six-unit militia called the First Battalion of Mountaineers, a Humboldt County volunteer organization. After the war his militia was disbanded so he joined the 32nd U.S. Infantry and served in Arizona. He became a captain in 1867 and was transferred to the 1st Cavalry in 1870. He retired in 1884 and became active in California politics. He died at Eureka on October 21, 1895. [*Encyclopedia of Frontier Biography,* Vol. 3, 1547–48.]

2   The Gatling gun, one of the first successful rapid-firing machine guns, was the invention of Richard Jordan Gatling (1818–1903). A prolific inventor, he had

produced sewing machines and agricultural devices before turning to armaments. He invented his gun in 1862, just in time for its use during the American Civil War. The gun consisted of ten rotating barrels operated by a hand crank. They were heavy and cumbersome, requiring two draft horses to pull each one. [*Oxford Encyclopedia,* 1998 paperback ed., 557.]

3   Quote from Whipple's report to Howard. [Howard, *Nez Perce Joseph,* 148–9.]

4   The tribes, for the most part, had adopted white men's time. [Author.]

5   Kawan means old, but old is a difficult word to define. In Nimiputimt, when used as a first name it usually indicates some characteristic of the person involved, not age. Kawan Chus'lum, for instance, means "old bull" but that does not necessarily mean aged bull; old bulls are generally smart, sly, crafty and hard to corral. Young bulls are usually lacking in such qualities. [Author's files.]

6   From the narrative of Chief Peopeo Tholekt. [McWhorter, *Hear Me My Chiefs,* 264–70]

7   Looking Glass was reported by a First Cavalry private, John Lynch, who claimed he had seen him at the Clearwater with some of his warriors during the time of the final battle. Lynch is the only one who claimed to have seen him. No Nez Perce ever mentioned his participation in the actual battle. [This claim was found in the papers of L.V. McWhorter, *Hear Me My Chiefs,* 319, fn 37.]

8   Howard to Whipple, July 3, 1877. [1877 US Army Continental Commands, entry 897, box1, part 3.]

9   Ibid.

10   His name can also be translated as Red Spy, as in the

Nez Perce language the word seeyakoon denotes both "scout" and "spy." [www.nezpercetrail.net/]

11   The two scouts were William Foster and Charles Blewett, both inexperienced youths. They had been sent out by Captain Whipple to scout ahead of his troop following his foolish raid on Looking Glass' peaceful camp. Blewett was killed but Foster escaped and reported back to Whipple who then sent Rains and his patrol, guided by Foster, to rescue or retrieve Blewett's body. [*Yellow Wolf,* 80–83.]

12   Three weeks later Red Scout would further add to his reputation. While leading a small war party he and his men ambushed and defeated a unit of army troops on the Lolo Trail. [Author's files.]

13   The story of Foster's escape has been often related with numerous variations. [Ibid.]

14   Preparations for battle meant stripping to near nakedness, applying paint to the face and body while quietly intoning hymns of praise to the Great Spirit. The warriors believed this ritual granted them protection in battle. [Many sources of Indian customs, including the excellent study "Save the Last Bullet for Yourself."]

15   This skirmish has become known as Rain's Encounter at Cottonwood. [Report #132 of the Secretary of War, 1877. Washington, DC: Govt. Printing Office, 1877.]

16   It is possible the soldiers might have managed an escape had they not been distracted by a solitary warrior (Strong Eagle, who had gained fame in the Battle at White Bird Canyon) on a hill some distance to the east, firing volley after volley into the fleeing riders. Obviously fearing that this warrior was not alone, they sought refuge among the rocks. [*Yellow Wolf,* 71–74.]

17   See Howard, *Nez Perce Joseph,* 151.

18 For a dramatic eyewitness narration of the pursuit and destruction of Rain's patrol see: *Yellow Wolf,* 80–83.

19 While Nez Perce warriors never scalped the dead, they were known to loot the dead of personal belongings. In this case, owing to their respect for bravery, they removed only badly needed weapons and ammunition. The only personal item taken that particular day was a small spyglass that Red Scout took from Charles Blewett, likely because he had never before seen such an intriguing object. [Perry, David, *The Battle of White Bird Canyon*, as cited by Brady, Cyrus, *Northwestern Indian Fights and Fighters*, 114.]

20 Some had argued the soldier be allowed "to live if he wanted to..." meaning if his willpower overcame the spirit of death. Others, seeing he had no chance of survival at all, felt he should be spared further misery. The majority eventually overruled the others. This incident is narrated with compassion by Yellow Wolf, an eyewitness to the scene.[*Yellow Wolf,* 71–74.]

21 The Nez Perce word for a cottonwood tree is cupcup. Its plural is cupcup pin [pronounced peen]. [Author's files.]

22 See: Sgt. Michael McCarthy's Diary and The Journal of M. McCarthy for full details of this ill-fated march. [McCarthy Papers, Manuscript Division, Library of Congress, Washington, DC.]

23 Letter to his father written by Lt. H.L. Bailey dated July 1877, pertaining to a crossing of the Salmon River on June 29. [Papers of 2nd Lt. Harry L. Bailey, 21st Infantry. Washington Archives.]

24 Much of Howard's lack of progress was due to bad information received from A" Chapman who on several occasions led him down trails found to be blocked or otherwise impassible. Either Chapman's scouts were inept or he was relying on outdated information. One

291
[CHAPTER 13]

such misdirection resulted in two entire days being lost. [McWhorter, *Hear Me My Chiefs*, 296.]

25 Named for two small brooks running past the ridge on separate courses until converging into one that eventually meets with the Clearwater River. [Author's files.]

26 Perry's report to McDowell is confusing with his reference to "my small party." His company numbered a full complement. Nonetheless, this is the message recorded on page 30 of Senate Executive Document No.256, 56th Congress, 1st Session under its sub-title: "Claims of the Nez Perce Indians." [Washington, DC: Government Printing Office, 1900.]

27 After Randall had been dismissed by Whipple following the Looking Glass attack, he had returned to Mount Idaho and formed his own group of seventeen which struck out on its own. He was not authorized but felt he could get back into Whipple's good graces.

28 See: Narrative of Lak'pee'a'loot in *Hear Me My Chiefs*, 289–291.

29 It is likely Randall had been the target of several shooters as he was a well-known and greatly disliked usurper of fifty acres of Nez Perce land besides having led the volunteers in the attack on Looking Glass' camp on July 1. [Author's files.]

30 Known as the Volunteers' Fight at Cottonwood. Randall, Howser and Evans were later buried in the Mount Idaho cemetery. [Records, Vital Statistics Department, Mount Idaho.]

31 Many tall tales of the valor exhibited by all groups of volunteers, as told by some of the survivors, were published in newspapers. Several of these tales can be read in the files of the July 7, 1877 issue of the *Lewiston Teller* in which the paper credits the volunteers as having

"killed 25 to 30 of the Indians." That same report tells of individual volunteers firing in excess of sixty shots and others firing over forty rounds. It also credits Captain Randall as having continued firing up to five minutes of the battle's end even though he was mortally wounded. That tale disregards the fact that Randall died within seconds of the first volley. Not to be outdone, the *Lewiston Tribune* in its July 3, 1927 issue quoted a Major Frank Fenn (who was not in that fight) that 200 Indians had fought the 17 volunteers. Fenn's claims were quickly disputed by several who had been there. [*Lewiston Teller* and *Lewiston Tribune* files, Boise Public Library, Boise, Idaho.]

32 This is an excellent example of dual names among the Nez Perces. There was even multiplicity of names. Names could change following a singular battle or a deed of significance. This presents a problem for researchers and has resulted in errors of identification from time to time. [Author's files.]

33 Plains and Plateau Indians often called off an attack when the party's number was reduced by injury or death. Cessation depended upon the size of the party, but rarely exceeded five casualties. In this particular case one casualty was the limit. The Nez Perce chiefs knew they could not afford losses in numbers and were, therefore, very prudent in their open attacks.

34 The Nez Perce name is Possossona (Water Passing), named for a small creek that burbled to the surface nearby. Army records refer to Possossona as Camp Misery. The army entrenchment was actually on Doty Ridge, a hill overlooking the Clearwater River. [Author's files.]

35 McConville was later appointed Superintendent of the Lapwai School System. He grew to admire his former foes and worked to better their situation. When the

Spanish-American War broke out he took the 1st Idaho Volunteers to the Phillpines. He was killed in the Battle of Santa Ana on February, 1899. [*Encyclopedia of Frontier Biography*, 893–894.]

36   As it turned out, the horses taken from McConville had been from the herd Whipple had stolen from Looking Glass' camp. These were returned to their rightful owners after the battle of the Clearwater River had ended. [*Yellow Wolf*, 79.]

37   As usual there were fictions made by members of the Lewiston Militia. According to one, he and 20 men had cut off a group of warriors, killing one and shooting a horse. This was later proven untrue. [Greene, *Nez Perce Summer 1877,* 74.]

38   Joseph was in no way either burning houses or bragging of his deeds. These claims were inventions by white settlers who were abetted in their disclosures by Howard's reports. [Claims of the Nez Perce. Senate document no. 257, 56th Congress, 1st Session, 331.]

39   Report of the Secretary of War, 1877, 1, 122–24. See also: Howard, *Nez Perce Joseph*, 164.

40   It is likely that Looking Glass and the bulk of his men were at Clearwater but did not engage in the Battle of the Clearwater. Most evidence points to their joining the group at Kamiah. His presence may have been supposed by early researchers because a party of his warriors under the leadership of Peo'peo'Tholket did take part in the fight. Those warriors, however, were a small advance party that arrived just in time to contribute their services. *[www.nezperce.com/]*

41   Sees'koomke lost both feet and one hand when his former master (reportedly a Snake chief) left him outside during a winter storm. His feet and one hand had frozen so badly a medicine man amputated them. The chief

then gave him his freedom and he eventually made his way into a Nez Perce camp where he was adopted and cared for. Because he had such trouble walking he became a superb rider. His Nez Perce benefactors never learned his origins and his ultimate fate remains unknown. [McWhorter, *Yellow Wolf*, 43.]

42 Shields, G.O., *The Battle of the Big Hole*, 16.

43 Bailey, Harry Lee, *An Infantry Second Lieutenant in the Nez Perce War of 1877*. [Manuscripts, Archives and Special Collections. Holland Library, Washington State University, Pullman, Washington.]

44 This evacuation, which the soldiers observed, was the basis for Howard's claim that the warriors had abandoned the fight with their many casualties. [McWhorter, *Hear me My Chiefs*, ch. XVII.]

45 McWhorter, *Hear Me My Chiefs*, ch. XVII, 314–16.

46 Author's files.

47 McWhorter, *Hear Me My Chiefs*, 316.

48 McWhorter, *Yellow Wolf*, 171; also deals with this refusal by the young warriors.

49 McWhorter. *Hear me My Chiefs*. P315–15.

50 Howard's reports were received by President Hayes as he was preparing his orders to relieve the general of his command and replace him with General George Crook, a personal friend of the president. Howard's aide, Major Harry Clay Wood, had dispatched the report directly to Hayes, thereby circumventing the proper chain of command, and this flagrant indiscretion has long been thought as having been done at Howard's suggestion. While Wood's disregard for protocol garnered him censure from General McDowell it did save his general's job and, possibly his career. [Jerome. *1877:Nez Perce Summer*. P 96.]

[CHAPTER 14]
THE WEIPPE CONFERENCE

Had General Howard followed the retreating Indians and moved his troops across the Clearwater he may well have forced the Nez Perce chiefs to surrender then and there. Why he did not remains unexplained. Instead he entrenched along the opposite bank. In his later writings on the subject of the Clearwater he remains silent except to gloat over his manufactured victory and the capture of Chief Temme Ilppilp[a] [Red Heart] and his small band of 28 persons.

Red Heart and his band were Treaty Nez Perces and had absolutely nothing to do with the uprising. They had just returned from Montana and Red Heart tried to explain, but Howard, in no mood to listen to the chief, confiscated the band's horses and property then had the band shipped to Fort Vancouver where they remained in confinement until the following April when they were returned to Lapwai.

None of Howard's reports indicate the date of the "capture," but a Captain Keeler mentions in a dispatch to his division commander, General McDowell, that the date was July 17.[1] Years later

---

[a] Not to be confused with the Temme Ilppilp who was with Joseph as a warrior chief throughout the trek. *[Author's files.]*

Colonel William R. Parnell (at the time of the action a 2nd Lieutenant with the 1st Cavalry) wrote of the capture. His article berates Howard for his action and his sarcasm shows clearly when he refers to it as "a stroke of military success." He questions Howard's real motivation because Red Heart and his band were legally on their own property within the Lapwai reservation. Howard claimed they had left the reservation to join Joseph, but Parnell insists they fell under the general's biased eye for no other reason than "their heathenish long hair was indictment enough in the eyes of the 'Bible General.'"[2]

Another "great victory" for the Christian Soldier was the apprehension of a Montana band under the leadership of a Sioux chief named Three Feathers. He and his small following had been visiting Looking Glass when the camp was attacked by Captain Whipple on July 1. Three Feathers and his party fled at the first assault and made camp near Kamiah. They were in the midst of making final preparations for their return to Montana but had not left before they were arrested.[3] Because they were Sioux (and were off their reservation with permission) they were allowed to return to Montana.

Because, as Joseph had hoped, Howard decided on only a short pursuit the Nez Perces were able, more or less leisurely, to move from Kamiah to Weippe, a distance covered in two days. Howard later wrote that he had briefly possessed a good chance to attack but decided not to because he would have needed 1,000 men or few would have returned alive.[4]

Meanwhile the rebels traveled across the reservation on their move from Kamiah to Weippe. They discussed the next move during a series of rest periods not, as some have maintained, in one long session at Weippe. What has been called the Weippe Conference could easily be renamed the Mobile Conference. The reasons for the sequential talks were partly because of the need to fight off Treaty Nez Perce raiding parties from Lapwai intent on stealing horses; another was that because of the ongoing indecision each chief had formulated his own agenda to present. The final session lasted less than two days, ending with the decision to go to Montana via the Lolo Trail. It also saw the appointment of Looking Glass as the chief in supreme command. This, without doubt, proved to be the worst decision made during the entire trek.

One of the beliefs long held by some historians when discussing the Weippe Conference is that Joseph championed a direct run to Canada. In fact, not only did Joseph not advocate going to Canada, there is no indication that he participated in the conference at all. In 1935, Yellow Wolf, Joseph's chief lieutenant, indicated Joseph had *not* been included in the talks. Yellow Wolf's averment is supported by Nez Perce historians, none of whom mention Joseph being part of that council. Further, none of the survivors disputed Yellow Wolf when they were interviewed by others in later years. None mentioned him being part of the discussions, and McWhorter was informed in his interviews the Weippe Conference was settled by war chiefs and warriors. Nonetheless, Joseph undoubtedly had his opinions voiced through Ollokot who was very definitely part of the discussions.

White Bird was almost alone in espousing the idea of a trek northward. Because he was without any real success, at each discussion his support diminished. The two chiefs who expressed the most opposition—Looking Glass and Tool'hool'hool'zote—did so primarily because they both had their own agendas. Some lesser chiefs, because their knowledge of the north country was limited, were opposed through fear of the unknown. None of the chiefs, including White Bird, had ever ventured into Canadian territory. Some of the warriors had hunted there on occasion, were aware the British Columbia mountain valleys were home to the Kootenai tribe about which they knew a little[5] and some knew of northern bands of the Selish Flatheads. While the southern Selish had generally been friendly to Nez Perce hunters, there were concerns northerners would object to a sudden influx of strangers. On the other hand, southern Alberta was known to all the buffalo hunters; but because it was home to the hated Assiniboine and the confederacy of Blackfoot, Blood, Peigan and (at the more northern fringe) the Sarcee, it could not be considered overly friendly. The Peigans and Bloods had been generally hospitable, but the Assiniboine were well known for hostility. Their fearsome reputation as jealous guardians of their lands (in the Maple Creek/Cypress Hills area) was obvious to all. None harbored any illusions that their intrusion into the foothills east of the mountains would be met with friendly enthusiasm.

In rigid opposition to a northward trek were Looking Glass and Tool'hool'hool'zote. Looking Glass was firmly convinced the Montana Crows, his long-time allies and friends, would not only offer assistance but would gladly share their lands. He based much of his argument on information he had recently received from Chiefs Rainbow and Two Moons. They had been informed by Indians returning from Montana that the Crows were planning war against the white oppressors. Both chiefs felt this was merely an unfounded rumor, but Looking Glass felt it might be true. Now, he argued, would be the opportune time to meet with the Crows and form an alliance.

> "We should seek help from the E'sookh'ha [Crows]," he advised. "They have long been our friends and will surely share their [vast territory] that will afford room for all. Listen to me, my chiefs! The Crows are the same as my brothers! If you go there with me you will be safe!"[6]

White Bird had also been in an occasional fight against the Sioux-Cheyenne coalition on the side of the E'sookh'ha, but his faith in erstwhile allies was very limited. To trust the Crows, he told Looking Glass, could prove a mistake. Also opposed were Wottolen, Two Moons, Five Wounds and Rainbow, none of the four being convinced the Crows were planning a war. They did, however, agree to go if the others voted in favor of Looking Glass' proposal.

Ollokot, Joseph and the Palu chiefs, Hahtalekin and Husis Kute, wanted to travel the Lolo Trail into the Bitterroot Valley then go south to what is today known as Nez Perce Pass. From there they could return to the area bounded by the Salmon and Snake Rivers. They knew, of course, a return would certainly result in eventual surrender, but they felt a fair treaty with Washington could be negotiated which would allow a return to the Wallowa Valley where the Palouse were more than willing to live.

Eventually Looking Glass was successful in convincing hawkish warriors his plan was the most advantageous. They could depend on the Crows, he insisted, and his argument was adopted. Thus the others, Ollokot, Husis Kute, White Bird, Two Moons, Tool'hool'hool'zote and Wottolen acquiesced to the war element. Then, in a final decision, they agreed to appoint Looking Glass as overall chief in command of the trek. The election of Looking Glass to overall command was to produce a series of ill-advised adventures and disastrous decisions that resulted in the group's misfortune at the Bear's Paw.

On July 16, as the sun was beginning yet another journey across the Idaho sky, camp was packed up and the great trek once again got under way. For the next seven days the laborious task of navigating the approaches to the Lolo Trail kept everyone busy. This phase of the journey was particularly difficult for the elderly, some of whom were very ill and were transported by travois. For others who were also in various stages of aches and pains that are part of advanced age, the journey was made worse by the titanic struggles against the elements and hazards of the narrow trail.

Joseph, concerned for his charges' safety, assigned five young warriors, volunteers all, to act as rearguards and remain at the campsite for three days. They were to watch for soldiers, scouts and potential hostiles who might approach. Should any be sighted, two were to ride in haste to Joseph with news of the danger. The remaining three would retreat slowly while keeping watch on the enemy and send word of the danger as it approached. This latter precaution was made in order to allow time to have a party of warriors assembled in order to hold off advancing troops. This would allow the families and the non-combatants to attain safer positions. After three days, if no danger was forthcoming, all five would return to the main group. Sarpsis Ilppilp [Red Mocassin Tops] was named group leader.[7]

On Tuesday morning, July 17 at 4:30 AM, Major Edwin C. Mason led a company of cavalry, twenty volunteers under Captain McConville, a howitzer detachment, and six Lapwai Nez Perce scouts to reconnoiter the area where the Weippe Trail meets the Lolo Trail.

Howard had told Mason to "confine the search to two marches [two days]," the object being to locate the Indians and determine the direction of Joseph's travel.[8] On the afternoon of the first day of the march they accomplished the first part of the mission in that they found the Indians—but it was not what had been expected. The Indians were waiting for them in a well-concealed ambuscade.

Mason had sent McConville and his volunteers ahead with six scouts as a reconnaissance party. They proceeded some twenty uneventful miles then stopped for lunch. After lunch they continued their march and at mid-afternoon came to open ground. Here McConville stopped and sent the six scouts ahead. The scouts moved toward the treed area and ran headlong into the guns of Sarsis Ilppilp and his team. One, John Levi [aka Sheared Wolf], fell dead and Abraham Brooks, Captain John [Jokais] and James Reuben were wounded. The other two ran back towards McConville's men, shouting to them to fall back. As the volunteers began to retreat, more firing commenced. This new fire was from a war party from the main group sent by White Bird. The rearguard had been watching the advance and one of the party had raced away to inform Joseph (who was only seven miles ahead) of the situation. White Bird's party had arrived just before the shooting started.

McConville's militia took refuge behind fallen trees and waited for the expected assault—but nothing happened. After a lengthy wait the men cautiously ventured forth while McConville went to find Mason, no doubt wondering why the major had not come rapidly when the shooting started.

Meanwhile, the militia entered the wood only to discover all the Indians had departed. They found Levis' body (riddled with forty-five bullets to the chest and abdomen) and the wounded Abraham Brooks, who died later from numerous wounds. Reuben was also wounded in the hand and thigh but was mobile. Captain John was missing but was later found unharmed. Of the unharmed scouts, all were critical of Major Mason who had departed even before the scouts returned from the woods. Many of the militia were equally critical as they, rightly so, had expected Mason and his cavalry to appear at any moment to help.

The details of this skirmish are described in reports written by Major Edwin C. Mason and Lieutenant Eugene Wilson of the volunteers (McConville's second in command) to the secretary of war. Mason's report reveals little more than that he had been sent by Howard, with a volunteer detachment under command of Colonel (*sic*) Edward McConville (of the Camp Misery defeat) to determine the route being taken by Joseph.

Lieutenant Wilson's report, on the other hand, is very detailed and extremely critical of Major Mason. He lists the personnel involved, including the scouts. They were "Ad" Chapman and six Nez Perces from Lapwai (including James Reuben and Captain John, both of whom would figure in the final phases of the rebellion). When the trail was located, McConville ordered Chapman to ride ahead with his Nez Perce scouts. Chapman hung back while the six rode directly into the ambuscade set up by Sarpsis Ilppilp.

In his report Lieutenant Wilson writes derisively,

> "When the scouts gave the alarm he [Chapman] put spurs to his horse and beat a hasty retreat back to where Mason and his men were trying to dismount a howitzer from the back of a mule."

Wilson's report to the Secretary is bitter in its criticism of Major Mason for abandoning the scouts and deserting his position instead of riding to their assistance. He has nothing kind to say of Ad Chapman. He claims members of McConville's volunteers waited and assisted the scouts when they straggled back to safety, carrying their dead and wounded. However, Seekumses Kunnin [Horse Blanket], one of the scouts, denied the volunteers had given any help at all, stating, "If they waited for us, they must have stood far away. I saw none of them."

General Howard's report to the secretary of war reads, in part, "One of the enemy was killed and two pack animals were captured." This is not true. No Nez Perce was killed and they had no pack animals with them.

In his 1907 book, *My Life and Experiences Among Our Hostile*

Indians, the general wrote on page 289, "Mason overtook Joseph's rearguard, had a skirmish near a forest glade not far from Kamiah, and returned in haste to me."[9]

The only truthful part of both his report and his book was the statement that Mason had "returned in haste to me."[10]

The ambush sent Mason and his entire company into hasty retreat. On reflection, it is surprising that White Bird did not unleash his entire force against Mason. His decision against a full attack may have been concern for the safety of the non-combatants who, at only seven miles distance, were still within the danger area.

On July 25, Joseph stopped his group at a place now called Lolo Hot Springs. It seemed a good place to rest for a day because the past week had been particularly difficult. It also gave everyone the opportunity to take advantage of the warm mineral waters that would soothe pains and ease aching bones. This was a safe stop, as Joseph's scouts had all reported no soldiers were near; and they also gave a full report on the July 17 action against the Mason's force and subsequent retreat.[11]

The next day Joseph led his group on what would be their final leg on the Lolo Trail. Unbeknownst to him, ahead lay a barricade manned by a contingent of army and militia personnel. That barricade would soon become famously known as Fort Fizzle.

[CHAPTER 14 ENDNOTES]

1 See *Claims of the Nez Perce Indians,* 42. This section suggests significant reasons why Howard makes no mention of the surrender of Red Heart in any of his reports or in his later writings on the campaign.

2 Parnell, WR, "The Salmon River Expedition" (pg 134) in Cyrus Brady's edited work, *Northwestern Indian Fights and Fighters* (1907).

3 McWhorter, L.V., *Hear Me My Chiefs,* 334.

4 This observance was probably because of the July 17

ambush of Colonel Mason's scouts on the Lolo Trail. Howard apparently feared he would also lose too many horses to White Bird and his rearguard fighters who had already given him more trouble than he cared to remember. Thus, he waited until the rebels were almost a hundred miles away before he even ventured across the river.

5   The Kootenai tribe was related to the Washington Territory Spokane tribe that had familial connections to the Nez Perce tribe. Nez Perce traders often bartered and traded goods with BC tribes and because of this they knew something of the Kootenai people.

6   McWhorter, *Hear Me My Chiefs*, 334.

7   Narrative of Sewattis Hihhih [White Cloud], *Hear Me My Chiefs*, 335–6.

8   Howard, Report to the Secretary of War, 1877, 124.

9   Howard, *My Life and Experiences Among Our Hostile Indians*, 289.

10 Howard, Report of Secretary of War, 1877, 1, 124; Mason, Report of Seretary Of War, 1877; Wilson, Report of Secretary of War, 1877, 1, 124]; narration of Seekumis Kunnin [Horse Blanket], Nez Perce scout, *Hear Me My Chiefs*, 338.

[CHAPTER 15]

FORT FIZZLE: *The* BATTLE *That* NEVER WAS

When Joseph and his allies resumed their northward march across the Lolo Trail they realized Montana—their perceived safe haven—was now attainable but they must continue to outpace Howard's force. The major problems were not knowing what Howard was planning at the moment, or if the general would pursue them beyond Idaho. Neither did they know if troops from eastern regions had been dispatched to intercept the migrants. Scouts were sent ahead while Ollokot and others deployed rearguard forces. Driving their horses before them, the rebels were moving at a good pace, but the horses, tired and deprived of their proper amount of nutrition, were becoming troublesome. Although necessary for survival, the horses were becoming a hindrance and causing no small amount of trouble. Because they had been without sufficient food for two days due to the enforced pace, the animals were fretful and unruly. In the chilling mountain air, and possibly able to scent grassland not far ahead, they wanted to move more quickly than the teenage drovers would allow. The situation, though not yet serious, was definitely showing signs of developing into a differing of opinions between men and beasts.

The sun had reached its apogee and the column was making good time when a scout galloped in from the north bearing news, none of it good. Soldiers, he reported, were busily erecting a huge log barrier across the trail some two miles distant. Joseph and his fellow chiefs were dismayed. They assumed Howard had anticipated their route of travel. Indeed he had, and had sent word to Fort Missoula to dispatch soldiers to stop the rebels. The soldiers seen by the scout had journeyed to a point their commanding officer, Captain Charles C. Rawn, had deemed the ideal spot to stop the Nez Perces. A wooden barricade, he decided, would suffice.

The chiefs drew some relief when the scout added the soldiers were few in number. Joseph quickly met with White Bird and Looking Glass. It was obvious to the three that retreat was not an option; the trail did not allow a detour through the woods and a continued advance might no longer be achievable. As the chiefs pondered the situation awaiting them, the line continued moving. The entire matter might have to be decided through battle, a last-stand encounter, at the barrier.[1] Either that or surrender, neither of which held any appeal.

Joseph and Looking Glass rode ahead to observe the situation first hand. What they initially saw elevated their spirits somewhat. Only a dozen soldiers were in evidence so, thinking they might be able to intimidate their way past the barricade, the two cautiously approached under a white flag. They were met by Captain Rawn,[2] who walked out to meet them. It was then, as they looked beyond the barrier, they felt the cold chill of dismay. The scout had seen only those who were busy with the construction of the barrier. The detachment numbered, not fifteen or twenty soldiers, but at least 200, perhaps more. Rawn's command was no small unit of barricade builders. It was two complete companies, a fifty-man company of regular soldiers from the 7th Infantry Regiment augmented by more than 150 riflemen of a Montana militia from Helena. Rawn's force was indeed formidable, standing as a invulnerable bulwark against the migrants. The chiefs realized there would be no intimidation here.

They were equally concerned upon seeing some two dozen members of a Bitterroot Selish[3] tribe in the camp. Because the Selish had always been generally friendly towards Nez Perce hunters, the chiefs could not help but wonder if these men had switched alliances and were now part of Rawn's command. It was revealed to them later the Selish, in order to earn some money,[4] had merely accepted work as laborers to haul logs from the forest to the construction site.

Looking Glass remained mounted as Joseph walked to where the officer stood with a civilian interpreter. He and Rawn shook hands and the captain gestured towards a wide-branched aspen tree, indicating it would afford shelter from the hot sun. The three walked to the tree where they were joined by Looking Glass. Joseph informed Rawn his people and their animals intended to proceed into Montana and asked permission to pass the barricade unhindered. Rawn replied he would be pleased to allow the band to pass providing they surrender all their rifles and animals. Joseph replied this could not be considered; the rifles were necessary for hunting and the horses were needed for riding and labor. He would however, as a gesture of good faith, surrender all the army mules they had captured. Rawn replied his authority was limited to allowing Joseph's people to pass only if they surrendered their rifles and animals, which of course included the captive mules. Joseph reiterated his intention was to pass with his rifles and animals.

Rawn then told Joseph he, on his own authority, could allow them to keep their rifles, but they must surrender the ammunition—and they must turn over the animals. Joseph replied such an issue was not negotiable, reminding Rawn empty rifles were of little use. The talks seesawed to an impasse until Joseph bluntly stated his people, their animals and the army mules would pass into Montana with their rifles no matter what the army directed. The women, the elderly and the children, he said, would commence passage the following morning under the protection of armed warriors. He asked only that Rawn command his soldiers not to fire upon the non-combatants as none would be armed.

Rawn had met chiefs in his time but never such a one as Joseph. As the conversation continued Rawn grew increasingly uncertain. He later confided to friends he felt he was being scolded, much as an errant student might be chided by a headmaster. To add to his discomfort he was also catching glimpses through the trees of what appeared to be many dozens of heavily armed warriors. He was beginning to feel nervous as well as intimidated.[5] He knew he would have to think of something—but what?

Rawn was aware General Howard was still a march of not less than three days away, and he also knew he could hold the upper hand only so long as he could delay the Nez Perce advance. Rawn, deciding his best option would be to prolong the talks, suggested the afternoon was growing late. Perhaps the band would see fit to make camp for the night so he and Joseph could continue their talk in the morning. Joseph agreed. Looking Glass nodded agreement.

This agreement spawned the first of many enduring fictional accounts of the proceedings at the barricade. By the time magazine writers began to publish their versions of the confrontation on the Lolo Trail, the log barricade had become a full-fledged fort, there had been a pitched battle, a hitherto unknown trail was discovered and a daring escape made. It is a myth that endures to this day in the lore and legend of the Old West. Exciting? Yes, indeed. Factual? Not at all.

The facts are these: Captain Rawn had certainly contrived to parley as long as he could, but Joseph had not for a moment entertained any such intention. Even Joseph's agreement to meet the following morning was a ruse. An overnight camp was all the delay he had in mind. Regardless of facts, that agreement sowed the seeds for an enduring myth.

The Myth

Legend holds that Joseph and Rawn met over a period of two days, talking while the warriors and non-combatants rested and their horses grazed in a nearby grassy field.[6] The legend portrays Joseph and Rawn continuing their talks in leisurely fashion until the afternoon of July 27 at which time Joseph told the captain he wished to confer with his chiefs. Returning to camp he met with the chiefs and warriors telling them Rawn was merely delaying and further delay would allow Howard to overtake them. He told them they would have to fight their way past the barrier.

Then, the legend continues, fate intervened. Even as they were formulating their battle plan a scout rode into camp to say he had discovered a hitherto unknown trail. Although nothing more than a narrow ridge high up the mountainside, it was passable. People and all the animals, he assured the chiefs, could manage, providing the undertaking was made with extreme caution. The chiefs saw this as the best chance to skirt the barrier, so the decision to proceed was quickly made. A narrow trail was less dangerous than an attack against a wooden barrier with two hundred rifles behind it. The decision was made: the entire band and all the animals would assault the ridge. The sure-footed army mules would be utilized to carry as much equipment as could be piled upon their backs.

As the myth unfolds it was during the night of July 27–28 when the band decamped as silently as humanly possible. The mules and horses were brought in from the field; the mules were laden to capacity. With all in readiness well before dawn, and only the waning moonlight to guide them, a long line of horses and mules began to move towards the pass. Shortly after, the people began their part of the trek. Some warriors remained in defensive positions while others concealed themselves further along as reinforcements should the first group be unable to repel the soldiers who were bound to try to overtake them.

The scout leading, the long file began the climb up the steep, narrow pathway with mules and horses in the front, the people in the rear. The Lolo Trail was soon far beneath them and was then quickly lost to sight.

As the sun's first rays broached the mountain peaks, Captain Rawn, puffing casually on his pipe, lounged against the wooden barrier awaiting Joseph's arrival for the third day of negotiations. Suddenly, a soldier ran to him, gasping in amazement and pointing upward. On a distant ridge high above the tree tops a long line of slowly moving tiny dots, barely visible against the blue-grey of the mountain was seen. Rawn grabbed his telescope, peered through it and discerned the dots were people and horses. He sagged in dismay and disbelief. He had been outflanked and outfoxed. Joseph had seen through his delaying tactic and rendered it ineffective with a pre-emptive maneuver. Hurriedly ordering his bugler to sound "assembly," Rawn rushed to his tent for his sword and rifle.

Rawn rushed his men towards the gulch and the trail leading to the ridge and ran directly into Looking Glass and his riflemen who unleashed a lethal barrage of gunfire. The soldiers fell back in disorder, retreating quickly to safety. Crammed together as they were in their rush to the trail, and with no stomach for an assault on the narrow ridge, they returned to the barricade. No one on either side had been killed.

The myth, as all good legends will, endured for decades, adding to Joseph's glory. From time to time various authors added pitched battles, and some included a vast herd of cattle. The "Legend of Joseph's Escape" is still believed by many to this day.

The Facts

The truth of the matter is simply this: there was neither a miraculous escape nor a hazardous nighttime march along a narrow mountain path little wider than a ridge. The only truth to the legend is that the route they followed traversed the Bitterroot Range into Montana and was very narrow. It was, however, wider than some reporters speculated. What is very true is that Joseph had once again outfoxed the army, again without suffering a single loss. Neither had any horses or mules tumbled from the supposed craggy ridge, and there were no cows or steers to cause added concern.

White Bird, for unknown reasons, was later credited by an admiring reporter with having charted the course along the trail. The reporter further embellished the legend when he described the journey as "treacherous" and dubbed the old chief "The Hannibal of the Bitterroots." His story was eagerly picked up by eastern newspapers whose readers were hungry for news of the exploits of Joseph, the upstart chief who was humiliating the great Army of the

Northwest. Their interest contributed further to the legend. White Bird, however, had neither blazed the trail nor led the way, and no scout had accidentally discovered it.

Although known to few white settlers, and apparently not at all to the army, the trail had long been familiar to Nez Perce buffalo hunters. They had utilized it for decades, perhaps centuries, as a shortcut to and from the plains' hunting grounds. In all likelihood it had been Looking Glass, well aware of its existence and its conditions, who suggested using it. Probably White Bird also knew of its location because no time had been wasted in debate. Obviously all considered it safe. Neither was it an epic crossing fraught with great danger calling for heroic measures; nor did it cause any real loss of time to Joseph or lessen Howard's time lag. The cost of leaving the Lolo Trail was an expenditure of a few hours, perhaps a day, but nothing else.

Joseph never had any intention of squandering two or three days in parley with Rawn, thereby giving Howard the chance to close the gap. He spoke with Rawn less than a few hours, and that was only in the hope of convincing the captain to allow passage through the barricade in safety. As for the battle, it simply never happened, although there may have been a shot or two fired during Rawn's brief attempt at trailing the Indians. The reason why the battle that never was is fiction is easily determined by reading Rawn's somewhat ambiguous report on the incident and the official "History of the First Cavalry Division," both of which testify to the non-battle.

Rawn, in his report stated, "all the volunteers had left me [except for] a dozen or twenty Missoula men..."[7]

In a segment covering the barricade and Joseph's part in it, the cavalry regiment's official historian mentions Rawn's force had suffered "considerable losses." Because he gave no explanation or details, many years passed before anyone realized the historian was disclosing, not casualties of battle, but mass desertion. Writing years later (c.1941) on his personal recollections of the incident, Charles N. Loynes, who had been present as a sergeant in the Seventh Infantry, revealed the facts behind the historian's reference to "considerable losses." As Loynes succinctly put it, "at the sight of so many Indians nearly all the volunteers deserted."[8]

When the bugler sounded "assembly," Rawn was shocked when only a handful of his militia volunteers answered the call. He was then informed many others had packed their gear during the night and returned to their homes "singly and in groups." Realizing at that point he had insufficient rifles to attempt a pursuit, Rawn merely ventured a short distance with the men he had before calling a halt.[9] There was no encounter, no intense shooting, no pitched battle and not a single casualty. Moreover, several of his remaining "dozen or twenty Missoula men" chose to leave at that time.

The rebels, having traversed the pass, entered Montana on July 29. Knowing they were out of Howard's jurisdiction, they rejoiced in their belief his authority had ended. They also thought the pursuit would end, so for two days they camped at the Indian village near Stevenville at the invitation of Chief Charo and his Selish band. During those two days Nez Perce women walked about freely in Stevensville shopping for needed supplies. Though they dealt mostly at Buck Brothers' General Store, other merchants were also happy to deal with them. Storekeepers happily reported sales were paid for with gold—dust and nuggets. While the women shopped and the warriors rested, the chiefs spent the time finalizing the details of the decision made at Weippe to go south to Crow country. None felt any compulsion to hurry as they all, including the usually skeptical White Bird, believed Howard had been vanquished and would remain in Idaho. They believed no one in Montana would take up the pursuit. One elated chief is reported as having shouted, "We have left the war in Idaho. General Two-Days-Behind can no longer pursue us."

It was during those spontaneous days of celebration that Joseph and his chiefs made their second serious error in judgment. Thinking they were safe they planned a leisurely trek to the land of the Crows, their longtime allies. Looking Glass volunteered that upon arrival he would personally locate the Crow chiefs who had been his allies. He would then arrange for Crow land on which to set up their individual villages. All agreed August 1 would be the day of departure.

During this stay at Stevensville the group was joined by Wawookya Wasaaw [Lean Elk] and his family. Lean Elk (known to Whites as Poker Joe) was a welcome addition. He knew the southern country better than anyone, and was familiar with every valley and trail they would encounter. Even Looking Glass, who normally brooked no competition from those less positioned in the hierarchy of rank, agreed Lean Elk's expertise should be used. This arrangement worked well until Lean Elk dared questioned a decision made by Looking Glass. The two had a falling out that would eventually have tragic effects on the entire group.

Sensing a successful end to their troubles, the chiefs sent riders to outlying areas, promising the settlers they would not trouble or harass anyone they met on the trail. The word was rapidly spread southward. A few days later the rebels left Stevensville and headed south. When Fort Owen, the first town, was passed without incident[10] all seemed to be well. The war was now behind them and ahead was a new land, a new future. The migrants trudged south, naively convinced Howard would no longer pursue them. They had no way of knowing he possessed all the authority needed to continue the pursuit and, moreover, he held authority to call out units from any of the Montana forts. In fact, he had already done so.

Thus the long files moved southward towards the Big Hole River and their first encounter that would produce disastrous results.

[CHAPTER 15 ENDNOTES]

1 His concern was only partly true. Howard, when it had become clear that Joseph was not going to Lapwai, had decided to block all possible routes in all possible direc-

tions and had dispatched troops for that purpose. One of his signals had gone to Fort Missoula. As the civilian Bitterroot Militia was attached to the fort when the fort commander, Capt. C. Rawn, moved out with the 7th Infantry to block the Lolo Trail, the militia went with him.

2   Charles Rawn (June 12, 1837–June 10, 1887) was born in Harrisburg, Pennsylvania and died in Lancaster, Pennsylvania. His army career was not exceptional, although he did achieve the rank of major. Following the debacle at Fort Fizzle he later came under unproven criticism by Wilson B. Harlan. In a 1921 article titled "The Fiasco at Fort Fizzle on the Lolo Trail" [see: Noyes, Alva, *In the Land of the Chinook*] Harlan maliciously wrote Rawn's failure to stop Joseph had been due to excessive drinking.

3   In recent years the original, proper, name of the Selish nation has been altered in spelling. Why, how, or even when this came about is uncertain, but at present the name is in general usage as Salish.

4   The Bitterroot Selish had not been relegated to a reservation to that point. They had avoided that when Chief Charo agreed with Washington to accept certain conditions, assist settlers and not enter into alliances with other tribes hostile to the government. Nonetheless, as were all tribes, Charo's Selish were eventually betrayed and forced into a reservation. The treaty signatures have since been proven to be forgeries.

5   The unsuspecting officer was never to learn that White Bird was using a ruse. Small groups of warriors were passing by in a continuous relay. The result produced the illusion by a few of being many.

6   In later years some soldiers wrote of the incident at the barricade. All commented on the poor condition of the horses and some vaguely recalled seeing a herd of cattle

as well, misinformation that eventually became the huge herd of cattle so many still believe had accompanied the Indians on their long trek. Not until 1932 would the truth emerge. That year, Yellow Wolf and others revealed to Lucullus McWhorter that during the first days of the exodus all their cattle had been lost to rustlers. According to Yellow Wolf, and known facts, all the cattle had been rustled from their pasture at the Salmon River. Even at the Tolo Lake gathering there had been had no cattle. [Many Sources including McWhorter, *Hear Me My Chiefs*; Greene, *Nez Perce Summer, 1877,* and *www.nezperce.com/*]

7   Rawn's Report, Report of Secretary of War, 1877, 1, 548.

8   Quoted from the *www.nezperce.com* website.

9   It is interesting to note that entries after June 17, whenever casualties number more than twelve, the cavalry's official historian never records figures. Invariably used is the blanket declaration "considerable losses." [U.S. Army Records, Reference: First Cavalry Division 1877.]

10 They stopped there long enough to assure frightened settlers no harm would befall them. The settlers agreed to make no effort to hinder the Indians. Several settlers later broke their agreement by joining Colonel Gibbon as scouts or militia members. [Author's files.]

[CHAPTER 16]
THE PURSUIT CONTINUES

The Montana newspaper editors, seeing in Joseph a circulation gold mine, spared few words in writing of what they perceived to be his elusive moves and tactics. Joseph's print value soon rivaled that allotted General Howard's latest setbacks and the army's impotence against its elusive foe. When a waggish reporter christened Captain Rawn's impassable barrier Fort Fizzle, the next edition of *The Helena Independent* appeared with the name emblazoned in large black headlines. Fort Fizzle caught the public imagination and remains famous to this day.[1] That the barrier proved useless against Joseph's wiles caused the publisher of the *Helena Daily Herald* such concern that he waxed eloquently in his July 30th edition about the ease in which the Nez Perce chief had so easily by-passed Fort Fizzle. He severely chided the army, in particular the infantry.

> *"How easy any Indian force, whether seeking pillage or only escape, could pass around, through and by our untrained troops. So far as the infantry goes, who can expect it to defend the larger towns or some fortified position."*[2] (sic)

Furious over the debacle at Fort Fizzle, Howard immediately assigned two new Montana groups to the chase. The largest, 7th

Infantry Regiment (Colonel John Gibbon commanding), was dispatched from Fort Shaw with orders to intercept Joseph. Also alerted was Colonel Samuel Sturgis (1821–89), stationed near the Crow Indian Agency farther to the south. Gibbon moved at once while Sturgis remained on standby. Howard, besieged and gloomy, then departed Kamiah. His advance was not as much to quiet the comments of his superiors in Washington as it was stop the increasingly snide remarks from newspaper editors.

While the complaints from Washington, at least temporarily, abated, the editors continued to carp. Howard, they growled, was allowing a handful of unmilitary, normally peaceable Natives to humiliate a large, fully equipped and ostensibly professional army. Howard worried that it would not be long before the press learned of the no small amount of rifles, ammunition, other equipment, field rations and valuable mules, formerly the property of his army, had been lost to permanent possession of the Natives. These were not happy days for the weary old soldier. Worse still, the situation was affecting his dispirited men.

Gibbon's scouts were able to quickly inform him Joseph was camped near Stevenville but could give no idea of which direction he intended to lead his people. Two perplexing questions then emerged to give Gibbon pause for thought: Would Joseph take his lead from Sitting Bull's 1876 exodus and head for Canada? Or was there any substance to a smidgen of information he had received indicating intentions of going south? Gibbon hoped to intercept his quarry before they departed, so he pushed his troops toward Stevensville. Colonel Gibbon, as did most others, considered Joseph the overall chief of the rebels and had he known Looking Glass, not Joseph, was masterminding the migration he might have changed tactics. Gibbon was aware of the friendship Looking Glass had with the Crows and that might have caused him to think Looking Glass was considering an alliance. Gibbon, of course, knew what Looking Glass did not: the Crows had already agreed to a treaty with Washington.

At the moment, though, because he thought Joseph was in charge, he felt Joseph was in the catbird[a] seat and would proceed northward. Gibbon's worry was that he would do so within a day or two, which would enable him to easily attain the border. He altered his route to north-northwest.[3] If Joseph was to proceed north he could be cut off before he had covered much distance.

Had Gibbon maintained his original direct course to Stevensville the advantage would have remained with him as the chiefs did not know he was now their immediate enemy. Neither did they know his troops were already on the way. Had they known they may well have abandoned thoughts of a Crow alliance and headed north without delay. Complacency however had the chiefs in its grip so none were considering unforeseen possibilities. Neither had there been thoughts of sending scouts to range east and south. All were thinking of Howard and this lack of concern caused their third serious error.

In their elation at eluding Howard they convinced themselves there would be no further pursuit. After all, General Two-Days-Behind was making no move to leave Idaho so it appears they had not considered the possibility of Montana-based troops taking up the chase. Had they considered this and dispatched scouts to the east Gibbon would have been quickly seen; but they remained unaware of the threat he presented until it was too late.

Whatever reluctance Joseph might have felt about the Weippe decision to appeal to the Crows remains unknown, but he accepted the judgment and sided with the majority. Looking Glass had advanced his plan eloquently enough to convince even the usually cynical White Bird the Crows would honor their 1873 promises. The more receptive Tool'hool'hool'zote had more quickly agreed. Looking Glass had delivered hope and Joseph and the others accepted as valid the Crows' promise because they wanted to believe in its cogency. While their optimism is understandable, it remains

---

a   *An enviable position, often in terms of having the upper hand or greater advantage in all types of dealings among parties.*

surprising both Joseph and White Bird should not have been able to see the Crows' promise for what it really was—a spontaneous commitment made in the heady euphoria of victory. Neither were any of the band chiefs or warrior chiefs aware the Crows had recently agreed to a treaty in which they surrendered nearly all their traditional land. The Crow chiefs had yet to sign the treaty[4] but reservation boundaries had been drawn, the acreage per family allocated and most of the tribe had already taken up residence. Nor were they aware a number of Crow warriors had accepted employment with the army as scouts. In fact, the scouts who had first observed the Nez Perces' entry into Montana had been Crows. It had been Crows who had alerted Gibbon to the camp at Stevenville.[5] Thus, on August 1, when the Nez Perce turned southward, the move was made under watchful eyes of Crow scouts, the erstwhile allies who had promised the deliverance that Looking Glass had only recently declared was assured.

The trail, winding and rugged, led to the Big Hole River on whose south bank was a camping ground long known as Eschuchilpan [Place of buffalo calves].[6] The rolling hills on the river's south bank were an ideal place with large groves of trees to shelter tepees, lush pastures of grass for animal grazing and plenty of fresh water. Plants and bushes provided roots, berries and vegetables in abundant harvest. Trout and other fish teemed in the river. Hunters had easy access to deer and elk without having to ride great distances. It was an idyllic setting for the people to rest a few days.

Though the trip from Weippe through the Bitterroots had gone well, some dissatisfaction was beginning to surface over the slow pace being budgeted by Looking Glass. Under Joseph's guidance the daily pace had rarely been less than twenty-five miles. Now the daily pace was averaging scarcely fifteen miles. White Bird and others told Looking Glass he was setting too slow a pace, while others were beginning to question his overall leadership. Anticipating their meeting with the Crows would end the odyssey, they were anxious to proceed faster. The dissenters also felt he was allowing too many rest periods and staying too long encamped. Several criticized him for impeding progress by demanding lodge poles be dragged along each day when they could be replaced easily each night. Looking Glass dismissed his critics out of hand.

As the Nez Perces approached white settlements, farms and ranches, Joseph, hoping to calm fears and avoid hostility, sent emissaries into each to assure the inhabitants his people meant neither harm nor mischief. Most had recently read of Joseph and his successes against Howard in Idaho while others were already acquainted with Nez Perce hunters from previous years. Few felt any reason for fear. Thus reassured by Joseph's messengers, merchants in towns and villages willingly sold and traded goods and supplies. Both sides mingled freely in bargaining, though some of the merchants charged exorbitant prices. Not once did any Nez Perce—not even impatient young warriors—loot or plunder, and never did any settler give them cause for concern.

Washington McCormick, a Missoula merchant, wrote in a letter to his friend, Benjamin F. Potts,[7] the governor of Montana, "The Indians have gold dust, coins and greenbacks. They are paying for all the supplies they select."

As is always the case, some of the population saw the large group not as harried nomads but as a potential danger and did not view the situation with the same enlightenment as had McCormick. Many, especially those who lived in large towns, were terrified. Hasty telegrams were sent to various authorities demanding the army do something to stop the migration. It was just such a message, dated August 1, giving details of the direction the Nez Perce were traveling, that gave Howard the information he needed. He was still at Kamiah when he received the message, but was about to decamp. His forced march through the Bitterroots saw his arrival in Montana on August 8.

Meanwhile, Gibbon had also been made aware of the latest developments and immediately turned south arriving at Stevensville on August 4. Two days later his scouts reported the Nez Perce camped at Carlton Creek, their tepees erected on a ranch belonging to John A. McClain. Gibbon left hurriedly, pushing his troops relentlessly, stopping only when darkness made further progress impossible.

John Gibbon (1827–96)[8] was a career officer who gained his commission as an artillery officer at West Point in 1847. After serving in the Seminole Wars (1849) he was appointed as artillery instructor at West Point. During his tenure, which lasted until the Civil War began, he achieved fame and recognition as an undoubted expert on the subject of artillery.[9] During the Civil War he was attached to "The Iron Brigade" in which he served as a corps commander.[10] He rose steadily through the ranks to that of colonel. During four major battles he was wounded twice. One was a serious leg wound that thereafter caused him to walk with a limp so conspicuous he was called "He Who Limps" by one of the Plains tribes. The name caught on among the tribes with whom he had dealings. In 1865, he was transferred west where he engaged in various battles against the Plains Indians.[11]

Gibbon's knowledge of tactical warfare had been learned during the Civil War, so he followed the example set by most professional soldiers of any era: he prepared for future wars by reliving the one just ended; his western experience, which, inexplicably, was as an infantry officer, showed this vividly. Following a term with the 36th Infantry Division, he was re-assigned in 1869 to the 7th Infantry Regiment as that unit's commanding officer. Though tenacious in battle and respected for leadership, by example he was never considered more than an average officer. His successes in the field came mainly because his troops always outnumbered the foe. He was not considered particularly effective in planning infantry tactics or strategy. He never studied new ideas, even those concerning artillery, his philosophy being that old methods worked so why change.

During the years preceding his retirement as a general he served as director of the Columbia District (1886–1891). During those five years he had many dealings with Joseph and the two former foes became very good friends, all animosity long since discarded. Such is the irony of war.

Gibbon, who to that point had biases normal for the age in which he lived, had never met an Indian he liked and he held none in respect. It is hardly surprising he considered Chief Joseph as just another naive savage ripe for defeat. After the Big Hole battle that bias changed and became tempered with time. Perhaps it is not surprising their friendship blossomed in later years.

Unaware that Gibbon was now the direct threat, Looking Glass decided to allow the women and children some additional rest. Joseph did not object, so they remained at Carlton Creek awhile longer. McClain, a long-time friend of Nez Perce hunters,[12] had for years allowed the hunters to camp on his land. He told Looking Glass to stay as long as he wished. For this Joseph was grateful, as many elders were not doing well. It had been a long, harrowing trek from the Cottonwood, and even with the stays at Weippe and Stevensville the rest periods had been insufficient for regaining health or strength. Adding to the stress had been the dangers in using rough trails, crossing swollen creeks and rugged forests. Many of the ailing had to be transported via travois dragged behind horses. These "A frame" contraptions bumped and jarred as they crossed ruts and rocks while tilting alarmingly in the process. No one objected to another delay as the last few days had been devoid of incidents.

On occasion, Whites would pass by and offer words of encouragement. To these people the Natives were friendly and accepted the good wishes. Even the usually truculent Looking Glass had been congenial when a group of militia volunteers—settlers and farmers returning to their homes—approached the camp. They asked permission to pass through the sprawling settlement of tepees. Looking Glass recognized some in the group as having been at Fort Fizzle.

When informed by one of his warriors these men were known to have deserted the barricade, he quickly granted permission. Nonetheless, he made it clear he knew who they were and chided them about having originally gone to the barricade intending to stop, and even kill, his people. Telling them disdainfully he knew they had fled before a fight had started, he could not resist giving them a short sermon on tolerance.

> "I bear no ill will towards you who had come to fight us. I could kill you now if I wished to but I do not. You can go to your homes. I give my word of honor that I will harm nobody."[13]

Two mornings later, as they were about to renew their journey towards Eschuchilpan,[14] several chiefs insisted on naming Lean Elk chief guide. This did not sit well with Looking Glass who considered guiding part of a commander's overall activities. Besides, Looking Glass considered himself a superlative guide. Lean Elk, however, was renowned as knowing every hill and valley in Montana. His arrival had been hailed as opportune and at that time a suggestion had been made to make Lean Elk the chief guide for the journey south. Looking Glass objected, and with the southern trip now the important order of business there was no time to discuss the matter. The matter was set aside and Looking Glass remained the guide when the Nez Perce vacated McClain's ranch to resume their long trudge southward.

They were still unaware Gibbon had picked up their trail but, while he had closed the gap to one day, he had again experienced difficulties. He was being hindered by both terrain and conflicting reports from scouts who had lost the trail. It did not take long before he realized that some settlers were deliberately giving false directions. He was also being hampered by the slow pace of his supply wagons. As they rumbled along the narrow trails, deep ruts caused wagons to occasionally overturn. These delays caused loss of pace until Gibbon feared he would be unable to close the gap.

On August 4, he was joined by Captain Rawn and his company who had left Fort Fizzle to join Gibbon. He immediately designated them as "I" Company. As the troops progressed they were joined, on August 5, by members of a hastily assembled group calling themselves the Bitterroot Volunteer Militia. These were civilians hastily assembled by Montana Territorial Governor Benjamin F. Potts [1836–1887]. All came from several towns, few had military experience, and all had signed on because their reward was to be Nez Perce horses and other chattels. Gibbon assigned them as reinforcements for "B" company under the command of Lieutenant James H. Bradley.

The volunteers began the journey with shows of elan and vigor, but most dropped out after a day or two when the going proved too tough. Others left when they were informed the Indians were without a great deal of goods and had fewer animals than they had been led to believe. By the fourth day several more left, having informed Bradley that, upon reflection, they had decided the Nez Perce had right on their side. Only thirty remained and another dozen departed during the night prior to arrival at the Big Hole. Of the eighteen who stayed to fight, six were killed by Nez Perce snipers; four others were wounded, some seriously. Though the wounded all survived, they, along with those who left the battle intact, were only too happy to return home. Many told family members in later days they had never encountered such a formidable group of marksmen. None had any horses to show for their troubles.

Some of Gibbon's delay had its cause in troubles he encountered while dealing with other Natives. Upon his arrival at Stevensville he felt Joseph was going to outdistance him completely, so he tried to enlist the aid of Chief Charlo and his Bitterroot Selish. He was motivated in this endeavor by his knowledge it had been Selish tribesmen who had joined Captain Rawn in the construction of Fort Fizzle. This caused him to believe the Selish were unfriendly to the Nez Perce tribe. In fact, inter-tribal differences had never entered into the Selish's reasons for aiding Rawn. They had helped only because he was paying them for their labor.

As events dictated, Gibbon squandered almost two days of valuable time in his attempt to contact Charlo, then lost two more days plus half of a third in presenting a proposal to the wily, old chief. Charlo listened politely while Gibbon explained why Charlo should join him in the hunt. To the colonel's dismay, Charlo, on the third day, not only turned him down but delivered a lengthy speech—more of a lecture—in which he described how and why Selish and Nez Perce bands had been on peaceful terms for many more years than white men had been in their land. He assured him the Selish would not impede the army's progress, but neither would they help in finding the Nez Perces. Charlo, an articulate speaker given to ornate phrases and colorful adjectives, in what was probably a deliberate ploy, spent several hours delivering his flowery address. Perhaps he relished the knowledge that with each passing minute the Nez Perces were opening the distance between themselves and the army. Gibbon, well aware of established protocol, was not daring enough to interrupt until the old chief had spoken his piece. He and his officers remained a captive audience until at long last Charo set aside the Talking Stick,[15] thus indicating he had spoken his piece. Gibbon thanked him for his hospitality, bade him good health, gave him gifts from his supply wagons and, totally frustrated, hastily left the camp with the great chief's words burning his ears.[16]

What Charlo had told Gibbon was not altogether truthful. His band members, though tolerant of the Nez Perces, felt no particular friendship toward them. They did, however, prefer them to the white men they were forced to countenance. Charlo and his people were living a provisional, uneasy freedom very much dependent upon the white settlers and townspeople for work and other favors. He had worked long and hard convincing his youthful tribesmen there must be no violence against either Whites or neighboring Indians. The wages of transgression, he had hammered into them, was life on a reservation under conditions and regulations enforced by the army. Charlo did not want to jeopardize either their tenuous freedom or the workable relationship he enjoyed with ranchers and townspeople. What Gibbon did *not* know was that Charlo, though he had shared his campgrounds with the Nez Perce, had expressly ordered his people to avoid trading with them. During those few days he had lived in fear the Nez Perce warriors might retaliate should his taboo on commerce be somehow discovered.[17]

From August 1 until they arrived at the Big Hole River on August 7, the Indians moved at an almost leisurely pace. The week was marred only once when, on August 4, a group of rogue warriors from Tool'hool'hool'zote's band swept down on a farm. The farmer, Myron Lockwood, was not harmed, but his house was ransacked and the raiders made off with sacks of flour, sugar, coffee and other supplies. When the raid was reported to Looking Glass he ruled the raiders could keep their plunder but demanded they return to the farm and give Lockwood their seven best horses as payment. Apparently Tool'hool'hool'zote agreed, for he did not object to the decision. The next day another small party of raiders rustled five steers from a ranch. These steers were butchered for food but it is not known if this incident produced a similar ruling of repayment.

On August 7, the Nez Perces arrived at the Big Hole River, crossed to the south bank to the Eschuchilpan grove and set up their camp among the trees. At this point Looking Glass made what turned out to be a grievous error. Considering how travel had gone smoothly so far and knowing Howard was so far behind, he decided scouts were no longer needed in the north. By that move he left the entire area devoid of surveillance and, as a result, there was no chance of an early warning of Gibbon's advance. He did this because there had been no hindrance from anyone, so he considered the agreement he had with settlers was holding firm. Meanwhile, as no further word had been heard of Howard's location, Looking Glass believed him to be still in Idaho. In fact, Howard would arrive at Stevensville on August 8. He would then be only four days behind.

Having set up camp at Eschuchilpan, the Nez Perces intended to rest a few days. There were, however, a number of warriors who had become decidedly uneasy, Five Wounds being one of them. Two members of Lieutenant Bradley's volunteers had been sent out for a reconnaissance mission and had been seen by Nez Perce hunters who were tracking deer. The distance had been too great for positive identification, but it was enough to cause concern. The hunters reported the sighting to Chief Five Wounds who went to Looking Glass during the morning of August 8. He relayed what the hunters had seen and asked permission to send scouts back along the north trail. He also told Looking Glass he had dreamed the night before of being involved in a great battle in which many children were killed. Five Wounds, a Dreamer, put great stock in dreams as omens. He told Looking Glass he feared they were being trailed by someone other than Howard. Looking Glass did not adhere to the Dreamer philosophy and had no belief in dreams as omens. He curtly dismissed Five Wounds' fears as groundless. He refused to consider sending scouts to cover ground he now deemed neutral. He reminded Five Wounds it was common knowledge that Howard was still in Idaho.

Looking Glass also had another reason for refusing the request—his sense of honor. To him sending scouts to recheck the way they had come would be a rebuke to the white settlers who had befriended them and granted safe passage. Such action, he told his unhappy warrior, would give the settlers the impression they were not trusted. Five Wounds replied that he did not mistrust settlers who had given their word, but he certainly did not trust the army. He also reminded his chief that dreams were omens. Looking Glass remained adamant. There would be no scouts. Five Wounds could not argue with his chief, saying only before he turned away, "Looking Glass, you are one of the chiefs. It is for you to make the decisions. I have no wife, no children to be placed in the danger I feel is coming to us. The gains or the losses will be yours."[18]

This decision by Looking Glass was but another of his many serious errors. His refusal to heed concerns of an experienced, competent warrior meant no rearguard scouts were deployed and, equally unpardonable, no sentries were posted. This decision, his second in severity, did more to doom the venture than any of the previous mishaps endured by the rebels. He was, however, not alone in his fallibility. Individual warriors had also informed White Bird, Joseph and Tool'hool'hool'zote that white men had been observed in the vicinity. All these chiefs believed the men to be settlers and dismissed the reports.

The one incident that would have derailed Gibbon in his tracks was a chance sighting of white men by two boys playing in the reeds along the river bank. During the afternoon of August 8, the two boys, one nine-year-old White Bird Jr.,[19] a nephew and namesake of Chief White Bird, saw two white men wearing grey blankets approaching. They hid in the reeds remaining very still. The men came by, looked around, paid particular attention to the teepee village, and then left, retracing their steps. When the two men were gone the boys ran to the village, but, perhaps afraid of being punished for being at the river, did not tell anyone what they had seen. Had either told his parents an alarm might have been sounded and Gibbon's approach could have been stopped.[20]

About the same time the boys in the reeds were watching the two white men, Gibbon and his 7th Infantry Regiment, numbering seventeen officers, 146 infantrymen (most mounted), plus some artillerymen lugging a howitzer,[21] were approaching a point five miles north the Big Hole River. The march was halted when scouts (either the men the hunters had seen or those the boys had seen) rode in to report the location of the Nez Perce camp. The men had also noted an absence of Indian scouts north of the river. This was good news to Gibbon. He had hoped to be afforded at least a modicum of surprise, so he stopped the march. His men could gain some much needed rest and the advance would resume at dusk.

When Gibbon and his army arrived at the Big Hole darkness had fallen. The horses, including those owned by the volunteers, were all tethered some distance away at a place now called Placer Creek. The horses were never committed to action except three horses utilized by Gibbon, his adjutant 2nd Lieutenant Charles A. Woodruff and an unidentified guide. All the horses became casualties when shot by a Nez Perce marksman during the ensuing siege. The final approach, made on foot, was difficult due to darkness and swampy ground, fallen trees and other hazards. It was made without detection and soon the troopers were on the river's north bank looking down on the quiet, unguarded village. They watched the shadows cast by the Nez Perces as they held their ceremonial night dance. Then the drums stopped, the dancers dispersed, the camp fell silent.

Gibbon, having no time to watch dancers, sat with his officers in his tent well back of the barriers. By the faint light of a candle he completed his final plans for the morning. He envisioned a two-pronged frontal attack, a maneuver that would surely catch the Indians as they slept. Just before dawn D and K companies would wade the river in order to be on the opposite shore when the bugle signaled the start of the assault. They would attack upon the first notes and the other companies would then cross the river in a second wave of attack. He felt assured of a quick, easy victory. With his strategy settled, he informed his officers of their roles in the order of battle and reminded them to tell their men to rest quietly through the night.

Under cover of darkness the troops moved silently to their assigned positions near the river below a sharply rising hillside directly opposite the tepee village. Separated only by the narrow bend in the river, they worked silently and hurriedly to dig sod which was piled up as barriers. Then they settled in for the rest of the night. There must be no fires, they were told, and absolutely no sound of any kind. Needless moving about would not be tolerated. Huddled as comfortably as possible behind the sod barriers they made the best of their cramped conditions. They could see eerie reflections dancing off the tepees' pale coverings caused by the flickering fires still aglow among the tepees clustered in a wide grouping. As the fires among the tepees turned to embers, gradually total darkness engulfed the area.

The disciplined regulars easily settled down to await the dawn, but the volunteers, many lamenting the prohibition of campfires, spent the cold night drinking whiskey to keep warm. The drinking was met with disapproval by a number of their fellow volunteers who complained to Bradley. However, he did not issue a "cease and desist" order and made no complaint to Gibbon,[22] who remained unaware of the drinking and was fortunate the group at least remained quiet and lit no fires. By dawn many were in varying degrees of drunkenness. From interviews given later by Nez Perce warriors it is clear the Natives were convinced many of the civilians were drunk when the attack began. Those interviewed felt the killing of women and children was mainly at the hands of these men. Most were convinced the wholesale killings were in retaliation for the deaths of Idaho settlers during the pillaging of ranches and farms by the young renegades lead by Red Mocassin Top, Shore Crossing and Swan Necklace.[23]

In the Indian camp, once the dance ritual ended, the people retired to their tepees and quiet descended. Obviously, most of the warriors—and all the chiefs—believed they were safe. It was this complacency that almost sounded the death knell of the Nez Perce revolt then and there.

It is unfortunate Five Wounds followed tribal protocol after he left Looking Glass. That protocol forbade him from seeking advice from either White Bird or Joseph, both of whom believed in dream-induced omens and would likely have been receptive to his warnings.

[CHAPTER 16 ENDNOTES]

1. Today "Fort Fizzle" is a tourist attraction. While the barrier no longer exists, its site is marked by a commemorative cairn and several signs. It is located about a mile north of hwy 12, some five miles west of hwy 93 south of Missoula, Montana. [Montana Road Map. Section D-2]

2. _*The Helena Independent*, July, 30 1877.

3. Gibbon had entertained a hunch that Joseph would go north to Canada so he marched on a line of interception. By the time he was informed the Indians had gone south from Stevensville he had to reroute. As a result he lost a day or two and did not arrive in Stevensville

until August 4. *[www.ourheritage.net/index_page_stuff/_ Following Trails/Chief Joseph]*

4   Although the Crows had already surrendered, their chiefs refused to sign a formal treaty until 1879. Washington seized on the delay to renege on the original agreement and without negotiations reduced the size of the reservation by considerable acreage. (See: *www.crownation. com*)

5   These same Crows scouted Gibbon's route during his tracking of the Nez Perces to the Big Hole, and after the battle ended and the Nez Perce had left, they exhumed bodies of the fallen from the shallow graves in order to take their scalps. [See: Appendix I.]

6   Referred to in some accounts as Ishkumsetauk (Place of ground squirrels). Nez Perce accounts use Eschuchilpan. [Author's note.]

7   No relation to Jerry Potts, horse trader and NWMP guide, who was famed in Montana as a very dangerous man and in southern Alberta as the bane of the Fort Benton whiskey runners. [Meyers, E.C., *Wild Canadian West*, 106–127.]

8   Born near Philadelphia, Pennsylvania, Gibbon grew up in Charleston, South Carolina. He graduated from West Point in 1847 and saw his first active service in the Seminole War (1849). He died in Baltimore, Maryland. [*The Harper Encyclopedia of Military Biography*, 280.]

9   In 1859 he wrote *The Artillerist's Manual*, which was received with high acclaim and widely used for many years. [*The Harper Encyclopedia of Military Biography*, 280.]

10 The Iron Brigade was composed of various units including the 2nd, 6th, and 7th Wisconsin Volunteers. It got its name, according to several sources, on August 28, 1862 (Gainesville) when, in a preliminary to the 2nd Battle of Bull Run, it held off a concerted attack of CSA

troops commanded by Stonewall Jackson. At the time, it was commanded by John Gibbon.

11 It was Gibbon's troopers who had found the bodies of Custer and his doomed comrades following the 1876 debacle at the Little Big Horn. [Ibid.]

12 Stories of the Nez Perce looting goods from McCain's barn were denied by McCain. The "goods," he said, was all equipment left over the years by Nez Perce trappers and hunters. He had simply returned to them what was theirs.

13 Source: *www.nezperce.com/html/looking glass.*

14 In some records this site is referred to as Iskum'tselalik Pah although the translation remains "Place of the buffalo calf." The difference may lie in differing dialects of various bands, but there does not appear to be a definite explanation. [Author's files.]

15 The Talking Stick, an ornately carved cedar branch (about a foot in length and four inches in width), was the Indian equivalent to *Robert's Rules of Parliamentary Procedure*. During council meetings it was passed from speaker to speaker serving as his authority to speak without interruption for as long as held the stick. There were strict rules of protocol where the Talking Stick was concerned. [Author's files.]

16 Charlo and his people were eventually forced onto a reservation. His and the other chiefs' signatures on the treaty are blatant forgeries.

17 Various letters in Montana Historical Society files all reflect the same sentiments.

18 Source cited from *www.nezperce.com*.

19 White Bird Jr. survived the war and eventually returned to Idaho. He related his adventures to McWhorter who

included them in several works. [McWhorter, *Hear me My Chiefs*, 375–79 & 419. Also, *Yellow Wolf*, 399–40.]

20 While there remains inconclusive proof of the validity of this incident, it was cited as being told by Yellow Bull to E. S. Curtis who published it in volume 8 of a 20-volume narrative. [Curtis, E.S., *The North American Indian*, Vol. 8, 167. These volumes were written between 1907 and 1930. Volume 8 was printed in 1911 by The Plimpton Press, Norwood, Mass.]

21 A short cannon with a small barrel, the Mountain Howitzer fired a 40-mm (1.75-in.) shell. (4th Artillery Regiment Records, U.S. Army archives, Washington, DC.)

22 Several volunteers deserted in disgust because of the drinking while others said later they had left because they felt the Nez Perce were right and should have been left alone. Accounts of the battle given later by Nez Perce warriors mention that many of the volunteers appeared to be drunk during the attack.

23 McWhorter, *Yellow Wolf*, 115.

Colonel John Gibbon. Defeated by the Nez Perce at the Battle at the Big Hole.

Colonel John Gibbon.

[Above] *General Oliver Otis Howard. Howard lost his right arm in the Civil War at the Battle of Seven Oaks.*

[Right] *Colonel Samuel D. Sturgis (1833-1889). Defeated and humiliated at the Battle of Canyon Creek.*

[Opposite] *Clark Expedition. The rifle is a .44 Henry Repeater and Alspotkit, though too old to ride with the warriors, undoubtedly used that rifle with good results in close-up fighting.*

[Above] *Chief Ollokot, brother of Chief Joseph. Ollokot was co-chief of the Wellamotkin Band.*

342

[Opposite] *In'who'lise (Broken Tooth), aka, Kot'Kot Hih'hi (White Feather).*

[Above] *General Nelson A. Miles (1839-1925). Defeated in two battles at the Bear Paw, he did accept Joseph's surrender five days later when the Nez Perces were no longer able to continue.*

[Left] *The Reverend Spalding was a tyrant who wanted to build an empire. He fled Idaho in fear of his life 1847.*

[Opposite] *Yellow Bull, Chief Joseph's trusted confidant and friend.*
Photo credit: Edward S. Curtis collection

[Below] *Unidentified warrior sits astride his war horse.*

[Above] *Chief Peopeo Thokelt [Bird Alighting]*
Photo credit: Edward S. Curtis collection

[Opposite, Top] *Nez Perce warrior.*
Photo credit: Edward S. Curtis collection

[Opposite, Bottom] *Unidentified Nez Perce war chief.*
Photo credit: Edward S. Curtis collection

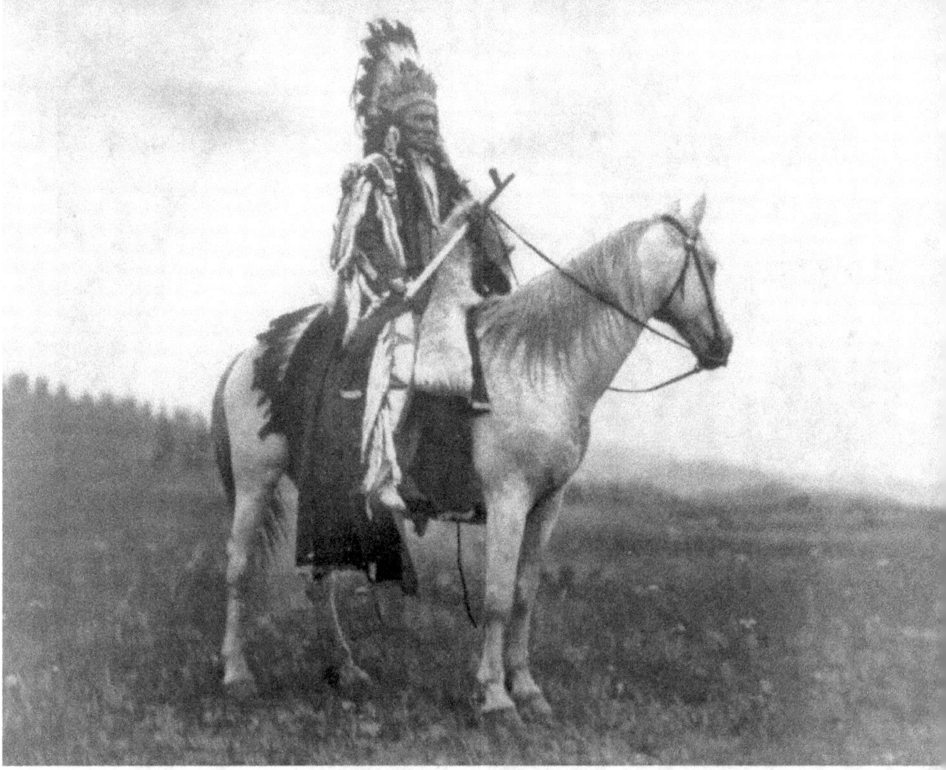

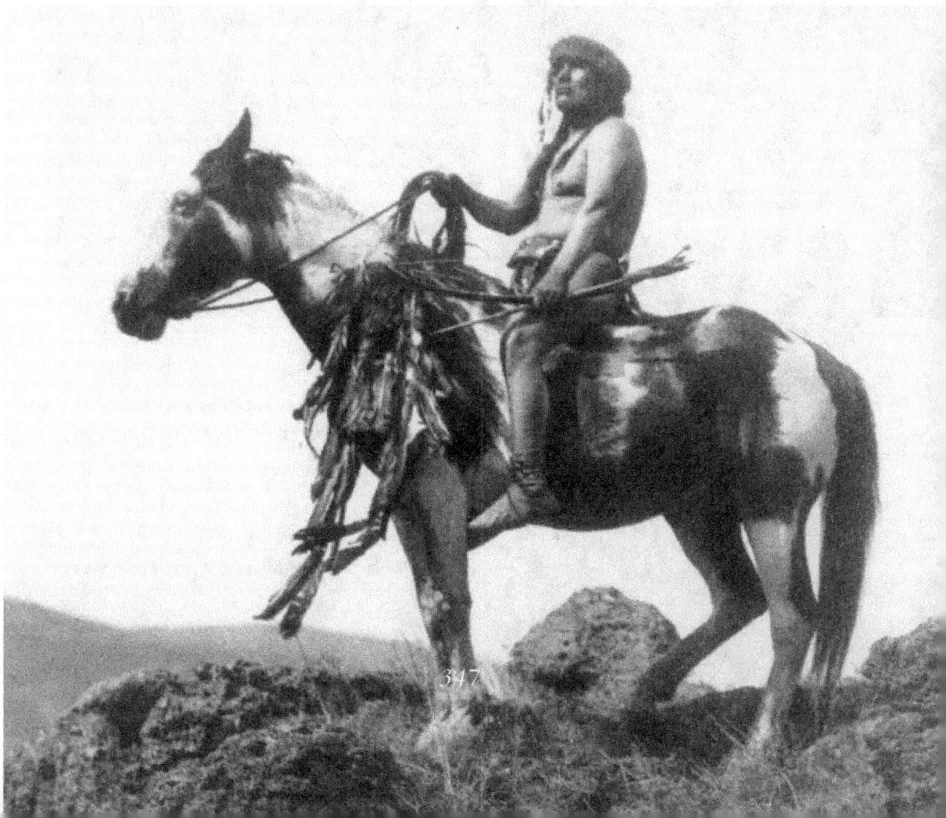

[Above] *Warrior with eagle feathers.*
Photo credit: Edward S. Curtis collection

[Left] *Chief Black Eagle.*
Photo credit: Edward S. Curtis collection

[Opposite] *Nez Perce night scout.*
Photo credit: Edward S. Curtis collection

[Above] *Waiting for the signal.*
Photo credit: Edward S. Curtis collection

[Opposite] *Chief Joseph c. 1911.*
Photo credit: Edward S. Curtis collection

[Above] *Chief Raven Blanket.*
Photo credit: Edward S. Curtis collection

[Opposite] *Chief Joseph, Nez Perce.*
Photo credit: Montana Historical Society, Helena.

[Above] *Peopeo Thokelt, c. 1910.*

[Opposite] *Two unidentified warriors in war regalia, c. 1885.*

[Above] *Steven Reuben, c. 1908.*

[Right] *Chief Looking Glass, 1871.*

[Opposite] *Kalkal'shuatash, Chief Timothy, 1868.*

[Above] *Left to right: Arthur Whiteman, unidentified warrior, Chief Joseph, Peopeo Tholekt. Photo taken at Colville WA in 1903.*

[Opposite] *Chief Peopeo Thokelt and his wife in 1900. Peopeo Thokelt was one of the most famous warriors in 1877. He was also the most wounded.*

[Above] *Patikhe' Ke'heci, 1908.*

[Opposite] *Chief Albert Waters, Joseph's successor in 1906.*

[Above] *Waaya'tonah Toesit'kahn (Blanket-in-the-Sun).
Became world champion rodeo rider in 1916 known as
Jackson Sundown. As an eleven year old in 1877, he was
Joseph's top horse drover.*

[Above] *Chief Lawyer (Alieya) prior to the signing of the 1866 treaty, c. 1865.*

[Above] *Nez Perce village, c. 1900.*

[Left] *Nez Perce children, 1903.*

[Opposite] *Unidentified warrior of the 1877 war. Photo c. 1912.*

[Above] *Chief Joseph with unidentified warriors at Colville, Washington, c. 1905.*

[Opposite] *Ahlakat, an 1877 warrior posed in 1907.*

Nez Perce warriors, c. 1895.

Bear Paw, Montana.

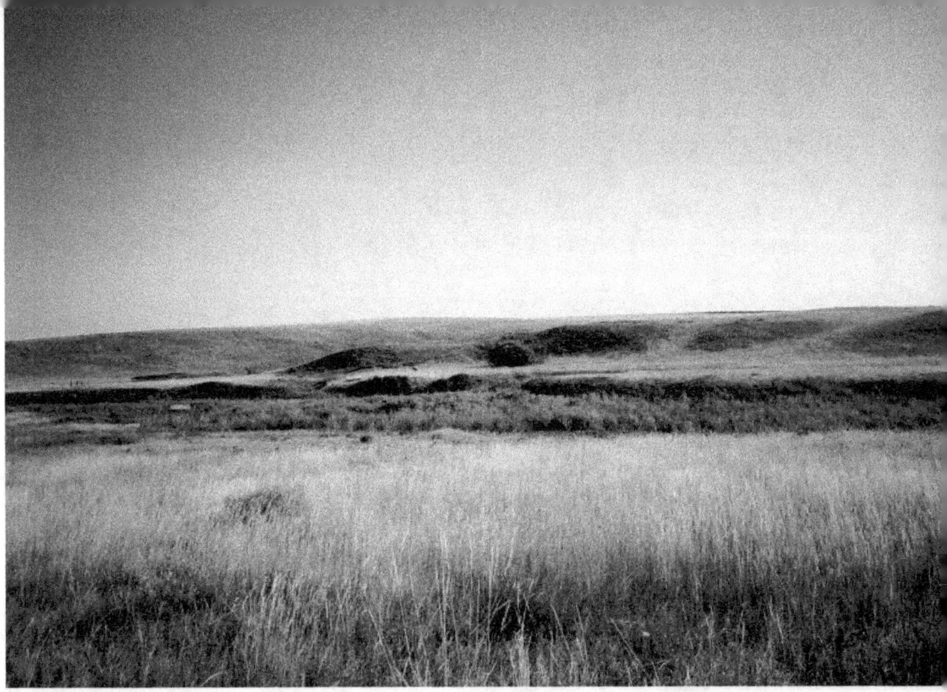

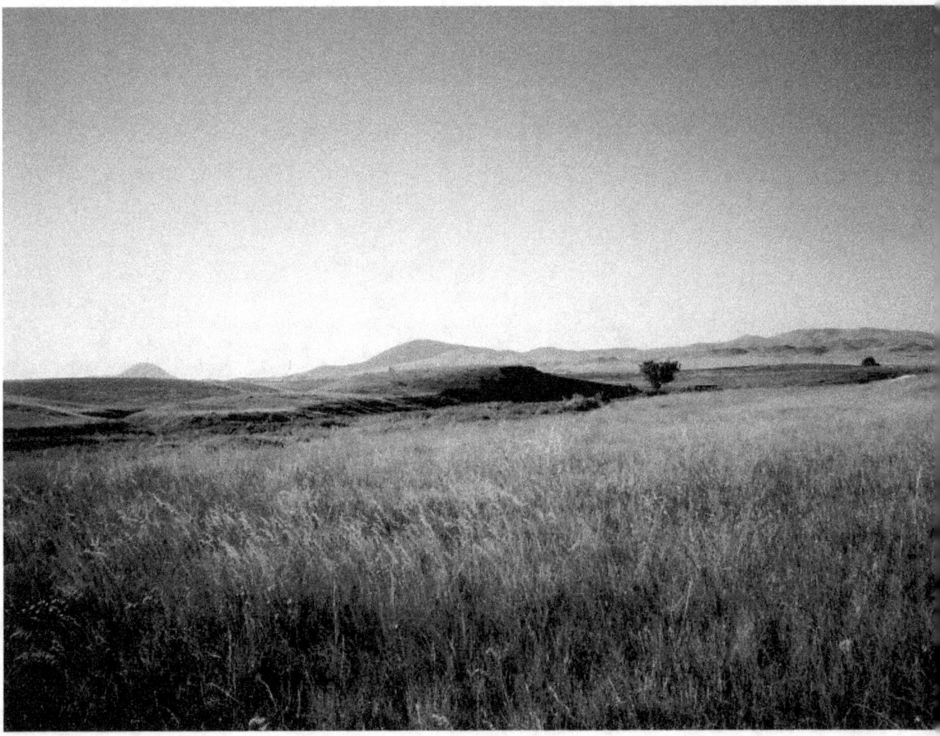

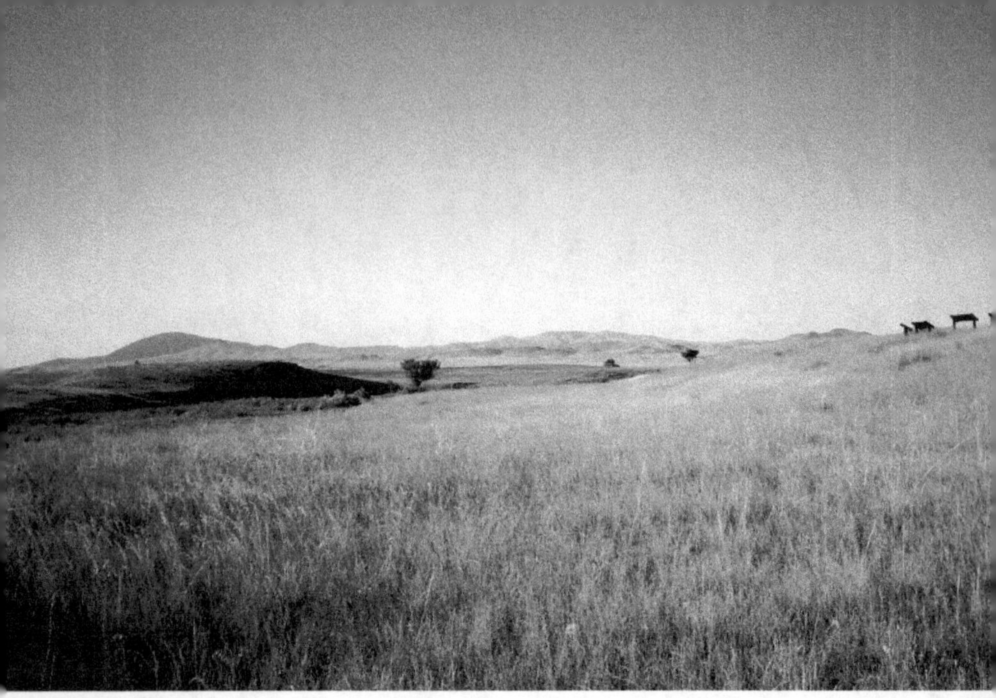

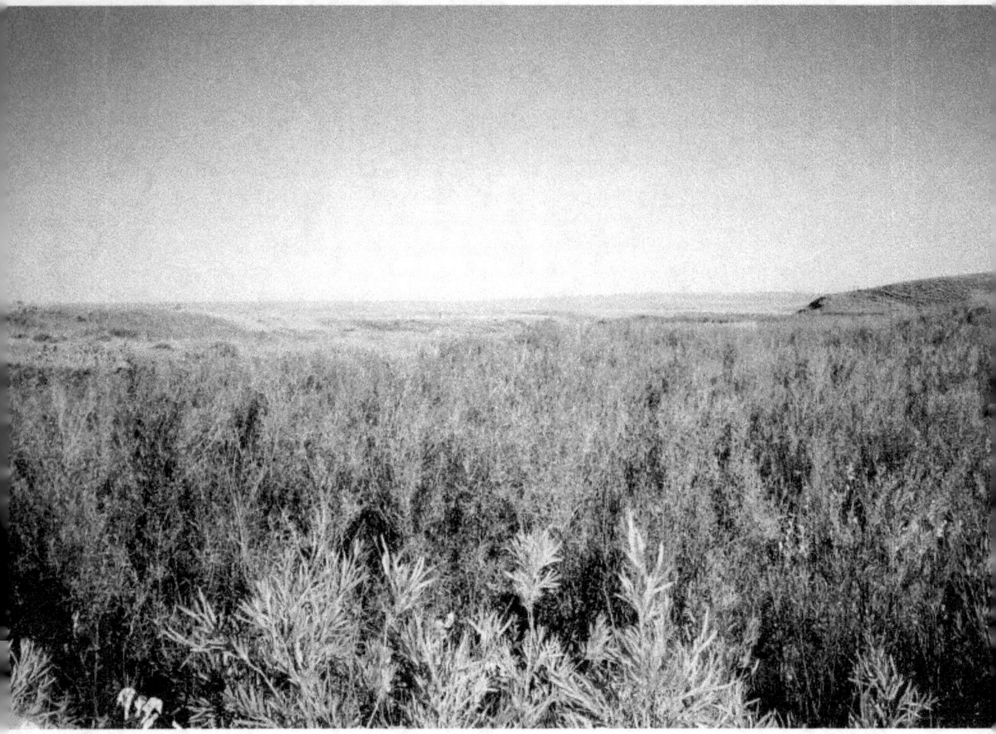

Bear Paw, Montana.

[Above] *Snake Creek.*

[Opposite, Top and Bottom]
Bear Paw. Warriors fought from this ridge. Rifle Pits.

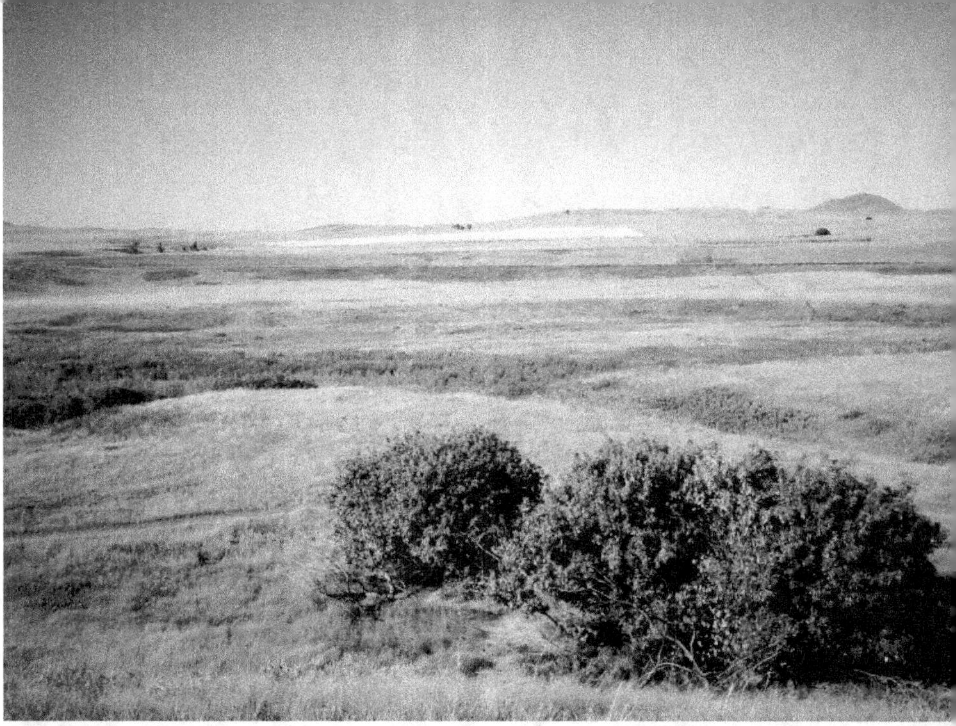

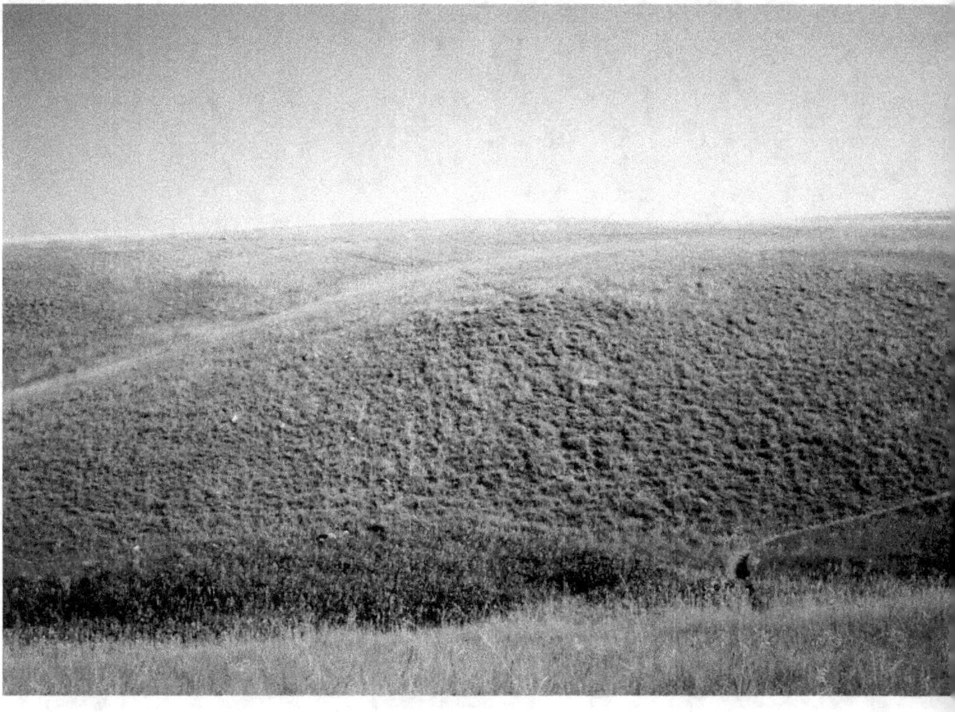

376

[Above] *Bear Paw. Soldiers' mass grave. Was later dug up and bodies were re-buried at the Military Cemetary at the Little Big Horn.*

[Opposite, Top] *Bear Paw. Gulley in which women and children were hidden. Shelter Pits.*

[Opposite, Bottom] *Bear Paw, Montana.*

[Above] *Bear Paw, Montana.*

[Opposite, Top and Bottom]
Big Hole battleground.

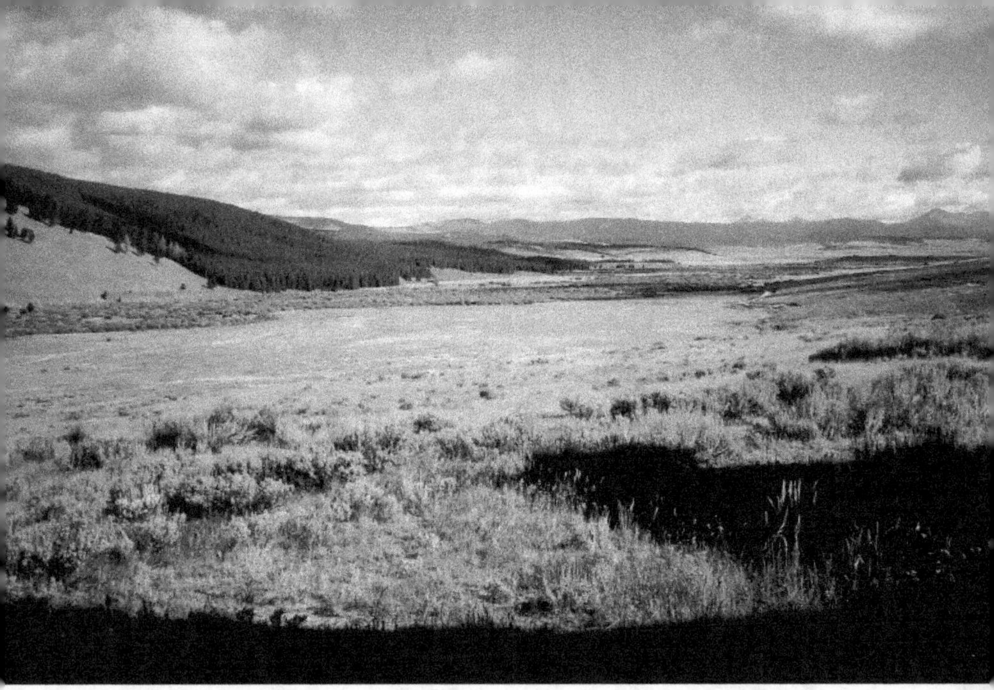

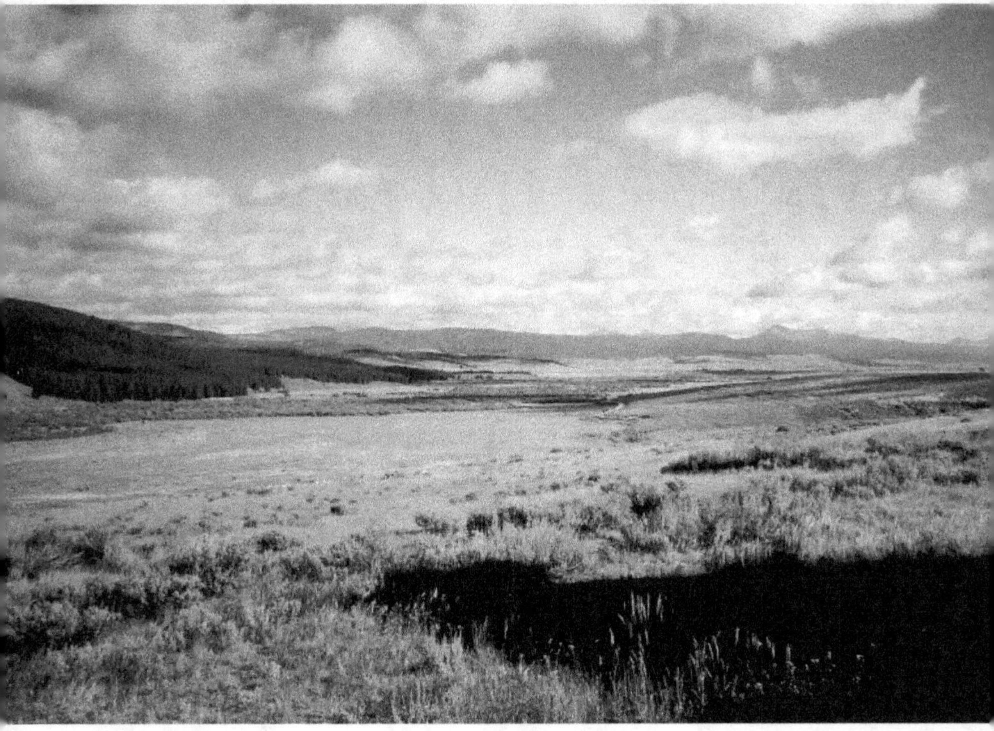

Big Hole battleground.

[no caption]

Big Hole battleground.

Big Hole Battlefield.

[CHAPTER 17]
DISASTER at ESCHUCHILPAN[1]

On August 9 at 4:00 AM in the silent half-darkness of early dawn, Captain James Sanno and Captain Richard Comba gave hand signals to their NCOs, who in turn relayed them to their troops. Quietly, silently, the men of D and K Companies waded into the cold water of the Big Hole River. Holding their rifles above their heads, they proceeded towards the tepee village lying quiet and darkened among the trees. At the same instance Lieutenant Bradley moved a few yards forward with B Company and his group of volunteers and dismounted cavalrymen. Companies F (Captain Constant Williams), G (Captain George L. Browning), and I (Captain Charles C. Rawn) formed into files. They would remain at full alert in their reserve positions. Captain Logan's A Company also in reserve, moved to bolster Rawn's right flank.

As the faint aura of daylight increased, Sanno stopped his troops as they reached the shore within yards of the village fringes. All was serene and quiet. Although drenched to their waists and shivering the men kept total silence as they reformed their lines in attack formation to await Comba's arrival. Luck had been with them, for they had not been seen. Sanno, surprised there were no guards, felt the endeavor was surely blessed.

Comba's company was still a few feet from shore when an

unexpected shot rang out breaking the dead silence. A sniper on the far bank had spotted an Indian leading a string of horses towards the river. With unerring aim he fired one shot and put an end to the possibility of total surprise. It is believed by some his victim was Hahtelekin, the aged and partly blind chief of the Palu, but other sources indicate the victim was a younger man, a warrior named either Wetistokaith or Wisookaankith.[2] According to Peopeo Tholekt, who spoke of the incident in 1928, Hahtelekin had been near the river at the time and had seen the soldiers on the opposite bank. He ran to the village, alerted those inside the nearest tepees and managed to arouse them. Wisookaankith, the other man mentioned, was on his way to tend to his horses when the sniper shot and killed him. Whichever account is true makes little difference as the shot put an end to Gibbon's hoped-for surprise.

The shot may have been mistaken for the order to open fire for it was quickly followed by Comba's men firing volleys into the tepees. Sanno immediately led his company in a headlong rush into the village. They were quickly followed by Comba and his troopers. At that moment the bugle, the intended signal, sounded—but the attack had already begun.

Captain Logan, realizing the element of surprise had been compromised, quickly led his men on the run through the tangle of brush and undergrowth to the river. They were followed from the far left flank by Bradley's assortment of volunteers and cavalry, no doubt all wishing they had their horses under them. Meanwhile, warriors and others, still half-asleep, confused and dazed by the unexpected attack, rushed from their tepees to begin returning fire.

Bradley did not get as far as the river when a bullet caught him. He fell, killed instantly, and immediately his command floundered. Uncertain of what to do next, the column inadvertently merged with A Company, an error that did not make the NCOs' tasks easier. The commingling instantly caused disarray, and to further complicate matters the civilian volunteers did not understand the hand signals. Bradley, a gifted young officer, was a loss sorely felt, particularly as the morning wore on, during the warriors' devastating counter attacks. Then his leadership qualities might possibly have made a difference.

Gibbon, who had been observing the advance from a hill, at first felt anger at the premature shot, but his wrath was assuaged by what appeared was going to be a quick, easy victory. Turning to Woodruff, he remarked the fighting would be over within the hour. His prophetic talents were quickly proven extremely circumscribed. Thirty-six hours later he and the remnants of his shattered command found themselves huddled behind barricades in complete disarray, no fight left in them and no means of escaping their confinement.

For the first twenty minutes of the initial attack the army did indeed hold the upper hand; and it was during this period in which the majority of Nez Perce casualties occurred. The soldiers seemed in such total control many thought the Indians had been whipped. They ceased shooting and set about the task of destroying the village. Some began running amongst the tepees intent on tearing them down while others attempted to set them ablaze, incendiary efforts that proved unsuccessful. Many of the hide coverings, sodden with heavy morning dew, did not ignite. Those that did flared briefly before turning from flame to smoulder.

Suddenly, to their complete surprise and total dismay, the rampaging soldiers were jolted into the realization they were nowhere near total victory. Despite the surprise and intensity of the initial attack, the warriors were neither in retreat nor about to surrender. What had seemed to the soldiers as being a full-fledged retreat had in fact been a withdrawal to areas where they rallied under their chiefs' directions. From those points they launched counterattacks from two points with a ferocity that quickly shattered Gibbon's plan of encircling the camp. Within minutes the only sector of the village under army control was the center. Now fully enabled, the Nez Perce sharpshooters concentrated their fire with the greatest effect. John Catlin, the leader of the civilian volunteers, later lamented so much valuable time had been lost trying to burn and destroy the tepees the Indians had gained the time needed to regroup. Regroup they had! Each chief had sprung quickly into action and the majority of warriors, having overcome the first reactions of unexpected awakening, became totally involved.

Joseph was one of the first to act. He wasted no time gathering up and leading women, children and elders from the village southward to a safe area. Through his superb leadership and the sheer courage from several elders and boys, the majority, despite the initial discouraging losses, were able to escape.

With Joseph busy in his endeavors, the warriors rallied around White Bird and Looking Glass. Others, mainly the Palu and their Cayuse allies, sought leadership from Tool'hool'hool'zote. He and his band had camped a short distance from the main camp. With his men and the Palu he hurriedly rushed to the village. They arrived within ten minutes of the first shots being fired. His was a well-organized force, battle-hardened from combat following the White Bird Canyon fighting and the two feverish days at the Clearwater. Taking up positions behind trees and bushes, they began laying down heavy fire. Because Tool'hool'hool'zote's sharpshooters had assembled at the west end of the village their accuracy caught the troops in a withering crossfire. Seeing the soldiers' confusion, White Bird called out orders that launched a massive counterattack. Vicious hand-to-hand fighting commenced.

Seeing his charges safe, Joseph left the elders to care for them while he and some older boys rushed back to the village to locate any who had become lost. The search, chaotic though it was and fraught with danger from errant bullets, encountered another danger. The horses, wild-eyed with fright at the pandemonium around them, were stampeding in panic, running in all directions. Some bowled over women and children who, having become separated from the main group, were lost in the woods and in reeds along the riverbank.[3] Joseph told some of his youthful helpers to calm the horses by herding them away. They did their task so well so that, once in calmer surroundings, the horses began herding together. The boys then drove them to safety.

Meanwhile, Joseph and others had rushed to the river where they rescued many more women and children who had sought refuge in the tall reeds. Hurrying here and there, they scooped small children from the river. Thrusting them into the arms of adults, they did their best to calm frantic mothers. Middle-aged men and young boys kept the group together until a semblance of order returned among them. Then Joseph moved them south towards the deep woods. That left only the horses to contend with. Determined the army would not capture the horses, he dispatched some of the boys to drive them further south.

Those warriors who had rallied around Looking Glass were concentrating their fire from the left of the camp's perimeter. He, it is reported, spurred his men to even greater effort when he singled out Red Moccasin Top, Swan Necklace and Shore Crossing, the three young hotheads responsible for instigating the uprising in the first place. It is said he soundly berated the trio with strong words.

> *"This is battle!"* he thundered. *"These men [the infantry] are not sleeping in their beds as were those you murdered in Idaho! Now it is time for you to show your courage and fight."*[4]

Nez Perce records attest that all three did show courage and fought bravely. Red Moccasin Top and Shore Crossing were killed in the fighting, but not before they had each taken down a number of soldiers. Fate dealt more kindly with Swan Necklace. He also fought in the subsequent battles, surrendered with Joseph at the Bear's Paw, survived the years of exile, returned eventually to Lapwai and lived into old age under an assumed name.[5]

Looking Glass and his warriors were soon joined by some older men and several women who had taken up rifles and rushed to assist. It was during this rush when Captain Logan was killed by a woman who ran from her tepee with her dead husband's rifle. Also among the fallen was I Company's Lieutenant William L. English, Rawn's second in command. Moments later Tool'hool'hool'zote directed his fighters to join those with Looking Glass. The warriors were more concentrated and better organized. Their bullets cut into the army ranks with devastating results. Still, the troopers held their ground another half hour before beginning to fall back.

This stand had been made possible by the quick action of the reserve units watching from the opposite side of the river. When the initial frontal attack faltered, Comba and Sanno were forced to order their troops to fall back. Rawn and Logan had then hurried their forces across the river in a counteraction. The added firepower was enough to keep the warriors from advancing against the faltering lines. Rawn and Logan had supplied enough reinforcement to stop the retreat and allowed the lines to steady. Finally, however, with their casualties beginning to mount, Sanno and Combo were forced to fall back further. As they began their cautious retreat, Rawn's I Company acted as rearguard while the remaining reserve companies, F and G came in. For two hours the battlefield remained in the tepee village.

The soldiers at the Big Hole were made of sterner stuff than those at White Bird Canyon. After two hours they were not yet vanquished. Eventually, however, the warriors' relentless attacks began to wear them down. Seeing their comrades falling around them, turmoil began spreading within the army ranks. Singly and in small groups they began abandoning their positions.

A group of warriors near the upper fringes of the camp had renewed hand-to-hand combat. One such encounter involved a volunteer and a warrior named Grizzly Bear Youth. The civilian was gaining the upper hand when another warrior fired a single shot, killing the civilian. However, the bullet passed through, hitting Grizzly Bear Youth in the upper arm. Despite his wound he fought on, survived the battle plus two others, surrendered with Joseph at Bear's Paw and lived into advanced years.

Gibbon's early elation turned to dismay as he watched his command in early retreat. His dismay became shock when he realized his men were being cut down in what appeared to be alarming numbers. Then, when they began to retreat, the colonel acted quickly to quell the withdrawal. He and his aide rode to the front where Gibbon rallied the troops by calling out, "Don't run men, or

I will stay right here and fight alone!" The retreat stopped and Gibbon launched the second assault. When that failed he led his men to a defensible point 800 yards from the tepee village.

This position, a fan shaped alluvial, had been created decades before by the wash from an ancient river or wide creek that had once cascaded down a hill situated slightly to the west. The soldiers quickly dug trenches and foxholes behind the natural barricades of rocks, trees and fallen timber. Though the retreat was made in orderly fashion it was not without casualties. Three groups of warriors inflicted heavy punishment on their adversary with their unerring aim and rapid fire. Gibbon was shot in the leg and his horse was killed. His adjutant was wounded when his horse was shot from under him.

At this time some of the warriors considered the battle over. They wanted to leave and join Joseph, who by now had proceeded a distance south with the non-combatants and the horses; however, White Bird and Ollokot managed to convince them to take up positions where they could continue their harassment of the troops. This they did and for the next twenty hours pinned the beleaguered troops down so tightly life was anything but pleasant.

Before Gibbon rode across to the river to rally his faltering troops he had ordered his howitzer brought into position atop a hillock a short distance away. He had hoped it would be an effective weapon but, being a matter of too little, too late, the cannon proved useless. The gun crew of five artillerymen did manage to fire two shells, neither of which had any effect, but they did not get the chance to fire a third shot. Chief Peopeo Tholekt had seen the crew manhandling the heavy gun into position. He led a small group of warriors to the gun,[6] where they circled to the rear, attacked and killed one gunner and wounded two others. The remaining two fled.

Knowing of a warrior in White Bird's band who was able to operate a howitzer, having gained that knowledge during a visit to a nearby fort, Peopeo Tholekt wanted to use it against the soldiers. The others, however, were interested only in retrieving the mules and ammunition wagon that had come with it. They took the mules and wagon and left Peopeo Tholekt with the gun. He tried to move it but it got stuck on a rock and could not be dislodged. So, to ensure the gun could not be reclaimed by the soldiers he tipped it over the embankment where it struck the rocks at the bottom, breaking the barrel loose from the framework. Just to be sure it could not be used again he also removed the breech mechanism lever, which he buried some distance away.[7]

During the final hour of the battle a number of boys, not knowing where to run, took up rifles. Some were too small to use a rifle so they contributed by reloading the warriors' weapons as they emptied. This ensured continuous fire from all points of the defense perimeter. Towards the final minutes, when the feeling of desperation and panic began to engulf the soldiers, several warriors realized the conduct of the battle was changing and took full advantage of the situation. They mounted horses and stormed from the woods in a three-pronged attack. Showing fearless disregard for their safety, with a blaze of gunfire and blood-curdling shouts they slammed into the rear ranks of the retreating soldiers. That ended the will to fight in what was left of Gibbon's shattered command. That single swift attack effectively ended the battle.

Now in full control of the field, the Nez Perce riders returned to the woods. One stayed a moment longer. Turning towards the soldiers he thrust a feathered lance into the ground with a shout of defiance. With a show of nonchalant indifference he returned to the shelter of the covering trees. The lance, the sign of victory, feathers gently fluttering in the slight breeze, remained there until after the warriors left the following morning. The Battle at the Big Hole was over.

During the two hours and thirty minutes of intense, brutal fighting the army managed two assaults before being forced to beat its final retreat leaving the field to the defenders. The soldiers and the twelve surviving members of the Bitterroot Volunteer Militia, fearful of an attack, bunkered down behind their barricades in the alluvial delta. For the remainder of the day and throughout the long, cold night, not daring to light small warming fires, they remained pinned down by Ollokot's sharpshooters. Unable to advance or retreat or even to safely raise their heads, they could not risk venturing to the river for water.

Gibbon also spent a very uncomfortable time. During the turmoil of retreat a Nez Perce rifleman had spotted him and, with a single shot, shattered the thighbone of the colonel's good leg. Gibbon collapsed with a shriek of pain. The sight of their commander on the ground had caused more panic within the ranks. As Gibbon writhed in the truly nauseous agony a shattered leg can cause, a lieutenant rushed forward and assumed command. Though lucky not to have died (the bullet had not pierced the femoral artery) Gibbon never regained full agility in the leg. As a parting insult he was renamed by the Nez Perce warriors. From that day forward he was referred to as "He-Who-Limps-Twice."

The survivors of Gibbon's badly mauled army spent the remainder of the day and all that night huddled behind their barricades in miserable anxiety, worrying what sunrise might bring. The wounded especially suffered, as there was no water to cleanse their wounds or to drink. There were no painkillers, and no expert medical help either, because Gibbon had not brought a medical team. Wounds, beyond the most rudimentary care, went untreated. Because heads had to be kept down, the soldiers could catch only quick glimpses of the women who had returned to see what they could salvage. Few tepees remained usable but those hides not beyond repair were packed for removal. Watching this final preparation of moving out was salt in the soldiers' wounds. Not only had the warriors whipped them, they were now going to escape once again. This was a bitter pill for Gibbon and his men to swallow.

The soldiers watched fearfully when a second group of warriors ventured onto the field. They watched them move among the dead and wounded. Because most were unaware that Nez Perce, unlike the Sioux, Crows and Cheyenne, did not take scalps they thought this was a scalping party. They were greatly relieved when it became obvious this was not a venture of retaliation. Working quickly and efficiently the warriors collected another fifty rifles,[8] many pistols and a number of cartridge belts, all the while reassuring the wounded no harm would befall them.

Soon more Nez Perce were seen in the woods. These had returned to find wounded family members and bury those who had died. Estimates vary but hardly a family did not lose one or more members.

As darkness descended, the women left with what they had saved. Ollokot and Tool'hool'hool'zote deployed men to keep the soldiers pinned behind the barricades to assure safe departure. Looking Glass, during a quick conference, advocated immediate departure. White Bird agreed, so warriors were assigned to Joseph as cover for the fleeing women and children.[9] Ollokot and his fifty men remained the remainder of the night, assailing the troops with accurate shooting. There was no need to ration their bullets for these were now an affordable luxury. They were, after all, using the army's rifles and ammunition.

If the soldiers thought they would receive some respite during the dark hours they were sorely disappointed. During that night Nez Perce snipers demonstrated their eyesight was almost as good in the dark as it was during the day. During the night some soldiers attempted to secure water from the river but, though they maintained utmost silence, one, a civilian volunteer, was killed. Ollokot's night operation, in reality merely a precaution to the retreating non-combatants, was thought by Gibbon a new tactic. It also served to keep Gibbon and his officers guessing, unable to determine how many warriors they were actually facing. As had Howard at the Clearwater, they also thought the Nez Perce force was many times larger than it really was.

When dawn broke over Gibbon's cold, thirsty, hungry soldiers, they realized escape from behind their barricades was now possible. They could leave and did so in orderly manner. They would have remained pinned down for another full day had Ollokot and his men not departed just before daybreak. They had left because word had been received from scouts that soldiers were approaching.[10]

Later that afternoon they rejoined the main band, which by then had covered quite some distance. Meanwhile the warriors had fully regrouped and the young men had recaptured nearly all the horses. The trek continued.

With the Indians now gone Gibbon was able to take stock. He was afraid his supply wagons and his horses had been plundered but this fear was mistaken. He sent a detachment of twenty-five men to retrieve them. The Indians had, however, captured two thousand rounds of ammunition from a wagon they had found. Gibbon's prized howitzer lay upside down on the rocks, a total wreck. The mules who pulled it were gone. Nonetheless, despite finding his supply wagons more or less intact, his force was in deplorable shape, worse than he had first thought. Twenty-two enlisted men and three officers, including Captain William Logan and Lieutenant James H. Bradley,[11] had been killed. Both young officers had been considered rising stars. Forty, including Gibbon and two of his lieutenants, had been wounded, two so seriously they died a day later. G Company alone had six dead and five wounded. In all, nine NCOs had died, with an equal number wounded. Among the eighteen Bitterroot Volunteers who had remained with Gibbon, six were dead and four lay wounded.

In all respects what should have been a brilliant victory had been a devastating defeat. As he viewed the ruination one wonders if perhaps he gave a thought to Abraham Lincoln who, thirteen years before, had said of General Ambrose Burnside, "Only Burnside could grasp Defeat from the jaws of Victory."[12] Gibbon didn't know it but he was soon to be considered by the nation's media a latter-day Burnside.

In excess of a third of the colonel's command was on the casualty lists. Some of the wounded who had been unable to make their way back to the barricades were in bad shape because of hypothermia. Chilled to the bone and in poor condition, they were treated and made as comfortable as possible. All his men were exhausted, thirsty and hungry. None had slept properly and there had been no sleep at all for those near the wounded. The hunger, thirst, cold, and the lack of medical attention, had denied them any rest. To add to the overall discomfort, the Natives had harassed them throughout the night; and the soldiers could not return fire as their supply of ammunition was so low it could not be wasted. The situation gave little hope to the bedraggled soldiers.[13] Worse, no relief was nearby and, despite his urgent messages, Gibbon knew replenishing supplies would take time to reach them.

As the morning progressed the surviving militia members decided to return to their homes. Gibbon let them go. He had enough worries without trying to hold back civilians. He was very concerned about what the press would say, and he had good reason for his concern. That bombshell would land on him three days later in large black headlines.

Aftermath

Although the Battle at Eschuchilpan is generally considered a victory for the Nez Perces, it was not. At best it could be considered a draw. It was the one single battle in which the Nez Perces suffered terrible losses, mostly among the women and children. The losses were estimated—but never confirmed—at between sixty and ninety. Many had gone missing. Among the missing whose identities are known are some whose fates were never verified. Many others have never been identified.[14] In contrast, the army losses, all confirmed, numbered fifty-nine. The civilian volunteers' casualties totaled an additional ten—56 percent, a high rate indeed.

Because the Nez Perce casualties remain incomplete and estimates vary so widely, the total could number up to 120. Nez Perce records indicate fifty-six dead and twenty-four wounded. That estimate s indicates a total of thirty-five men (including about fifteen warriors) were lost, the remainder being women and children. Most non-combatants died in the initial attack. These include Ollokot's wife and young daughter. Warrior casualties inflicted during the remaining ninety minutes of fighting were six confirmed dead and fourteen wounded. Among the known dead were three prominent warriors, Pahkatos (Five Wounds) who had prophesied the disaster, Chief Rainbow and Black Owl, a sharpshooter, all killed defending their positions. Others suffered wounds of varying severity. In all, known Nez Perce male casualties were twenty-three killed on the field with three dying of wounds a day or two later and fourteen wounded of which several were elders. Among the women ten are known dead and six wounded. Many however went missing and were never accounted for, while other non-combatants, all elders, were left on the trail in the days ahead.

It must be explained that no Nez Perce elder was ever forcibly abandoned. Nez Perce philosophy was such that a mortally wounded person, or one whose death from other causes was imminent, would voluntarily leave the group rather than hinder progress. This was common practice among many aboriginal societies, although some did apply enforced abandonment. No Nez Perce was ever callously abandoned. All who were left were given some form of shelter, water and food. Reports by army officers and civilian scouts in Howard's army tell of coming across lone elders encamped near the trail. Their reports all mention they were left unharmed to die in peace. One report, a narrative a civilian scout wrote, mentions a very old woman he discovered had asked him to shoot her to spare her further suffering. He refused as he could not bring himself to grant such a request. However, he wrote, he had not proceeded very far down the trail before he heard two shots. "It seems," he wrote, "one of my Bannock scouts had no compunction against acquiring an easy scalp."[15]

Using total casualties as a benchmark, Joseph lost more heavily than Gibbon. However, Nez Perce losses being mainly among non-combatants places warrior losses considerably less than those in Gibbon's force. His losses, excepting the civilians, were all professional soldiers, including three highly valued officers and no less than ten top-flight NCO's. In addition, because of the severity of their wounds, a further three officers and seven NCO's were rendered incapable of continued fighting. Technically speaking, if the benchmark is a ratio of fighting men, the outnumbered Nez Perce fighters had indeed defeated the army handily and had thereby won a military victory.

In addition, the ratio of material losses needs to be considered in evaluating victory vis-à-vis defeat. Many, nearly all, tepee coverings were damaged beyond salvage value, many cooking vessels were broken and some food supplies destroyed. Several horses among those recaptured were injured or in such poor condition as to be considered useless. They were turned loose to fend for themselves.[16]

The army's losses were also great. Dead were two cavalry horses. Several mules, a wagon and a vast quantity of rifle ammunition were missing. The cannon was destroyed (the Indians buried its shells which were never found). Soldiers, killed or wounded and left on the field, had been plundered of their rifles and ammunition belts and pouches. When material losses are factored into the benchmark the Nez Perces and the army stand about even. Also to be considered is the fact the Nez Perce losses were not replaceable, whereas the army's losses were.

On the other hand, Nez Perce morale never wavered to the same degree as the army's. The blow to army morale was not easily repaired. The army had once again been soundly whipped in combat and not a soldier among the survivors ever denied that. It is worth noting that Gibbon himself gave tribute, however grudging it may have been, to the warriors when he acknowledged Nez Perce marksmen were far superior to any of his. Gibbon said his troopers had been,

"totally out-classed. Almost every time one of their rifles went off one of our party was sure to fall."[17]

In overall terms, Joseph and his allies may have won the battle but, as was the victory at White Bird Canyon, it was a pyrrhic victory. Further, it was an omen of what would be the final conclusion to the long trail that would end at the Bear's Paw. The final outcome was predicted at Eschuchilpan.

When news of the battle was made public, Montana newspapers, still grumbling over the debacle at Fort Fizzle, continued their ridicule of the army in deadly earnest. Banner headlines, which were quickly picked up by eastern papers, fairly shouted the bad news. In its August 12 edition the vociferation of Helena's *Daily Independent* came in giant, black, print:

BIG HOLE BATTLE
Gibbon Makes A Desperate Fight And Is Overpowered

HELP! HELP! Send Us All The Relief You Can
We Are Cut Off From Supplies

It was at this point that editorial writers, needing a prime figure to capitalize upon, anointed Chief Joseph as overall warrior chief.[18] As they composed their lurid accounts of the battle, brandishing quotes from Gibbon's desperate messages to headquarters as if wielding a club, their critical and stinging prose questioned the tactical abilities of both Howard and Gibbon. They commented on the radical strategies being employed by Joseph as they informed their readers the Nez Perce warriors numbered less than 200, then adding the scathing fact that Joseph's progress was encumbered by upwards of 600 women, children and old people. Gibbon joined Howard in getting no easy ride from the press.

Fortunately, the army was temporarily spared an even further embarrassment which the media, had it been informed, would have gleefully reported. The highly critical *Independent* had not yet learned the reason why Gibbon was without supplies. The editor would have ripped him mercilessly had he known that Joseph not only captured guns and ammunition, he had also taken several mules. And the howitzer was never mentioned.

In time, Colonel Gibbon lived down the defeat, but not without undergoing the usual board of enquiry held to look into such matters. He also endured criticism from the public, for by now many in white society were beginning to side with Joseph and his followers. The principal question to emerge was why so many women and children had been killed.

The board of enquiry, unlike the press, did not question why mounted soldiers had not been used. It had no quarrel with the tactics Gibbon used at the onset of the attack. The board members demanded to know why so many of the victims were women and small children. They wondered why, despite orders from their officers not to target women and children, some soldiers seemingly did not obey the orders. Why did some choose targets randomly, not caring who they had in their sights? Some privates and volunteers called as witnesses said Gibbon's words countermanded the officers' admonition against shooting non-combatants. Others, such as Sergeant Loyne, steadfastly insisted there had been no orders that prisoners were not to be taken. One of the volunteers, Tom Sherrill, recalled no orders concerning prisoners were ever issued. Sherrill said he had asked the volunteer commander, John B. Catlin, about it and Catlin had asked Gibbon. The reply, according to Sherrill was, "We don't want any prisoners."[19] As well, many in the command insisted he had clearly given a "no prisoners be taken" order in his *verbal* instructions to the troops prior to the battle. While the official enquiry declined to find Gibbon accountable, the unofficial court of public opinion took a somewhat different view.

The army's defenders had their own explanation and countered by stating soldiers shot only women and older children who had attacked them with guns, hatchets and knives. While there was a modicum of truth in this claim, the number of casualties among the non-combatants was disproportionate to the witnessed instances of such attacks. Gibbon, not altogether convincingly, defended himself by insisting he had not meant his statement to sound the way some had interpreted it. He was backed by surviving officers who had given orders against random killing. The army chose to agree his words had been misunderstood and he was not to be blamed for the misunderstanding. Nonetheless, it was never proven exactly what he had meant. The wording can be considered ambiguous.

"The Indians," he had told his men, "will fight fiercely and *I do not expect that any prisoners will be taken*."[20] [italics added]

Had Gibbon issued a "no prisoners" edict? Or was he stating a belief the Indians would never surrender but would fight to the last breath? Such edicts—and misinterpretations—were all too common during the so-called Indian Wars.

Meanwhile, as the battle had raged, Howard, having lumbered slowly northeasterly along the Lolo Trail, had finally crossed into Montana. He was distressed at the news of the rout at the Big Hole; and he was even more appalled when he read the casualty list. His anguish increased when he learned of the loss of the rifles and mules. The general was a deeply troubled man. He immediately set out on a forced march. He was still well behind his quarry and now the entire mission appeared to be on the verge of collapse.

[CHAPTER 17 ENDNOTES]

1 Official US Army documents refer to this battle as The Battle at Big Hole.

2 There is some controversy about who was shot by the sniper. Greene and others claim it was Hahtalekin, chief of the Palu. Chief Peopeo Tholekt [Bird Alighting] told McWhorter in July 1928 that it was a man named Wetistokaith who was killed by the sniper and that Hahtalekin died later during the battle. A warrior named

Wisookaankith is listed in the files of those killed. Similarity in the names indicates the same man. Either Bird Alighting's memory in 1928 was faulty or Mr. Greene's sources are incorrect. It should be remembered that Bird Alighting was at the battle while Greene's sources were not. [Author's files.]

3. Joseph's daughter was among those who became lost. She was eventually found, made her way to Canada with White Bird then later returned to Lapwai. Many children went missing or were killed.

4. There are others who credit the tirade to both White Bird and an unnamed warrior. Looking Glass, however, is the one most likely to have said it. [MacDonald, Duncan, *Nez Perces*, 260.]

5. See: Appendix H.

6. Old Yellow Wolf, Weyatan'atoo Latpat (Sun Tied), Pitpill'ooheen (Leg's calf), Ketalk'poosmin (Stripes Turned Down) and Temet'tiki were the others in the party. [*Nez Perce Summer 1877*, page 136.]

7. A replica of the howitzer is on display in the main building of the Big Hole Memorial Center that overlooks the battlefield.

8. See *www.nezperce.com* a particularly good source of the history of the Nez Perce with excellent coverage of the 1877 Nez Perce War. Also, *The Official History of the First Cavalry, 1877*.

9. For an excellent description of this battle see, *Yellow Wolf: his own story*. McWhorter, Lucullus V. (Caldwell, Idaho, 1940).

10. This group was a patrol from Fort Smith. By the time it arrived it was too late to be of any help to Gibbon, and Ollokot's warriors had already departed.

11. Bradley had been the first soldier on the scene after the

Battle of the Little Big Horn and had discovered Custer's body.

12 General Ambrose Burnside was the recipient of Abraham Lincoln's wrath following the Battle of the Crater (July 20, 1864) during the Civil War. This was a battle that, for all intents and purposes, had already been won, a certain victory for the Union, until Burnside blundered his incompetent way to a crushing defeat. Upon hearing the news Lincoln is reported to have remarked, "Only Burnside could grasp Defeat from the jaws of Victory." [Credited to Lincoln, but possibly apocryphal.]

13 See: Woodruff, *Battle of the Big Hole*, 111.

14 Three of the casualties were from Grey Eagle's family. Grey Eagle died on the trail the following day from wounds. His fifteen-year-old daughter, called Lucy, died in the first assault. Grey Eagle's eldest daughter, Peopeo_Hih'hi_[White Feather]—today more widely known as In'who'lise [Broken Tooth]—was wounded but escaped with the others. At Bear's Paw she was separated from her friends and escaped with White Bird intending to go to Canada. Several of the missing later showed up and were returned to Lapwai. One of the missing whose fate remains unknown was Grey Eagle's wife, called Mary. She is thought to have ventured away on her own to find refuge with an Indian band. There is some thought she might have eventually made her way back to Lapwai but this is not verifiable. [Garcia, *Tough Trip Through Paradise,* 218–6; 234–61; 406–9. Also, Appendix H].

15 Reddington, J.W., *Scouting in Montana*. [Montana Historical Society manuscript archives.]

16 Nez Perces did not kill incapacitated horses. They set them free to survive on their own and some invariably found a herd of wild mustangs. However, if hostile Indians were in the area they would cut a tendon in

one front leg. This rendered the horse useless for work or riding but allowed the animal to live in the wilds. [Author's files.]

17 *History of the First Cavalry Division.*

18 It is likely the editors singled out Joseph because he was known to the public through his previous well-publicized efforts to gain some justice for the non-Treaty Nez Perce bands. He was a ready-made model for the press. Looking Glass and White Bird were not well known to the general public. Tool'hool'hool'zote, where he was known, was disliked by nearly everyone. [Author's note.]

19 Cave, William, *Battle of the Big Hole*, 15.

20 Woodruff, *Battle of the Big Hole*, 114

[CHAPTER 18]

THE BATTLE at CAMUS MEADOWS

ESCAPE FROM ESCHUCHILPAN

Upon departing the Big Hold River area, the survivors of the latest battle still could have turned north to Canada. The distance to the border, though still days away, could have been covered in fifteen had haste been made. No army food rations had been captured from Gibbon, but other rations plundered along the way were still plentiful enough to ensure the journey could be made if austere rationing was imposed. Hunters could be depended upon to augment existing supplies with buffalo (of which there were still reasonable herds). Gibbon's army, in no condition to give chase, was no longer even a minor threat. The Bitterroot Volunteers, sadder but wiser for their ordeal, harbored no desire for a second encounter and had already dispersed to their homes. Scouts with information of Howard's traversal of the Lolo Trail had arrived so the chiefs now knew Howard had reached Stevensville. To Looking Glass and the others that meant he was still several days distant; in fact, he was now but a day behind. Still, by angling northeast for two days and then turning due north they could have easily skirted his army.[1]

However, the Nez Perce chiefs were still unaware of Howard's forced march approach and none knew of General Miles, the commanding officer at Fort Keogh[2] who would soon become their main threat, or that he had received orders to prepare for entry into the hunt. Miles, still at less than full strength and not fully supplied, was in no way ready to leave Fort Keogh. Therefore, had the Nez Perces turned north immediately following the battle at the Big Hole, he would not have been able to intercept them. Even had a northward march forced Miles out within a week he still might not have had enough time for interception. The Nez Perces would by then in all likelihood have been close enough to the border to cross in safety. Had Miles located the Nez Perce warriors he very probably would have met the same fate as Gibbon. Miles had no need to hurry. He would not leave Fort Keogh until September 18, still a month away.

Nelson Appleton "Old Bear Coat" Miles (1839–1925) was a career soldier. Born in Westminster, Massachusetts, he moved to Boston at age eighteen to complete his education, and while there he raised enough money to form a volunteer militia group in time for the Civil War outbreak in 1861. His group joined the 22nd Massachusetts in which he was appointed a lieutenant. Ha was assigned as an aide de camp to General O.O. Howard, was promoted to Lieutenant Colonel at Fair Oaks for bravery, won promotion to colonel at Antietam, and at Chancellorsville was promoted to brigadier general where he also was awarded the Congressional Medal of Honor. His Civil War record was outstanding, but it was marred by his treatment of the captive ex-president of the CSA, Jefferson Davis, who he kept shackled in a dank cell when Davis was sent to Fort Monroe where Miles was the commanding officer.

When the war ended he remained in the army as a colonel. Sent west, he fought in the wars against the Plains Indians, defeated Chief Crazy Horse and was instrumental in subduing the Sioux in Montana Territory. He gained the nickname from the press who found him difficult to deal with. They began referring to him as "Old Bear Coat" for the fur-lined coat he wore during the winter. It was a heavy coat he had tailored from the hide of a grizzly bear.[3]

Not far south of the Big Hole, Joseph's group quickly regrouped with the warriors to resume the march south. In sorrow and despair, mourning their dead and missing, they trudged southward. They had not gone far before scouts reported Howard's troops, having departed Stevensville under forced march, were now within two days of contact. The news came as a total surprise to the chiefs, particularly Looking Glass who had not anticipated such a change in the situation. Joseph and his fellow chiefs were undecided how to cope. They briefly considered the eastern trails that would take them to the Dakotas, but Looking Glass reassured them the Crows, their friends and allies, would welcome them and give aid in their quest for freedom.

Always the cynic, White Bird raised a voice to the validity of the promises, but once again the chiefs listened to Looking Glass who stood unwavering in his belief. Indeed, the Asotin chief was so absolutely convinced they would be given sanctuary he volunteered to journey ahead to seek out the Crow chiefs and make the arrangements. His offer was approved, so Looking Glass chose three of his top warriors, laid plans to depart and said they would leave as soon as Crow country was within riding distance.[4] Placing their immediate future in his assurances, they opted to continue to Absaroke territory. They were yet to learn the Crows had signed treaties and were cooperating with the army.[5] Meanwhile however there was still a distance to travel.

When Howard arrived at Stevensville on August 8 he received reports Joseph and his people were camping at the Big Hole River. Putting his faith in Gibbon, who was within a day of overtaking the

Indians, he decided to stay in bivouac to rest his tired men. With all confidence he awaited word of Gibbon's anticipated victory. In the afternoon of August 10 he was informed of Gibbon's devastating defeat. He immediately ordered his troops to decamp and, after a forced march south, arrived at the Big Hole River on August 12. He stayed two days while his troops assisted in burying the dead and he arranged for transportation of the wounded, among them Colonel Gibbon, to Deer Lodge for hospital treatment.[6] On August 14 he proceeded south, taking with him fifty of Gibbon's men (Capain. George L. Browning, commanding).

The Nez Perces, though looking Glass was still in overall command, were now being guided by Lean Elk. They continued southwesterly under greater distress than any had anticipated. The soldiers in their short rampage of burning and demolition had destroyed cooking utensils, food, and burned or damaged a number of tepees and their contents. Though some tepee coverings had been retrieved, many had holes and rips severe enough to allow rain and wind to enter. Damage to most coverings was such that only superficial repairs could be managed. Everything deemed beyond repair had been left behind.[7]

The trail from Weippe had been one of optimism and anticipation. At the Big Hole River it became a trail of heartbreak and hardship, and it was soon to merge with the trail of sorrow.

Under Lean Elk's expert guidance the group began once more to make excellent time. Although the hierarchy of command remained as usual, Lean Elk had the confidence of the people. According to Wottolen, the old warrior who related this part of the journey to various interviewers between the years 1926 to 1935, Lean Elk had the group up before first light. No longer hindered by Looking Glass' previous insistence of bringing the encumbering lodge poles each day they were on the move by sunrise. He kept them moving until about 10:00 AM and then stopped for a few hours during which time cooking was done and horses were allowed to graze unhindered in grassy fields. About 2:00 PM the trek resumed without stops until just before sunset. Under Lean Elk's regimentation an average distance upwards of twenty-five miles per day was maintained.[8] During this period discipline was upheld to a high degree among the non-combatants, but not so much among some young warriors. Whereas among the older warriors Ollokot, White Bird and Tool'hool'hool'zote gained in stature Looking Glass was beginning to lose influence, particularly with his own young warriors.

The Horse Prairie Raid

On August 12, now two days away from the Big Hole, the refugees reached Horse Prairie, an area near Horse Prairie Creek. That evening a group of young warriors, mostly Asotins, defied Looking Glass' direct orders not to leave the encampment. In what was obviously a rage-induced retaliation against the attack at the Big Hole, they rode out and went on a rampage in which they killed five farmers, ransacked their houses and stole their horses. All the chiefs were furious at the senseless act that did nothing to improve the Nez Perce cause. The killing of settlers greatly angered the entire group and also caused a weakening of endorsement among an increasing number of Whites who had begun to voice support for Joseph and his people.

The renegades first attacked the nearby Montague-Winters Ranch. Fortunately, when it had become clear the Nez Perces were heading in their direction, the women and children who resided there had been evacuated to Bannack City. The renegades killed W.L. Montague, Thomas Flynn, James Farnsworth and James Smith. Daniel Winters and two others escaped, fleeing to Bannack City where they sounded the alarm. The renegades ransacked the houses before leaving the ranch with many horses. A few miles further along they attacked another farm, killing one of the four men who were there before leaving with several more horses. Overall, the renegades netted close to forty horses. On their way back to their camp they came across a deserted ranch, property of John and Thomas Paine, and destroyed its house and out buildings. All six who had escaped arrived safely in Bannack.

On August 13, Lean Elk's trail experience came to the fore when the Indians departed Horse Prairie. He led the group across the Continental Divide through Bannock Pass and reentered Idaho not far from the Lemhi Reservation, passing along the Lemhi River.

Settlers in the Lemhi Valley, aware the Nez Perce were approaching, hastily erected palisade forts, but Joseph met with them near Timber Creek and assured the frightened settlers no harm would come to them. Being aware their age-long adversaries, the Lemhi Shoshones, were not in the least receptive to their presence, the Nez Perce chief, possibly to show his contempt, had his people pause for a rest of several hours before moving eastward to a canyon where they stayed the night. Joseph was, however, careful to assure safety, having rifle pits dug in a defensive pattern. Later that evening a small party of Nez Perce warriors rode out and killed some of the Lemhi's cattle, which they butchered for food. The next morning, having had neither attack nor contact with their unwilling hosts, the group moved on along the Lemhi Valley towards Birch Creek.

The Birch Creek Affair

On Wednesday, August 15, a large group of warriors attacked a six-unit mule train freighting goods to the Idaho towns of Salmon City and Leesburg. After subduing the teamsters, the warriors ate the remainder of the men's' supper and then pillaged the wagons of their cargos of tinned goods and general merchandise (which included some whiskey). Some drank a portion of the whiskey after which they burned the wagons and the material they did not want. Two

Chinese cooks who had been with the train were spared. They later said about the raid,

> "We camped for dinner on Birch Creek, had finished dinner and were lying under the wagons when we heard the clatter of horses' hooves. [We saw armed Indians all mounted galloping towards us]. The men [the mule skinners] all started for the wagons to get their guns but...[the Indians leveled their rifles and demand surrender which they did]. I counted them and there were fifty-six of them...The Indians after eating [the remainder of the prepared meal] made us hitch up the teams and drive them to their camp about a mile away, where they made us go into camp. The men started with some Indians to drive the animals out to feed. I never saw any of them again. The other Indians broke open the wagons and helped themselves to goods. The Indians said they were Nez Perces and belonged to Joseph's band."[9]

Whether the two cooks were let go or escaped is unclear, but during the night they made their way to Junction City where they told their story.

The next night (August 16) the Lemhi Chief Tendoy and some of his braves, having tracked all day, located the Nez Perce camp. They did not attack, choosing instead to wait until night. Taking advantage of darkness they made off with seventy-five horses, forty of which had been the plunder from the Horse Prairie ranch.

The following day a party led by Colonel George L. Shoup of the Idaho Volunteers arrived at the site of the mule train wreckage where they found five dead teamsters and buried them. They had all been shot.

When the Nez Perces left the canyon the morning of August 16, Lean Elk returned to an easterly direction. Lean Elk guided the group through forests and when they reappeared on the 17th it was at a point sixty miles south of Virginia City, well away from the Virginia City volunteers who had been searching for them.

The disappearance bothered Howard, but he was convinced

the Indians would reappear on Camus Meadows where he would be in good position to corner them. It may have wishful thinking on his part, but as events transpired he was partly correct. On the evening of August 18, Howard, who had actually been ahead of the Indians a day or two previously, received word the Nez Perces were nearing Camus Meadows. The distance between the two now was less than eighteen miles. Howard, upon advice from his officers, agreed the cavalry horses were too tired to endure a night march. He decided to camp for the night.

The following morning the army resumed the march and soon found the trail the Indians had taken.[10] It was easy to follow and along the way fresh graves were discovered, which the soldiers determined were more of those who had been wounded at the Big Hole. During that day Howard was joined by several fresh cavalry companies, so by nightfall his force had increased to more than 260 men. Among the newly arrived was a militia group, the Montana Volunteers and some Bannock scouts. Throughout the day the soldiers could see the dust columns the Indians caused as they progressed. From time to time they also saw Nez Perce scouts in the distance, whom Howard thought were keeping tabs on his troop's progress. More likely they were determining the number of new troops and the positions being assigned the various units. It was information White Bird and Looking Glass needed for what they were planning for Howard that night.

On August 15, Tool'hool'hool'zote and White Bird were forewarned of Howard's approach by two scouts named Gosawyiennight [Bull Bait] and Lakochet Kunnin [Rattle Blanket]. They had been shadowing Howard's troops and experience told them that if he stayed with the route he was on, it would lead him directly to Camus Meadows. This would intersect the new route Lean Elk was taking. The two scouts located White Bird and told him their news. Intent on holding Howard's pace to a minimum, White Bird sought out Tool'hool'hool'zote and launched a series of rapid attacks by mounted warriors. In this the attacks were successful in catching Howard's troops by surprise and achieved their first goal: Howard's progress slowed. Following the attacks, and never knowing when or from where the next would come, the soldiers were not having an easy time. White Bird and his warriors gave them little respite and the narrow trail forced the soldiers to proceed in long columns. This was not conducive to defense but perfectly adapted for hit and run tactics. The almost daily attacks ended the day before Howard reached Camus Meadow on August 19.

There, Howard felt compelled to rest his tired men as well as his horses. That was what White Bird had wanted. He and Looking Glass hatched a plan, and that night warriors launched a major raid on Howard's campsite.

The Raid at Kamisnim Takin[11]

As darkness began to fall, the general called a halt; the pack mules and the bell mares[12] were hobbled and left to graze in a grassy field. For the first time in weeks the weary soldiers and their officers enjoyed a hot supper. They then settled in for what they anticipated would be a restful night. After all, they told each other, Joseph and his Indians were on the run and not in any position to cause trouble. Some decided to sleep under the wagons while others chose to pitch their shelter tents. Many were so confident of a good night's sleep they shed their dusty uniforms before going to bed.

That night clouds guaranteed enough darkness for a peaceful sleep, and though an occasional light rain fell, it was not enough to awaken anyone. The horses and mules remained quiet and the soldiers slept soundly. But not far away all was not still; three groups of Nez Perce raiders were riding quietly towards the slumbering camp. Among the riders were Chiefs Ollokot, Looking Glass and Tool'hool'hool'zote. The principal warriors were Teeweeyownah [Over the Point], Too Moon and Espowyes [Light in the Mountain]. Several sources indicate Joseph was also there, but this is not true.[13]

At about 2:00 AM one group of three men slipped quietly away and rode ahead in order to arrive at the camp before the others. At 3:30, when the night was at its darkest, the other two groups approached from the north. As they neared the picket line a sentry, perhaps thinking Lieutenant George R. Bacon was returning from Tacher's Pass from an assignment[14] with his forty-man unit, called the normal challenge. The riders did not reply, but drew closer. Suddenly a shot rang out and immediately the riders surged forward at full gallop. With rifles blazing they bowled over the sentry and crashed into the sleeping camp. Captain Randolph Norwood, commanding officer of the 2nd Cavalry's L Company, described afterwards the startling impact the shots had upon the camp, "[the camp] was startled and hurriedly aroused by a volley or heavy discharge of fire arms and loud yelling and whooping from the hostile Indians."[15]

While some warriors, firing randomly, galloped between the tents and wagons, then through the volunteers' area, others scattered the mules and horses. The animals—all of which had been unhobbled previously by the trio of warriors, Peopeo Tholekt, Chapowits [Plenty Coyotes] and Chtwiweyunaw [no translation available], who had earlier snuck into the camp—stampeded into the night. Those warriors then turned to the cavalry horses in an attempt to drive them away as well.

In the first moments of the assault some volunteers ran into the icy waters of the nearby creeks seeking to hide, while others ran to the main camp in an attempt to reach protection from regular soldiers. By this time soldiers, hurriedly donning some clothing, were crawling from their tents and from under the wagons. Mostly on hands and knees they tried to shoot into the warriors who were riding at breakneck speed through the camp. Afraid of hitting the volunteers who were rushing towards them, they stopped firing. Some soldiers managed to get to the cavalry horses, thus thwarting the attempt to drive off those animals.

Then, as quickly as they had come the warriors were gone, leaving behind dazed, confused soldiers and thoroughly frightened volunteers. A quick count revealed two civilians and one soldier had been wounded. When last seen the raiders were heading northeast, driving before them the large herd of pack mules and many of the volunteers' horses. Twenty-eight Indians had deprived

Howard of almost his entire mule train and many volunteers were now without mounts.

With the dawn came a disappointing discovery for the raiders. What they had thought to be their intended plunder were in fact dozens of pack mules and a few dozen horses. Still, the mules would serve well as food and the horses would replenish some of those Chief Tendoy had stolen a few nights previous.

THE BATTLE OF CAMUS MEADOW

The raid had been a prelude to an all-out battle known in army histories as the Skirmish at Camas Meadows. From its beginnings as a raid at 3:30 AM until its end as a firefight about 9:30 AM, it was another defeat for General Howard.

During the night raid soldiers and volunteers became scattered, and because of the darkness regrouping took nearly two hours. Howard then ordered Major George B. Sanford, the commanding officer of the 1st and 2nd Cavalry regiments, to pursue the Indians. Sanford dispatched 1st Cavalry's Company B (Captain James Jackson, commanding). The other two were the 2nd Cavalry's Company I (Captain Camillus C. Carr commanding), and Company L (Captain Randolph Norwood commanding). He kept two companies, K and C, back to guard against another attack.

The Indians' direction was quickly ascertained by the dust cloud they and their captured animals were raising. Sanford estimated the distance at three to four miles. The Indians, because they were herding captured animals, were not moving quickly, so the pursuing cavalry managed to close the distance in short time. About three miles from the bivouac Norwood's company located some of the herd that had managed to stray and retrieved seventy-five mules and horses. However, in the rounding up process fifty escaped again and ran towards the main herd, which allowed the warriors to reclaim them. Norwood wisely chose not to go after those horses, but took what animals he could and rejoined the main force.

Meanwhile, the warriors continued leading their pursuers until they reached a point about six miles from the army camp. While a few carried on with the stolen herd to where Joseph was with his group, the others took up positions behind ridges and outcroppings of lava. Their chosen battlefield was a flat land between heavily timbered lava ridges to the west, bordered to the north by rolling foothills and to the east by lava formations that were further sheltered by timber growth. The area was well known to the warriors, as they had camped there between their raids on the army during the previous few days.

The advancing cavalry had lost sight of the warriors. As Captain Carr's company, which was a short distance ahead of the other two, approached the lava ridges the hidden warriors opened fire. . Quickly dismounting, they began to return fire, but no enemy is as difficult to ward off as one unseen. Norwood and his troop then appeared and his company also dismounted. The horses were quickly rushed to the rear out of danger. The two companies formed up "in line" to meet what appeared to be a well-planned ambush. Then Captain Jackson's troops, having dismounted a few yards back, rushed up to form a line on Norwood's right.

The three companies were now behind cover of lava rocks, but still in great peril; they were able to hold off any attacks, but could do nothing to stop the warriors from advancing closer. In what was soon a pitched battle, Jackson's bugler, Bernard A. Brooks, was killed in a volley of shots. Jackson and a couple of his men bravely rushed out and recovered the body. Privates Harry Trevor and Samuel Glass also received wounds that ultimately killed them. Lieutenant Benson, Jackson's second-in-command, was wounded, and by the time the battle ended, four more soldiers and one civilian had received injuries that took them out of the fight.

After an hour, Sanford, seeing the fight was not going well, ordered a retreat. Carr and Jackson were able to withdraw, but Norwood could not move because of very heavy fire being concentrated against his company. He did, however, manage to gain a slightly better position on higher ground. Major Sanford then sent a messenger to tell Norwood to withdraw but Norwood replied he would have to stay where he was until he could figure a way to withdraw safely. Norwood, unable to advance or retreat, had his soldiers dig in and pile up earthen breastworks.

Howard was still back at the bivouac when he received word of Sanford's predicament. He knew this would be a tragedy akin to that of White Bird Canyon unless Sanford could hold out long enough for help to arrive. Howard quickly assembled two of his reserve force, the 1st Cavalry's C Company (Captain Henry Wagner) and a company from the 8th Infantry (Captain Daniel T. Wells), plus a howitzer cannon and its gun crew (Lieutenant Harrison G. Otis). Howard arrived with his reinforcements at around 8:30, and, apprised of the situation, immediately placed the howitzer and the infantry on Sanford's flank and pushed forward. Attaining Norwood's position, they effected the rescue, but the warriors, having seen the cannon, had quickly departed.

Captain Norwood later expressed bitterness over what he perceived to have been overly hasty actions of the other two companies in withdrawing. The withdrawal had, he thought, placed his company in grave danger. He felt, "had not his troops been so well sheltered by the rocks…the company must have been annihilated." He further suggested that "had he been vigorously supported they would have emerged victorious."[16] This of course was pure conjecture on his part because another, unidentified, individual who survived that perilous day later wrote, "it must be admitted that Joseph worsted us."[17]

After the battle, Norwood reported—or at least Howard in his reports claimed he had—that L Company had imposed equally severe losses on the attackers. Howard claimed Norton told him the Nez Perce casualties were at least six dead. This remained unconfirmed until 1932 when it was revealed by Chief Peopeo Tholekt that he had been the more serious of only two casualties.[18] He had received a head wound which put him out of action for quite some time. While his recovery was slow it was fully complete and he was able to fight again in the siege at Bear's Paw.[19] Wottolen had received a slight hip wound that did not keep him from the Canyon Creek fight two weeks later.

Howard still had many soldiers, but was so depleted in field rations and ammunition he had to order severe rationing, not only of food but also of ammunition. He was compelled to issue an order that no more than a few rounds of ammunition be issued to each man. Because there was such a shortage of rations, he also had to tell the men they must supplement their shortage by living off the land as best they could. This was no easy task for men with little knowledge of edible roots and berries. To make matters worse, the area, though it held some rabbits and sage hens, was almost bereft of big game. Over the next several days he whiled away his time considering his next move while Joseph and his followers disappeared deeper into the heavy timber.

Howard's frustrations at the defeat at Camus Meadowns were further aggravated by his belief that his losses now exceeded those of Joseph, whom he now considered to be operating at minimal risk. He was not correct in this assumption. He had no way of knowing the severity of Joseph's casualty list, or that with sickness and fatigue beginning to affect the elderly, and women and children, progress was drastically slowing. Howard's anxiety heightened because once more he was in the unenviable position of having to make excuses to Washington. He could not conceal his own losses: eleven dead and wounded soldiers, plus one dead civilian volunteer, plus nearly all his mules and many horses; but he could—and did—exaggerate Nez Perce losses. As he had done in his report following the Battle at the Clearwater River, he fudged the results.

Though he was quite factual in reporting that the Indians had infiltrated the horse compound and had awaited the chance to break out with his mules and horses, for the most part his reports are fictional accounts. In the camp raid, he wrote, a party of mounted Nez Perce warriors imitated a cavalry company by approaching the Camas Meadow camp at a slow trot in a column of fours. He tells of how the posted sentry, thinking it was a returning cavalry unit, called out the challenge and when it was not answered he fired a warning shot which awoke the entire camp. In the pandemonium that ensued those Indians who were hiding in the horse compound ran off with the horses and mules while the mounted warriors, breaking their column, rode headlong through the camp shooting at random. This, wrote Howard, was the cause of the casualties and animal loss the army had suffered.[20] His report was mainly fiction.

Nez Perce accounts of the entire affray reveal a greatly different picture. In 1932 several old warriors told their versions. There had been no "column of fours" and the surprise shot had *not* been fired by a startled sentry. All interviewees agreed Nez Perce warriors would never have tried such a ploy because their methods so completely differed from those of the army.

Chief Peo'peo'Tholket stated, "We rode the Indian way, in three different bunches. Waiting for us to cut the horses loose, all three companies were in place waiting for the signal."

Wottolen and Yellow Wolf added to their comrade's statement. Wottolen said, "Indians do not ride like that. We were divided into three groups and rode in Indian style."

Yellow Wolf agreed. "Indians did not teach themselves to ride in rows like soldiers. Soldiers have one-way fighting, Indians have own way fight."[21] (*Sic*)

Accounts written later by individual soldiers, and also documents from Howard's adjutant, Charles E. Wood and Sargeant Harry J. Davis of Norwood's company, support the Indians' revelations.[22] None of the military writers reported anything about a "four-horse column" and all reported the shot had not come from the north picket line but from an entirely different direction. None could identify the source. The Indians, however, knew the source because according to Peo'peo Tholekt, the shot came from the rifle of an undisciplined Asotin warrior named Otskai [Go Out]. He had stupidly (or perhaps deliberately) disregarded orders from Looking Glass not to fire until the proper signal had been given. What that signal was Peo'peo Tholekt could not recall but said it would have been one of the usual—an owl's hoot or a wolf's howl. In any event, Otskai cost Peo'peo Tholekt and his group the time they needed to capture *all* the cavalry's horses and the mules.[23] The shot had so greatly hindered the Indians in the horse compound they managed to run off very few of the animals they had selected. Though greatly disappointed at dawn when they tallied the results and found most of the animals were mules, they gained some satisfaction when they realized the horse count was relatively higher than first thought. This was because many of the volunteers' horses had joined the stampeding mules when that herd crashed through the volunteers' camp after crossing the creek.

The victory at Camus Meadow did much to improve Nez Perce morale, but, as important, it bought them time. On August 23, Joseph led his people through Tacher's Pass (now known as Targhee Pass) into the newly opened Yellowstone National Park.

[CHAPTER 18 ENDNOTES]

1. While still some distance west of Montana, Howard had anticipated the possibility the Nez Perce might turn east towards the Dakotas. He reasoned they could easily hide in the rolling hills and valleys of that vast territory for quite some time; and perhaps he secretly hoped they would turn east. Should they have done so they would be far beyond his jurisdiction and someone else would have had to take up the chase. At that moment Howard was every bit as apprehensive about his next move as was Joseph, so he decided to wait until he knew which direction Joseph and his fellow chiefs would turn. Meanwhile he would proceed to Weippe and bivouac there until word arrived as to which direction Joseph would lead his people. [Author's files.]

2. Fort Keogh was also called the Tongue River Cantonment. The TRC was established in 1874 but was relocated in 1876 when Fort Keogh was built. Both

names were used in army reports during the time of the 1877 uprising.

3   Miles received more credit for the surrender of the Nez Perces at the Bear's Paw than he rightly deserves. He gained the credit mainly from the report he exaggerated and enhanced his role in the surrender while downplaying the part played by General Howard. Perhaps his conscience troubled him, as he later became a champion in Joseph's quest for fairness and justice.

4   Many historians dispute the notion of Looking Glass having volunteered to seek out the Crows, and they may be correct. The fact of the matter is he did not depart to find the Crows because several Crow warriors came upon the band. They were friendly (one even briefly contemplated joining the revolt) but they bluntly advised the Nez Perce chiefs to surrender to Howard and accept resettlement at Lapwai. Whatever version is correct it remains that the Crows had no intention of honoring the 1873 promise. They were no longer in a position to offer assistance of any kind because they had already signed a treaty. [Camille Williams, Nez Perce tribal historian quoted by McWhorter in *Hear Me My Chiefs*, 459–60.]

5   The Crows were not the only Indians willing to betray their Nez Perce brothers. In August, acting on behalf of the army, General George Crook visited Chief Crazy Horse who at the time was a prisoner at Camp Robinson, Nebraska. Crook asked Crazy Horse if he would be willing to lead some of his Lakota Sioux warriors against the rebellious Nez Perce. Speaking through an interpreter, Frank Grouard, Crazy Horse replied that he would be willing to fight "until not a Nez Perce was left." Grouard, who is thought to have had a personal grudge against Crazy Horse, twisted the words to mean Crazy Horse had said he "would fight

until not a white man was left." Crook left in anger and Crazy Horse was led back to his cell. Possibly not comprehending what had happened, he struggled and was shot by his two Indian guards. Mortally wounded, he died several hours later. Since then many legends have sprung up concerning the death of Crazy Horse. ["The Death of Crazy Horse: Fables and Forensics," *Wild West*, Feb 2009, 22–3.]

6   Because Gibbon had no medical personnel, he and his wounded received only basic treatment. Some of the wounded were very seriously wounded and they spent the cold night in dire agony. Two died before help arrived. [Woodruff, *The Battle at the Big Hole,* 111.]

7   In many cases, because their tepees had been destroyed, families had to be accommodated with others. There being only limited room in each tepee families had to split up. This caused hardship as well, especially where small children were involved.

8   McWhorter, *Hear Me My Chiefs*, 406–7.

9   Claim made by Fred Philips, owner of the train, but not with it on that day. Testimony was that of one of the two cooks, Charles Go Hing. [Claim no.1782, 13 April 1878. Entry 700, Indian Depredations, US Bureau of Indian Affairs.]

10 The soldiers were discovering horse droppings all piled neatly into pyramids on the side of the trail. They thought the piles might be directional signs to other Indians. When asked what the mounds might mean the Bannock scouts were hard-pressed to hide their amusement when they informed the soldiers the droppings were indeed signs—of contempt. They had been assembled by Nez Perce boys as symbols of scorn for their pursuers. [Author's files.]

11 Literally, "Many camus." Named by the Nez Perces for

the abundance of camus roots, a staple food in the Nez Perce diet, available in the meadows. White settlers called it Camus Meadows.

12 Bell mares were female mules, horses or donkeys used as leaders in mule trains. They wore a bell around their necks and the mules would follow where they led. [*Merriam-Webster Dictionary*.]

13 Joseph barely mentions the fight at Camus Meadows in his later accounts, and Yellow Wolf, Wottolen and Peopeo Tholekt also denied his presence. Those sources claiming his presence were perhaps caught up in the legend or assumed, because he was a chief, he was at the battle. [Greene, *Nez Perce Summer, 1877,* 154.]

14 Lieutenant Bacon and his unit had been sent to Tacher's Pass (now called Targhee Pass) to apprehend the Nez Perce should they decide to use it. Bacon stayed only a day or two before deciding Joseph was not coming his way. Howard later accused Bacon of not showing enough courage by leaving early, but the accusation went no further. In fact, had Bacon and his forty men met Joseph they would likely have met total annihilation. Howard was often too quick to pass judgment on subordinates. [McWhorter, *Hear Me My Chiefs,* 414.]

15 Norwood report to Gibbon, August 24, 1877. [Nez Perce War Papers. Item 6154, roll 338.] Author's note: Because Norwood had been seconded from Fort Keogh to Howard's force, his reports all went to Gibbon, his commanding officer.

16 *Virginia City Madisonian,* August 25, 1877. See also, Davis, H.J., *An Incident of the Nez Perce Campaign,* 563–4.

17 *New York Herald,* September 10, 1877.

18 McWhorter, *Hear Me My Chiefs,* 419–420.

19 Peopeo Tholekt was the most wounded warrior of

the entire campaign. A fearless fighter, he was in every major battle (from the Clearwater) and most skirmishes. His wounds, though often severe, never kept him from the next battle. In this regard he was the Nez Perce equivalent to the army's Captain W.R. Parnell of 5th Cavalry fame. [Author's files.]

20 Report of Secretary of War, 1877, I, 129. "Howard to Kelton" August 27, 1877.

21 McWhorter, *Hear me My Chiefs*, 416–417.

22 McWhorter, *Hear me My Chiefs*, 413–426.

23 McWhorter, *Hear Me My Chiefs*, 418.

[CHAPTER 19]

YELLOWSTONE

Following the victory at Camus Meadows, Joseph pushed his charges eastward with no respite as the warriors remained as rearguards at the aforementioned Camus Meadows to hold off the troopers who had given chase. Wottolen said in a 1932 interview,

> "The soldiers follow and we stop to have a fight. Back of a ridge we dismount to await their coming. We do not stop too close to that ridge. Soon soldiers appear on that ridge top, but do not stay. Immediately they drop from sight. We do not charge or follow them."

Instead they relied on their rifles. With long-range shooting they pinned the troopers down until Howard appeared, whereupon the warriors left.

Wottolen continued,

> "Soon all shooting stopped. The soldiers could not be driven from the woods and the captured herd was now out of danger so we also left. We left a few mules on the trail that could not travel fast enough for us."

Thus assured the non-combatants and the purloined horses and mules were well ahead, the warriors rejoined the main group.

On August 23 the entire band entered Targhee Pass into what was totally unfamiliar territory, a little-known wilderness that is now Yellowstone National Park.[1] Joseph, knowing he could not go back, but unsure of the trail ahead, was forced to delay while he pondered his next move. White Bird and the other warrior chiefs also held back, because they did not want their warriors to get ahead of Joseph's people; nor did they want to chance losing each other in the heavy timber. By delaying, Joseph knew he was flirting with danger but he dared not venture further until scouts had sent word of the best trail to follow.

Then, to add to the problems a more immediate trouble appeared. The chiefs were informed of the presence of exceptionally large numbers of white people in the immediate area. This came as a surprise for they had no way of knowing they were in the newly opened national park. In order to avoid contact with these groups, plans were revised to ensure the people kept well off the trails and remained in the deep woods. Joseph and the other chiefs hurriedly discussed the situation, and a unanimous decision quickly made: in order to keep Howard as far behind as possible they must immediately make haste to locate the Crows; and the Crows' land was still some seventy-five miles distant through rugged forest and rivers.

Even the well-traveled Lean Elk knew little of this strange, wondrous locale in which great plumes of hot water and steam shot high into the air, where herds of elk abounded and wolves and cougars lurked in the heavily treed forests.

In an ironic twist, one of the white people in the area was General William Tecumseh Sherman (1820–1891), known as "Cump" and "Uncle Billy" to his idolizing troops, and whom the Plains Indians had named "Old Warrior Sherman." Sherman had been long considered the best general in the US Army,[2] and had been sent from Washington on a fact-finding mission to determine how Chief Joseph was managing to make Howard and his officers appear blundering fools. Usually a forbearing man, Sherman had begun to lose patience with his officers, and in particular Howard. That Joseph and his warriors had so far won every encounter was particularly infuriating to Sherman. Also concerned was General Philip Henry Sheridan [1831–1888], whose district Joseph and his Nez Perces had recently entered.

Sherman and Sheridan, along with most of their fellow generals, had never held any Indian in anything but the lowest contempt, so it was galling to be forced to reassess their erstwhile opinions of the Nez Perce chiefs' military expertise. Equally irritating was to have to admit that during the past two years their army had been beaten in humiliating fashion at every turn.

For his part, Sherman had tried to retain optimism that Howard, once he came into direct contact with the Indians, would put a quick end to the uprising. With this as his mindset—and knowing Howard had closed the gap to a day or two—he had decided to allow Howard that chance. Meanwhile he would enjoy a few days exploring the new park and its amenities before starting to work on his assignment. But his mood quickly changed when he was informed of Howard's defeat and the losses at Camus Meadows.

For awhile following that humiliation Sherman considered taking personal charge of the entire operation. How serious had been Sherman's notion to take overall charge? That is not fully known, but it seems likely it was reaction at finding himself seriously embarrassed by an incompetent army led by a seemingly incompetent commander. His chagrin only increased with the knowledge his officers and soldiers were being out-foxed, out-maneuvered and out-fought by small groups of Nez Perce warriors led by war chiefs who knew relatively nothing of established military tactics.

However, when rumors that Joseph and his band had entered Yellowstone became fact, Sherman found himself thrust into the position of having to take immediate charge.[3] The tourists were understandably frightened, so Sherman did his best to convince them there was no need for concern. Indians, he assured them, were so superstitious they would never come close to the main tourist areas because they feared geysers and large pools of boiling mud. He added to his guarantee by attesting to a commonly held belief that Indians feared darkness and the evil spirits that dwelt therein. He assured them a night attack would never occur unless the moon was full. Sherman actually believed in this myth, widely known by its Texan term, Comanche Moon.[4] Those tourists who were veterans of life on the plains scoffed at the general's assertions, but did so quietly so as not to further alarm the Easterners.

Sherman was either trying to soothe the tourists' fears or he knew less of the Nez Perce community than they knew of him. Of all the Indian nations, the Nez Perce was among the least of any influenced by superstition and taboos. Spouts of gushing hot water, bubbling mud and evil night spirits had never been among their fears. Evil spirits were sometimes used to keep disobedient children in line. "Be good," Nez Perce mothers warned naughty children, "or the evil night spirits will capture you and you may never be seen again." It was the Nez Perce version of the European bogeyman and the Florida Seminole's Whompus cat, a wild creature that carried away bad children during its nighttime forays. Neither were the Nez Perces shy about fighting at night, although they had not practiced it to any great degree prior to the present situation. The warriors knew nothing about a Comanche Moon. They would fight when they had to, moon or no moon.

One group's concerns proved justified when, on August 24, twelve tourists from Radersburg,[5] a small mining community situated just south of Helena in western Montana, wandered into an area occupied by a scouting party at rest. They were quickly overpowered. Some of the younger warriors waved their rifles in the tourists' faces saying they intended to kill them in vengeance for Gibbon's surprise attack at Big Hole. Perhaps they would have, but Red Scout, the war party leader, told them to release the tourists unharmed. His edict caused some muttering among the warriors, several of whom wanted to disobey Red Scout but dared not as they would then have had to face the wrath of both Red Cloud, their warrior chief as well as White Bird and the other band chiefs.

However, during the argument one of the tourists, George F. Cowan, made a run for the trees. A shot rang out and Cowan fell dead, a bullet in his head. His wife, Emma, fainted, as did another woman. Several others turned to run but were quickly re-captured. The shot brought Red Cloud and Lean Elk to the scene. Red Cloud, with assistance from Red Scout and Lean Elk, convinced the young warriors to release the tourists. The Indians then left quietly.[6] Later another group of tourists were captured by another war party but they were also released.

Rankling under Howard's failure to corral the Nez Perces before they arrived in Yellowstone, Sherman sent him a message roundly criticizing the general for his latest failure to subdue the Nez Perces at Camus Meadows, citing Howard's unfortunate propensity for losing his quarry for days and weeks at a time.[7] Sherman was of the opinion Howard could have ended the uprising back in Idaho and could not understand why Howard had not seen the opportunity that had presented itself at the Clearwater.

Howard held a different viewpoint. As Joseph had managed to lead his Nez Perces into Montana they were no longer in the Department of Columbia. Thus, Howard thought Sheridan, the general responsible for the Department of Montana, could assign Miles or Crook to chase them down. For that reason Howard had remained almost three weeks in Idaho bivouacked at Kamiah. He resumed the chase only because no orders to quit the pursuit had been forthcoming from General McDowell.[8] It was with clear reluctance he had resumed his march eastward. His late departure, the casual pace taken to reach Montana and the layover at Stevensville denied Colonel Gibbon any assistance at the Big Hole River. To Sherman that was another lost opportunity. Then Howard's army had been ambushed and beaten at Camus Meadows. The humiliation of a relatively small raiding party taking nearly all his mules and then beating three companies in a fight at the lava rocks cemented his desire to quit the chase.

Leaving Camus Meadows, Howard had bivouacked once

again, at Henry's Lake, to await replacement wagons and mules. From there Howard had dispatched the message to Sherman in which he attempted to explain his delays. Part of his message read, "My command is so much worn [by fatigue] that...I may stop... and in a few days work my way back [to Fort Boise]."⁹

Sherman would have no part of it. In order to alleviate any criticism that might be directed against him should Joseph escape from Yellowstone Park, he moved quickly to counter Howard's intention. Part of his response to Howard included what can be seen as an ultimatum.

> *"[you] should pursue the Nez Perce [letting them] lead where they may. May I suggest that if you are tired [you should] give your command to some energetic younger officer and let him follow [Joseph]. No time should be lost."*¹⁰

Sherman's undisguised irritability offended Howard so deeply he immediately dispatched one final message.

> *"Sir: You misunderstand me. You need not fear for the campaign. Neither you nor General McDowell can doubt my pluck and energy. [I and my troop] are on the heels of the enemy...We will...continue to the end."*¹¹

Sherman did not bother to reply but did institute several changes. The minute he was informed of the Nez Perce entry into Yellowstone, Sherman sent orders to the commanders of other forts in the area; they were to ready their troops for deployment. His hope was to trap the Indians within the park's confines.

Cowan's death forced more immediate action, so on August 26th he telegraphed Colonel Samuel D. Sturgis (1833–1889),¹² commander of the 7th Cavalry, to set out for Yellowstone by the fastest means possible. The commandant, who was a Fort Keogh, dispatched troops via forced march to Clark's Fork in hopes of mounting an ambush.

Bypassing Sheridan, General Sherman sent a direct signal to

General Nelson A. Miles (1839–1925) who was at Fort Keogh awaiting orders. Sherman anticipated that Joseph intended to break out of Yellowstone to try for an escape to Canada (he did not know of the Nez Perces' hopes to gain sanctuary with the Crows) so he ordered Miles to undertake a forced march to an area just below the US-Canada border. There he could intercept the refugees and bring them to bay. Miles set out from Fort Keogh on September 8th on the northerly route that he felt would intersect Joseph's.

Another signal brought General George Crook (1929–1890) and General Alfred H. Terry (1827–1890) to alert status. Crook, who was then in the Department of the Platte, did arrive but lost the trail when White Bird's warriors outfoxed him. They led him to a trail that ended in a dead-end, and by the time he returned the Nez Perces had gone. He soon returned to his home base. Terry, who at the time was the commander of the Department of Dakota, might have been making arrangements to join the pursuit, but no records show his participation in the campaign. Regardless, he would not have arrived before the Nez Perces had departed.

Sherman, now convinced he would have to replace Howard, dispatched a message to Lieutenant Colonel Charles C. Gilbert (1822–1903)[13] on August 29th informing him that he was to immediately take command of E Company, 7th Cavalry and proceed to Howard's camp at Henry's Lake. He was then to assume command, whereupon Howard was to return to the Department of the Columbia. Sherman could not have chosen a more inept replacement. He got as far as taking command of the cavalry unit, which at that moment was poised to march to where its commander, Lieutenant Gustavus Doane (1840–1892), was certain Joseph would appear next.[14] Doane was a complete plainsman, experienced in the ways of Indians and familiar with western landscape and topography. It had been his intention to head westward to the Musselshell River where he was convinced the Nez Perce would go after leaving Yellowstone. Doane explained his plan but Gilbert overrode him, cancelling his plans. Doane was, after all, a lieutenant and was not expected to suggest advice to a senior officer. Had he listened to Doane he could have easily overtaken Joseph.

A day or two later Gilbert had another opportunity to encounter Joseph had he heeded some timely intelligence from a scout who knew what he was talking about. Gilbert ignored him, also.

Gilbert instead took the unit back along the Yellowstone River—away from the Nez Perce line of march—and then followed an old trail and became hopelessly lost in the process. By the time he disentangled himself from the maze Howard had already left Henry's Lake and had headed into the park. Unable to proceed further, Gilbert called a halt, abandoned his mission and returned to Fort Ellis by mid September.[15] Gilbert never did contact Howard nor did he report to Sherman.[16] He simply vanished into the limbo of office jobs that claim inept and failed military officers and was heard of no more until he retired in 1886.[17]

Meanwhile, if Colonel Sturgis had hoped to arrive unnoticed at Clark's Fork he was disappointed, for his columns had been under constant surveillance by scouts for hours prior to their arrival. Within hours of departure from Fort Keogh, the long columns of cavalry and foot soldiers were seen by far-ranging Nez Perce scouts who wasted no time in reporting the route of march to White Bird and Joseph. Both chiefs increased the pace along their own route foiling any hope of Sturgis setting up an ambush. Sturgis moved on to the Yellowstone River.

The scouts also deprived him of valuable intelligence that would have helped him. General Howard had dispatched a courier with a message containing the latest intelligence received from his army scouts concerning Joseph's route, direction and an estimate of the remaining numbers of Nez Perce warriors; the rider never reached Sturgis. Over the next few days Howard sent more riders, none of whom reached their destination. Sturgis never learned of the weakened state of the Nez Perce warriors, nor did he learn the locations of Joseph's non-combatant group until he rendezvoused with Howard.

On September 8, Sturgis and his cavalry reached the Yellowstone River, and, outwitted once again by the Nez Perces, travelled south and reported to Howard at his new camp on September 11th. Howard immediately delegated a segment to return north to join

Miles. They never reached Miles in time to give him information he could have used, nor did they see any Nez Perce scouts, although the scouts certainly saw *them*.

With Miles moving north-northwest[18] and his own numbers now well reinforced by Sturgis and some smaller units that had reported, Howard once again began plodding doggedly forward.

Joseph and his chiefs were at last in common agreement that the band must make all haste to make contact with the Crows and the freedom they believed awaited them. But first they had to find the quickest way out of this alien forest, no easy task because none of the trails seemed to lead where they wished to go, and Lean Elk was not familiar with this particular area.

Deliverance appeared at noon on August 24 in the person of one John Shively who had been prospecting the area for many years and knew both the land and the Indians who inhabited it. He wintered with various tribes and got along well with those he dealt with. Fluent in several Indian languages, he was equally at home with their dialects. He was not unduly concerned when a group of mounted warriors emerged from the forest and surrounded him; however, he became worried when he suddenly realized these riders were of a band he did not know.

Using a sign language the riders understood, he learned they were Nez Perce, and that he was their captive. At first he resisted; but heroism was not a sound idea under the circumstances, so he agreed to go with them. Brought before Chief Joseph, he was assured he had nothing to fear; all Joseph wanted of him was assistance. He was to help Lean Elk guide the band through the area. Shively agreed to do this.

Within a day the mountain man guided the band directly to a northern trail he said would lead them to more familiar country. Shively was told he could leave but he decided to stay a few more days to act as guide for the women who were serving as the pack train. On August 31, Lean Elk recognized the terrain and Shively again was told he would be free to leave the following morning and would be given several mules and a couple of good horses as payment for his troubles. However, unsure if the Indians intended to keep their promises and might kill him, Shively snuck away that night and escaped.[19]

Joseph was leading his people towards Clark's Canyon, but not at the desired pace, as the number of sick elders was increasing with each passing day. The need to transport them by travois slowed the pace. As had happened along the trail from the Big Hole River, several reports from army scouts informed Howard of individuals found dead or dying along the trails. Again, several of the elderly had chosen to remain behind rather than delay or slow the others.

To add to the refugees' overall miseries, the night temperatures were beginning to drop to chilling degrees, a discomfort especially felt by the children. Because of the destruction at the Big Hole, and few supply wagons taken from the army had included blankets or clothing, these items were now in short supply. Food was also beginning to run low. The loss of the cattle before the trek had started meant the lack of protein was an increasing problem. The warriors managed to locate small buffalo herds, but the kill was not enough to assure full rations for all. The few vegetables harvested earlier were nearly depleted, and with the growing season over, few berries were available. Plants with edible roots were falling dormant and no longer easy to spot. Still, the band struggled onward with spirits buoyed in the knowledge the Crows' land would soon be within reach.

The Nez Perces broke out of Yellowstone on September 6 and began heading up Clark's Fork, a tributary of the Yellowstone River, to Crow country, unaware of impending betrayal.

[CHAPTER 19 ENDNOTES]

1   In 1872 the US government proclaimed Yellowstone the first national park, but did not open it to the public until

1877. When, on August 22, the Nez Perce invaded the area, the first curious tourists, unaware of the Indians' presence, were admiring the scenic grandeur. The new park's existence was due to the efforts of Canadian-born Seth Bullock [1847–1919] who, as its first sheriff, had tamed the lawless town of Deadwood, Dakota Territory. He was later elected a senator for Montana. Bullock introduced the bill that decreed certain areas be reserved as national parks. [Author's files]

2   Sherman's full rank was general-of-the-army. The rank was abolished when Sherman died (1891) and was not re-instated until 1944. [*Harper Encyclopedia of Military Biography*, 680–81.]

3   There was no fort in Yellowstone, so General Sherman was in the area called the Lower Basin where tourists camped out in tents (the first hotel, Marshall's, was not built until 1880). Sherman and his staff would have been in tents among the tourists.

4   The greatly feared Comanche (and their more northern cousins, the Shoshone) had developed the tactic of night fighting in Texas because Texans were very good shots, making daylight raids very risky. As a result, the Comanche never raided a Texan settlement except at night, and then only under a full moon. Thus the term Comanche Moon came into the American lexicon. [Author's files.]

5   Radersburg, in the 2000 US census had a population of 70. In 1877 it was only slightly larger and depended on its gold mining activities for survival. [Author's files.]

6   C.E. Woods, in his *Century Illustrated Monthly* article, claimed two tourists had been killed. There is no evidence to substantiate this claim.

7   Greene, 164.

8   General Irvin McDowell (1818–85) was the director

of the Columbia District, and Howard's immediate superior. The Nez Perce came under his directorship. Gibbon eventually became his replacement.

9 Report of the General of the Army, dated 7 Nov., 1877 to the Secretary of War. [File is in Report of the Secretary of War, 1877, 12. National Archives, Washington DC.]

10 Ibid, 13.

11 Ibid, 12–13. [See also: Carpenter, John, *Sword and Olive Branch*, 254–57, for a complete and in-depth interpretation of the Howard-Sherman-McDowell messages.]

12 Samuel Sturgis was born in Shippensburg, Pennsylvania. He graduated from West Point in time to fight during the final days of the Mexican War (1846–48) during which he was captured but was released after the Battle of Buena Vista. He stayed in the west, fought in various campaigns and in time was promoted to colonel. He had no use whatsoever for George Custer who he considered "a brave but very selfish man." Sturgis, though he had success in the Apache campaigns, was no match for the Nez Perce chiefs. He retired in 1886 to St. Paul, Minnesota where he died in 1889. [*Encyclopedia of Frontier History*, Volume 3, 1384–85.]

13 Charles C. Gilbert, at fifty-five, was eight years older than Howard, so was not likely the "younger, more energetic officer" Sherman had in mind when he sent Howard his scathing message. However, he was available and had experience gained in the Mexican War and the Civil War. However, despite his credentials, he made a poor showing. He mismanaged Doane's cavalry unit so badly from the start many horses fell from starvation and twenty-five animals had to be shipped to Fort Ellis to recuperate. [Scott, Hugh, *Some Memories of a Soldier*, 68.]

14 As events transpired, Doane had been correct in his

assumptions because the Nez Perces did cross that area a day or two later. Doane would have been in the perfect position to engage and possibly subdue them. As it was, they crossed safely and proceeded to Canyon Creek with no interference at all. Despite this setback at the hands of the inept Gilbert, Doane continued in the army although he never achieved the glory that might have been his had he been able to meet Joseph at the crossing he had foreseen. [Various files. See also, *Nez Perce Summer 1877*, 194–96; and *Encyclopedia of Frontier Biography*, 407.]

15 Gilbert mismanaged his very brief part of the campaign so badly he wore out all his horses. By the time he got back on the proper course his troops were no better off either. His horses, some of which were on the verge of starvation, had to be ferried by boat up the Madison River to Fort Ellis. [Greene, *Nez Perce Summer 1877*, 167–168, 194–200.]

16 Phinney, Mary Allen, Jirah Isham Allen, *Montana Pioneer*, 99.

17 Whether Lieutenant Doane regained command of E Company upon Gilbert's sudden departure is unknown. The company received no further mention in army records pertaining to the remaining weeks of the Nez Perce War. As the Crow Agency was E Company's main assignment, it is possible, indeed probable, it returned to the agency. [Author's files.]

18 In retrospect, had he swung to the southwest he would have been in position for interception at the Musselshell River. However, Miles had no way of knowing if the Nez Perce chiefs might avoid the area as being too obvious for an ambush and move to a more easterly route. As it was, his decision proved correct when he took the calculated risk by heading north on the route he had chosen. [Author's files.]

19 Shively narrated his account of his Nez Perce adventure

to Edwin J. Stanley, who included it on pages 177 and 178 in a book he published the following year. Shively's account may be flawed, as he told Stanley he had stayed with the Nez Perces for thirteen days and escaped a day or two after Frank Carpenter, a tourist who had also been captured, had been released unharmed. This would have meant Shively escaped several days before August 31. [Stanley, E.J., *Rambles in Wonderland,* 177–78. Doubleday, NY, 1878.]

[CHAPTER 20]

CLOSE CALLS at CANYON CREEK

"My heart was just like fire. I do not understand how the Crows could think to help the soldiers. They were fighting against their best friends!"

—YELLOW WOLF.[1]

For many decades, writers and researchers remained convinced that on September 11 Looking Glass departed on his previously agreed mission to seek out the Crows. Some were of the opinion that during his absence Joseph took Looking Glass's place as overall leader while Ollokot led the Wallowa band. Some were further convinced Joseph served exclusively as the overall warrior chief even after Looking Glass returned. To these writers his genius as a military strategist was proven during intense fighting during three days of encounters between September 13 and 15. None of this is true.

In 1932, evidence emerged proving Looking Glass did not meet with the Crow chiefs. Had he gone on that mission he would have ridden out with a light heart only to return a few days later crestfallen with all hopes dashed. The Crows, he would have told Joseph and White Bird, had not only refused assistance, but had themselves already surrendered and accepted reservation status. He would have told them the Crow chiefs had advised him to surrender. As it was, he had no need to seek the Crows; he saw them plainly enough when their warriors launched an attack on the Nez Perce horse herd just prior to the bands' arrival at Canyon Creek.

An even more grievous blow than the Crows' failure to assist their former allies came after Canyon Creek when they learned a large number of Crow warriors had scouted for Gibbon prior to and during their stay at the Big Hole. Perhaps forgetting the participation of Lapwai Nez Perce warriors with Perry's army at White Bird Canyon, Joseph and the other chiefs had remained convinced that no Indians except Bannocks and Shoshones (who were longtime enemies and therefore expected) would turn against them. They had joined Looking Glass in his optimistic belief in the Crows' assistance. At Canyon Creek they realized that without the Crows' help the task at hand had become not only more difficult, but perhaps impossible. Even the most naive among the band members now knew there was no hope of settlement in Crow land. They also realized safety in Montana's Buffalo Country was unattainable.

Yellow Wolf had been among those who believed Looking Glass' averment of the Crows' involvement as allies. He bitterly recalled the moment they learned the Crows had broken their promise in the book he co-authored with Lucullus McWhorter.

> "Crows! Many snows the Crows had been our friends. But now [they had become] our enemies. I do not understand how the Crows could think to help the soldiers. They were fighting against their best friends. Some among us [Nez Perce warriors] had helped them whip the Sioux who came against them only a few snows before."[2]

What Yellow Wolf and the others, including Looking Glass, had not known until the fighting at Canyon Creek dashed their hopes was that at least 200 Crow men were on the army's payroll as scouts and as warriors. Looking Glass, Tool'hool'hool'zote, Ollokot and the sub-chiefs who did not survive the long trek never learned that Crow warriors had also launched a number of attacks within the Yellowstone area against straggling women and children. Joseph and his fellow survivors of the Bear's Paw siege would not learn until months later it had been Crow warriors who had scouted them for Gibbon from when they entered Montana, and that they were now assisting Colonel Sturgis because he had promised they could keep as war prizes all Nez Perce horses they could capture. The survivors of the Bear's Paw siege would also eventually learn that, following the Battle at Big Hole, Crow warriors had disinterred Nez Perce dead women and children for their scalps. Until that time they had blamed only the Bannocks.

Though the Crows' treachery was a terrible blow to all, none could have felt it more than Looking Glass. It had been on his advice and persuasive talents that Joseph and the others had rejected the offer made at Kamiah by Duncan MacDonald to would lead them to safety in Canada. Once they knew the Crows were now also against them, their rejection of his proposal caused great anguish.

To others, such as Two Moons, the news had not come as a great surprise. They had already taken into account the number of other tribesmen—Shoshone, Bannock, Sioux, Cheyenne—seen with the soldiers. As Two Moons said, "If all the others were against us, why not the Crows as well?"

The answer lay in tribal distrust, animosity and deceit that had been ongoing for hundreds, perhaps thousands, of years (see: Appendix I). Nonetheless, they were determined to press on. The devastating news forced the decision to try for escape to Canada, so now the chiefs moved quickly to put this plan into operation.[3] Joseph and company had no time to ponder the situation. They and Colonel Sturgis were about to clash; and they still had to worry about Howard, who at last had resumed his own push forward.

Howard was still smarting from his embarrassments at the hands of the Nez Perce chiefs. The recent engagement with the sharpshooters at the lava rocks and the raid at Camas Meadows had not helped his demeanor. The sharp rebuke from Sherman had been more salt in his wounded ego. Still, he could do nothing but remain in his rearguard bivouac awaiting the arrival of the resupply wagons. He began to see some hope with the arrivals of replacements for losses suffered at the lava rocks by Major Sanford's cavalry group. There also was a small group of Bannock scouts under command of Captain Stanton G. Fisher.[4] His spirits took another turn upwards when Sturgis arrived with his detachment of the 7th Cavalry on September 11. Howard assigned several of his own units to Sturgis and tasked him with continuing the pursuit. Sturgis, having been informed the Nez Perces were slowly making progress toward the Canyon Creek area, saw this as his best chance to interrupt their flight. Perhaps, he thought, he could defeat them once and for all.

On September 12, leaving some units in reserve, Sturgis took 6 companies—F, I and L under Major Lewis Merrill (1834–1896) and G, F and H under the command of Captain Frederick W. Benteen (1834–1898)[5]—and headed north. Sturgis, barely pausing to rest, pushed forward at a blistering pace on a forced march he felt would pay dividends when he reached the Nez Perce main group. Without regard for himself, his men or the horses, he moved along almost at a trot for twenty hours before calling a halt. They had covered an astounding sixty miles.[6]

While Sturgis was moving at best possible speed, the Nez Perces were also moving at an extremely brisk pace. Joseph and his people, once they crossed the Yellowstone River, made good time as they plodded westward along the dry creek bed to a flat area near the mouth of an unnamed canyon that during millennia past had been carved out of the yielding soil by a raging river. Over time the river diminished, so when the first white explorers saw it they named it Canyon Creek. By 1877 the creek had also dried up, leaving only a sandy bed and isolated pools of alkali water. The canyon, however, was a gateway through the Absaroke Mountains, offering a chance to widen the gap from Howard's cavalry. The following morning the Nez Perces moved to enter the canyon, but they had left it a little late to assure safe entry. As a result Benteen came very close to cutting them off and ending the flight then and there.

As the sun was setting on September 12, Sturgis sighted a group of Nez Perce warriors. About the same time several of his scouts returned to report the location of Joseph's main camp. Sturgis, thinking his approach had been unseen, made camp, but his approach had been observed. Joseph and the war chiefs were well aware of his arrival.

While his troopers were tending horses and pitching tents, Sturgis retired with his officers to his tent to outline the next move. As did many commanders of that era, Sturgis paid little attention to the thoughts and proposals of his subordinates. He would have been wise to have listened to Captain Frederick W. Benteen, who was well versed in the whys and wherefores of fighting Indians. Benteen proposed a plan that probably would have proven successful had not Sturgis chosen to disregard it.[7]

Although conversant with the fighting qualities of most tribes of the Plains Indians, Sturgis knew basically nothing of the Nez Perces or their military prowess. Thus, he laid his plans to his own standards and assumptions, gave his orders to the unit and company commanders, dismissed the officers and retired for the night. At dawn he moved his forces against a foe about whom he knew little and paid dearly for it.

Joseph, concerned mainly with the safety of his non-combatants, entertained no thought of risking precious time before starting them towards the canyon. White Bird and Looking Glass were equally concerned about further diminishing the warrior ranks in an all-out battle. Quick agreement was reached when White Bird proposed a series of ambushes by small war parties positioned at strategic points along the trail. It was this tactic that ultimately allowed the entire group to once again outpace the pursuers with few casualties or loss of horses beyond those already stolen by marauding Crows.

So it was that even before the onset of pre-dawn light Joseph sent the horses ahead with the now well-experienced youths as drovers, and before the sun had dispersed the darkness he led the women and children to the canyon. Once within reach of the canyon he left them in the care of elders whose orders were to enter the canyon, make haste northward with no stops until darkness fell. They would then wait, well hidden, until the warriors arrived, probably the following morning. Joseph, seeing his people on their way, returned to White Bird, Looking Glass and Tool'hool'hool'zote. All would be in readiness when the first troopers arrived.

A series of war parties under command of Ollokot, Red Cloud and other war chiefs moved quickly to their appointed ambuscades with Tool'hool'hool'zote and his band of snipers. White Bird, Looking Glass and their warriors took up positions in the heavy timber. One such position was approximately one mile south of the creek bed along the crest of a long sloping butte that rose some 300 feet above the rugged terrain.

THE BATTLE AT CANYON CREEK

The facts of the battle's preliminaries, based on interviews by Nez Perce survivors between 1927 and 1935, indicate the warriors had not been adequately aware of the troops' approach until September 12, which was almost too late. This oversight has been interpreted to some degree by researchers as failure to post scouts along the approaches, and, more so, to excessive interest in foraging and raiding by some war parties. Indeed, much of Sturgis' first days on the trail had been spent despatching small groups[8] to investigate raids against farms and arranging protection for farmers not yet raided.

This duty was later taken up by Howard's troops when he again moved forward. There is much to be said for these suppositions and, in fact, had Joseph not insisted his people remain ready to move on the shortest notice possible it is highly probable Sturgis might have been enabled to attack and wrest a final victory.

What may have saved the refugees was Yellow Wolf's fortunate sighting of soldiers crossing the Yellowstone River. These were advance scouts for Sturgis' main force checking out possible crossing sites, but Yellow Wolf interpreted the advance as a prelude to an attack. He quickly sent word to White Bird who sent a large war party under Ollokot's command to stop the soldiers before they could reach the creek.

Bannock scouts had, meanwhile, informed Sturgis that Joseph and his group were already moving west along the north bank of Canyon Creek. They gave him enough information to allow him to guess an estimated time of arrival. Sturgis, as had Howard at the Clearwater, assumed this to be the entire group in full retreat. He hurried his force along a northwesterly course that would put him put him at the canyon's mouth in time to intercept the Nez Perces. Four miles later, about noon, the troop arrived at the aforementioned bluff at the foot of rising ground terminating in a sharp ridge rising some 300 feet. Now, less than six miles from the canyon, they were beginning to skirt the bluff when heavy rifle fire from the top of the ridge stopped them in their tracks. Sturgis quickly signaled Major Lewis Merrill to take Companies F, I and L up the slopes of the ridge. Benteen's three companies would remain in reserve.

When Merrill and his troops reached higher ground they could see the creek in the distance and the line of Nez Perces on its far side moving quickly towards the canyon's mouth. Also noting the terrain upward was too rough and tangled for horses to move across easily, he signaled "dismount." The troops were formed into skirmish patterns. The horses were led back to the bluffs by handlers while the troops continued upwards on foot. The warriors, meanwhile, kept up a steady barrage, while slowly retreating into the broken, rocky terrain that afforded them good cover.

Sturgis, realizing this delay was preventing him from reaching the canyon before the Indians, ordered Benteen to take G and M Companies and continue the approximately 5.75 miles (9.25 kms) to the canyon and intercept the Indians before they could enter. The remainder of H Company would remain in reserve with Sturgis in case Merrill needed them.

Shortly after Benteen's departure Merrill gained the top of the crest only to find the warriors had disappeared into the ravines and wadis. The plateau was clear and Sturgis realized he had been lured there. The ridge was not the crest of the canyon, as he had thought, nor were the two connected. The ravines into which the warriors had entered were not a means of escape, but traps. Sturgis was not about to be tricked a second time, so he signaled Merritt to return his men to the bluff and ride to rejoin Benteen. The skirmish had wasted much valuable time and it now appeared the Indians and their horses would enter the canyon. The outcome of his plan now rested in Benteen's ability to stop them and how quickly Merritt could join him. Thus had a sour note sounded against Sturgis in the contest of strategies pitting the traditionally unmilitary Nez Perce against the experience of U.S. Army tacticians.

While Merrill was being lured up the slope, Benteen made his way rapidly to a point where he crossed the creek just west of the canyon's entrance. His orders from Sturgis were clear. According to Sturgis' plan (he had thought the encounter at the ridge would be brief) Benteen was not to attack the Indians until Merrill's force had entered his area. Benteen would then charge across to the canyon entrance cutting off as many of the horses as possible from the Indians. When Benteen began his charge, Merrill's companies would split, some to act as rearguard for Benteen, the others to charge into the main group of Indians and to move against sharpshooters the Indians would have positioned on the ridges and buttes above the entrance. On paper it looked good and should have worked; on the field it was not so good and didn't work.

Benteen's men had made good time as they moved towards the canyon. They were ahead of the Indians as they neared their intended position, although some of the leading horses were already entering the canyon. As they made their way onward they flushed some warriors from a sheltering wadi; they quickly ran to refuge behind an outcrop of rocks. It was then Sturgis' plan began to unravel. The small group he had chased from the wadi had been placed there to lure any patrol of soldiers into range of Ollokot's mounted riflemen behind the rocks that Benteen thought held only a few Indians. As the troopers crossed the creek bed and drew close they were met by a blistering volley that dropped several soldiers from their saddles. Following a short skirmish Benteen retreated back across the creek bed to a safer position at the base of a butte.[9] A few warriors remained to hold the troopers down as the others left to rejoin White Bird. It was here that Sturgis' well-laid plan to deny Joseph and his people entry to the canyon went completely awry. The horses and Joseph's group, protected by warriors on the ledges and in crevices along the canyon's walls, entered the canyon unmolested and proceeded on their way.

Two warriors, Teeto Hoonod, a sharpshooter, and Yellow Wolf, equally adroit with a rifle, remained in well-hidden positions, pinning down Benteen's force until their comrades were safely positioned within the confines of the canyon.[10] Leaving Teeto Hoonod[11] to hold off the soldiers, Yellow Wolf rejoined White Bird who had already moved to where the canyon began to narrow. There he positioned his men on one side in thick bush while Joseph placed his smaller force on the other. By the time Merrill came on the scene, Joseph and his people were two miles into the canyon.

While Benteen was unable to move from his position, Merrill advanced, but arrived too late to be of any assistance to him. Sturgis later reported the skirmish on the ridge had so much fatigued his soldiers they had been unable to cover the distance in better time. He blamed the fatigue on the three miles of very rough terrain with which his skirmishers had to contend on the way up the slope as well as on their return. The duplication was because the horse handlers had failed to bring the horses to them. Those tending the horses explained their failure by stating a large group of Indians had suddenly appeared. The handlers prepared to defend their charges, but by the time it had been revealed the Indians were Crows (who had arrived to capture the Nez Perce herd) Merrill was already

[CHAPTER 20]

on his way back. When the Crows moved on they were unable to capture any horses and had to be satisfied with those they had captured a day or so previously. That number was not nearly as many as Sturgis claimed later. His reports were greatly exaggerated in other particulars as well. Crow warriors remained in the background at Canyon Creek, taking no part in the battle.

While Benteen was holding the butte to the west, two of Merrill's companies moved to the canyon's entrance.

Meanwhile, unaware of Benteen's encounter and retreat, Sturgis pushed forward supremely confident in his plan for a two-prong attack. Sturgis had told Benteen only to delay the Indians' progress while awaiting his arrival, as Sturgis wanted both forces to attack at the same time.[12] When Benteen and his bedraggled force rejoined Sturgis they become part of the main force and turned once again towards the canyon.

Upon reaching the canyon Sturgis, for no reason ever specified, made what would prove a serious blunder: *he ordered his cavalry to dismount.* He had decided to attack in skirmish formation. Obviously he had not studied the results of Captain Perry's dismounting of his cavalry in his defeat at White Bird Canyon, or of Gibbon's fate at the Big Hole a few weeks previously when he emulated Perry. As White Bird watched the cavalry dismount he could hardly believe his good luck; now the fighting ceased being at close range, with all the advantage going to the mounted warriors. Having expected the cavalry to ride headlong into the canyon, his delight at seeing them approaching on foot can be imagined. He took full advantage of this unexpected situation. From about 11:30 in the morning until 4:30 in the afternoon they harassed the dismounted soldiers as the stragglers in Joseph's group made their escape complete.

Meanwhile, back at the canyon mouth, Sturgis assumed the Indians had all retreated and he pressed his dismounted men forward. As they approached the narrowing arroyo they were forced to close ranks. Suddenly one side of the canyon erupted in rifle fire. Sturgis had encountered Ollokot's warriors. A few seconds later White Bird's men opened fire. Sturgis had blundered into an ambuscade. The crossfire disrupted his ranks and as the sun began to set on what had become a disastrous day Sturgis ordered his bugler to sound "the retreat."

Joseph then departed to find his non-combatants, intending to push them as far as he could in order to ensure they would get far ahead. Locating the main group, he shepherded them in a brilliant retreat. With Joseph's people now far enough within the canyon and darkness beginning to fall, the mounted warriors rode away into the depths of the canyon, joining the group the following morning.

Nez Perce accounts of the Canyon Creek encounter are modest. Few gave more than minor details of, and none attached importance to, the battle. They did acknowledge the wounding of three warriors: Eashlokoon, who was shot in the right leg; Silooyleam who was hit in the left ankle; and Elaskolatat [Animal Entering a Hole] who was wounded in both the left hip and thigh by a single bullet. (This was his second leg wound, the first having occurred at Clearwater). They also mention one fatality: an elder, Tookleiks [Fish Trap], was shot by a Crow as he tried to stop the theft of horses. Their accounts also admitted the loss of horses was severe enough to hinder their future rate of travel.

Sturgis' reports and future accounts of the battle were greatly exaggerated.[13] He claimed sixteen warriors killed, many wounded and nearly the entire Nez Perce herd captured by his Crow allies. What his official report mentions is that his 250 Crows did not engage in the fighting. Their skirmishing consisted of action against one Nez Perce warrior, Teeweeyownah [Over the Point] and two unarmed elders, all of whom were killed. How many Crows were killed or wounded is unknown, but there must have been enough to cause the remaining Crows to decide the Nez Perces were too tough. They took what few horses they had captured previously and fled hurriedly. The officer who had charge of them reported sardonically, "They [the Crows] fell back, then retreated. Most continued the retreat until they were safely back in their own reservation."

It was no easy battle for either side, although the outnumbered Nez Perce, because of the experience they had gained at White Bird Canyon and the near-tragedy at the Big Hole, held the edge.

As the casualty lists came in Sturgis realized, to his total dismay, how badly he had been defeated. His casualties, although comprising only two dead on the field and twelve wounded, indicated he had fared very badly at the hands of a handful of warriors. Not only had he suffered defeat, he had been humiliated, a crushing blow to a proud officer.

Leaving the wounded and dead to the administrations of Lieutenant Charles A. Varnum, the regimental quartermaster, Sturgis and his men departed the following day, September 14. Varnum awaited the arrival of Howard's column who were bringing rations, water and wagons to transport them to Fort Keogh (also known at this time as the Tongue River Cantonment[14]) for proper treatment.

Sturgis returned his straggle to the original campsite while steeling himself for the unpleasant task of facing Howard and writing reports of the proceedings. In what had become a routine practice, he exaggerated his reports by indicating he had inflicted deaths and many injuries among the enemy. In another report he included a mention of 900 to 1,000 horses having been being killed or captured by the Crows in a separate two-day skirmish. He did not mention for several months that of the 250 Crows he started with, none had stayed in the fight long. Over the two days of skirmishing, eventually all but twenty had taken the horses they had managed to capture and fled to the sanctuary of their reservation. Howard's report shaved the number of captured horses. He approximated "400 have fallen into our hands, most of them worthless for use."[15] Howard's figure is more in keeping with Nez Perce accounts, which indicate lame and useless horses were abandoned along the trail. So much for reports.

Mercifully, possibly owing to the reports he submitted, Sturgis was spared an encounter with Sherman, and Howard was too busy with his own problems to deal with his subordinate. His fighting role in the war would likely have ended at Canyon Creek had not

Howard dispatched him and most of his troop to continue his pursuit of the Nez Perce. Sturgis left during the afternoon of September 14 along the trail leading to the Musselshell River. However, it soon became apparent the Indians were now at least two days ahead of him. Besides, their horses were worn out and rations were in such short supply his soldiers were killing their weakest horses for meat. Though there were occasional sightings of Nez Perce scouts, no contact was made. On reaching the river, Sturgis decided that further pursuit was hopeless. Joseph was well ahead, his rations were gone, his horses were fatigued and his men weary. For the second time in ten days the hapless colonel was forced to admit defeat. His entire part in the overall campaign had been a tragedy of errors; he had been out-foxed at every turn and Joseph's fighters had out-classed and out-maneuvered his. He returned to Fort Keogh knowing his part in the war was over.[16]

During the early morning of September 17 Joseph's group crossed the Musselshell River with intentions to stop, make camp and await reunion with White Bird and the other warriors. However, because it was still so early in the day, Joseph decided to continue the fifteen miles further to the Missouri River to camp and rest for two or three days. While there a scout informed Joseph of the location of a nearby Crow hunting camp. He quickly dispatched a war party. The party arrived on September 21. They rode through the camp at top speed, shooting down several Crow defenders. The others surrendered.

The war chief[17] informed his disarmed victims the raid was retaliation against the Crows for refusing to assist their long-time friends and allies. Chief Dumb Bull, the Crow leader, was pointedly told he and his companions must return to their reservation to relate the events of the raid—and the reason—to his fellow chiefs. He was told he and his companions must leave immediately because it would be a long walk. To emphasize the point, the Crows' horses were rounded up and their rifles, ammunition, blankets and food were collected. When the raiders departed, the horses and all their goods went with them. The blankets would provide warmth for the children and the food would assure the Nez Perce campers a more hearty supper that evening.

[CHAPTER 20 ENDNOTES]

1   Greene, *Nez Perce Summer, 1877,* 232. See also: McWhorter, *Yellow Wolf: His Own Story,* 187–189 and 194.

2   McWhorter, *Yellow Wolf: His Own Story.*

3   What is undoubtedly a fiction originating with Howard's 1907 publication of his book, *My Life and Experiences Among Our Hostile Indians,* is the story that Joseph had happened across a Crow hunting party. These men were friendly and professed sympathy with Joseph but said they could not join him. They did, however, give directions to a trail enabling the Nez Perces to go via Clark's Fork, cross the Yellowstone River, and then follow the dry riverbed of Canyon Creek which would lead them directly into the canyon where they defeated Sturgis. As the Crow leader explained the situation, Howard wrote, Crows, though now under government dominance, were still sympathetic to the Nez Perce cause. These hunters promised to assist the Nez Perces by watching for the army and firing shots as a warning. Significantly, the general did not include his unlikely story in his 1877 reports. Sturgis never mentioned hearing of such an encounter nor did any Nez Perce survivor. Nez Perce survivors insisted there was no need to use Crows as guides as Lean Elk knew the land very well and found the trails required. [Howard, O.O., *My Life and Experiences Among our Hostile Indians,* 294–5.]

4   The term "captain" was strictly honorary. Fisher was a civilian scout, though he was considered the best of all.

5   Benteen had been a principal subordinate to Custer at the Little Bighorn, but because of his perceived refusal to commit his company to rescue Custer he became snarled in controversy that dogged him for the rest of

his life. He and Sturgis did not get along but managed to serve together during their time in the Yellowstone campaign. Benteen, although a very brave officer, tended to complain on a chronic basis and was critical of anyone he thought inferior to himself —which included almost everyone. [Heitman, *Historical Register & Dictionary*, 1:212; Carroll & Price, *Roll Call on the Little Bighorn*, 117; Mills. *Harvest of Barren Regrets*.]

6   Goldin, Theodore W., Biography MS. [Brinstool Collection, H.B. Lee Library, Brigham Young University, Provo, Utah.]

7   Benteen, who knew more about fighting Indians than Sturgis, recommended certain tactics which, as history has proven, would have caused the Nez Perce severe casualties and perhaps a sound, if not final, defeat. Sturgis rejected the proposals mainly because he believed that Benteen had been responsible for Custer's defeat at the Little Bighorn and, therefore, was also indirectly responsible for the death of his son, 2nd Lieutenant James C. Sturgis who had fought and died there. Sturgis was one of many who considered Benteen's failure to go to Custer's assistance at the Little Bighorn the previous year was due to fear and cowardice. [Greene, Jerome, *Nez Perce Summer 1877*, 206. See also the writings of other notable researcher/historians, including Colonel W.A. Graham and Fred Dustin.]

8   Between September 11 and 13 there were encounters between war parties and Crow warriors intent on capturing the horses; also several skirmishes with units of Sturgis' command that had been dispatched in various directions to seek out the Nez Perce main group. One such unit was tricked into chasing a dust cloud. Its commander, Captain Stanton G. Fisher, was convinced the dust was being raised by Joseph's main group hurrying *away* from the canyon. Fisher sent word

to Sturgis of his surmise which did, temporarily, cause Sturgis to change his course somewhat. He quickly corrected the alteration when he received word from Fisher his unit had reached a high point near Dead Indian Pass and the realization of trickery set in. The dust cloud had been caused by Nez Perce riders dragging bundles of sage brush behind their ponies, which they were galloping in increasing circles. Many years later the subterfuge was expanded by fiction writers into a major defeat for Sturgis at the hands of the wily Joseph. The ruse was true enough, but the scope was hardly that of a major coup. [*Nez Perce Summer:1877*, 210–11.]

9 Despite his initial defeat and subsequent losses, Captain Benteen was cited for gallantry at Canyon Creek. [*History of the First Cavalry*, 1877.]

10 *Yellow Wolf*, 185; also, Redington, John W., *The Frontier*, November 1932, 60.

11 Teeto Hoonod's valiant stand very much pleased White Bird. Though not part of his initial plan, it served to delay as long as possible the need to engage the troops fully. It also meant the main body of non-combatants, the escorts and the horses could get closer to a safe area. [McWhorter, *Yellow Wolf*, 181–194.]

12 Sturgis' official report concerning the operation at Canyon Creek is undated. [Report of Secretary of War, 1877, 1, 508–512.]

13 Sturgis exaggerated greatly when he reported sixteen warriors killed, many more wounded and many horses captured. William Connolly wrote in his diary of seeing "4 dedd (*sic*) Indians…" on the battlefield. Thomas Sutherland, a reporter, increased that number to six. None of these accounts are corroborated by other sources. [Sturgis' letter, dated December 5, 1877 is in Secretary of War Report 1877, 512. William Connolly

Diary, dated September 13, 1877. Sutherland, Thomas, *Howard's Campaign,* 41.]

14 The Tongue River Cantonment and Fort Keogh are the same places. Established in 1874, the TRC was relocated in 1876 when Fort Keogh was built. During the time of the 1877 uprising either name was used in army reports.

15 Report of Secretary of War 1877, Vol.1, 624.

16 Sturgis did have one more venture into the war. During the Bear's Paw siege he was ordered to leave Fort Keogh with some troops and wagons. He thought for awhile he would get back into action, but soon discovered he and his men were to act only as an ambulance convoy transporting wounded to hospital. [*Nez Perce Summer,* 307.]

17 It was thought for several years the leader was Rainbow, but later information (discovered about 1935) determined the war chief was Red Thunder. Chief Rainbow, whose Nez Perce name was Wahchumyas, had been killed at the Big Hole, but that detail had not emerged owing perhaps to a case of confused identification. [Greene, *Nez Perce Summer, 1877,* Appendix B, 374.]

[CHAPTER 21]
HUMILIATION at YELLOWSTONE: an ANALYSIS

The pursuit through Yellowstone Park lasted twenty-four days, each one hazardous for both sides. Over that time, continuous skirmishes culminated in a major defeat for the army. Principal details have been well documented in several excellent studies,[1] but little known incidents of importance have been uncovered. Also recently discovered are facts concerning strategies used by the warrior chiefs that confused, confounded and ultimately defeated General Howard's and his subordinate officers' efforts to subdue the Nez Perces before they could escape from the park.

On August 22, when Joseph led his people through the Targhee Pass into Yellowstone National Park he once again become "lost" to Howard's scouts. Howard, once again with no idea where his quarry might be, decided to encamp at Henry's Lake (just outside the park's boundary) to rest his soldiers and search for, and perhaps recover, at least some of his purloined horses and mules. Besides, he had also to await badly needed resupply wagons as he had run out of basic rations and other necessary material. This latest setback forced him to tell his troops they must live as best they could "off the land," no easy task considering wild game had fled upon the influx of so many strangers. The soldiers killed some of the weakest and worn-out horses for meat and ate buffaloberries,[2] the only edible berries growing in great abundance in the area at the time. During his enforced inaction, Howard kept his troops as busy possible in easy tasks and dispatched a number of small units in various directions to see if Joseph might be relocated.

On August 27 Howard was made aware of the Nez Perce presence within the park. He decamped from Henry's Lake, entering Yellowstone Park the following day. On August 31 he arrived at Mary's Lake where he made camp. Shortly after arrival he was joined by six companies of the 7th Cavalry under command of Colonel Samuel D. Sturgis. The newcomers were put on alert, ready to move out on one hour's notice.

About the same time another notable officer, Captain William F. Spurgin (1838–1907) arrived from the north with a group of fifty-two laborers specially hired for the purpose of hewing roads through the dense forest. Road and bridge building was necessary because the park's trails either came to an abrupt end or were too narrow; as well, the Nez Perce warriors had burned several bridges along the trail. Repairing or rebuilding these structures took time. It was a Herculean task for the roads had to be wide enough to accommodate Howard's supply wagons and allow better than single file for the cavalry. The accomplishments of Spurgin and his men, dubbed "Spurgin's Skillets" by the soldiers[3] earned him a citation "for conspicuous and arduous service..." Part of his citation included his personal service. During the entire chase he had remained with Howard from Lapwai to the Bear's Paw.

Lieutenant-Colonel Charles C. Gilbert, who had been sent from Fort Ellis to take command of Company E, 7th Cavalry from Lieutenant Gustavus C. Doane, proved to be the most incompetent officer in the entire command. His mismanagement of Company E came under severe criticism. Set in the routines and procedures common to the Civil War, he listened to no one.

One of the greatest problems in the army's chain of command at the time was a prejudice held by many officers above the rank of captain: an age-old refusal to listen to anyone they considered below themselves in rank or social status. That bias had its genesis in European armies and had seeped through to the Americas. In the west it was aimed directly at scouts, many of whom were part Indian and were therefore of little account.

There are no accounts of what Howard or Sturgis thought of Gilbert; and Sherman made no further mention of him either.

None of Sturgis' six companies were to achieve any success. Although Benteen proposed an excellent plan to stop Joseph at Pelican Creek, he was unable to convince Sturgis to give it consideration. Benteen had gained much knowledge of Indian warfare[4] and had added to it the year previously at the Little Bighorn. However, Sturgis and Benteen had long held a mutual dislike. Sturgis, whose son had been killed at the Little Bighorn, was one of those who considered Benteen cowardly because he had not rushed to help Custer. As a result, he refused to act on any suggestion put forward by Bentee. In retrospect, however, at least one of the three ideas he put forward was of sufficient worth to have perhaps turned the tide against the Nez Perce warriors. Sturgis simply would not listen to him.

During these weeks of confusion and personal conflicts besetting Howard's overall command, Joseph truly came into his own as a leader. Although he had never been a war chief, during the next dangerous weeks he showed he knew the finer aspects of strategy—not so much of tactical warfare but of guile, deception and evasion. Time and time again soldiers were enticed (when they were allowed to come close enough) down trails leading nowhere. Then, as if by magic, Joseph and his band would disappear. He avoided needless skirmishes by adhering to the fine art of outwitting the enemy. By so doing, aided mainly by White Bird and Tool'hool'hool'zote, and to a lesser degree by Looking Glass who had his own agenda, he made the army look foolish and ill-prepared. In Joseph and his allies they met a foe whose cunning far surpassed theirs.

The chiefs, however, were also hindered by their undisciplined warriors, mostly young ones acting independently without the knowledge or authority of their chiefs. As the band picked its way through the park, several random attacks were waged against settlers' farms by small groups of renegade youths angry at their dispossession. In these raids several settlers were killed, houses looted and ransacked, horses stolen, crops burned and wagons destroyed. Joseph spoke later about these proceedings, denouncing them.

Meanwhile, Howard had also resumed his advance. From September 1 to 9 he kept his army moving, allowing little rest until he reached Dead Indian Pass where he made camp at the foot of Dead Indian Hill. During this march several skirmishes and engagements took place, and all were handled expertly by White Bird, Looking Glass, Ollokot and Tool'hool'hool'zote. None of the Nez Perce warriors who took part in those encounters, when interviewed as late as 1935, considered them memorable. Few could recall them in great detail.[5]

The one battle to which several attached importance was the decisive victory over Sturgis at Canyon Creek. When Joseph and his group were some five miles north of the Yellowstone River one of Benteen's scouts saw them heading along Canyon Creek towards Clark's Fork.[6] The scout instinctively knew their goal was Clark's Canyon. Benteen forwarded a plan to Sturgis indicating an attack on the main group would succeed if launched as the band emerged from the creek's narrow outlet. Sturgis saw the perfect chance for a final victory.

On September 12 Colonel Sturgis, who had led his cavalry force within four miles of Joseph's main group, realized if he could overtake them they could be attacked as they passed between the canyon to the north and a high butte just south of the creek. The entire area was rugged terrain, difficult to traverse for a large army but perfect for smaller troops. He ordered Benteen's cavalry to proceed at the gallop to head off the Indians as they approached the pass. At the same time he sent Major Lewis Merrill[7] (1834–1896) with three companies of the 7th to a ridge two miles to the north. The intent was to stop a large party of warriors from joining Joseph. With his flanking forces underway, Sturgis swung westward, intent upon arriving in time to reinforce Benteen.

Meanwhile, scouts under Yellow Wolf had informed Joseph and White Bird of the six troops of cavalry approaching. The two chiefs saw immediately the best defensive position was to gain the pass before the army. Joseph forced his group forward at an increased pace while warriors positioned themselves between the oncoming cavalry and the fleeing Indians. As the main group scurried to safety, the warriors hidden behind rocks and any shelter available within the numerous gullies began a steady barrage of fire into Merrill's companies. Pinned down, Merrill was kept from advancing to the canyon for several hours.

It was also a time of singular acts of heroism, one of the most notable being that of Teeto Hoonod who singlehandedly (with some temporary help from Yellow Wolf) held off an entire line of Benteen's company attempting to intercept Joseph's large group.[8]

On September 10, while passing the base of Hart Mountain, scouts rode in with word for Joseph that a large force (six companies)[9] was marching toward Clark's Basin, the major fording point of Clarke's Fork River's six crossing points. Joseph, of course, not knowing this group was under the command of Colonel Sturgis, a new foe he was not yet acquainted with, assumed these troops were Howard's. If that was so, he reasoned, Howard had caught up with him and was much closer than he had thought. Soon other scouts arrived to report that five of the companies had control of all the fords but one. Only Clark's Basin, a wide spot on Canyon Creek remained open. To Joseph these reports were nothing short of appalling, as he would now have to abandon his initial plan of crossing at different places and shepherd the entire group across the river at a single point. Not only would this be a task that would take longer, but, more importantly, it meant he had to reach Clark's Basin before the soldiers were within interception distance.

In order to accomplish this Joseph pressed his group forward at an advanced pace regardless of the strain it put on elders and the boys herding the horses. With everyone's full cooperation they managed this formidable task with time to spare. The crossing of Canyon Creek was made successfully without loss or mishap. For the time being, though they were safe, there was no time to rest so Joseph pressed his charges towards the Canyon entrance.

The canyon's entrance resembles the spout of a giant funnel. During millenniums past it had been the exit point of a torrential mountain river that had eroded its course into high, vertical walls. These steep precipices appear almost man-made—a roofless tunnel. This canyon, Joseph had been assured by Lean Elk, would lead them north to comparative safety within the Absaroke Mountain range. The large band was almost at the entrance when Joseph was informed soldiers had entered the canyon some time before and had not re-emerged.

Alarmed, Joseph quickly directed his people into the woods to take shelter in the dense forest. The entire group, including the horses, remained there but, although well hidden, it was a tense and trying time. Joseph and White Bird then met to ponder how to lure the soldiers from the canyon into an ambush without raising a warning to the main body of troops already too close for comfort. A brief discussion followed, a plan was made and, as Joseph ushered his people deeper into the forest, White Bird assembled some warriors who re-crossed the creek and rode away towards an area known as Dead Indian Plains. They were about to cause Colonel Sturgis an embarrassment he would not soon forget. Neither would his superiors.

Sturgis, although he knew he was closing with the enemy, had not yet reached a position where he could see them. Had he paid better attention to a report received from a scout, J.W. Reddington,[10] who had actually seen the main body as it progressed along Clark's Fork River, he would not likely have fallen for White Bird's ruse. But Sturgis was not one to pay much attention to those he considered subordinate. Prior to Reddington's report he had ignored a suggestion from Captain Benteen that would have placed him at an advantage to stop Joseph and end the flight once and for all.[11] As he crested a hill he saw large clouds of dust on the horizon. This told him Joseph had decided against going to the canyon and was moving *away* from the river. This about face made sense to Sturgis because, for some reason, he believed the canyon to be a dead end, certainly a place Joseph would avoid unless he had chosen it as the site for a final, last-ditch stand. The sight of dust clouds convinced him Joseph had turned to avoid the advancing troopers.

Sturgis didn't know it, but White Bird was, as usual, several steps ahead and had devised an ingenious ploy. He had sent warriors south to a dusty plain a short distance away. When they reached the plain they tied bundles of sagebrush to ropes then, dragging the bundles behind their horses, rode at a rapid pace around the fringes as others milled about in the center in an ever-widening circle. A great cloud of dust was raised as the riders, still dragging the brush, rode to the south edge of the plain at top speed. The illusion caused to distant onlookers was of a great many people rapidly proceeding south. This dust was what Sturgis had seen and believed to be the entire Nez Perce band. In reality it was less than fifteen mounted warriors dragging bundles of sagebrush in circles.

Sturgis wasted much time pursuing the dust cloud. The companies he had dispatched had traveled some distance before an advance scout, Stanton G. Fisher, returned with depressing news. He had crested the ridge at Dead Indian Pass and immediately realized the dust had been a trick. By turning many of his troops toward it, Sturgis had allowed the enemy a victory without a shot being fired. He had accomplished nothing; all he had to show for his effort were bundles of sagebrush the riders had left as a memento.

The warriors employed such ruses because Joseph needed as much time as possible in order to allow the non-combatants to stay ahead of his pursuers. Sturgis, in deciding to do battle with a dust cloud, had left the escape route totally open. With the outfoxed Sturgis temporarily delayed, Joseph, his group and the horses drew closer to the canyon that would allow then to escape into the Absaroke Mountains many miles to the north.

Thus, the battle at Canyon Creek became somewhat of an anti-climax. When Sturgis eventually arrived they were defeated by the warriors. Though the battle itself was hard-fought, Sturgis suffered only fourteen casualties—ten more than the warriors had suffered. Sturgis' casualties included four dead, whereas Nez Perce had one fatality which may not have occurred in the canyon fighting.

For Sturgis the setback proved serious. When the news of his defeat reached General Sherman he was furious. He informed Sturgis he was to await the arrival of Howard's army and join that force in a reserve status. This was a severe blow for Sturgis, an ambitious colonel who had long envisioned promotion to general. Now he saw the promotion dissipating as quickly as the dust he had chased.[12]

During the afternoon of September 23 Joseph and the non-combatants, having advanced steadily northward averaging twenty-five miles each day, were joined by the warriors and crossed the Missouri River near Cow Island. They stopped for a planned lengthy rest at place the Nez Perce knew as both Seloselo Wejainwais [a shade of colored paint] and also as Attish Pah [Place of the Cave of Red Paint].

The warriors were pleased to rejoin the main group as it meant a respite from fighting—at least it seemed so. From the 12th until the 14th, they had been engaged in skirmishes with Crow warriors under Sturgis' command. During these skirmishes one Nez Perce warrior, Teeweenowyah (Over the Point), was killed and two unidentified elderly men, unarmed, were shot down. On the other hand, the Crows fared badly. They suffered a disastrous defeat and fled the area. Sturgis later stated in his report to the secretary of war the Crows had killed or captured 900 to 1,000 horses during the two days of fighting,[13] but the Crows never claimed such a coup. The Nez Perce stoutly denied the loss of any horses in the battle, insisting horses the Crows had captured had been several dozens released because they were in such poor condition they could not keep up. Whatever the number of horses the Crows might have captured, all would have been useless (except as food) because the Nez Perces always assured uselessness by cutting one foot of any abandoned, worn-out horse that might fall to an enemy. If no battle was involved a worn-out horse was simply released to fend for itself. Howard also joined in this blatant exaggeration, but tempered it in his reports to about 400 horses and never mentioned it again.

It was during the two days leading up to the Canyon Creek battle that the full impact of being deserted by the other tribes hit home the hardest. To all, warriors and non-combatants alike, it seemed the entire world had turned against them. Yellow Wolf later said it was then that his heart had been set afire at the treachery of their supposed friends. They held no such resentment against the Bannocks who were scouting for S.G. Fisher, for they were long-time enemies. In fact, the Nez Perce held them in such contempt they had no fear of them whatsoever.

Fisher would have agreed with the Nez Perce on their opinion of the Bannocks. Fisher, a first-class scout had captained a forward party of eighty Bannocks sent out by Howard on September 7. Though he had come close to the Nez Perce warriors on occasion, he had no luck at all in convincing his Bannocks to engage them. Within a few days, Fisher reported, because no dead Nez Perces were found to scalp, they all deserted. Apparently none of the Bannocks actually wanted to earn the scalps through battle, so Fisher returned to Howard to report that scouts had deserted, no Nez Perce had been killed or found dead, and no worthwhile horses had been captured.

Another noted captain who did not fare well during those two weeks was Captain Fred. W. Benteen. Because of Sturgis' dislike of him, Benteen was given tasks difficult to carry out. His was the unit that suffered the most casualties: one man killed, five wounded, forty-one horses killed or lost. More salt was poured into the wounds when he was unable to report having killed or wounded a single Nez Perce warrior or captured any horses.

If the Crows and Bannocks were being accused of less than heroic service, Colonel Sturgis and his soldiers were not having a good time, either. While they awaited General Sherman's displeasure they huddled in their uncomfortable camp near the canyon's mouth. Though they were no longer engaged in fighting, their suffering was no less harsh. They were out of supplies and were reduced to killing their worn-out horses for food. The wounded suffered the most for they had insufficient water and no extra blankets for warmth. On the morning of the 14th, Howard arrived, but he was also so short of supplies (wagons from Fort Ellis had reached Howard on the 13th but they contained insufficient supplies for two forces). Howard's men shared their rations with Sturgis' troops who supplemented with the horsemeat left over. Shortly after, Sherman's orders also arrived informing Sturgis he would remain with Howard's force.

Howard immediately assigned Sturgis to a reserve position, but Sturgis and pleaded with Howard for one more chance to overtake and capture the fleeing Indians. Howard, after due consideration, agreed to allow Sturgis another chance. Two days later Sturgis, finally having received much needed supplies, resumed the journey with his reassembled troops. He proceeded northward but made no contact with the warriors. On September 27 he reached the Musselshell River only to learn the Indians had departed the day before. He decided to quit the chase and returned to Fort Keogh.

[CHAPTER 21 ENDNOTES]

1   Three of the best works are L.V. McWhorter's *Hear me My Chiefs* and *Yellow Wolf: His Own Story*, as well as Jerome Greene's *Nez Perce Summer 1877*. All three narratives go into great detail while McWhorter includes extensive interviews with survivors of the revolt. [See bibliography for publication details.]

2   Buffaloberries (*Shepherdia argentea*) are very rich in vitamins. They are best ingested when boiled. When steeped in very hot water for twenty minutes or so they produce a nourishing tea. Buffaloberries can be eaten uncooked but it is not recommended as they have an insipid taste. Raw buffaloberries rank among the more astringent of the many "pucker inducing" berries on earth. [Meyers, E.C., *Basic Bush Survival*, 37.]

3   Organized as a company of engineers, the group was armed as an infantry unit and paid three dollars a day plus rations. The official title of this special group was Spurgin's Skilled Laborers. The troops coined the term "Skillets" as a shortened form of a description given by Spurgin when he referred to his squad as "[while they] are not engineers, as bridge repairers and road builders they are highly skilled." [Brown, Mark H., *The Flight of the Nez Perce,* 241; and author's files.]

4   An interesting account of this phase of Sturgis' defeat is to be found in letters written in 1891 by Major Fred W. Benteen to Thomas Goldin. At the time Benteen was a captain recently transferred from Montana. Because of his experience in fighting the tribes of northern plains, he made several suggestions to Sturgis about how Joseph could be apprehended, but Sturgis dismissed him quite curtly on all occasions. Benteen felt the snubs were probably because he was becoming a prominent figure in the previous year's disaster at the Little Bighorn. Already facing numerous accusations that he and Major Marcus A. Reno (1834–1889) had more or less deserted Custer and his men to their fate by failing to come to their assistance, Benteen was not held in high regard. However, an equally logical answer to the snubs was that one of the soldiers who had died at the Little Bighorn was Lieutenant James Garland Sturgis, twenty-two-year-old son of Colonel Samuel D. Sturgis. The colonel in all likelihood felt Benteen at least partly responsible for his son's death. [Graham, W.A., *The Custer Myth,* 157–214.]

5   McWhorter, L.V., *Hear Me My Chiefs,* 427–468.

6   This canyon was known to the Nez Perce as Tepahlewam Wakuspah [little Split Rocks] because it was similar to the sacred place at Tolo Lake. [Author's files.]

7   Lewis Merrill was an officer of much experience. He had served in the Civil War and had received many

commendations for bravery. At the war's end he remained in the army and served in the southwest before being assigned to 7th Cavalry. He missed the battle at the Little Bighorn because he had been sent east on duty a few weeks prior. [Author's files.]

8   Reddington, *The Frontier,* November, 1932, 60.

9   A company normally comprised one hundred men.

10 Reddington, J.W., "Scouting in Montana in the Seventies," *The Frontier,* 1932, 57–59.

11 For an excellent and detailed narrative of this aspect of Sturgis' folly see: McWhorter, *Hear Me My Chiefs,* 460–466.

12 Sturgis never got his promotion. He retired, embittered, in 1886 and died three years later.

13 Report to the Secretary of War, 1877, Vol. 1, 507. The part of the report that was written by Sturgis is undated and has no notation of where it was written or its point of dispatch.

[CHAPTER 22]

THE TIGHTENING NET

Following the September 21 encounter with Chief Dumb Bull,[1] Joseph led his people into a concealed valley in which they again made camp. During a short stay he and the other chiefs decided on a safe route that would lead them to Canada. On September 23, at approximately 2:00 PM, Joseph and his people, flanked by warriors, arrived at Judith Basin on the Missouri River. Here was a safe fording place that Whites called Cow Landing but was known to the Nez Perces as Seloselo Wejanais [Soil-Tinged-in-Red].

The arrival was observed by the interested and watchful eyes of a twelve-man infantry unit commanded by Sergeant William Molchert. The sergeant and four infantrymen, accompanied by a team of four civilians headed by Michael Foley, Chief Disbursing Clerk for the Josephine Steamboat Line, had arrived from Fort Benton the day before. The civilians were employees of George Clendenin, a former colonel of the Union Army who, upon retirement, had become chief agent for the JSL. They were there to arrange forwarding of fifty tons of freight, comprised of government supplies and commercial goods, to various parts of the region. A vast array of material was stacked and piled on and near the pier. Molchert and his twelve-man squad were multitasked; besides protecting the clerks, they were to sort and segregate the government supplies for transport to various army posts; they were also to select listed goods and rations assigned to a team of engineers clearing obstructions from the Judith River at a place upstream called Dauphin Rapids. The engineers, also from Fort Benton, were under the protection of B Company of the 7th Infantry regiment from which eight of Molchert's soldiers had been detatched. There was a certain apprehension felt by the onlookers as the vast numbers of Indians began to wade through the water. Molchert quickly dispersed his men to pre-selected defensive positions while the clerks took cover.

However, neither warriors nor non-combatants gave the soldiers any perceivable notice as they passed. The entire group seemingly ignored the tents and piles of goods completely as they rapidly moved out of sight to an open area two miles away where they encamped. Molchert and his men breathed a sigh of relief, thinking they would not see the Natives again. They were wrong.

An hour later two riders returned to the landing. Foley, who had a working knowledge of several tribal languages, walked out to meet them. To his surprise, he was to say later, one "spoke English as well as anyone could…," expressed friendship, and then asked to speak with the officer in charge of the soldiers. Foley left to relay the message to Sergeant Molchert. When the sergeant came forward the spokesman declared he wished to purchase food and some other supplies. He said payment would be in gold nuggets, but Molchert, a man short of diplomacy and tact, stated he would never supply food to renegades. He then turned to walk away, but the spokesman called him back and asked once more for some food. Molchert told him to wait, went back to his defense position, retrieved a half sack of hardtack biscuits and a side of bacon, returned and gave it to the Indian whom he later insisted was Joseph.[2] The two men shook hands and the Indians withdrew. Years later Molchert wrote a letter to a friend describing what happened during the next hours.

> "a while [later we saw] an Indian coming between our breastworks and the foot hills…[he was] stripped naked [which we knew] means fight. Having previously distributed ammunition and giving each man his place, we were

standing around taking our supper as I jokingly remarked [that] this might be [our last supper of bacon and hard tack], when without any warning they [the Indians] commenced to fire from the hills...but luckily nobody was hurt. This was sun down (sic) *and from that time on till* (sic) *day break* (sic) *we were fighting for our lives. Of course the freight we could not save as it was piled right up against the bluff. [A hospital tent] with 500 sacks of bacon piled against it [the Indians] set on fire that lit up the country for miles. They charged us three times during the night through high willows, impossible to see anyone."*³

THE PLUNDERING OF COW ISLAND

In his letter Molchert omitted mentioning the two civilians, George Trautman and E.W. Buckwater, who were wounded in the first volley of shots. The accounts of the fight as accredited to Chiefs Peopeo Tholekt and Yellow Wolf differ greatly from Molchert's. Both stated the approach was through a coulee opposite the landing and the attack was undetected until the first shots were fired. Both considered the subsequent plundering justified as an act of war. As Peopeo Tholekt put it, "We had privilege to do this. It was in the war." However, both denounced igniting the fires, claiming the fires were set against the wishes of the chiefs. The fires, as Yellow Wolf put it, were started by "bad boys" who disobeyed the directions of their leaders. Michael Foley, on the other hand, credited the blazes as having saved the soldiers and civilians. "I believe," he said later, "the fire was what saved us."⁴ He also managed to compose and send a message to his boss, Agent Clendenin.

Rifle Pit at Cow Island.
September 23, 1877, 10 A.M.
"Col: Chief Joseph is here, and says he will surrender for two hundred bags of sugar. I told him to surrender without

the sugar. He took the sugar and will not surrender. What shall I do?"ᵃ

Agent Clendenin, who did not receive the signal until the morning of the 24th, never replied so far as is known. His reply would have been moot at any rate, for the fighting had stopped, the camp had been pillaged, and what goods had not been taken had been torched. After the soldiers and their civilian companions had retreated to safety in the woods, the Nez Perce women arrived to take what they wanted. According to Peopeo Tholekt,

> "We took whatever we needed, flour, sugar, coffee, bacon and beans. Anything whoever wanted it. Some took pots and pans for the cooking. We figured it was soldiers supplies, so set fire to what we did not take."[5]

Eventually the chiefs put an end to the looting and ordered everyone to return to the camp to prepare for departure early the next morning. Unknown to the chiefs, word of the looting had reached Fort Benton. Word had been quickly dispatched to Major Guido Ilges (1835–1918)[6] the fort's commander, who at the time was on a patrol to the east at the head of a small force. Thus, word did not get to him quickly. Ilges had left Fort Benton on September 21, with a squad of thirty-eight citizen volunteers and one soldier (Private Thomas H. Bundy of F Company, 7th Infantry). It had been Ilges' intention to assist the occupants of Fort Clagett (near the junction of the Missouri and Judith rivers), who had reported being threatened by a large Nez Perce war party.[7] When Ilges and his troop arrived late afternoon of the 22nd they were informed the Nez Perces had not attacked the fort but had continued toward Cow Island. On September 23, Ilges moved on to Cow Landing, arriving shortly after the Nez Perces had resumed their trek north-

---

a   Foley was likely very nervous when he sent his message. The time was undoubtedly 10:00 PM. [Author's note.]

ward. Amid the wreckage of the depot the fires still smoldered and goods unwanted by the women lay scattered over a wide area. Ilges was pleased to learn Molchert and his supply party had escaped with only two casualties. He learned this when a small force led by Second Lieutenant Edward Hardin (who had in tow a small howitzer) arrived from Fort Benton. He had with him Molchert and his men whom he had found on the trail as they proceeded towards Dauphin Rapids.

Meanwhile, Ilges had learned the Nez Perces had traveled northward up Cow Creek Canyon where they had encountered an oxen-drawn wagon train. The slow-moving wagons were quickly overtaken and looted. Three teamsters, determined to protect their property, resisted and were killed. The others fled into the hills.

The looting of the wagons delayed the warriors long enough for Ilges and his small troop to come within sight of the Indians, who saw the troops at about the same time. Shots were fired. In the ensuing fight, which lasted about two hours, one of the civilians was killed, causing Ilges to withdraw. Knowing the Nez Perces could easily outflank his small force, he made a gradual retreat, returning to Cow Landing at 6 PM. When Ilges retreated, the raiding party resumed their looting. They set all the wagons ablaze before riding to rejoin the main group.

The next day, deciding to return to Fort Benton by way of Cow Creek Canyon, Ilges and his men inspected the remains of the burned wagons and searched for the teamsters who had escaped. Turning then to the Cow Creek Trail they came across the body of a man who had been killed near Birch Creek,[8] which they took as further evidence of Nez Perce raiding. On September 29 Ilges returned to Fort Benton to wait for Howard, whom he knew to be nearby and approaching rapidly.

From Ilges' point of view, though he considered his retreat from Cow Canyon, the looting of the Cow Landing depot and failure to overtake and stop the Nez Perces a military defeat, he took some consolation in knowing he had delayed Joseph's progress. From Joseph's perspective, the Cow Island battle, though a victory in that badly needed food and goods had been taken, had been costly in its delay on the road to freedom. The outcome of wars, of course, can often be measured more in defeats and delays than in victories.

AFTERMATH OF COW ISLAND: THE SETTLERS' REACTION

When news of the Cow Island raid became known to the public, some Whites were very frightened; but an equal number applauded, spurred no doubt by editorials and accounts in newspapers from Missoula and Helena. The incident gave editors the opportunity to renew their ragging of what they considered their inept army. Readers began to cheer for Joseph when large headlines, depicting Howard, Sturgis and Gibbon as blind men groping after shadows in the dark, made sport of the situation. It was an extremely unhappy time for the commanders and men of the Army of the Northwest.

However, as unhappy as the army was in its distress, it hardly equaled that felt by the Nez Perces. They were worn out and tired of running. Most of them had little idea of where they were going, but continued their northward trudge only because they had faith in their chiefs. Their spirits remained buoyant with the knowledge their warriors had defeated the army at every turn. Now, sustained by Sargeant Molchert's bacon, beans, biscuits, sugar and coffee (and the prospect of fresh buffalo meat), they prepared to slog their way northward, giving thanks to the Great Spirit Chief because they had been unmolested for four days in a row. Since the retreat of Major Ilges following the departure from Attish Pah there had been no sightings of soldiers.

Joseph and White Bird began to see a ray of hope as the border drew ever closer. Then they made yet another error. They agreed with Looking Glass who, informed by scouts that Howard had dropped back to three days distance, had decided a two-day rest was in order. Joseph agreed because, while he did not want to stop for long, he was concerned about driving his people harder. There were now among the numbers too many sick elders and too many tired women and children. Some of the people suffered from cuts, lacerations and broken limbs sustained in the many rushes for safety. His decision, regrettably, simply tightened the impending noose.

Had Joseph been less concerned with the discomfort of his charges and more concerned with the tactics of his foe he might have been able to clearly see what Lean Elk had seen: Howard, having noticed a particular trait in his quarry's routine, began dropping his march to a slower pace. He did this, not because his troops were tired, but because his scouts were reporting the Nez Perces also reduced their rate of march each time Howard dropped back two or three days. When Howard resumed his advance so did the Indians. Howard, not one to miss such an opportunity, took advantage of this intelligence because he knew Miles, who was already on an angling course, would use any delay to close the gap. Howard was deliberately keeping his distance, opening and closing the gap as he saw fit. Lean Elk had seen through this ploy, but Looking Glass, Joseph and White Bird had not.

Looking Glass' Penultimate Error

The Indians moved on from Cow Island, but because of the time lost with the wagon train attack and the fight with Major Ilges' patrol, Chief Looking Glass ordered an early camp be made. This was not a popular decision, but was carried out for several reasons: the majority of the people were tired, the grueling trek had weakened the sick and elderly, and the days were darkening earlier with the onset of autumn. Added to that, earlier in the day Lean Elk had been replaced in his role as the chief guide when he got into an argument with Looking Glass who complained the Lean Elk was pushing onward at too fast a pace. Lean Elk, who did not get along well with Looking Glass at the best of times, told Looking Glass he should lead if he thought he could do better.

Lean Elk's[9] expertise in tracking and guiding told him what Howard was doing. He went to Looking Glass, who was still the overall chief, with his concerns. He outlined Howard's tactics, explained how the general was manipulating the pace. When Howard stopped, so did Looking Glass. By quickening and slackening his own pace he had lured Looking Glass into making needless stops. Looking Glass, unable to understand Lean Elk's logic, dismissed his concerns. Instead, he criticized Lean Elk for hurrying the people, thereby causing the elders needless discomfort. He reminded him he was not a chief and that he, Looking Glass, should be the guide. Lean Elk, upset with the chief's indifference and criticism, angrily turned on Looking Glass. In a 1932 interview, Chief Many Wounds (Hohots Ilppilp) described the confrontation.

> "Looking Glass upbraided Poker Joe [Lean Elk] for his hurrying, for causing the old people weariness, told him that he was no chief, that he himself [Looking Glass] was a chief and that he would be the leader. Poker Joe replied, 'All right, Looking Glass, you can lead. I am trying to save the people, doing my best to cross into Canada before the soldiers find us. You can lead but I think we will be caught and killed.'"[10]

Had Lean Elk gone to White Bird or Joseph instead of pouting after being rebuffed by Looking Glass he likely would have averted the forthcoming tragedy. Lean Elk had no need to answer to the Asotin chief for he was not of the Asotin Band. He was, as noted previously, the son of a Nez Perce mother and Delaware father. Many years before he had married into the Delaware tribe and, in keeping with custom, had gone with his wife to her Delaware band. Unfortunately, he did nothing following his talk with Looking Glass. He simply relinquished his position as lead guide and returned to the warrior ranks.

For the second time Looking Glass had refused to heed advice of an experienced warrior. His first rebuff had caused the disaster at the Big Hole and this latest one would result in yet another tragedy. Looking Glass assumed the guiding, and, because he felt safety was closer than it actually was, for the next four days he moved at too leisurely a pace. Under his flawed leadership a daily march of twelve miles, less than half the previous twenty-five miles, became the average.

Regardless, the Nez Perces remained ahead of Howard and on September 28 hunters located a small herd of buffalo, a supply of badly needed hides and meat.[11] The chiefs sent hunters after the animals while the main group moved on to Snake Creek in order to make camp and spend one day there. This was a good camping area well known to Nez Perce hunters. It had abundant fresh water, hills to act as natural barriers and lookout points, plus large treed areas to shelter the horses. Because it lays in the shadow of the Bear's Paw Mountains, the siege that was about to fall upon them became known as The Battle of the Bear's Paw.

A one-day rest would have provided adequate respite before their final push to the border. Looking Glass, however, was about to blunder yet again. Because they were within forty-eight miles of the border he decided a two-day rest was in order. What he had no way of knowing was that Snake Creek was also now within forty-eight hours of General "Old Bear Coat" Miles, who was pushing his troops hard and closing the distance with each passing hour.

While the people rested it was decided that a party of scouts should be sent north to determine the most favorable route to the border. Two riders were also dispatched to the "Land of the Grandmother" in search of Sitting Bull's camp. The hope of, course, was Sitting Bull might send warriors to help the Nez Perces in their final push northward. The Sioux might even fight should Howard's army somehow overtake the fleeing band. Riders set out along separate trails early the following morning.

While the scouts were gone, Looking Glass explained to the chiefs his plans for a successful conclusion to the exodus. He told them departure would start two mornings hence. He felt the border scouts would have their part of the assignment well in hand by then, and while it would take longer to find Sitting Bull, with luck the Sioux would meet them either very close to the border or soon after the crossing had been made.

Just as hope was appearing to take an upward turn, the fates dealt a terrible blow. Three scouts who had been sent earlier to the north rode into the camp to report the border was but a day and a half at normal walking pace. They also reported they had met, and had camped the night with, a group of northern Assiniboine[12] hunters. The Assiniboine [Walk-around-Sioux], the scouts said, had agreed to lead the Nez Perce to a Sioux camp north of the border.

White Bird felt uneasy when he heard this report. The Assiniboine, he counseled, were not well known to the Nez Perces, but were very well known to the Sioux. In fact, he cautioned, those two tribes had long been traditional enemies. White Bird had also heard the Assiniboine were noted for treachery and said so; but Looking Glass thought no harm would come if a small group met with the Assiniboine to arrange for their assistance. Allies were needed if Sitting Bull's camp was to be found easily. A group of six riders, including White Bird's stepson, Tipyahalahnah Kapskaps [Strong Eagle], set out. Near dusk the following day a member of that party raced his lathered, near-blown horse into camp. He gasped out a tragic story to his brothers.

The group, he told them, had found the Assiniboine and had been greeted as brothers. They had parleyed at length and had smoked sweet grass in a spirit of friendship.

"Suddenly," the survivor related, "they turned and fired on us. The others are all dead. I alone escaped."

If Joseph was sickened by the news, Looking Glass was devastated. It had been he who had argued most convincingly for meetings with potential allies, first with the Crows then with the Assiniboine. Both had betrayed his good faith. For Joseph and his people the choices now were very limited: they could await Howard's arrival and fight one final battle, or depart at first light to make a desperate dash for the border and hope there would be no great assemblage of Assiniboine in their way. Surrender was not yet in their minds.

Joseph and his chiefs met in council late into the evening to decide the best course of action. Since June the band had traveled hundreds of miles, had suffered great hardship and had seen many of their people killed or wounded. All the elderly were so fatigued many were being transported via travois. Also, summer was rapidly turning to autumn, so the nights were cold. There were not enough buffalo robes left to give the women and children proper covers for the cold nights. That the warriors had won every battle seemed small compensation for the plight in which they now found themselves.

In fact, the five valiant bands had covered upwards of 1,700 miles (2,736 kms) of the west's most rugged terrain, had eluded the searching armies for 118 days, had fought—and won—no less than seventeen battles and skirmishes, including one on the Lolo Trail against a group of Treaty Nez Perces. Two of the battles had been major full-scale encounters. They had humiliated the 1st Cavalry Division and had decimated many companies of infantry. They had defeated every volunteer militia that had dared challenge them. They had knocked Colonels Gibbon and Sturgis out of the fight, in the process reducing Sturgis to a laughingstock. They had humiliated the 7th Cavalry Regiment, had caused General Sherman no end of embarrassment, and had left Howard in the dust.

To date, September 29, Joseph, his fellow chiefs and their warriors, outnumbered four to one, had soundly whipped the cream of the U.S. Army of the Northwest. They had inflicted upon an army of hundreds 175 casualties—in excess of 10 percent *(of which 101 were fatalities)*. They had captured dozens of mules and horses, had seized many hundreds of pounds of rations and supplies, dozens of rifles and thousands of rounds of ammunition.[13] Now they were down to a few hundred horses, had no cattle, possessed just over eighty tepees—and worse—had less than ninety-five healthy fighting men.

Joseph and his chiefs decided that night on a final bold plan. In the morning at first light the final rush to Canada would commence. It would be a forced march, estimated at two days; sufficient they felt because Howard was still at least two days to the south. No one in the Nez Perce camp had any idea that General Miles was less than thirty miles distant and moving quickly.

[CHAPTER 22 ENDNOTES]

1. Not to be confused with Perish Dumb Bell, the Flathead chief who had been in charge of the party of buffalo hunters of whom Lean Elk was a member when he joined with Joseph.

2. Molchert is clearly wrong in his identification. Joseph, though fluent in several Indian languages and dialects, was never described by anyone as being able to speak English "as well as anyone could." Whether Foley thought the man was Joseph is unknown.

3. William Molchert's versions of the meeting and subsequent raid are detailed in a letter to David Hilger, dated November 13, 1917. [Montana Historical Society Archives, SC491. Helena, Montana.]

4. Foley does not explain how or why the fires saved him and his companions. It has been conjectured he meant the brightness had prevented the warriors from approaching closely or entering the camp until after the defenders had withdrawn. [Author's files.]

5. Quoted from interviews with Peopeo Tholekt. [McWhorter, *Yellow Wolf*, 62.]

6. A very interesting narrative on Guido Ilges, his background, his record as Fort Benton commandant and his uneasy relations with Inspector James Morrow Walsh, commander of the NWMP in Canada's northwest territory (now Alberta and Saskatchewan) is found in Guy Vanderhaeghe's historical novel, *A Good Man*.

7. There is no evidence in Nez Perce narratives indicating such a war party had ventured near that fort. [Author's files.]

8. Not to be confused with the Birch Creek, as described in a previous chapter.

9   George Oliver Shields (1846–1925), in his book, *The Battle of the Big Hole* (Rand McNally, Chicago, 1889) falsely described Lean Elk (on page 27) as a disreputable renegade Nez Perce chief named Kiniknik Squalsac [Little Tobacco]. Shields wrote, "Joseph was reinforced in this valley The Bitterroot Valley] by eighteen lodges of renegade Nez Perces, who lived off the reservation, under the leadership of the disreputable chief, Poker Joe."

10 Many Wounds in conversation with L. V. McWhorter, August 1935. [McWhorter, *Hear Me My Chiefs*, 473–4.]

11 The Nez Perces cattle had been lost at the Salmon River, but beef had never been a preferred part of their diet. Buffalo was preferred because it did not require a tenderizing period of several days. Freshly killed beef is generally tough and quite unpalatable.

12 The Assiniboine, part of the Blackfoot Nation, resided mainly in the Cypress Hills in what is now southern Saskatchewan. A southern Assiniboine band resided in Montana. In almost every regard the two were separate tribes.

13 Report of the First Cavalry Division 1887. [US Archives, Military Section, Washington.]

[CHAPTER 23]
THE LAST BATTLE: SIEGE at SNAKE CREEK

It is officially known as the Battle at the Bear's Paw, a short mountain grouping adjunct to the Rocky Mountain range in northwestern Montana.[1] It was, in fact, fought several miles to the east. The "battle"—in reality two separate attacks by the army—was fought over one day of bitter fighting. In both attacks the army was repulsed, with heavy losses by the defenders. The first, a major assault, was launched in the early morning hours of Sunday September 30. It resulted in the army suffering a humiliating defeat. The second attack was smaller in scope because the severe casualties suffered in the morning attack had diminished the troop strength by nearly 30 percent. It was launched at 3:00 PM and also ended with the soldiers retreating in disarray.

There followed four and a half days of sporadic gunfire and a few attempted encroachments by Cheyenne warriors, all of which failed. It was, in effect, a siege during which the army, held at bay by the unerring Nez Perce sharpshooters, was unable to advance. The battle lines extended along the eastern bank of Snake Creek and in the swales and hills on the creek's northern flank. The entire group, pinned down in three villages with the Piquinins in the upper north end, the Asotins near the center and the Wellamotkin and Palu bands to the west, was confined mainly to the heavily wooded areas that afforded protection to some extent for the few tepees still in the Indians' possession. (Nearly all their tepees had to be abandoned at the Big Hole and very few replacements had been made along the remainder of the trek.) For the first day huddled within were elders, women and children. By the second day, shelter pits had been dug and the people moved into them. The warriors remained strategically positioned in rifle pits along the perimeters to deny entry into the encampment area by soldiers and the army's Cheyenne allies.

As any attempt at a mass escape was now out of the question, escapees, if they were to have any chance of success, would have to leave alone or in small groups. White Bird, aided by several warrior chiefs, set about planning such attempts, finally settling on a plan that was to prove successful. The defensive entrenchments prevented the army from advancing close to the area, but the warriors were also unable to launch any sort of attack. They were satisfied in holding their own positions.

Snake Creek today is much diminished from the fairly wide waterway it was in 1877, but its narrow course still meanders between the same rolling brown hills and grassy knolls, albeit not as fast flowing as in 1877 and for centuries before. In 1877, still wide and swiftly flowing, it provided a watering place for antelopes, wild horses, deer and smaller animals. The buffalo grass grew thick and abundant, providing nourishing fodder for ungulate animals. It also had long served as a camping site for countless groups of Nez Perce, Sioux, Cheyenne, Peigan and Blackfeet hunters, as well as white trappers and buffalo hunters who stopped there as they ventured in search of furs and the buffalo herds.

In the waning days of the 1877 Nez Perce trek it seemed the perfect resting place for weary men, women and children. The long days over many weeks had granted little rest. There had never been enough time to repair tattered clothing, let alone make new ones.

Blankets, despite the number plundered from the defeated army, were in short supply, and new ones were not attainable. Because buffalo, deer and elk had been scarce, few hides were available for clothing of any type. Moccasins had been worn threadbare, so, many children were already running barefoot. With summer now ending there were no longer enough berries for food, and harvesting vegetable roots along the hurried way had not been possible to the extent needed to feed close to 800 hungry people. As a result of the shortages, each family had imposed strict rationing. Snake Creek, with an abundance of buffalo still ranging in the nearby foothills and a surrounding topography ideal for defense was, therefore, ideal.

The rolling hills protected the dales and glens in which grew heavy bush and copses of fir trees that provided both shelter from the Montana wind and shade from the heat of the afternoon sun. Aspen and poplar trees provided stout poles for tepees. The hills, high enough to serve as good lookout posts, provided views of the countryside for miles around. No enemy could sneak up to any encampment if those encamped were suitably alert. The only natural dangers were rattlesnakes[2] that might occasionally venture along the camp's outskirts.

On the 27th and 28th a number of buffalo were killed and butchered, fresh meat quickly prepared for the travel north. Now the people began to feel safer. In two days, their chiefs told them, they would resume their journey, a short two-day trek to the medicine line beyond which was, "The Land of the Grandmother." There they would be free, safe from the long knives of General Howard's sapporo[a] soldiers. Thus, in a spirit of jubilation and anticipation, the women erected the few remaining tepees in copses in the dales between the hills while warriors dug rifle pits—just in case...—and youths herded the horses into the aspen and poplar groves a short distance to the west. Then all settled in for what was expected to be a restful period of two days.

---

a *Sapporo is a Nez Perce word meaning "long knife" used to name the sabers used by cavalry soldiers.*

The most optimistic was Chief Looking Glass, who was soon to make the first of his final three fatal errors. Looking Glass, confident in his knowledge that Howard was still two, perhaps even three, days behind, despite advice from others, did not dispatch scouts to the north and east. Thus, he remained totally ignorant of the great threat bearing down on his band of migrants. General Miles and his large army were at that very hour only a few miles to the north and less than a day away.

The Army Arrives

"Enemies right on us! Soon the attack!"
—Unidentified scout's blanket warning.

"From the south came a noise—a rumble like stampeding buffaloes."
—Yellow Wolf

General Miles had lain his overall plans well enough that, had they transpired accordingly, the Nez Perces would have been tightly contained. Murphy's Law, however, as so often happens during military campaigns, quickly made itself known. Miles was soon to learn—as had Perry at White Bird Canyon, Howard at the Clearwater and Camus Prairie, Gibbon at the Big Hole and Sturgis at Canyon Creek—that the Nez Perce reputation for peaceful co-existence was exceeded by their fighting prowess. Although communication procedures were well in place by 1877, there seems to have been an abysmal lack of information passing between individual armies and their commanders. So lacking was communication that no two commanders seem to have known what had happened in the major battles already fought. All they seemed to know was that Nez Perce warriors had laid fearsome beatings on each of the commanders involved.

Miles, as had the others, had made his plans around a surprise encounter, and for that reason he proceeded on the northwesterly course he thought would put him ahead of the migrants. Until September 29 all had gone according to plan. The tactic, based as it was on surprise, had a good chance for success, and by late afternoon of September 29 his army had proceeded to a point just northeast of his quarry. Although Miles did not know the exact distance between them, he was, in fact, in perfect position where the two forces would have met head-on.

The General had, however, failed to consider two possibilities: he was much closer to his target than he thought (his Cheyenne scouts had failed to locate the migrants), and his men were greatly tired from their forced march. Also, most of the cavalry units' horses were nearing their limits of exhaustion. Obviously Miles had not been apprised of the Yellowstone fiasco perpetrated by the inept Lieutenant Colonel Charles Gilbert when he so exhausted his unit's horses through non-stop travel that most of them had to shipped back to their base by river steamer.

On the morning of the 30th when the troops, in order to get underway by 4:00 AM, were roused from their tents a half-hour earlier, they were met head-on by a bitterly cold north wind that chilled one and all to the very marrow of their bones. To further compound their misery, all had endured a sleepless, miserable night when an unseasonably cold rain, driven full force by a north wind, pelted their tents. By morning the tents were sodden canvas sheets. The troops hustled to begin what they were sure would be just another miserable day on a seemingly endless trail. None was fully prepared for the battle soon to be thrust upon them.

Even before dawn had fully broken the morning of September 30 the Nez Perce camp was alive with activity. The migrants, too, were feeling the effects of the bitter cold, but it was partly offset by the knowledge of being within a few hours of beginning the final leg of their long journey north. Their understanding that Howard's army was still at least two days to the south gave them a feeling of security. While the women set about their chores of packing and preparing the children and elders for travel, the men went to the horse herds a short distance away to choose animals for use as pack animals and to be used for hauling the numerous travois. Some travois would be laden with material while others would provide transportation for the wounded and for sick elders. The men would also select horses to be ridden. The remainder would be herded by older boys chosen as wranglers. Among the selecting group were Joseph and his daughter, twelve-year-old Kapkap Ponmi [Sound of Running Water]. She was a skilled horse handler, so, possibly because of this talent which was unusual in a Nez Perce female, she was Joseph's favorite child.

Back in the camp, small children were trying to keep warm by running around playing a noisy game, a sort of frontier hockey involving sticks and a ball made of matted grass sewn inside a rawhide cover. Ambulatory elders were having breakfast, while those who were ill were being fed prior to being secured on the travois that would carry them the forty-three bumpy miles to their final destination.

Suddenly, two scouts on lathered horses raced into camp shouting that soldiers might be approaching. When the two had dismounted and caught their breath, they explained they had been watching a buffalo herd sedately munching on grass, and while they were planning the best way to swoop down and cull a few from the herd, the animals suddenly bolted and stampeded. The scouts had not noticed any discernible reason for the herd's sudden action, but a few minutes later they heard a commotion similar to the thunder of many horses' hooves and the growling of wagon wheels in need of grease. Fearing the worst, the two raced to the camp to sound the alarm.

Looking Glass, true to form, made little of their fears. General Howard, he pronounced, was still far to the south. Whatever had spooked the buffalo it was not the army. The people had plenty of time to continue their preparations for departure. It was later revealed that only an hour earlier Looking Glass had dismissed a warning from Wottolen, a noted warrior, who had told the chief he had dreamt that night of a sudden attack on the camp.[3] Looking Glass, who had no respect for the Dreamers beliefs and none at all for their omens, dismissed Wottolen with a curt wave of his hand. His action was eerily similar to his rejection of Five Wounds' warning prior to the Big Hole disaster. Thus, the work continued at a leisurely pace.

About an hour later some of the women and children had begun to move northward from the village, leading horses laden with the final supply of prepared meat. They were progressing along the creek's east bank when a scout on a high bluff waved a red blanket. The signal meant "Enemies right on us! Soon the attack!"[4] The women quickly increased their pace while the camp sprang to action. Quickly arming themselves, some warriors rushed to the rifle pits while others, aware the greatest threat would in all probability emerge from the south, ran along the flats and gullies toward the higher ground. The boys, who remained with the horses, hurried to secure the animals.

THE FIRST ATTACK

Years later Yellow Wolf described the army's approach as "a rumble like stampeding buffaloes." Much of the rumble was caused by companies B (Captain Andrew Bennett), F (Captain Simon Snyder) and G (1st Lieutenant Henry Romeyn) and I (1st Lieutenant Mason Carter) of the 5th Infantry Regiment and its supply wagons. The rest was from the rapidly advancing 2nd and 7th Cavalries. The 7th, in three lines with Company A (Captain Myles Moylan) on the left flank and Companies D (Captain Edward S. Godfrey) and K (Captain Owen Hale) in the center and right flank respectively, had taken a position to the right of and slightly ahead of the 5th Infantry. This force was advancing northward as the right flank of a three-prong pincer movement designed to sweep around the perimeter of the Indians' camp.

The 2nd Cavalry had already split away to the west as the second prong. The 2nd was comprised of companies E (Captain George L. Tyler), G (Lieutenant Edward J. McClernand) and H (Lieutenant Lovell H. Jerome).

At center-rear were the four companies of the 5th Infantry. This was the plan of battle; an attack Miles had quickly devised upon learning from his scouts the Nez Perce had at last been sighted. He had then swung his troops south and as he rode he consulted with Lieutenant Marion Maus, commander of the Cheyenne scouts and Luther "Yellowstone" Kelly,[5] leader of the civilian scouts. Along the way Miles had devised the plan of attack he felt certain would end the Nez Perce War of 1877. All would be soon resolved, he told his officers.

Approaching the Indian encampment, General Miles felt justified in envisioning a complete and easy victory. However, depending solely on information garnered by his civilian and Cheyenne scouts, he had no idea the Nez Perce warriors had received warnings and were now, more or less, waiting for the attack. He made some final amendments when he saw the camp and had noted women engaged in preparations for departure. He also saw other non-combatants seemingly busy and unhurried. What the general did not know was the seemingly unhurried pace had been the women herding their children towards the safety pits. He had also been fooled by the line of approach that appeared so smooth but was, in fact, a rise that ended in a sheer cliff with a drop of several yards to the creek. His scouts had not dared a close reconnaissance so they had missed this very important feature which would figure greatly in the defeat he was about suffer.

When Miles gave the order to charge, the 7th Cavalry, amid shouts and loud huzzas, thundered along the broad, smooth descending plain. Suddenly they reached a point where their view was obscured in all directions by rising ground. Their view of the village was now lost as they rode up the moderate slope that to them appeared to be a gentle crest that would lead them unencumbered directly into the village.

The 7th Cavalry, led by K Company with the undeniably brave Captain Hale in command on the right, A Company only yards behind on the left and D Company in the center, charged toward the top of the hill. Without warning the field suddenly narrowed, as a coulee to the right crowded the command together. Hale's riders were forced to deviate slightly, a move that required them to ride through two swales. Companies A and D stayed the course, but what had been a unified charge was now broken.

What happened next happened swiftly. K Company, having passed through the swales, found itself on a flat ridge. Suddenly bullets began swirling all around them. Had the warriors hidden in coulees and wadis waited but a few more seconds before opening their devastating fire, K Company would not have stopped in time to avoid a calamitous disaster. As it happened, the warriors had not opened fire on Hale's men at all, but rather on D and A Companies, both of which had arrived on the bluff a second or two before K Company emerged from the swale. The scathing barrage stopped all three companies just in time for K Company to avoid a plunge over the cliff into the creek below. It was, in fact, the horses of A and D Companies that had saved them. Sensing an unseen danger, those horses had simultaneously ground to a sudden halt.

Before the riders had a chance to react, a group of warriors sprang up from below the crest of the bluff. With deadly fire at almost point-blank range it was hardly possible for any warrior not to hit at least one target. Horses reared and panicked. Riders fell from their saddles, some already dead or wounded. Several horses were shot. Others panicked, ran directly to the edge of the cliff and tumbled over. As Private John McAlpine would later recall,

> *"Those Indians stopped our charge cold. The bullets flew fast and thick. My horse went down...when I pulled myself free a slug took my hat off. A man riding beside me [whose horse was also shot] got to his feet but a bullet caught him square in the forehead. I took his hat...a fur one."*[6]

There being no chance of further engagement, the order to retreat was sounded.

Meanwhile, totally unaware of the difficulties the 7th Cavalry was experiencing, the 2nd Cavalry had advanced to the westerly area where the Indians' horses were being protected. They had better luck, as they managed to round up a great many of the animals, but it was no easy task. Mounted warriors who had remained when the others rushed to the campsite began to charge back and forth firing enough to keep the cavalrymen in turmoil much of the time. The warriors' actions diverted the cavalry's attention, enabling those who had been attending the selection of horses to escape back to the camp. Among them were Chief Joseph and his daughter. For Joseph it had been a very close call. As he raced his horse to where his wife stood ready to toss him his rifle, he felt several bullets tear through his jacket. Later, Joseph noticed his jacket had received no less than three bullet holes. Closer inspection revealed the bullets, when passing through the loose flaps of the cloth, had all missed hitting him by mere fractions of inches. Joseph's daughter had run the distance to the camp, dodging from tree to tree to escape the bullets that were being aimed her way. She rushed to a shelter pit.

To add to the 2nd Cavalry officers' frustrations, the previously mentioned contingent of women and children were rapidly disappearing further northward with their meat-laden horses, protected by sharpshooting older teens. Second Lieutenant Edward McClernand's G Company was detached to pursue them. McClernand managed to overtake the group, but some determined youngsters, all with rifles and mounted, closed on him and drove his troopers back. Twice G Company tried to overtake the group and twice the young men forced them to retreat. Their action assured the group, numbering a little more than twenty adults, would escape with an undetermined number of children. The group later split into two, with both eventually finding refuge with various bands. One group went directly to Canada where they found help from Peigans who took them to Sitting Bull; they joined White Bird's band when he arrived at Sitting Bull's camp. The other group found help from friendly bands of Kootenay and Flathead hunters from British Columbia and northern Idaho respectively. Some eventually returned to Lapwai and others assimilated into these bands.

One of those who reached Canada was Eelahweema [About

Sleep] who, with his little brother hanging on tightly behind him, galloped his horse through a line of soldiers and Cheyenne warriors. He later described the ordeal to L.V. McWhorter.

> *"Our warriors are passing shots with the cavalrymen. They were close together, mixing up. Soldiers continue sending shots at us, but they cannot stop us. My little brother, holding tight to me, has one braid of hair shot off close to his ear. Two soldiers pursue us but are driven back before they catch us."*[7]

Another youngster, Suhmkeen (later known as Samuel Tilden), also escaped with the group, succeeded in eluding the pursuers and continued northward. He related his adventure to Rowena and Gordon Alcorn, who printed his account as an article for *Montana: The Magazine of Western History*, (October 1965).

> *"I looked and saw the high bank back of the camp was black with soldiers [G Company, 2nd Cavalry]...We camped that night...and that afternoon we killed two buffalo and roasted the meat that night and had plenty to eat. All of us were mounted [so] the next night we camped on the Milk River and from there we went on into Canada."*

The Indians' escape did nothing to boost the 2nd Cavalry's morale, although it did improve somewhat when they managed to herd and capture nearly 350 horses from the Nez Perce herd; but overall their efforts accomplished little else. In his first report, Miles, in what had become the army's penchant for exaggeration, praised the efforts of the 2nd Cavalry and announced they had captured horses numbering 600. Three days later the number increased to 700 and finally, in his official report to the secretary, he set the number at 800. None of these totals were correct. According to Nez Perce sources no more than one-third (350) of the herd was captured by the army on that first day. Several hundred remained in the camp proper and were used in the final escape efforts; and those that did not go with White Bird were confiscated by Miles after the surrender. Some of the herd had run away during the army's attempts to capture them, escaping into the wilderness to wander here and there. While some were later recaptured, others would certainly have joined wild herds. How many of the total numbers of the once vast herd actually got to Canada remains unknown, but Northwest Mounted Police accounts estimate White Bird's escapees had close to 300 horses when they arrived at the Sioux refuge.

While the cavalry units were fighting and losing their battles, the four companies of the 5th Infantry, B, F, G and I, were slowly pushing forward. Upon hearing the first shots fired, those infantrymen who had been mounted quickly dismounted. Leading their ponies they continued on foot to the bluff recently vacated by the decimated 7th Cavalry. From this vantage point, though forced to lie in the prone position, they could view the camp below. They were also able to fire a few shots into the bluffs where warriors were positioned. This was blind firing, not at all effective, but it did allow the harassed cavalry to retreat out of range.

At this point G Company deployed to the right flank hoping to gain a more advantageous position. According to Lt. Henry Romeyn,

> "The bugler was ordered to sound the deployment. 'I can't blow sir, I am shot,' said the brave fellow, and a glance toward him showed him on the ground with a broken spine. Another man lay still so [when the move forward began] a Sergeant...was directed to have him move along. 'He can't do it, sir, he's dead,' was the reply."[8]

The infantry's position was somewhat improved shortly after by the arrival of a Hotchkiss gun, one of two cannons Miles had included in his supply train. It was trundled to the bluff with the intention of using it to bombard the village below, but its muzzle could not be lowered sufficiently to have the desired effect. Within minutes a group of warriors opened fire on the gun crew, who hastily abandoned the gun. It remained there unattended for some time but the warriors were unable to gain access to it, so, though temporarily useless, it remained in commission, was eventually rescued and used later. The other, a twelve-pound Napoleon cannon, was used during the final two days of the siege. Fortunately for the Indians, Miles had been able to bring only twenty-four shells for this destructive high-explosive weapon. It produced a degree of terror amongst the women and children and possibly caused two fatalities.

With 5th Infantry now immobilized, the shooting stopped from both sides, a lull that enabled Miles to assess the situation. What he saw was not what he had envisioned a few hours earlier. All three companies of the 7th Cavalry were in tatters, the 2nd was still wildly riding about in running gun battles with hard-riding warriors, and his four infantry companies were tied down to the point of being ineffective.

The leadership situation had also been rendered a serious blow. Many of his finest officers and NCOs were either dead or wounded. Because some of the units were now virtually leaderless, he hastily deployed several junior officers from different companies to fill the breach. He called a cessation of fighting and summoned his remaining officers for a conference to discuss the next move.

Their initial assessment of the outcome of the first battle did nothing to return anyone to an optimistic view of the situation. Still, Miles felt the day could be won, despite the initial setback, if he could launch another attack after a well-organized regrouping, which began at once. At 3:00 PM Miles launched his second attack. This time the remnant of the 7th, unhorsed, was placed alongside the 5th Infantry. It was, however, so reduced in strength it was only an augmentation to the infantry's G Company. Both units were placed under command of Lieutenant Romeyn. This small combined force moved to the ridge just beyond the ravine to the right of the 5th Infantry. As Romeyn rose to give the signal to move forward in skirmish formation a volley of bullets from the warriors' positions several hundred yards away struck him down. He fell to the ground and then crawled some seventy yards to the rear before losing consciousness. He was fortunate a private who had seen him go down called for the assistance of two others. They dragged the stricken officer further to the rear and laid him amidst the wounded from the first attack. He was later diagnosed as having a collapsed lung.

Romeyn was one of the lucky ones. For him the war was over, but he did eventually recover.⁹

Meanwhile, having seen Romeyn's signal, the command began their advance. Then, with deadly accuracy, Chief Joseph's Wellamotkin warriors began to take a further toll and several men fell. The advance halted. The battalion hurriedly withdrew to their original position. As a result only one other combined force, a small one with a total of twenty-five men of I and F Companies of the 5th Infantry, moved forward. This small unit, under command of Lieutenant Mason Carter, actually advanced a few yards into the village—and were stopped dead in their tracks. Joseph had positioned some of his men in rifle pits on rising ground to the right, and when they opened fire the troops turned and swiftly retreated to a nearby deep gully. Eight of Carter's men (of whom two died later) had been wounded.

The charge, having failed, was not tried again. Carter and his men, unable to retreat further but safe enough providing the warriors did not launch an attack, remained pinned down in the gully. For some four anxious hours they and the warriors exchanged random but ineffective shots. As darkness began to fall Carter and his men began a successful withdrawal to the safety of the army lines. Still, it was a dicey and slow retreat for the troopers, hampered by the need to drag the seriously wounded. They were forced to keep their heads well down as they belly-crawled the entire length of the ravine. Occasional bullets, blind-fired by warriors, whistled scant inches above them.

Miles, in a subsequent report,¹⁰ praised Carter's overall attempt as courageous. He noted the Nez Perce marksmen had disabled Carter's force by 36 percent owing to their adroit use of repeating carbines. The irony of the situation was not lost on him. He was well aware those rifles and their deadly bullets had been pillaged in previous encounters with Howard's army. He did, however, include his usual exaggerations by stating Carter's men had "inflicted heavy losses..." on the Nez Perce defenders. In truth, three non-combatants were killed.¹¹

Following Carter's defeat, Miles finally decided further attacks were impossible because of losses and the lack of intelligence pertaining to the numbers of warriors within the camp. He dispatched his intentions to General Howard, Colonel Sturgis (who was proceeding north to guard the ambulance wagons) and Captain David H. Brotherton (who was awaiting further orders at Forchette Creek with an auxiliary supply train). His message is confusing. His listing of an estimated twenty-five warriors in the enemy camp seems obviously in error, possibly made by the dispatcher, or perhaps the zero was simply omitted, because Miles jotted it down hurriedly. It seems likely he had meant to write 250 because twenty-five warriors would seem an easy target for yet another attack. He omitted mention of his large number of casualties, although he did admit his inability to become mobile was "on account of my wounded." He wisely advised Howard and others who might be progressing to his sector to advance with extreme caution.[12] Obviously he felt the Nez Perce warriors were capable of extending their field of operations.

Confronted with the inescapable fact he had been soundly whipped in both attacks, Miles took stock. The result of his appraisal was discouraging. The 7th Cavalry had taken a severe drubbing:

- Company K, a company of forty-four men, had suffered nine fatalities including its commander, Captain Owen Hale. He had been shot through the neck. Also dead was Hale's second in command, 2nd Lieutenant J. Williams Biddle. Three of the unit's senior sergeants and four privates had been killed. The wounded numbered fourteen, for a total of twenty-three casualties—a 53 percent loss.

- Company A, with thirty men, had four dead and twelve wounded including the company's commander, Captain Myles Moylan, and his two senior NCOs, one of whom (Sargeant Otto Durselen) died later. That loss was 51 percent.

- Company D had lost four to fatal bullets and nine wounded, one of which was the commander, Captain

Edward S. Godfrey. That percentage was above 39 percent.

- The 5th Infantry had taken the least casualties, with three killed and thirteen wounded, of which one (Private Joseph Kohler) died the following day.

- The 2nd Cavalry, because they had engaged only a small band of warriors, got away with the lightest number of casualties: one killed and one wounded.

Realizing he could not dislodge the warriors, and not willing to suffer more than the sixty-six losses he had already compiled, Miles wisely decided to remain content with what little he had gained. He now held the high ground, the Hotchkiss gun had finally been re-positioned where it could do some damage, he was awaiting the arrival of the Napoleon cannon, and he had captured a sizeable number of horses. He set about repositioning his various companies and the civilian and Cheyenne scouts to strategic sites (see map) in order to lay siege to the village. Meanwhile, he would await Howard's arrival. Only then would he perhaps consider a third attack. He also decided to send an envoy under a white flag to see if Joseph might be willing to negotiate surrender. He would do that within a day or two when the situation became more settled.

Behind the Indian lines Joseph, White Bird and Looking Glass watched the troops retreat to their newly assigned positions. He, too, had taken stock of his situation. Although his people had not been hit as hard as he knew Miles had been, his casualty list was no less the cause of distress. Among the twenty dead were eight Nez Perce warriors[13] among them three noted warriors, Kowyehkown, Kowwaspo and Peopeo Ipsewahk [Lone Bird]. Of equal loss were two very important chiefs. Tool'hool'hool'zote, and Ollokot had both been killed in the initial assault. Another great loss was the important guide, Lean Elk. Five non-combatants (never officially identified) had also been killed. A further twenty-five were unaccounted for, but these were later identified as those who had escaped during the initial attack by the 2nd Cavalry. The total number of wounded remains unknown to this day, but is believed to be about twenty.

With the deaths of Tool'hool'hool'zote and Ollokot, only Joseph, White Bird and Looking Glass remained to direct the order of battle. Joseph was now more and more becoming looked upon as the prime leader. White Bird was already considering escaping with as many warriors and non-combatants as would choose to accompany him. He was also planning to take as many of the remaining horses as he could. White Bird was looking to the immediate future and was, therefore, no longer interested in planning battles. Disillusionment among the warriors against Looking Glass had quickly set in following his brusque, even rude, dismissal of Wottolen that morning and his disinterest in the warning given by the two hunters. The warriors were tired of both his delays and refusals to heed warnings. As a result, Looking Glass was, for all intents and purposes, losing his position as overall chief. He was now mostly limited to the affairs of his own diminished band, the Asotins.

Joseph was seriously considering surrender. Though it was an unpleasant thought, he did not want the women, children and elders who would remain with him subjected to further attacks. He was to say later he had not wanted to surrender. He knew the majority could have escaped to Canada had they left behind all those were unable to walk at a quick pace. That included most of the elderly men and women, all the sick and injured and a number of small children. This he was unwilling to consider. Of course, he did not know Miles had already given up the idea of further fighting and no longer had the mobility required to give extended chase. Neither did he know Miles had decided to do nothing more than lay siege with occasional harassing rifle fire from the various positions. He was now content to await Howard's arrival.

So, as the sun disappeared over the western mountains, the scene was set for the events which were to develop over the following five days.

Four Days of Terror and Treachery

October 1 dawned on yet another cold day. During the night almost five inches of snow had fallen, but the wind had diminished, which somewhat relieved the discomfort felt by the refugees huddled in fireless tepees and shallow shelter pits. Their ragged clothing and shared blankets did little to stave off the bitter chill of night. To help fight the cold, the chiefs conscripted all able-bodied men and women to dig deep shelter pits along the creek's shore. These deep pits were deemed safer than the tepees because they provided more protection from rifle fire and cannons that Miles had ordered be fired on a sporadic basis. While the Hotchkiss gun did little damage and caused no casualties, it did cause terror among the inhabitants. The newly arrived Napoleon cannon was more frightening because its shells exploded high above the ground showering fragments of red-hot shrapnel. In a 1932 interview, Red Elk, a survivor of the siege, spoke about seeing many who were required to move about in the camp during the day "holding buffalo hides above themselves for protection [against shrapnel]."[14]

More rifle pits were dug above the creek, in low bluffs and on higher ground so the riflemen could have more command of the entire area. This strategy stopped members of the 7th Cavalry from taking positions that would deny the refugees access to water. They were driven back by rifle fire and the attempt was never tried again. One woman (never identified) who had been engaged in the digging of the various pits said later,

> "We digged (sic) the trenches with camas hooks and knives. With pans we threw out the dirt...Dried meat and some

other grub would be handed around. If not enough for all, it would be given to the children first. I was three days without food. Children cried with hunger and cold. Old people suffered in silence. Misery everywhere. Cold and dampness all around."[15]

Such tales of hardship, hunger and discomfort abound throughout the pages of the many interviews conducted with survivors. All speak of the time spent shivering in the shelter pits, of intense hunger and the crying of children. The warriors, for the most part, stayed in their rifle pits. No men except the aged, the very sick or wounded stayed in the shelters. They, however, kept their fully loaded rifles at their sides at all times. They were the final line of defense should the warriors be driven from their rifle pits. For five days these shelters served as home to all. Non-combatants did not venture out unless they absolutely had to. During the nights the able bodied dug deeper while others cautiously crept out, some to fetch water from the creek, others to bury the dead from the two attacks. Several bodies, Tool'hool'hool'zote's among them, remained unburied as they were too close to the army lines. Those who had tried to escape and had been killed also went unburied.

Despite the lack of immediate knowledge within the camp of who had died or been wounded, one old man named Alahoos [Elm Limb] kept a summary of casualties and events of each day. Although no longer a warrior but still strong and active, each day he moved throughout the area gathering information of those who had disappeared, were missing or injured. He then informed Joseph of what he had learned. It was through his accounting that it was learned that of the twenty-five killed at the Bear's Paw, twenty-two had died on September 30 during the first attack, and three were killed during Carter's attack on Joseph's sector during the second siege. Three more deaths were recorded by Alahoos, all during the first day of the siege.

On that first day the conduct of battle changed greatly. Because Miles had decided against any further general attacks, fighting amounted to sporadic shooting between army and Nez Perce sharpshooters. The army riflemen hit no one and there is no evidence the Nez Perce sharpshooters hit anyone on the army's line. The shooting was effective mainly in assuring that all kept their heads down. Not until the evening of the fourth day was the final death in the encampment recorded.

From the first day of the siege General Miles had been thinking of ways to induce Joseph to agree to surrender terms. His progress, however, was slowed by his reluctance to approach the encampment without drawing fire. About midday he displayed a white flag of truce and a voice from the army line called out in Chinook jargon, "Miles wishes to speak with Joseph." Tom Hill, a warrior of mixed Nez Perce-Delaware lineage, who spoke both the jargon and English, replied saying Joseph was willing to talk. Thus, the basis was set for a discussion and Hill went over to the army lines to speak with Miles. During their conversation Hill gained Miles' assurances the talks would proceed under the provisions of fairness and equality. Hill said Joseph would agree to meet the general at a half-way point. Hill returned to the camp, relayed Miles' message and Joseph agreed.

That afternoon Miles and two officers walked under a white flag to the meeting place to await Joseph's arrival. After a short wait Joseph and two warriors came forward. Joseph and Miles shook hands whereupon Joseph, as a token of Nez Perce sincerity, surrendered several rifles and some ammunition to Miles. The discussion commenced amicably with talk of peace, terms of surrender and guarantees of honorable treatment of the Indians. Miles led Joseph to believe the Indians would be returned to Idaho for residence at Lapwai, though he later denied making such a promise. Miles then began to show his true colors by insisting Joseph's people surrender immediately and turn all their weapons over to the army. Joseph refused this demand, telling Miles the other chiefs would have to be consulted to determine if all were of a mind to surrender. He also insisted at least half the rifles would have to be retained in order to shoot game for food upon which they would depend for survival during their journey to Lapwai.

At this point the discussion broke down. Joseph and his companions started back toward their own lines. It was at that moment Miles displayed the treachery he probably had been considering all along. He called Joseph back on some pretext. When Joseph returned Miles ordered his officers to take him prisoner. He told the escorts to return to the Indian lines and tell the chiefs they must surrender if Joseph was to remain safe. Joseph was then escorted to the army lines and placed under guard in conditions that appear to have been previously planned.[16]

In his official report, which he wrote later, Miles made no admission of having asked for the parley, stating only, "On the morning of October 1st, I opened communications with the Nez Perces, and Chief Joseph and several of his warriors came out under a flag of truce."[17] (*sic*)

Miles subsequently denied originating the talks or of promising to return the Indians to Lapwai. He was supported by Lieutenant Jerome of H Company, 2nd Cavalry. Though Jerome later insisted the Nez Perces had been the first to unfurl the white flag, his averment seemed unlikely to nearly everyone. Most observers agreed Joseph had nothing to gain by initiating surrender talks because he and the other chiefs were still hoping Sitting Bull and his Sioux warriors would come to their assistance. Miles, on the other hand, was impatient to terminate the matter before General Howard arrived so he could garner all the credit. Miles had no desire to share the glory with Howard.[18] This points to Miles as the instigator of the truce talks.

Jerome was asked years later why Miles had taken Joseph prisoner if some agreement had been achieved. He replied, "That was Miles' way. When he could get hold of a chief or some other prominent person, he would grab him on some pretext. He did this with Geronimo in the Apache affair."[19]

Jerome was very soon to play a leading, but unintentional, role in a culmination of Joseph's capture.

With Joseph being held as a prisoner, the mood within the Indian camp was not conducive to further dealings with Miles, whom they now considered a man of two faces who spoke with the forked tongue of a viper. Looking Glass and White Bird held council with their warrior chiefs, discussing what retaliation for this breach of protocol might be appropriate. Suddenly, most unexpectedly, a ray of hope appeared in the person of the abovementioned Lovell Jerome.

Following Joseph's capture, Jerome had walked across to the Indians' lines. Though this was clearly a very unwise venture he always claimed he had done so with Miles' permission. His actual reasons remain to this day obtuse, if not downright asinine, but he may have thought it possible to gain a quick reconnaissance of the strength of the warriors' positions. He got too close, stayed too long and found himself suddenly in the strong grip of two of Yellow Bull's warriors. He was unceremoniously dragged to the council circle where the astonished chiefs quickly realized this officer might be the answer to the subject of discussion. It did take some persuasion to restrain the immediate urge to kill him, a desire held by several Wellamotkin warriors. Sound arguments by Wottolen and Yellow Bull convinced them otherwise when they stated Jerome could be traded for Joseph. Miles, they argued, would likely be willing to trade Joseph for Jerome. Miles would be informed his alternate choice would be to watch his young officer shot in plain view of his entire army.

White Bird and Looking Glass, and eventually Joseph's warriors, agreed that Miles would have a difficult time explaining to his superiors why he had allowed one of his officers to be killed instead of agreeing to a prisoner exchange. Jerome was then led away to an underground shelter pit where he was held under guard pending the outcome of the proposal that would soon be presented to General Miles.

All of Jerome's later accounts insist he had been treated very kindly and humanely as befits a prisoner of war. Not only was he was permitted to keep his revolver, he was also allowed to send a communication to Miles. Further, he was allowed food be brought to him from the army's field kitchen.[20]

Conversely, Joseph was not being treated at all well. According to all accounts, including army reports, Miles feared he would attempt to escape or an attempt would be made at a rescue. He kept Joseph not under shelter, but in the open. Rolled up in two heavy blankets, tied hand and foot, he was placed in a secluded corner of the mule corral. He endured those conditions until the following morning when Miles, upon being informed by Jerome of the good treatment he was being afforded, relented. Miles then had Joseph released from the blankets and untied. He also allowed him to walk about within a confined area of the camp.[21]

That same morning White Bird sent an ultimatum to Miles. The message was terse. Miles must agree to exchange Joseph for Jerome or the officer would be brought into full view of his comrades and shot. Miles saw no recourse but to comply, so he agreed to meet with Tom Hill halfway between the two lines. Agreement for the exchange and the points of release was reached. At the appointed hour Joseph, General Miles and Lieutenant Marion P. Maus, the commanding officer of the Cheyenne scouts, left the army lines under a white flag. At the same moment Jerome and three warriors appeared from the opposite side to proceed to points previously agreed upon. Joseph and Jerome[22] were simultaneously released to walk the distance of open ground between the parties. Because both sides held suspicions of treachery afoot, several very tense minutes elapsed as the two men walked toward each other. When they met, both men stopped for a brief moment of conversation. What they spoke of was never recorded. They shook hands, probably wished each other well, then walked to join their respective escorts and retreat to their own lines. To the relief of all concerned the exchange had gone smoothly.

For the next two days the truce continued. The white flag continued to flutter above the Nez Perce entrenchments, possibly as a silent message that no attacks would be launched from that side.

Occasional shots were fired for no discernible reasons, but neither side made any move that could be considered a prelude to attack. Miles, possibly in the hopes of confusing the warriors, moved his troops from position to position, mostly upstream well out of range of the sharpshooters in the rifle pits. The warriors simply moved some of their own positions to counter those of the soldiers. From time to time interesting colloquies were shouted across the lines between the combatants. Most were minor insults, but one report mentions an officer (suggested as being the general himself) who, becoming annoyed at the conversations, shouted to his men that if the warriors didn't stop the harangues the cavalry should, "Charge them to Hell." This evoked an indignant reply from a Nez Perce who called back in clear English, "Charge to hell. You goddamned sons of bitches. You ain't fighting the Sioux."[23]

So the siege wore on with the respite enabling the defenders to improve their positions. The shelter pits were deepened and reinforced with timbers. The few tepees that remained were dismantled to deny the cannon gun crews visible targets. Their poles were cut up and distributed to the inhabitants of the pits to be used for warming fires.

On the third day, however, the situation again shifted. Lieutenant Brotherton arrived with his supply wagons and with them was the Napoleon cannon. Miles immediately positioned it where he thought it might do the most damage and began sporadic fire. Because he had only twenty-four shells, the gun produced nothing in the way of casualties with a possible exception. On the fourth day a shell from one of the cannons exploded above a shelter pit. The explosion caused the pit to cave in on the six occupants, a small boy, a girl and four women. The boy and three of the women were dug out in time to assure survival, but an elderly woman and her granddaughter, a twelve year old named Astipeeten, were found dead. Whether the two were killed by the explosion or smothered under the dirt was never determined. Neither was it ever known if the cave-in had been caused by the explosion or through poor construction, but it did have some effect on morale and caused much apprehension. Regardless, morale remained high enough that the camp remained divided in thoughts of surrender. Joseph, though with much reluctance, advocated surrender, but White Bird and Looking Glass were both vehemently opposed, as were most warriors and a surprising number of non-combatants, including many older persons.

During the afternoon of the fourth day (October 4) a council was held to further discuss the issue. The three chiefs and the warriors plus their leaders openly discussed the matter together. It was held mainly to gain a final consensus of the numbers who planned to attempt escape and those who would surrender. It was not a matter of gaining a decision, either unanimous or majority, because under tribal law each chief and each individual had the right to do as he saw fit. They did, however, intend to use powers of persuasion to influence those final decisions. They all knew none of the five bands would likely act as cohesive units.

Looking Glass, in his final say in the matter, tried to convince Joseph to go with him and White Bird. He warned him that surrender to Miles would only result in regret and sorrow. Miles, he said, was a man of two faces and two tongues.

Joseph, however, was only concerned with the welfare of his own people as well with those of the other bands. Since the death of Tool'hool'hool'zote he felt he had to now look after the Piqunin. He told Looking Glass he did not want to surrender but he had to think of the women, sick elders and children, all of whom were suffering, hungry and cold, in the dampness of the safety pits.

As the council drew to its close Looking Glass is reported as saying to Joseph, "I will never surrender to a deceitful white chief." Joseph turned to him and replied, "For myself I do not care. It is for them [the women and children] I am going to surrender."[24] With this statement he made it clear to all his intention was to notify Miles the following morning (October 5) that he would surrender during the afternoon. The matter was settled.

White Bird and most of the warriors supported Looking Glass. The two chiefs then set about informing those who would hazard the difficulties of the escape that they would leave that night during the darkest hours. Less than three hours later only White

Bird remained as the principal chief. At twilight Chief Looking Glass was killed, picked off by Milan Tripp, one of "Yellowstone" Kelly's scouts.

Looking Glass was in a shallow rifle pit on the high ground with some Asotin warriors going over details regarding the escape plans. He was also hoping for the return of one of the scouts he had dispatched during the evening of September 30. That night, in the hopes of contacting Sitting Bull, he had sent riders north. Each carried a request for assistance. Now, on the final night before the surrender and the escape attempt, he peered above the rim of the pit to see a rider furtively approaching. Thinking one of his scouts was returning (or he might have thought the rider was an advance scout from Sitting Bull) he rose up and waved a greeting. Too late he recognized the rider as a Cheyenne. Before he could drop back into the pit the sharp-eyed Milan Tripp, from a distance of several hundred yards, snapped off one shot. The bullet found its mark and Looking Glass fell back into the pit. He was dead, killed instantly by the single shot that had struck him directly in the forehead. Tripp's remarkable shot is described in a letter dated November 15, 1927 written to L.V. McWhorter by Charles A. Swick, one of Miles' civilian packers.[25] Looking Glass was the last Nez Perce killed by an army bullet at the Bear's Paw and the first since September 30.

WHITE BIRD ACTIVATES HIS ESCAPE PLAN

During the morning of Friday, October 5, while Joseph was engaged in the formalities of the impending surrender, White Bird assembled his escapees, an estimated 233, of which 140 were men and boys, plus ninety-three women and girls. Even as those who were about to surrender were preparing to leave the camp for the final time, those contemplating escape stayed in hiding. White Bird's single fear was that Miles would send soldiers to the camp to assist in the surrender so he herded his flock into the camp's farthest recesses to hide until darkness fell. Luck was with him, for not all those planning to surrender intended to leave that afternoon. With darkness falling, Miles, who was in no hurry anyway, decided they could be left until morning. At that time he would send in soldiers to hurry them along and to convince White Bird to report to him. Because no soldiers appeared, White Bird and his charges remained safe.

After the sun had fully set and darkness engulfed the land, his followers were given last-minute instructions, with warnings and admonishments of the dangers ahead. They then divided into three pre-arranged groups and started the hazardous journey north to "The Land of the Grandmother." White Bird's group would go first, and if they were successful in eluding the sentries the other two would follow, each in turn. White Bird, his two wives Kate and Wyanato'tampip, some twenty-five women with their children, and several dozen horses whose hoofs had been wrapped in cloth and whose muzzles had been tied shut, slipped out. The group was protected by twenty-eight warriors.[26]

By stealth, and some good luck, the group eluded the sentries.[27] One of the escapees later said sentries had seen them but did nothing. Whether this was a true observation or a product of a frightened imagination is unknown. Once well clear of the area they broke into a run, keeping a rapid pace for some time. Finally, feeling safe, they slowed to a walk until dawn when they rested. In that first group were Looking Glass' widow Wetanonmi and daughter Martha.[28]

Once it was determined that White Bird's group had successfully eluded the pickets, the second group departed with Yellow Wolf leading. This was also a large group made up of warriors, healthy elders and a great number of horses. He was also accompanied by a number of women and children, among whom were Joseph's senior wife, Hey'oom'yo'yish [Bear Crossing], and their teenage daughter, Kepkop'ponmi.²⁹ This group also eluded the sentries without incident and, after quietly moving a good distance, began their rush for the border.

Then the third group, the smallest, an estimated seventy, mostly women and children, under the leadership of Chief Black Eagle, slipped out of the camp to begin its flight toward the border. They would also be under the protection of warriors who had left first leading many horses. When Black Eagle and the remainder silently filed from the camp they had no difficulty at all. Scouts and army pickets appear to have returned to the army camp for the night. Black Eagle and his charges quickly disappeared into the inky blackness of the moonless night.

The three groups all safely escaped from Snake Creek, but not all reached Canada intact; and none did so without enduring a difficult journey. There were losses of people and horses over the two days that passed before they reunited, and it was another day before they crossed into Canada where the three merged into one, with White Bird recognized as the band chief. All were exhausted and hungry. None was in good shape, but they were safe. Many bore wounds suffered at the hands of Assiniboine attackers. Many had cuts to their face, hands and arms, some of which were bleeding, and several of the children had broken an arm or sprained an ankle. Seven adults of the second group had been killed by a large Assiniboine war party.³⁰ One woman in that group had been struck by an Assiniboine bullet but managed to struggle on after a warrior put her on a horse. Though very weak she rode to safety by holding tightly to the animal's mane. She recovered over time.

Several in the third group who had become separated from their companions wandered around for days before meeting a friendly band who gave them shelter. Some of those lost ones stayed with their adoptive families for some time and eventually returned to Lapwai. Two or three, after wandering alone throughout the night, encountered Chippewa hunters who gave them food and blankets and later took them to Sitting Bull's camp. One of those women, Mrs. Husis Owyeen [Wounded Head], had high praise for the Chippewas. One hunter, seeing she was barefoot, gave her a pair of moccasins. She was to say years later, "Next day we come to see some Chippewa Indians. They are nice people. They give us food. I am given a pair of moccasins. Then I feel better."[31]

Late in the afternoon of October 11, White Bird met the Sioux warriors who had been sent by Sitting Bull to find the refugees and offer assistance. They took the refugees to Sitting Bull's camp where they were made welcome and were reunited with the twenty who had arrived earlier after eluding and fighting off the 2nd Cavalry during the first attack of October1. A few days later White Bird met with Inspector Walsh of the Northwest Mounted Police who explained the conditions for sanctuary in Canada. White Bird made to Walsh the same promises Sitting Bull had made a year before.

The Sioux treated the refugees kindly and with generosity. Over the winter, which was bitterly cold even for the prairies, they lodged them in a camp of 300 tepees near Sandy Hills in what is now southern Saskatchewan.[32] By March the Nez Perces had made their own tepees and had formed a village not far away. Inspector Walsh and his men also helped the Nez Perces with food and blankets from their own supplies. Walsh met with local merchants and arranged credit for them until spring arrived.

White Bird managed to keep his camp intact until June, at which time some families decided to go north to trap. A few decided to risk a return to Idaho. Many of the men had found work with local farmers and ranchers. Many ranchers, impressed with the Natives' ability with horses, offered them steady work and a steady wage. Many accepted the offers but, rather than travel back and forth, left the village, moving their families and tepees to the ranches.

With his band slowly diminishing, White Bird eventually moved those who remained with him to a rich bottomland near the Peigan Reserve near the town of Pincher Creek in what is now Alberta. That group remained there until the final blow was struck in the early evening of March 6, 1892. (See: Chapter 25 Aftermath.)

The Final Surrender

On the morning of October 5, two Nez Perce scouts who had arrived the day before with General Howard approached the Nez Perce camp under a white flag. These men were well known to Joseph and the others, so they were allowed safe conduct. These men were Jokais [Lazy] but known by his Anglicized name, Captain John, who had recovered from injuries received in the Lolo Trail ambush, and Meopkowit [Old George]. They had been sent ahead by Howard in the hopes they could persuade Joseph to surrender. Because each man had daughters who had joined the rebels in Idaho, Howard felt they would receive favorable attention. They were to inform the chiefs that Howard was already in Miles' camp awaiting his army, expected to arrive that afternoon. Joseph was to be told surrender meant no trials or executions and all the people would receive honorable treatment as prisoners of war. Joseph was also told Miles had said the people would be returned to their homes. While most understood that to mean Lapwai, others, among them Roaring Eagle, testified years later General Miles had promised a return to Wallowa; but the widow of Chief Ollokot distinctly remembered hearing, "If you will surrender you can all go back to Lapwai." Either way, for those who had misunderstood, the feeling of betrayal and of Miles having lied remained with them the rest of their lives.

Miles had not lied. Both he and Howard had understood from the messages they had received from General McDowell that Joseph and his people were to be detained within the District of the Clearwater (Idaho). Miles stated in his report that he had acted on what he supposed was the design of the federal government. He thought he was to place the Indians on their own reservation [Lapwai] and he had so informed them. However, Miles also denied that statement on several occasions, and his reports are filled with contradictions and denials. He did think the federal government intended to return them to Idaho. However, in a treacherous move Sheridan, abetted by Sherman, later convinced Washington officials not to abide by the terms of the surrender.

On the morning of surrender, Joseph and several warriors went with Captain John and Old George to meet with Miles and Howard. Exactly what transpired remains in doubt. Miles is reputed to have said he would take them to a safe place for the upcoming winter and in the spring they could all go home. According to Yellow Wolf, Joseph then replied to the effect that he considered Miles their protector (Howard obviously was still not trusted) so they would surrender to Miles. Miles concluded the meeting with the promise of food and good treatment. He and Joseph shook hands and Joseph and his companions returned to their own lines.

It was almost mid-afternoon, according to Howard's adjutant, Lieutenant Charles E. S. Wood's, description of the surrender, when Joseph rode out of the Indian camp. He rode slowly up the incline to the place where he was to formally present his rifle as a token of surrender. According to Wood,

> "His scalp-lock was tied with otter fur. The rest of his hair hung in a thick plait on either side of his head. He wore buckskin leggings and a woolen shawl through which were the marks of four or five bullet holes…"[33]

As Joseph and his escort approached, Wood was to write later, he rode slowly. His attendants, five warriors on each side, walked beside his horse. They were speaking to him softly but intently. Some clung to his legs as they proceeded toward the six-man army delegation. Wood noticed that Joseph sat stiffly upright with his hands crossed on the pommel of his saddle, his rifle lying across his knees. Wood glanced at his watch and noted it showed 2:20 when the entourage stopped. For a moment, Wood recorded, Joseph sat looking at the two generals then swept his eyes across their companions. These were Wood, 2nd Lieutenant Oscar F. Long (an engineer officer with Miles' army), Arthur "Ad" Chapman, designated by Howard as the official interpreter, and one unidentified orderly on Howard's clerical staff. As Joseph dismounted he raised a hand, whereupon the warrior escort stepped back a few paces leaving Joseph to walk alone to face the two generals. There he extended the rifle in surrender—but the manner in which he presented it has been the subject of conjecture ever since and has never been fully resolved.

Some thought Joseph extended the weapon toward Howard who graciously stepped back while motioning it should be presented to Miles, who then received it without comment. Others believed Joseph deliberately snubbed Howard by first extending the rifle to him but, when the general reached to take it, he turned handed it to Miles, saying to Howard, "No, I am not surrendering to you. This is the man who whipped me. You are an old woman."[34]

One of several who claimed to have witnessed the surrender, Ami Frank Mulford, a private in the 7th Cavalry, later wrote a pamphlet,[35] in which he claimed Joseph "passed by General Howard without paying any attention to him, walked deliberately to Miles and said, 'I want to surrender to you.'" There is, however, much doubt if Mulford's claim of having been among the witnesses has validation.

Another who claimed to have witnessed the surrender was a William Bent. He was quoted by A.J. Noyes, on page 97 of his 1917 book, *In the Land of the Chinook,* "Bent says, 'Joseph handed his gun, muzzle first, to Howard who refused it saying, 'No, that is the man who won it.' Then Joseph handed it butt first to Miles."

According to Noyes, Bent believed Joseph would have shot Howard had he actually accepted the rifle.

Some Nez Perce accounts of the surrender are in general agreement with Bent and Mulford. They indicate Joseph did indeed refuse to give his rifle to Howard. According to their statements his was clearly a symbolic gesture, emphasized by walking past Howard and going directly to Miles.

None of the negative accounts, including those of the Nez Perces, came from people who have been proven as having been present at the actual time of surrender. It appears Wood's version should be accepted as it seems closest to the truth of what actually transpired.

According to Wood's account, when Joseph extended the rifle, Howard indicated it should go to Miles. Joseph then turned to

Miles and handed him the rifle. Then he stepped back, adjusted his blanket to leave his right arm free, and began his speech, which has been famously titled by historians as "From Where the Sun Now Stands." Speaking slowly, and distinctly he directed his words to Chapman who translated them in like manner.

> *"Tell General Howard I know his heart. What he told me before I have in my heart. I am tired of fighting. Our chiefs are killed. Looking Glass is dead. The old men are all killed. It is the young men who say yes and no. He who led the young men is dead.*[36] *It is cold and we have no blankets. The little children are freezing to death. My people, some of them, have run away to the hills, and have no blankets, no food; no one knows where they are, perhaps freezing to death. I want time to look for my children and see how many of them I can find. Maybe I shall find them among the dead. Hear me, my chiefs. I am tired: my heart is sick and sad. From where the sun now stands, I will fight no more forever."*[37]

From where the sun stood at that point in time the Nez Perce War of 1877 ended. Joseph was turned over to the care of Lieutenant Wood who was to take him to a tent where he would be kept in comfort and treated with dignity and respect. Before he left he shook hands with each officer, all of whom later commented how sad he looked but how he managed a smile for each of them. As Joseph was being led away, the warriors, women, children and elders who could walk began emerging from the encampment. In twos and threes they make their way to the army lines. The warriors carried their rifles with the muzzles pointing in reverse, the sign they had no intention of using them. They each surrendered their weapons to a party of soldiers who counted and stacked them in neat piles. The parade continued until dusk. Fires were lit, hot food from the army kitchens was distributed and blankets were given out. The children were all restrained from eating too much. The medical officer, Dr. Henry R. Tilton, feared too much food all at once could cause severe stomach cramps and might even result in death amongst the very young.

The surrender, however, was anything but spontaneous or unanimous. Joseph had, in effect, spoken only for his own people, the Wellamotkins of the Wallowa Valley. Those who had not agreed with him tended to hang back. Husis Kute, chief of the Palu band, led nearly all his followers and the handful of Cayuses who had been with them to join Joseph, while others, mainly Piquinin and Asotin, who had followed Tool'hool'hool'zote and Looking Glass stayed in the encampment to contemplate their next move. As a result of their contemplations a number belatedly joined White Bird and went to Canada. The remainder came out the next morning and surrendered.

The following morning soldiers were dispatched to the camp to bring out those elders and wounded who were unable to walk. They also intended to convince White Bird to bring out his followers. Miles and Howard, neither of whom knew of the escape, were enraged when informed that White Bird, a large number of rebels, and most of the horses had escaped. As noted earlier, Howard had never bothered to acquaint himself with Nez Perce laws or societal customs, and had never learned that chiefs were independent and not bound by the wishes of others. He felt White Bird's escape had been abetted by Joseph who had stalled the surrender, thus buying time to engineer the escape. To his way of thinking Joseph was in violation of the terms and agreements of the surrender. Miles was unsure of what to think. He had never dealt before with Nez Perces but should have known the customs of Plains Indians. Yellow Wolf tried to explain the situation.

> "All who wanted to surrender took their guns to General Miles and gave them up. Those who did not want to surrender kept their guns. The surrender was just for those who did no longer wish to fight. Joseph spoke only for his own band, what they wanted to do."[38]

In all, the initial surrender netted 184 women, 147 children, and eighty-seven men, for a total of 418. Only fourteen warriors surrendered, the others having opted to go north with White Bird. Over the next few days the total increased to 448 as another thirty Nez Perce women and other non-combatants were found in shelter pits, including one wounded man who was found at the end of a long tunnel burrowed from the wall of a shelter pit. He was found with a good supply of roots and berries. He had obviously been waiting for friends to rescue him.

Lieutenant Long, the engineer officer, took great interest in the safety pits the Nez Perces had built. He marveled at the twists and turns that had been employed. It was obvious to him why cannon fire had failed to inflict any damage. One of his men commented, "These entrenchments consisted mainly of a series of rifle pits dug deeply into the earth, and they were arranged in some respects with a skill which would have done credit to an educated military engineer."[39]

Lieutenant Wood, who had also taken a keen interest in the defenses, later wrote in an article, "the ravines were so crooked as to prevent enfilade [cannon] fire and so protected by hills as to be safe from our sharpshooters."[40]

Upwards of 700 Nez Perces had begun the long trek from Idaho in June. Their fatalities in the various encounters, battles and skirmishes are considered to be about ninety-six, of which thirty-six were women, elders and children—all non-combatants. The injuries suffered are estimated to about one hundred, but it is not possible to determine the total number because the Nez Perces never counted wounds not considered serious. Warrior Chief Peopeo Tholket, for example, suffered several wounds but only three were considered serious enough to be counted. The total number of casualties, therefore, can be estimated at about 190. The number of warriors killed numbered fewer than forty, far fewer than their professional counterparts in the army. White Bird escaped to Canada with at least 233, which included seventy to eighty actual warriors and the rest able-bodied young men and older teenage boys who had not attained the status of warrior through the various tests and rites required, but were able to—and did—fight.

On the army side, the total number of troops engaged throughout the war numbered about 1400 officers and men. One hundred fourteen were killed, 115 were wounded, for a total of 229 casualties, all combat soldiers. Among the civilian and Indian scouts, the casualties numbered sixteen, of which six were fatalities. Had the Nez Perce combatants been comparable in number to those of the U.S. Army there is little doubt the victory would have gone to the Nez Perce warriors. As it was, even discounting the blunders and rash decisions made by Looking Glass, a Nez Perce victory came very close to becoming reality.

The cost of the campaign to the government treasury was $1,873,410 (excluding the value of destroyed private property), but the cost to the Nez Perce bands involved was also high. Their vast herds of cattle had been lost; their horses were gone, as were their caches of food and gold dust. They had lost nearly all their tepees at the Big Hole with only a scant few replaced as the trail went on. Along the way they lost most of their camp supplies and utensils. In the surrender their guns were taken from them. The five bands had gone in four months from rich and powerful to impoverished, their people forced to depend on their conquerors for support—and it all fell short by forty-three miles, due in great part to the errors in judgment by the chief they had appointed to lead them. As the years passed, the survivors, when asked who had been mostly to blame for the defeat, almost as one and with no hesitation replied, "Chief Looking Glass was to blame."

[CHAPTER 23 ENDNOTES]

1   The battlefield is now an area of National Historical Interest, located forty-five miles south of the border near the town of Havre.

2   Rattlesnakes are timid by nature and go to great lengths to avoid contact with intruders. They will not attack, but will most certainly defend. In 1877 at Snake Creek,

the Nez Perces (who were well aware of snakes) walked cautiously while the snakes either left the area or hid in crevices or under flat rocks. Today visitors to the battlefield park are warned about rattlers but are told there is no danger if they stay on the pathways. Should they wander off the paths any distance, they are told they must keep an ear open for the noise of the warning rattle, and never stick their hands under rocks.

3   Wottolen's account as described to McWhorter. [*The Last Battle,* McWhorter's notes: NP12, 46]

4   Ten-year-old named Suhmkeen (later known as Samuel Tilden) years later related, "the man yelled, then fired his rifle in the air while at the same time waving a blanket in a signal—soldiers are coming—soldiers are coming." [Alcorn, Rowena L. and Gordon D., "Aged Nez Perce Recalls the 1877 Tragedy," *Montana: The Magazine of Western History,* October 1965, 71.]

5   "Yellowstone" Kelly became famous in later years as a Hollywood created legend and TV hero.

6   McAlpine, John, *Memoirs of a Frontier Soldier.* Unpublished. 1938.

7   Eelahweema's full account is extremely interesting. [McWhorter, *Hear Me My Chiefs,* 484–84.]

8   Romeyn, *Capture of Chief Joseph,* 288.

9   Henry Romeyn never recovered completely from his wound. Though he continued in the army he was subjected to frequent bouts of intense pain, which often clouded his judgment. In 1897 he made slanderous remarks about a junior officer's wife then, when the man objected, struck him. He was court-martialed for that offence and found guilty. He appealed the sentence, which was remitted on condition he retire. In 1913 he was admitted to Walter Reed Hospital where he died. [Romeyn, Henry. Commission and Personal File.

Records of the Office of the Adjutant General, National Archives, Washington, DC.]

10 "Miles Report" in Report of the Secretary of War, December, 27 1877. [Washington Archives, Government Printing Office, 1877.]

11 "Ten or twelve soldiers charged into our camp and got possession of two lodges, killing three Nez Perces and losing three of their men who fell inside our lines. I called on my men to drive them back. We fought at close range, not more than twenty steps apart and drove them back upon their own lines. We secured their arms and ammunition." [Chief Joseph, *An Indian's Views*, 428.]

12 Dispatch to Howard, Sturgis and Brotherton, September 30, 1877. [Nez Perce War folder, box 3. Sladen Family Papers. MS Div. US Army Military History Inst. Army War College, Carlisle, Pennsylvania.]

13 Kowyehkown, Kowwaspo and Peopeo Ipsewahk were the three fallen warriors who had been shot accidently by Husis Kute, the Palouse chief. Lean Elk had been shot when he advanced too far forward and was misidentified as a Cheyenne scout. [Greene, *Nez Perce Summer*, 291.]

14 Red Elk as quoted by McWhorter. [*Nez Perce Notes*, 38–42.]

15 From the narrative of an unidentified woman.

16 Tom Hill's affidavit concerning this incident was sworn before the Congress of the United States. [Senate Document No 97, 1st Session of the 62nd Congress, 31–32.]

17 Miles' report to Secretary of War. [Report of Secretary of War, 1877, 1, 528.]

18 Miles, an ambitious officer, was hopeful of being promoted to brigadier-general, to which a Nez Perce defeat at his hands would certainly contribute. He was

fearful he would be superseded in command and thus forfeit the honor of receiving the surrender. [Wood, C.E.S., *The Pursuit and Capture of Chief Joseph,* and quoted by C.A. Fee in his book, *Chief Joseph,* (New York 1936), 324–26.]

19   Robert Bruce. Comments of Lovell H. Jerome, December 13, 1932. [Archives and Special Collections, Holland Library, Washington State University, Pullman WA.]

20   Reported in the *Otsego Journal* (Otsego, New York), July 17, 1930.

21   Miles makes no mention of the incident, save for a short statement in his official report that Joseph remained his prisoner for the same period Jerome was held in the Nez Perce camp. [Report of the Secretary of War, 1877, 1, 528.]

22   Jerome's military career ended twice, both under near-tragic circumstances. The first occurred shortly after his highly controversial adventure within the Nez Perce camp. In 1879 his drinking habit got out of hand and he faced a court-martial, which forced him to resign his commission. He appealed to a relative with influence in high places and Jerome was allowed to enlist—as a private—in the 8th Cavalry, which at the time was posted to duty in Texas.

Determined to win back his commission, he served well for awhile and was promoted to corporal. This allowed him to take exams, which he passed. He was recommended for promotion to 2nd Lieutenant, but before the commission could be processed he regressed to old habits. Cited for frequent drunkenness, he was reduced in rank to private and spent some time in confinement. His final discretion occurred on October 30, 1881 when he appeared at a parade inspection so drunk he could not saddle his horse. At that point his father, in order to avoid disgrace for the family, requested the secretary of war release his son from the service "as speedily as possible," and Jerome was discharged on January 31, 1882.

He fared better as a civilian. He found employment with the US Customs Service, became involved in the McKinley-Roosevelt election campaign of 1900 and founded Alumni Day at West Point. He died in 1935. [Johnson, Barry C., "Solved: The 'Mystery of Lt. Lovell Jerome," *Montana The Magazine of Western History*, Autumn edition 1969, 167–170.]

23 This incident was reported in the *New York Herald*, October 11, 1877. The suggestion the "Charge!" comment was made by Miles, or any officer for that matter, is suspect. According to Private John McAlpine in his "memoirs," no officer ever came to the front for the entire five days of the siege. Wrote McAlpine, "I never saw an officer for the whole five days of the battle. They stayed in the rear with the grub and hot coffee." [Greene, *Nez Perce Summer*, 309.]

24 McWhorter quotes this exchange from a letter he received from Duncan McDonald dated December 15, 1929. [McWhorter, *Hear Me My Chiefs*, 496.]

25 Swick's letter. [McWhorter, *Hear me My Chiefs*, 495.]

26 Only fourteen warriors surrendered with Chief Joseph. The remaining seventy to eighty had joined White Bird in the breakout.

27 Miles, possibly thinking all the Nez Perces were surrendering, had not increased the pickets. In fact, he may have actually decreased their number for the same reason.

28 Martha lived in Canada nine years before returning to

Idaho where she married a Nez Perce man. Wetanonmi remarried and lived until 1934. Martha died in 1945.

29 Kepkop'ponmi later returned to Idaho, married a Nez Perce man and settled at Lapwai. Both lived long lives.

30 Miles, upon discovering the escape, sent messengers north to Gros Ventre (Atsina) and Assiniboine camps informing them that arms and horses could be kept if any of the escapees were captured or killed. He also offered a reward of tobacco for information regarding the whereabouts of any escapees. The Assiniboines managed to recapture some of the army horses and mules previously taken from Howard's army and claimed they had killed seven escapees and captured four more. [*Fort Benton Record*, October 12, 1877.]

31 Quoted from the description of the first breakout as told by Wounded Head's wife. [McWhorter, *Hear Me, My Chiefs*, 510–11.]

32 Quoted from the description of the first breakout as told by Wounded Head's wife. [McWhorter, *Hear Me, My Chiefs*, 510–11.]

33 Wood, C.E.S., *Chief Joseph, the Nez Perce*, 142.

34 Charles A. Smith, private, 7th Cavalry, in an interview with McWhorter, November 28, 1935. [McWhorter, *Hear Me My Chiefs*, n19, 497.]

35 Ami Frank Mulford wrote the account in a pamphlet, "Fighting Indians in the Seventh United States Cavalry." It was published in Corning, New York (no date given) and was later republished with a new title. ["Fighting Indians! In the Seventh United States Cavalry, Custer's Favorite Regiment," 123. Rev. ed. Corning, NY. Paul Lindsley Mulford, 1925.]

36 Joseph is referring to Ollokot. When speaking in the Nez Perce language, names of close family members

were rarely used. The individual's station or position of authority within the band was most often used.

37 Joseph's words, written *verbatim* by Lieutenant Charles E. S. Wood, as translated by interpreter Arthur Chapman on the afternoon of October 5, 1877. [Report of Secretary of War, 1877, I, 630.]

38 McWhorter, *Yellow Wolf,* 225–27.

39 Zimmer, *Frontier Soldier,* 130.

40 Wood, *Harper's Weekly*, November 17, 1877.

[CHAPTER 24]

AFTERMATH

> "The Great Spirit Chief who rules above seemed to be looking some other way and did not see what was happening to his people."
> —Chief Joseph, Washington, 1897.

When the soldiers entered the Snake Creek camp at the Bear's Paw and discovered a large number of Indians had made a break for the border, they thought the breakout had taken place over a period of several days. How, they wondered, could so many people slip past the pickets? It was a question both Howard and Miles wanted answered. The overall count later revealed over 300 had escaped—and had also managed to take with them at least 300 horses. Howard was furious; however, expecting the escapees had already crossed into Canada, he did not order a pursuit. Miles issued messages to other tribes that rewards would be paid to any Indians who captured Nez Perce escapees or horses. When further investigation revealed that Chief White Bird, women and 124 children and about seventy-five heavily armed warriors had all quietly left during the night of October 5, Howard accused Joseph of breaking the agreement of the surrender. Howard never understood the Nez Perce laws that forbade any chief from overriding the wishes of another, or that a band chief could impose his law on his people.

After a few months in Canada several, including Joseph's daughter, decided to risk a return to Idaho. They departed as a group but were apprehended in Montana by an army patrol. Most were captured, but Joseph's daughter and five others escaped and quickly returned to Canada. Those captured were sent to Kansas where they rejoined Joseph. Over the next months others still in White Bird's village grew homesick and departed in hopes of getting to Lapwai. White Bird did his best to stop the reverse exodus, but had little success.

In late summer a fairly large group went west to the Rockies where they found refuge with the Kootenay tribe in British Columbia's Creston Valley. While some chose to remain there, others continued south where they made contact with the Spokane tribe in western Washington. They were made welcome and were not discovered until the Spokane and Kalispel bands were relocated to the Colville reservation at Nespelem. At that point they were identified as Nez Perce. Some were transferred to Lapwai while others stayed in Colville.

Meanwhile, the American government requested of Ottawa an opportunity to meet with White Bird's people to discuss a return. Ottawa, quite happily, approved the request; so, during late June of 1878, White Bird, Yellow Wolf, Tookka'licktsema [Never Hunts] plus three others were escorted by a North-West Mounted Police patrol commanded by Lieutenant Colonel James F. Macleod to Fort Walsh for talks with U.S. Army delegates.

The American delegation, headed by General Miles' aide de camp, Lieutenant George W. Baird[1] (no relation to Sergeant A. Baird of the White Bird Canyon battle), included three members from Joseph's camp, at the time situated in Leavenworth, Kansas where the Nez Perce had been forced to move after the surrender. Washington hoped Baird, with the Indians' assistance, could convince White Bird to return to the States. The three Nez Perces were Yellow Bull, Espowyes [Light on the Mountain] (who had been the principal war chief in the Camus Field battle) and Palu

Chief Husis Kute. It transpired, however, the three had journeyed north with their own agenda[2]—to inform White Bird of the truth of Joseph's exile to Kansas.

On July 1 the meeting commenced, Macleod and his Mounties watching as silent observers. A North-West Mounted Police officer, working with a Canadian translator, recorded the minutes. The meeting was doomed from its beginning. Baird started out with a blatant lie in which he stated that Joseph was *insisting* White Bird and his people return. Apparently Baird was another American in authority who thought Joseph was the "chief of chiefs," and was also lacking in knowledge of the Nez Perce laws forbidding enforcement of wills. He then told White Bird he and his followers would likely be sent directly to Lapwai. Baird was obviously unaware White Bird had already heard of the treacherous refusal by Generals Sheridan and Sherman to abide by the terms agreed to by Miles and Howard. White Bird also knew about the hardships endured by Joseph and his people on their trek to Kansas; and he was well aware of the sickness and intolerable living conditions in the Leavenworth camp. Moreover, White Bird had immediately seen through the first of Baird's falsehoods. The meeting began to unravel and Baird suggested a recess for the remainder of the day.

That evening White Bird and the three Nez Perce emissaries held their own meeting under the watchful eye of Macleod. They dissected Baird's statements and discussed the conditions in Joseph's camp.

The following morning Baird compounded his blunders by presenting White Bird with a statement that he claimed Joseph had signed in which he agreed with the countermanding of the Bear Paw agreement. The statement contained an order from Joseph for White Bird to return. At that point White Bird and his entourage angrily walked out.

The following morning the meeting resumed during which White Bird replied to Baird. His reply was direct and to the point, and he even engaged in some verbal sport at Baird's expense. He reminded the lieutenant that in view of the insinuation that he and his band would likely go to Lapwai, a move to Kansas would be a waste of time and expense. The Nez Perce refugees in Canada,

White Bird remarked, were already closer to Idaho than were the prisoners in Kansas. Thus, he continued, considering Baird's statement the previous day that Joseph and his people would likely be returned to Idaho upon White Bird's surrender, it made much better sense that they should join Joseph in Lapwai. He told Baird he would return to the United States under no other agreement except that which had been made with Miles and Howard at the Bear Paw surrender. The day he and his people would leave Canada and return to the US would be the day the original agreement was implemented and Joseph had been returned safely to Lapwai. White Bird then told Baird,

> "Now...I am waiting Joseph's return to Idaho. He was promised by General Miles that if he surrendered he would be taken there [to Lapwai]. If the Government sends him back to his home in Idaho I will go at once...I want justice from the Americans and if I cannot have it I will remain in the north and do the best I can."

He completed his statement by discounting Baird's offer of a safe return. The meeting dissolved completely when Baird reluctantly admitted that all the promises made by Howard and Miles had been broken.[3] The Americans returned south the following day having accomplished nothing except to cement in White Bird's mind his belief that Washington and the U.S. Army could never be trusted.

Upon his return to the Sioux camp at Sandy Hills, White Bird moved his people, in what was not a wise decision, east to a valley in what is now Manitoba. There was no bison, very little game and poor soil so deficient in nutrients that cultivation of vegetables was impossible. Family after family departed for other sites. Within a year White Bird's village had been reduced to ten tepees.

Canada was difficult for White Bird and his band of Nez Perces. By 1880 the once great herds of buffalo, whose numbers had once extended over the prairies, were all but gone. Only a few hundreds of the great beasts, spread far and wide in small, scattered groups, now remained. Once again White Bird's people were in dire straits, but the Canadian government still adamantly refused anything other than sanctuary. Ottawa insisted they were American Indians and were not entitled to either assistance or a reservation in Canada. White Bird, probably on the advice of North-West Mounted Police members who had befriended him, took his remaining followers to a site close to the town of Pincher Creek, in southern Alberta.

The new site was ideal. It had rich, loamy soil, fresh water in abundance and large herds of antelope. Steady work on ranches was available, hunting was good and nearby Peigan bands made them welcome.[4] It proved a fine place for settlement. The women harvested more than enough cultivated and wild vegetables and berries to feed their families during the long winters. The surplus harvest was such that it could be sold for cash in the nearby town. The children attended school with the Piegan children. Ottawa still refused to recognize them for the purposes of negotiating a treaty, nor would they grant them a deed to the land they occupied. By now, though, assistance was no longer needed. Local ranchers made no effort to claim the acreage the group occupied. The Nez Perces were making their own way and enduring.

White Bird and his Nez Perces adjusted so well that in 1885, when Joseph was returned to the northwest, only a few ventured south to join him.[5] Those who stayed did so because they had found steady work with Alberta ranchers who, appreciative of their work ethic and skills with horses, were happy to hire them. It appeared they had at last found a home where they could be free if not altogether happy.

Then, on March 6, 1892, tragedy struck the little community when Lamnisnim Husis [Shriveled Head] authored the final Canadian chapter in the saga of White Bird's little Nez Perce band. Lamnisnim Husis had been a ten-year-old (known by his mission name, Charley) when he fled north with White Bird's survivors. Now twenty-six, he had abandoned his mission name and had married and built a small wooden house in which he lived with his wife Sara and their children.[6] Because of his skill with horses he held the respect of the ranchers and was never unemployed. Unable to easily pronounce his name, the white populace simply called him Nez Perce Sam, and soon the name fell into common usage even among his fellows. Then, when all seemed to be going so well for him, he began to exhibit signs of mental derangement. He began to denounce White Bird with harsh words. On the evening of March 6, as the sun was setting, Lamnisnim Husis ambushed the elderly chief and murdered him with blows from an axe.

White Bird, the reluctant chief, shaman, renowned ceremonialist, proven warrior, military tactician and field general par excellence was then about eighty-five years of age. Enfeebled by arthritis and nearly blind, he may not have seen his assailant. He certainly would not have been able to evade him. The old warrior was felled with one blow from the axe—and then his assailant hacked him into several pieces.

White Bird's distraught followers carried their beloved and venerated chief's remains to a remote place, sang the mournful ceremonial songs of the dead and buried him. They did not mark the grave.[7]

North-West Mounted Police officers investigating the case quickly discovered the bloodied axe. After questioning many they arrested Nez Perce Sam and charged him with capital murder—a hanging offence.[8] Sam never denied killing White Bird. He had to kill White Bird, he insisted; it was a deed he was required to do.

At his trial Sam told the court White Bird was an evil man who had been using "bad medicine" to treat illnesses. The old chief, Sam insisted, was systematically destroying his family and his friends, and said, "Four years ago [White Bird] diseased one of my sons and he has diseased others in the camp."[9]

The interpreter could not determine what was meant by "diseased" until Sam explained White Bird had been using supernatural powers to steal a person's spirit. At that point the translator realized Sam was implying the old chief was "possessing" souls. The Nez Perce had no word for the phenomena of spirit possession; of all the prairie Indian nations only the Cree language had a word for what Sam was trying to describe. The interpreter, fluent in Cree, informed the court

Sam was describing a Windigo, an evil spirit. Crees believed the Windigo possessed the power to steal human souls.

Sam's lawyer put forth a vigorous defense. He had attempted to convince Sam to plead "not guilty by reason of insanity," but Sam had refused. The jury, therefore, had but two verdicts to consider—"guilty as charged" or "not guilty"; and because Sam had admitted the killing, a "not guilty" verdict would be difficult to warrant. Nonetheless, the twelve jury members were obviously discomfited because they deliberated many hours before returning the only verdict open to them. Nez Perce Sam, the likeable young man and noted horse wrangler, was declared guilty. An equally reluctant judge sentenced him to hang. He also had no choice. In 1892 there was no alternate sentence for a verdict of guilty in a case capital murder.[10]

However, Sam had many friends within the white community and among North-West Mounted Police personnel. They, including the presiding judge, rallied to his side. Following appeals to the Supreme Court, the death sentence was commuted to life in prison.

Sam's life, however, was already nearing its end. Tuberculosis had ravished his lungs and death was hastened under the heartbreak of enforced confinement. In late August 1893, he became so ill he stopped eating. On October 1 he died.[11]

Chief White Bird's brutal murder proved to be the final blow for the remaining members of the distraught band. Now, with no chief to lead them, the band split up. Two or three families settled on a stretch of bottom land near the Piegan River; several moved their lodges to the Piegan reservation and assimilated with that band. The remainder, perhaps five families, returned to Idaho where they were allowed to settle at Lapwai.

Joseph's anguished statement, "the Great Spirit Chief seemed to be looking some other way…" surely appears to have applied to the Lamtama band of the Salmon River. Truly the Great Spirit Chief had lost sight of those who had fled to "The Land of the Grandmother" in search of the justice they never found.

On October 9, 1877, Chief Joseph formally surrendered and was taken into custody with his followers. According to the terms of surrender, discussed the previous evening and agreed to by both Howard and Miles, Joseph and the Nez Perces would be considered prisoners of war, would be treated with all due respect and would to be returned safely and quickly to Idaho for settlement at Lapwai. The agreement closely paralleled the original dictates presented by Howard in his effort to obtain agreement the previous May.

With Miles' approval, Joseph gave Chief Yellow Bull responsibility for the well-being of the women and children. The group was then removed to an area some distance from the warriors who were being confined under tight security. While Joseph was assigned to a tent in solitary, he was under the authority of Lieutenant Charles Scott Wood, who saw to it every respect was afforded the chief. Joseph had made a great impression on the pursuing army and such was the admiration held for him that all the officers and men extended him every courtesy. It was during this initial confinement that Joseph talked at length with Lieutenant Wood who very quickly became Joseph's good friend and confidante. Wood left the army shortly after to return to university where he acquired a law degree. For years after he worked tirelessly to champion the Nez Perce cause, as well as those of other minorities.

Despite the promises made by Howard and Miles, the Nez Perce were not returned to Idaho. This was not the doing of either general—at least not directly. Rather, it was a flagrant betrayal in the classic sense of treachery perpetrated by General Philip Henry Sheridan (1831–88) and General William T. Sherman, his immediate superior; but the two would have been unable to succeed in their perfidy had they not been supported by the bureaucracy within the Department of Indian Affairs and Secretary of War George W. McCrary. Sheridan was no champion of Native people[12] and he held in total disdain all who were. Sherman, the commander of the army, shared his views. Already on record was his opinion the Nez

Perce prisoners should never be allowed to return to the northwest. In his view no Indians who had fomented or partaken in rebellious actions should ever be allowed to remain in their home areas. To this end he had already persuaded Washington to relocate several tribes. The transplants included the Peorias, Modocs, Poncas and Miamis, all of whom went to the so-called Indian Territory.

Miles also showed he possessed a degree of treachery within his bosom. This was stirred, not by bigotry, but by personal ambition. He also was somewhat envious of Howard, although they had been friends since their days together during Civil War. Following the surrender at Bear's Paw he dispatched a mandatory primary report to Sheridan. It was a brief, terse report. After Howard's departure he sent a second, detailed account in which he took sole credit for the surrender. Downplaying his own failures, he magnified Howard's by emphasizing his delays in the pursuit and his failure to capture Joseph weeks earlier despite having had several chances to do so. He commented on Howard's late arrival at the Bear's Paw and omitted all reference to any influence Howard may have had in convincing Joseph to surrender. Neither did he acknowledge that Howard had purposely relinquished his right of seniority which had enabled Miles to remain as officer-in-charge.

An interesting omission in this report is the absence of any mention of Joseph's refusal to surrender his rifle to Howard. Miles made no mention of this, stating simply that it had been he who accepted the rifle from Joseph. This omission clearly indicates such an exchange occurred. Miles surely would not have missed the chance to further embarrass Howard. As noted earlier, Howard was already under the gun in Washington by those who could not, or did not wish to, understand the reasons for his failures. In Miles' self-serving report Sheridan saw the opportunity to throw his support behind any thoughts Washington might have to renege on promises made by Howard.

Howard was not entirely blameless in Sheridan's interpretation of the surrender agreement for he had made an off-hand remark indicating that Joseph, technically at least, had violated the terms of surrender. Howard was convinced Joseph had used the lapse between the first talk in the morning and the afternoon session to give White Bird the time he needed to prepare his escape. When Sheridan read Howard's statement in Miles' report he immediately saw it as yet another excuse to renege.

Howard learned of Miles' second report when he read it in the Chicago *Tribune*. Incensed, he authorized Lieutenant Wood, to write a rebuttal.[13] Wood did so and sold it as an article to the *Chicago Times*. Howard, accompanied by Wood, journeyed to Chicago to meet with Sheridan who was there. Coincidentally, Sheridan had arrived shortly after the *Times* published Wood's article. Now it was Sheridan's turn to be furious. The moment he learned of Howard's arrival he immediately ordered him to his hotel room for a meeting.

The meeting was heated and acrimonious. Sheridan threatened to have Howard court-martialed whereupon Howard replied he would welcome the procedure. It would, he stated, present him an opportunity to relate the truth about Joseph's surrender. Sheridan, well aware that during such a hearing the entire story would be fully revealed, knew he could ill afford to accept Howard's challenge. Changing tactics, he threatened instead to court-martial Wood for writing the article he had found so offensive. Howard again stopped Sheridan in his tirade by reminding the general that selling the article was not only legal under military law,[14] but that Wood had merely transcribed Howard's words and opinions to paper. Again Sheridan was stymied.

Howard argued valiantly in an effort to convince Sheridan that Joseph and his band be returned to the Department of the Columbia. He reminded Sheridan of Joseph and his people having been promised resettlement at Lapwai as a term of surrender. He also told Sheridan that had Joseph decided to continue resistance the army would have suffered many more casualties and—even worse— might well have induced Sitting Bull and his Sioux to enter the fray. Howard had known, and had worried about, the Sioux warriors massed near the border. He had no way of knowing Sitting Bull did not intend to join the battle. The Sioux were near the border only because Inspector Walsh of the North-West Mounted Police had given them permission to go there to assist any Nez Perce who crossed into Canada.

Howard's efforts failed. Miles had given Sheridan—and hence Sherman and the Washington bureaucrats—all they needed to break yet another promise. Miles, to his credit, also pleaded Joseph's case to Sheridan and later to Sherman. His appeals also fell on the same deaf ears that had rejected Howard. There was no way Sherman or the determined bureaucrats in the Department of Indian Affairs were going to honor any promise made to an Indian. Sherman, in a letter to Secretary George W. McCrary, was particularly emphatic that Joseph and his followers never be returned to the northwest. He suggested Joseph's situation be used as leverage against other chiefs contemplating refusal to enter reservations. He advised McCrary, to immediately send the Indians to Leavenworth, Kansas to await furtherance to Indian Territory.[15]

Meanwhile, even as Sherman was arranging with McCrary plans for the disposition of the Nez Perces, the prisoners were already on the road from Bear's Paw to the Tongue River Cantonment (Fort Keogh), the first leg of what was to prove a dreadful eight-year period. They arrived at Tongue River on October 23 expecting to be there until spring when they would be returned to Lapwai. Joseph still believed the promises made by Howard and Miles would be kept.

At the Cantonment they were provided tepees that they erected near the river. Accompanying soldiers treated them kindly[16] and doctors saw to it that medical attention was administered. Over the next days, John H. Fouch, a distinguished frontier photographer, photographed many of them. Talk of a return to Lapwai was plentiful.

Then, their hopes began to unravel. A directive arrived from Sherman ordering Sheridan to move the group to Fort Lincoln in Dakota Territory. Sheridan opposed the move; he replied, proposing the Nez Perces be accommodated at Yankton, a much larger fort, for the winter to await their disposition. Sherman's directive, and Sheridan's proposal, also met with opposition from Miles. He was obviously unaware of Sherman's plans, already being formulated, to send the Nez Perce to Indian Territory. Miles immediately sent off a letter to Command HQ recommending the prisoners remain at Tongue River until they could be returned to Lapwai. He noted in his letter,

> *"three (3) died on the road [from Bear's Paw], two (2) on arrival and others cannot live. I consider it inhuman to compel them to travel further at this season of the year."*[17] [italics added]

A letter of rejection informed him the decision to transport the group had already been made. Miles was bitterly disappointed. On October 29, word was received from McCrary informing Sheridan to proceed with the move to either Yankton or Bismarck [Fort Lincoln] as he saw fit. This allowed Sheridan to choose for himself where the stop would be made, with the understanding the stay was to be only long enough to arrange transportation to Leavenworth. Sheridan opted for Bismarck and on October 31 the trek began once again.

After a relentless march with little rest they reached the Missouri River where the group was split. Prisoners of able body would ride horses while others would ride in wagons over the nineteen days it would take to reach Bismarck. The sick, the children and the women, some 200 in all, embarked to a fleet of large wooden boats, called Mackinaws.[18] At one point the soldiers had to use force to quell a disturbance when some of the Nez Perces panicked at the sound of the steam whistle from an approaching riverboat. Having never before seen such a vessel, they were greatly frightened by the whistle and several were hurt in the panic that followed the first blasts.[19]

They endured a long journey to Bismarck in the crowded Mackinaws, and on the way several of the weaker Indians died. All suffered from the cold, overcrowding, poor food and little water. The journey was a ghastly experience made worse because they had no idea of where they were going. One of the escorting officers, Lieutenant Frank Baldwin, wrote to his wife of the journey as being "inhumane, and if the public [were to learn of it] they would raise a glorious row."[20]

However, at least in the first phases, the travel was without incident, which may have given Joseph some glimmers of hope. As they passed through various towns and settlements, residents extended diverse acts of kindness. They offered gifts of food and toys for the children. When the overland travelers reached Bismark on November 21 (those who traveled in boats arrived two days earlier) the citizens laid on a lavish buffet assortment of pre-cooked food for the Indians and escorting troopers.[21] Later, a parade was staged to honor Miles and his troopers. Joseph was extended, and accepted, an invitation to join the parade. A few days later, at the town's largest hotel, ironically named The Sheridan House, a banquet was held for Joseph and his sub-chiefs. Those three events were reported by the media and were perceived by many ordinary Americans as an attempt to tell Washington officials to honor the terms of surrender.

The gestures failed to make any impression on Washington and on November 23, in despondency and tears, Joseph and his followers broke their encampment and with their equipment and personal belongings boarded a train of freight cars and day coaches to begin the journey to Leavenworth, far to the southeast. Escorted by two companies of the 1st Infantry, they arrived three days later only to find the fort had no accommodation for them and no space for a proper camp. The commandant, Major-General J. Pope, wanted to send them on to Fort Riley, but Sherman rejected his request. Pope issued small army tents and did the best he could under the circumstances, but those circumstances only increased the misery.

According to army records, Fort Leavenworth personnel processed 418 Indians,[22] supplied them with the 108 small tents on hand in the quartermaster's stores and issued as many rations as could be spared. Then the soldiers escorted them to a narrow tract of land about one square mile in area near a river. Some two miles from the fort, it had once been the site of a racetrack, but had been abandoned years before. The ground, packed hard by the hooves of countless horses in thousands of races and the boots of multitudes of spectators, was useless for tilling. The adjacent area had nothing to offer as it was bordered on one side by the Missouri River. With only swampy bottomland, the area was totally unsuitable for cultivation of edible plants. It was also unlikely any seeds planted there would ever grow. Land further from the river was overgrown with weeds and bush; there were no wild plants with edible roots or stalks. The surrounding area had neither game to hunt nor smaller animals to trap. With no fields to till the 400 wretched souls were informed this was their new home, albeit temporary. They were then left to fend for themselves.

Thus, dependent on the meager rations and basic supplies that would be given them by the army, they prepared to meet the winter. Within a few months four died and almost half their numbers were sick from a variety of ailments caused by the unsanitary conditions and stagnant drinking water. Washington seemed in no hurry to move them elsewhere.

There was another brief flurry of problems with the arrival of three young Nez Perces, converts from Lapwai, all ordained Presbyterian ministers. One was Archie Lawyer, a nephew of Chief Lawyer, Joseph's one-time nemesis. They had been sent for the purpose of converting their Nez Perce brethren from the Wéset religion to Christianity. They remained with the band for the duration of the exile, including the years in Indian Territory. They had no impact while at Leavenworth; only when the band reached the Indian Territory did the three begin to make some headway. They started a school for the children and were instrumental in arranging resettlement at Lapwai for twenty widows and orphaned children. Over the next five years nearly half the group, mostly women, who believed conversion would help them gain entry to Lapwai, embraced, with varying degrees of enthusiasm, the Presbyterian faith.

While at Leavenworth, however, Joseph and his people largely ignored the three young men and endured their troubles with quiet dignity. They made their tents as comfortable as possible, constructed some tepees with the few bison hides they had managed to bring with them, constructed a sweat lodge for healing purposes, held regular rites and ceremonies to honor the Great Spirit and treated their many visitors (some of whom were mere annoyances) with hospitality and friendly tolerance. The women, quickly realizing money could be earned from these visitors, established a cottage industry for the sale of baskets, moccasins, mittens and other artifacts they could manufacture from river reeds and other materials at hand. The artifacts found a ready market. Joseph was also kept busy during this time by the many reporters and others with historical interests who sought his company and counsel. He spoke with all who came, relating his account of the war and its causes. He spoke of the suffering of the elders, the women and the children. He told the reporters of the sadness his people had felt at the realization that Treaty Nez Perce men had scouted for the army. He spoke of the perceived treachery of the Crows who had only a few summers before promised enduring friendship for their Nez Perce allies. The reporters, most for the first time, learned that Crow and Cheyenne warriors—all supposedly allies—had not only scouted for the army, but had inflicted indignities upon many Nez Perce dead following the battle at the Big Hole. Joseph spared no details, so when his listeners left it was with a better understanding of the sorrow the Nez Perces had and were enduring.

When eastern papers began to run copy sent by their various reporters, and when various visitors began to publicize the conditions of the Leavenworth encampment, Washington was hard-pressed to ignore the situation. For six more months they did just that until so many compassionate groups became involved indifference could no longer be sustained. In early July 1878, officials of the Bureau of Indian Affairs visited the encampment and were appalled at what they beheld. The delegation chairman sent a scathing report in which he condemned the location of the camp deeming it "the worst possible place that could have been selected." In his report, a doctor with the party denounced the conditions under which the people were living, describing rampant sickness. He reported that everyone in the camp was afflicted with infections and various ailments and that at least half their numbers could be deemed to be showing serious symptoms of malaria.

Unfortunately, the science of medicine had not yet connected mosquitoes to malaria so, instead of taking measures to control the insects through such means as oiling nesting areas and draining stagnant pools, nothing was done to forestall the cause. The only treatment known was quinine but, as the doctor noted in his report, that medicine was not being supplied by the army's medical branch in sufficient quantity to treat all the victims.

The two reports so embarrassed the secretary of the interior he was jolted into immediate action. Within weeks the band, now numbering only 410, was told permanent land had been found for them in the northeastern corner of Indian Territory. In the waning days of July, with little notice, they were told to gather their belongings and equipment, and board a train for a fourteen-hour journey to a Kansas town called Baxter Springs. There they would leave the train and ride in wagons the short distance to the Quapaw Reservation. They were about to enter their second phase of hell. This time their nemesis would appear in the person of an Indian agent named Hiram W. Jones.

Eeikish Pah: The Hot Place

When the train arrived at Baxter Springs, a large crowd of townspeople were on hand to get a look at the now famous Chief Joseph. Curiosity quickly turned to shock and dismay at what they saw. The 400 Natives, sick, weary and showing signs of illness, struggled in their efforts to leave the coaches which had been so overcrowded that getting up to stretch or move about had been impossible. Insufficient food and inadequate water had been supplied for the journey. The heat within the coaches plus lack of ventilation had aggravated the conditions. No effort had been made to segregate the seriously ill from the others, so several new cases of fever had already appeared by the time the train arrived at Baxter Springs. Three children had died en route and two more were so seriously ill no hope was being held for their recovery.

Some of the townspeople, seeing how few of the disembarking passengers possessed the strength to descend the steps, moved forward to help. Several wanted to do more but were ordered away by Indian Agent Hiram W. Jones and Indian Inspector John McNeil, who had been assigned to escort the Indians from Leavenworth to the Quapaw reservation. The Indians were told to make camp in the railway freight yards, as darkness was prohibitive for wagon travel. The remainder of the journey they were told, a relatively short trip, would be completed the following morning. The bodies of the three children who had died en route were then buried near the freight yards. The following morning in the light of early dawn the other two children, who had died overnight, were also buried beside the three others.

Adding further to their misfortune, Washington had decided to release them from the army's jurisdiction to that of the Bureau of Indian Affairs. The decree removed their prisoner-of-war status and placed them into the less-than-tender mercies of Hiram Jones, the agent in charge of the Quapaw Agency. Much of the despair that was to befall Joseph and his people during their first year in Oklahoma can be placed squarely upon Jones. Within a few months more than 100 more Nez Perces died from a variety of illnesses. Some were such that even medicine could not cure but most were caused by the negligence of the man who was supposed to help them.

Jones had been appointed to the post of Indian agent by his church, The Society of Friends, also known as Quakers. Under the terms of governance drawn up during the Grant administration, several Christian denominations had been assigned reservations for the purpose of "educating and civilizing" the Indians into the ways of the white man. The churches did little to educate them in formal academics as their principal intention was to show them the way to eternal salvation through the doctrines of Christianity.[23] Jones, ostensibly a devout Quaker, was in fact intolerant, arrogant and blatantly corrupt. Unfortunately, it was not until after 1879 that the ongoing suspicions of fraud resulted in hearings and the eventual laying of charges.[24] In 1878, however, Jones was still considered "a fine agent..." and was that year lauded by the Board of Indian Commissioners as a man of "wise management" who "long and faithfully administered the affairs of the Quapaw Agency."[25] Joseph very quickly realized Jones could not be trusted.

The Nez Perces' land, allotted to them by Jones, was an almost barren area adjoining that of several bands of the Modoc (Maklac) tribe[26] that had been involved in a rebellion for which they had been exiled from California, their traditional homeland, to the Indian Territory. The acreage was only a little less foul than that just vacated; and in fact it was to prove worse for it was so heavily infested with the deadly anopheles mosquito that malaria, against which the Nez Perce had no immunity whatever, quickly struck. Some 260, including Joseph, fell prey to the deadly insects, and during the first three months 100 people died—with worse to come. Unaccustomed to the intense humidity and heat, the Nez Perces christened their new home Eeikish Pah[27] which translates as "The Hot Place."

Joseph and Jones clashed many times over various matters, not the least of which was Jones' opinion of religious freedom. Joseph was concerned by Jones' insistence that the Nez Perces convert to the Quaker religion. The continuous proselytizing became more than Joseph could tolerate, considering he was also having to contend with the three ministers from Lapwai. To Joseph it was an attempt to divide his people, thereby weakening his leadership. He was also critical of Jones' efforts to proscribe the Wéset rites and ceremonies, in particular the Sun Dance. Joseph and his followers frustrated Jones' prohibition efforts by attending Sun Dances on neighboring reserves where Jones had no control or influence. To Jones' dismay, none of the Nez Perces converted despite his efforts, and Joseph and the others continued following the Wéset beliefs. Worse, they continued with their traditional ceremonies, including the Sun Dance. After the band was transferred to the Oakland Agency in 1881 their new agent made no effort to thwart rites or ceremonies.

Meanwhile, the three Presbyterian missionaries who had accompanied the band from Leavenworth quietly worked at setting up a school and building a small church. They made no attempts at coercion and Joseph did not interfere with them. Joseph, however, was always very concerned in the welfare of his people so he did attend some of the mission services, sitting quietly off to one side listening and watching. While he and the majority of his fellow Dreamers declined to accept conversion by Reverend Lawyer and associates, several, mostly women (not of the Wellamotkin band), did convert.[28] The resulting conversions, as might be expected, eventually divided the Nez Perces to a degree that determined a final disposition. Division, however, never lessened Joseph's leadership while the Nez Perce were in the Indian Territory.

On October 1, 1878 a delegation from the Bureau of Indian Affairs arrived at Quapaw to negotiate with Joseph on a permanent settlement in a better part of the agency. It was the BIA's intention to relocate the Nez Perce away from the Modocs in the area assigned to the Miami and Peoria bands of the Illinois tribe, both of whom had also been banished from their homelands. Joseph, with Yellow Bull, attended the meetings but withheld agreement to the changes, partly because it meant displacing some of the Peorias and Miamis, but mainly because he remained adamant that his people must be relocated at Lapwai in accordance with the agreement he had made with Howard and Miles. While his reluctance to negotiate greatly distressed the BIA officials, their final report praised Joseph highly. They were particularly impressed with his ability to discuss the situation with logic and sound argument. That he and Yellow Bull were so eloquent amazed them. Their annual report states,

> "Seldom have we been in councils where the Indians more eloquently or earnestly advocated their side of the question. Joseph's arraignment of the army for alleged bad faith to him after the surrender of himself and his people to General Miles was almost unanswerable."[29]

Despite the "almost unanswerable" eloquence of Joseph's linguistic abilities, the commissioners pressed on to their preconceived decision. Following the usual procedures of browbeating and promises of large payments in dollars, the commissioners persuaded the Peorias and Miamis to relinquish a large parcel of their land to the United States for the purpose of reassigning it to the Nez Perces. Those two tribes agreed to the terms and the commissioners, pleased with their work, invited Joseph to travel with them on a survey of the lands which, in the words of the commissioners' report, "are prairie and timber, with springs of water abundant, and with good natural boundaries, two sides being bounded by Spring River and Warrior Creek."[30] Joseph, who was ill with malaria, declined the invitation.

Considering their job done, the commissioners prepared to leave and duly informed Agent Jones that the Nez Perces were "to be moved to their new lands as early as possible."[31] This edict did nothing to ease the strained relations between Joseph and Jones. The two had clashed so often that Joseph wanted nothing more to do with him. Most of the chiefs within the agency despised Jones, who was equally disliked by leaders of the white communities bordering the agency. Indians and Whites alike saw the graft, mistreatment, shortening of provisions, withholding of medicines and the nepotism which prevailed as his staff was top-heavy with his immediate relatives. All saw Jones as a bigot who considered Indians as nothing more than savages who, as he himself put it, had to be "straightened out" by "corrective methods" which included severe punishment[32] for violations of even the most minor agency rules. Jones was particularly strict in matters involving gambling, which he perceived as one of the more glaring weaknesses of the Nez Perces, who loved games of chance. He was particularly appalled at their devotion to horseracing, long a cherished sport of the tribesmen. Jones' abhorrence of alcohol also brought him into repeated conflict with the young men who had developed a taste for whiskey.[33] Joseph had been concerned with the disastrous effects of alcohol for years and tried to curb its use, but without a great deal of success.

Eventually, having endured enough of Jones, Joseph unilaterally and without permission moved his charges as far eastward as he could without leaving the confines of the reservation. The new camp was made on the banks of the Spring River near a place called the Blue Hole.[34] Unfortunately, while they had temporarily escaped Hiram Jones, the mosquitoes could not be avoided. Many more of the band sickened and several more died. During the stay at Quapaw not a single newborn baby survived beyond a few days.

While the band was at the Blue Hole, Joseph was invited to Washington under the auspices of interested groups. While there he,

Yellow Bull and Ad Chapman (who had been hired by the federal government as official translator) met with these groups. Joseph addressed government officials, had a meeting with President Hayes, attended a few gala events and thoroughly impressed everyone he met, especially the ladies, some of whom appeared more than casually attracted to the handsome chief. Joseph, it is reported, enjoyed the social gatherings, was noted as being particularly charming towards the women and once even accepted, albeit with obvious reluctance, a shot of whiskey which he drank in one swallow.[35]

However, at the end of his visit, despite all the good intentions of his supporters, no assurances or promises of a return to the northwest were forthcoming. From Joseph's point of view at least, the trip was not a success. Nonetheless, he had discussed the situation with a total of not less than forty senators and representatives and had made an impression on so many people that very soon moves began behind the scenes, moves which would eventually decide the issue of a return to the northwest. The views Joseph expressed in Washington received more support for his cause when one of his most notable speeches was published in the prestigious *North American Review*,[36] a widely read magazine of the day.

In Quapaw, with Joseph away in Washington, his people were not idle. Because their new camp was in such close proximity to Baxter Springs, they quickly discovered ways to improve their lot along diverse avenues. The women resumed their Leavenworth industry of making artifacts and clothing and were soon spending long hours in town actively selling their wares and dealing with merchants eager to promote the items on a consignment basis. The artifacts became top sellers, with pairs of beaded moccasins and mittens fetching $2.00 and $0.75 respectively (about $30.00 and $15.00 at present day monetary values). The women and older girls also sold baskets of freshly picked berries and wild fruit door-to-door to Baxter Springs homemakers.

Nor were the warriors idle. Local farmers were so greatly impressed by their handling of horses they taught the Nez Perces how to handle teams of two, four and six horses and how to operate teams of six to twelve mules. The men quickly learned to hook up whippletrees, apply traces, use the long reins and to care and maintain wagon wheels and axles. The Nez Perces, whose experience with horses had always been limited to single animals, quickly became capable teamsters. It was the first time in many months the warriors had handled horses and they appreciated the opportunity to again work with the animals. Then, the farmers and teamsters hired their erstwhile students. When Joseph returned from the east he was greatly pleased with the progress his people were making. He and Yellow Bull, accompanied by Ad Chapman, also began spending much time in Baxter Springs talking to reporters and other interested persons of influence who sought them out.

Joseph, refusing to leave the industry of Baxter Springs, persistently refused to move his people to the Peoria/Miami lands. His camp remained at the Blue Hole while he played a waiting game. This refusal meant he and Jones remained at odds, but this time Joseph emerged the winner in the battle of wills. Hiram Jones was running out of luck and out of time.

The many complaints against Jones (underscored by those from the white communities) had reached a degree where they could no longer be ignored. Early in the new year, Federal Inspector Arden Smith, without advance notice, visited the Quapaw Agency for a firsthand investigation into the situation. Over a period of several days he interviewed chiefs, tribesmen, white traders, community leaders and finally agency staff members. His report, dated February 6, 1879, detailed the many blatant irregularities that existed. He also pointedly commented on how Hiram Jones immediate supervisors in the Quaker Church were greatly influencing Jones' activities. This activity, he felt, was not only interference in agency affairs, but a direct violation of President Hayes' Executive Order abolishing such activities. Hayes' recently issued Executive Order had countermanded President Grant's edict governing church-appointed agents. Smith's report caught the attention of those in authority and, although Jones was not immediately suspended, he was fired shortly after. He was replaced by Special Agent James Mahlon Haworth (1831–85)[37] who assumed control of the Quapaw Agency on a pro tem basis.[38]

With Haworth's arrival, policy changes were quickly made, numbering the Nez Perces' days at the reservation. Haworth soon arranged for Joseph and his people to move from Quapaw to the Oakland Agency near the town of Tonkawa. In April Joseph was notified the move would take place in May to Cherokee Outlet where they would be assigned good land near the Ponca Reservation. The new lands, altogether a better area, had both arable and grazing land. There they could farm and resume the raising of horses and proceed to rebuild their once massive cattle herds. The move indeed proved more favorable and, although the band was confined there for five more years, life improved so greatly under the honest administration of Agent William H. Whiteman[39] no trouble of major importance was ever recorded.

Although the situation was vastly improved, it was not totally ideal, as the adamantine Joseph would not budge in his insistence the Nez Perces be returned to the northwest. While he cooperated with each agent in turn, he often showed displeasure by refusing to sign for supplies or failing to report on the progress of various undertakings. When these displays of rebelliousness taxed the agents' patience, Yellow Bull quietly signed the papers in his capacity of sub-chief.

Small issues notwithstanding, the farms were producing well, the herds of horses and cattle, though still small, flourished, and the band raised what was considered a very reasonable amount of money, which they put towards their own subsistence. Each agent reported favorably on the Nez Perces, all expounding on the intelligence and work ethic of the band in general. Several of the tribesmen were hired as constables for the reserve's police department. Though the salary of five to eight dollars a month was less than half of what a wagon driver could earn, with less danger, all committed themselves diligently during their terms as constables. Only one, Wa'tas'tsis'kum [Earth Blanket] could be said to have faltered. He did well for several months and then was fired by Agent Thomas J. Jordan on a flimsy excuse.[40] He then began to do very poorly in all respects. Twice he was arrested on serious charges, once for assaulting his wife (she suffered a broken arm) and later for the rape of a fifteen-year-old girl. He was confined to the agency jail for two weeks but was released to the band on the understanding that Joseph, Yellow Bull and two others would guarantee future good conduct. Whatever punishment the band meted to him must have been severe enough to ensure the desired affect (under Nez Perce law, rape was punishable by public flogging and/or exile) but no record of his punishment exists. Nonetheless, Wa'tas'tsis'kum, though not exiled, never ventured into trouble again.

During those five years Joseph never eased his efforts for the return to Oregon, and while he never revisited Washington, he was in constant touch with those who championed his efforts. General Miles, meanwhile, had written to both President Hayes and Secretary Schurz lobbying for the Nez Perce to return to Lapwai, but there was no immediate movement. Hayes, who did not seek a second term, was replaced as president by James Abram Garfield in 1881. He received further petitions, but his assassination ended their progression. Garfield's vice-president, Chester A. Arthur, succeeded him in the White House, but he had no interest in Indian affairs. Not until 1885, when Democrat Grover Cleveland was elected was there any movement in matters pertaining to the Indian situation. Cleveland reopened the files, forced changes in the Bureau of Indian Affairs, tightened the reins on Indian agents (particularly in the matter of nepotism) and took a long look at conditions in the Indian Territories.

Meanwhile, the Nez Perces, despite the disinterest in Washington, were not forgotten. Joseph was visited many times by many persons, some just ordinary people interested in seeing real Indian tribesmen and buying authentic trade goods made by the women. Bureaucrats began checking on the conditions under which the Natives were living. There also came a new class of people who had very different interests. These were social activists and liberal politicians who were just beginning to make headway in Washington affairs. While none managed immediate results, their reports eventually reached the channels where such messages struck chords. During the later years of captivity in the Indian Territory, Joseph was championed by more and more associations who advocated

Indian rights. Those efforts finally came to partial fruition. During those years, however, the Nez Perces continued to be plagued with illnesses and a feeling of abandonment by those in authority who held the final say on their fate.

Besides Cleveland's election, possibly the one single effort that swung the balance in favor of Joseph was that made by his former adversary, Nelson Miles. In 1884 General Howard was relieved as commander of the Department of the Pacific and was replaced by Miles. While Howard generally had been in favor of placement at Lapwai, he had steadfastly opposed the return of Joseph and his band to the Wallowa Valley[41]; Miles, however, vigorously lobbied on Joseph's behalf. In the autumn of that year he was successful in obtaining a decision to return Joseph and the remnants of his band to the northwest. Although the decision was made, the wheels of government still moved so slowly that it was not until 1885 that the funds necessary for such an undertaking were made available to allow the Nez Perces to return to the northwest. There were, however, many conditions attached.

Lapwai, it was decided, could be home only to the 118 tribesmen who had converted to Christianity. Joseph and the 150 Wéset followers would be assigned to Colville, in Washington State. Over the years several opinions on why Colville had been chosen have been advanced. One insists the army leaders in Washington (Sheridan and Sherman still led the pack) had been so opposed to the move they unilaterally split the group by interpreting the order to suit themselves. The order only specified the army must arrange "to return the band to the northwest…." As "the northwest" encompassed a huge area, the generals decided to split the band as a guarantee that Joseph could never again be in a position to foment another uprising. Although debunked by recent research, this popular opinion remains part of the legend of the 1877 War. The facts are quite different.

Though Joseph lamented the splitting of his band, he agreed to it because he knew that many white settlers in Oregon had no intention of returning even a part of the Wallowa Valley to him, and many in Idaho were contemplating vengeance against him and his people—through legal means or vigilante action—as reprisal for the original uprising. Many Idaho settlers, particularly those who had suffered at the hands of Swan Necklace's renegades during their run of terror in June 1877, were unaware of the true facts of the case. None knew that Swan Necklace and his gang had all been from White Bird's band; and all were convinced that Joseph had been solely to blame for the uprising. Thus, Joseph and the rest of the Wéset Nez Perces, thinking in terms of safety, opted for Colville, which was as far from Oregon and Idaho as was possible to send him and those who chose to remain with him. On May 22, 1885, the 268 remaining survivors of the Bear's Paw surrender went to Arkansas City where they boarded a train for the long journey home.

That journey, while it ended without serious incident, was not a smooth undertaking because certain problems were encountered along the way. On May 26, when the train arrived at Pocatello, Idaho, the situation took on a dark and somber tone. Idaho settlers, their politicians and most of the area's newspaper editors had made it clear the exiles were not wanted. So, when the train arrived at Pocatello it was met by a hostile crowd. The situation was considered dangerous enough that officials decided to depart as quickly as possible for Wallula Junction in Washington where the group would separate. At Wallula Junction the band split. Old friends said tearful farewells as families went their separate ways according to their religious status. Those bound for Lapwai continued to Lewiston where they were met by friends and a large number of horses. They rode the remaining distance to Lapwai. Joseph and his group remained on the train to Spokane Falls in Washington.

Arriving at Lapwai, the 185 returnees were greeted by no less than 500 relatives and friends. Nevertheless, the greeting was by no means unanimous. Many of Lapwai's established residents feared the newly converted intended to quickly revert to the old ways. They advocated newcomers be isolated in a northern area of the reservation. Among those most worried was Kate McBeth, the principal missionary and Joseph's soon-to-be opponent. McBeth was particularly worried that Joseph would somehow inveigle his way to Lapwai and resume leadership of the entire tribe, for she was well aware of Joseph's popularity. McBeth was also envious of Archie Lawyer, stemming from his ordination as a minister while she, because of her church's refusal to recognize women as ministers, was prohibited from that lofty station. Charles D. Warner, the agent in charge, however, refused to even consider the idea of segregating the group; and when Tom Hill [Husis'tool] assured the community that the newcomers were determined to live within the law and worship the Christian god, acceptance began. Eventually, when the supposed fears were seen to be groundless, full integration became a fact and no longer presented a problem.

COLVILLE: EIGHT UNEASY YEARS

When Joseph and his band members (103 adults, thirty-four teenagers, thirteen younger children) arrived in Colville they found their troubles far from over. Families had been shattered by the war and the years in Oklahoma. Now only thirty-one families remained intact. Three bachelors were alone and several single men were caring for elderly parents and grandparents. Six single women were in charge of daughters, sons, nephews and nieces, and were also looking after each other. There were three orphans—two boys and one little girl—who had no one in charge. One boy, Willie Andrews, was adopted by Joseph and his wife, while the other, Red Elk, was adopted by Yellow Bull, the boy's widower uncle. Yellow Bull was also looking after his widowed sister. The orphan girl, of whom little is known, was adopted by a childless couple.

No well-wishers greeted the wagons carrying the Nez Perces upon arrival at Colville. Rather, the newcomers were looked upon as invaders, extra people with whom to share the land and, worst of all, a group alien to the residents with almost nothing in common in the way of language, customs or legends. That they shared the Wéset religion seems to have made no impact because of slightly differing versions. Among those most displaced were Indian Agent Sidney Waters and Skolaskin, chief of the San Poil tribe. He saw Joseph as a political rival.

Waters was furious that his agency had been chosen to house the Nez Perces. He was extremely vocal in his complaints and intense in his criticisms of the Bureau of Indian Affairs. His several suggestions included sending his unwanted charges to Lapwai or, better yet, returning them to the Indian Territory. He railed against the eastern liberals who had championed Joseph's cause. He forecast a bitter future for the Nez Perces due to the lack of sufficient rations and supplies, implying that none would be forthcoming from his storehouse. This latter complaint prompted the army to issue sufficient rations to tide the band over the winter. Waters' constant nagging became such an irritant the BIA replaced him within three months. The new agent was Benjamin Moore who improved conditions to some extent. Moore's first annual report told a bleak tale of the situation, which he claimed had not been helped when the army placed the band on only one-quarter rations until the following summer (1896). Moore's report persuaded the BIA to increase the rations to one-half and then to a full quota.[42]

Skolaskin (c1839–1922) caused much trouble in the settling of the Nez Perces. The first troubles arose when Skolaskin complained when some San Poil land was given to the Nez Perces. Skolaskin, a Wéset prophet and an original disciple of Smoholla, had been instrumental in spreading the Wéset religion[43] and may have seen Joseph as a rival for the Dreamer leadership. Whatever his reasons, he chose lack of cooperation as a means of defeating Joseph. Only the quiet diplomacy of Moses, chief of the Columbians, smoothed the waters sufficiently to keep Skolaskin at bay. Moses had convinced Agent Waters to divide the land proportionally so no one tribe would be given a greater share.

In 1889 Skolaskin was alleged to have ordered his followers to maim and kill the Nez Perces' cattle and destroy their fences. The allegation was never proven, but when shots were fired "by persons unknown" at a group of Nez Perces who were rounding up cattle, the army stepped in. No one had been hit, but Skolaskin was taken into custody without trial or due process on orders of Colonel Gibbon, who was then in charge of the army. Skolaskin was sent to the army's Presidio on Alcatraz Island. There he sat in lonely confinement steadfastly denying any involvement in the troubles. Perhaps it was coincidental, but the attacks and other incidents abruptly ceased upon his departure. When he was finally allowed to return in 1892 he found a further portion of his land had been given to white settlers. Though he felt betrayed by federal authorities, he caused no further trouble and shortly after moved to the Yakima reservation to be with Smohalla. He died at the estimated age of eighty-three years.

Skolaskin notwithstanding, the troubles for the Nez Perces were further acerbated by the Spokane band who complained to the agent (by that time H.J. Cole) that preferential treatment was being afforded the Nez Perces. Cole managed to smooth ruffled feathers, but not to the Spokanes' full satisfaction.

As 1884 drew to a close only 287 of the Wellamotkin, Lamtama and Asotin survivors of the Bear's Paw surrender (plus the surviving Palu of Chief Husis Kute, and the Cayuses who had joined the Palu in the uprising) remained alive in the United States. Many were too young to remember the previous life of freedom and the older ones were too heartsick to care any longer.[44] None had any reason to look hopefully to the future.

Indeed, Joseph's primary years at Colville were not smooth and many difficulties were met. As the years passed, however, the various bands at Colville began to work together and by 1894 better relationships and cooperation had been attained and these continue to this day.[45]

If Washington had learned anything from the 1877 uprising, its attention span proved short indeed. The habit of expropriating Indian land continued, which caused Joseph great anguish even when it was not Nez Perce land being grabbed. Although he continued to speak out against the practice, he embarked on no further personal entreaties in Washington until 1892 when Washington announced yet another betrayal would be finalized. The Federal government announced on March 30 of that year that 1,500,000 acres of the Colville reservation had been "ceded" for $1,500,000 in a deal ratified by 506 residents of that reservation. The acreage would be opened to settlement by white farmers.[46] On April 24, North Dakota's *Bismark Daily Tribune* wrote about a land rush.

> *"Spokane, Wash., April 24 — The proposition to open the Colville Indian Reservation, which was discussed at a large meeting of the citizens of Stevens county at Kettle Falls, has created a great deal of excitement here. A rush will now be made for the reservation and it is likely that 2,000 claims will be filed in less than a week. It is held by good lawyers that the Indians are merely tenants of the reservation by sufferance (sic) and that whites have a perfect right to the land."*

Joseph was among the dissenters and he went to Washington to plead the case. His entreaties fell on deaf ears, including those of Benjamin Harrison, the incumbent president.

Joseph spent his remaining nineteen years of life at Colville aiding his people. He became friends with reformers and those interested in social justice. He had learned to cooperate with missionaries but, remaining true to his faith in the Great Spirit Chief, he never accepted their teachings. He helped authors write books pertaining to Nez Perce history and travails. He set straight the record of the skirmishes and the three major battles. He told them of the role he had played in the great drama, and of the mistakes he and the other chiefs had made as the trek progressed.

Joseph helped biographers write unbiased accounts of his life and times. He never once attempted to claim glory that was not his due and downplayed that to which he was fully entitled. It was during this period that he disclaimed the generally held assumption that he had been the principal war chief of the Nez Perce War. He admitted that some of the strategy used had been his, but he gave full credit to Looking Glass and White Bird for their share of the tactics that had humiliated the army. He told those who inquired that he had not done as much as some seemed to think. He never claimed to be the military genius writers wanted him to be. However, legend had already overridden fact and had become so deeply entrenched that people, as is their custom, preferred to believe the legend.

He traveled with Wood and others on several occasions to speak on behalf of his people, and was also an invited speaker at Pacific Coast venues. He was honored by the citizens of Vancouver, Washington who commissioned the famed sculptor, Plan L. Warner, to engrave a bronze medal of his likeness.[47]

Because he and his family preferred to live in a large tepee in the old ways, Chief Joseph declined to accept the wooden house that had been built for him. While he twice went to Washington and New York, during his years at Colville for the most part he remained busy with tours and lectures in western venues. During his stays at home he gave audiences to numerous reporters, educators, missionaries, writers, government officials and hundreds of people just interested in meeting the famed chief. Always cordial, he turned no one away, even those he may have considered having more curiosity in him than interest in what he had to say. By 1903, now approaching his sixty-fifth year, Joseph was beginning to feel the aches and pains of old age. He spent more time in front of the fire for the warmth that afforded relief to his arthritic knees.

His spirits had been buoyed in 1900 when the federal government rekindled an interest in returning to his band several square miles of the Wallowa Valley. Joseph was encouraged by the news and elated when Washington commissioned Indian Inspector James McLaughlin to investigate the feasibility of such an allotment. McLaughlin took Joseph, Yellow Bull and Peo'peo'Tholket with him on a visit to their beloved valley. A visit to the senior Joseph's grave was arranged and Joseph had thought his chances of regaining the land for his people seemed favorable, even though he had previously been told by Oregonians he could never return. All hope was dashed, however, when McLaughlin's final report was decidedly adverse. The government shelved the proposal. This final denial was devastating to the aging chief, but still he continued in his efforts for justice. Support for his cause continued to be steadfast and extensive, but his supporters could make no headway in Washington. The lobbying campaign by Oregon commercial interests and their political allies was too strong.

In early 1904 he made one final trip east when he traveled to Pennsylvania to the Carlyle Indian Industrial School for a celebration in his honor. He spoke to the students, praised their work, encouraged them to continue their education and thus attain goals that would benefit themselves and their children. Part of the ceremonies was a special supper attended by his old enemy, General Howard. Joseph, always the diplomat, chose the occasion to mend fences and heal old wounds. After supper Howard rose and proposed a toast to his old enemy in which he referred to Joseph as "the greatest Indian warrior I have fought against." Joseph's response to the toast did not mention the general's military abilities. Instead he simply stated he was happy to at last be able to meet the general as a friend.

> "I meet here my friend. I used to be anxious to meet him. I wanted to kill him in war. Today I am glad to meet him, and am glad to meet everyone here, and to be friends with General Howard. We are both old men, still we live and I am glad..."[48]

Upon his return to Colville he was invited to Seattle as the guest of James J. Hill, the railway tycoon. Hill was attempting to restore part of the Wallowa Valley to the Nez Perce, whom he considered the rightful owners. Joseph accepted and spoke to an overflow audience in the city's largest auditorium. The following day he gave a short lecture to the faculty and student body of the University of Washington. At the end of his speech he left the dais to mingle with his audience and shake hands with one and all. That afternoon he attended a football game at the university, the first football game he had ever seen and he showed great interest. This was his last public appearance.

After he returned to Colville he remained quietly at home, but still entertained friends and visitors. Quite plainly, though, he was growing tired. During a mid-summer visit by an old confederate he turned to him and quietly said to his friend, "Halo Manitah" [I will not see another winter] which proved to be a prophecy of his impending death. During the early hours of Wednesday morning, September 21, 1904, while enjoying the warmth of the fire, he suddenly fell forward and died. By Nez Perce calculation of time the day fell during The Moon of the Turning Leaves.

The agency physician, Dr. Edwin Latham, who knew and liked the valiant chief, prepared the death certificate. In the space marked CAUSE OF DEATH, a small rectangle routinely filled with such terse comments as "old age," "natural causes," "heart failure," etc., Doctor Latham printed in large, black letters: A BROKEN HEART. In those three words Doctor Latham had summarized Chief Joseph's years from 1877 to 1904.

Joseph was buried in a temporary grave so that on June 20, 1905, he could be reburied in the graveyard at the town of Nespelem below a monument that had been made in his honor. The ceremony was in the Wéset rites in which only Natives could participate. The wails and songs of the grieving women brought tears to the eyes of old warriors and also to those of the many Whites standing in respectful silence a short distance away.

Later that afternoon the people again assembled, this time to dedicate the monument. This time Whites and Natives stood together. The principle speakers were Yellow Bull, Espowyes and the newly elected chief, Albert Waters.[49] A professor from the University of Washington, Dr. Edmond Meany, spoke on behalf of the white community, the Washington University State Historical Society and Samuel Hill, who had donated the monument.

It is a beautiful monument. A white marble shaft, it stands ninety inches high. On the front within a circular frame is an accurately carved likeness of Joseph's head and shoulders. At the base in large raised letters is his name: CHIEF JOSEPH. On the right side of the shaft is his Nez Perce name: Heinmot Tooyalakekt. Below is its English translation: Thunder-Rolling-in-the-Mountains. On the left side is the inscription: "He led his people in the Nez Perce war of 1877. Died 21 September, 1904, age about 60 years." On the back of the monument is inscribed: "Erected 20 June, 1905, by the Washington University State Historical Society."[50]

The following day at noon a banquet was held in the reserve's large council lodge. In attendance were many Indians and Whites. All had come to see the distribution of Joseph's worldly possessions. Joseph left something for almost every band member. His main beneficiary, of course, was his widow, to whom he bequeathed his herd of fine Appaloosa horses. The herd was of sufficient size to guarantee financial security for the remainder of her life.

Chief Joseph was never defeated in battle by the Army of the Northwest. He surrendered to save his people and in fact it can be said he won the final battle when his people, the survivors, were returned to the northwest. But his victory was pyrrhic. Most of his nine children had died at early ages, he never regained his peoples' ancestral lands in the Wallowa Valley, and he was never allowed to rejoin those who lived at Lapwai, although he was granted two visits. On those two occasions he was hailed by many—but not by all. Among those who did not welcome him were the missionaries; they feared both his Dreamer philosophy and his political prowess.

He was allowed two visits to his father's grave in the Wallowa Valley, the first in 1897. At that time he proposed a deal in which he and his band could buy a sizeable acreage in the valley where they could live. His proposal was rejected and he was told he would never be allowed to live there.

He made one trip to New York at the invitation of Buffalo Bill Cody. In full regalia he rode with him in a parade. One wonders what were his thoughts as the parade passed Grant's Tomb, wherein lay the remains of the president who had at first supported his claim to the Wallowa Valley, even to issuing an Executive Order granting the valley to his people, only to treacherously repeal the order a short while later. Whatever his thoughts may have been, he did salute the tomb as he passed.

Grant was but the first of seven successive US presidents who would either betray or ignore his pleas for justice. The last was Theodore Roosevelt, who in 1904 met with Joseph in Washington. It was Joseph's final attempt to reclaim for his people at least a portion of the Wallowa Valley. Roosevelt—already on record as having no sympathy for Native claims—not surprisingly declined to intervene. The only president to help the Nez Perce chief in any way was Grover Cleveland, and that help proved of little importance.

The regard in which Joseph is held by present-day Nez Perces is decidedly mixed. Those in residence in and around the Colville reservation consider him the greatest among their many heroes, while regarding Chiefs James, Timothy and Lawyer as traitors. On the other hand, there are many in residence at Lapwai who consider Joseph a manipulative, self-serving opportunist. The detractors will, with some emphasis, explain their views that Joseph gained fame only because he survived, where Looking Glass and Tool'hool'hool'zote did not, and because White Bird remained in self-imposed exile in Canada. They tell how he used that fame to continue in his efforts to regain the Wallowa Valley. They maintain he was concerned only with the well-being of his own band and cared little for the Nez Perce tribe as a whole. They will tell the listener he never made a single effort to gain benefits for anyone other than his own band. There is a certain irony in that. The same Lapwai Nez Perces, though not greatly disposed toward Chief Joseph are often less disposed to extend praise toward the three chiefs Lawyer, James and Timothy.

There is another ironic twist to his story. Chief Joseph did not win his war but the honors bestowed upon him were those normally accorded to victors. Today Joseph's name is commemorated in more historic sites located throughout the American northwest than *all* his 1877 foes combined. Very few honors were bestowed upon those who officially won the war. Only General Nelson Miles has a town—Miles City, Montana—named after him (and that was named pre-1877)[51] because he was responsible for its founding. General Howard garnered no important accolades. Neither did Sherman, Sheridan, Gibbon, Sturgis or Crook. Most of the sites honoring Joseph were chosen through the initiative of Whites with co-operation and, very often, encouragement of latter day Washington bureaucrats, plus the efforts of the Nez Perces who revere him.

Joseph's eulogy should perhaps have included the following words he spoke during an address before a gathering of senators on one of his visits to Washington.

> "All men were made brothers. The earth is the mother of all people, and all people should have equal rights upon it. You might as well expect the rivers to run backward as that any man who was born free should be penned up and denied liberty to go where he pleases."

[CHAPTER 24 ENDNOTES]

1. Baird's request to visit the Nez Perce in the Sandy Hills camp was refused because the NWMP commander (Lieutenant Colonel Acheson G. Irvine) did not wish to raise any problems with the Sioux who shared the area and were highly distrustful of American soldiers.

2. These three were selected by the Americans, who mistakenly thought they would convince the Nez Perce to return to Leavenworth with them. This idea originated because Yellow Bull was related through marriage to White Bird and Espowyes was his uncle. Husis Kute was included because, as a gifted orator, he could convince White Bird to return. What they overlooked was the fact that Yellow Bull was now Joseph's second-in-command and confidant and knew his wishes, that Espowyes had argued against the surrender at Bear's Paw (and remained convinced Howard intended to execute the chiefs who returned from exile) and that both had lost sons in the war. When asked to accompany the delegates, all three agreed on the condition the refugees decide for themselves and not be coerced. [Pearson, *The Nez Perces in Indian Territory*, 96–99.]

3. Interesting descriptions of the White Bird-Baird

interchange can be read in the following references: MacDonald, Duncan (a NWMP interpreter for the White Bird-Baird conference) in his article printed in the *Deer Lodge New Northwest,* August 9, 1878; Pearson, J. Diane, *The Nez Perces in Indian Territory,* 98–9; and Greene, Jerome A., *Nez Perce Summer 1877,* 344–47.]

4   As the years passed, some assimilated with the Piegan, Sarcee and Blood tribes of the Blackfoot Nation. Their descendants live in southern Alberta to this day.

5   Bear Crossing and Kepkop'ponmi, Martha and Wetanonmi were among those who returned. Bear Crossing and Kepkop'ponmi rejoined Joseph at Nespelem. Martha stayed in Canada until 1886 when she returned to Idaho and entered a mission school at Lapwai. Unfortunately, nothing is known of Wetanonmi after her return to Lapwai.

6   Sara remained in Canada until her death, from tuberculosis, in 1899. Her daughters then moved to Lapwai. A year prior to her death Sara was regarded as being the last of the original Nez Perce women remaining in the settlement.

7   White Bird's grave site remains unknown. There is but one clue to its location: in a field on a farm near Pincher Creek. In 1997 a group of Nez Perces from Idaho visited the farm hoping to locate the grave. They searched diligently over two days but failed to find it. [Lindsay Moir, Glenbow Archives, Calgary, Alberta.]

8   The term was later changed to "murder, 1st degree." Though still a hanging offence, the change made the appeals process easier. By the mid-1960s the death penalty had been abolished in favor of "life in prison" with a provision for a parole hearing after twenty-five years. [Criminal Code of Canada.]

9   Court records, "Regina vs Nez Perce Sam," National Archives, Ottawa.

10 Laws were eventually changed to accommodate exceptional circumstances by allowing a judge to instruct a jury on the legalities of considering verdicts to lesser charges such a non-capital murder and even manslaughter (sometimes referred to in US courts as 3rd degree murder). Manslaughter today also contains provisions such as "involuntary" and "reckless endangerment."

11 *The Beaver*, Feb/March 1993, 28.

12 "The only good Indian is a dead Indian" is a quote often attributed to Sheridan, supposedly uttered in January 1869 in a reply to the Comanche chief, Toch-a-way [Turtle Dove] who had said to Sheridan, "Me good Indian." Sheridan, according to several witnesses, replied, "The only good Indians I have ever seen were dead." Sheridan repeatedly denied making such a statement (and he certainly did not coin the phrase), but his affirmed reputation as a bigot and Indian hater made his denials hard to accept. The remark was synonymous not only with his attitude towards Indians, but was the prevailing attitude throughout most of the military and much of the civilian population.

Sheridan's statement is mild compared to that of Theodore Roosevelt who, fifteen years before his election as president of the US, made the following statement in a January 1886 speech in New York. "I suppose I should be ashamed to say that I take the Western view of the Indian. I don't go so far as to think that the only good Indians are dead Indians, but I believe nine out of every ten are, and I shouldn't like to enquire too closely into the case of the tenth." [For Roosevelt's full statement see: Hagedon, Hermann, *Roosevelt in the Bad Lands*, 355.]

13 Woods, "The Pursuit and Capture of Chief Joseph."

14 Wood sold the article to augment his salary, which was allowed by the US military. The federal government had denied the army's requisitions for expenses to officers so some officers took to writing accounts of campaigns in which they served. Newspapers paid well for such articles.

15 In an unusual twist, Sherman later denied Howard's request that thirty-nine of the Bear's Paw prisoners being held in Montana and Washington forts be sent to join the others in Leavenworth. Sherman directed those prisoners be sent to the Indian agent at Lapwai and released. His reasons were that they had already cost the government too much in money and trouble and further costs were unreasonable. [Nez Perce War Papers, item 7685, roll 339. Sherman's annotation to Howard's letter to the Adjutant General, Military Division of the Pacific. Howard's letter dated November 14, 1877. Sherman's annotation dated December 14.]

16 The soldiers fed the children cooked food, slices of meat and gave them blankets so they would be warm. These kindnesses pleased the children to the point where they decided the soldiers were not all that bad after all. Thereafter the soldiers had no trouble getting the children to obey orders and do as they were told.

17 Miles to Asst. Adj. General, Dept of Dakota. Oct 27, 1877. [US Army Continental Command 1877 files, part 3, box 3, entry 107.]

18 Mackinaws were wide and long and had evolved from the big freighter canoes used by fur traders of the 17th century. Because they were outfitted with a sail they were ideal for the Missouri River when wind was favorable, and they were light enough to be paddled upstream and when there was no wind. It is thought

these boats were developed for use in the Mackinac Straits, hence the name they came to be known by. Mackinaws, all various lengths, are still used on the Great Lakes by fishermen and campers. *[www.ccmhg.org/ Dronfheims/MackinawBoats.htm]*

19   Woods, "The Pursuit and Capture of chief Joseph."

20   Quoted in Steinbach, *Long March*, 132.

21   During this time Miles made one more attempt to convince Washington of the error they were making. He requested he bring Joseph and some of his chiefs to the capitol so they could plead their case. He was turned down. [Adjutant General File, Item 7053, roll 339, November 14, 1877, Nez Perce War Papers.]

22   Miles reported 448 had been captured at Bear's Paw, but this number is not verified. It may, however, account for some of those who died prior to arrival in Kansas, but that number also remains unaccountable. [Commissioner of Indian Affairs. Report 1887, entry xxxiii.]

23   For information on the reservation distribution and denominations involved, see Appendix J.

24   Jones was charged with corruption and hearings were conducted to that effect. [Investigation of Charges against Hiram W. Jones, Quapaw Agency, 1874–78. Special Files, M574, roll 63, case no. 221.]

25   Annual Report of the Board of Indian Commissioners, 1878. Reports no. 47–50.

26   Although there was never any serious trouble between the two bands, the Modoc and the Nez Perce bands did not make good neighbors because the Nez Perce had been assigned land originally ceded by Jones to the Modoc, and, though the land was no good, the transfer to newcomers was resented.

27   In some reports and articles this is referred to as Ecash.

This appears, though, to be more likely a dialectic abbreviation of the proper Nez Perce pronunciation. [www.nezperce.com]

28 Joseph's band, the Wellamotkins, had been greatly increased by members of Looking Glass' and White Bird's bands who had chosen to surrender rather than attempt the escape with White Bird. He also had a number of Piquinins whose chief, Tool'hool'hool'zote, had died in the first attack on September 30. The Palu, though under the leadership of Husis Kute, also looked to Joseph for leadership.

29 Annual Report of the Board of Indian Commissioners December 1878, Item 47.

30 Ibid. Article V, 41C.

31 The chief commissioners, Clinton B. Fisk and William Stickney, however, later wrote a letter to Joseph wherein they expressed their disappointment that he had not been able to accompany them on the survey and that he had declined to enter negotiations with the Peorias and Miamis. The letter praised Joseph for his ability and concern for his people and expressed the hope he would come to realize that he should lead his people to prosperity in their new home. They signed the letter "Faithfully, your friends." There is no evidence that Joseph was impressed. A copy of the letter can be viewed at: *www.archive.org/stream/annualreportindian00unitrich*

32 No reference books mention the forms of punishment Jones imposed, but in other reservations the Indian agents' punishments would include withholding rations, banning attendance at events, detention in the reservations' jails and in some cases imposing what is nowadays called "house arrest." Jones would have used the same methods. [Author.]

33 Despite the zealous efforts of a long list of Nez Perce

chiefs, alcohol had gained a hold on young warriors from the time of the earliest encounters with trappers during the seventeenth century. Joseph discouraged its use, but this was one battle he had little hope of controlling.

34 The Blue Hole is a deep pool in the river below a falls. Intensely blue in color local legend has it that the pool has no bottom. [Courtesy of Larry O'Neal, a Kansas historian of Indian affairs.]

35 It is believed the whiskey was offered to him more to see how he would deal with the gesture, as it was accepted fact that Joseph never drank liquor. Even the Lapwai missionary Kate McBeth, who held no liking for Joseph at all, is quoted as saying years later, "Joseph had one good thing about him. He was a temperance man." Others who knew him well also averred that he did not use alcohol. He likely accepted the drink in order to be polite. [Pearson, J. Diane, *The Nez Perces in the Indian Territory*, 143.]

36 "An Indian's View of Indian Affairs," *North American Review* (1879), Issue 128, 412–34.

37 James Mahlon Haworth was a much respected special agent. Following his clean-up of the Quapaw Agency, he went on to become the first superintendent of Indian schools. Headquartered in Albuquerque, New Mexico, he died there March 12, 1885 after suffering a massive heart attack in his office. *[www.archive.org/stream/indianagents/]*

38 Special agents were federal employees tasked with overseeing the activities of the Indian agents. In cases such as the firing of Jones a special agent would assume control of the agency until a permanent agent could be appointed. Eventually, all church-appointed agents were replaced by government employees. While this did not totally eliminate graft, it did minimize it and other

practices considered as being not in the best interests of the reservation residents.

39 Indian agents were replaced on a regular basis, so, as a result of this practice, the Nez Perce dealt with five agents during their stay on the Ponca Reservation in the Oakland Agency. Whiteman was replaced in 1880 by William Whiting, who was replaced in 1881 by Thomas J. Jordan. In 1882 the agency was managed by Lewellyn Woodin, but he resigned in 1884 following unproven charges of corruption. He was replaced by John W. Scott, who oversaw the departure of the Nez Perce for Lapwai and Colville. [Records of the BIA: Index of Letters 1881–86, Ponca Agency, Indian Territory Files, National Archives & Records Administration, Washington DC, reel 2.]

40 Agent Jordan stated Earth Blanket was fired from the force because he had failed to learn sufficient English to carry out his duties. This is disputed by many who feel the firing (as were five others from the Ponca Tribe) was based on religious bias. Those fired had not converted to Christianity, as Jordan considered this necessary for employment with the police force. The firing was a great loss of face to Earth Blanket. He quickly fell into depression and turned to a way of life quite out of character to the usually dependable warrior. [Pearson, J. Diane, *The Nez Perces in The Indian Territory*, 201.]

41 Howard was very contradictory at times, as his reports and books clearly show. He was opposed to Joseph's return to the Wallowa Valley, but he did not oppose a placement at Lapwai. That was an acceptable solution in his opinion, but any other area in the Northwest was not. [Author.]

42 None of the agents succeeding Waters appear overly fond of the Nez Perces. In his 1877 report, Richard Gwyder lauds Joseph for his leadership and industry, but

the following year does a complete about-face when he accuses Joseph of thinking "that the government is bound to support him in idleness." He then went on to write, "It is expecting too much from a naturally indolent savage to be industrious when he gets all he wants without any exertion on his part." It appears bias was still prevalent among agents when, in 1891, Hal J. Cole lamented that "the majority of Joseph's band would, I think, when it comes to receiving their lands in severalty, oppose the scheme, and would be entirely willing to content themselves by having the government furnish clothing and rations for them." [Agents' Reports for 1887, 1888, 1891 and 1893 for the Colville Reservation. *www.lib.uidaho.edu/mcbeth/governmentdoc/comagt.htm*]

43 The Dreamers continued their rites and ceremonies after Skolaskin's death in 1922 when his son assumed the mantle of leadership. As late as 1975 their ceremonies were being observed in various reservations within the northwest region, but little has been heard of them lately. [Author's files]

44 The last of the Nez Perce survivors, Josiah Red Wolf, died at Spalding, Idaho, on March 23, 1945 at the age of ninety-nine. Red Wolf had been a five-year-old child during the odyssey of 1877. [McDermott, *Forlorn Hope,* 162.]

45 J. Diane Pearson, *The Nez Perces in the Indian Territory,* 290–293.

46 An article in the *Bismark Daily Tribune,* April 8, 1892, Bismark, North Dakota.

47 That medal is today in the Metropolitan Museum at New York.

48 Wood, *Lives of Famous Indians,* 525.

49 No relation to the disliked Indian agent of the same name.

50 Joseph has two monuments in Nespelem. The second is in a park just a few yards off the highway.

51 The Montana town of Miles City (population 2800) was created in 1874 when Colonel Miles, a straight-laced temperance man, was commandant of the nearby fort. He ordered all gamblers, saloon owners and brothel keepers from the fort property. These worthies moved about 1700 yards down the trail and set up a shack town which they named Miles Town. Whether this name was chosen as a sardonic reference to the blue-nose colonel or because it was located a mile from the fort is not certain. Miles could not stop his off-duty soldiers from attending the "services" the shack town offered, and eventually it grew into a town in its own right.

Appendix A:
The Treaty of 1863

Over a period of seven years, three signs from Washington clearly indicated the Treaty of 1855 had been but a prelude to what the government had long intended. First, Congress delayed ratifying the treaty for four years; and second, only two partial payments of the promised annuities had been forthcoming; third, between 1855 and 1861 numerous attempts were made to convince the Nez Perces to willingly give up their Oregon and Salmon River holdings. All entreaties were met with flat refusals, but Washington was determined, so bureaucrats set about seeking ways to reduce the huge Nez Perce reservation. Normally, as had been done in the past, Congress would have been asked to pass a bill enforcing amendments, but Indian Affairs officials, well aware of the size of the Nez Perce tribe and its great number of warriors, decided instead to wrest amendments through persuasion. They knew that despite the tribe's peaceful ways, it had a well-earned reputation as being superb fighters. They also knew war could easily erupt if unilateral tactics were employed. Added concerns were that ongoing troubles with the Apaches and Comanches in the southwest were nowhere near settled, and secession threats by southern states were moving towards reality. Thus, because Washington's original intentions were delayed by circumstances, the Nez Perces gained some time. The 1863 land grab—for that is what it was—could not be a smash and grab operation.

Lessons the government had learned in the latest Creek and Seminole Wars, and in earlier series of conflicts with other eastern tribes protesting the treatment they had received, had not been forgotten. Determined to avoid another Indian war, the bureaucrats, carefully planning their tactics before introducing any amendments to the 1855 treaty, decided to employ allies upon whom they had relied heavily in 1855. In that instance, they had contacted various missionaries who had been working, with some success, to convince bands to renounce their old ways of nomadic hunting and turn to sedentary agriculture. Those involved with the Nez Perce bands, particularly those at the Lapwai Mission, were eager to promote the principle of a smaller reservation. They turned once again to the three reliable chiefs: Tamootsin aka Timothy [1808–1891], chief of the Alpowai Band; Kalkalshuatash aka Jason [c.1805–c.1900]; and Hallalhotcuut[1] aka Aleiya[2] and Lawyer [1896–1876], chief of the Stites-Kamiah Band. With the promise of further rewards, the trio was swayed into expounding the advantages of a reduced reservation.

The three chiefs, the first major converts of Henry Spalding, had remained loyal to him even after his ignoble flight in 1847. They were now staunchly allied with the missionaries who had replaced Spalding. The trio agreed to roles as emissaries and was sent east to meet with representatives of the government in both New York and Washington, where they were wined and dined in lavish fashion. In their absence, the missionaries prepared their congregations to heed the advice of the three "wise" chiefs upon their return. Once back from their junket, the trio embarked on their part in the project of persuasion.[3] Their work this time, however, was not as easy as it had been in 1855.

By 1863, a large number of the chiefs who originally had been won over to the idea that reservation life would hold advantages were now opposed to any thought of more restrictions. Few, if any, were concerned about the loss of the two Oregon valleys and the Salmon River areas. They were happy in the Lapwai area because they were in no danger of losing their original hunting grounds, so the two valleys and southern Idaho areas were of little concern. Their objections concerned the delayed and non-payments of the promised annuities, and the probability of further restrictions. Nonetheless, they listened to the three chiefs and agreed to attend the proposed conference. Once again the trio had done yeoman service, despite the opposition of Old Joseph and his allies.

Among the 58 Nez Perce chiefs involved in the talks and signing of the treaty, many considered some terms to be of little benefit. All, however, acknowledged the smaller area was adequate. One concession the federal agents made to the chiefs was continuing access to traditional fishing locations long used for the harvesting of salmon. They would be outside the new boundaries but would be retained for seasonal use. This was a particularly important concession, as salmon netted during the annual autumn spawning was a major food source. The terms also allowed unrestricted access outside the new boundaries to several lakes that teemed with fish year around.

The major stipulation, so far as Washington was concerned, was that each band would settle permanently within its own area. This condition effectively eliminated seasonal changes of location. This upset Old Joseph because it meant his band would no longer be allowed access to their traditional winter camp with its sheltered area that made winter conditions less rigorous. Old Joseph decided to ignore the residency rule, as did his son when he became band chief. The rule, though never enforced, became a major point to accentuate Washington's 1877 decision to force the Wallowa valley band to resettle at Lapwai.

The principal cause of discord among all the chiefs was the treaty's denial of access to age-old hunting grounds east of the Bitterroot Mountains. Washington was adamant about denying Nez Perce hunters access not only to Montana and its buffalo, but also to Utah[4] and Wyoming for trapping and associated activities. Despite strenuous objections to the prohibition of freedom to go where they pleased when they pleased, the government negotiators would not budge. They explained the term "on the reservation" meant exactly that; travel beyond the specified boundaries, except where otherwise stated, was expressly forbidden. In rare and unusual circumstances, they said, travel beyond the boundaries could be permitted—but special permission was required in advance. From the Nez Perce standpoint this prohibition spelled the end to the buffalo hunt, which had always been their mainstay for meat and hides. There were, after all, no great buffalo herds in Oregon and northern Idaho. The chiefs who disagreed with that prohibition solved the problem by simply ignoring it. For the most part the annual buffalo hunt continued for another dozen years.

The Nez Perces, although technically not nomadic, had always been free ranging. Accustomed to unfettered access to what is now Oregon, Washington and Idaho,[5] they wintered in certain places and spent summers in others. Because they had always been free to go where they pleased, they naturally objected to Washington's insistence that they must now remain always and forevermore within a specified area.[6]

The few American authorities who understood the ways of Indians realized travel restrictions would never be obeyed by the Nez Perces, least of all the buffalo hunters. They were also well aware of the near impossibility of enforcing the restrictions. They were correct on both counts, for the Wallowa Band continued its annual moves from summer to winter grounds and the Asotin under Chief Looking Glass continued hunting buffalo far afield. The hunts continued until the issue was settled when the buffalo disappeared into near-extinction. Until that happened, though, the experts were proven correct in their belief the restrictions were unenforceable. At no time was any great effort made to stop the buffalo hunters.

By signing the new treaty, the chiefs agreed to reduce the original reservation by 90 percent, leaving them with about 9,000 square miles [14,400 sq km], approximately 7,000,000 acres. Once again the government promised *for all time* to prohibit settlement by Whites *without the express permission of the Nez Perces.*

[APPENDIX A ENDNOTES]

1. Hallalhotcuut, [Shadow of the Mountain] aka Lawyer, was chief of the Stites-Kamiah band. Born in 1796 he died January 3, 1876. He was an astute survivor who always seemed able to align himself with the winning side, despite the cost to his people. Washington bureaucrats considered him a progressive leader, and, upon the death of Chief Ellis, transferred to him the illegal and artificial title of Head Chief of the Nez Perce. Because he was basically a timid man, missionaries easily manipulated him as an influential ally. The acknowledged leader of the Big Three, he was called "Lawyer" by Whites because of his cognition of Native laws. Although named as head of all the chiefs by Washington, the appointment was never recognized by the Nez Perce. While he wielded influence in his day, his present-day standing among the Nez Perce is open to extremely differing opinions. [Author's files]

2. "He who knows the laws." Whites compressed the original meaning to "Lawyer." Joseph always referred to him Aleiya.

3. Within the Nez Perce community, depending upon whom you talk to, these three chiefs were either great chiefs or irresponsible rascals. [Conversations with Lapwai residents in 1995.]

4. In 1855, a group of Utah Mormons attempted to enlist Nez Perce bands in a proposed Indian revolt by Columbia Basin tribes against territorial citizens in the northwest. Old Joseph convinced his fellow chiefs to stay neutral. [Report of Secretary of War, 1858–9, Vol. 1, Pt 2, Doc. 1, 335, 338 and 339. Also, Splawn, A.J. *Kamiakin: the Last hero of the Yakimas*, p. 43; and Haines, *Red Eagles of the Northwest*, p. 148.]

5   The one area they studiously avoided was the area inhabited by the Snake tribe, as the two tribes were long-time foes. By mutual consent they avoided contact as much as possible. [Letter from Indian Agent John Montieth, Lapwai, to H. Clay Wood, dated April 24, 1876. Idaho State Historical Library, Boise, Idaho.]

6   Washington's reasoning for this prohibition was basically segregation. The entire purpose of the reservation system was to sequester each of the various tribes into confined areas to keep them isolated from the others. This, Washington felt, would eliminate tribal warfare, stop any chances of affiliations and also discourage assimilation with Whites.

In British North America the reasoning was even more sinister. Prior to 1867, Britain's posture, unofficially of course, towards Native tribes (particularly to those west of the Rocky Mountains) had been more or less "Ignore the Natives. Perhaps they will simply die off." The British attitude emerges as more malevolent when latter day Canadian historians discovered the number of Indians hanged for "criminal offences" far exceeded that of Whites. Indians were hanged for offenses that would have cost white offenders a short term in jail. When the totals are taken into account it certainly was not an attitude to invoke pride in British justice.

In 1867, when Canada attained independence from Britain and embarked on her own course, Ottawa tried to undo some of the injustices of Britain's policies by passing The Indian Act. Unfortunately, in general The Indian Act and the ministry that superintends it has failed, at times miserably, and should be abolished. [Mercredi, Ovide, *In the Rapids,* 59–79. See also: National Archives, Ottawa. Statistics pertaining to Indian Crime and Punishment in the Colony of BC 1775–1867.]

Appendix B:
A Tense Night at Fort Walsh

During the siege at Snake Creek neither Joseph nor any of his chiefs knew that one of their scouts had located Sitting Bull's camp near Fort Walsh (in what is now Saskatchewan) 100 miles northeast of The Bear's Paw. The scout had ridden into camp to be immediately surrounded by Sioux warriors. Sitting Bull was alerted and brought to the scout, who blurted out his story. He had been sent, he informed Sitting Bull, to seek assistance. He feared the American army might already have overrun his people.

Sitting Bull was aware the attack had begun and knew the Nez Perce camp was encircled, as his own scouts had kept him apprised of the situation. He had also known of General Miles' approach as the Nez Perces rested, oblivious to the threat, and his heart was saddened at his inability to warn them. He had regained some optimism when he learned Miles' offensive had bogged down under the intensive defense the Nez Perce warriors had mounted, and he was pleased to learn Miles had failed to dislodge the Nez Perces from their defensive positions. Perhaps he could still help.

It was all well and good that Sitting Bull desperately wanted to help the Nez Perces, but his hands were tightly bound by the agreement he had made with Major James M. Walsh (1840–1905)[a] the North-West Mounted Police commander. According to NWMP records, when Walsh had met the Sioux chief at the border he had extracted a promise from Sitting Bull that Sioux warriors would break no laws while within the confines of Canadian territory.[b] That included a prohibition on returning to Montana for any reason[c] unless it was a permanent return.

Sitting Bull, an honorable man, had given his word to Walsh,[d] and he kept it all the time he remained in Canada. Now the great chief was truly distraught—torn between his wish to help Joseph and his promise to Walsh. He called an immediate council of sub-chiefs to resolve a plan of action. The chiefs urged offensive action be taken. Sitting Bull, unwilling to renege on his promise, refused.

Pressured as he was from his own people, he requested Walsh to come to his village to counsel his chiefs with good advice. When Walsh, accompanied by several Mounties and an interpreter, arrived

---

a   Anderson, *Sitting Bull's Boss*, 70–87.

b   *On occasion, younger Sioux broke a law or two, but Walsh and his constables dealt with the matter with a firm but fair hand and experienced very little trouble doing so. In one famous case, a warrior had rustled several horses from a nearby ranch. A Mountie investigated, trailed the horses to one of Sitting Bull's camps and confronted the thief who had the horses tethered together in a line. The officer ordered the horses be turned over to him. The warrior refused and others gathered as if to give him support. For a few minutes the scene was very tense; but suddenly the Mountie knocked the rustler down, took the horses and without a further word turned and rode out of the village. No one tried to stop him. [NWMP files, National Archives, Ottawa.]*

c   *This included all hunting, skirmishing against the Americans and scouting the terrain south of the border. [Ibid.]*

d   *Walsh was dubbed "Sitting Bull's Boss" in an editorial in the Fort Benton (Montana) Times, which was quickly picked up by Canadian papers; the name stuck. However, who was really the boss is open to conjecture, as Sitting Bull, on occasion, gained the upper hand over Walsh.*

at the village he was greeted with mixed reactions that told him the general mood among the warriors was hostile—not against him, but against the American soldiers, the detested "long knives." Walsh, of course, had his own informants so he knew Miles had the Nez Perce contingent pinned down. He also realized the Sioux warriors felt this was the time to assist the Nez Perces by launching a revenge attack on the hated cavalry. He could not miss noticing the warriors had already painted their faces and bodies and, with coup sticks in hand, were in full war regalia. Many were already dancing around a fire to the beat of war drums. Ignoring them, Walsh strode to Sitting Bull's tepee, entered, greeted Sitting Bull then shook hands with the assembled chiefs. He seated himself on buffalo robes to face the great chief.

"Would Wahonkeeza,[e]" Sitting Bull asked, "allow a party of Sioux warriors to meet the Nez Perce at the border? They will neither fight the "blue coats" nor will they venture across the Medicine Line."

"If any of your people go to help the Nez Perce," Walsh bluntly replied, "they risk the peace and security you have found in the country of the Great Mother." He spoke slowly to give the interpreter plenty of time to put emphasis to his words.

"The Sioux," Sitting Bull countered, "would only gather in the Nez Perce that will cross the Medicine Line. The Sioux would give shelter to the Nez Perce and welcome their tepees into our camps."

While the two men conversed inside the tent, the evening air outside was rent with the thump-thump of dozens of war drums, howls of warriors and the sound of stamping feet as impatient dancers circled ceremonial fire in preparation for battle. Walsh knew there was no way those warriors would stand idly by watching a running battle between the Nez Perces and Bear Coat Miles' troopers. They would charge headlong across the border, fully intent on repeating their recent victory at the Little Big Horn. Walsh had to

---

[e] "White Forehead," the name the Sioux gave to Walsh. [Anderson, Sitting Bull's Boss, 144.]

be firm in his resolve, yet he fervently wanted to help any Nez Perce who succeeded in crossing the border.

He was also fully aware Ottawa wanted no further influx of southern Indians. It was a touchy situation, as his personal ethics and empathy with Indians had already run full force against the wishes of the Canadian Federal Government. His orders, never official but undeniably resolute, had long been clear: he must convince the Sioux to return to Montana. To drive home the point, Ottawa had assured the Sioux that the "Great Mother" had received from the American president a promise that pardons and forgiveness awaited all returning Sioux warriors. To encourage acceptance of the American terms, Ottawa continuously—and coldly—denied the Sioux both land and sustenance.

Walsh, through experience, knew the American promises were every bit as worthless as those so often made before—and he was well aware Sitting Bull was not fooled either. A compassionate man, Walsh had risked censure many times by giving the Sioux food and arranging credit for them at trading posts.[f] Now, carefully choosing his final words on the subject, he gathered the entire assembly of chiefs within his steady gaze.

"If any of the Sioux go to help the Nez Perce," he warned, "you risk losing the protection of the Great Mother. Anyone who crosses the Medicine Line intending to fight the blue coats will lose forever the shelter you now have."

Walsh had tacitly, but pointedly, told the chiefs he would not stop the warriors from going to gather in any Nez Perces who managed to cross the border—but they must stay north of the Medicine Line and they must not become involved in a fight with the U.S. Army. He could do no more than hope his words were fully understood.

---

f At one time Walsh was threatened with court-martial on charges of defrauding his own men by issuing rations from NWMP stores to help destitute Sioux families. The charges were quickly dropped when the "defrauded" constables hastened to assure Ottawa the supplies had been given voluntarily. [RCMP files, NAC, Ottawa.]

Without a further word, Walsh rose, shook hands with Sitting Bull and each of the chiefs in turn, then strode out into the chill night air. He and his men rode from the camp to a knoll some distance from the camp, let a fire for warmth, set up their tents and settled in to spend the remainder of what they knew was going to be a long, anxious night. With nervousness and no small amount of trepidation, they watched the scene below. Walsh hoped he had given the chiefs sufficient reason to rethink their plans.

As the chiefs talked on into the night the young warriors continued their war dance. The first fingers of sunlight were groping through the purple haze of dawn when a weary rider, his horse almost spent, thundered out of the gloom into the Sioux camp.

"The Nez Perce have escaped the blue coats' circle. Many women and children, one hundred warriors, approach the Medicine Line. With them are hundreds of horses."

Pandemonium engulfed the camp. Warriors rushed to their ponies, made ready to mount and ride. Walsh, knowing immediate action was needed, rushed with his men to Sitting Bull who had joined the melee.

"Give us your permission to ride to the Nez Perces who have broken from the blue coats' trap," Sitting Bull pleaded. "Many are wounded; there are sick children and injured women."

"The American soldiers will not cross the line in pursuit," Walsh told him. "Go and gather up those Indians who have crossed the line, but you must stay far enough away that the blue coats will not fire at you."

"And," he added before any of the Sioux could get out of earshot, "none of you shall cross the line or fire at the blue coats. If you do not heed my words..." He left the final sentence dangling. It would give them something to think about as they rode. Sitting Bull ordered his warriors to ride as hard as their horses could carry them. The warriors mounted and thundered away westward. They had close to a hundred miles to cover, an extremely long, hard ride, with stops required to rest the horses. Two days later they met White Bird's Nez Perces. It was Thursday, October 11, 1877.

Appendix C: Authenticated Battle Casualties

Nez Perce Casualties

White Bird Canyon, June 17

Killed:
None

Wounded (2)[a]:
Cheloyen—side wound, superficial.
Espowyes—slight abdomen wound; quickly recovered.

---

a   White volunteers claimed five Nez Perce warriors were wounded. This was a false report.

Clear Creek, July 1

> *Killed:*
> None
>
> *Wounded (4):*
> Red Heart—right thigh
> Tahkoopen—leg wound
> Peopeo Tholekt—leg wound
> Black Raven—wounded; died later

Cottonwood, July 5

> *Killed:*
> None
>
> *Wounded (1):*
> Weesculatat—died a few days later.

Clearwater, July 11–12

> *Killed (4):*
> Wayakat
> Yoomtis Kunnin
> Red Thunder
> Lelooskin (a Palouse chief)
>
> *Wounded (6):*
> Howwallitis—injured in howitzer barrage
> Kipkip Owyeen—torso wound
> Pahkatos Owyeen—shot in hand
> Old Yellow Wolf—head wound
> Yellow Wolf [Heinmot Hihhih]—left arm & below left eye
> Elaskolatat—leg wound

Big Hole, August 9–10

Killed (32)[b]:
Black Owl
Chemih
Ellisyacon
Hahtelekin
Heyumtananmi
Ipnasapa'hyutsan
Ipnan'yetama Lilpith
Lucy, daughter of Grey Eagle
No Heart
Otsilwah (female)
Oyema (female)
Pahka Tahtahank [Five Fogs]
Pahkatos [Five Wounds]
Patsakonmi
Red-Headed Woodpecker
Red Heart
Sarpsis'Ilpilp [Red Moccasin Top]
Tahkinpalloo
Tewit'Toitoi
Tokta'wetisha (female)
Tosciahpoa
Tsaiyah
Wahchumyas [Rainbow]
Wahkinkinno Ilppilp
Wahlitits [Shore Crossing] and Wife of Shore Crossing
Watisto Kaiikth
Watyetmas Liklienen and Wife of Watyetmas Liklienen
Wayatanatolatpath (female)

---

b   *Another eight, including children, remain unidentified. Others went missing and also remain unaccounted. Total fatalities may have numbered between 75 and 90.*

White Hawk (female)
Wisookaankth (female)

Wounded (8):
Elaskolatat—leg wound
Grey Eagle—head wounds; died later
Howwallitis—injured in howitzer barrage
In'who'lise (daughter of Grey Eagle)—shoulder and face wounds
Kipkip Owyeen—torso wound
Pahkatos Owyeen—shot in hand
Old Yellow Wolf—head wound
Yellow Wolf [Heinmot Hihhih]—left arm & left eye

Camus Meadows, August 20

Killed:
None confirmed. (The army claimed six warriors died here, but could produce no official records as proof).

Wounded (1):
Peopeo Tholekt—head wound
(Possibly two or three others were wounded, but no accounts are available for proof.)

Canyon Creek, September 13

Killed (1):
Tookleiks [Fish Trap]

Wounded (3):
Eashlokoon—leg injury
Elaskolatat—hip & thigh
Silooyleam—lower leg wound

Cow Island, September 23

> *Killed:*
> None
>
> *Wounded (1):*
> Husis Owyeen—head wound (wood splinter)

Bear's Paw, September 30–October 05[c]

> *Killed (16):*
> Eagle's Necklace, the Elder
> Heyoomee'kahlikt [Grizzly Bear on his Back]
> Imnawaha
> Kow'waspo
> Koyehknown
> Lakoyee
> Lean Elk [aka Poker Joe]
> Looking Glass
> Lying
> Ollokot
> Peopeo'Ipsewahk [Lonely bird]
> Red Leg
> Sookoups, the younger
> Timhillpoosman
> Tohtohalikan

---

c   *Indian scouts in the employ of the US Army killed at least 15 Nez Perce. Several were killed at or near Bear's Paw by Crow, Cheyenne and Sioux scouts. As well, three warriors who had been sent north to locate Sitting Bull's encampment were infamously—and treacherously—murdered (one escaped to tell the details) by an Assiniboine hunting party near the border. However, the overall number killed by Indians may number upwards of 17. Imnawaha was killed by an unknown scout some distance from Bear's Paw, under obscure circumstances.*

Tool'hool'hool'zote

Wounded(3):
Eagle's Necklace, the younger
Rainbow, the younger
Tomyahnin

(Several unidentified women and children were killed or wounded, but their identities were never recorded.)

Total Army Casualties by Regiment

Regiment	Rank	Killed	Wounded[1]
1st Cavalry	Officers	2	1
	Enlisted	47	9
2nd Cavalry	Officers	0	0
	Enlisted	0	6
7th Cavalry	Officers	2	5
	Enlisted	21	46
4th Artillery	Officers	0	1
	Enlisted	10	2
5th Infantry	Officers	0	3
	Enlisted	0	11
21st Infantry	Officers	0	1
	Enlisted	6	15
7th Infantry	Officers	3	1
	Enlisted	34	0
		125	101
Militia/Civilian		10	8
Indian Scouts		1[2]	4
TOTAL		136	113

[APPENDIX C ENDNOTES]

1. Several army personnel who were wounded died later from their wounds.
2. Four scouts believed killed. This is unconfirmed.

Appendix D: Rogue Missionaries Amid the Nez Perce Bands

> "It is the Nez Perce elders who teach the young. They teach them in the ways of the Great Spirit Chief. His way is the Nez Perce way. Missionaries mean churches. Churches teach the people to quarrel about the missionaries' god and the Great Spirit Chief. It is all right for men to quarrel about things of the earth from time to time, but it is not good to quarrel about their god and the Great Spirit Chief."
> — CHIEF JOSEPH.[1]

> "When missionaries came we were told they were going to do us much good. Many summers passed before we realized they were doing little good for us but were doing very well for themselves."
> —WILLIAM LOUIE.[2]

Washington bureaucrats were by no means a singular force behind the theft of the Indians' traditional land, including that of the Nez Perce. While they completed the deed by whittling away boundaries and breaking promises made in original agreements, it is unlikely they could have managed without able assistance from an army of eager helpers. Their allies were settlers, ranchers, miners, territorial politicians and countless lobbyists who besieged the nation's elected representatives on Capitol Hill. The most fervent of all—groups with a very special agenda—were missionaries of various churches, cults and sects who converged upon the Native tribes, intent on convincing the people to convert to their version of "the true religion." Among these were rogue missionaries. They went about the task of religious conversion, but their methods employed coercion, carefully planned confidence games and fiscal misdeeds. While exhorting Natives to sign treaties with Washington "in order to protect Indian lands...," many were securing vast acres of that same land for their own profit. They succeeded by taking full advantage of the Indians' natural friendship, their susceptibility to supernatural mysteries and a naïve belief that what these men in black were asseverating was the absolute truth.

One of the most influential among the rogue missionaries was Reverend Henry Harmon Spalding (1803–1874), an ordained minister. He and his wife, an authorized missionary-teacher, Eliza Hart Spalding (1807–1851), arrived in Idaho (to the area that later became the Lapwai Reservation) during 1836.

This unusual man was born out of wedlock in a New York State village called Bath.[3] Under the narrow moral standards of the day, his illegitimate birth hung over his head like a stigmatic cloud for many years, and was particularly harsh during his youth. The taunts and barbs he endured as a boy produced a bitter and stern man incapable of showing friendly affection to others. The records indicate his father was one Howard Spalding, his mother a village woman identified only as Lucy.

Howard either would not or could not marry Lucy, but he did support their son for almost fourteen months before deciding to move on. Since his departure was intended as a solo endeavor it meant leaving Lucy alone in her disgrace, burdened with raising the child. Howard was not without some honor, so he fostered his son to a local farmer. The farmer and his wife raised Henry more as an indentured servant than a family member. He attended the local school where he attained marks sufficient to earn him admission to a theological college. At age seventeen he left both the farm and

Bath to enter the college from which he graduated as an ordained minister in the Presbyterian faith. During his time at the college he had also met Eliza Hart, a devout member of the Presbyterian congregation in the nearby town of Prattsburg. In keeping with the times, a formal courtship ran its course and they were married.

The newly ordained minister's first assignment was to a mission on an Osage reservation. Armed with strict spiritual convictions, his prayer books, the Bible and a religious fervor described by one contemporary as "fanatically sincere..."[4] he stayed among the Osages long enough to gain a reputation of being a martinet, an attitude that earned him no favor with his flock. Complaints were made about his strict discipline, but before any action could be considered he was enticed by an acquaintance to make application to join a mission party being assembled for assignments in Oregon and Idaho. The American Board of Commissioners for Foreign Missions controlled such ventures, and after interviews with Henry and Eliza the commissioners agreed a move was desirable and gave approval.[5] Thus it was that Henry and Eliza traveled west in 1836 as members of the Methodist Missionary Party, an integrated group of Congregationalist, Methodist and Presbyterian ordained missionaries, assistant missionaries, missionary-teachers and medical practitioners. Also in the party, perhaps to Henry's surprise, was Narcissa Prentice, newly married to Marcus Whitman, MD.[6] Before Henry met Eliza he had proposed to Narcissa, but she rejected him.[7]

When the company reached Mission Headquarters at Willamette, Oregon the Spaldings left to continue their journey to the Nez Perce territorial land in Idaho. The ill-fated Dr. and Mrs. Whitman were assigned to the Waiilaptu Mission near Walla Walla, Washington, to administer to the Cayuse Indians.

The Spaldings were mandated by the Board of the Presbyterian Church to set up a mission complete with a school. This they did. Henry preached that the only way to salvation was to renounce "heathen ways," while Eliza taught the way to worldly happiness was through adoption of the ethics and morals of white society. Both methods meant giving up semi-transient life which, though mentioned only in very oblique terms, was the first step towards the

Natives' acceptance of a treaty-invoked reservation. The Spaldings' primary intention was to convert the Nez Perces to Christianity by ending all rites and ceremonies they considered pagan, which Henry labeled "heathen worship." They also tried, but with little success, to end secret societies that attracted young warriors. Spalding, determined to use whatever means he considered necessary to achieve his aims, set about his enterprise by draping himself in the mantle of God's Crusader. This included the role of leadership and brandishing a rawhide whip, which he had no qualms about using. In the beginning Spalding's aims were not transparent, but it did not take long for the more astute to realize his true intentions.

At first there was cooperation between the Natives and the Spaldings and various assistants who arrived at the mission. The Nez Perces, eager to learn better ways to enrich their well being, including matters of the spirit, embraced the Spaldings. They willingly listened to the long-bearded man dressed in black who spoke with such passion. He convinced them he had been directed by a divine power to give them a book he called The Bible and which the Natives came to call The Sky Book. He further impressed various chiefs favorably by introducing their people to agriculture through cultivation of vegetables, grain and corn. He had them build a gristmill where they ground the harvested kernels into flour. He also had a lumber mill constructed, which large numbers of Nez Perces looked favorably upon, as they liked the idea of living in wooden houses. Spalding also introduced his flock to the cultivation of carrots, beets, turnips and tubers previously unknown to them.

For quite some time the Natives supplied meat and fish to the missionaries and also provided labor to cut trees with which to build the mission's log homes and buildings. Later, when they began to seek payment for their goods and services, Spalding followed the examples of missionaries in Oregon and Washington Territory. He flatly refused. He was God's representative, he told them, so food and labor was really their payment to God.

When Mrs. Spalding's school opened its door, at least seven Nez Perce bands enrolled all their children, some as young as two years of age. The adults attended Spalding's religious services where they learned hymns and the required gospel verses. Some, in order to learn English, attended day classes as well. As an added feature of their benefice, the Spaldings provided medicines and performed minor medical services, which of course were greatly limited because neither were doctors. However, they could tend to cuts, treat abrasions, burns and perform the treatment of bloodletting, the popular method of "healing" almost anything during that era. Spalding cleverly sought the assistance of the tewats, tribal medicine men whose expertise lay in the healing qualities of herbs and roots.

Despite early successes, not all went according to plan, for within two years matters began to turn sour. Because Spalding thought it an unnecessary nuisance, he never learned even rudimentary Nimiputimt, the Nez Perce language. The Natives, he decided, must learn English. This insistence caused misunderstandings, whereupon incidences arose. Though at first small, these slowed the pace of his success, as Spalding was not only stern, he was also impatient and short of temper.

He was also embittered by unpleasant memories from his troubled youth. He regressed to the authoritarian personage he had displayed at the Osage reservation; conditions in the mission began a downward spiral and quickened as his intolerance mounted towards those he considered beneath his station. It was not long before his prejudice towards Nez Perce traditional beliefs and rituals, which he viewed as Satanic sorcery and evil in concept, overcame common sense. He commenced harsh measures to wipe them out.

All rituals came under his sights including the nightly drumming, singing and dancing that were all part of the Sunset Ceremony of which he did not approve. Committed also to end gambling, he tried to ban the age-old games of chance Nez Perce men played. He came down hard on horse racing, the highlight of the annual summer celebrations. Those who followed such practices, he would thunder at every service, were doomed to spend eternal damnation in Hell,[8] a place of fire and suffering. Non-compliance to his gambling edicts brought about increased use of the whip. Fiery pits of brimstone and sulphur fumes were a new—and profoundly disturbing—concept to the Indians, and many refused to buy into it. Refusal served only to enrage him, and his wrath became legendary.

Not all of Spalding's attempts to win converts succeeded. His methods of persuasion were often so bizarre they did nothing to endear him to the as-yet unconverted. One example was his distribution of potatoes that had sprouted. Each sprout, he informed his flock, was evidence of God's power and would turn one potato into many. He gave the sprouted potatoes to his converted flock, showed them how to cut each into small pieces so each piece had a sprout. He showed them how to plant them in prepared mounds of soil. He told his pupils the sprouts were "eyes" through which the potato pieces saw the blessings God would bestow upon them. The eyes, he said, would receive those blessings, which would enable them to become many new potatoes.

He also gave potatoes to "the heathens" with the same instructions. However, he had carefully removed all the sprouts. As any gardener knows, sproutless potatoes will not reproduce. Thus, while the gardens of the converted flourished, nothing was produced in those of "the heathens." Weeks later, Spalding was able to point out the lush gardens of his flock and also point to the empty gardens of the heathens. He proclaimed God favored the labors of Christians while refusing to shower his blessings on heathens.

Spalding played this and other types of cozenage on many occasions, but eventually friendly white settlers and mountain men revealed his subterfuge. The revelations alienated many. Such games, when combined with his attacks on cherished traditions and customs, served to drive away several of the converted, including entire bands. Two such bands were those of Wala'mute'kint and Iname-toom'shila, powerful chiefs of the Wallowa Valley Band and the Lapwai Valley Band respectively. With their withdrawal Spalding lost half his congregation.

Preaching the concept of settling in one confined area with restricted travel proved neither a major problem nor one even as difficult as he may have feared. Most bands stayed within a fairly limited area, so objections came mainly from those whose hunters ventured far afield in search of buffalo and other game, and bands that occupied summer and winter camps, often many miles apart. The hunters were away most of spring and summer, and in some cases for upwards of two years. On the other hand, many elders and most women found cultivating grain and potatoes provided a quiet contentment. Spalding was pleased to see those plans for the Nez Perces falling quietly into place.

The converted had willingly placed their children under the teaching influence of this man and his woman; but as time passed they also expressed misgivings about the rawhide whip Reverend Spalding carried at all times. They viewed the whip with grave suspicion but, because it was not until later their aversions proved correct, it was not easy to break the spell this brooding man held over them. There were also those who had remained, to some degree, unconvinced in his teachings. They were confused because the God of whom Spalding preached was portrayed as three benevolent gods in one form. The chief god, called Father by Spalding, was benevolent but stern. The most forgiving and beneficent god, called Jesus, was God's son. The third god was a mysterious spirit who seemed to have very little to do. This trio sharing a single entity puzzled them greatly. Han'ya'wat, their tradition told them, was not a god but a powerful spirit who had neither wives nor sons. Many grew skeptical.[9]

Spalding also told them of God's three worlds, two of which were in the afterlife. One, which he called Heaven, was a wondrous place of joy and contentment where eternity would be spent by the righteous. The other, which he called Hell, was a world of fiery torment where the father-god cast sinners into fire pits when they died. There they would forever remain to repent their sinful lives. Even the son-god could not pardon them. Many came to have misgivings about the benevolence of Spalding's god. In Han'ya'wat's afterlife only one world, Ahkinkenekia [Place of Happiness] existed. Most also noticed how Spalding often flew into a rage threatening to whip anyone who asked questions about the afterlife which did not please him. In such rages Spalding said and did things that defied Nez Perce traditions that had endured for centuries; and the outbursts began to cause many to feel less secure in this new belief. Perhaps changes were not so good after all.

Eventually Wala'mute'kint (who had allowed Spalding to pour water on his head and rename him Joseph) spoke with his friend, Inametoom'shila (who had also allowed Spalding to pour water on his head and rename him James) about the doubts both were beginning to have. Both had enrolled their bands' children in the school so Mrs. Spalding could teach them the white man's way of life. Then one day Spalding whipped one of the children for an indiscretion that Spalding refused to discuss, a refusal that distressed Inametoom'shila. He spoke of the event with his son-in-law, a white man named William Craig. The next day Craig spoke with Spalding but received neither an explanation nor an offer to apologize. It was at this point both chiefs began to lose feelings of friendship for Spalding.

Those Spalding punished with the whip included small children and women. That had never been part of Nez Perce life. Maleficent men were occasionally whipped for serious crimes, but never had women or children been so ill treated. More chiefs complained, but Spalding not only refused to change his ways he told them bad people could be hanged for serious crimes. This revelation caused more concern, as execution had never been part of Nimipu punishment. The worst punishment imposed—one greatly feared—was permanent exile. No exiled man could ever find welcome anywhere within Nez Perce society. He was doomed to wander alone and friendless.

As time went by there arose more difficulties with some of his flock because Spalding had convinced himself they were his personal laborers. In one instance he decided to move his house from its original location near the Clearwater River to high ground closer to the mission. He had his "laborers" take the building apart and move it to its new place. There were many complaints, as most of the rough-hewn boards were heavy and the distance far. Their complaints were ignored; instead they were threatened with punishment. There is no doubt he worked them too hard by Nez Perce standards. Nez Perce men were in the habit of working when, where and if they felt like it, whereas Spalding insisted his orders be obeyed without delay. It was inevitable that differences would occur in deciding which of the two definitions of the work ethic was correct.[10]

While Spalding, steadily decreasing in reverence, supervised his laborers in the building of mills, digging of gardens and planting grains and vegetables, Eliza operated the school. With her gift for languages she had quickly learned the basics of the difficult Nez Perce language. She translated Matthew's gospel and some English school texts into Nimiputímt as teaching aids for her students. Fluent in Greek and Latin, she translated classical literature to Nimiputimt in order to teach her students some history of the Classical Period, but the success of this project is difficult to determine. Nonetheless, she was a gifted teacher and, had some of her niceties rubbed off on her husband, things might have turned out differently for all concerned. Under her tutelage many children, and some adults, learned conversational English.

Regardless of how Spalding had envisioned his progress as a missionary, not all went the way he had foreseen. Trouble began in earnest in 1842 on receipt of a notice of dismissal from the Board. His appointment, he was informed, was being terminated because of numerous complaints and allegations concerning his treatment of his charges. The complaints originated from various sources—including fellow missionaries—and all expressed alarm over the draconian rules he was implementing, as well as his heavy-handed dispensation of overly harsh disciplinary measures.

He dutifully left the mission property but appealed his dismissal, remaining on his farm pending a final decision. A few months later the Board, having reviewed the case, granted him reinstatement. Feeling absolved, Spalding returned to the mission only to find his flock was not in agreement with the decision. The mission's numbers further diminished and would soon become even less. It seemed that 1842 might see an end to the Lapwai mission.

The years 1837 to 1841 had seen Spalding's greatest success. During that time the rolls had increased to several hundred names, mostly members of six large bands and several smaller ones. By 1841, Chiefs Wala'mute'kint and Inametoom'shila [Big Thunder][11] were beginning to have second thoughts, and in 1845 both departed. Their apostasy further depleted the rolls because 1844 had seen the defection of Twvish Sisimnen [Sparkling Horn], another influential chief Spalding had baptized and renamed Ellis. Sparkling Horn had been one of Spalding's most ardent followers and his departure was keenly felt. In 1840, Spalding had asked Elijah White, a previously disgraced rogue missionary who had since finagled appointment as Indian agent for the entire territory, to name Ellis[12] Head Chief of the Nez Perces. The appointment was made by White and confirmed by Washington shortly after. Thus these had been the good years for Spalding.

By 1843, having grown smugly self-righteous, he drew up a list of punishments for every sin imaginable, including those against him and the mission. He submitted it to White for approval. White not only approved but published it as a booklet under the title "Book of Rules"[13] and adopted it for use throughout his jurisdiction. Basically copied from the American penal code, punishments included death by hanging for several crimes, including arson. The death penalty applied also to dogs that killed lambs, harassed sheep or chased cows. Jail terms and heavy fines were meted out for lesser crimes; one such was owning a dog if you were not an authorized hunter. All non-capital offenses rated lashes, fines and/or imprisonment, or such other punishment as would be deemed fitting by "the authorities." The authorities were, of course, White and selected missionaries and band chiefs.[14] Spalding never went so far as to hang anyone, possibly because his time at Lapwai was soon to come to an abrupt and ignoble end, but the threat was there. When added to his other outrages, his list of punishments brought no small degree of resentment followed by desertion from the mission by recent converts.

Chief Ellis was among those who resigned from Spalding's mission because of his increasing cruelty and the introduction of the Book of Rules.[15] He abdicated the title of Head Chief and departed for Montana in self-imposed exile. He died there in 1848. When Ellis left, only Chiefs Timothy, Lawyer and Jason stood by Spalding. The mission would have failed entirely had they also left, but these three, driven by ambition, kept enough spark of interest glowing that it managed to survive through the period of Spalding's suspension and subsequent reinstatement. In gratitude for their loyalty he appointed Chief Lawyer [aka Aleiya] to the position of Head Chief and gave unspecified rewards to the others.

Despite reinstatement, there were still lean months ahead for the Spaldings, owing to the drop in numbers. Henry and Eliza struggled on, hoping fortunes would begin to increase.[16] Spalding had, however, learned nothing from his ordeal and, adamant in his belief that Nez Perce culture was the spawn of Satan, refused to abate his regime of harsh discipline and severe punishment, which now included public whippings that exempted no one.

Whipping, though not unknown to the Nez Perces,[17] had always exempted women and children. Under Spalding, exemptions were nullified. One of his reports contains the dismaying information that he "had been required to whip three children for stealing corn." Their crime had been taking three ears of corn, one from each of three stalks, when passing a field and eating the kernels as they walked home. To emphasize to his flock the necessity of such punishment, he told them it was a requirement of God's forgiveness. Spalding insisted his sentences be administered by adult followers, but found none willing to comply.[18] This expectation was mainly the cause of Chief Ellis' rebellion and the cessation of his friendship with Spalding.

Spalding's refusal to extend equal punishment to his assistants and teachers for their infractions of the infamous rules was especially repugnant to the Natives and their white supporters. One supporter was William Craig, who became famous as a highly respected Indian agent. In one well-recorded, ill-famed case the mission blacksmith, a man named Williams, continuously physically abused the Nez Perce woman to whom he was married. (Spalding had performed the ceremony.) Finally, having suffered enough abuse, she ran away to her family. Spalding flushed her out and returned her to Williams. Before he returned her, though, he publicly administered seventy lashes to the unfortunate woman's back, doing the deed himself because no one else would obey his order. He spoke not a word of admonishment to Williams for his abusive behavior. Many were of the opinion Williams was the one who deserved the seventy lashes. This incident not only offended the Nez Perces, but also a number of Whites. It so enraged William Craig he unleashed harsh words on Spalding who merely replied that God had one set of punishments for Natives and another for white men. Spalding considered the woman had reverted to her former heathen ways when she fled from her abusive husband.

Not only did Craig intensely dislike Spalding as a man, he had no respect for his religious zeal. Craig, though himself a nominal Christian, believed Indians should be left to follow their own religion and traditions. He saw nothing wrong in the Wéset and had long argued for the Indians' right to worship as they pleased. That was an issue no missionary could countenance.[19] He championed their cause, and during his tenure as an Indian agent decried the coercion used by various missionaries to gain converts. His complaints went nowhere. The missions, being sanctioned by Washington, were considered self-governing entities.

Spalding's mission began its final downturn when he lost his influence over the several bands that ultimately became known as the non-Treaty Nez Perces. Without doubt his arrogance and intolerance, traits possessed by both he and, albeit to a lesser extent, Eliza, were overriding factors. Her weaknesses of character remain exhibited in her reports and letters, many of which are on file in the archives of the University of Idaho and others in the University of Idaho Library's Special Collections Department. Both, located at Boise, are available to researchers and interested students of northwest history.

In contrast to her husband, Eliza was liked. She employed kinder methods to convert the Nez Perces and was patient in convincing them to shun their long-established, semi-transient lifestyle. Until 1842 she enjoyed better than moderate success. The respect many of her students felt toward her would probably have quickly diminished had they known what she really thought of them. Eliza's reports show she did not reciprocate her students' love or respect. Her reports show her seeing them as being "too lazy to learn much." She was particularly disappointed in the women who, to her way of thinking, lacked initiative. This was mostly because they showed no inclination to do housekeeping the same way as white women. Her reports describe Nez Perce women as "savages" and one includes the comment, "the more savage an Indian woman the better is her bead work and embroidering." Her personal bias also shows through in letters to friends. Eliza,[20] however, did not escape criticism from several of those friends. Many thought she was "too critical of her charges" and she was also considered by one contemporary as being "aloof, unworldly, and almost nunlike in her naiveté..." while others considered her "belief in the sanctity of the Sabbath is much too deeply ingrained..." because "she abstains from labor of any sort in order to spend the entire Sunday in solemn prayer"[21]

Chief Big Thunder, undoubtedly encouraged by his son-in-law, William Craig, had been the first important chief to rebel. Big Thunder steadfastly supported the non-Treaty bands, although he did not join them in 1877 insurrection.[22] When he withdrew from the mission, the removal of his band's children from the school gave cause for Spalding to express anger in his records and reports. He wrote equally angry reports following Chief Wala'mute'kint's defection and departure from Lapwai with his band to return to the Wallowa Valley.[23] Spalding steadfastly refused to relent in his methods even though the defections were greatly felt.

Spalding's tenure at Lapwai came to an abrupt and final end following the destruction of the Waiilaptu Mission near Walla Walla at the hands of enraged Cayuse warriors. During their rampage on Monday, November 29, 1847, they killed Marcus and Narcissa Whitman plus several others who worked with them. Spalding, who had been on his way to Waiilaptu, was very near his destination when he received word of the raid. Fearing the Cayuse warriors also wanted him dead, he made a quick about-turn and hurriedly returned to Lapwai where he sought and was granted refuge with William Craig. (Though many see a certain irony in Craig's benefice toward the man he so intensely disliked, his animosity could never extend to refusing to save a life.) The next day Craig went to Eliza to help her depart to safekeeping, but she refused to leave. It was Sunday and, in keeping with her beliefs, she would do nothing but pray on the Sabbath. Craig left several warriors as guards. The next morning he returned, took her to his farm and a day or two later assisted the Spaldings to flee Idaho.

Whatever respect the Nez Perces might still have had for Spalding was lost by his sudden departure. His flight was regarded as cowardice. The Nez Perce views of Spalding's departure were two-fold. Many saw his panicky flight as his own lack of conviction in the powers of his God to protect him. Many cited in their observation that Spalding's God had done nothing to save his friends, the hapless Whitmans. Others saw it as either blatant cowardice or a wise decision considering his growing unpopularity among his flock. Whatever his reasons, he was wise to leave. Years later, Many Wounds[24] summed up the situation when he was quoted as saying,

"Spalding did not elevate himself heroically with the Nez Perces when he ran away."[25]

Several days later a raiding party of Cayuse warriors did arrive at the mission. Over a period of a few hours they looted and burned several buildings and caused other damage. They appear to have been looking only for Spalding, because they did no harm to the Nez Perce inhabitants. On the other hand, the Nez Perces did not a single thing to repulse the raiders, which in itself speaks volumes.

Spalding stayed away from the northwest for seventeen years.[26] When he did reappear, in 1864, it was not to Idaho, but to Oregon. In 1871, as a member of the Presbyterian Board of Foreign Missions, he reluctantly visited Lapwai. He did so only because he had been ordered to embark on a church-sponsored tour of Oregon and Idaho missions, of which one was Lapwai. One of his apologists has written that he had been welcomed by the Lapwai Indians "with enthusiasm" and had traveled through the area "drawing great crowds." Spalding later claimed that during that tour he baptized 1,000 persons, but not a single one of his biographers—including the aforementioned apologist—mention it, and no records show this to be a fact. His enthusiastic welcome is also conjecture.

Three years later, on August 3, 1874, he again visited Lapwai. This was his final visit, as it was there that he died following a sudden, massive heart attack. He was buried there. He is remembered by Lapwai Nez Perces but, although memories of his despotism have diminished in the mists of time, few speak of him favorably. Most describe him as a man whose accomplishments were far overshadowed by the great harm of his evil deeds. None are inclined towards generous praise. His memory evokes cynical opinions, as attested in the remarks of one Nez Perce who, when discussing the man, bitterly remarked, "When Spalding came to Lapwai he gave to my people the Bible and as payment he took their land." His is a very similar lament to one so often heard in the Polynesian Islands, South America and other places where missionaries plied their trade.

The point is true, for as time went on Reverend Spalding became less interested in religious conversion and more in determination to advance his personal concept of the latest American aspiration. He was a devotee to the conviction—he believed it was God's plan—that America was destined to rule North America from Atlantic to Pacific. In this he followed his immediate predecessors and associates, the rogue missionaries Jason Lee (b. Quebec 1803; d. New York 1845) and Dr. Elijah White (b. New York 1805; died California 1879).

Spalding believed wholeheartedly in the popular concept that Americans must rule the land, and white men must own the land. The idea had been around for some time. It was the reason Thomas Jefferson made the Louisiana Purchase deal with France and had then sent Lewis and Clark on their historical cross-country expedition. Not until 1845 was the term Manifest Destiny[27] coined to justify the war to liberate Texas from Mexican occupation. Manifest Destiny became a tidy name for the exploitation that was in vogue long before Spalding decided to go west.

Continental expansion, as a general intention, recognized that total control could succeed only if the original inhabitants ceased their nomadic life as hunters and embraced farming. The reasoning behind this, of course, was if Indians stopped roaming freely they could be more easily convinced to give up their traditional lands and that would safely open an extremely vast area to White settlement.

Spalding ventured west with two thoughts in mind: He would save the souls of the heathen Indians and lead them to a sedentary agricultural life. He realized that in order to achieve such aims the Indian population would have to settle—and stay put—in restricted areas, embrace Christianity and adapt to the ways of the white man. It was this that prioritized his personal agenda when, in 1836, he went west in the belief his legacy would be the acknowledgment that he had done his share convincing Idaho Indians to renounce their transient lifestyle and settle on reservations. In other words he intended to see them become compliantly dependent upon the masters of a continent-wide America.

Unlike Lee and White,[28] both of whom proved more interested in the profits of land speculation than the prophets of the Bible, Spalding never actively recruited colonists to settle on Indian land. This might have been owing to his relatively short tenure at Lapwai and his panicked abandonment of both mission and converts. Nor did he place excessive personal claims on land, as had White and Lee. His friend Marcus Whitman has been accused of having dabbled both in land claims and in encouraging hundreds of settlers to claim homesteads on Indian land. There is, however, no viable proof that he ever profited from either. Two years before he was killed, Whitman is quoted as having admitted that he "had done nothing for the teaching of the Indians, because they would not listen to him."[29] Obviously the Cayuse warriors thought he was working against their interests.

Spalding's wife was not as determined as her husband to invoke Manifest Destiny, possibly because she did not fully understand the concept. Her determination was to turn the Nez Perces into Presbyterians as devout and dour as was she. That meant they must cease gambling, stop racing horses in wild contests, abstain from smoking kinnikinik leaves[30] and renounce alcohol. The latter was a most commendable undertaking on her part, although she seemed naively unaware the whiskey traders were merely following the trail she had already blazed. Despite her harangues against gambling, racing, drinking and smoking, Nez Perce males tended to overlook her strict rules-for-life. Most Nez Perce males greatly enjoyed such "evils."

Eliza Hart Spalding[31] was apparently liked—perhaps even loved—by her young students, and many adults respected her. She showed genuine kindness to children—a trait her husband never displayed—but their love was not her objective. She wanted obedience.

Both Spaldings shared a determination to curb both the Nez Perces' earthy humor and their taking more than one wife at a time. The interdiction against earthy humor failed totally (Nez Perces still enjoy a blue-tinged joke) and the anti-polygamy crusade succeeded only years after both Spaldings had died and the Nez Perces had settled down for good.

Neither of these two adherents of parochial religion realized polygamy had come among the Plains and Plateau tribes through attrition caused by years of intertribal warfare. Attrition had reduced the male population to a point where males were greatly outnumbered by females. While no one knows the exact ratio, the estimates of 5:1 to 8:1 are considered reasonable. A tribe, therefore, because its survival depended on population increase through natural means, found polygamy a workable solution. It also partly explains inter-tribal marriages,[32] which occurred even during periods of ongoing hostility and wars.[33]

Because the women never appeared concerned about sharing their husbands, an assortment of wives (on average three) and their various children were able to live in a man's tepee in amazing degrees of familial harmony. The only checks on multiple marriage were tribal laws that limited the number of wives to a man's ability to support them, and tribal tradition. In all tribes, custom insisted the proposed bride's father be presented with suitable gifts, such as a good rifle, a horse or two of top quality and/or several fine blankets. Eliza Spalding could never understand this and, although determined to abolish polygamy, she never achieved any appreciable success.[34]

If Eliza enjoyed respect and love of many Lapwai Nez Perces, Henry Harmon Spalding had neither, despite his lofty claims of achievement. That he was feared is unquestioned, but he was never generally respected. He cared not. His primary objective was obedience, with respect a distant second.

When the Spaldings departed Lapwai for the final time many of the precedents they had instituted remained. These had settled in firmly enough that those who followed them made few changes of any substance. Spalding's harshest methods of punishment were quickly dispelled, but firm discipline remained for several more years.

Strict rules had lessened greatly by the time the McBeth sisters, Sue (1830–1893) and Kate (1833–1915) arrived years later as missionary-teachers. Sue arrived in 1873, and by the time Kate followed, in 1879, Sue had made a number of changes in the school routine. She could not, however, change rules made by ordained missionaries. When several Nez Perce converts were ordained as ministers and took over the mission's administration, they quickly put an end to the severe discipline.

Kate, it turned out, would have enjoyed working for Reverend Spalding. She looked upon Indians as a lower class[35] and was critical of Sue, who leaned towards tolerance. Kate had no use for Nez Perce traditions or customs, although she did transcribe a few legends that were related to her by one of her students. Her bias shows clearly in her translations. She cast a particularly unfavorable eye upon the Wyakin, the personal guiding spirit all Nez Perces believed was with them always.[36] She wrote on the subject, but the views she expressed indicate clearly she had no idea of what a Wyakin was or even what it signified. She continually upbraided students who carried the symbol of their own Wyakin with them. She saw the symbols only as proof her students were still pagans at heart. All she knew about the Wyakin was that it was not part of her version of Christianity[37] and, therefore, had to be abolished.

As a teacher, Kate McBeth's qualifications also emerge as questionable. Her reports, archived at the University of Idaho, are poorly written with many spelling errors and flawed grammar. Her personal letters (also in the university's archives) plainly show her prejudices never changed. She constantly refers to adult Indian men as "boys" and uses other terms and derogatory descriptions. McBeth also held deep resentment toward the number of Nez Perce men, some of whom had been her students, being accepted into the Presbyterian Church as ordained ministers. This, she lamented, was terribly unfair when she, because she was a woman, was denied any chance of ordination.[38]

She particularly disliked Chief Joseph, and was instrumental in convincing Washington to deny him permission to visit Lapwai. The fact of the matter was that she was afraid of the influence she erroneously believed he wielded over the Lapwai Nez Perces. She was certain, should even a short visit to Lapwai be allowed, ultimately he would find a way to stay. Such an event she believed would allow him to influence her students. Thus, she managed to block all but two of his few requested visits. All of Joseph's requests had been made only in order to visit his eldest daughter. She had escaped to Canada with White Bird in 1877, but later returned to Lapwai where she married a Nez Perce man. Joseph personally had no desire to live at Lapwai, and both approved visits were of short duration.

Unfortunately, missionaries and teachers neither understood the Nez Perce traditional religion nor did they consider it worth examining. To their way of thinking Wéset was a Satanic invention, and Han'ya'wat was a pagan god who had to be eliminated. They had never bothered to find out traditional Nez Perces *never* worshiped Han'ya'wat as a god. The Wéset, in fact, recognized no gods, only spirits, some of which were benevolent and others malevolent. Han'ya'wat had greater powers than any of the others, but at times he needed assistance from other powerful spirits. Two had adopted for their earthly roles Coyote and Raven. Han'ya'wat rarely appeared, for he was a solitary entity, but when he did it would be as a small bird or a shy animal, such as a rabbit. In no way did he resemble mortals. He had no parents, no brothers, no sisters, no uncles or aunts, no cousins. He had no wife—and he had no son to send to the Nez Perces on his behalf.[39] Han'ya'wat had no son for one simple reason: Nez Perce shamans, who for thousands of years had interpreted lore and legends, had never been inclined to fabricate such a being.[40]

In his dealings with the Nez Perce, Henry Spalding personified the typical missionary of the 19th century. He would neither tolerate discussion with those who held opposing views, nor would he deign to consider differences of religious opinion.[41] His only authorities—which he considered absolute—were the Book of Common Prayer, the New Testament and his church-edited Bible. These, in his opinion, were the only recognized documents to be used in dealing with religion—and the Bible was to be interpreted literally in all matters, which explains his "eye for an eye" philosophy. Harold Harmon Spalding, as did the missionaries and teachers who worked with and for him, failed to realize the Nez Perce traditional religion, Wéset (or Seven Drums as it has also been called) embraced most of the ethics and moral examples found in Christianity and other leading religions. Wéset laws included kind treatment of others, sharing with those less fortunate, honesty in word and deed, respect for parents and the honoring of ancestors. Kindness towards the elderly and children was paramount. Honesty in trade matters and keeping of promises was dominant. A man's word was expected to be his bond. Forbidden were pride, lying, adultery, murder, greed, lust and envy. Wéset differed from Spalding's concept of religion mainly in that it did not teach of two worlds in an afterlife. There was the suggestion that following death the spirit of a virtuous person entered a hallowed state where it would rest easily for all eternity, but there was no place called heaven. It suggested the spirit of an evil person would be denied such rest and would roam aimlessly until the evil of past deeds had been swept clean,[42] at which time the spirit would attain eternal rest.

 It would be incorrect to consider Spalding as being alone in the role of a rogue missionary, for he was by no means alone. Those who had gone before, as well as his contemporaries, had the same views toward physical and mental abuse of Natives who refused to comply with their wishes. Of those who succeeded him, all vying for souls, nearly all repeated the mistakes in varying degree that singled out Spalding, Whitman, Lee and White. Where a new way of life was acceptable to a number of Nez Perces, to others it was not. Discernible divisions within the missionaries' own ranks in their variegated interpretations of the Sky Book did not go unnoticed either; and the missionaries' insistence that everything must change to their way of life caused a schism amongst individuals, and often entire bands. This split had begun, virtually unnoticed, with the appearance of the first missionaries and led to the ultimate division of the once united Idaho-Oregon Nez Perce tribe. In 1855 the rift widened and in 1863 it became final.

The unhappy, disastrous experience with Spalding, Lee, White, Whitman and others was by no means unique to the Nez Perce and other northwest tribes. Through the histories of nearly every tribe in the United States and Canada there runs a similar thread. Exploitation, fear and coercion were practiced by most of those authorized by Washington and Ottawa to administer to the acculturation and education of the Indian population. As is so often the case with edicts that seem like good ideas at the time, both Ottawa and Washington erred in authorizing church groups administrative powers over reservations. The only differences were the methods employed.

During the first of his two terms, President Ulysses S. Grant authorized the Bureau of Indian Affairs to appoint various church groups to take over the control of services in a number of reservations. Where the BIA had previously appointed Indian agents, the new regulations allowed the churches to appoint their own agents. It was an edict they eagerly jumped at. Missionaries, once in full authority, zealously forbade totems, the keeping of emblems of historical value or even prohibited the speaking of Native language.[43] Before long the experiment began proving itself a total disaster.

Government-appointed Indian agents were for the most part honest men who worked hard to improve the Indians' lives and to familiarize them with the laws they were expected to obey. Their counterparts, the church-appointed Indian agents, also worked hard—at proselytizing on behalf of their religion. Many were thieves, intent only on increasing their own fortunes. Few cared about improving lives or upholding laws. Those who were caught feared no punishment beyond dismissal from their posts; as often as not they were simply transferred to another reservation.

When Grant left the White House, his successor, Rutherford B. Hayes, eventually realized how badly the situation had eroded. Following investigations, Hayes rescinded the churches' authority and the BIA resumed control through special agents who brought back some of the mutual trust that had been lost during the years of church control—and by men like Henry Spalding. (See Appendix J.)

[APPENDIX D ENDNOTES]

1. Chief Joseph, "An Indian's Views of Indian Affairs," *North American Review,* April 1879, 412–13.

2. Conversation with William Louie, an elder of the Okanagan Tribe. [Author's files, 1996.]

3. Bath was incorporated by the City of Wheeler. A marker to Spalding's memory stands in the area where Bath was once located. Because the facts of Spalding's early years are fragmentary, his actual birthplace is open to question, but he always said it was Bath, New York. A recent biographer claims new evidence has come to light indicating he was born either at Troy, Pennsylvania or at Prattsburg in New York State's Steuben County. Bath, however, seems correct. Spalding's father was from Pennsylvania, which may be the reason behind the speculation.

4. Full text of Henry Harmon Spalding available for viewing at *www.archive.org/*

5. It is not known whether or not the members of the board were aware of the Osages' complaints, but it seems likely. Very rarely were novice ministers transferred so readily.

6. Though Whitman, a medical doctor, was not an ordained minister, he was authorized as an assistant missionary. This enabled him to hold informal services and teach classes in religion. His profession, however, was in the field of medicine so his main concern with the Cayuse Indians was as a healer. His work with the Natives earned him accolades within his church, which gave rise to the myth that he was a "Father of Oregon statehood..." The accolades did not extend to the Cayuses, many of whom thought he was giving their land to white settlers. In 1842 he was unable to stem a cholera epidemic that swept through the Cayuse tribe, killing

many. Cayuse warriors and chiefs blamed him, claiming he was poisoning the Indians. The warriors rampaged, destroyed the mission, killed Marcus and Narcissa and many mission workers. The four major leaders were later hanged. [McWhorter, *Hear Me My Chiefs*, 69–71.]

7 There had been some initial concern about Henry joining the company because prior to his marriage with Eliza he had courted Narcissa most ardently. When she refused his proposal of marriage Henry took the rejection hard. Obviously, though, Eliza soothed his pains and later he and Narcissa renewed their friendship on a most respectable level. However, Marcus may have harbored a jealous streak within his saintly bosom. The two men remained cool towards each other and at times their friendship was strained. [McWhorter, *Hear Me My Chiefs*,. 69–71.]

8 "Time was when the Sioux, a brave people, were not afraid to die. But then the missionaries came among us with their story of the Christian endless hell and now they are afraid to die." [Chief <u>Mochunozhin</u> [Standing Bear], Oglala Sioux, 1868–1939.]

9 "They [the Nez Perces] have learned enough to fear the consequences of dying unforgiven, but not sufficient to embrace the hopes and consolations of the gospel." [Rev. Samuel Parker, *An Exploring Tour Beyond the Rocky Mountains* (New York, 1843) 283.]

10 McWhorter, *Hear Me My Chiefs*, 50–74.

11 White men shortened and anglicized his Nez Perce name to Big Thunder. The full interpretation actually reads: Thunder-sounding-loudly-in-the-distance.

12 Spalding nominated Ellis in 1842 for appointment by Washington as the designated Head Chief of the Nez Perce. However, the Nez Perce did not generally recog-

nize the title. Ellis died during his self-imposed exile in Montana.

13 The list of punishments is astounding. Drawn up as a code of laws, it lists the crimes and punishments in eleven articles. [Drury, *Spalding*, p 296; also McWhorter, *Hear Me My Chiefs*, 65.]

14 Allen, *Ten Years in Oregon,* 205.

15 Narcissa Whitman was so very much alarmed at the introduction of the Book of Rules she begged her husband, Marcus Whitman, not to impose its contents on the Cayuse people. Whitman disregarded her concern. He was never disposed to cruelty or severe discipline, as was Spalding, but he saw no harm in holding the book over his charges as a tacit warning. This error in judgment might have influenced his eventual fate to some degree.

16 For a time, the Spalding resorted to selling artifacts and ornamental garments made by their students to individuals passing on their way to settle new farmlands in Oregon and Washington. This further diminished their luster in the eyes of the uncommitted Nez Perce, who thought it unbecoming to resort to such wayside bargaining.

17 The Nez Perce employed only two punishments: whipping with a birch rod for major crimes, or the punishment of exile. Women and children were exempt from both.

18 Among Plains and Plateau Indians, indeed among all the tribes of the northwest, children were treated with kindness almost to the point of being spoiled. Small children were considered very special beings, and those who had physical or mental handicaps were given special attention and treated most kindly.

19 Missionaries kept a firm grip on their biased approach to Native rights until 1922, at which time, under the en-

lightened administration of Indian Commissioner John Collier, Indians were granted the Right of Freedom of Religion; and later Collier convinced Congress to grant them recognition as American citizens. [McWhorter, *Hear me My Chiefs*, 86.]

20 Those interested in the troubled life of Eliza Hart Spalding are advised to search the archives at the University of Idaho rather than rely exclusively on biographies already written, most published many years ago by friends. [Frazier, Julia, *Peaha Soyapu*.]

21 In 1847 an attack on the Lapwai mission by the Cayuse warriors who had killed Whitman was looming as a distinct possibility. Eliza refused to flee to the safety of William Craig's farm because it was Sunday and travel was forbidden on the Sabbath. That interdict had not deterred Henry. Nonetheless, Craig and several Nez Perce warriors remained to defend the mission. On Monday they escorted her to Craig's farm and safety.

22 Big Thunder had no need to participate in the war as his traditional lands were within the reservation proper, even after the treaty of 1863 had reduced the area allotted in the 1855 pact. His only real objection was the limitations of travel, the authority granted to missionaries, and the addition of bands to the reservation.

23 A long-held belief that Wala'mute'kint left Lapwai because of a disagreement with Big Thunder is incorrect. Those two chiefs never had any falling out. The disagreement, such as it was, had been with a medicine man with a similar name, Loud Thunder, from another band. Loud Thunder had expressed an opinion that the Lapwai Valley was not large enough to support three bands. Wala'mute'kint, not wanting to become embroiled in an inter-band squabble—and planning on leaving anyway—moved his departure time ahead by several days. [McWhorter, *Hear Me My Chiefs*.]

appendix d

24 Many Wounds (also known as Bloody Chief) had been one of Spalding's followers until he turned against the mission to join the Dreamers. His personal history reveals a man who taught in a Methodist Bible-study group, knew scriptures well and was able to quote them when discussing secular subjects. He left the mission because he disagreed with the missionaries' attitudes towards his people. During the 1877 uprising he fought in all the major battles and surrendered with Joseph at Bear's Paw. He eventually returned to Lapwai where he served as interpreter for many interviewers. [Author's files.]

25 McWhorter, *Hear Me My Chiefs,* 72.

26 Spalding's influence among the Nez Perces had so diminished by 1847 that only twenty warriors could be found willing to escort him to safety. An ironic detail of this arrangement was that the warriors had to be asked by Spalding's enemy, William Craig. In contrast, no less than forty warriors escorted Eliza to Craig's farm a day or two later. [Ibid.]

27 The term, Manifest Destiny, was coined on December 27, 1845 when a newspaperman named John O'Sullivan, editor of the *United States Democratic Review,* wrote an article in which he outlined his vision of the nation's future. [O'Sullivan, John, "The Great Nation of Futurity." *United States Democratic Review,* Vol.6, issue 23, 426–430.]

28 Both Lee and White came under intense criticism during their respective tenures in Oregon-Idaho. According to Clifford Drury, the leading historian of Protestant missions and missionaries of the northwest, Lee was "a good man but he made mistakes of judgment." He quit his mission in 1845 and returned east where he died in 1847. In 1906, his remains were returned to Oregon for reburial at Salem. [Thrapp, Don L., *Encyclopedia of Frontier Biography,* Vol. 2, 831]

In 1860, White was denied reappointment as Indian agent following intense complaints by settlers and Indians alike. He went to Washington to plead his case. He returned to Oregon in 1861 with a paper issued by President Lincoln naming him a "Special Indian Agent." However, because Lincoln's paper defined neither his mission nor his responsibilities, no one paid any attention to him. Shortly thereafter he moved to San Francisco where he resumed his medical practice. [Thrapp, Dan. L., *Encyclopedia of Frontier Biography*, Vol.3, 1549.]

29 Quoted from the testimony of one John Toupin, as recorded by J.H.A. Brouillet. Author's note: Brouillet was highly prejudiced against Spalding and associates and may have embellished Toupin's testimony somewhat. [House Executive Document No. 38, 35th Congress, 1st Session, 18–19.]

30 Kinnikinik (the leaves from what today is called the bearberry plant) gives a mild, pleasant smoke. Because it contains no nicotine or tars, it was a harmless pastime that caused no ill health. Even after tobacco became available from trappers and others, Nez Perces rarely smoked genuine tobacco, but on occasion a shred or two would be mixed in with the Kinnikinik. [Author's files.]

31 Eliza died January 7, 1851, four years after she and Henry had fled from Lapwai.

32 One interesting fact about intertribal marriage is that upon his first marriage the groom would move to his bride's tribe. Chief Joseph, for instance, was the second son of Wala'mute'kint, a Cayuse who had married a daughter of a Nez Perce chief, then moved to the Wallowa Valley band and eventually became the band chief. [Nez Perce History files.]

33 Inter-tribal warfare is a study in itself, but a simple explanation is found in the Indians' concept of warfare. War

and hostility were not exclusively tribal, but could be between bands only or even between individuals. This partly explains why, during the latter days of the 1877 uprising, Nez Perce scouts near the Canadian border where lured to their deaths by Assiniboine hunters showing kindness while at the same time Assiniboine families gave refuge to many Nez Perces who were attempting to escape the siege at Bear's Paw. [Author's files.]

34   Missionaries were generally unable to check polygamy on either side of the border. It was not until police in charge of law and order within the reservations or the resident Indian agents began (often reluctantly) to enforce federal laws that an end was brought to the practice. Even this took time, as enforcement varied from state to state and province to province. [Author's files.]

35   Kate adhered to the views prevalent at the time within the society of which she was part that non-white races were of limited intelligence and needed white guidance for their own good and betterment. Given also the circumstance of having been born and raised in England, this prejudice was even more deep-rooted. On the other hand, her older sister, Sue, had worked longer in the field (on Choctaw and Cherokee reservations) and had adopted a more enlightened view. [See: *K&S McBeth Allotments,* Special Collections, University of Idaho Library. Boise, Idaho.] See also Frazier, Julia: Peaha Soyapu.

36   The Wyakin, in many ways similar to the Christian concept of guardian angels, was a personal spirit that every Nez Perce had as a guide and protector. When Nez Perce boys and girls reached their tenth year they would venture alone to some sacred place. There they would seek their Wyakin through meditation and prayer. If the prayers were accepted, a Wyakin would appear to them as a symbol, often a bird's feather or a bone of some

small animal. The recipient would keep the symbol all his or her life (sewn into a shirt or some item of clothing, or worn as a necklace or bracelet). The Wyakin would guide and protect the Indian so long as the symbol remained with the person. While Wyakins were under no obligation to protect their humans at all times (such as during stupid or foolish acts) for the most part they did an admirable job. [Author's files.]

37 In this she was incorrect. Her own religion also held to the tenet that each person possessed a guardian angel and, had she studied the matter in a less biased spirit, she would have learned that any differences between her students' Wyakins and her own guardian angel were really not that dissimilar. Such, however, is the cost of prejudice and intolerance. [Author's files.]

38 Like most religions of that era, the Presbyterian Church would not admit women to the ranks of ministers, a prohibition McBeth fought against all her life. She must have made some good points in her ongoing arguments, however, for eventually women were accepted for ordination. The first female minister in the US was ordained October 24, 1956, an event that undoubtedly caused the body of John Knox to spin wildly in his grave and that of Kate McBeth to stand up and shout. It would certainly have given Kate a deeper degree of eternal rest.

39 When the Great Spirit did at times intercede on behalf of humans, he usually did so through Coyote, the greatest of the lesser spirits. Most Plains and Plateau Indians held Coyote in high esteem as a good spirit. Pacific Coast tribes generally considered Raven or Thunderbird as the mightiest of the lesser good spirits. No Indian tribe, so far as is known, actually "worshiped" the Great Spirit. [Meyers, E.C., *Children of the Thunderbird,* passim.]

40 At first "They [the Nez Perce] were not inspired toward Christianity, nor did they have need to seek a higher

moral standard." This observation is made in numerous documents and publications. [Haines, Francis, "The Nez Perce Delegation to St. Louis in 1831," *Pacific National Review,* vol. 4, March 1937. Later, Haines expands his observances in *Red Eagles of the Northwest,* 59–60, The Scholastic Press (Oregon, 1939).]

41   Spalding did not win all his arguments. In one well-documented discussion he insisted all warriors must cut their long hair. The warriors disagreed and one stated, "If God is so opposed to the length of a man's hair why did he not have had us all born bald?" Spalding quickly dropped the subject. His sermon in which he railed against men having two or more wives was dropped from his Sunday repertoire when a chief pointed out that the "Sky Book" tells the story of King Solomon "who had a thousand wives." [Nez Perce Historical site: *www.nezperce.com*]

42   Most northwest tribes subscribed to similar ideas. Tribes along the Pacific coast believed in the Land of Mists where spirits of the good find happiness and eternal rest with the Supernatural People. Others imagined the dead would be welcomed into a sort of parallel universe guarded by the Keepers. Some Plains Indians had a Happy Hunting Ground, but The Nez Perces did not subscribe to such a place. That denoted the killing of animals and in an afterlife there was no need for food; and because all creatures lived together in harmony there would be no need to kill animals or anything else. [Meyers, *Children of the Thunderbird,* 17–126; and *Totem Tales,* 54–63.]

43   In the US, English became compulsory, while in Canada English or French became mandatory depending on the reservation's religious authority.

Appendix E: Arthur "Ad" Chapman— A Villain of the Piece

To this day most researchers consider it a great mystery why Chief Joseph, who at first regarded Ad Chapman as his friend, remained loyal to him for some time after Chapman had been exposed as an absolute scoundrel. Certainly Joseph's suspicions should have been aroused at White Bird Canyon after it became common knowledge that Chapman had fired upon Nez Perce riders approaching under a flag of truce. Perhaps he accepted Chapman's later explanation that he had fired out of surprise when the riders emerged suddenly from behind a rise—although few others believed him. Chapman was, by far, too trail-wise to be snuck up on.

The fact that Chapman was commanding a small group of volunteers he had recruited should have revealed him to be untrustworthy then; and events over the next six years certainly proved he was hardly a man of integrity. Even though the loose standards of the era applied to many white men, Arthur Chapman was a man who exceeded the definitions of treachery and deceit.

Arthur "Ad" Chapman was one of two sons born to William Williams Chapman and his wife, a woman of French extraction. Although no birth date for baby Arthur is on record, he is believed to have been born c.1840 in Burlington, Iowa. He was named for his maternal grandfather, Arthur Ingraham. In 1847 William moved his family to Oregon, where his work was instrumental in the founding of Portland. In 1861 he was named the first surveyor-general of Oregon, a position he held for many years.

Arthur's boyhood, normal for the times, was spent mostly in the woods where he learned survival, trapping, hunting, shooting and riding. He also learned to tell mammoth lies, not only in English but also in several native languages and dialects. He learned to speak fluent Nimiputímt, the Nez Perce language that is both difficult to master and to speak eloquently. This was the sole important attribute that eventually ensconced him in Chief Joseph's world. Another, albeit of lesser importance, was that Chapman's first wife was one of Joseph's cousins. Before he rid himself of her, Chapman fathered her five children.

He was fourteen years old when he was first mentioned as a government employee for services rendered during the 1855 Rogue River Indian War. He had been hired to run dispatches between the army camps at The Dalles and Walla Walla.

Chapman also learned as a youth that it was easier to attain worldly goods through treachery than honest endeavor, lessons that guided him throughout his life. When he was twenty-one he acquired land near White Bird Canyon. A small creek meandering through his land that he named after himself still bears his name. Within a year he had expanded his holdings to a ranch of reasonable size and had acquired sizeable herds of cattle and horses. How many had been obtained legally remains unknown.

Chapman grew to be a mean, hot-tempered, brutish man of low morals and few ethics. He thought nothing of whipping Native children who displeased him. He was not above strong-arming men who withheld information he wanted. In 1882, when he was a translator to the Nez Perce exiles, he finagled employment as an assistant to Hiram Jones, the corrupt Indian agent at the Quawpa Reservation in the Indian Territory. Jones was pleased with his new assistant because he got results. On one occasion he strung up an Indian by the thumbs to force him to disclose the names of several Indians that Jones suspected of drinking. In the same year he also impregnated a thirteen-year-old Modoc girl, but denied knowing her and brushed aside her parents' accusations. Jones refused to investigate the charges. Chapman had no regard for women considering them mere servants and objects for his sexual desires—and age meant nothing.

Over the years Chapman was the subject of numerous accusations and denunciations that ranged from suspicion of horse theft, cattle rustling to embezzlement of Indian funds.[a] He was accused of murder, fraud, bigamy, spousal abuse, harassment, and sexual misconduct, which included rape and child molestation. Such behavior and lifestyle ultimately exacts a price, and Chapman's cost was a total loss of respect from Whites and Indians alike. He cared not at all, as he apparently considered such accusations as nothing more than the cost of doing business. Among the Palu, Cayuse, Modoc and Nez Perce tribes no one could be found who had a good word to say of him. He was equally hated by Sioux and Blackfeet tribes whose paths he had crossed.

His several wives were mostly Indians, but two were white. He treated none of them kindly, although his first came out better than any of the others; when he sent her and three of their five children back to her family, he gave her a herd of good horses. Perhaps he did this because she was Joseph's cousin, as this was prior to 1875 when he still feared Joseph. However, he kept the two oldest boys to work on his ranch. As for his other wives, except for his last who survived him, he simply abandoned them or sent them home to their families when he tired of them.

How Chapman acquired his nickname, "Ad," is not verified, but is generally thought to have come about through a business venture. For several years he owned and operated a ferry crossing on either the Salmon River or the Snake River (reports differ, but favor the Salmon River). His customers took to calling him "admiral," which obviously pleased him as he kept it, eventually shortening it

---

[a] *In a blatant con game, h was charged with taking money from several naive Nez Perces on the pretext of arranging their return to Lapwai. As usual, he denied the charges.*

to "Ad." The idea of possessing a military rank became an obsession, because in later years he used a variety of ranks at various times in his efforts to acquire government positions.

In 1877, when the uprising by the non-Treaty Nez Perce bands had become a fact, he wrote a letter to General Howard in which he offered his services as commander of a large unit of volunteers he said he intended to recruit. To gain some capital, he signed the letter Captain Arthur Chapman, assigning to himself an army rank despite having no regular army service time. Howard probably knew no evidence existed of him having served in *any* military capacity beyond running messages during the Rogue River War and later serving as a scout during a Palouse uprising. General Howard declined the offer.

Chapman's offer of a squad of militia volunteers was later accepted by Captain Perry during the battle at White Bird Canyon, but his volunteers were so few in number they were assigned a rear position. Undaunted, Chapman later claimed he had conducted the campaign at White Bird Canyon. This claim has been dismissed by everyone as just another of his many tall tales. His sole claim to celebrity at White Bird Canyon is his infamous cause of starting the battle. In later years Chapman promoted himself to "colonel," a title of strictly honorary rank cherished mostly by ex-Confederate officers who would not accept the CSA's defeat in the Civil War. Chapman, however, had never served the CSA in any capacity; nor had he made any effort to serve the Union.

Following Joseph's surrender at Bear's Paw, Chapman inveigled an appointment as official federal interpreter. He was hired because he had served as Howard's intermediary with Joseph, was one of the few Whites fluent in the Nez Perce language, and Joseph did not mention to anyone that he distrusted him. The position ensured him steady employment at a decent salary and an expense account. More importantly, it gave him the opportunity to indulge in self-serving situations, which he worked to full capacity.

As an official translator he accompanied the exiled captives to Leavenworth, Kansas and then to the Quawpa Reservation in Indian Territory. Quawpa was ruled over by Hiram Jones, a Quaker-appointed Indian agent, one of the most corrupt agents in the history of the Indian Territory reservations. During his tenure he shortchanged the Indians on their beef and medicine allotments, and hired crooked contractors to work on the reservation and greedy merchants to supply goods. His share of this graft was a percentage of the gross profit. Chapman, immediately seeing great opportunities, arranged to be hired as an assistant agent. It was not long before he and Jones were in a power struggle.

Chapman spread word that Jones had shortchanged the Nez Perces 5,000 pounds of beef, all in one week. Jones retaliated by firing Chapman, who then immediately went to his friend, Alfred Meacham, a rights activist. He told Meacham about Jones offering to arrange a return to Lapwai for any Indian who would become a Quaker. Meacham talked to Joseph about this but Joseph, while he didn't deny it, dismissed it as a rumor. No Nez Perce, he told Meacham, would give up his faith in the Wéset to become a Quaker. Meacham, apparently considering Joseph's statement biased, supported Chapman. Shortly afterwards, Chapman was reinstated on the order of the chairman of the BIA Standing Committee, Ezra Hayt.

One afternoon a BIA commission arrived unexpectedly at the reservation. Jones was informed he was under investigation by the Bureau of Indian Affairs, and the commission would conduct an investigation into several charges. Always the opportunist, Chapman quickly joined those bringing charges of corruption and fraud against the agent. Chapman testified before the commission that he had been aware that Jones had shortchanged the Nez Perces, and reiterated his belief that in one week alone Jones had stolen 5,000 pounds of Indian beef. He stated it was his belief Jones was corrupt. As a result of the investigation, Jones was removed from office and replaced by a new agent who quickly fired Chapman. However, his dismissal did not bring charges of anything criminal against him. He kept his job as translator, as that was not under BIA jurisdiction. By then the Nez Perce no longer trusted Chapman, but there was no way to get rid of him. In June 1879, when the Nez Perces, Cayuses and Palus were transferred to the Ponca Reservation near Oakland Indian Territory, Chapman went with them as translator. During that final trek he later claimed to have been the wagon master, a partial lie. Officially he was, but none of muleskinners and oxen handlers, either Native or white, would follow his directions. They turned for advice and leadership to Joseph, Yellow Bull and Husis Kute, the Palu chief; Chapman was never considered.

Chapman's appointment as translator remained permanent in Oakland, but his downturn was continuing, albeit slowly. One of his final assignments was to accompany Joseph and Yellow Bull to Washington in the winter of 1879 for meetings with members of the Senate. The trip was taxing on all involved as Chapman was already thoroughly hated by Chief Yellow Bull, who had seen through his machinations long before. Several references have been made to Yellow Bull's efforts to distance himself from Chapman. He even refused to stand next to him at photo sessions. While in Washington, Chapman is known to have misinterpreted several statements made by both Joseph and Yellow Bull; but his greatest transgression occurred the morning of the party's departure.

Just prior to leaving Washington, Chapman presented the authorities with a document, purportedly a written translation of the previous night. It was "signed" by Joseph and Yellow Bull. In the letter the pair ceded to Washington all the territory they disputed. The letter gained no credence, as the two signatures were such blatant forgeries that no one considered them authentic. While there were some who gave him benefit of the doubt—because by then Chapman was known to be very ill and probably should not have been at the meeting at all[b]—everyone agreed he had forged the document for his own purposes, which he had, indeed, done. Because neither house of government ever got around to ratifying the document (probably intentionally) much potential damage was avoided. What Chapman had hoped to gain from his subterfuge remains obscure, but it is known he had expressed hopes of obtaining a grant of substantial acreage in the disputed area the two chiefs had supposedly ceded to Washington.

---

[b] . Pearson, Diane J., *The Nez Perces in the Indian Territory,* 156–59.

Then, in 1882, already hated by all, he virtually sealed his own fate when he wrote a self-serving letter to a New York newspaper. In it he declared himself the true champion of the downtrodden Indians. He heaped praise upon himself for his tireless efforts to bring justice to the Nez Perces. Among other self-aggrandizing assertions he claimed to be the real leader of the Nez Perces, with Chief Joseph merely a figurehead who spoke the words Chapman wrote for him. When a copy of the letter arrived at the reservation, a group of warriors, many still angry over his actions in the 1877 uprising, drove him from the agency. They trailed him clear across the Salt Fork River as far as Arkansas City where they cornered him and told him he should never return to the reservation.

Chapman, however, was nothing if not determined, He went to the nearest army fort and complained that young warriors had threatened him and a rancher named Dean; and then, after Dean's escape, they stole several horses and chased him to Arkansas City. The army was alarmed and a Lieutenant Scott and eight troopers rode to the reservation. They found no unrest and no stolen horses. A visit to Dean's ranch showed he was safe and none of his horses were missing. Somewhat confused, Scott and his men returned to Arkansas City, anxious to talk with Chapman. He was nowhere to be found, having skipped town.

Surprisingly, Chapman returned to the agency within three weeks. Once again the situation became nasty when Chapman claimed the young men who had driven him away had threatened to kill him. Agent William Whiteman called a meeting with Joseph, Yellow Bull, some of the Modoc chiefs and Chapman. James Reuben, a Treaty Nez Perce who was also serving in the dual roles of the agency's church deacon and the schoolmaster, also attended the meeting. Reuben listened quietly while Chapman made his accusations about the plot to kill him. Then Reuben rose and called him a liar.

This brought forth an immediate outburst from the enraged Chapman. He turned on Reuben and told him in blunt, profane language that he would be wise to remain quiet or he would end up the next dead Indian. Reuben said nothing further, but he didn't have to. Agent Whiteman had heard enough and ordered Chapman to leave the reservation immediately and never return. Chapman's profane outburst had decided and sealed Whiteman's verdict.

Joseph had already given Agent Whiteman his personal guarantee that, despite ill-feelings towards Chapman, the warriors never had any intention of killing him. Nonetheless, Whiteman grew uneasy following Chapman's outburst against Reuben, as he now realized that Chapman was the most detested man in the entire territory. He feared that if the Nez Perces did not kill him the Modocs would; he was aware of Chapman's rape of the young girl. Both situations might have hastened his decision. By banishing Chapman permanently from the agency then and there the agent may well have saved Chapman's life. Chapman left, never to return.

With Chapman out of the way, agency routine began to stabilize. Joseph and his people began to trust those who acted kindly towards them. By 1885, when Joseph and his followers were returned to the northwest, Arthur Chapman had been three years out of the picture.

Years later, in interviews with researchers such as McWhorter and Elsensohn, notables such as Yellow Bull, Tom Hill, Many Wounds, Eagle Blanket and Joseph revealed that Ad Chapman had been the bane of their existence during all the years of the exile. None of these men, and no small number of women who were also interviewed, were able to relate a single good word about him. Some of those conducting the interviews were surprised because they had been led to believe through earlier accounts that the Natives had considered Chapman a friend. Apparently the earlier writers never bothered to ask the people of the Nez Perce, Cayuse, Palu or Modoc nations what they thought of him.

One of the most telling denunciations of Ad Chapman can be found in *Pioneer Days in Idaho County*, Volume 2, a lengthy history of Idaho written by Sister M. Alfreda Elsensohn, (1897–1989), a nun of the Benedictine Order. She tried hard to find something good to say about Arthur Chapman, but everyone she interviewed told basically the same story: Arthur Chapman was not only despised and hated by those who had personally known him, but all described him as a fraud, cheat, coward, wife beater, sex offender and child molester.

The good sister's normal propensity to find even fleeting value in everyone failed in this case. In fact, despite her outward displays of tolerance and goodwill towards all, a very certain—albeit latent—bias clearly emerges in her paragraphs when she deals with the subject of Arthur Chapman. She, perhaps unintentionally, repeatedly refers to Chapman as "the squaw man."[c] Finally, she was compelled to write the truth of the man's relationship with the Indians.

> *"They [the Nez Perces] considered him to be a coward and a bad man who had given them nothing but trouble, and was not thought of as a friend, a reputation which had sometimes been given him."*

Nonetheless, Chapman lived a relatively long life. When he died in 1924 at around eighty-four years of age, he was living on the reservation at Lapwai because he had married yet another Nez Perce woman—his fifth or sixth, but final, wife—which gave him the right to live on the reservation. Arthur "Ad" Chapman died unlamented, unforgiven and friendless. That he was quickly forgotten is attested by the unknown location of his grave. Wherever it may be, it is without identifying markings of any kind. One may wonder if the old man often awoke during dark nights on hearing the crack of a twig or an unexplainable noise, afraid someone intent on murdering him in his bed was approaching his house.

> Note: The term "squaw man" was not necessarily derogatory, as the emphasis was on "man," not squaw. The word squaw is not derogatory, although some believe it is. According to Professor Margaret Bruchac of the University of Connecticut, a member of the Abenaki tribe and a

---

c   *This term, now rare in the general vocabulary, depicted white men who took Indian women as wives in what was then known as a "frontier marriage." See "note" at end of appendix for expanded discussion.*

recognized authority on Native Studies, "squaw" was a phonetically altered version of the Algonquin word Esqua, which means woman in the totally feminine manner.

The Edmonton, Alberta-based Institute for the Advancement of Aboriginal Women (IAAW) is on record as stating, "From the colonists' inability to pronounce esquao, the northern linguistic equivalent of the Algonquin esqua, the word squaw came to be a degrading term. The IAAW is claiming back the term for all aboriginal women to stand proud when we hear esquao applied to us." The IAAW further informs us that esquao is a word meaning "total femininity" and has nothing to do with anatomy. Neither does it mean simply "wife" as used in some Indian dialects. In recent years, in a case of political correctness run amok, moves have been set afoot to remove squaw from any usage. Some of this effort involves Indian societies, but mostly it is the high-handedness of misinformed white liberals. Some years ago a move to rename Squaw Creek, in Washington State was rejected when several Indian bands objected to the proposal to change the creek's name. To date, none of the many place names employing the word squaw has been changed, altered or eliminated.

The misuse of proper and legitimate words is nearly always the inability of diverse societies trying to assimilate or at least get along together. For instance, there are those who see derogatory connotation in the word "Yankee" without realizing the word came about because the Iroquois, although they had allied themselves with the redcoats, could not properly pronounce the word "english." They called their new friends "yanglace," which in turn became "yankee." [Excerpts used with permission, from the article by Professor Margaret Bruchac appearing on *www.nativeweb.org/pages/legal/squaw.html,* and from the author's files.]

Appendix F:
Chief Joseph Speech to US Congress during 1879 Visit to Washington

At last I was granted permission to come to Washington and bring my friend Yellow Bull and our interpreter[a] with me. I am glad to be here. I have shaken hands with a great many friends, but there are things I want to know which no one seems able to explain to me. I cannot understand how the government sends a war chief to fight us, as it did General Miles, and then breaks the word he gave to us. Such a government has something wrong with it. I cannot understand why so many chiefs are permitted to speak so many differing ways and promise so many different things.

I have seen the great father chief,[b] the next great chief,[c] the commissioner chief,[d] the great law chief[e] and many of the other law chiefs.[f] They all say they are my friends. They all say they will do justice for me. But while their mouths speak right, I do not understand why they do nothing for my people. I have heard talk upon talk, but nothing is done.

---

a   Arthur "Ad" Chapman.
b   President Hayes.
c   The secretary of the interior.
d   Head of the Bureau of Indian Affairs.
e   Chief justice of the Supreme Court.
f   Congressmen and senators.

Good words do not last long unless they amount to something. Words do not pay for my dead people. They do not pay for my country now overrun by white men. Words do not protect my father's grave. Words do not return my stolen horses and cattle. They do not give me back my children. Good words will not make good the promises made to me by your war chief, General Miles. Good words have not given my people a home where they can live in peace and look after themselves.

I am tired of talk that comes to nothing. It makes my heart sick when I remember all the good words and all the broken promises. There has been too much talk from men who had no right to talk. Too many misunderstandings and too many misinterpretations have come between the white men and the Indians. If the white man wants to live in peace with the Indian he can do so. There need be no trouble. Treat all men alike. Give them the same laws. Give them all a chance to live and grow. All men were made by the Great Spirit Chief. They are all brothers. The earth is the mother of all people, and all people should have equal rights upon it. You might as well expect the rivers to run backward as that any man who was born a free man should be contented if penned up and denied the liberty to go where he pleases. If you tie a horse to a stake do you expect him to grow fat? If you confine an Indian to a small plot of earth and expect him to stay there he will not be contented nor will he grow and prosper. I have asked some of the great war chiefs where they get their authority to say to an Indian that he must stay in **one place** while he sees white men going where he pleases. None have been able to tell me.

All I ask of the law chiefs is to be treated as all other men are treated. If I cannot go to my own home,[g] let me have a home where my people will not die so fast. I will go to a Bitter Root Valley.[h] There my people would be happy. Where they are now, they are dying.[i] Three have died since I left them to come to Washington.

---

g   *The Wallowa Valley in Oregon.*
h   *Here Joseph asks for his people to be given one of the many valleys within western Montana's Bitter Root Mountain Range.*
i   *Joseph is referring to the Quapaw Reservation in the eastern area of what is now Oklahoma.*

When I think of our condition my heart is heavy. I see my own race treated as outlaws and driven from country to country or shot down like animals. I know we must change. We cannot hold our own with the white men as we are. We ask only an even chance to live as others do. We ask to be recognized as men. We ask that the laws shall work alike on all men. If an Indian breaks the law, punish him by the law. If a white man breaks the law, punish him also.

When the white man treats the Indian as they treat each other then we will have no more wars. We will be alike as brothers of one father and one mother, with one sky above us and one country around us and one government for all. Then the Great Spirit Chief who rules above will smile on this land. He will send rain to wash away the blood spots made by brothers' hands upon the face of the earth. For the arrival of this time the Indian race is waiting and praying. I pray no more groans of wounded men and women will ever again go to the ear of the Great Spirit Chief above and that all people will be one people.

Heinmot'tooyalakekt has spoken for his people.

> Note: The speech was delivered to Congress in January and was printed as an article by *The North American Review* in its February edition. The article caused interested groups to begin campaigning on Joseph's behalf, and in March the Bureau of Indian Affairs was ordered to investigate the Quapaw Agency to determine the conditions under which the Nez Perce were living. In April, H.W. Jones, the Indian agent, was suspended (fraud and graft charges were laid) and later fired. In June, Joseph's band was transferred to the Oakland Reserve where their conditions improved greatly. By 1885 the entire group had been relocated to Lapwai, Idaho and Colville, Washington.

Appendix G:
Anatomy of Treachery and Deceit

The federal government was no stranger to interpreting "give and take" as meaning "give-now-and-take-later," so the course it was following in 1855 and again in 1863 was by no means new. Treaty treachery had made its successful debut in 1778 with a treaty made with an eastern tribe, the Lenni Lenape [Delaware]. Within a year the treaty was broken when Congress took back a sizable piece of the reserved land, which it then assigned to white farmers. When the Delaware protested, a vigilante group attacked a Delaware village and killed Chief White Eyes.[a] The protest died with the chief.

In 1778, a treaty with the Wyandotte was signed, only to be broken two years later. A large section of Wyandotte land was appropriated and given as battle gratuities to a number of Revolutionary War veterans. The Wyandottes, like the Delawares, had not been consulted. Their protests were ignored.

In 1791, the Treaty of Echota was signed with the Cherokee

---

a   *The Delaware were never compensated for their losses, but following the attack by the frontiersmen they allied themselves with British North America. Following the end of the War of 1812 the British abandoned them. Shortly thereafter the American army subdued them.*

tribe, only to be amended in 1798 with the expropriation of a huge tract of Cherokee land in eastern Tennessee. Again there was no consultation, but a small token payment of $5,000 was later paid to the Cherokees. Treaty amendments sometimes resulted in such token payments, but usually neither consultation nor payments were part of the proceedings. Washington alone decided the courses of action to be taken.

In several cases Acts of Congress broke treaties. The Indian Removal Act (1830) and the Dawes General Allotment Act (1887) put the final degrading touches on treaties signed in good faith by the Nez Perce chiefs. One of the most infamous cases concerning The Indian Removal Act involved the State of Georgia. When that state moved to force the entire Cherokee nation from their reserved land, the Cherokees appealed to the US Supreme Court. In a 9–0 decision the court unanimously upheld the Treaty of Echota, thereby nullifying the removal order—but not the act itself. President Andrew Jackson, who had absolutely no consideration for indigenous persons, ignored the court's order, as did the pro-south US Congress. Georgia proceeded with the removal.[b] The entire Cherokee tribe was forced into exile in a perfidious case of classic treachery. The case, exile, and relocation in Indian Territory (now the State of Oklahoma) are all well documented. The journey to Indian Territo-

---

[b] Jackson is often—and mistakenly—quoted as saying upon hearing of the Cherokee verdict, "John Marshall [chief justice of the Supreme Court] has made his decision. Now let him enforce it." Jackson never said that about the Cherokee verdict and, in fact, he never said it at all. He has been widely misquoted in various instances concerning a statement he made about an 1832 verdict in a case [Worcester vs Georgia] that concerned the State of Georgia and two New England missionaries. The lengthy statement he made about that particular verdict, however, made it easy to apply to the Cherokee case because it nicely summed up his attitude towards Indians in general and the Supreme Court in particular. [Boller, Paul, They Never Said That: Famous Misquotes, 53.]

ry came to be known as the Trail of Tears.[c] Cherokee accounts refer to the tragedy of the relocation as Nu'na'hi'du'no'tlo'hi'lu'i [The Place Where the People Cried].[d]

Emphasis on how merciless the practice of amending treaties can be is seen in the experience of the Oneida tribe of New York. At one time (c.1800) the Oneidas possessed a reservation of some six million acres. Through a number of orderly and regulated amendments and Acts of Congress, over a period of 118 years the treaty was pared away. By 1919 all that was left to the Oneidas was 32 acres.

By 1890 every tribe had seen its original reservation systematically reduced, while some had lost their reservations entirely. The Cherokee of Georgia, the Peoria of Illinois and the Modoc of California were just three of many tribes forcibly exiled to Indian Territory. Others were moved to reservations held by other tribes. A few were simply abandoned to become extinct. Such was the case of an isolated Palu band in Washington State. Treaty makers, perhaps deliberately, had overlooked the band and it was left on its own. The land the band called home was deeded as homesteads to white farmers. By the early 1900s the landless Palu had been reduced to less than two dozen members living in abject poverty. They found shelter wherever they could and scraped out a meager existence. By 1930, the few remaining members of a once-proud band had disappeared entirely. What happened to them or where they went no one knows.

---

c   There are many excellent published works covering the Cherokee tragedy. Most are available through public libraries and major booksellers. [For one of the best see: Ehle, John, Trail of Tears: The Rise and Fall of the Cherokee Nation, Anchor (1997).]

d   The Cherokee exile, however, did produce an ironic twist of fate. During the early 20th century the Cherokees realized the reservation that had been forced upon them was fairly floating on a vast ocean of Oklahoma's oil. The Cherokees, as a result, became a wealthy tribe and with the oil royalties constructed casinos which brought in more returns. [Author's files.]

The 200-year history of treaties between Washington and Native Americans is a study in shame and abjection.[e] Over a period of twenty decades no less than 750 treaties were made law by Congress, although in several cases the chiefs' signatures were later proven to have been blatant forgeries. All 750 were broken outright or amended by Washington in order to accomplish land grabs of varying sizes and importance.[f] What is interesting to note is that no treaty was ever broken by a Native tribe or a single band. The chiefs who signed the treaties had all acted in good faith—and those whose marks had been forged simply complied with the order to move to a reserve. In many cases where government negotiators had signed with honorable intentions, Washington bureaucrats, politicians and presidents proved themselves bereft of scruples, ethics and morals.[g]

Lest Canadian readers smugly say that Ottawa never broke a treaty or took away land, it can only be suggested they read their nation's history. Ottawa's record is not much better than Washington's. Although no troops were ever sent to attack villages or kill women and children, treatment of Native people in Canada was neither fair nor equitable. Ottawa never reduced the areas of reservations for one simple reason: the lands originally ceded to the various bands

---

[e] *Ottawa's history of treaties with Canadian Indians is no less dismal. While the procedures adopted by authorities on both sides of the border are dissimilar, they gained equivalent results. [Mercredi & Turpel, In the Rapids, 80–95. Penguin Books International, Toronto (1994).]*

[f] *New York Times, June 25, 2000. Also: Deloria, Vine Jr., Behind the Trail of Broken Treaties; Long Chain of Abuses: Broken Treaties. www.native-namericanfirstnationhistory.com*

[g] *Two honorable negotiations were made by Isaac Stevens in 1855 and General Oliver O. Howard who, in 1872, signed a mutually acceptable treaty with Cochise of the Chirichaua Apaches. Both treaties were decimated in Washington, Stevens' over a period of years and Howard's in a few pen strokes by Columbus Delano, Secretary of Indian Affairs in Grant's administration. He changed the terms and wording of his own volition.*

were rarely worth taking back. Instead, Ottawa saddled the tribes with The Indian Act, a nefarious piece of legislation that doomed the Natives to an existence of penury and dependence. All that The Indian Act accomplished was to reduce a proud people to the status of being wards of the state; in effect, children who depended on handouts and hand downs.

When Chief White Bird and his Nez Perce refugees arrived in Canada in 1877, he asked only for some land on which to settle. Ottawa not only refused the request, but also declined to help them survive the oncoming winter. Only members of the North-West Mounted Police and some settlers and traders gave assistance. Canadians have nothing to be smug about in Ottawa's treatment of Native people.

Appendix H:
Six Not Forgotten

ALSPOTOKIT

Among those who surrendered with Joseph was an ailing, seventy-year-old elder named Alspotokit [Daytime Smoker], more commonly known as "Clark." His graying hair still had wisps of what had obviously been a full head of hair so light in color it was almost blond. His eyes were blue, unusual for a person of his race. None of the white men knew at the time that this man was the son of William Clark who, with Meriwether Lewis, had blazed the trail to the Pacific in the now-famous Lewis and Clark expedition of 1804–06.

During their return from the Pacific coast in 1806, the expedition members wintered in a Nez Perce camp where William Clark married a Nez Perce woman in what frontiersmen at that time called a "blanket ceremony." A few months after Clark departed, the woman gave birth to a healthy boy. She named him Alspotokit after Clark's habit of smoking his pipe during leisure periods in the afternoons. There are conflicting reports of whether Clark ever learned of his son. While some say he never knew, others insist he did and intended to have his son come east to be educated. Regardless, his death in 1838 put an end to whatever plans, if any, he had for his son.

Alspotokit grew up in the manner of any normal Nez Perce boy. He did well in his lessons in hunting and riding and passed all the rituals from which he emerged a full-fledged warrior. Whether he ever engaged in warlike activities is unknown; but he is known to have been a respected buffalo hunter, and as he grew old younger men looked up to him. He probably married, although nothing is known of that phase in his life. Neither is it known if he had children.

There is no record of Alspotokit actually engaging in fighting during the 1877 trek, but a photo taken in 1863, when he would have been about fifty-seven, features him holding a heavy caliber long gun—and he is known to have been an acknowledged marksman. Thus, it is quite possible he did take up arms during the trek from the Wallowa Valley to Bear's Paw. Many elders are known to have fought at the Big Hole River and even more during the Bear Paw siege.

Alspotokit was fully aware, and was truly proud, of his lineage. Always, whenever asked his name, he would stand proudly, touch his chest and reply, "Me Clark." He surrendered with the others at Bear's Paw and went with Joseph to Leavenworth. He did not survive long enough into the ordeal to get to Oklahoma. Alspotokit, son of William Clark, died, possibly of malaria, in 1878 or early in 1879.[a]

Kot'kot Hihhih

Kot'kot Hihhih [White Feather] (1860–1880), the eldest daughter of Tomupsi Upokpok [Grey Eagle], was in her seventeenth summer when the war started. A member of White Bird's band, she started the trek from the Salmon River with her father, her fifteen-year-old sister (identified only as Lucy), and a Lapwai woman named Mary, whom Grey Eagle had married after his first wife died. The four

---

a   Halsey, Cheryl, *Lewis & Clark Across the Midwest*, 91 and 95. (Hancock House, 2006.)

survived the battle at White Bird Canyon, the battle at the Clearwater River, the journey along the Lolo Trail, the risky crossing of the Bitterroot Mountains and the journey to the Big Hole River.

Tragedy struck the family during the battle of the Big Hole when soldiers' bullets struck Grey Eagle, Lucy and Kot'kot Hihhih. Lucy was killed in the first assault, but Grey Eagle, although mortally wounded, continued to fight through the battle. One bullet, the fatal shot, had struck him in the abdomen and he died in great pain during the second day on the escape trail. The bullet that struck Kot'kot Hihhih knocked her to the ground. A soldier grabbed her and struck her in the mouth with his pistol butt. The blow cut her lip, bloodied her nose and broke a front tooth. She fought back, struggled free and managed to escape to where Joseph was rounding up the non-combatants.

When Grey Eagle died Mary fled, apparently alone, in hopes of rejoining her original family in Lapwai.[b] Her departure did not seem to bother Kot'kot Hihhih, for it seems Mary had never liked either of her stepdaughters, a dislike mutually shared. Mary's desertion left the girl on her own, but another family took her in. With them she shared the rigors of the harrowing trip through the Camus Meadows, Yellowstone Park, Canyon Creek, Musselshell and finally Bear's Paw. Kot'kot Hihhih survived the Bear's Paw siege and during the final hectic days decided to go with those who accompanied White Bird on his run to Canada. She escaped the army's pickets north of the encampment but never reached the border. About twenty miles from the border Assiniboine warriors attacked. She was wounded and fell from her horse. In the confusion she lost contact with the others.

The next day, wounded, lost and disoriented, she was rescued

---

[b]   No evidence exists to determine whether Mary reached safety in Lapwai, if she is among the unidentified dozens killed at the Big Hole, whether she was killed at some point during her escape, or if she was absorbed into some other village along the way. The latter is always a possibility as that happened often in those days. [Author's files.]

by hunters from a Gros Ventre band. After tending to her wounds they took her to their village where she was adopted into a family. They gave her a new name, In'who'lise, which in the Gros Ventre language means "Broken Tooth," a reference to her injured mouth. She retained the name, apparently by choice, and that is the name by which she is remembered to this day. In'who'lise stayed with the Gros Ventre family until early 1878 when she met a young mountain man named Andrew Garcia [1856–1943]. It is at this point in her life that the plot, as the saying has it, begins to thicken; it also becomes very muddied in detail.

When Garcia was nearly eighty years of age he wrote a lengthy, rambling account of his life and the adventures it had held. In it he included accounts of his two years with In'who'lise. Those details, from 1878 until her death in 1880, were included years later in a book, *Tough Trip Through Paradise*. Based on Garcia's autobiographic musings, edited by Bennett H. Stein, the book was published in 1967. Several chapters are devoted to the adventures of In'who'lise during her two years with Garcia. There are however some rather intriguing contradictions—and not a few revisions.

Thirty-five years previously, a noted Montana reporter, William H. Banfill, interviewed Garcia and published the interview in the June 17, 1932 edition of *The Philipsburg Mail*, a Montana newspaper. In the interview Garcia revealed, among other things, In'who'lise's Nez Perce name, Kot'kot'Hih'hi, and that a Lapwai missionary had renamed her Susan. Stein relied on Garcia's spelling of her Nez Perce name. However, White Feather in the Nez Perce language is Tu'u'ynu_Hihhi, but Stein did probably not know that. There may even be other spellings, a not uncommon situation in Indian language translations.

According to Stein's heavily edited version, Garcia and In'who'lise, who he affectionately calls Suzie, were married in late 1878 by an itinerant Catholic missionary named Father Landre,[c] an account similar to that which appears in the 1932 interview but with more detail. However, research has failed to uncover any actual proof that Fr. Landre did perform the marriage ritual in accordance with Catholic doctrine. He would not have done so had he known Garcia already had five wives, all living. The authenticity of the edited version of the Garcia/In'who'lise nuptials depends upon whether one prefers Garcia's original writings or the generally accepted edited version.[d]

The edited version also gives a very tame account of In'who'lise's troubles when she and her new husband went to live in a Pend d'Oreille village. The book claims two women, both asserting Garcia as their husband, roughed her up. The facts, as described in Garcia's writings, are vastly different. The two women, with whom Garcia was indeed involved, were Sow'set and Kat'a'lee. Both were opposed to In'who'lise, who had made it known she believed in monogamous marriage and had no intention of sharing her husband with other women. The two plotted against her but

---

[c] *In that year Fr. Landre is known to have been traveling through Montana with a group of Manitoba Crees and that they stayed a few weeks with the Gros Ventres. Whether he actually performed a marriage rite between Garcia and In'who'lise is not recorded.*

[d] *The 2001 edition of Tough Trip Through Paradise, edited by Bennett R. Stein, is highly criticized by his son, David Stein, also an author. Stein carefully studied Garcia's handwritten original manuscripts and states his father's heavy editing overly romanticized the original. He suggests Garcia stretched his imagination in many instances—and he may have been responsible for In'who'lise's death. Stein has a point, because Garcia's original writings have no less than three versions of that event, each different and in conflict with the others. David Stein's essay on this subject is extremely interesting. Readers wishing to learn more of Garcia and his version(s) of the eventful two years with In'who'lise are directed to:* www.mtpioneer.com/2009-November-Cover-Tough-Trip.html. *It is well worth the trip.*

she found out about their plan and demonstrated her ability to look after herself.

In fact, in the melee that followed, In'who'lise proved herself to be an above-average knife-fighter.[e] Sow'set escaped while In'who'lise was busy stabbing Kat'a'lee three times in the abdomen. Kat'a'lee survived her wounds, following a lengthy recuperative period, but the incident turned all the Pend d'Oreille women against In'who'lise. They plotted to poison her, but that went nowhere when realization sank in that she was not only a survivor but was more than capable of looking after herself. Nonetheless, Garcia took great pains to never leave In'who'lise alone in the village. On this there is agreement in either account.

At one point in 1879 the two returned to the Big Hole River to search for the graves of Lucy and Grey Eagle. Lucy's grave was not found, but In'who'lise believed her sister's spirit had come to her in a dream a night after the search ended. They later found Grey Eagle's grave on the south trail where he died. It was empty. The Nez Perces had buried Grey Eagle, but Bannocks later dug up his body when scavenging graves looking for scalps. She and Garcia found the body nearby in a bush where the Bannocks had discarded it. Garcia then gave him a proper burial.

After they left Big Hole, In'who'lise and Garcia wandered from place to place hunting, trading horses and staying at various Indian camps. He wanted to go to Lapwai but she refused, saying the Nez Perces living there would never accept her because she was a member of White Bird's band whom they blamed, along with Chief Joseph, for the uprising.

In'who'lise was not yet twenty-one when she died. How is not absolutely known, but all versions agree she died violently. Garcia always insisted she met her death at the hands of a Sioux renegade, but kept muddying the waters by changing the circumstances of the attack and the weapon used. Those changes have caused many to believe Garcia killed her. Some think he became convinced she was

---

e   *Garcia mentions in his writings that In'who'lise had previously defeated a Gros Ventre assailant in a knife duel. [Author's files]*

being unfaithful to him. The truth will never be known, so an individual's decision will have to depend on which version is believed. However, all versions agree her two years with Garcia were exciting.

Although Garcia married three more times, his writings would have us believe In'who'lise had been his true love. Nonetheless, because of his many inconsistencies one cannot help but wonder. Also, he never told In'who'lise he had served as a scout for Colonel Sturgis during the pursuit of Joseph at Canyon River and Clark's Fork River. He would never have dared confess that to her knowing how adroitly she had carved up Kat'a'lee. Andrew Garcia died in Montana in 1943.[f]

Charles Scott Erskine Wood

Arguably, Joseph's greatest champion during the long ordeal and beyond was Charles Scott Wood, Howard's erstwhile aide de camp and the interested confidant of Chief Joseph during the days following the surrender at Bear's Paw. Wood, then a lieutenant, grew disillusioned with the army and the hypocrisy of Washington's bureaucrats and high-ranking army officials. He eventually resigned his commission to return to university. He emerged with a degree in law, and moved to Portland, Oregon where he set up practice specializing in maritime and corporate law. He earned respect and renown as a lawyer, often appearing to argue cases before the US Supreme Court. He also became active in civic affairs and developed his interest in the plight of minorities. His thoughts easily returned to the one man he considered the noblest he had ever met: Chief Joseph.

It had been Wood, while still in the army, who had arranged for Chief Joseph and Yellow Bull to visit Washington to meet several top officials. (Wood is thought to have polished Joseph's speech to

---

[f] *Garcia, Andrew, Tough Trip Through Paradise, 1878–1879*, Bennett H. Stein, ed., 1967. University of Idaho Press (Moscow, Idaho). 2001 printing]

Congress for publication as an article in the *North American Review*.) During that visit, in which Joseph spoke many times to many audiences about the history of abuses the Nez Perce tribe had suffered since signing the 1855 Treaty, he had made but one request. He asked that the Nez Perce of the Wallowa Valley be returned to Idaho in keeping with the promises made by Generals Miles and Howard. This promise, he reminded his audiences, had also been previously made by others, only to be broken by the government in Washington. He spoke to them of freedom, justice, rights, freedom to choose one's own religion and the need for Whites and Indians to live together in peace. Wherever Joseph spoke, Wood was usually there to assure the translation was honest. He had dealt with translators such as Ad Chapman on other occasions and was well aware of their knavery.

When Joseph would finish speaking Wood reminded the audience it had been Nez Perces who had befriended the first Whites who had come to their lands, how they had saved the lives of Lewis and Clark and their men during the great expedition. He reminded them of the trust the Nez Perces and trappers of bygone years had enjoyed and nurtured. Wood spoke of justice and the need for tolerance.

Joseph's speeches and Wood's discussions with the officials were reported in the press, and historians who replied to the articles agreed with Wood. The Nez Perces, they wrote, had always been friendly to Whites—and often had been their only friends. Washington officials were reminded that until the killings of the rustlers and settlers near Idaho City and the settlers at Horse Prairie no white men had ever been killed—or even harmed—by the Nez Perces.[g]

No one in authority appeared to listen, so Joseph and his people, still considered prisoners of war but without the dignity afforded such prisoners, languished in sordid conditions in Indian Territory. For six more bitter years Wood continued to plead his

---

g   *Prior to 1877 a Nez Perce had killed only one white settler. According to General Howard, the killer's name was Sa'poon'mas. [Howard, The True Story of the Nez Perce War.]*

case through articles and general lobbying of politicians in Oregon and Washington. He spoke to groups interested in civil liberties and human rights, as well as various church groups that expressed interest in the welfare of Native people.

Wood had often been discouraged, but he continued in his quest. In early autumn 1885 he felt the heady joy of success when the federal government announced the Nez Perces must be returned to the Department of the Columbia. The army was ordered to carry out the transfer as quickly as possible—or as military terms put it, forthwith. Wood, the soldier turned lawyer turned civil rights champion had won his greatest case.

Besides being a champion of the Nez Perces, he later supported the causes of Tom Mooney and Sacco and Vanzetti, which resulted in his becoming known as a "philosophical anarchist." During his long life he wrote many books and articles and became a painter of note. One of his more notable articles, "Chief Joseph, the Nez Perce," appeared in the May 1884 issue of *Century Magazine*. His only book with a western theme, published in 1901, was titled, *A Book of Tales: Being Some Myths of the North American Indians*.

Wood was born in Erie, Pennsylvania on February 20, 1852, and died, 30 days short of his ninety-second birthday, on January 22, 1944 at his home near Los Gatos, California.

Wetyemtmas Wahyakt

Although he was one of the original three renegades who caused the uprising, Wetyemtmas Wahyakt [Swan Necklace] survived the war. He apparently fought bravely at the Battle of the Big Hole, showed great courage at The Bear's Paw and then surrendered with Joseph, going with him into exile. While in exile in Indian Territory he was befriended by James Reuben, a Treaty Nez Perce who had become a Presbyterian minister. Swan Necklace's conversion by Reuben allowed him to resettle at Lapwai. In the interests of his safety he had foresworn his Nez Perce name of Wetyemtmas

Wahyakt and was baptized as John Minthon. As Idaho settlers were still determined to bring the White Bird Canyon renegades to trial, his true identity remained known only to a few residents at Lapwai. The Nez Perces, having obviously forgiven him for his youthful escapades, no doubt feared Idaho settlers would take revenge on him regardless of how much time had elapsed. Thus, none ever revealed John Minthon was Swan Necklace. Swan Necklace lived out the remainder of his life as a farmer respected by the white community. He died on his farm during the late 1920s.

WAAYA'TONAH TOESIT'KAHN

Another youngster who would achieve fame after the 1877 uprising was Waaya'tonah Toesit'kahn [Blanket of the Sun]. Born in 1863 in the Wallowa Valley he was a nephew to Chief Joseph and a cousin to Suhmkeen [Shirt On]. When the war started he had not yet turned eleven years of age, so was not eligible to be proclaimed a warrior or allowed to participate in a buffalo hunt. He was, however, an accomplished rider and horse handler, talents that were to serve him well during the long trek and for many years beyond.

When Joseph led his people from the Wallowa Valley he detailed his young nephew as a drover in charge of horses; and when Joseph joined the other bands at Split Rocks, the chiefs and warriors of the other bands, recognizing the eleven-year-old's ability, had no reluctance in allowing their horses to join the Wallowa herd. Waaya'tonah Toesit'kahn soon became the "go-to" man for advice in the herding of horses. Each morning he and several young companions arose early to tend to their charges, and if it was a moving day they began early to move the great herd along the trail. It was a formidable task keeping over a thousand horses under control. Over the many hundreds of rugged miles traveled, the drovers lost a few horses, most of which were cut loose intentionally due to injuries or other reasons that kept the animals from keeping up. Some were traded to settlers along the way, and at Bear's Paw some were used as food.

When the surrender at Bear's Paw appeared inevitable, the youngster joined White Bird's refugees and herded many of their horses into Canada. It was not long before local settlers and ranchers learned of his expertise with horses. He was soon in great demand by ranchers who readily hired him to tend their livestock and break wild horses to the saddle and harness. He was never unemployed and as his fame spread he was invited to enter local rodeos in which he won prize money on a regular basis.

In 1879 he returned to Montana to live secretly on a Flathead reservation. He worked quietly on a ranch whose owner kept him from being discovered by authorities. He was now calling himself Jackson Sundown. In 1910 he returned to Lapwai, took an allotment of land and built a cabin.

He also resumed his rodeo career, and it was not long for Jackson Sundown to become a crowd favorite. In 1911, in the finals for the world championship saddle bronc event at the Pendelton Round-Up, he placed third, a decision the crowd considered robbery. They felt he had earned first place and loudly protested, but the decision stood.

In 1912 he married Cecilia Wapshela and they moved to Jacques Spur, Idaho (near Lewiston) where he built up a ranch. He continued in rodeo competition, winning so often that others, not wanting to risk their entry money, refused to compete against him. However, the inevitable injuries that are part of rodeo riding were beginning to take a toll. By 1915 he was thinking of retiring, but entered the Pendelton Oregon Round-up for one final try at the world championship. He again placed third and announced his retirement. Fate, however, had another plan.

Alexander Proctor, who had hired Sundown as the model for a sculpture he was working on, told him he would pay the entry fee if Sundown would try once more. So, in 1916, Sundown entered the event. Over the grueling week that followed he beat out all the top riders until only he, Rufus Rollen and Bob Hall, both top riders, were left for the final rides.

Sundown drew a vicious brute of a horse facetiously named "Angel." The horse had previously thrown 127 riders, so no one thought the fifty-three-year-old Sundown had much of a chance against him. When the chute door swung open, Angel exploded into the arena in a series of leaps, twists, circles and bone jarring landings. Again and again the horse tried to dislodge the rider, but Sundown stayed in the saddle until some watchers came to believe horse and rider had melded into a single entity.

In those days the ten-second rule had not yet come into being, so a ride continued until the judges saw fit to call a halt—or the rider ended up in the dust, whichever came first. No one remembered how long that ride continued, but it was far in excess of ten seconds. When the judges finally signaled an end to the ride, Jackson Sundown was still in the saddle but "Angel" was a thoroughly subdued horse, broken of spirit.

The cheering lasted a long while as the horse was led meekly from the arena and Sundown walked slowly to the railing. Then a hush fell over the crowd. For a long moment the 20,000+ spectators remained silent, perhaps expecting the judges to declare yet another robbery. Then came the judges' decision: Jackson Sundown, first place! The hitherto silent crowd erupted in thunderous cheers. It was the first standing ovation ever seen at the Pendleton Round-Up. Jackson Sundown, age fifty-three, survivor of the Nez Perce War, nephew of the legendary Chief Joseph was now the world saddle bronc riding champion. That evening he retired.

In 1923, Waaya'tonah Toesit'kahn died of pneumonia. He was buried in the Slickpoo Mission Cemetery near Jacques Spur. A monument to his achievements was raised later. In 2006 he was inducted into the Rodeo Hall of Fame at Fort Worth, Texas.

Suhmkeen

Suhmkeen [Shirt On], a cousin of Jackson Sundown, was born in the Wallowa Valley, Oregon in 1867. When the war broke out he was only ten years of age, but was already an accomplished horse wrangler. Because of these talents, Chief Joseph assigned him the task of assisting his older cousin in tending the great herd belonging to the band. From the meetings at Split Rocks until Bear's Paw he helped with the entire herd of the five bands. It was an enormous responsibility, but the two cousins, with the help of some others and a couple of older men, did an admirable job.

Suhmkeen and his family escaped to Canada with White Bird from the Bear's Paw rather than surrender. They lived there until about 1880, when he and his parents returned to Montana, but they stayed very close to the Alberta border. They worked for ranchers until they went to a Flathead reservation where Suhmkeen was enrolled in the Carlisle Indian Residential School. In 1910 he returned to Lapwai with his parents; but when he graduated he returned to Montana. Now known as Sam Tilden, he joined the Flathead Reservation Police Force, serving twenty years. When he retired from the police force he returned to Lapwai to manage the family farm.

In 1940, Helen A. Howard and Dan McGrath, who were collaborating on their book, *War Chief Joseph,* approached him for an interview. They were searching for eyewitnesses from 1877 in hopes some would reinforce their theory that Joseph had been the overall chief during the flight. Sam Tilden agreed to talk with them and they later claimed he had substantiated their theory. Perhaps he had, but he was a seventy-three-year-old reaching back for memories from 1877 that were those of a child. Joseph, his uncle, would likely have stood out to a ten-year-old boy as being the bands' war leader. In fact, the young people who had been part of the 1877 uprising did indeed think Joseph was the leader. In'who'lise, another famed Nez Perce teenager, certainly thought he was.

When old age caught up with Sam Tilden he took residence in an old folks' home near Washington State's Tri-Cities. He died there on Friday, January 29, 1965, aged ninety-eight. Suhmkeen was one of the last remaining survivors of the 1877 Nez Perce War.[h]

---

h   *Tri-City Herald,* Richland, Washington, January 31, 1965.

Appendix I:
Inter-tribal Animosity and Distrust: Contributions to the Ultimate Defeat of the Indian Nations in the West

The North American Indians had little hope of defeating the European flood of settlers bound for western expansion. This was not because the possibility was not there, but because the Indians simply could not get along together. Millennia of inter-tribal animosity, distrust, suspicion and prejudice made such a victory impossible. The Indians themselves had forced entire tribes from traditional lands in their own expansion.

The Carriers had lived for centuries in what is now northern Alberta. Anthropologists and historians now believe they were driven from their traditional lands by hostile tribes, and, as a result, presently inhabit northern British Columbia. A second case concerns the Inuit of the Arctic. Scientific evidence indicates the Inuit, always peaceful to a fault, once occupied lands some distance to the south, perhaps as far as southern Alberta, but were steadily pushed northward by stronger tribes coveting their hunting grounds.

The Cherokees were generally considered as having been the occupiers of the land area now known as Georgia for centuries. Treacherous lawmakers, with the connivance of President Andrew Jackson, forcibly displaced them during the 18th century. The language spoken by the Cherokees, however, is a variance of Iroquois, indicating they were once inhabitants of northern New York or southern Ontario. Expansion of tribes now resident in that area indicates the Cherokee tribe was driven south by their more militant cousins, the Cayugas, Oneidas, Iroquois and/or Ticonderogas.

The Apaches of the southwestern United States quite likely originated in what is now Manitoba, a far distance from their present homeland. How did this come about? Their language is a variance of Athapaskan, the root of many northern languages. In probability, the Crees and Ojibways, in their separate advances, drove the Apaches from Manitoba. Unable to find a welcome in Minnesota, and then Kansas, the Apaches continued southward, ending up in Texas and Arizona.

Disputes over territory and hunting grounds usually led to inter-tribal warfare, which forced weak tribes to move on. Occasionally a weak tribe would assimilate with a stronger one, unless they located a tribe of lesser strength, whereupon they would drive them out and take their land. Many strong tribes were engaged in ongoing warfare over so many decades that by the 17th century even tribal elders had no recollection of the beginnings of hostilities. Chronologies of hostilities between Apache and Hopi, Sioux and Crows, Iroquois and Huron are murky, the genesis of each having been lost in the mists of time.

Often tribes were so greatly reduced through the attrition of warfare the various bands were forced to disperse and integrate with others or face extinction. Among all tribes the resultant loss of young men through wars became so inordinate that females came to outnumber males. This gave rise to the necessity of plural wives in order to keep the population at a viable level.

It is not that no one ever thought to abolish war, the cause of the deficit. There were tribal prophets and visionaries over the centuries who made attempts to unify various tribes, but most failed; and on occasion when an effort succeeded, it rarely lasted long. None was ever fated to combine great numbers into one united nation.

There was a real Hiawatha, but several others are also remembered as historical personages in the quest for unity. There were undoubtedly others, most of whom are forgotten, while some have been relegated to obscure legends. Probably the best remembered is an Onondaga shaman named Ayenwatha who lived during the early years of the 12th century. He is immortalized in the epic poem *Hiawatha* by Henry Wadsworth Longfellow, who exercised a great deal of poetic license in his poem's composition, including changing Ayenwatha's name to Hiawatha. Ayenwatha was a disciple of a Mohawk mystic named Deganawida.[a] He managed to unite several eastern tribes into an alliance from which the Six Nation Confederacy eventually emerged.

Other factual idealists to gain prominence over the years were Black Hawk, Tecumseh, Joseph Brandt and Pontiac, all of whom had political leanings. Others, such as Smoholla, Sitting Bull and Skolaskin, were of spiritual inclination. They prophesied the coming of a great chief, a messiah who would unite the tribes and drive the Whites from the lands. Sitting Bull, the Hunkpapa shaman, proselytized the belief for some years prior to 1876 through the dogma of the Ghost Dancers. Whether he really believed the concept is difficult to say. Following the 1876 Sioux-Cheyenne victory over the U.S. Army at the Little Bighorn, he never mentioned it again.

Over the centuries other alliances were formed. The little known AHT confederacy of the northern Pacific coast was primarily a commercial pact between Nootka and Kwakiutl tribes.[b] Another was the Blackfeet Confederacy of several tribes whose lands ranged from southern Alberta into central Montana. None flourished for long, nor did any produce workable defense pacts. Nez

---

a   *Deganawida was a prophet who became known as the Great Peacemaker. He preached that an evil spirit, a foe of Manitou, the Great Spirit, would introduce white serpents into the land but that Manitou would do battle against the serpents and emerge victorious. At that point Deganawida would return to rule over the entire land in benevolence and peace. [A Mohawk and other Six Nations legend.]*

b   *During the AHT Confederacy, capturing slaves continued, indicating it was not taken seriously by either partner.*

Perce and Selish tribes made trade agreements (c.1600). Blackfeet and Cree chiefs agreed (c.1860) to a peace treaty that finally ended decades of their devastating wars.

No inter-tribal alliances and confederations produced anything other than loose unions. Because no binding obligations were placed on member bands, there were no commitments for one or more tribes to come to the aid of any other—and few ever did. Even within individual tribes there were known differences that sometimes led to inter-band clashes. Few tribes possessed either central leadership or a central authority to prevent such behavior. The pressure rested with the individual band chiefs to avoid such occurrences. Trade agreements faltered through backsliding and non-cooperation. Such an apolitical system could never regulate or direct the conduct of individual bands within the tribe; ergo no tribe had truly genuine cohesion. Few systems work well without some degree of central direction. Unfortunately for the Indians of the northwest, none of their tribes had any cooperative system at all. Theirs was very similar to the 20th century hostility among Europe's Balkan states and the short-lived United Arab Republic of the 1960s. Both are modern-day examples of tribalism.

Through long centuries of existence, bands were autonomous entities, aligned with their tribes only through language, customs, legends and religion—and even these were often subject to variance. Band chiefs were not bound by decisions made in tribal councils, nor for that matter were individuals bound by decisions made by their band chief. There were no set rules for warfare and few for social intercourse, of which one interesting aspect was marriage. In most western tribes, a man who married outside his tribe or band was expected to leave. He would move to his wife's camp, becoming in the process a member of her band and tribe. This meant a change of allegiance, a practice that seemingly caused no great rancor, but did little to extinguish, or even alleviate, animosity between tribes.

It was this type of enmity and distrust that hindered the non-Treaty Nez Perce chiefs in their quest for freedom in 1877. The Nez Perce bands that had signed the contested treaties were domiciled at Lapwai under the Treaty of 1863. They refused to support the Nez Perce bands either morally or militarily. The Crows, whom the Nez Perce warriors had helped defeat the Sioux only four years before, had promised their Nez Perce allies lifelong assistance if ever it was needed. The Crows not only turned against them in 1877, but advised them to surrender and accept life on a reservation. Then, pouring salt into that wound, Crow warriors assisted the army in locating their trail, and at Canyon Creek assisted the army in attacking their former allies.

The Crows' betrayal had stung, but the worst anguish felt was when many Nez Perce warriors from the Lapwai reservation joined Howard's army as scouts. Some assisted the militia in the fighting at White Bird Canyon, a demonstration of the concept of brother against brother. Such behavior was, and is, considered at least morally wrong, but it was part of North American Indian philosophy.

During their flight from the Snake Creek battlefield at Bear's Paw, Assiniboine and Gros Ventre warriors attacked many escaping Nez Perces for no other reason than they were from another tribe. Ironically, members of those two tribes also helped Nez Perces. The most help offered was from Sitting Bull's Sioux followers, even as Sioux scouts working under Miles' command were trying to track them down. Meanwhile, in Nebraska, another Sioux chief, Crazy Horse, was offering his help to the army against the Nez Perce.

Following his own surrender, Chief Crazy Horse of the Oglala Sioux told General George Crook he was more than willing to lead his followers against the Nez Perces. "I will fight until not a single Nez Perce remains alive," he told Crook. The translator (many historians believe intentionally) repeated Crazy Horse's words as, "I will fight until not a single white man remains alive."

Crook, furious, ordered Crazy Horse be returned to his cell in the fort's stockade. Crazy Horse, not knowing his statement had been mistranslated, was confused and puzzled. Why, he wondered, was he being he denied the chance to fight the Nez Perces? He struggled with his two guards, who were also Sioux tribesmen, and they shot him. A microcosm of treachery from a greater sphere? Tribe against tribe, brother against brother, warriors against a chief points to this. While this remains a hypothesis there seems no other explanation.

The reasons for the lack of inter-tribal cooperation seem to lay in distrust, animosity and hatred. There was no advantage to any single tribe to turn against their kindred beings who, though not of the same tribe, were certainly of the same race. That they turned against their brothers who were in rebellion against the white interlopers is not easily explained and is perhaps inexplicable. Many would consider it reprehensible. The rebels were in protest against the same mistreatment giving despair to all the tribes. In the overall scheme of things, and the turn of history, the North American Indians hastened their own defeat and decline.

Appendix J:
Religious Denominations in Charge of Reservation Agencies

Missionaries and their regulating authorities directly and indirectly caused much of the trouble leading to the 1877 Nez Perce War. Prior to 1874, individual chiefs regulated missionaries among the Indians, barring them if they did not trust them or their message, and sometimes because of conflicts between the different groups vying for converts. The Grant Administration (1869–77) dealt with this confusing state of affairs by signing an accord with the diverse denominations. Each denomination would be given one or more reservations to which they would send missionaries to administer religious and educational affairs, and also assign members of their faith as Indian agents to supervise the reservations' fiscal affairs.

This arrangement was certainly not approved by the Indians, as no Indian bands were consulted prior to the edict, nor were they considered in any way; however, this issue was totally overlooked. The only objections raised were those by several of the religious groups because the reservations were not allotted equally. The complainants were denominations that had been bypassed, as well as those who considered themselves shortchanged. The Roman Catholic Church, for instance, felt snubbed because it was assigned only seven reservations, whereas the Methodists were allotted fourteen. Episcopalians groused at the Unitarians being included because they were not considered full adherents of the Christian faith. In retrospect, it does seem the method of allocation was more than disproportionate.

Also never regarded were the Indians' opinions about which denomination would prevail over their spiritual well being. It mattered not to Washington which ones they might have accepted—or refuted, as would undoubtedly have been the case in some instances. They simply had no say in the matter. This caused ill feeling in many tribes that had no use for missionaries bent on downgrading their traditional beliefs in their Great Spirit. Chief Joseph was paramount among the dissenters.

It was not long before evidence arose indicating that many of the church-appointed agents were dishonest, and that not a few of the missionaries were petty tyrants. Washington, of course, paid no heed to the Indians when they complained; but when a number of concerned Whites took up the cause, Washington began to pay attention. The Bureau of Indian Affairs took notice, but nothing was done until 1877 when Grant's term ended.

When Grant left the White House and Rutherford B. Hayes took the presidential helm, the BIA began to take action, chiefly because Carl Schurz, Hayes' secretary of the interior, was a genuine humanist and vocal champion of minorities. At least he tried to be until Hayes shut him down. Hayes personally had little, if any, concern for the Indians' plight, but was inclined to listen to complaints by white settlers and merchants who were also being victimized by dishonest agents.

When it became obvious that agents with sticky fingers were reaching deeply into the tills and wallets of merchants, while at the same time cheating ranchers supplying beef to the Indians, Hayes cancelled the Grant Agreement, probably the only action he ever took to benefit Native people in any way. Secretary Schurz quickly ordered the BIA to undertake a far-reaching investigation and take corrective measures. It was the only good thing he was able to do for the Natives during his term as secretary because Hayes blocked all his other good intentions.

The BIA set about replacing the church-appointed agents, but the clerics fought back, delaying the process to such a degree Hayes' term was a fading memory before BIA investigators managed to oust all the dishonest agents. The investigators, however, were nothing if not doggedly determined to appoint government agents; so, by 1890, all church-appointed agents had been replaced by federal Indian agents.

The BIA agents quickly cleaned up the reservations' fiscal problems while investigative committees followed. Their findings resulted in several high-profile prosecutions. Among those charged was Hiram W. Jones, the notorious agent who had operated his own little empire on the Quapaw Reservation in Oklahoma where Joseph and his Nez Perce followers had spent two years of their exile. Joseph was continuously at odds with Jones during those years.

By 1895 all reservation affairs were under direct supervision of BIA Indian Agents.[a] Eventually, Natives were released from the grip of religion-by-mandate, and residents of many reservations debated other viewpoints. Several returned, at least in part, to their traditional ways of worship.

---

a   See: *Frantz, Klaus,* Indian Reservations in the United States, *21–23; and Prucha, Francis Paul,* Documents of United States Indian Policy, *141–43.*

Church-assigned Indian Agent Operations in 1877

Denomination	Principle Area	Number of Reservations
Presbyterian	Southwest	9
Presbyterian	Northwest	2
Methodist	Northwest	14
Lutheran	Texas	1
Dutch Reformed	Northeast	5
Episcopalian	The Dakotas	8
Baptist	Nevada	5
Unitarian	Colorado	2
Unitarian	Southeast	1
Congregational	Midwest	4
Roman Catholic	Washington Territory, Oregon/Montana Territory, The Dakotas	7
Quaker (Orthodox Friends)	Kansas & Nebraska	1
Quaker (Hickside Friends)	Indian Territory	6
Christian (non-denominational)	Washington Territory, New Mexico	2

Appendix K: Original Tribal Names of Western Tribes Mentioned in the Text

Original Names in Correct Languages & their Meaning	Names Today [with origins]
A'aninin [White Clay People]	Gros Ventre [Big Bellies]. Named by French-Canadian trappers for their physical appearance.
Absaroke [Bird People]	Crow [Anglicized from original name translation]
Asanaki or Ksunka [Mountain People]	Kootenai. A Blackfoot word meaning Beyond the Mountains [so called by the Blackfeet who objected to their hunting on prairie buffalo grounds]. In Canada spelled Kootenay.
Bana'kwut [See: Panaili]	Bannock. A segment of the Panaili. Named by Scottish trappers for the flat breads they baked that reminded them of cakes popular in Scotland.
Dakota & Lakota [The Allied People]	Sioux. Misnamed from an Ojibwa word meaning Little Snakes.

Dzitsista [Our People]	Cheyenne. Misnamed through Whites' misunderstanding of Tsitsistas, a Sioux word meaning "relatives of the Cree."
Illiniwek [The Best People]	Peoria. Misnamed by white settlers from the area in Illinois they inhabited.
Ininiwok [The People]	Cree. Misnamed by French-Canadian trappers but the word has an uncertain origin. The Sioux called them Cheyenne.
Kalispel [Camus Gatherers]	Pend d'Oreilles [Ear Pendants]. Named by French-Canadian trappers for the ear pendants the people wore.
Kootenai [See: Asanaki]	
Myannmia [Allies or Friends]	Miami. A corruption of their original name by early settlers. Not a Florida tribe.
Ndee [The People]	Apache. Anglicized from a Zuni word meaning "enemy."
Nesilextch'n [Salish People]	Sans Poil [without body hair]. Named thus for no known reason by French-speaking Canadian trappers.]
Newe (pronounced Nuh'wuh) [The People]	Shoshone. The Shoshone do not know why or when the name was changed.
Nimipu [The People]	Nez Perce [pierced noses]. Misnamed by French-speaking Canadian trappers who mistook some other tribe's habit of piercing their noses for ceremonial purposes. The practice was not a Nimipu custom.

Nuut'siu (also Nuntzi) [The People]	Ute. Thought to be a corruption of the tribal name.
Palu & Naham [People of the Rock]	Palouse. Anglicized from Palu, probably by trappers.
Panaili [Northern People]	Bannock. Named by Scottish HBC trappers because the flat bread the Panaili and the Bana'kwut made greatly resembled their own, which they called bannock.
Pikunin [Short Robes]	Peigan.
Ponca [The People]	Original name was kept.
Qwulhwaipum [Prairie People]	Klickitat. A Chinook word meaning "Beyond the Mountains" and so named by the Chinooks. It was assumed by Whites to be the proper name.
Selish [proper spelling of Salish]	Flatheads. Misnamed by trappers. These Selish flattened only the foreheads [through a long but painless procedure and then only those of their royal babies].
Sihgomen [The Sun People]	Spokane. Named by trappers, probably for the nearby river.
Siksika [People with Black Feet]	Renamed "Blackfeet" from English translation. Reference to their practice of darkening new moccasins in campfire smoke.
Snake	No original name known. This is a branch of the Shoshone tribe.
Tetawken [We People]	Cayuse. Named by French-Canadian trappers for the gravel terrain on which they lived. *Cailloux* is French for stones.

Tsitsistas [Our People]	Cheyenne. Whites misnamed this tribe as they misunderstood the Sioux name for the Cree.
Tukuaduka [Sheep Eaters]	Shoshone.
Ugakhpa [Downstream People]	Quapaw. Anglicized from pronunciation.
Walla Walla [People of Many Rivers]	One of the few tribes to keep its original name.
Wanapum [River People]	Another tribe that kept its original name. It is the only tribe that never accepted a treaty with Washington and managed to survive. To this day they remain independent.
Waptailnsim [People of the Narrow River]	Yakima. Probably from trappers' name for the river.

Nez Perce Band Names

Alpowai [People of the Butterflies]	Named for their place in Lapwai.
Asotin [Clear Water People]	Named for their Clearwater River location.
Lamtama [Of the Lamtama River]	Named for a tributary of the Salmon River.
Piqunin [People of the Snake River]	Named for location. Not of the Snake Indians.
Wellamotkin [Wallowa Valley People]	Named after their Chief Wellamotkin

Appendix L:
Names of Warriors & Some Others of Note Involved in the 1877 War and/or its Prelude and Aftermath

Nez Perce Name	English Translation
Aihits Palojami	Fair Land (Ollokot's wife)
Alahmoot	Elm Limb
Alla'koliken	Buck Antlers
Alspotokit	Afternoon Smoker
Apis Wahyakt	Flint Necklace
Chellooyeen	Bow and Arrow Case
Chuslum Hahlap Kanoot	Naked Foot Bull
Chuslum Moxmox	Yellow Bull
Eapaleckt Ilppilp	Red Cloud
Eashlokoon	[translation unknown]
Eelahweema	About Sleep
Elaskolatat	Animal Entering a Hole
Elootpah Owyeen	Shot in the Belly
Eoye Kam	Shell Rock
Espowyes	Heavy Weapon
Gosawyiennight	Bull Bait

Hahtalekin	[translation unknown] (Palu)
Heinmot Ilppilp	Red Thunder (Chief)
Heinmot Tosinlikt	Bunched Lightning
He'mene Moxmox	Yellow Wolf
Heyoom Bakatimma	[translation unknown]
Heyoom Moxmox	Yellow Grizzly Bear
Heyoomekahlikt	Grizzly Bear on his Back
Hohots Ilppilp	Red Grizzly Bear
Howlis Won'poon	War Singer
Howwallits	Mean Man
Husis Owyeen	Wounded head
Husis Kapsis	No Hair
Husishusis Kute	Naked Head (Palu)
Ilatakut	Bad Boy
In'who'lise[1]	Broken Tooth (Gros Ventre)
Jouwolkonton	[translation unknown]
Kapoochas	[translation unknown]
Ketalkpoosmin	Stripes Turned Down
Kipkip Owyeen	Wounded Breast
Koklok Ilppilp	Red Raven
Kool'kool Si'yah	Spying Raven
Kool'Kool'Snehee	Red Owl
Kot'kot Hihhih	White Feather
Lahpatupt	Bone Twice Broken
Lah'peeah'loot	Geese Three Times Landing
Lee'peet Hessem'dooks	Two Moons
Lelooskin	Whittling
Mimpow Owyeen	Wounded Mouth
Moositsa	Four Blankets
Nennin Chekoostin	Black Raven
Ollokot	Frog (Chief)
Otskai	Go Out
Pahkatos Owyeen	Five Wounds
Pahkatos Qohqoh	Five Ravens

Pe'nah'wehmon'mi	Helping Another
Peo'peo Ipsewahk	Lone Bird
Peo'peo Hih'hi	White bird
Peo'peo Tholekt	Bird Alighting
Sarpsis Ilppilp	Red Moccasin Tops
Seekumses Kunnin	Horse Blanket
Sees'koomke	No Feet
Semu	Fiery Coals
Sewattis Hihhih	White Cloud
Silooyam	[translation unknown]
Suhmkeen	Shirt On
Tahkoopen	Shot Leg
Temme Ilppilp	Red Heart
Teeto Hoonod	[translation unknown]
Teetouton	[translation unknown]
Teewee'yownah	Over the Point
Tettus Telumtikt	Last Time on Earth
Timlihpoosman	[translation unknown]
Tipyahalahnah Kapskaps	Strong Eagle
Tip'yah'lah'nah Siskan	Eagle Robe
Tomupsi Upokpok	Grey Eagle
Tomyahnin	[translation unknown]
Tookleiks	Fish Trap
Waaya'tonah Toesit'kahn	Blanket of the Sun
Wahchumyus	Rainbow
Wahlitits	Shore Crossing
Waptas Wahhaikt	Feather Necklace
Wattes Kunin	Earth Blanket
Wawookya Wasaw	Lean Elk
Wayakat	Going Across
Wayouh'yuck	Blue Leg
Weesculatat	Wounded Mouth
Welweyas	Coulee (or Dry Gulch)
Wetti'wetti Howlis	Vicious Weasel

Wetyemtmas Waahyaht	Swan Necklace
Wetyetmas Yahonyeen	Three Feathers
Weyatanatoo Lapat	Sun Tied
Why'lim'lex	Black Feather
Wi'yyu'kea' Ilppilp	Red Elk
Wottolen	Hair Combed Forward
Yahtteen'cilu Kitaniyin	Metal-eyed Crane
Yoomtis Kunnin	Grizzly Bear Blanket
Zya Timenna	No Heart

[APPENDIX L ENDNOTES]

1   See: Kot'kot Hihhih. She was renamed by the Gros Ventre family who rescued her from Assiniboine hunters.

Appendix M:
Recent Thoughts on Joseph's Motives

In the years following the 1877 uprising, writers, scholars and historians of Old West affairs gave a great deal of thought to the causes of the war and the effects of the surrender. Ultimately, a number of survivors of the trek and the Siege at Snake Creek (officially known as Battle at Bear's Paw) were interviewed from time to time about the journey and their ordeals, but none of the interviewers ever asked their subjects for their opinions of what—indeed, if anything—had been achieved; and none seemed overly curious about the personal views their subjects might have held concerning the chiefs involved. Neither did any ask about their own understanding of the motives that had sparked the uprising. This lack of curiosity also precluded them seeking opinions from Joseph about his motives for extending beyond the defeat his failed crusade for regaining the Wallowa Valley. Had they done so, the number of books written and theories expounded may well have been fewer.

More importantly, the legend that built up around Joseph might never have expanded and flourished as it has. But no one asked the Nez Perce survivors until 1927 when L.V. McWhorter took an interest, lasting many years, during which time he delved deeply into the subject. Eventually, the activities in 1877 became an old issue. Most profess disinterest in the subject and others decline to make any comment at all.

Those who will comment are, as might be expected, either dedicated to, or very much opposed to, the Joseph legend. In fact, the Nez Perces themselves have always been very much at odds on the subject, the divisions being mainly within the two reservations of Lapwai and Colville. The descendants of the Nez Perces who, for varying reasons, remained in Oklahoma rather than return to the Northwest,[a] and those who no longer keep close ties to either reservation are, by and large, disinterested. These people prefer to keep their own counsel or, as one elderly man told this writer, "Who cares? Both sides lost."

Kent Nerburn in his recent (2005) book, *Chief Joseph and the Flight of the Nez Perce: The Untold Story*, which is based on Joseph's life and times, suggests the truth of the matter is that Joseph was less a champion of a just cause than a self-serving opportunist. Nerburn's findings appear to be almost equal in proportions of pro and con, as he apparently conducted a "straw census" among residents of both Colville and Lapwai. He found that the majority of Joseph's admirers—who are mostly descendants of those who followed Joseph in 1877 and are a small percentage of the overall Nez Perce population—reside in Colville. Most of the Lapwai residents have no kinship or connection to Joseph and are either indifferent to him or do not agree with his efforts to be returned to the Wallowa Valley. Nerburn implies that only when Native "pro" votes are merged with votes from white supporters does Joseph emerge a bonafide hero. His book is an interesting study in complexity, yet holds irony in that both views can manipulate opinion.

In Nerburn's judgment (and this writer tends to agree), the many complex reasons for this difference date back prior to the war and continued well into its aftermath. Unfortunately, he does not include any "block" quotations nor does he identify the Nez Perces

---

a   Contrary to common belief there are many Nez Perces in Oklahoma. [Pearson, J. Dianne, *The Nez Perces in Indian Territory*. See Foreword.]

with whom he spoke. Thus, without the benefit of an official survey it is impossible to determine the accuracy of his observations. Nonetheless, this writer also found serious differences in opinion, although I could not uncover many reasons supporting as great a difference existing as Nerburn suggests.

Joseph's Nez Perce admirers are found mainly in the Colville reservation area[b] located near the Washington town of Nespelem. This is hardly surprising considering the reservation's Nez Perce residents are, for the most part, descendants of the non-Treaty Wallowa Band who, because they were followers of Joseph, were denied residency at Lapwai.[c] His detractors are found mainly at Lapwai, whose ancestors were mostly descendants of those who had accepted both the 1855 and the 1863 treaties. They tend to view Joseph with a jaundiced eye. His admirers among Whites garner their information mainly from the legend that grew over the decades until it became larger than life. They find little opposition within their own society.

The reasons for the disparity are simple to define. The argument generally stems from Joseph's long struggle to overturn what he felt was an injustice to his people. The root cause of the uprising was Washington's order to three Nez Perce bands to give up their lands in the Wallowa Valley and the Salmon River area. Then, after the surrender, Washington refused to honor the terms of surrender agreed to by Howard, Miles and Joseph. Those terms would have seen the rebels returned to Idaho for resettlement at Lapwai. Instead, officials in Washington, out of force of habit one suspects, tore up the surrender document and sent the dissidents to Kansas and later to Oklahoma. That injustice was further increased when Washington decided Joseph and his followers should be moved from Oklahoma to Colville after first indicating resettlement would be at Lapwai. That Joseph agreed to settle at Colville was more a matter

---

b   It is a touch of irony that Colville is located a very short distance from the Canadian border, Joseph's original destination.

c   There are Nez Perce descendants among the Piegan band of southern Alberta. For the most part they express little interest in the legend.

of personal safety than desire. As explained in the main text, Idaho settlers had erroneously labeled Joseph as the war chief responsible for the Idaho outrages. Army telegraphers with lazy fingers caused much of this belief.

Originally, bureaucrats in Washington on the whole had few objections to sending Joseph and his followers to Lapwai, but they were dissuaded through intense lobbying by the two surviving chiefs of the original triumvirate, Timothy and Jason and Chief Lawyer's son (who had inherited his late father's position), their allies the Lapwai missionaries and Kate McBeth (Lapwai's resident tyrant missionary-teacher). All were vocal in their disapproval of Joseph's return. Adding to the lobbying were Generals Sherman and Sheridan and other military officials who were still smarting from the humiliation they had suffered at the hands of the dissident Indians. They did not want them returned to Idaho. In fact they did not want them returned anywhere near the northwest.

What becomes obvious is that all concerned greatly feared Joseph. The army feared further insurgence. The Lapwai chiefs were certain he would exert behavioral and political influence on the reservation's restless youth, and although not sure to what extent Joseph would influence the people as a whole, were certain his influence would weaken their authority. The missionaries feared a resurgence of the Dreamers, and (particularly Miss McBeth) greatly feared losing the grip they held over their flock; the allure of Christian spiritual values was still tenuous with many Nez Perces not far removed from the animist tenets of their forefathers. All groups in opposition feared Joseph's residency in Lapwai would undoubtedly disrupt the status quo they had so painstakingly established since 1855. The Washington bureaucrats were duly convinced and Joseph was resettled at Colville where he would have no influence beyond his own band members. In this they were proved correct.

The Natives already at Colville, as they themselves quickly pointed out, were so diverse and varied they had no interest in the tribulations of the Nez Perces or their wish to return to the Wallowa Valley. As a result, Joseph found himself seriously limited in the pursuit of his dream. Nonetheless, he continued his quest aided by a gathering force of white supporters.

As interest in the unfair settlement of the 1877 war increased, so also did Joseph's legend. Books, in the form of novels and dime magazine fictions, became popular and very soon he became popularly regarded as having been *the* Nez Perce tribal chief. Adding to the legend were various appellations, such as Napoleon of the Plains and The Red Napoleon, bestowed upon him by white writers. These provided emphasis to the adulation that sustained his efforts to regain title to the Wallowa Valley. It is also here that his detractors find common ground for their accusations that he was first and foremost an opportunist whose only real concern lay not with the Nez Perce tribe as a whole, but with the remnants of the non-Treaty bands in general and those of the Wallowa Valley Band in particular.

Joseph's detractors point mainly to one irrefutable fact: Joseph never once denied or offered any amendment to the belief held by so many that he was the de facto chief of the Nez Perces or that he was a brilliant tactician and field general. Indeed, if anything, he encouraged the legend, albeit in a decidedly tacit manner, by simply making no comment whatever on the claims. That his friends and allies among the Nez Perce bands also remained silent convinced detractors that a conspiracy of silence existed. While conspiracy is highly unlikely, it is a fact that only rarely in the many interviews with the survivors of 1877, including important chiefs such as Yellow Bull and Yellow Wolf, did any mention that it was White Bird, Tool'hool'hool'zote and Looking Glass, and not Joseph, who had devised the tactics that had so humiliated the Army of the Northwest. With Joseph not denying the claims—and no others offering disputation—his legend and reputation inevitably grew.

So the question arises: are the detractors correct in their surmise? The answer appears to be both yes and no. It is true that Joseph was never head chief of the Nez Perce, for there was no such position until the department of the interior unilaterally crowned Hallahotcuut [Lawyer aka Aleiya] to their newly minted position of head chief. Washington's naive bureaucrats, in their belief that no nation could exist properly without a senior executive, could not understand how the Nez Perce had existed successfully for many hundreds of years without a grand chief at the helm. Jason and Timothy paid lip service to the appointment because it assured them security in their own small demesnes. Joseph, moreover, was the only major chief to survive the war and his band was the largest of the five involved. These are the only real factors that produced the basis for the legend of Joseph, Chief of the Nez Perces.

The second argument presented by detractors contains absolutely no truth at all. Joseph, despite their efforts to lay the blame squarely on his shoulders, was *never* the major instigator behind the uprising. He, in fact, had spoken most vocally against it. He and his brother Ollokot had been lonely voices advocating a pacifist approach to relocation. Joseph would have gone to Lapwai but was drawn into the war by well-recorded circumstances over which he had no control.

Their third argument holds some truth, for Joseph was not the all-important essential architect of the tactics employed by the Nez Perce warriors during the battles with the army. In fact, his input was limited in the extreme. The accolades, and rightly so, belong to White Bird and Tool'hool'hool'zote, for those two were initially the major war chiefs. White Bird (and later Looking Glass) was without doubt the prime architect of the unusual tactics. Joseph, because he aided in the deployment of the warriors at the onset of the various battles and encounters, certainly had input in their development and implementation. After Weippe he had little voice in the meetings and was basically charged mainly with the safety and well-being of the women, children and elders. Evidence indicates he played only minor roles in the fighting. It was at Bear's Paw that he took on the role of primary chief, following the demise of Looking Glass, Ollokot and Tool'hool'hool'zote, and White Bird's successful escape to Canada.

Therefore, because Joseph chose, deliberately or otherwise, to allow his legend to grow uncurbed with no restraints it can be said he used it to serve his own purposes. He was indeed a man of shrewd intellect and firm commitment, but to what degree he intentionally exploited it for his own purposes depends greatly upon which side of the argument one accepts. As in all such debates, when the legend overruns the facts the verdict must rest with the individual.

Timeline of Joseph's Life and the Nez Perce War

1836	Henry Spalding establishes a mission at Lapwai.
1837	Chief Old Joseph becomes a follower of Spalding; enrolls his village children into the school.
1840	Joseph born; named Heinmot'tooyalakekt.
1842	Heinmot'tooyalakekt given the Christian name Joseph and is enrolled in Spalding's school.
1845	Old Joseph and Chief Big Thunder (James) break with Spalding. Old Joseph removes the children from the school and resettles his band in the Wallowa Valley.
1855	The Walla Walla Treaty (ratified by Congress in 1859).
1860	Gold discovered at Clearwater.
1863	Looking Glass the Elder dies. His son becomes chief.
1863	Washington proposes amendments to the 1855 Treaty. Old Joseph, White Bird and others oppose the amendments. Old Joseph leaves the conference after condemning Lawyer and Spalding, whom he accuses of causing all the troubles.
1863	Chief Lawyer forces through the revised treaty which surrenders 90 percent of the 1855 reservation.
1864–7	Although these years were peaceable, ongoing problems arose from time to time that caused unrest.

1865		Joseph's older brother, Sousouquee [Brown], is killed.
1868		First settlers arrive in the Wallowa Valley.
1871		Old Joseph dies. Heinmot'tooyalakekt (Chief Joseph) becomes co-chief with brother Ollokot.
1873		Wallowa Reserve established by President Grant.
1874		Nez Perce council held at Lapwai.
1875		Wallowa Reserve dissolved by Grant.
1876		Wilhautyah murdered by two settlers. Charges dismissed (lack of evidence). Much unrest. Rutherford B. Hayes elected president of US in November.
1877		
January	06	Nez Perce informed by General Howard of a conference at Walla Walla scheduled for April.
March		Hayes inaugurated as president.
April	01	Ollokot meets Gen. Howard at Walla Walla.
	20	Ollokot meets Lt. Boyle at Walla Walla.
May	03	Howard meets with Joseph et al at Lapwai.
	07	Howard arrests Tool'hool'hool'zote.
	07	Chiefs tour Lapwai for four days.
	10	Chiefs agree to move to Lapwai. Tool'hool'hool'zote released from stockade.
June	01–10	Nez Perce begin move to Lapwai.
	10–12	Chiefs Council at Tolo Lake.
	13–14	Settlers killed by three enraged braves avenging a mass horse theft. Fifteen warriors ride out to retrieve horses; up to 11 settlers killed.
	14	Howard sends Perry to arrest the three braves.
	16	Perry arrives at Norton's Ranch; short rest.
	16	8:00 pm: Perry arrives in Grangeville.
	16	10:00 pm: Perry decides to move on to White Bird Canyon.

	16	Chiefs decide to fight, if necessary.
	17	4:00 am: Perry arrives at White Bird Canyon with his dead-tired troops.
	17	Joseph sends team for truce talks.
	17	"Ad" Chapman treacherously fires on team Shots exchanged.
	17	Battle at White Bird Canyon. Army defeated.
	18	Nez Perce move to Horseshoe Bend.
	19	Nez Perce cross Salmon River; camp near Craig's Ferry.
	18–27	Army bury dead; find wounded and missing.
	25	Howard arrives with 700 reinforcements.
	29–30	Howard's troops cross Salmon River.
July	01	Lt. Whipple attacks Looking Glass's village. Looking Glass joins rebellion.
	02	Nez Perce re-cross Salmon River.
	01–08	Joseph evades Howard. White Bird fights series of rear-guard actions.
	03	Lt. Raines and his 12-man unit wiped out near Cottonwood.
	04–05	Battle of Cottonwood. 113 soldiers pinned down unable to retreat or advance.
	05	Militia reinforcements defeated.
	05	Lt. Randall defeated at Camus Prairie.
	06	Looking Glass joins Joseph.
	07	Howard finally crosses Salmon River; loses much equipment in the effort.
	09–10	Battle at Misery Hill. Nez Perce capture army's horses.
	10	Howard surprises Joseph. Battle of the Clearwater begins. Army loses.
	12	Battle at Clearwater ends as Nez Perce withdraw safely to Kamiah.
	13–31	Howard's troops stalled at Kamiah on south side of Clearwater River.

	15	Skirmish at Weippe. Militia defeated.
	16	Howard sends scouting party to search for Joseph.
	16–27	Nez Perce travel the Lolo Trail.
	17	Howard's scouting party killed by Joseph's rear-guard warriors.
	25	Nez Perce reach barrier that will later become known as "Fort Fizzle."
	26	Joseph parleys with barrier's officer, Capt. Rawn. Band camped safely at Grave Creek Meadows.
	27	Fort Fizzle by-passed through subterfuge. Nez Perce cross Bitterroot Mountains into Montana.
	28	Col. Gibbon at Fort Shaw gets orders to intercept Joseph; prepares troops.
	29	Nez Perce camp near Salish village of Chief Charlo. Spend next two days buying supplies in Stevensville. Pay with gold.
	31	Howard prepares to depart Kamiah.
August	01	Lean Elk and family join the group.
	01	Nez Perce depart Stevensville heading south.
	01	Howard moves on to Soldier Meadows, Montana.
	04	Gibbon arrives at Stevensville.
	07	Nez Perce arrive at Big Hole River.
	09–10	Battle at Big Hole River. Colonel Gibbon loses the 36-hour battle; the Nez Perce take serious casualties, but escape.
	11	Howard reaches the Big Hole.
	13	Nez Perce stop near Bannock for short time.
	15	Howard reaches Bannock.
	19	Howard camps at Camas Meadows

	20	The Nez Perce stage a lightning raid on Howard's camp; make off with many supply wagons and the mules hitched to them. All Howard's supplies now in the hands of the Nez Perce. The Battle of Camus Meadows commences; the army loses again.
	23	Nez Perce cross into Yellowstone Park.
	23–31	Nez Perce moving steadily northward.
	26	Colonel Sturgis ordered to intercept Joseph.
September	01	Sturgis positions his troops near mouth of Clark's Fork Canyon. His plan is to ambush the Nez Perce.
	06	Nez Perce exit Yellowstone Park.
	08	Col. Sturgis eluded at Clark Canyon through a ploy. He heads his troops towards the Yellowstone River; once again finds he has been tricked.
	11	Sturgis finds Howard; reports failure.
	12	Sturgis ordered by Howard to begin a forced march in order to overtake the Nez Perce.
	12	Colonel Miles at Fort Keogh directed to ready his troops to intercept Joseph who is now decidedly heading north.
	13	Sturgis encounters the Nez Perce only to be soundly whipped in the Battle at Canyon Creek. Sturgis abandons the pursuit.
	23	Nez Perce cross Missouri River. Army supply depot at Cow Island raided and sacked.
	25	Col. Miles arrives near Musselshell River.
	26	Miles crosses the Missouri River and heads north.
	29	Nez Perce arrive at Bear Paw; camp at Snake Creek.
	30	Miles attacks. His troops are driven back.

October	01	The Snake Creek Siege at Bear Paw begins. Weather turns cold with rain, then snow and Joseph realizes the end is soon to come. During this day Ollokot, Lean Elk ol'hool'hool'zote, and other important chiefs are killed.
	02	Joseph meets with Miles but is arrested. Capt. Jerome is captured by Nez Perce and held hostage for Joseph.
	03	Miles releases Joseph for Jerome. General Howard finally catches up. Negotiations begin.
	04	Joseph agrees to surrender. White Bird and 200 others begin an escape during the night. Looking Glass shot and killed by a scout, Millen Tripp, in the evening.
	05	Joseph formally surrenders. Nez Perce are declared prisoners of war.
	08	Joseph's group leaves for Fort Keogh.
	11	White Bird and followers arrive in Canada at Sioux camp at Sandy Hills, Northwest Territories.
	23	Joseph's group arrives at Fort Keogh.
	31	Leave for Fort Buford in two groups, one overland, and the other by riverboats.
November	05	River Group arrive Fort Buford.
	07	Overland group arrive Fort Buford.
	09	Boat group departs for Bismarck.
	10	Overland group departs for Bismarck.
	16–19	Both groups reunite at Bismarck. Greeted warmly by population and feted at lavish banquets. Washington revokes the terms of surrender; orders Nez Perce exiled to Indian Nations in Oklahoma. Both Miles and Howard are furious, but helpless.
	23	Departure for Leavenworth, Kansas by train.

| | 27 | Arrival at Leavenworth. For eight months they are encamped in squalid tents near a swampy bottom land two miles from the fort. |

1878		
July	05	A visit by officials of Bureau of Indian Affairs (BIA) prompts removal from present location.
	21	Depart Leavenworth, Kansas.
	21	Arrive Baxter Springs, Kansas
	22	Depart for Modoc Reservation at Quapaw Agency, Indian Territory

October — Forty-seven people die from malaria.
Indian Agent Hiram Jones accused of various crimes by contractors and suppliers to the agency.

1879
January — Joseph and Yellow Bull visit Washington DC. Joseph talks with President Hayes and speaks to the Senate; addresses social groups and civil rights associations.

April — Joseph moves, unilaterally, closer to Baxter Springs, Kansas and camps near Spring River in order to distance his band from Jones.
The *North American Review* publishes article authored by Joseph.
Agent Hiram Jones is fired amidst charges of fraud and other crimes against Indians in his Agency.

June — Joseph's people are relocated to the Ponca Indians' Oakland Reserve (near present day Tonkawa Oklahoma). There they engaged in farming and ranching.

1880 — Miles promoted to command the Department of Columbia. Increases his efforts to have Joseph returned to the Northwest.

timeline

1882	Arthur "Ad" Chapman banished from Nez Perce reservation.
1883	Twenty-three widows and orphan children relocated to Lapwai.
1885	One hundred eighteen Nez Perce transferred to Lapwai, Idaho territory. Joseph and his followers transferred to Colville, Washington Territory. Joseph continues his ongoing attempts to convince Washington to return his people to the Wallowa Valley. He continues this quest until his death.
1887	The Dawes Act enacted. This reduces the Lapwai Reservation agreed in Treaty of 1863 by a further 542,000 acres.
1892	Chief White Bird murdered in Alberta, Canada by "Nez Perce Sam", a demented young man who believed White Bird possessed his soul through black magic. Sam also believed White Bird had possessed his sons, both of whom had died. White Bird buried at an unmarked site.
1893	"Nez Perce Sam" sentenced to hang. Many lobby for commutation. Ottawa commutes to life. He dies of TB after six months in prison.
1894	Several of White Bird's followers go to the Kootenay Valley in BC while others return to Idaho. The remainder stays in Alberta and assimilates into the Peigan and Blood tribes.
1899	Joseph allowed to visit the Wallowa Valley.
1902	Joseph visits Washington for final time. Has audience with Theodore Roosevelt.
1903	Joseph visits Carlisle School. Speaks to students; attends a special banquet held in honor of both him and General Howard. The two men exchange toasts and speak of old, long-forgiven antagonisms.

1904
September 21 Joseph dies at Colville, Washington.

1906 Albert Waters elected as his successor. Monument to Joseph erected in a Traditional Nez Perce Ceremony.
1926 Old Joseph's remains reburied at Wallowa Lake. Monument erected.
1995 Hundreds of Idaho Nez Perce gather at Brocket, Alberta for a historic reunion with Nez Perce-Peigan relatives and to search (unsuccessfully) for Chief White Bird's grave site.

Bibliography

BIOGRAPHIES & HISTORIES

Allen, A.J. *Ten Years in Oregon: Travels and Adventures of Doctor White E. White and Lady.* Ithaca, NY: Andrus, Gauntlet and Company. 1850.
Anderson, Ian. *Sitting Bull's Boss: Above the Medicine Line.* Surrey, BC: Heritage House, 2000.
Andrist, Ralph K. *The Long Death: The Last Days of the Plains Indians.* New York: Collier Books, 1964.*
Binns, Archie. *Peter Skene Ogden: Fur Trader.* Portland, OR: Binsford & Mort Publishers, 1967.
Boller, Paul F. and John George. *They Never Said It: A Book of Fake Quotes, Misquotes, and Misleading Attributions.* New York: Oxford University Press, 1989.
Brady, Cyrus Townsend. *Northwestern Fights and Fighters.* New York: Doubleday, Page & Co., 1907.
Brown, Mark H. *The Flight of the Nez Perce.* University of Nebraska Press, 1982.
Carroll, John M. *The Benteen-Goldin Letters on Custer and His Last Battle.* New York: Liveright, 1974.

Carroll, John M. with Byron Price. *Roll Call on the Little Big Horn*. Fort Collins, Colorado: Old Army Press, 1974.

Carpenter, John A. "General Howard and the Nez Perce War of 1877." *Pacific Northwest Quarterly* 49 (October 1958): 129–45.

———. *Sword and Olive Branch: Oliver Otis Howard*. Pittsburgh, PA: University of Pittsburgh Press, 1964.

Cebula, Larry. *Plateau Indians and the Quest for Spiritual Power 1700–1850*. Lincoln, NE: University of Nebraska Press, 2003.

Clark, Robert. *River of the West: A Chronicle of the Columbia River*. New York: Picador Press, 1997.

Cline, Gloria Griffen. *Peter Skene Ogden and the Hudson's Bay Company*. Norman, OK: University of Oklahoma Press, 1974.

Cohen, Kenneth. *Honoring the Medicine: The Essential Guide to Native American Healing*. Ballantine Books, 2006.

Cruise, D. and A. Griffiths. *The Great Adventure: How the Mounties Conquered the West*. Toronto, ON: Penguin Books, 1996.

Curtis, Edward S. *The North American Indian*. Vol. 8, pg. 164. Norwood, MA: 1911.

Davis, H.J. "The Battle of Camus Meadows." In *Northwestern Fights and Fighters,* pp 191–197. New York: Doubleday, Page & Co., 1907.

Debo, Angie. *A History of the Indians of the United States*. London: The Folio Society, 2003.

Deloria, Vine, Jr. *Behind the Trail of Broken Treaties*. University of Texas Press, 1985.

Dunn, J.P. *Massacres of the Mountains*. New York: Harper & Bros., 1880.

Dupuy, Trevor N. *Harper Encyclopedia of Military Biography*. Edison, NJ: Castle Books, 1995.

Ehle, John. *Trail of Tears: The Rise and Fall of the Cherokee Nation*. Anchor. Reprint Edition, September 1977.

Elsensohn, M. Alfreda, Sister (OSB). *Pioneer Days in Idaho County*. 2 vols. Caldwell, ID: Caxton Press, 1947 & 1951. [A rambling account but fairly valuable in local history.]

Finerty, John F. *Warpath & Bivouac*. Chicago, IL: self-published, 1890.

Frantz, Klaus. *Indian Reservations in the United States*. Chicago, IL: University of Chicago Press, 1999.

Garcia, Andrew. *Tough Trip Through Paradise 1878–1879*. Edited by Bennett H. Stein. University of Idaho Press, 2001.★

Graham, W. A. *The Custer Myth: A Source Book of Custeriana*. With Part IV added by historian Fred Dustin, pp 360–405. New York: Bonanza Books, 1953.★

Greene, Jerome. *Nez Perce Summer 1877*. Helena, MT: Montana Historical Society Press, 2000.★

Guie, Heister Dean and L. V. McWhorter. *Adventures in Geyser Land*. Caldwell, ID: Caxton Printers, 1935.

Hagedon, Hermann. *Roosevelt in the Bad Lands*. Boston: Houghton Mifflin, 1921.

Haines, Aubrey. *An Elusive Victory: the Battle of the Big Hole*. West Glacier, MT: Glacier Natural History Assn., 1991.★

Haines, Frances. *The Nez Perces: Tribesmen of the Columbian Plateau*. Norman, OK: University of Oklahoma, 1955.

Halsey, Cheryll. *Lewis & Clark Across the Midwest*. Surrey, BC: Hancock House, 2006.

Heitman, Francis B. *Historical Register and Dictionary of the U.S. Army from its Organization, September 1789 to March 02, 1903*. 2 vols. Reprinted by Urbana, University of Illinois Press, 1963.

History of Montana. Chicago: Warner, Beers & Company, 1885.

History of North Idaho. San Francisco: Western Historical Publishing Company, 1903.

Hodge, Franklin Webb. *Handbook of American Indians North of Mexico*. 2 vols. Washington DC: Government Printing Office, 1910.

Hook, Jason. *American Indian Warrior Chiefs*. Dorset, UK: Firebird Books, 1989.

Howard, Helen Addison. *Saga of Chief Joseph*. Lincoln, NE: University of Nebraska Press, 1971 reprint.★

Howard, O. O. *Nez Perce Joseph: An account of His Ancestors, His Lands, His Confederates, His Enemies, His Murders, His War, His Pursuit and Capture*. Boston: Lee and Shepard, 1881. [A good study of military tactics and conditions in 1877, but Howard's interpretation of Nez Perce motives and battle tactics contain many flaws, excessive speculation and flights of fancy.]

———. *My Life and Experiences Among Our Hostile Indians.* Hartford, Connecticut: A.D. Worthington Co., 1907.

———. "Nez Perces Campaigns of 1877." *Advance* (Jan–Oct 1878): serialized.

———. "The True Story of the Wallowa Campaign." *North American Review* (July 1879)

———. *Chief Joseph: His Pursuit and Capture.* Boston: Lee & Shephard, Publishers, 1881.

———. "General Howard's Comments on Joseph's Narrative." In *Northwestern Fights and Fighters*, 75–89. Cyrus Brady, editor. New York: Doubleday, Page & Co, 1907.

———. *Famous Indian Chiefs I have Known.* University of Nebraska Press, 1989.

Hutchens, Alma R. *A Handbook of North American Herbs.* Shanikala Press, 1992.

Hutton, Paul A. *Phil Sheridan and His Army.* Lincoln, NE: University of Nebraska Press, 1985.

Josephy, A.M., Jr. *The Patriot Chiefs: A Chronicle of Indian Leadership.* New York: Viking Press, 1961.★

———. *The Nez Perce Indians and the Opening of the Northwest.* New Haven, CT: Yale University Press, 1965.

Lang, George. *Compendium of Culinary Nonsense and Trivia.* Avenel, NJ: Wings Books, 1994.

Lee, Chester Anders. *Chief Joseph: The Biography of a Great Indian.* Wilson-Erickson, 1936.★

MacDonald, Duncan. *The Nez Perces: The history of Their Troubles and the Campaign of 1877.* Wrangell, AK: Mountain Meadow Press, 1993.★

Marquis, Thomas. *Save the Last Bullet For Yourself.* Algonac, MI: Reference Publications, 1987.★

McWhorter, Lucullus V. *Yellow Wolf: His Own Story.* Caldwell, ID: 1940.★

———. *Hear Me My Chiefs.* Caldwell, ID: Caxton Press, 1952 ed.★

McDermott, John D. *Forlorn Hope: The Nez Perce Victory at White Bird Canyon.* Caldwell, ID: Caxton Press, 2003. ★

Mercredi, Ovide and Mary Ellen Turpel. *In the Rapids.* Toronto, ON: Penguin Books, 1994.

Meyers, E.C. *Wild Canadian West.* Surrey, BC: Hancock House, 2006.

Mills, Charles, K. *Harvest of Barren Regrets: The Army Career of William Frederick Benteen, 1834–1898.* Glendale, CA: Arthur H. Clark Co., 1985.

Morril, Allen Conrad. *Out of the Blanket: The Story of Sue and Kate McBeth.* University of Idaho Press, 1978.

Nerburn, Kent. *Chief Joseph and the Flight of the Nez Perce: The Untold Story of an American Tragedy.* San Francisco: Harper Press, 2005.

Noyes, Alva J. *In the Land of the Chinook: the story of Blaine County.* Helena, MT: State Publishing Co., 1917.

Pearson, J. Diane. *The Nez Perces in the Indian Territory.* Norman, OK: University of Oklahoma Press, 2008.★ [A must read for anyone interested in the survival history of Joseph and his followers after the surrender. This perhaps is the definitive work on the subject to date.]

Prucha, Francis Paul, ed. *Documents of United States Indian Policy.* Third ed. University of Nebraska Press, 2000.

Rasky, Frank. *The Taming of the Canadian West.* Toronto, ON: McClelland & Stewart, 1967.

Rickey, Don Jr. *Forty Miles a Day on Beans and Hay.* Norman, OK: University of Oklahoma Press, 1963.

Shields, George Oliver. *The Battle of the Big Hole.* Chicago: Rand McNally, 1889. [This book is filled with suppositions and false claims. It is, however, interesting for these errors alone as an example of the inadequacies of the early researchers.]

Thrapp, Dan L. *Encyclopedia of frontier Biography.* vols. 1 A–F; 2 G–O; 3 P–Z. Norman: University of Nebraska Press, 1988.

Touchie, Rodger D. Bear Child: *The Life and Times of Jerry Potts.* Surrey, BC: Heritage House, 2005.

Warren, Eliza Spalding. *Memoirs of the West: The Spaldings.* Portland, OR: Press of the Marsh, 1916.

★ **Recommended reading.**

Articles

Baughman, Benjamin, "Such Deeds of Darkness: William Craig at the Spalding Mission 1840–1848," *Idaho Yesterdays*, vol. 46 no.2 Spring/Summer (2005): 6–20.

Davis, H.J., "An Incident of the Nez Perce Campaign," *Journal of the Military Service Institution of the United States* May & June (1905): 560–64.

Dempsey, Hugh A., "The Tragedy of White Bird," *The Beaver* February/March (1993). [An excellent article about the tragic murder of White Bird by "Nez Perce" Sam and subsequent developments.]

Howard, Oliver O., "The True Story of the Wallowa Campaign," *The North American Review* (1879). [General Howard gives his version of the events leading up to the onset of the Nez Perce War of 1877.]

Woodruff, Charles A., "Battle of the Big Hole," Montana Historical Society, contributions to the Miscellaneous Library, vol. 7 (1910): 95–135.

Woods, E., "An Account of the Nez Perce War—1877," *Century Illustrated Monthly Magazine* vol. 27 (1884): 136–42. [An article written by Private Woods (not to be confused with Lt. Charles Wood), one of General Howard's foot soldiers. It gives Howard undue credit, many situations are inaccurate and many dates are incorrect. The article's real value lies in its portrayal of the prejudice held by soldiers and bureaucrats against native people during that era.]

Chief Joseph, "An Indian's Views of Indian Affairs," *The North American Review* vol. 125 (1879). [Available in the reference section of most large libraries, usually by special request only.]

Wood, Charles Erskine Scott, "The Pursuit and Capture of Chief Joseph," appendix to Chester Anders Lee's biography of Chief Joseph.

DOCUMENTS

Annual Report of the Board of Indian Commissioners, report nos. 47–50, 1878, *www.archive.org/stream/anualreoprtsindianaffairs.*
The Dawes Act, February 08, 1887.
The Indian Removal Act (1830)
The Indian Reorganization Act, 1934. [This repealed the Dawes Act.]
Investigation of Charges Against Agent Hiram W. Jones, Quapaw Agency, 1874–78, Special Files, M574, Roll 63, case No. 221, Bureau of Indian Affairs Archives, Washington.
McCarthy, Michael, journals and papers, located in Library of Congress, Washington DC. [Included in the papers is his diary for the period of 6 May to 6 August 1877.]
The Merriam Report, 1928.
Nez Perce website, *www.nezperce.com*
Peo'Peo Tahlikt, stories about Indians as told to Many Wounds, February 1935. Located at the University of Washington Library Archives, Pullman, WA.
Reports of Indian Agents at Lapwai & Colville from 1878 to 1906, *www.lib.uidaho.edu*
Samples, John. Letter dated 25 November 1927 to David Hilger, Montana Historical Society, Helena MO. File SC 715.
Secretary of War Reports—1877. National Archives, Washington DC.
US military files, *www.usarmy.mil.com/1875-80/*
Wainwright, R.P. Page, Capt. US Army, "History of The First Cavalry Regiment." Washington, 1899. [A biased account of the 1877 battles. Capt. Page presents only the First Cavalry Regiment's point of view. He does not mention or give credit to Nez Perce tactics for the cavalry's defeats and records only a fraction of the regiment's casualties.]

MAGAZINES

American Heritage, February 1958. [An account of *Inwholise* from the files of Andrew Garcia.]
The Beaver, Canadian historical magazine, Winnipeg, Manitoba. [Report of the trial of Nez Perce Sam.]
Century Illustrated Monthly.
Idaho Yesterdays.
Harper's.
The American Quarterly Review.
The Frontier, November 1932, Missoula, Montana.

NEWSPAPERS

Avant Courier, 1877, Bozeman, MT, 1877.
Baxter Springs Times, Baxter Springs, KS, 1879.
Calgary Herald, Calgary, AB, 1893.
Daily Herald, Helena, MT.
Daily Independent, Helena, MT.
Daily Times, Leavenworth, KS.
Macleod Gazette, Fort Macleod, AB, 1879, 1892, 1893, 1903.
Madisonian, Virginia City, MT, 1877.
Miner, Butte, MT, 1878.
Morning Oregonian, Portland, OR.
New North-west, Deer Lodge, MT.
New York Times, New York City, June 25, 2000.
Portland Oregonian, Portland, OR.
Record, Fort Benton, MT, 1877–8.
Regina Standard, Regina, SK.
San Francisco Chronicle, San Francisco, CA.
Statesman, Boise, ID, 1877.
Teller (The), Lewiston, ID, 1877.
Times, Bozeman, MT, 1877.

Tribune, Chicago, IL, 1877.
Washington Statesman, Walla Walla, WA.
Winnipeg Times, Winnipeg, MB, 1878, 1892, 1893.
Winnipeg Free Press, Winnipeg, MB, 1892, 1893.

Index

A

About Sleep, [Eelahweema].
 Warrior *223, 236n2*
Absaroke Mountains *443*
Absaroke People [Crows] *32*
Alberta (Canadian Northwest Territory.), gives refuge to White Bird's refugees *299*
Allalimya Tanakin. [Fairy] *See: Looking Glass, the younger*
Allan, Frank *216*
Alspotokit [Afternoon Smoker] aka Clark. Claims to be son of William Clark *641-642*
Animal Entering a Hole. *See: Elaskolatat 277, 287*
Assiniboine Indians *587 fn "c"*
Apash Wyakaikt [Flint Necklce]. *See: Looking Glass (the elder) 81, 134*
Appaloosa horses. Attributed to *32, 67, 51n32*
Arenoth. Old Joseph's wife. Mission name bestowed by Spalding *61n3*
Army of the Northwest (Columbia Div.) *16*
Asotin band. At Lapwai *152n6*
Attish Pah. [Place of the cave of red paint]. *See: Cow Island raid 464*
Ayenwatha. *See: Appendix I 657*

B

Bacon, George R. (Lieut.) *414*
Bailey, H.L. (Lieut.) *282, 283*

Baird, A. Sgt. Killed at White Bird Canyon *210*
Baird, George W. (Lieut.) At Canada conference *526, 528*
Baldwin, Frank. Lieut. Letter to wife *536*
Bannock City, Montana Territory *409*
Battles. *See: battles individually listed*
Baxter Springs *540*
Bear's Paw Mountains *483*
Bennett, Andrew. (Capt.) At Bear's Paw *429*
Benson, Henry M.(2i/c B coy.) At Camus Meadow *416*
Benteen, Frederick, W. (Capt.) At Canyon Creek *442, 446, 446, 447, 453n7*
Big Hole River. Failure to post rear guards *330*
Big Hole, battle of *385-388*
Big Thunder, Chief (aka James). *See: Inametoom'shila*
Birch Creek, Idaho. Raids by Joseph's warriors *410–411*
Bitterroot Mountains *191*
Black Owl, (warrior) *397*
Blewett, Charles. (Scout) *267*
Blue Hole. (Okla.) Joseph moves his people *544*
Boyle, William F. (Lieut.) At Umatilla conference *119*
Bradley, James. (Lieut.) *395*
Brave Seventeen, the *276–277*
Brown's Pass *250*
Brook, Bernard A. (Bugler.) killed at Camus Creek *416*
Brooks, Abraham *302*

C

Camas Prairie *213*
Camas Meadows Raid on Howard's troops *411-417*
Canada. White Bird arrives in Alberta. Ottawa's attitude toward the refugees *15*
Carr, Camillus C. Lieut. Commanding 2nd Cav. I coy *415*
Carter, Mason. 1st lt. At bear's Paw *489*
Cayuse Indians. Mission revolt *81*
Canyon band *105n16*
Canyon Creek, battle of *463*
Captain John. *See: Jokais*
Chandler, Zachary (Secretary of the Interior). replaces Delano Attitude towards minorities *115*

Chapman, Arthur "Ad" *232, 151-155, 621-630*
Chapowits [Many Coyotes] at Camus Meadows *414*
Charlo, Salish Chief *327-328, 335n16*
Chellooyeen [Bow and Arrow Case]. Warrior *233*
Chinook Jargon *69n5*
Chtwiweyunaw. Warrior at Camus Meadows *414*
Cheyenne Indians *32*
Chuslum Moxmox [Yellow Bull] *173, 531, 533*
Clark's Fork Canyon *434*
Clark's Basin *461*
Clear Creek *171*
Clearwater River *29*
Clearwater River, battle of *261*
Columbia River *29*
Comba Richard, (Lieut.) at Big Hole battle *385*
Company "F", First Cavalry, at White Bird Canyon *224*
Company "G", seconded officer Theller *224*
Company "H", First Cavalry, at White Bird Canyon *224*
Concerns of Nez Perce chiefs about Army *194-195*
Cornoyer, Narcisse A. (Agent) Umatilla Conference *116, 123*
Cowards, the *287*
Cow Island, the Nez Perce raid on supply depot *471*
Coyote-god. Second to Han'ya'wat, the Great Spirit *146*
Craig, William. Indian agent *66, 68n8*
Crazy Horse, Sioux chief *155n26, 659*
Crook, George, (General) *155n26, 431, 659*
Crow Indians. Promises and betrayals. Employed by army. Raid on Nez Perce herds, scalps dead women and children after the battle at Big Hole *61, 320, passim*
Cupcup. [Cottonwood] *271*

D

Daganawida. *See: Appendix I 657fn"a"*
Davis, Harry J. (Sgt.) *419*
Davis, Jefferson C *41, 58, 59*
Deer Creek *249*
Delano, Columbus. Secretary of the Interior (1870-75)
    Attitude towards Indians. Involved in scandals. Dismissal for fraud *113*

Devine, Richard *185*
Doane, Gustavus. (Lieut) *441*
Dreamers. Religion. *See: Smoholla Smokellers 139, 145*
Dug Bar, Oregon *161*
Dumb Bull. Crow Chief. at Cow Island, horses stolen. Given message by Joseph *451*

E

Eagle Robe *188*
Eashlokoon, Warrior *449*
Eeikish Pah, the Hot Place, (Oklahoma) *542*
Eelahweema, [About Sleep] *236n2*
Elaskatat, Warrior *277, 449*
Elfers, Henry *189*
Elsensohn, Sr. M. Alfreda. Biases. Errors in historical writings *236n2*
Espowyes {Light in the Mountains; also Heavy Weapon] *413*
Elaskolatat. *See: Animal Entering a Hole 233*
Evans, Phillip [Bow and Arrow Case] See: Chellooyeen *233*
Eewatham. *See: Lake Tolo*

F

Farnsworth, James *409*
Fifth Cavalry *463*
Fifth infantry, at Bear's Paw *490*
First Cavalry: Company "E", Company "L" *232*
Fisher, Stanton, B. (Capt.) Militia leader *463*
Five Wounds. Warrior *269*
Flathead Indians, *492*
Flynn, Thomas. Killed in Asotin raids *409*
Fort Fizzle *304, 317*
Fort Keogh, Montana *406, 450*
Fort Lapwai, Idaho *175*
Fort leavenworth, Kansas *537*
Fort Misery. *See: Misery Hill*
Foster, William. (Scout) *267*
Fort Walsh *377*

G

Garcia, Andrew. Army scout. *See: Appendix H 643-647*
Gibbon, John. Loser at Big Hole
Gilbert, Charles C. (Lt.Col.) 7th Infantry. Slated to replace Howard. Ineffective leader *431-432, 334n8*
Glass, Samuel A. Pvt. Wounded at Camas Meadows (Lava Rocks)
Godfrey, Edward, S. Capt. Wounded at Bear's Paw
Gosawyiennight [Bull Bait]
Grande Ronde River, Idaho *29*
Grant, U.S. (President) *91, 103n11, 106n21, 106n23, 106n25*
Great Sprit. Defined *55n46*
Grover, Lafayette A. (Oregon governor) *92, 96*
Gunn, Patrick (Sgt.) *210*
Gwyder, Richard *567n42*

H

Hahtalekin, Chief of the Palu (Palouse) *171, 385*
Hale, Owen. Capt. Killed at Bear's Paw *489, 490*
Hallalhotsoot [Shadow of the Mountain] *178*
Han'ya'wat [Great Spirit Chief] *59*
Harrison, Benjamin *554*
Haworth, James Mahlon. (Special Agent) *566n37*
Hayes, Rutherford.B. US President. Sends Gen.Howard to parley with Joseph. Issues ultimatum to non-Treaty Nez Perce bands *100, 110, 111*
Heinmot Tooyalakekt [Thunder travelling to mountains].
  See: Chief Joseph the Younger
Helena Daily Herald, newspaper *703*
Helena Independent, newspaper *703*
Hemackkis Kaiwon [big Morning] *189*
He'mene Moxmox [Yellow Wolf] *287, 299, 418, 461, 489*
Henry's Lake, Montana *431*
Heyoom'ekahlikt [Grizzly Bear on his Back] *587*
Hey'oom Moxmox [Yellow Grizzly Bear] *187*
Hey'yom'yo'yisk [Bear Crossing]. Joseph's senior wife *509*
Hiawatha *656, 657*
Horse Prairie *409-410*

Howard, Oliver O. (General) *111-113, 117, 120, 121, 133-134, 149n2, 149n4, 206, 207, 279, 278, 281, 288, 549, 556*
How'wallits [Mean Man] *284, 286*
Hunter, George, militia leader *245*
Husishusis Kute [Naked Head], Palu leader *115, 123, 516*
Husis Owyeen [Wounded Head] *256*
Husis Owyeen, Mrs. (Wife of Husis Owyeen.) *256*

I

Ilges, Guido (Major) *472-473*
Inametoom'shila [Big Thunder] Chief *66, 146*
Indian tribes (American): Apache, Cayuse, Crow, Modoc, Sioux, Snake, Umatilla, Yakima. (Canadian): Blackfeet, Morley, Assiniboine, Gros Ventre, Kootenai, Blood, Sarcee, Piegan *659-665*
In'who'lise, [Broken Tooth]. *See:Kot'kot Hihhih 642-647*

J

Jackson, James L. (Lieut.) *415*
Jackson Sundown. *See: Appendix H 650-652*
James. *See: Big Thunder.*
Jacques Spur. *See: Appendix H 651*
Jason [Kalkalshuatash]. Chief of 1855 treaty *78, 145*
Jerome, Lovell H., at Bear's Paw; Captured by White Bird; aftermath of service and discharge for unbecoming conduct *488, 490, 521n22*
Jokais [Lazy] aka Captain John *512*
Jones, Hiram. Indian agent, at Quapaw, vs. Joseph, in disgrace, fired as agent *540-542*
Jones, John M. Pvt *226*
Jordon, Thomas, J. (Indian agent) *567n40*
Joseph,Chief *88, 90, 96, 97, 512-517, 556, 557, passim*
Joseph the Elder (father of Chief Joseph) *65*

K

Kalkalshuatash. *See: Jason*
Kamisnim Takin. *See: Camus Meadows*
Kamnaka. *See: Looking Glass's camp*

Kapkap Ponmi[Sound of Rushing Water].Joseph's 12 yr old daughter. Escapes to Canada *488, 510*
Kelly, Luther "Yellowstone" *490*
Ketalkpoosmin [Stripes Turned Down] *402n6*
Khapk'naponimi, Joseph's mother *59*
Kipkip Owyeen [Wounded Breast] *287*
Kot'kot Hihih {White Feather} See: In'who'lise
Kootenai Indians. trades with Nez Perces *492, 526*
Kowwaspo. Warrior *520n13*
Kowyehkown. (Warrior) Killed at Bear's Paw *498, 520n13*

L

Lah'peeah'loot [Geese Three Times Landing on Water], Joins renegades, leaves renegades, rejoins Joseph, surrenders at Bear's Paw *190*
Lake Tolo. Meeting place *139*
Lamtama band. White Bird's band *233*
Lamniswin Husis *529*
Lakichet Kunnin *412*
Latham, Edwin MD. Signs Joseph's death certificate *557*
Lapwai Conference *137-144*
Lapwai reservation *549, passim*
Lawyer, Chief. Influenced treaty of 1855 *78, 81, 144*
Lawyer, Archie *551, 538*
Lean Elk *313, 408, 411, 429, 434, 476*
Lee'peet Hessem'dooks [Two moons] *187, 224*
Lee, Jason. (Missionary). in land dealing *56n48, 57n50*
Lee, Roman. Cpl. Killed at White Bird Canyon *210*
Lelooskin [Whittling]. Warrior *286*
Lemhi settlers. Build parapets against Nez Perce *410*
Lemhi reservation *410*
Lewis and Clark expedition *29-31, 152n7*
Liquor, abuses of. Chiefs' efforts to suppress use *33*
Lolo Trail, *246, 257n10*
Looking Glass, Asotin chief *134-137, 147-148, 409, 508, passim*
Looking Glass's camp *263*

M

MacDonald, Duncan. Befriends Nez Perce *286, 401*
Macleod, James F., NWMP Inspector. Befriends and assists hite Bird in Canada *526*
Malaria. Kansas and Oklahoma *539*
Marksmanship evaluated *282-283*
Mason, Edwin C. (Major). Lolo skirmish *301*
Maus, Marion. (Lt.) At Bear's Paw *490*
McBeth, Kate. As Joseph's nemesis. Biased reports *90, 550*
McBeth, Sue (Kate's sister), in conflict with Kate *90*
McCarthy, Michael (Sgt.) Keeps diary *209, 243, 250-252, 278, 279, 280, 281*
McClernand, Edward. (2nd Lt.) *490*
McConville, Edward. Militia leader *280, 278-279, 243*
McLaughlin, James. Negative report on Wallowa Valley *555*
McWhorter, Lucullus V *287, passim*
Meopkowit [Know Nothing] *See: Old George 512*
Merrill, Lewis. Major. At Canyon Creek. F,I & L coys
Miles City, Montana *567n51*
Miles, John [Weyeehwahtsiskan] *230*
Miles, Nelson A. "Bear Coat". (Gen.) *406, 433, 490, 496*
Mi'min *(See: Appaloosa horses) 32, 54n31*
Mimpow Owyeen [Wounded Mouth] *277*
Minthon, John. *See: Weyatemtmas Wahyakt*
Misery Hill, Ollokot leads raid on *278-290*
Missionaries. Damage done *56n41*
Mitchell, Frank *225*
Modoc Indians *542*
Molchert, William, at Cow Island *470*
Montague, W.L. Killed in Asotin raid *409*
Montieth, John B. (Indian agent) at Lapwai *119, 153n16*
Moylon, Miles. (Lt.) At bear's Paw *489*
Mount Idaho, Idaho *210*
Mount Idaho Militia, at White Bird Canyon *233*
Mount Idaho Volunteers, at White Bird Canyon battle, criticism of, in Cottonwood engagement *233*
Musselshell River *451*

N

NimiPu. (Nez Perce). Meaning of and pronunciation *25*
Nennin Chekoostin [Black Raven]. Warrior *265*
Nez Perce Indians, Treaty and non-Treaty differences *78, 89*
Nez Perce casualty lists, *App. C 583-588*
Nez Perce lands *29*
Nez Perce langiage [Nimiputimt] *595*
Nez Perce Sam [Lamnisnim Husis} (Shrivelled Head), kills White Bird, trial, imprisonment, death of *529-531*
No Feet. *See: Seeskeemko*
North-West Mounted Police *639*
Norton's Ranch *267*
Norwood, Randolph. (Capt.). Describes, Camus Meadow raid *414, 415, 417*

O

Ogden, Peter Skene *54n43*
Ollokot, Joseph's uncle, helps name young Joseph *64*
Ollokot, [Frog] Joseph's brother *87, 88, 117, 499, passim*
Old Joseph, father of Joseph and Ollokot *72*
Otskai [Go Out]. Asotin warrior at Camus Meadow *419*
Old Yellow Wolf *287, 401n6*
Ott, Lawrence *188*

P

Pahk'atos Owyeen [Five Wounds] *286, 585*
Pah'tis'sah. Daughter of Big Thunder *66*
Painter, W. Charles. Capt. At Umatilla Conference *119*
Palmer, Joel (Gen.) *84n4*
Palouse Indians, Also known as Palu *145*
Parnell, William R *208, 298*
Peo'peo Ipsewahk [Lone Bird] *498*
Peo'peo Kiskiok Hih'hi. *See: White Bird 123, passim*
Peo'Peo Tholekt [Bird Alighting], Asotin chief, hero warrior, many times wounded *414, 419, passim*
Perry, David (Capt.) *181, 205-242*
Piquinin Indians *157*

Poker Joe. *See: Lean Elk*
Ponca Indians *547*
Pope, J. (Major-General) Commander of Fort Leavenworth *537*
Possossona [Misery Hill] *274-280*
Potts, Jerry. NWMP Scout, avenges father's murder, saves NWMP patrol. Kills whisky runners. Death of *334n6*
Potts, Benjamin F. Montana Governor *327*

Q

Quapaw Reservation, Indian territory *547*

R

Rainbow, Chief. Killed at Big Hole *269, 397*
Rains, Sevier McC. (Lieut.) *268*
Rain's Patrol. Ambushed *269-271*
Randall, D.B. Militia leader *266*
Rawn, Capt. Charles, C. At Fort Fizzle *308, 310, 316n2*
Red Cloud *429, 424*
Red Elk *551*
Red Wolf, Josiah *568n44*
Red Heart *297*
Redington, J.W. (US Scout). Unbiased reports *462*
Romeyn, Henry. Lt. Wounded at Bear's Paw *489, 519n9*
Rueben, James. Ordained Nez Perce minister. Role at Bear's Paw and in Okla. Disputes with Kate McBeth *303*
Ryan, Thomas. (Sgt.) *210*

S

Selish Indians [aka Salish}. Eastern Washington *316n9*
Salmon River (Idaho) *249*
Salmon River Band. *See: Lamtama band*
Sanford, George B. (Major) *415, 416*
Sarpsis Ilppilp [Red Moccasin Tops] *187, 231, 301, 302*
Scalps, taking of *14, 21n1*
Schurz, Carl. Secretary of Interior. Turns from reformer to biased bureaucrat *99*

Sees'koomke. *See: No feet*
Seven Drums Religion. *See: Weset*
Seventh Cavalry *430*
Sheridan, Philip H. (General) *427, 532*
Sherman, William T. (General) *426, 532*
Shively, John *433*
Shoup, George. (Colonel) *411*
Sik'em. Nez Perce war horses *10, 67*
Silooyeam, warrior *449, 586*
Sitting Bull. Sioux chief *14, passim*
Skolaskin, Sans Poil chief. Joseph's bete noir *72, 74n6, 357*
Smith, James. Killed in Asotin raid *409*
Smohalla, [Preacher] Dreamer prophet *39, 72, 74n6*
Smokellers. *See: Dreamers 39, 72*
Snake Creek. *See: Bear's Paw, Siege of 484*
Snake River *158*
Snyder, Simon (Capt.) *489*
Sousouquee [Brown]. Joseph's older brother *87*
Spalding, Eliza. Establishes Lapwai school *602*
Spalding, Henry H. (Missionary) history of, alienates James and Old Joseph, at odds with David Craig, flees Lapwai, death of *50, 66, 69n7, 599-607*
Spurgin, William, E. (Capt.) *458*
Spoils of war *234-235, passim*
Stevens, Isaac. (Governor) *79, 80, 84n1*
Sturgis, Samuel D. (Colonel) *320, 430, 432, 443, 443, 448, 449, 455n16, 463, 466n4*
Suhmkeen [Shirt On] *See: Samuel Tilden 652-653*
Sul'in mox-mox. *See: Yellow Bull*
Sun Dance. Rite of passage *542*
Swan Necklace (warrior). *See: Weyatmtmas Waahyaht*
Swartz, Theodore D *231, 237n9*

T

Tamootsin. *See: Timothy. Influenced 1855 Treaty*
Tackers Pass (now Targhee Pass) *414, 426*
Teeto Hoonod. Warior. At Canyon Creek *447*
Teewee'yownah [Over the Point] *449, 463*
Temme Ilppilp [Red heart] *265*

Tel'lik'leen *187*
Tendoy. Lemhi chief *411*
Tepahlewam [Split Rocks] *159*
Teukakis. *See: Old Joseph 61*
Theller, Edward R. Cavalry officer *209, 229*
Thompson, David. Canadian explorer, mapped Columbia R.
  Opens BC-Idaho north route *47n12*
Thompson, Frank. *See: Wap'tas'wa'tiekt*
Thompson, John. (Cpl.) *210*
Timothy, Chief. Influenced treaty of 1855 *78, 145*
Tip'yah'lah'nah Siskan, [Eagle Robe] *188*
Tip'yah'alah'nah Kapakaps [Strong Eagle] *231*
Tomyahnin. warrior *588*
Took'ka'lickt'se'ma [Never Hunts]. Warrior *526*
Tookleiks [Fish trap] Sniper at Clark Canyon *449*
Tool'hool'hool'zote [Sound] Chief *115, 123, 137, 283, 489, passim*
  Treaties of 1855 & 1861. Amended by Washington *83*
Trimble, Joel Graham. (Capt.) *208, 226*
Tripp, Milan. Scout. Kills Looking Glass *508*
Tuetakis, a spade for digging Camus roots *60n1*
Twenty-first Infantry: Coy. "B", "C", "D", "E", "G", "H","I". At Bear's Paw *224*
Two Moons. Warrior *269, 441*
Twvish Sisimnen [Sparkling Horn}. (Aka Ellis) *83, 85n8*
Tyler, George, L. (Capt.) *490*

U

Umatilla Indians *78, 116*
United States Army of the Nortwest. Casualty List *588*

V

Vicious Weasel. *See: Wetti'wetti Howlis*
Varnum, Charles A. (Lieut.) At Canyon Creek *450*

W

Waaya'tonah Toeait'kahn [Blanket of the Sun] *650-652*
Wahchumyus. *See: Rainbow*

Wahlitits [Shore Crossing] *187, 230*
Wala'mute'kint. *See: Old Joseph*
Walla Walla councils of 1877 *116, 121*
Wallowa Valley 26 *136*
Wallowa Valley Band *26*
Walsh, Jamess, A. NWMP *578*
Waters, Sidney. (Indian Agent) at Colville Res *551, 552*
Waters, Albert. Chief, succeeds Joseph in 1906 *557*
Wawookya Wasaw [Lean Elk] *See: Poker Joe 315*
Wayakat [Going Across] *286*
Wayouh'yuck [Blue leg] *101n2*
Weesculatat [Wounded Mouth] *277, 291n32*
Weippe. Conference at *299*
Wellamotkin Band. *See: Wallowa Valley band 59, 233, passim*
Weset. Nez Perce Traditional religion *71n2*
Wetti'wetti Howlis. See: Vicious Weasel *225, 236n5*
Wetyemtmas Wahyakt [Swan Necklace] *188, 649-650*
White Bird, (Chief). *See: Peopeo Kiskiok Hihih*
White, Elijah. Missionary. steals land *37, 57n51*
Whipple, Stephen G *262-265, 288n1*
Wiy'yukea' Ilppilp [Red Elk] *551*
Wottolen [Hair Combed Forward] *287, 417, 489*
Wood, Charles E.S. *419, 514-515, 647-649*
Wyakin. A personal spirit guide of each Nez Perce *63, 68n2*

X

Y

Yakima Indians *78*
Yellow Bull. See: Sul'in'mox'mox *173, 551, 557*
Yellow Grizzly. See: Heyoom Moxmox
Yellow Wolf. See: He'mene Moxmox *287, 299, 418, 461, 489*
Yoomis Kunnin [Grizzly Bear Blanket] *256, 284*
Young Chief. Umatilla chief *46*

Z

Acknowledgements

This book could not have been written without the help of many people I met or had contact with along the way. Many thanks to Robert M. Brown, PhD, of Montana whose information concerning Captain Charles C. Rawn was of great help. Also thanks to Vernon Carroll of Montana State Parks, Missoula, Montana for his assistance. Thanks to the two delightful Nez Perce ladies who were managing a gasoline station at Nespelem, Washington the day I stopped to ask directions to Chief Joseph's grave. They not only directed me there but answered many questions about the man. It was from them I learned that many of the non-Nez Perce residents in the Colville Reservation had been less than pleased that he had been resettled there. They initially feared he would begin another insurrection, but soon realized he wanted only to be left alone to live a peaceful life and work towards the betterment of his people.

Many thanks to the research staff at the National Archives of Canada, Ottawa for information pertaining to the Nez Perce refugees and their relationship with Inspectors Walsh and Macleod of the NWMP. Also, many thanks for the photos of Nez Perce warriors and chiefs in the NAC collection that had been taken in Idaho by the famed frontier photographer, Edward S. Curtis [1868–1952]. Although the photos were posed, they, as closely as possible, re-enact the activities of various battles and incidents during the summer of 1877.

Thanks to US Army archivists for their assistance in locating maps, documents and reports pertaining to the officers and men who participated in the 1877 campaign.

Thanks also to residents of Lapwai and Colville who made me feel welcome and who generously shared their accounts of the long trek. Many related narratives told them by parents and grandparents who had contemporary knowledge of the events of 1877. Special thanks to Ms. Amelia Marchand, a Nez Perce archivist at Colville, who was extremely helpful in my search for details of Joseph's fortunes and misfortunes of the years between 1885 and 1904.

Thanks is also extended to Mr. Jim Magera, a seasonal park ranger and tour guide at the Bear's Paw Battlefield (south of Chinook, Montana). Mr. Magera was very helpful in describing to me the layout of the Nez Perce camp, the siege area and numerous other points of interest, including the area where their vast herd of horses had been pastured. Mr. Magera also informed me that Chief Looking Glass had been no stranger to the area, having often dealt with the Sioux. Mr. Magera also told me Looking Glass was well known among the Blackfeet who thought so highly of his singing talents they called him Chief Meadowlark.

Mr. Donald Wagner, a guide at the Big Hole Battlefield (near Wisdom, Montana) was particularly helpful with his information about how that battle was fought. It is his opinion, as is mine, that although the army took a beating, the battle must be considered a draw because the Nez Perce defenders suffered many dead and wounded, especially among the women and children. These casualties came about because the soldiers fired randomly and wantonly into the tepees housing the non-combatants.

As usual I thank the editing, layout and production staffs at Hancock Publishing for their patience and assistance for which I am very appreciative but perhaps have come to take for granted.

— E.C. Meyers
Victoria, BC, 2013

About the Author

Ted Meyers has had a fascination with Old West History for most of his life, having spent much of the past fifty years researching and uncovering details about the lives of many western characters. He is the author of *Wild Canadian West,* published by Hancock House in 2006, and five other books covering topics from bush survival to naval history and North American Native legends. He lives in Victoria, BC.

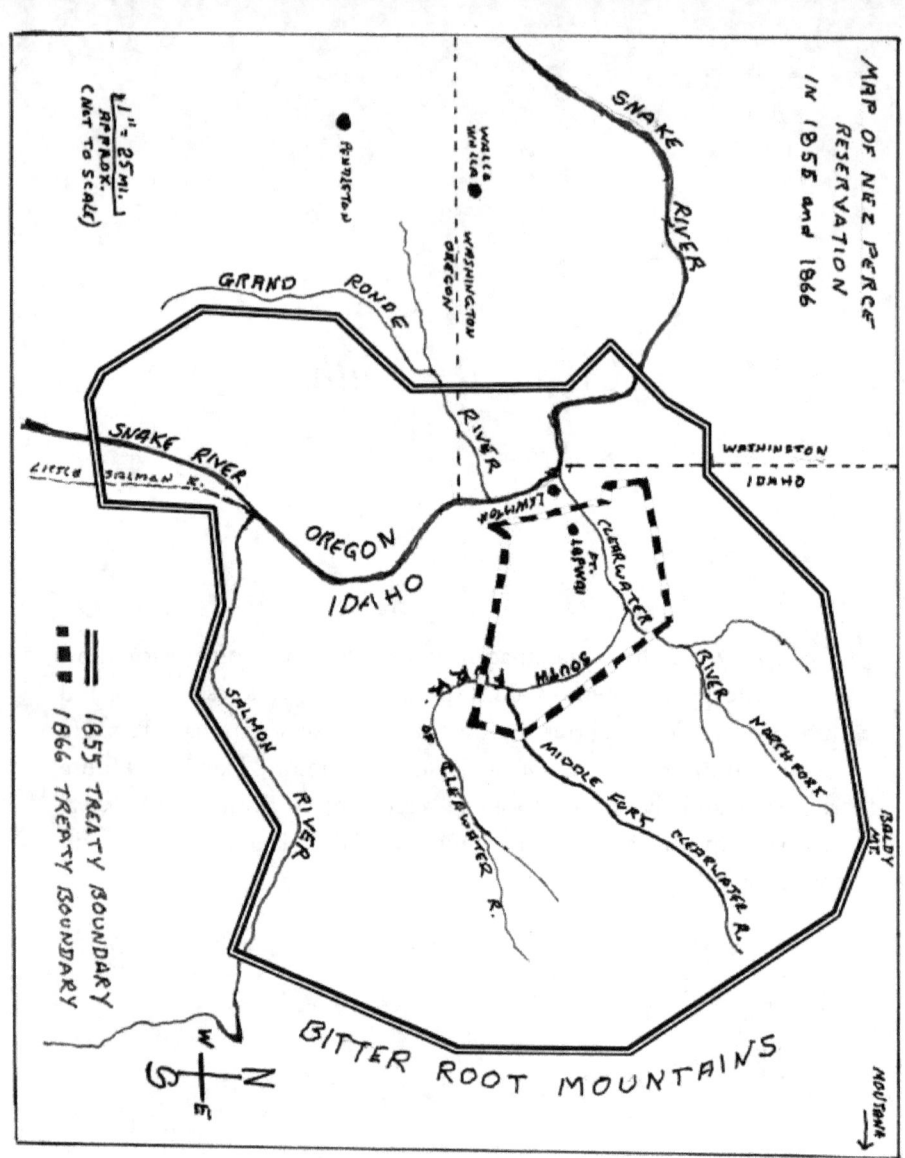

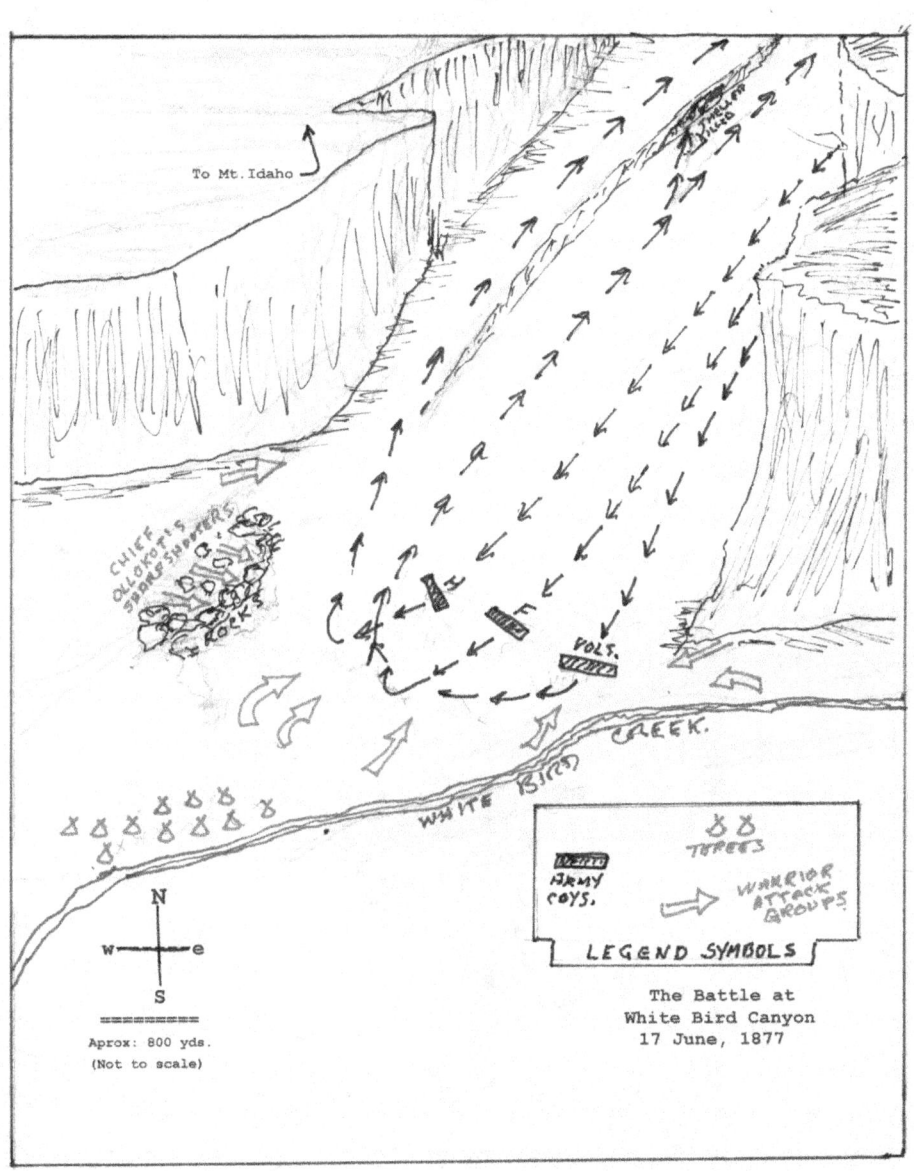

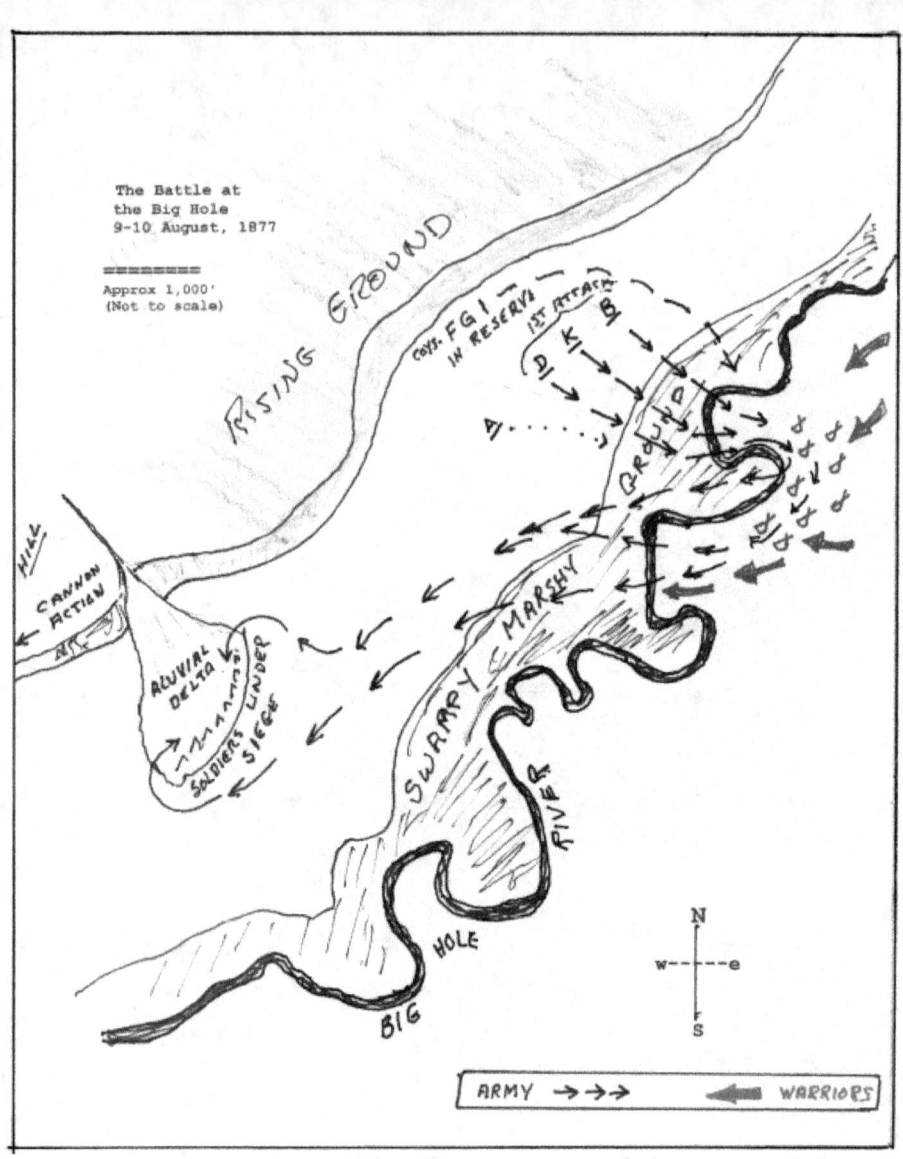

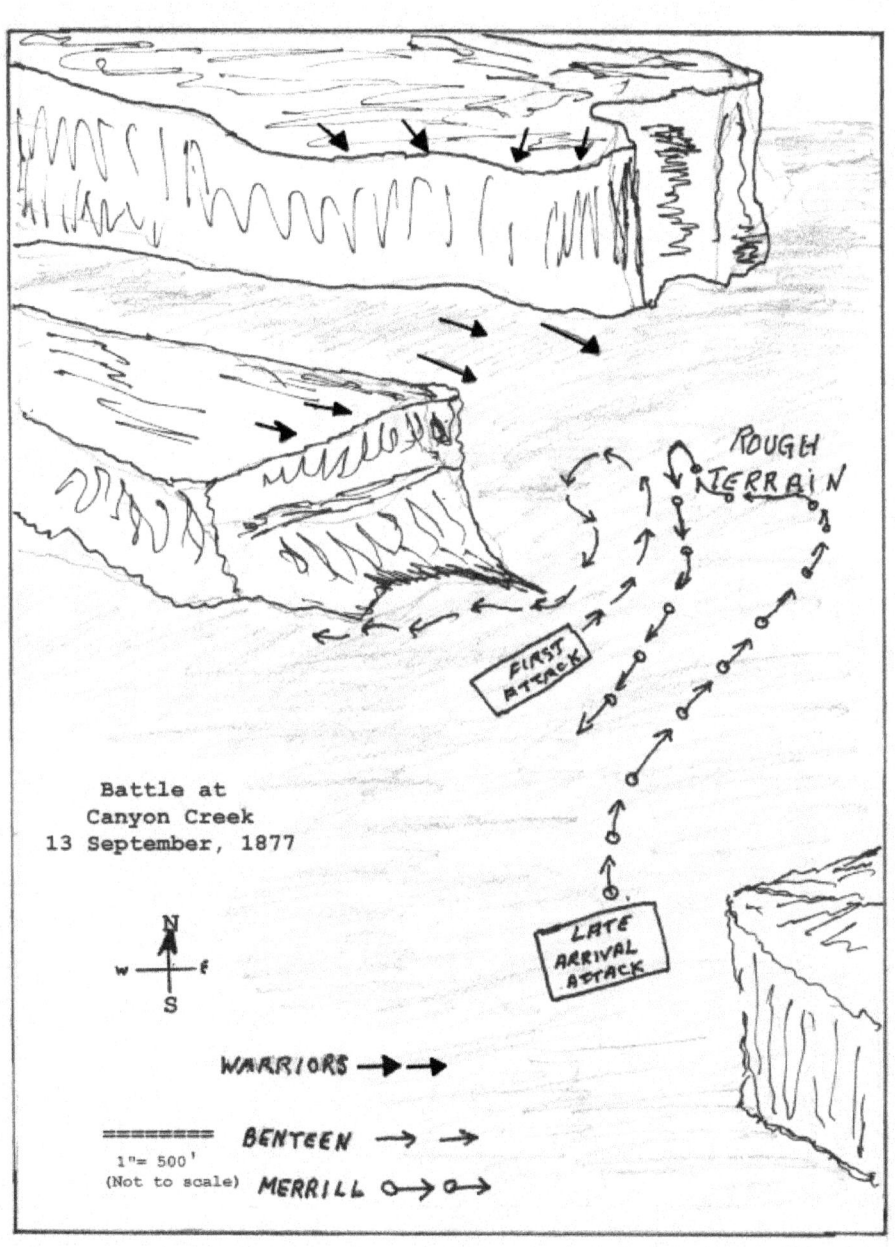

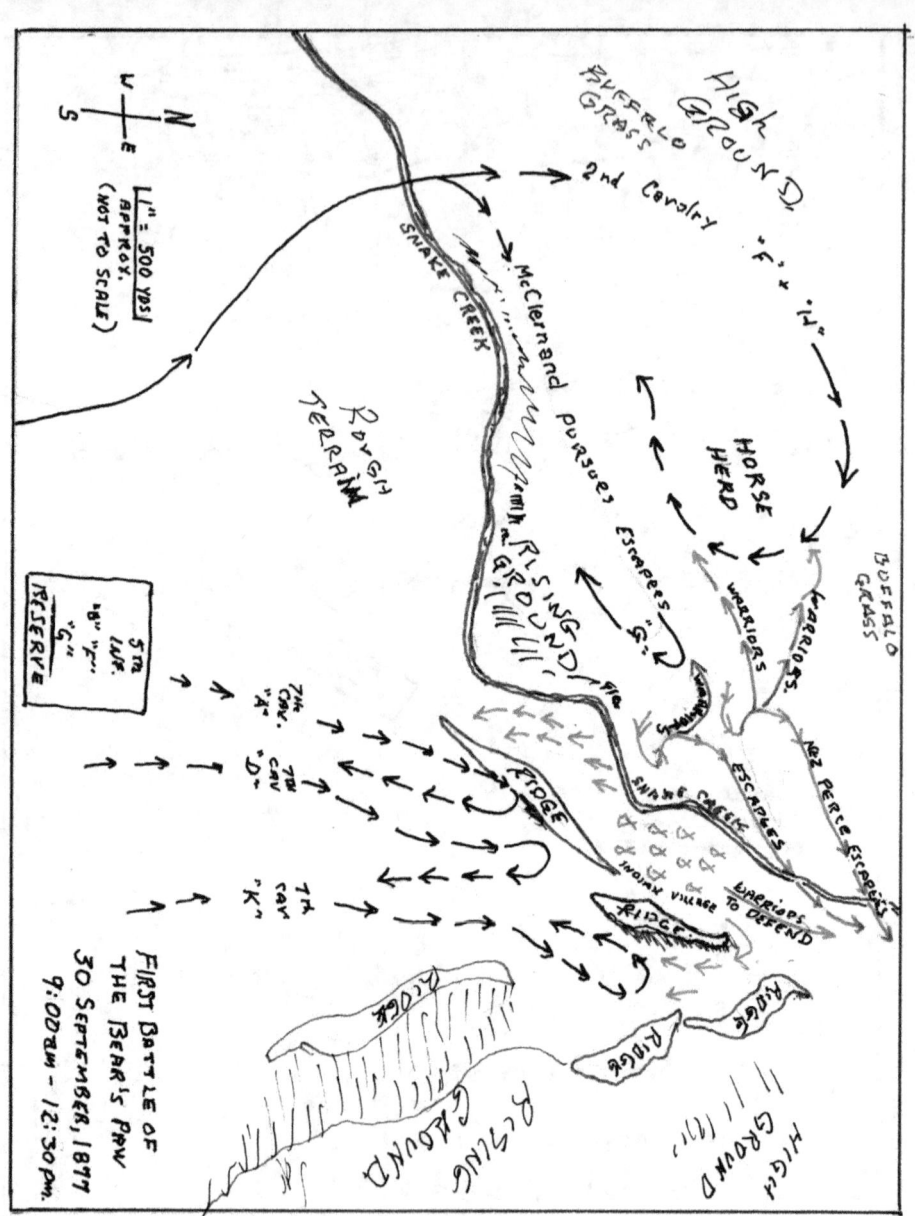

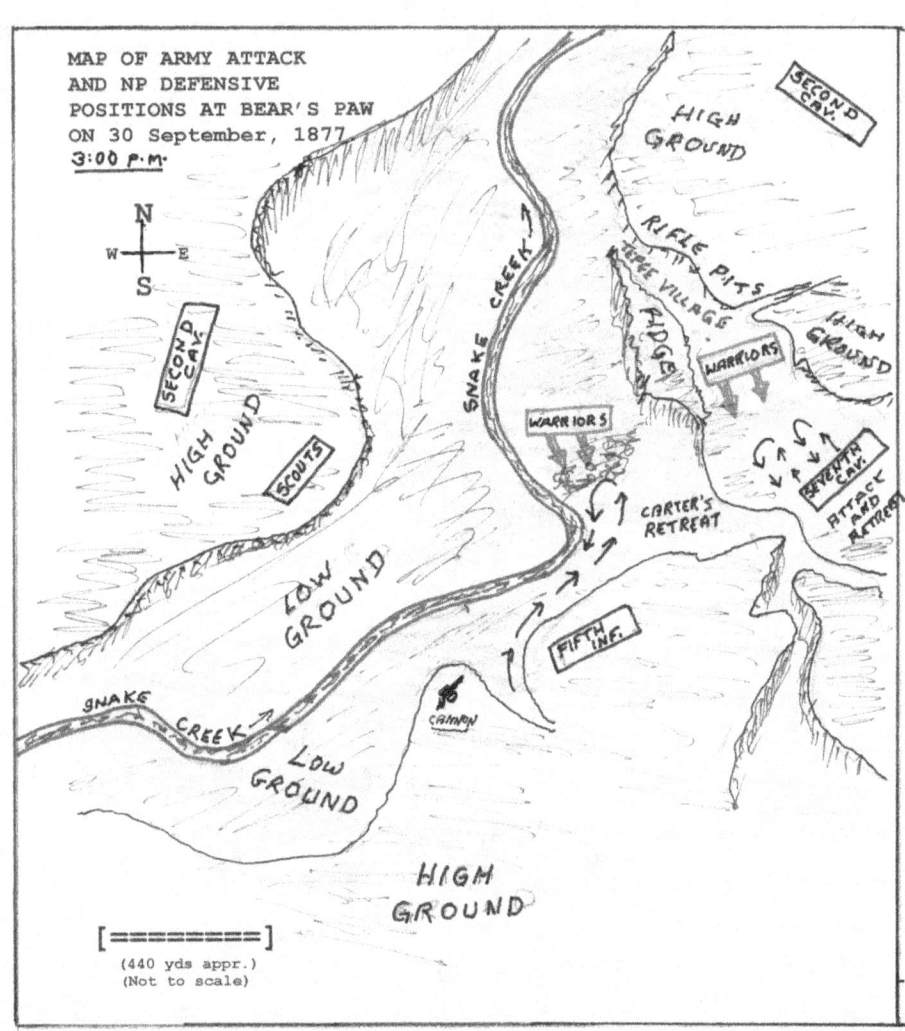

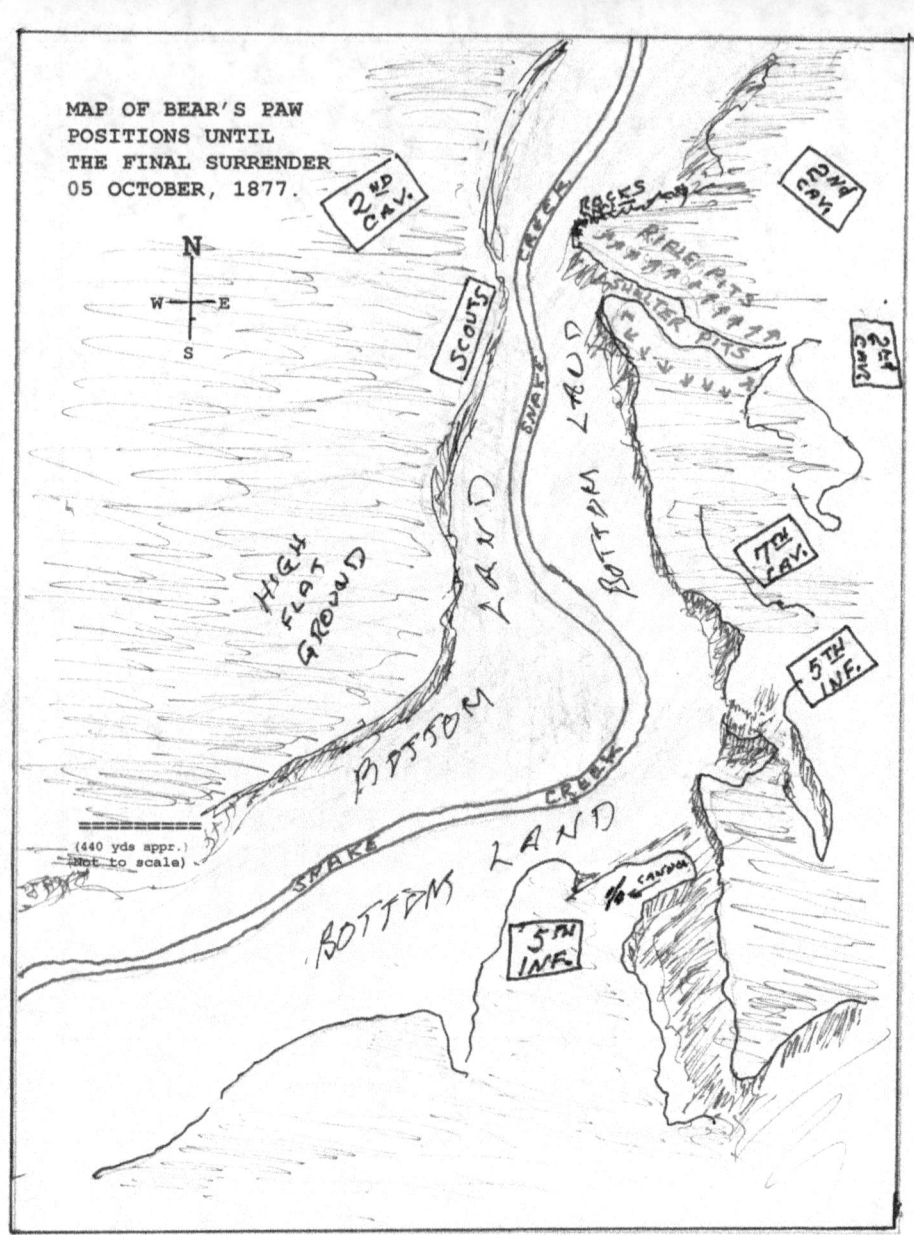

www.ingramcontent.com/pod-product-compliance
Lightning Source LLC
Chambersburg PA
CBHW071229300426
44116CB00008B/969